Employment in
Britain

Industrial Relations in Context

General Editor: George Sayers Bain

Titles (available or in preparation)

Industrial Relations in Britain
George Sayers Bain (ed.)

Labour Law in Britain
Roy Lewis (ed.)

Employment in Britain
Duncan Gallie (ed.)

Personnel Management in Britain
Keith Sisson (ed.)

Employment in Britain

Edited by
Duncan Gallie

Basil Blackwell

Copyright © Basil Blackwell Ltd

First published 1988
First published in USA 1989

Basil Blackwell Ltd
108 Cowley Road, Oxford, OX4 1JF, UK

Basil Blackwell Inc.
432 Park Avenue South, Suite 1503
New York, NY 10016, USA

British Library Cataloguing in Publication Data

Employment in Britain
    (Industrial relations in context)
    1. Employment. Sociological perspectives.
    I. Title   II. Series
    306'.36

    ISBN 0–631–16019–1
    ISBN 0–631–16021–3 Pbk

Library of Congress Cataloging in Publication Data

Employment in Britain / edited by Duncan Gallie.
    p. cm. — (Industrial relations in context)
    Bibliography: p.
    Includes index.
    ISBN 0-631-16019-1
    ISBN 0-631-16021-3   (pbk.)
    1.   Industrial sociology—Great Britain. 2.   Labor supply—Great Britain—Effect of technological innovations on. I. Gallie, Duncan. II. Series.
HD6957.G7E46 1989
306'.36—dc19
                                                                    88–16774
                                                                    CIP

Typeset in 10 on, 11½ pt Times
by Gecko Limited, Bicester, Oxon
Printed in Great Britain by Page Bros. Ltd, Norwich

In memory of Eric Batstone

Contents

List of Contributors

David Ashton, Director of Research, Labour Market Studies Group, University of Leicester.

Eric Batstone, until his death in 1987, Fellow of Nuffield College, University of Oxford, and University Lecturer in Industrial Relations.

Richard Brown, Professor of Sociology, University of Durham.

Shirley Dex, Lecturer in Economics and Management Science, University of Keele.

P.K. Edwards, Principal Research Fellow, Industrial Relations Unit, University of Warwick.

Duncan Gallie, Official Fellow in Sociology, Nuffield College, University of Oxford.

Richard Jenkins, Lecturer in Sociology, University College of Swansea.

Christel Lane, Lecturer in Sociology, University of Aston.

Catherine Marsh, Lecturer at the Social and Political Sciences Committee, University of Cambridge, and Fellow of Newnham College.

Roderick Martin, Teaching Fellow, Management Centre, Templeton College, Oxford.

Lydia Morris, Lecturer in Sociology and Social Policy, University of Durham.

Kate Purcell, Senior Research Fellow, Industrial Relations Unit, University of Warwick.

Michael Rose, Reader in the Sociology of Economic Life, University of Bath.

Jill Rubery, Senior Research Fellow, Department of Applied Economics, University of Cambridge, and Fellow of New Hall.

John Scott, Reader in Sociology, University of Leicester.

David Winchester, Lecturer in Industrial and Business Studies, University of Warwick.

Foreword

'Industrial Relations in Context' is a new series of books which complements the well-established 'Warwick Studies in Industrial Relations'. The latter continues as a vehicle for disseminating research undertaken at Warwick University's Industrial Relations Research Unit, while the new series is designed for the purposes of teaching and wider dissemination. Its rationale is the need for an analysis of current problems and issues in British industrial relations which is systematically informed by the relevant research and scholarship, and by an awareness of recent trends and developments and the wider social, economic, political and international contexts of industrial relations.

The series aims at providing a clear, comprehensive, authoritative, and up-to-date analysis of the entire field of employment relations. It is intended for students doing diploma, undergraduate, or postgraduate courses in personnel management and industrial relations at colleges, polytechnics, or universities, as well as for those studying industrial sociology, labour economics and labour law. It should also be of interest to those in adult education, to those seeking membership of professional bodies like the Institute of Personnel Management, to industrial relations practitioners in both unions and management, and to the general reader who wants to find out more about industrial relations in Britain today.

The hallmarks of the series are clarity, comprehensiveness, authoritativeness and topicality. Each chapter of each volume is an original essay that brings together the relevant theoretical and empirical work. Each is stamped with the views of the authors who are leading experts in the field. Each emphasizes analysis and explanation as well as description. Each focuses on trends over the past two or three decades (unless a longer time perspective is required to develop the argument) and says something about likely future developments. And in each case the complete text is welded into a coherent order for teaching purposes by an editor who combines a distinguished research record with a proven ability to communicate to a wide audience.

The series began with the publication in 1983 of *Industrial Relations in Britain*, edited by George Bain, a general text covering trade unions, management, collective bargaining, industrial conflict, the labour market, labour law, and state intervention in industrial relations. It continued in 1986 with the publication of *Labour Law in Britain*, edited by Roy Lewis, a specialist text of 20 chapters covering virtually every aspect of its subject. *Personnel Management in Britain*, edited by Keith Sisson, is in the process of preparation.

Employment in Britain is the latest volume to be published in the series. Its appearance is most timely. The last two decades, as Duncan Gallie points out in his Preface, have seen dramatic changes in both social structure and social theory. The authors of the following chapters survey these changes as they affect people's experiences of work, the labour market and the wider pattern of social stratification. In doing so, they offer new perspectives on the topics they discuss as well as the most up-to-date, comprehensive, and authoritative account of the employment relationship in Britain.

George Sayers Bain

Preface

Over the last two decades, sociological research into the employment relationship has been substantially transformed as a result both of changes in the employment structure of society and of internal theoretical development. In the past, under the label of industrial sociology, it was concerned primarily with the experiences of manual workers in manufacturing industry; indeed, typically, it was restricted to the study of male manual workers. The increasing importance of non-manual work, the growth of the service sector, the expansion of women's employment, the rapid spread of new technologies among both manual and non-manual employees, and the rise of unemployment to levels that have not been experienced since the inter-war period, combined to underline the need for a far more comprehensive definition of the field of enquiry.

At the same time, there has been a considerable renewal of the theoretical frameworks used to analyse the employment relationship. The earlier deterministic traditions – whether of a neo-liberal or neo-Marxist variant – have been increasingly replaced by an explanatory framework that gives central importance to historically conditioned forms of managerial culture and to the institutionally structured pattern of power relations between management and employees. Further, it has been increasingly recognized that social relations at work have to be understood in the context of the way in which labour markets operate. The types of labour recruited, the aspirations of employees, the nature of alternative work opportunities and the relationship between employment and family life have been increasingly seen as fundamental to the pattern of social inequality at work and to the nature of relations between employers and employees.

The very fact that sociology of employment has been one of the richest and most dynamic areas of new theory and research has made it increasingly difficult for both student and specialist to remain fully abreast of its most recent developments. The objective of this volume is to provide an overview of recent work in the subject, and each chapter has been written by a person who has made a significant personal contribution to the particular area of work. The authors' brief was to give an account of the development of research and of the major theoretical controversies in their field. They were encouraged, however, to give their own personal interpretations of where the debates had reached, and this they have done.

The volume is organized in three parts. The first is concerned with the implications of the changing nature of employment for people's experiences of work. After an initial chapter outlining the major theoretical debates about the character of the employment relationship, there are chapters assessing the significance of the extensive changes occurring in the technology of work for the working lives of both non-manual and manual employees. These are followed by chapters addressing the major debates about the changing nature of attitudes to work, and the significance of gender for people's experience of the work situation. Finally, this part of the book closes with a discussion of the sources of different types of employee resistance at work and the factors that determine the frontier of control between management and the workforce.

In the second part of the book, the focus shifts to the labour market. The approach here is one that views the labour market as the result of social organization, rather than of the operation of some set of universal and impersonal laws. The character of the demand for labour is seen as the result of the types of labour-force policies that employers develop in the context of the institutions regulating the labour market, while labour supply is seen as moulded by the prevailing forms of family organization, the character of local community structures and the nature of the educational system. A central concern of this part of the volume is to assess the extent to which the social processes involved on both the demand and the supply sides generate systematic inequalities of condition and opportunity in ways that are difficult to account for in conventional economic terms.

The third and final part of the volume examines the relationship between the changing structure of employment and the wider pattern of social stratification in society. This addresses the sustained controversy about the nature of change in the pattern of ownership of industry and its implications for management policies. It takes up the debates about the ways in which changes in the nature of work and the labour market may be modifying the traditional lines of social division in British society. Finally, it examines the problems posed by changes in the employment relationship for the strength and structure of trade-union organization.

I am grateful to Teresa Davidson for her invaluable help in typing chapters and in administering the extensive correspondence that goes with such a book. My thanks too to Mary Robinson for her work as desk editor and to Jacqueline McDermott for preparing the index. They were both confronted with timetables that I am sure would have made many others flinch.

The volume is dedicated to Eric Batstone. Eric was writing his chapter on the evening of his tragically early death. He was already widely respected in both Britain and Europe as one of the leading sociologists in this field. His work made a major contribution to the drawing together of the traditions of industrial sociology and of industrial relations that was one of the central developments in the subject over this period. He was a close personal friend of several contributors to this volume and the memory of his personal warmth and intellectual vivacity will stay with us.

Duncan Gallie

1 Introduction

Duncan Gallie

The chapters in this volume chart the major developments in sociological research into employment in Britain over the last two decades. The central theme of research has remained the way in which employment relations contribute to and are affected by the structure of social inequality. The period has, however, witnessed a major reformulation of what is involved in this research agenda and of underlying assumptions about the central influences on economic processes. In the 1960s, it was a subject that was primarily concerned with the experience of employment of male manual workers in manufacturing industry. More recently, it has extended its frontiers to focus more centrally on non-manual workers, on female employees and on work in the service industries. This has led to a deeper exploration of the way in which work organizations influence, and are influenced by, the dynamics of labour markets. At the same time, there has been a marked movement away from the view that it is possible to establish general theories of the evolution of employment relations in capitalist societies and an increasing awareness of the way in which processes of economic change are mediated by institutional structures that are heavily moulded by past patterns of historical development. These changes have altered fundamentally the character of research into employment relations in the enterprise, labour markets and the implication of economic change for the class structure.

Employment Relations in the Enterprise

While research in any given period consists of quite diverse agendas of work, the dominant influences in the 1960s and 1970s were those that sought to develop general theories of the evolution of work and of the nature of work organizations. It was believed that it was possible to isolate a decisive causal mechanism that produced broadly similar effects throughout the advanced capitalist societies. In the 1960s, such interpretations were mainly of an optimistic type. The experience of work was believed to be becoming a source of greater personal enrichment and conflicts around the employment relationship were thought to be in steady decline. By the 1970s, however, this perspective had been replaced by one that emphasized the increasingly exploitative nature of the employment relationship and the growing impoverishment of the experience of work. The accumulating problems of these two theoretical traditions were to lead to a widespread rejection of the deterministic assumptions about social change that they embodied.

The Optimistic Scenario of the Future of Work

The optimistic scenario of the evolution of work and of work organization received its most powerful general formulation in *Industrialism and Industrial Man* (Kerr et al., 1960). This argued that social structure has been determined increasingly by the requirements of an advanced industrial technology developing inexorably in the direction of greater complexity and greater technical sophistication. As a result the skill structure of society has become increasingly differentiated and the general level of skills progressively higher. This change in the character of work tasks has had profound implications for the nature of work organizations. With higher levels of skill, employers have become increasingly dependent on the ability and willingness of employees to use their initiative. It has become dysfunctional to manage the work process through authoritarian forms of decision-making and control; rather, to be effective, work organizations must be designed in a way that allows employees greater discretion at work, thereby increasing their motivation and making the best use of their knowledge and skill. At the same time, the broader decision-making processes in the firm become more pluralistic, allowing for greater participation of employees and their representatives in the formulation of work rules.

An important development of the thesis with regard to manual work was that by Robert Blauner (1964). Blauner believed that the decisive development was the emergence of advanced automation which reversed the historic tendency towards an ever increasing division of labour and transformed the very nature of manual skills. Instead of manual dexterity being the key criterion of skill, the new skills were of a more conceptual type. The new emphasis on judgement, rapidity of decision-making and the ability to assume responsibility requires substantial experience and on-the-job training. Automation, then, involves a substantial rise in skill levels, albeit of skills of a very different type, and restores meaning and satisfaction to work. The major British contribution to theory and research in this perspective was the work of Joan Woodward and her team at Imperial College (Woodward, 1958; Woodward, 1965; Woodward (ed.), 1970). This came to conclusions that strongly reinforced Blauner's conception of the impact of automation on the nature of skills. Similarly, Wedderburn and Crompton (1972: chapter 4), comparing different types of technological setting, showed that workers in the most highly automated settings found work more interesting than traditional machine operators, were much more likely to feel that they could try out their ideas on the job and had better relations with their supervisors.

The research of Woodward and her team also led – albeit by a rather different route – to similar conclusions to those of the theorists of industrialism about the way in which the nature of managerial control over work would change. Indeed, as the research developed, the nature of the control system became increasingly central to their explanatory framework and appeared to have some claim to being the underlying variable linking organizational behaviour with technology. There was, Woodward argued, a necessary link between the type of technology and the nature of the control system. In large-batch pre-automated systems, the mechanisms of control are personalized in a managerial structure that is itself highly fragmented. In this type of system, workers are likely to be exposed to contradictory managerial pressures to give priority simultaneously to both quantity and quality. This introduces a permanent potential source of friction between management and the work-force. In the highly automated setting, however, the balance between these different types of objective has to be determined when the production system is first designed. As a result more of the pressure is taken off supervisors in the everyday work setting, their role changes from a repressive to a consultative one and the quality of their relations with employees correspondingly improves.

Thus, by the later 1960s, there was a growing body of research that suggested that technological change would, at least in the longer run, bring about a transformation of manual work involving higher skills levels, greater discretion in work and more participative forms of organization. However, the 'optimistic scenario' of the theorists of industrialism was not based uniquely on the changing character of manual work. Even more fundamentally, these authors pointed to the great expansion that was occurring in non-manual work. With advanced industrialization, they argued, an ever greater need exists for scientific and technical staff, while the growing complexity of organizations increases the requirement for educated non-manual employees to ensure effective co-ordination. This part of their argument was developed by Daniel Bell (1974) into one of the central pillars of his thesis that a major transition was occurring in the advanced societies from an 'industrial' to a 'post-industrial' form of social structure. In the decades after the Second World War there had been a progressive change from an economic structure based primarily on manufacturing industry to one that was dominated by the service sector. This expansion of the service sector, he concluded, inevitably brought about a major expansion of non-manual occupations.

These arguments were largely based upon trends in the occupational structure in the USA. Such changes, however, were also evident in Britain. Inter-census comparisons show that whereas clerical workers constituted only 4.8 per cent of the occupied population in 1911, they had risen to 14.8 per cent in 1981 (Routh, 1987: 74). In the post-war period, the growth in the professional and managerial categories has been even more remarkable. Routh (1987: 69) estimates that professional workers increased from 4.6 per cent in 1931 to 14.7 per cent of the occupied population by 1981. Between 1971 and 1981, when the occupied population grew by only 1.5 per cent, the number of professionals grew by 34.4 per cent (1987: 67). While precise estimates of the size of the professional and managerial categories are very sensitive to the particular methods of occupational classification, the overall picture of the direction and magnitude of change remains remarkably consistent. It is clear that in the period 1951 to 1981, the professions and the managerial and administrative categories have been by far the fastest growing sector of the work-force (Routh, 1987: 28, 37–8; IER, 1987: 30). While the non-manual categories were rapidly expanding, the manual work-force was declining in both relative and absolute terms. The combined effect of these changes was to transform the occupational structure of British society. On the eve of the First World War nearly 80 per cent of the occupied population were manual workers. By 1987 the active population was roughly evenly divided between the manual and non-manual categories: 48 per cent were non-manual and 52 per cent were manual workers (Routh, 1987: 28, 38).

Bell argued that this type of shift in the occupational structure was necessarily associated with rising levels of skill and education in the work-force. Further, he believed that it contributed to other significant changes in the nature of the typical forms of work organization. The work situation of the rapidly expanding non-manual strata, he suggests, is distinctive because of the small size of the units of employment. Even where they are large – as in hospitals and colleges – they are characterized by the greater autonomy of their smaller constituent units. Particularly important, it is a work setting governed not by hierarchically structure forms of management, but by more egalitarian forms of professional control (Bell, 1974: 162). Instead of dominance by the rhythm of the machine and the consequent dehumanization of work, the new pattern of work is inherently personalized: 'what is central to the new relationship is encounter or communication . . . the fact that individuals now talk to other individuals, rather than interact with a machine, is the fundamental fact about work in the post-industrial society' (1974: 163). Overall the evolution of work was likely to eliminate its more alienating characteristics and to make it a greater source of personal enrichment.

The Pessimistic Scenario

During the 1970s the view that there was a necessary long-term evolution towards higher levels of skill and more participative types of work organization came under increasing criticism. This was largely associated with the re-emergence of a distinctively Marxian approach to the analysis of work organization. The most detailed and sophisticated development of this perspective had been by the great French industrial sociologist, Georges Friedmann (see especially Friedmann, 1955). However, for British sociologists – who were largely unfamiliar with the classic French literature – the major influence came rather later with the work of Braverman (1974). Following closely Friedmann's argument, Braverman posited an inherent dynamic in capitalist societies towards an ever increasing division of labour that led to the deskilling of work tasks and tighter managerial control over work performance.

Braverman was sharply critical of the view that advanced automation was leading to an improvement in the conditions of manual work. Rather, it merely accentuated the long-term trend towards the degradation of labour. The deskilling of work, he suggested, was evident from the decline of pre-job training time in the automated setting. His argument relied heavily on Bright's (1958) research, which, for the greater part, provided rather imperfect examples of highly automated work situations. However, there are a number of studies that can be seen as providing independent support for a more pessimistic reading of the impact of automation (Naville et al., 1961; Naville, 1963; Chadwick-Jones, 1969; Nichols and Beynon, 1977). Chadwick-Jones (1969: 75–107) concluded that, despite higher levels of worker satisfaction with automation, a substantial proportion of workers found the more work more boring, offering fewer opportunities for promotion and more tiring than their previous experience of work in a batch production factory. Nichols and Beynon (1977) also drew a largely negative picture of the quality of work life in the advanced automated setting. They concluded firmly in favour of the deskilling thesis: 'during this century the working classes of Europe and America have been systematically deskilled by the "progress" of capitalist production' (1977:17).

It was, however, Braverman's extension of the general argument to the growing strata of non-manual workers that formed the most interesting part of his thesis. In sharp contrast to Bell, who associated the change in the occupational structure with an increase in skill levels, Braverman argued that non-manual work – albeit with a significant time lag – was subject to precisely the same general law of the capitalist division of labour as manual work. The process, he argued, is one of an uneven development of the labour process. In the initial stages in which knowledge is extracted from craft workers and monopolized by management, there is a growth of the white-collar work-force to facilitate the transfer of knowledge and the restructuring of manual work. In this phase, white-collar workers do indeed have much more favourable working conditions than those of the manual workers whose positions they are undermining. However, as white-collar workers become increasingly central to the efficient operation of the production process, they at the same time acquire greater power to disrupt it. Hence they too come to constitute a problem for management and are subjected to the same strategies for enhancing employer control that had been developed in relation to manual work. Non-manual work is increasingly subdivided and the office is mechanized. This undercuts non-manual workers' skills and autonomy, until eventually their employment conditions become virtually indistinguishable from those of manual workers.

The major British study developing this argument has been that of Crompton and Jones (1984). Contrasting clerical work in three organizations at rather different levels of technical development, their conclusion was emphatic: 'Our case-study evidence indicates that as far as clerical work is concerned, computerisation "deskills" tasks, enhances the level of functional specialisation, and centralises control within the organisation' (1984: 53). Moreover, it was the organization that had the most sophisticated type of computer system (and hence presumably represented the pattern for the future) that had the lowest clerical skills (1984: 73). Whatever their official classification, clerical workers' skills, they argued, are effectively equivalent to those of unskilled or semi-skilled workers.

Problems in the Skill Debate

The striking feature of these attempts to develop general theories of the evolution of work is the sharp contradiction in the conclusions they reach. One explanation for this is the tendency of their proponents to underestimate the heterogeneity of work tasks in any given historical period and to assume that it is possible to generalize from the characteristics of a limited set of jobs to the overall skill structure. By selectively focusing upon different types of jobs, theorists can conjure up quite different pictures of the long-term evolution skill. For instance, in the analysis of trends in manual work, it is notable that Braverman's argument that there was a general process of deskilling in the first half of the twentieth century depends upon the characterization of the typical manual worker of the nineteenth century as a skilled craftsman; conversely, arguments about upskilling more frequently focus upon the prevalence in that period of unskilled labour. In the discussion of automation in the post-war period, it is significant that Blauner (1964: chapters 6, 7) focuses almost entirely on the work tasks of the most privileged production operators, while Nichols and Beynon (1977: 11–18) develop their thesis of the continuing degradation of work by giving a vivid description of the heavy labour of unskilled sack packers.

Much the same problem re-emerges with the discussion of the implications of the growth of non-manual work. Bell links this firmly to the growth of the service sector. However, despite occasional qualifications, he understates the extent to which the 'service sector' embraces what are in fact a very heterogeneous set of activities. Browning and Singlemann (1978) have stressed the importance of distinguishing between the producer services which provide the service requirements of other industries (for instance, banking, accounting and legal services); distributive services that are concerned with transport, communications, storage and sales for other industries; social services which provide for collective needs such as health, education, postal services, and law and order; and finally, personal services which cater for individual service requirements such as cleaning, catering and recreation.

These different types of services involve crucially different types of work task and sets of social relations. For instance, daily interpersonal contact with clients is likely to be a central feature of the work situation in the social and personal services but peripheral for many working in producer services. The different types of services are also differentiated by the extent to which they are constrained by market pressures. While some are fully exposed to competitive market pressures, others – in particular those provided by the state – are more sheltered. The frontier between marketed and non-marketed services can shift over time and differences in protection from the market are likely to be ones of degree. Nevertheless the nature of employment relations may be rather different in the two sectors. In practice, Bell constructs his model of the social dynamics of the service sector from what is in fact a limited part of it: professional and technical occupations in the non-marketed sector of the services industries. In contrast Braverman concentrates on the changing work situation of clerical and retail workers in sectors integrally related to the market.

The selective choice of examples, and the failure to take seriously the problem of assessing change across a very heterogeneous work-force, accounts then in part for the very confused picture that emerges from the literature about the evolution of work. But the difficulties clearly lie even deeper than this and relate to the problems involved in conceptualizing skill itself. The issues involved in the conceptualization of skill are taken up in detail by Richard Brown in chapter 2. For the moment it is sufficient to note that the 'optimistic' and 'pessimistic' scenarios frequently use the concept of skill in rather different ways. For instance, the key measure of skill for Braverman would appear to be the extent to which a task requires prior training. It is, then, premised on the craft model of skill. The essence of the position advanced by authors such as Blauner and Woodward, however, is that the nature of skill is changing in a way that makes this type of measure altogether misleading. When, as in the automated setting, skill primarily involves the capacity to assume responsibility and to exercise judgement in the face of relatively unpredictable problems, the expertise required must be drawn partly from general educational skills and partly from experience acquired on the job. If the nature of skill has changed in this fashion, however, there are evident difficulties for theorists of both camps in finding the type of common measure that would be need to make convincing claims about trends in skill levels between different historical periods.

An analagous problem arises with the issue of 'tacit' skills. With the growth of interest in the problem of the occupational classification of women's jobs, it has been argued that women formally classified by their employers as semi-skilled or as unskilled are often deploying quite complex skills acquired in the domestic sphere. The most common examples are sewing, wiring and social skills. Employers, it is maintained, take for granted such skills and fail to recognize them. They are encouraged in this by trade unions which are primarily concerned with protecting the employment conditions of full-time male workers. The relative ranking of such tacit skills, however, would appear to pose major difficulties for sociologists as well as for employers. It is notable, for instance, that Crompton and Jones (1984: 66, 254), who emphasized strongly the importance of tacit skills, none the less based their empirical work on an 'objective' measure of skill that largely discounted them. Somewhat paradoxically, they concluded that female clerical workers were largely unskilled, despite the importance of contact with the public in such jobs and the fact that this could require 'the exercise of considerable tact and social skills – for example, dealing with the recently bereaved' (1984: 146).

In short, there appears to be little consensus between analysts about what consitutes skill or how it is to be measured. The term covers a number of distinct capacities that are difficult to compare directly. A more refined analysis might focus on the evolution of different types of skill rather than on skill *per se*. The very complexity of the task of defining skill, however, makes it implausible that skill classifications in industry reflect in an unproblematic way some objective hierarchy. Rather, they are likely to be the product of a continuous negotiation between employers and employees, in which both relative power resources and prevalent cultural beliefs will influence the grading structure. Moreover, the scope for such negotiation is not confined to the value to be attached to tasks predetermined by the character of specific technologies or by some inherent law of the capitalist division of labour. As will be seen, the major development in research has been to emphasize the extent to which there can be choice about the way in which work tasks can be structured. The analysis of skill trends therefore leads inexorably into a consideration of employer policies with regard to work organization and of the structure of power relations in which these are formed.

Management Strategies and Worker Resistance

A common aspect of these general theories of the evolution of work is the deterministic nature of their causal assumptions. In the optimistic scenario it is the nature of technology that narrowly determines the character of work tasks and the pattern of work organization, whereas in the pessimistic scenario it is the single-directional and universal law of the capitalist division of labour. There have been, however, long-standing currents within the British research tradition that have pointed to a very different way of understanding the issues of skill and control. The first of these placed a strong emphasis on managerial choice in structuring work organizations and the second, largely represented in the separate discipline of industrial relations, linked the analysis of the internal dynamics of work organizations to trade-union power. By the early 1980s there was growing criticism among industrial sociologists of deterministic theories of the evolution of work and, in elaborating this, they came to broaden considerably the scope of inquiry into the determinants of work organization.

From the late 1940s, the research carried out by members of the Tavistock Institute was significant for its emphasis on managerial choice in the structuring of work tasks and the implementation of control of work performance. Although largely rooted in traditions of industrial psychology, their lengthy programme of empirical research in the coal-mining industry led them into a consideration of the linkages between technology, work organization and worker satisfaction. Their findings, brought together by Trist et al. (1963) ran counter to the central assumptions of the thesis that Braverman was later to advance in a number of crucial ways. First, they suggested that a system of work organization based on a high degree of division of labour and a low level of worker autonomy generated deep-rooted dissatisfaction without being conducive to any very high level of efficency. Secondly, they indicated that 'composite' group systems that provided workers with a wider range of skills and gave work teams substantial autonomy in selecting their membership, allocating work tasks and determining work pace were likely to improve output and, at the same time, to replace job alienation by 'task-oriented commitment' (1963: 214).

Methods of work organization, they concluded, while constrained by the technology and the financial position of the firm, were none the less significantly open to managerial choice.

While the work of the Tavistock School was virtually ignored by the new generation of British labour process theorists of the 1970s, their basic insights were assimilated into the debate through Andrew Friedman's influential *Industry and Labour* (1977). Friedman's central criticism of Braverman's argument was that employers could deploy and indeed had deployed quite diverse strategies in their attempts to control worker performance. Friedman's work echoes the distinctions drawn by the Tavistock School by pointing to the viability of two broad types of strategy. The first, 'direct control', is essentially the strategy that Braverman viewed as universal; the second, the strategy of 'responsible autonomy', involves giving workers status, authority and responsibility by establishing small work teams with some degree of decision-making power. For Friedman, the development of capitalism has been associated, not with intensification of direct control, but with an extension of the scope of managerial choice (1977: 74–101).

Friedman's conclusions were based on an historical study of the policies of British employers in three industries. However, the same general conclusions about the range of viable managerial policies emerged just as clearly from cross-cultural studies carried out at this time. For instance, Dore (1973: chapter 9) documented the very different managerial policies in the British and Japanese engineering industries, emphasizing the distinctive role of the internal labour market and a team ethos in generating employee commitment in larger Japanese companies. Similarly, research on employment relations in the French and British oil industries (Gallie, 1978: chapter 9) revealed that, even with virtually identical types of technology, the forms of managerial control could be altogether dissimilar. In an advanced automated setting British management had decentralized control over the immediate work process to the work groups, while French management exercised tight supervisory control, gave its workers little discretion and undercut the cohesion of work groups through a highly individualized salary system.

One development that might be thought to have called into question the conclusion of these studies is the rapidity of technical change. By the later 1970s, it was becoming clear that the application of microprocessors was making possible the extension of automation to most types of production. Developments in robotics and direct numerical control meant that automation could be introduced not only in most forms of large-batch production, but also in small and medium-batch manufacturing. At the same time the diffusion of word processors and other types of electronic equipment was producing a rapid transformation of office work. The 1980s, saw a major growth of research into the implications of new technology. The evidence about the way in which new technology has affected the nature of clerical work is surveyed in detail by Christel Lane in chapter 3, while Roderick Martin examines its impact on manual work in chapter 4. Those engaged in this research appeared often to have little familiarity with the accumulated body of knowledge on earlier phases of automation, yet the conclusions that emerged from their work were remarkably similar. The introduction of automation itself has few clear implications for either skill levels or patterns of work organization. Rather, what would appear to be decisive are the organizational philosophies that underlie the way in which automation is introduced. In short, the view that there is a single logic of control looked increasingly implausible in the light of the empirical studies that had been carried out; rather it was clear that analysis needed to focus on the causes and implications of quite diverse strategies of control (Gospel and Littler, 1983; Knights and Willmott, 1986).

A second current within the British research tradition that conflicted with the deterministic assumptions of the general theories of change was concerned with the nature of shopfloor power. In the post-war period ethnographic studies (Lupton, 1963; Beynon, 1973: chapter 6) gave a detailed view of the way in which work groups could under certain conditions, impose their own controls over management systems that had been originally introduced with a view to individualizing workers and maximizing effort. At the same time, the 'Oxford School' of Industrial Relations, and its later incarnation in the Industrial Relations Research Unit at Warwick, focused attention on the growth of shop steward power and the development of complex systems of joint regulation in the workplace (Clegg, 1979; Flanders, 1970; Batstone et al., 1977, 1978). While the longer term implications of the growth of shop steward power were a subject of much dispute (Hyman, 1975; Batstone, 1984), at lease in the shorter term it clearly constituted a substantial constraint on management's capacity to impose its policies unilaterally (Flanders, 1964; 1970). As industrial relations research revealed, the 1960s and 1970s witnessed not only a major extension of shop-floor organization across British industry, but also a substantial increase in the range of workplace bargaining that was to prove remarkably resilient even in the difficult economic context of the 1980s (Brown (ed.), 1981; Daniel and Millward, 1983; Batstone, 1984; Millward and Stevens, 1986).

In their work in the late 1970s and early 1980s, British industrial sociologists brought together the earlier insights into the range of variable patterns of work organization that could be deployed with any given technology with the knowledge acquired from industrial relations research about the extensiveness of informal work group job controls and shop steward bargaining power. The critical thrust of their criticism of the general theories of skill and control was that employers' strategies were likely to vary, not only because of differences in managerial philosophy, but also because they had to take into account the capacities of resistance of the work-force. Thus Friedman suggested that Taylorite techniques tended to increase worker dissatisfaction and facilitate collective resistance, leading employers to respond to organized worker strength by shifting to strategies of 'responsible autonomy' (1977: 79–81, 945). Gallie (1978) argued that the more coercive forms of control to be found in French factories reflected the deep internal divisions between the French trade unions and their consequent lack of strike power, while the greater reliance on decentralization to the work group in British factories was a response to much more powerful forms of workplace trade unionism. Penn (1982, 1985) pointed to the capacity of craft workers in the British engineering industry to resist deskilling and to use their organizational strength to maintain their market power through strategies of exclusion and Jones (1982) pointed to the importance of the character of trade unionism in influencing decisions about task design and skill levels with the introduction of numerical control in engineering.

There was, then, growing support for a 'power model' of the employment relationship that took account not only of the variable character of employer policies, but also of the influence of worker resistance. Given the important explanatory status now given to worker resistance, there was remarkably little research into its forms and dynamics. Indeed, there was a notable lack of systematic empirical evidence of the extent to which it did in fact influence managerial policies towards work organization or of the conditions under which such influence might vary. A new research agenda, however, had been set that involved exploration of the changing nature of employee expectations and demands, of the sources of variation in patterns of resistance and of the determinants of different levels of employee control. A number of chapters in Part I of this book take stock of what is currently a highly fragmentary body of research.

The nature of viable patterns of employer control and the level of employee resistance are likely to be heavily affected by the attitudes and expectations that employees bring to the work situation. A common argument is that there has been a long-term change in work attitudes, characterized by the decreasing importance of an internalized work ethic. As intrinsic interest in and commitment to employment has slipped away, dissatisfaction with an essentially coercive work situation has increased and resistance to authority has become more systematic. In chapter 5, Michael Rose underlines the poorly substantiated nature of this argument and its crucial dependence upon weakly based assumptions about work attitudes in earlier historical periods. More credible, he suggests, is the view that there has been an increased diversification of work values – with a stronger emphasis on individualism and self-actualization. Such value changes do not necessarily generate increased resistance at work, but they do have considerable implications for the types of work organization with which people are likely to be satisfied.

In a period in which women have come to constitute a much higher proportion of the work-force, one of the major issues that an analysis of work attitudes needs to confront is the extent to which expectations differ by gender. A number of studies have suggested that women have rather different priorities in employment from men and that they show higher levels of satisfaction with objectively less satisfactory employment conditions. This, together with the possibly lower importance of employment to their overall life interests, is arguably a source of lower participation in trade unions and greater deference to managerial authority. Kate Purcell takes up these issues in her discussion of women's experience of employment in chapter 6.

She casts a sceptical eye on the existing evidence for major differences in work values. Apparent differences, she suggests, reflect primarily a recognition of the objective nature of the opportunities that are available rather than any fundamental difference in aspirations. The main differences in women's experience of work derive not from differences in work priorities, but from the way in which gender affects social interaction in work – reinforcing women's sense of subordinate status, generating distinctive gender-based patterns of tension and making it more difficult for them to participate fully within their organizations. Such problems affect relations with fellow workers as much as with management. If women are less likely to participate in trade unions, she suggests, this is not due to greater docility or to higher levels of satisfaction, but to the poor welcome they receive from the unions. Women resist their employers, but their resistance is likely to take less conventional institutional forms.

Certainly a notable feature of the literature is the tendency to use the concept of 'worker resistance' in a global way, without distinguishing the different forms it might take or trying to understand the conditions under which the particular types of resistance emerge. The importance of taking into account the full range of patterns of resistance is emphasized by P.K. Edwards in chapter 7. The literature has focused heavily on the strike as the acid test of levels of resentment. But, in practice, resistance can take forms as varied as individual fiddles, pilfering, sabotage, individual bargaining, quitting and absenteeism, as well as organized collective resistance. The meaning of particular actions - indeed whether they actually constitute resistance – depends crucially upon the type of bargaining context in the firm. Conflict, Edwards argues, is inherent in the employment relationship and the supresion of resistance in one form may simply lead to its re-emergence in another. He examines the way in which the particular form that predominates is influenced by the wider structure of workplace relations, the extent to which the technology and employment conditions promote group awareness, the nature of the product and labour markets and the type of workplace culture that has developed over time.

There is little evidence, then, that long-term changes are occurring in employee attitudes either as a result of value changes or of changes in the composition of the work-force that are likely in themselves either to intensify or reduce levels of resistance to employer authority. Rather, changes in work values and changes in the composition of the work-force may be altering the sources of friction and the forms of resistance that emerge. However, there is no necessary transition from resistance, even of a collective type, to control over aspects of managerial decision-making. The analysis of the complex set of factors that do account for the level of employee control is the focus of Eric Batstone's discussion in chapter 8. Batstone shows that the view that the frontier of control is determined by the type of production technology is implausible in the light of the evidence. He also argues that there has been a tendency to overestimate the significance of labour market conditions; rather, over the longer period, union control has become increasingly immune to adverse labour market conditions. The reason for this, he suggests, is that there is an internal logic to the process of institutionalization, whereby once initiated it gains its own momentum, influences the attitudes and actions of those involved, and is thereby protected from short-term fluctuations in contextual conditions affecting the balance of power. Finally, he underlines the central importance of the character of employer organizations, the internal structure of trade unions and the role of the state in establishing and consolidating the broader institutional system that conditions the influence that workers can wield within the workplace.

The Social Organization of the Labour Market

One central development, then, in industrial sociology from the mid-1970s was an awareness of the need to take account of variations in employer strategies and the extent of collective worker power. At the same time, however, there was a growing realization that an analysis of the dynamics of social relations in the workplace required a more systematic analysis of the structure of labour markets. Indeed by the 1980s this had changed in a fundamental way the nature of research in the subject. Until the late 1960s, it was usually assumed that the dynamics of social relations within the workplace could be understood primarily in terms of factors internal to the establishment. The implications of new types of technology, specific modes of supervision, types of work group and procedures of industrial relations were treated as though they were largely unaffected by the recruitment patterns of firms, the prior labour market experiences of individual employees or the broader conditions of local and national labour markets. Two developments were particularly important in undercutting these assumptions. The first was the emergence of an 'action theory' approach that emphasized the importance of worker expectations; the second was the growing interest in the nature of women's employment.

The Orientation to Work of Manual Workers

A major challenge to 'closed system' assumptions came from *The Affluent Worker* study in the 1960s (Goldthorpe et al., 1968, 1969). This was to have a substantial influence on research for the next decade through its powerful development of the thesis that the intrinsic characteristics of the work situation were in themselves wholly indeterminate. In sharp contrast to approaches that argued that workers' attitudes were primarily determined by technology, the authors maintained that attitudes to any given type of technology would depend crucially upon the prior orientations that workers brought to the workplace. Their own study included what was normally held to be one of the work settings that was most likely to generate resentment with the production process – the car factory assembly line. Yet their empirical findings showed that workers were largely satisfied with their employment conditions. The explanation for this, they argued, was that workers were self-selected. They were people who were primarily concerned to maximize income and who had deliberately chosen employment in these firms to achieve this objective. By implication processes of recruitment, worker preferences and the nature of the available pool of labour become crucial for understanding the social relations of production and the patterns of work organization that were viable without generating high levels of resistance.

Although not systematically developed, many of the underlying assumptions about the operation of the labour market in this study appear to be close to those of neo-classical economics. The broad stratum of the labour market in which job opportunities were available was decisively influenced by people's educational achievement (although the authors were very conscious of the social as distinct from the individual determinants of education success). Within the manual sector, however, individual preferences were becoming increasingly important in determining the types of jobs that workers occupied. In the past, the closed and static nature of communities had restricted people's knowledge of the range of options open to them. However, the general trend in the developing structure of industrial society was towards the disintegration of traditional communities and much higher levels of geographical mobility, thereby increasing the possibilities for rational job choice. At the same time, income maximization was becoming the dominant factor in worker preferences – as the growing importance of family life and consumer values undercut the centrality of work to people's identities. Increasingly, 'workers act as "economic men", seeking to minimize effort and maximize economic returns; but the latter concern is the dominant one' (Goldthorpe et al., 1968: 38–9). In short, however inadequate a market model was for the analysis of the past, it was thought to be increasingly appropriate as societies reached more advanced levels of industrialization.

The work of Goldthorpe et al. was a powerful stimulus to extending the definition of the field of inquiry of industrial sociology to include the operation of the labour market. The outstanding empirical study that came out of this phase of research was Blackburn and Mann's *The Working Class in the Labour Market* (1979). Combining a detailed study of the objective character of non-skilled jobs in the Peterborough labour market with a survey of workers' attitudes, the authors challenged the neo-classical assumptions of the 'orientations to work' approach on a number of points. First, they pointed to the relatively closed nature of access to the 'better' jobs even in this sector of the labour market. Far from workers being free to shift from one job to another in an attempt to maximize their interests, they were confronted with a situation in which access to more interesting jobs was dependent upon movement upwards through an internal labour market. Moreover, these moves were determined not so much by skill as by demonstrating to employers a high level of compliance and co-operativeness (Blackburn and Mann, 1979: 102–9). Secondly, their data cast doubt on whether workers had the type of stable, well-ordered preferences that were assumed in the 'calculative' model of job selection advanced by *The Affluent Worker* studies. Only about half the workers they interviewed show substantial stability in the criteria they used in assessing different potential employers. Moreover, orientations were rarely of a 'strong' type in which one or two types of job reward were of predominant importance. Rather, workers attached importance to a whole range of factors in weighing up a job, making the calculation of the overall advantages of any specific job relative to another inherently difficult (1979: 136, 141–76). Finally the exercise of choice was made difficult by the very restricted nature of workers' knowledge of the details of the terms offered by different employers in the labour market – a result partly of the limited information that employers themselves made available (1979: 112–25). Given this very low visibility of the pattern of job rewards on offer, it was implausible that workers could select jobs rationally in terms of the multiple criteria to which they attached importance.

Mann and Blackburn's study cast major doubts about the value of an analysis of labour markets that placed primary emphasis on worker preferences as the determinants of job allocation. However, while their work pointed in a fragmentary way to some of the crucial processes that an adequate theory of the operation of labour markets would need to take into account, they offered little in the way of a systematic alternative approach to labour market structure.

The Growth of Female Employment

The second major impetus to the development of a sociology of the labour market lay in the major expansion of female participation in the labour force. Between 1951 and 1986 the female participation rate rose from 34.7 per cent to 46.8 per cent (Joseph, 1983: 126; IER, 1978: 20). Moreover, by the late 1970s, female participation had become the dynamic factor in the growth of the labour force: between 1971 and 1986, the entire increase of the labour force by 1.8 million can be accounted for by the increase in the number of women in the labour force (*Social Trends*, 1988: 67–8). Differential trends in participation rates were associated with a marked change in women's share of overall employment. Women constituted around 39.4 per cent of all employees in 1986; compared with 29.8 per cent in 1954 (IER, 1987: 98). In short, it was clear that a striking change was occurring in the gender composition of the work-force. Why this was occurring and with what consequences now became a central issue of debate. In good part due to an unusually ambitious and imaginative research programme launched by the Department of Employment, research in this area was to be one of the major contributions to the sociology of employment in the 1980s (Martin and Roberts, 1984; Joshi, 1984; Dex, 1984; Cragg and Dawson, 1984).

The major expansion of women's employment also altered significantly the terms of the research agenda with regard to the organization of work. In part this was because female employment had certain distinctive characteristics. This was particularly evident in the extent to which women were involved in part-time work. Moreover, the increase in part-time work was striking: in 1951, part-timers represented only 4 per cent of total employment, by 1987 they constituted 23 per cent (Hakim, 1987: 556). To some extent this could be related to the fact that the most significant source of the rise of women's labour force participation had been the increased involvement of married women. Part-time workers were drawn principally from married women, in particular married women with dependent children (Martin and Roberts, 1984: 15). In comparative perspective, however, it is clear that an adequate explanation would need to be a good deal more complex. Britain has exceptionally high levels of part-time work, and the reasons for this posed a central issue for the analysis of the interrelationship between patterns of work organization and the structure of labour markets (Beechey and Perkins, 1987; Rubery, 1988). It focused attention on the different ways in which employers could seek to achieve flexibility, on the influence of legal and fiscal systems and on the variations between societies in the availability of childcare provision.

A second issue that was highlighted by the growth of women's employment was the extent of gender segregation. If the market was competitive, as neo-classical theory postulated, and the sellers of labour power were individual decision-makers primarily concerned with income maximization, it seemed strange that the pattern of job allocation should be one that involved such a very high level of occupational concentration. For instance, in 1986 women employees represented 79.8 per cent of all clerical and secretarial occupations and 69.5 per cent of sales and personal service workers. On the other hand, they constituted only 36 per cent of managers, 39.9 per cent of professional and related workers and 22.9 per cent of operatives and labourers (IER, 1987: 29). Similarly, there were marked variations in women's level of employment in different industrial sectors. They represented only 29 per cent of the work-force in manufacturing (disproportionately concentrated in specific industries such as textiles and clothing), but an overall majority of (58 per cent) of the work-force in government, health and education (IER, 1987: 28). Moreover, there was even more striking evidence of gender segregation at the level of particular establishments: fully 63 per cent of women were in a work setting where only women did their kind of work (Martin and Roberts, 1984: 26).

In short, once the centrality to the employment structure of women's work was recognized, it became markedly more difficult to ignore the need for a thorough exploration of labour market processes. It heightened the awareness that levels of labour market participation required explanation and more specifically focused attention on the determinants of the rise in women's participation. At the same time, the changing gender composition of the work-force posed new issues about the character of work organizations. It highlighted aspects of the employment contract and of the distribution of tasks by gender that had been left largely unexamined. The early 1980s, then, saw a major growth of interest among British sociologists in the analysis of the labour market. This brought them, however, none too self-confidently, into a terrain that had been conventionally left to economists and, indeed, which had been a central war-zone between different groups of economists.

Conceptualizations of the Labour Market

The difficulties for sociologists were compounded by the overwhelming dominance in British economics of neo-classical theory. Despite its awesome powers of calibration, it rapidly became clear that its central assumptions fitted rather poorly with the empirical evidence that sociologists had been accumulating about labour market processes. In neo-classical theory workers are allocated to particular jobs on the basis of their natural endowments or of their investment in human capital in the form of education and training. Mobility between jobs is assumed to be largely unproblematic and the market therefore offers equality of opportunity. It is a conception that focuses primarily on differences of pay as the factor that distinguishes jobs and guides job choice and it assumes that there is a tendency for the pay rewards of workers at any given level of skill to become increasingly similar under the pressure of market forces. Labour is essentially regarded as homogeneous and differences relating to factors such as sex or ethnicity should not in themselves affect market outcomes. It was wholly unclear how assumptions such as these could be accommodated to the growing evidence about the nature of employer recruitment criteria, the importance of internal labour markets in firms, the limited nature of employees' knowledge about job rewards in other firms in the local labour market, the weakly defined character of their own preferences and the importance of social constraints on educational attainment. Moreover, neo-classical theory appeared to offer little in the way of explanatory ideas for some of the key problems that had originally drawn sociologists towards this area of inquiry, in particular the very variable nature of employment contracts and the striking levels of gender segregation in the employment structure.

In this situation, the developing body of theory on labour market segmentation appeared to offer an attractive alternative conceptualization of labour market processes to which sociological concepts and research could be related much more easily. The major early influences were the work of the American economists Piore and Edwards (Doeringer and Piore, 1971: Berger and Piore, 1981; Edwards et al., 1975; Edwards, 1979). The importance that they attached to employer policies in the determination of job structures, their awareness of the constraints on individual choices and their concern with the structured nature of inequality fitted closely with sociological concerns. However, their insistence on a highly simplified model of labour market structure, with its critical distinction between a primary sector of highly paid and secure jobs offering significant promotion opportunities and a secondary sector of insecure, poorly paid and dead-end jobs, was ultimately to prove of limited value for understanding empirical patterns of employment. For, in Britain at least, internal labour markets were not particularly extensive in firms that on other criteria would usually have been allocated to the primary sector, while there was little evidence that women's work, despite its marked disadvantages in terms of pay and promotion, was associated with the type of insecurity that was fundamental to the theory of the secondary sector.

For British sociologists in search of an analytical framework that could grapple with the evident complexity of labour market structures, a particularly helpful body of work was that by Labour Studies Group at the Department of Economics at Cambridge (Rubery, 1978; Wilkinson, 1981: Wilkinson, 1983; Labour Studies Group, 1985). Indeed, among British researchers, they made perhaps the most important contribution in the early 1980s to the development of a sociological conceptualization of the labour market. While retaining a sharp critique of the assumptions of neo-classical theory, they at the same time rejected any simple model of the boundaries of labour market segments. Employer policies, and changes in industrial structure, were still regarded as the major determinants of employment opportunities rather than labour supply conditions. However, employer policies were not determined in any simple way by the capital intensiveness of firms, by the nature of the product market, or by some universal logic of the capitalist division of labour.

Instead the Labour Studies Group have focused on three major influences on employer labour force policies. The first is the role of the trade unions in regulating employment conditions. This, they argued, is heavily affected by the historically conditioned character and structure of the trade-union movement and of national systems of collective bargaining. In Britain, where legal regulation has been weak and workplace bargaining strong, the unions have played a crucial role in defining labour market boundaries and determining the nature of employment conditions. The second major institutional influence is the state – both because of its ability as a major employer to establish models of acceptable forms of labour organization and through its legislative impact on the system of labour market regulation. Again the character of state intervention differs markedly between societies, generating quite distinctive modes of labour market regulation with different patterns of incentives and constraints for employer labour force policies and for labour market participation. Finally, they underline the significance of the 'system of social reproduction'. At one level this involves the social organization of the family: the way in which patterns of socialization influence aspirations for particular types of employment and the domestic division of labour constrains choices in ways that generate a source of relatively cheap labour irrespective of the level of skill. At another, it focuses attention on the role of the educational system and the processes of selection within it that determine the social distribution skills.

In short, it is a conception of the labour market that rejects the search for simple universal laws of labour market structure and development in favour of an analysis of the interplay of the historically conditioned institutional structures that generate specific systems of labour market regulation. It places a central emphasis on the empirical investigation of the nature and sources of change rather than the development of complex deductive models based upon highly simplified assumptions about the determinants of human behaviour.

Empirical Research on the Labour Market in the 1980s

Alongside these efforts to develop a broader interpretative framework, there was a growth in the 1980s of empirical projects examining specific aspects of labour market processes. These focused in particular upon the changing character of employer labour force policies, upon the extent and stability of labour market disadvantage due to gender, race and unemployment, and on the influence on the labour market of changes in the household and in the educational system. The chapters in Part II of this book provide an overview of the current state of research on these issues.

The role of employer policies. One central debate has been whether changes are occurring in employer strategies that are fundamentally restructuring the types of job opportunities available. The initial impetus came principally from the various versions of 'dualist' or 'segmentation' theory, directing attention to whether British employers were developing internal labour markets for their core workers, while creating secondary sector jobs to handle fluctuations in demand. By the mid-1980s, however, the terms of debate had shifted to whether employers were seeking to implement more generalized policies of flexibility which embraced both the core and the secondary work-forces. This view is particularly associated with the work of Atkinson (1985) who suggested that, given the increasing uncertainty of product markets, employers have been reducing and restructuring their core work-forces, as well as seeking to maximize numerical flexibility through the use of temporary workers, part-time workers and subcontractors.

In chapter 9, Jill Rubery assesses the evidence about the impact of, and direction of change in, employer policies. She concludes that there can be little doubt about the importance of employer policies for determining job structures, pay, and employment conditions. However, the distinctive characteristic of the labour market in Britain is the relative absence of national institutional regulation and the importance of workplace industrial relations. This implies that employer decision-making is highly decentralized and the nature of employer policies correspondingly diverse. Overall, there is little sign of a major shift towards the creation of internal labour markets. Similarly, while there have certainly been a number of highly visible cases of employers seeking to implement much higher levels of flexibility, and accumulating evidence about the prevalence of different forms of non-standard employment, there is little evidence of the type of generalized drive for change that Atkinson had anticipated.

Patterns of labour market disadvantages. A second major body of research has focused on the persistence of structural inequalities in the labour market. Shirley Dex, in chapter 10, outlines the striking differentials in pay between men and women and emphasizes that these have largely survived attempts at legislative intervention. While human-capital theorists have substantially elaborated their theories to account for these differences, the evidence suggests that these can at best offer only a partial explanation. Of major importance are the disadvantages that women suffer from their high level of concentration in part-time work and from the fact that employers define skills in ways that systematically underestimate women's skill levels. Dex examines the research that has sought to account for the high level of occupational segregation, which is also an important factor underlying inequalities of pay. While one explanation lies in the socially conditioned nature of women's occupational choices, it is also clear that employers structure opportunities – particularly through part-time work – in ways that are likely to generate or at least reinforce segregation. Finally, she addresses the debate about whether female employment also involves the disadvantage of heightened job insecurity. On one interpretation it has constituted a 'reserve army' that has been highly vulnerable to fluctuations in demand. Dex finds the evidence in support of this view weak. The fact that women are disproportionately concentrated in part-time jobs in the service sector, while reinforcing many other aspects of labour market disadvantage, has none the less sheltered them from the worst effects of the recession.

A second major source of labour market disadvantage that has been examined in recent research is ethnicity. In chapter 11, Richard Jenkins focuses upon the situation of black people in Britain and of Catholics in Northern Ireland. Both are disproportionately crowded into the lower ranges of the occupational structure and, most notably, both suffer from exceptionally high levels of unemployment. The unemployment rate of black people is about twice that of white people; and Catholic men are more than twice as likely to be unemployed as Protestant men. The major legal reforms of the 1970s were largely unsuccessful in reducing inequalities. Instead, recession sharpened them by decimating the industries to which the ethnic minorities had been recruited and by increasing competition in the labour market. The disadvantages of the ethnic minorities, Jenkins argues, cannot be attributed primarily to educational differences. Even at similar educational levels their opportunities are still markedly worse. Rather it is the nature of the recruitment process and the criteria used for selection that are decisive. In the first place, research has revealed substantial employer discrimination in recruitment. Secondly, with the recession, there has been an accentuation of the tendency to rely on informal methods of recruitment, utilizing the social networks of current employees. This increases social closure and gives priority to the kin and friends of the more securely placed workers of the dominant ethnic group.

The most dramatic increase in labour market inequality in the 1980s has been due to the rise in unemployment. Even on the official count, whereas 5.6 per cent of the active population had been unemployed in 1979, by 1982 this had risen to 11.9 per cent and by 1984 to 13.2 per cent. It affected particularly sharply the ethnic minorities, young school leavers, older workers and non-skilled manual workers. The analysis of the nature of the unemployed and the consequences of the experience of unemployment became a central focus of research in the 1980s and the literature is reviewed by Catherine Marsh in chapter 12. One of the most controversial issues has concerned the severity of the impact of unemployment. For some unemployment was seen as a choice on the part of people who found that benefit payments secured them a standard of living comparable with that in employment (Minford, 1983). Marsh concludes that the great majority of the unemployed suffer from a sharp decline in income when they lose their job, while a major programme of research into the social psychological consequences of unemployment has demonstrated the severity of its impact on psychological well-being. The view that unemployment has been chosen by any significant proportion of those affected seems implausible in the light of the evidence. Overall, the impact of unemployment has been greatly to increase inequalities of labour market experience by class, ethnicity and region.

In short, research into patterns of labour market disadvantage has concluded rather heavily against the view that these can be ascribed to the choices or deficiencies of individuals. Much more important would appear to be factors such as cultural norms affecting job allocation, the overall level of demand in the economy, the spatial distribution of industry, the nature of employer recruitment policies and the forms of national institutional regulation of the labour market. In addition, there has been a growing interest in the influence on labour market behaviour and opportunities of supply-side factors such as the household, local social networks and educational institutions.

The household, social networks and educational institutions. The influence of cultural norms governing the division of domestic responsibilities has long been recognized as a major influence on women's labour market choices and opportunities. They help to account both for the discontinuous nature of women's employment experiences and for their preference for, or acceptance of, part-time work. What has been more controversial is whether there has been a long-term trend of change. The view that there has been a tendency towards a redefinition of gender roles, involving a more egalitarian distribution of household responsibilities, was elaborated most influentially by Young and Willmott (1973). By the early 1980s, however, this evolutionary thesis had been replaced by a perspective that emphasized the wide potential variation in 'household work strategies'. Households were now viewed as largely independent decision-making units, making consensual choices about the distribution of different kinds of work (Pahl, 1984).

The assumptions behind both these approaches are analysed by Lydia Morris in chapter 13. Recent research has revealed the persisting strength of gender norms and the importance of external constraints in structuring household 'decisions'. Even in the context of male unemployment, the extent of change in the household division of labour is in practice very limited. This reflects both the importance of traditional roles to personal identity and the way in which supplementary benefit rules penalize women's employment in a situation in which the main type of work available is low-paid part-time work (Harris, 1987). In general, while there is some evidence of changes in general roles in the household, the primary responsibility for both housekeeping and childrearing remains with the women and there is little sign of the disappearance of this constraint on their labour market choices and opportunities.

A second developing area of research has focused on the role of social networks. The traditional emphasis on the individual decision-maker in the labour market would appear to be doubly incorrect. It fails to take into account that individual decisions are made in the context of the social relations of the household and it neglects the fact that the relationship between the household and the labour market is mediated by the nature of people's social networks. As Morris shows, there is now substantial evidence that these can be a vital source of information about job opportunities, influence in obtaining jobs, and support in undertaking them. They can be a significant source of financial and moral support in the context of unemployment and they may affect the strength of cultural constraints on employment choices. With high unemployment the role of social networks appears to become more important in the operation of the labour market. The work of Harris and his team on the labour market careers of redundant steelworkers in South Wales suggested that the degree of integration into local social networks affected both the speed with which new employment was acquired and the type of work obtained (Harris, 1987). Morris's own work showed that a highly developed and interconnected social network was likely to reinforce traditional gender norms about household roles and employment, whereas more privatized households found it easier to renegotiate gender roles. Moreover, in chapter 11, Jenkins emphasizes the importance of recruitment through social networks in reinforcing ethnic disadvantage in a period of recession.

Finally, there has been a renewed interest in the role of educational systems in structuring labour markets. The view that the willingness to invest in human capital through education was in any sense an ultimate explanation of later labour market careers was already implausible in the light of the extensive literature on the social determinants of educational success that emerged in the 1960s. This emphasized the central importance of family socialization for aspirations, knowledge, linguistic resources and the ease of integration into the culture of the school. While it is still too early to draw firm conclusions about the impact of the introduction of comprehensive education, the evidence collected in the 1970s showed that the growing importance of qualifications in labour market allocation did not significantly affect the probabilities of inheritance of class position between fathers and sons. Rather, education appeared to be primarily a mechanism through which prior class inequalities were reproduced (Halsey et al., 1980; Goldthorpe, 1987).

As David Ashton shows in chapter 14, the major development in research in the 1980s was to extend the analysis of sources of educational disadvantage to the situation of women and to the ethnic minorities. At the same time the focus was widened to include not only the school system itself but also the rapidly expanding systems of vocational training. The 1980s witnessed a major restructuring of the transition from school to work in the context of high youth unemployment; by the mid-1980s over a quarter of all 16 year olds were being channelled into government training schemes. However, this restructuring of training provision would not appear to have significantly altered the underlying patterns of labour market allocation. Indeed, in part because the schemes relied heavily on work experience, they have tended to reproduce existing forms of occupational differentiation. Research both on women and on the ethnic minorities suggests that the schemes consolidate rather than undermine the wider patterns of labour market disadvantage.

Economic Change, Social Stratification and Collective Organization

The 'optimistic' theories of the 1950s and 1960s had a bold vision of the way in which patterns of economic change would affect the structure of social inequality in the wider society. They would lead to the transcendance of the essentially capitalist nature of the system through a fundamental restructuring of the power structure of the enterprise, they would bring about the decline of traditional class resentments and the social integration of the employed population within the existing framework of society and they would lead to the growing acceptance and institutionalization of the trade-union movement. Each of these predictions has unleashed a fierce critical literature and has generated a substantial body of research.

To begin with, it was argued that with advanced industrialization there has been an inexorable shift in the nature of the groups that dominate the major economic institutions. The power of the private owner – whether an individual or family – has been undercut and economic control has passed to a stratum of professional managers. In a situation in which major advantages accrue to capital-intensive development and large-scale production, the capital of individual families becomes insufficient for further expansion and has to be augmented by the conversion of the firm into a joint stock company. Through successive phases of expansion, the share of capital of the founding family dwindles until ultimately it becomes merely one among many others. At the same time the atomization of the ownership interest that this involves gives effective power to those who have direct managerial control of the enterprise. Given the increased sophistication of the task of managing the giant corporations of an advanced industrial society, such executive management must be increasingly recruited on a meritocratic basis, thereby severing the links between the economic decision-makers and any specific social class background. Thus, through an evolutionary process, the specifically capitalist nature of the economic system is dismantled and power is placed in the hands of people who will be concerned with the collective interest rather than with short-term personal profit.

This general interpretation has been heavily contested from quite diverse directions. The common point, however, of these criticisms is that, while major changes have occurred in the the decision-making structures of the major enterprises, these still operate primarily in the interests of enriching the small stratum of the wealthiest people in the society. Whether directly or indirectly, ownership interests remain dominant and where these conflict with the wider collective interest – say in the provision of employment or in the quality of work life – the collective interest will be ignored. One version of this argument – that of Baran and Sweezy (1966) – accepted that effective power had been passed to managers of firms, but argued that these were compelled both by their social conditioning and by the impersonal forces of the market to continue to serve essentially capitalist interests. An alternative view rejected the underlying thesis of a separation of ownership from control, and maintained that what had occurred was an institutional restructuring of ownership control. In chapter 15, John Scott assesses the current state of this debate and in particular examines the organization of ownership interests in British industry. He argues that while, for a period, there may have been a tendency for the type of dispersal of ownership that lay at the centre of the managerialist thesis, this trend was set in reverse from the 1960s. There was now a reconcentration of ownership, but in the hands of financial institutions – such as insurance companies, investment trusts, pension funds and unit trusts – rather than of individuals. This has generated a structure of control over a wide sector of the economy that is neither 'minority control' in the traditional sense nor managerial control. It is control through a 'constellation of interests' in which the powerful shareholders have delegated their power to representatives drawn from the banks.

This creates a system in which the boards of directors have unusual autonomy from shareholder control and in which bank directors exercise far greater influence than is warranted on the basis of direct bank investment in companies. The inner circle of multiple directors is virtually exclusively male, comes from highly privileged social backgrounds and is bound by extensive kinship links. Tightly connected to the City, it uses its influence to press for high share prices at the cost of longer-term productive investment. It is mode of control that differs sharply from that in many other capitalist countries. On Scott's analysis, the strategic centres of the British economy remain not only firmly capitalist, but quite exceptionally constrained by the demand for short-term profit.

If the structure of power over the major economic institutions has remained fundamentally similar in type, how has economic change affected the nature and organization of the wider work-force? The theorists of industrialism drew a picture of an increasingly differentiated work-force in which the major traditional demarcations between types of occupation were becoming decreasingly salient as determinants of identity and as bases of collective organization. The technical transformation of traditional work tasks was undercutting the distinction between manual and non-manual work in favour of a much more finely graded stratification of the work-force by skill level. Moreover, such skills were seen to be increasingly the products of firm-specific classification systems. Thus collective identifications were being weakened both by increased vertical differentiation within employing organizations and by the increased horizontal differentiation of occupations between firms. This transformation of the stratification system was seen as leading to heightened social integration within particular enterprises and to the decline of types of collective organization that seek to bring together employee interests between firms and across different sectors of the economy.

Two major challenges to this view of the growing social integration developed in the 1970s. The first, premised on Braverman's theory of deskilling, argued that large sectors of the middle classes were being proletarianized. While the precise implications of these developments for employee identities and attitudes were left tantalizingly unspecified, the implication was that an increasingly extensive and homogeneous working class was still likely to remain resentful of the exploitative nature of society and to be favourable to more extensive class forms of union organization. The second scenario largely accepted that there was a progressive integration of the bulk of the employed population, but argued that a major new line of social division was developing between the employed on the one hand and the unemployed and underemployed on the other. This led to the fragmentation of the traditional working class, it reinforced the conservatism of its relatively privileged elements, and it created powerful new sources of social radicalism within society. These very different arguments about the impact of economic change on the pattern of social divisions are examined in chapter 16. The thesis of an emerging underclass is criticized on the grounds that it conflates social categories with quite distinct labour market situations, underestimates the degree of heterogeneity within each category and, in particular in the analysis of the unemployed, fails to take account of the high levels of turnover of the population affected. Social inequalities have certainly accentuated in the 1980s, with particularly severe implications for the ethnic minorities and for non-skilled manual workers. But, with the possible exception of the long-term unemployed, it is difficult to argue that these changes have created a qualitatively different labour market situation, generating distinctive social attitudes.

The extent to which change is thought to have occurred among those in stable employment is crucially dependent upon assumptions about the attitudes and life-styles of occupational groups in the past. For the period for which we have adequate data, the evidence for any long-term shift in the social attitudes of manual workers is decidedly thin. British workers have shown consistently very low levels of resentment of inequalities of income and wealth. But there is little sign of a decline in their attachment to trade unions for achieving their instrumental objectives. The principal change affecting manual workers would not appear to be a change in social values, but a longer-term decline in their relative weight in the occupational structure. The more significant development has been in the non-manual strata, where the 1970s saw a sharp increase in levels of unionization. However, the evidence suggests that this had little to do with the processes of deskilling that underlie the proletarianization thesis. Rather it reflected the interaction of labour market tensions with a political environment highly favourable to trade unionism. Moreover, the unionization of non-manual workers reflected faithfully the high level of fragmentation characteristic of manual unionism, thereby contributing to perpetuate lines of labour market differentiation and the difficulties of trade-union co-ordination at national level.

It is clear that the extent, modalities and strength of collective employee organization cannot be accounted for solely by reference to developments in the nature of work and of the labour market. Hence many of the theoretical accounts of trade unionism provide little purchase on the variations between trade-union movements in different capitalist societies. While there has been a general tendency towards increased occupational differentiation, the growth of non-manual occupations, the relative decline of the manufacturing work-force and the increased labour market participation of women, these changes have had rather different implications depending on the unions' historically derived structures.

As David Winchester shows in chapter 17, these changes have taken place in Britain in the context of a trade-union movement characterized by a low level of central co-ordination and by weakly defined frontiers between spheres of union influence. While the British unions adapted in the 1970s to changes in the structure of the employed population relatively succesfully in terms of membership levels, they did so at the cost of an intensification of internal competition. At the same time, the competitive federal structure of the British unions meant that they were notably unsuccessful in developing the type of central power resources that could have sustained their influence at national level at a time when government intervention in the direction of economic life had become greatly heightened. Indeed, their brief period of significant involvement in national economic regulation in the 1970s was terminated by the growth of sharp internal tensions that a decentralized structure was unable to contain. As a result organized labour entered the 1980s ill-equipped to bring pressure on an unfavourable government to modify its policies or even to develop a sustained and co-ordinated programme to influence public opinion. While union strength at workplace level remained largely intact, the balance of power at national level was heavily modified with major consequences in terms of the accentuation of class inequalities and the pursuit of a form of economic restructuring that involved exceptionally high levels of unemployment. Recession in turn undercut many of the traditional bastions of union strength and led to a severe decline in overall membership. The scenario facing the British unions in the mid-1980s was not one of progressive institutionalization, but of a struggle to prevent the erosion of their organizational strength.

Conclusion

The last decade, then, has seen two major trends in the development of sociological research into employment. In the first place, there has been a significant extension of the frontiers of the discipline. A relatively narrowly defined 'industrial sociology' became a broader based 'sociology of employment'. It became increasingly evident that an adequate analysis of the nature of work and of work organizations required a framework that embraced the influence of industrial relations and of labour market structure. This led to growing interest in authority relations in the firm, the forms of resistance and control in the workplace and the wider character of employer and trade-union organizations. At the same time, there was a growth of research into changes in the nature of employer recruitment policies, the extent and determinants of persistent forms of labour market disadvantage, and the influence of the household, local community structure and the educational system on labour market processes.

Secondly, these research developments in turn produced a significant shift in underlying assumptions about the way in which the employment relationship was structured. In was increasingly realized that work organizations could not be understood in terms of the inherent requirements of specific technologies, some simple law of the capitalist division of labour or the need to meet a set of psychological needs that were universal to all employees. Rather, employers could exercise choice in the types of work organization they wished to introduce and quite different models of work organization appeared to be viable. They could choose between different strategies of control of work performance and they could vary the character of work organizations by decisions about recruitment – for instance by decisions about the gender composition of the work-force. Research into employer policies and the constraints upon them led inexorably into a recognition of the importance of cultural and institutional factors. Moreover, these could not be seen as a mere reflection of the level of economic development, but had their own internal logics and were heavily influenced by the pattern of historical development. Hence there was a growing interest in the variability of institutional patterns between societies and the way in which these affected the character of employment relations and their wider social implications.

References

Atkinson, J. and Meager, N. 1985. *Changing Working Patterns*. London: NEDO.

Baran, P.A. and Sweezy, P.M. 1966. *Monopoly Capital*. New York: Monthly Review Press.

Batstone, E. 1984. *Working Order*. Oxford: Basil Blackwell.

—— et al. 1977. *Shop Stewards in Action*. Oxford: Basil Blackwell

—— et al. 1978. *The Social Organization of Strikes*. Oxford: Basil Blackwell.

Beechey, V. and Perkins, T. 1987. *A Matter of Hours*. Cambridge: Polity.

Bell, D. 1974. *The Coming of Post-Industrial Society*. London: Heinemann.

Berger, S. and Piore, M. 1981. *Dualism and Discontinuity in Industrial Societies*. Cambridge: Cambridge University Press.

Beynon, H. 1973. *Working for Ford.* London: Allen Lane.

Blackburn, R.M. and Mann, M. 1979. *The Working Class in the Labour Market.* London: Macmillan.

Blauner, R. 1964. *Alienation and Freedom.* Chicago: University of Chicago Press.

Braverman, H. 1974. *Labor and Monopoly Capital.* New York: Monthly Review Press.

Bright, J.R. 1958. *Automation and Management.* Boston: Harvard Business School.

Brown, W. (ed.) 1981. *The Changing Contours of British Industrial Relations.* Oxford: Basil Blackwell.

Browning, H.C. and Singlemann, J. 1978. 'The Transformation of the U.S. Labour Force: The Interaction of Industry and Occupation'. *Politics and Society,* 8, 481–509.

Chadwick-Jones, J. 1969. *Automation and Behaviour.* London: Wiley.

Clegg, H.A. 1979. *The Changing System of Industrial Relations in Great Britain.* Oxford: Basil Blackwell.

Cragg, A. and Dawson, T. 1984. 'Unemployed Women'. Research Paper No. 47. London: Department of Employment.

Crompton, R. and Jones, G. 1984. *White-Collar Proletariat.* London: Macmillan.

Daniel, W.W. and Millward, N. 1983. *Workplace Industrial Relations.* London: Heinemann.

Dex, S. 1984. 'Women's Work Histories'. Research Paper No. 46. London: Department of Employment.

Doeringer, P. and Piore, M. 1971. *Internal Labour Markets and Manpower Analysis.* Lexington, Mass: D.C. Heath.

Dore, R. 1973. *British Factory–Japanese Factory.* London: George Allen & Unwin.

Edwards, R. 1979. *Contested Terrain: The Transformation of the Workplace in the Twentieth Century.* London: Heinemann.

—— Reich, M. and Gordon, D. (eds) 1975 *Labour Market Segmentation.* Lexington, Mass: D.C. Heath.

Flanders, A. 1964. *The Fawley Productivity Agreements.* London: Faber.

—— 1970. *Management and Unions.* London: Faber.

Friedman, A.L. 1977. *Industry and Labour: Class Struggle at Work and Monopoly Capitalism.* London: Macmillan.

Friedman, G. 1955. *Industrial Society: The Emergence of the Human Problems of Automation.* Glencoe, Illinois: The Free Press.

Gallie, D. 1978. *In Search of the New Working Class.* Cambridge: Cambridge University Press.

Goldthorpe, J. 1987. *Social Mobility and Class Structure in Modern Britain.* Oxford: Clarendon Press.

—— Lockwood, D., Bechhofer, F. and Platt, J. 1968. *The Affluent Worker: Industrial Attitudes and Behaviour.* Cambridge: Cambridge University Press.

—— Lockwood, D., Bechhofer, F. and Platt, J. 1969. *The Affluent Worker in the Class Structure.* Cambridge: Cambridge University Press.

Gospel, H.F. and Littler, C.R. 1983. *Managerial Strategies and Industrial Relations.* London: Heinemann Educational Books.

Introduction 29

Hakim, C. 1987. 'Trends in the Flexible Workforce'. *Employment Gazette.* (November).
Hasley, A.H., Heath, A. and Ridge, J.M. 1980. *Origins and Destinations.* Oxford: Clarendon Press.
Harris, C.C. 1987. *Redundancy and Recession.* Oxford: Basil Blackwell.
Hyman, R. 1975. *Industrial Relations: A Marxist Introduction.* London: Macmillan.
Institute of Employment Research. 1987. *Review of the Economy and Employment.* Coventry: Institute of Employment Research.
Jones, B. 1982. 'Destruction or Redistribution of Engineering Skills'. *The Degredation of Work?* Ed. Wood, S. London: Hutchinson.
Joseph, S. 1984. *Women at Work,* Deddington, Oxford: Philip Allan.
Joshi, H. 1983. 'Women's Participation in Paid Work'. Research Paper No. 45. London: Department of Employment.
—— and Owen, S. 1984. 'How Long is a Piece of Elastic? The Measurement of Female Activity Rates in British Censuses 1951–1981. Discussion Paper No. 31. London: Centre for Economic Policy Research.
Kerr, C., Dunlop, J.T., Harbison, F. and Myers, C.A. 1960. *Industrialism and Industrial Man.* Cambridge, Mass. Harvard University Press.
Knights, D. and Willmott, H. (eds) 1986. *Managing the Labour Process.* Aldershot: Gower.
Labour Studies Group. 1985. 'Economic, Social and Political Factors in the Operation of the Labour Market'. *New Approaches to Economic Life.* Eds Roberts, B. et al. Manchester: Manchester University Press.
Lupton, T. 1963. *On the Shop Floor: Two Studies of Workshop Organization and Output.* Oxford: Pergamon.
Martin, J. and Roberts, C. 1984. *Women and Employment: A Lifetime Perspective.* London: HMSO.
Meager, N. 1986. 'Temporary Work in Britain'. *Employment Gazette,* 94, 1.
Millward, N. and Stevens, M. 1986. *British Workplace Industrial Relations 1980–1984.* Aldershot: Gower.
Minford, P. 1983. *Unemployment: Cause and Cure.* Oxford: Martin Robertson.
Naville, P. 1961. *L'automation et le travail humain.* Paris CNRS.
——1963. *Vers l'automatisme social?* Paris: Editions Gallimard.
Nichols, T. and Beynon, H. 1977. *Living with Capitalism.* London: Routledge and Kegan Paul.
Pahl, R. 1984. *Divisions of Labour.* Oxford: Basil Blackwell.
Penn, R. 1982. 'Skilled Manual Workers in the Labour Process'. *The Degradation of Labour?* Ed. Wood, S. London: Hutchinson.
—— 1985. *Skilled Workers in the Class Structure.* Cambridge: Cambridge University Press.
Robinson, O. and Wallace, J. 1984. 'Part-time Employment and Sex Discrimination Legislation in Great Britain'. Research Paper No. 43. London: Department of Employment.
Routh, G. 1987. *Occupations of the People of Great Britain.* London: Macmillan.
Rubery, J. 1978. 'Structured Labour Markets, Worker Organization and Low Pay'. *Cambridge Journal of Economics,* 2 (March).
—— (ed.) 1988. *Women and Recession.* London: Routledge & Kegan Paul.

Social Trends. 1988. London: HMSO.

Trist, E.L. et al. 1963. *Organizational Choice.* London: Tavistock.

Wedderburn, D. and Crompton, R. 1972. *Workers' Attitudes and Technology.* Cambridge: Cambridge University Press.

Wilkinson, F. (ed) 1981. *The Dynamics of Labour Market Segmentation.* London: Academic Press.

—— 1983. 'Productive Systems' *Cambridge Journal of Economics,* 7 (September/December), 413–29.

Woodward, J. 1958. *Management and Technology.* London: HMSO.

—— 1965. *Industrial Organization: Theory and Practice.* London: Oxford University Press.

—— (ed.) 1970. *Industrial Organization: Behaviour and Control.* London: Oxford University Press.

Young, M. and Wilmott, P. 1973. *The Symmetrical Family.* London: Routledge & Kegan Paul.

PART I
Employment

2 The Employment Relationship in Sociological Theory

Richard K. Brown

Introduction

Almost everyone who lives in an industrialized society will be an employee at some time during their lives. Getting a job and being employed are so commonly part of the experience of people in the industrialized world, whether 'capitalist' or 'socialist', that the status of employee and the institutions of employment are very much taken for granted. Such a situation, however, is a relatively recent development in human history. Hunters and gatherers, peasants, independent artisans and craftsmen, merchants – and slaves – all have a longer pedigree. Employment as the dominant institutionalized way of organizing work in society is a phenemonon of the last two or three centuries; and initially that was the case only in the minority of societies in Western Europe and North America, which went through an 'industrial revolution', a 'great transformation' from an economy based primarily on agriculture to one based on manufacturing industry, with all that that implied.

It can be argued that sociologists have not given the social relations of employment the close attention they deserve in view of their centrality in industrial societies of all sorts. Such a claim, somewhat modified, could certainly be derived from the discussion in this chapter. There is, however, a considerable body of material in sociology which directly or by inference provides an account of the employment relationship or of some aspect of it. Analyses of workers' attitudes and behaviour, of work organizations, and of management–worker relations inevitably imply, even if they do not explicitly state, a view of employment relationship. In the first half of the twentieth century these views were initially formulated as largely critical reactions to the assumptions of others – economists, engineers, employers, managers – and of 'common sense' about employment. Subsequently the debates about the nature of relations between employer and employee developed more autonomously within sociology itself, and drew more explicitly and to good effect on the contributions of some of the 'founding fathers' of the discipline. There is as yet no agreed account of how employment should be conceptualized and understood, and indeed it may be mistaken ever to expect such agreement. Nevertheless the discussion in this chapter of sociological approaches to the employment relationship will show the importance and relevance of the ideas developed so far, and provide some basis for a claim that the debates are progressing towards some agreed common ground rather than continually circling the same familiar points of contention.

The Early Development of Industrial Sociology

The nature of the employment relationship is clearly an issue of central importance to industrial sociology, whether or not this is explicitly acknowledged in the writings of industrial sociologists. The development of industrial sociology as a distinctive area of work, first in the USA in the 1930s and 1940s and then in Britain and Western Europe in the period immediately following the Second World War, took place largely as a response to an accumulation of empirical investigations and findings, and without much reference to the main traditions of social theory. The main theoretical preoccupation was a critique of notions of 'economic man' and the advocacy of an alternative model of 'social man'. While the criticisms were often well founded, certain assumptions were built into the alternative conceptualizations, especially that which came to be known as the Human Relations movement, which have been widely, and rightly, criticized in their turn.

'Economic Man'

Marsden (1986: 19–24) has helpfully identified five 'postulates of the mainstream neo-classical model of the labour market' within economics. the first of these, 'methodological individualism', provides the essential basis for the notion of 'economic man':

> Methodological individualism is one of the key principles under-lying neo-classical models of the labour market, and it states that the explanation of labour market processes should be sought in the interaction of individual workers and employers, each with their own set of preferences. Within each of their preference sets they are treated as utility maximisers, although this is often simplified to treating them as wealth maximisers. Economic man is an individualistic utility maximiser . . . (Marsden, 1986: 20)

There are two important elements contained within this account: that workers, and employers, should be seen as isolated individuals, and hence by implication that the employment relation is a relationship between individual actors which can be understood largely without reference to the network of other social relations in which such actors might be involved; and that such actors will act in a 'self-interested' way as utility maximizers. As Marsden indicates, this latter assumption has often been interpreted as meaning that actors will pursue their *economic* interests, narrowly conceived. However, restriction of the notion of utility to narrowly economic costs and benefits is not logically necessary, and, for example, Becker and other economists have introduced the notion of 'tastes' to provide for situations, such as discrimination on grounds of race or sex, where actors' behaviour is apparently against their narrowly economic interests (Marsden, 1986: 68–9).

Both these elements – the isolated individual and motivation by self-interest – were emphasized in one of the most well-known critical statements of the assumptions of neo-classical economics, Mayo's description of what he termed 'the rabble hypothesis'. Referring to the work of Ricardo, Mayo argued:

> I think it may be said that he bases his studies upon three limiting concepts. These are:
>
> 1 Natural society consists of a horde of unorganised individuals.
> 2 Every individual acts in a manner calculated to secure his self-preservation or self-interest.
> 3 Every individual thinks logically, to the best of his ability, in the service of this aim. (Mayo, 1949: 36–7)

He went on to assert that 'For many centuries the rabble hypothesis, in one or other form, has bedevilled all our thinking on matters involving law, government, or economics' (Mayo, 1949: 40).

Whether or not 'bedevilled' is a defensible judgement, there is no doubt about the pervasiveness and influence of the notion of economic man in considerations of employment relations right up to the present day. The idea that employment is governed by a contract freely negotiated between an individual employer and an individual employee is, for example, central to the understanding of the employment relationship in English law (Wedderburn, 1986: 106). Industrial sociology, however, and more specifically the Human Relations movement, developed in opposition not so much to the formulations of economists as such, as to the embodiment of the same basic assumptions in the ideas and activities of managers and engineers, and in particular the interpretations of industrial attitudes and behaviour offered by 'Scientific Management'.

Braverman (1974: 87) has argued that the fundamental features of the scientific management movement (what he termed 'Taylorism') 'have become the bedrock of all work design'. In contrast, Rose (1975: 32) implied that such ideas often failed in application, and other studies (e.g. Littler, 1982) have shown that in many industries the organization of work and the management of labour developed in rather different ways from those suggested by Braverman. What is clear, however, is that 'Taylorism' as an ideology incorporated assumptions about the employment relationship which were very influential at the time and have remained so, with modifications, among many engineers and managers ever since. The core features of the approach of early scientific management have been described as follows:

The worker was seen as a source of labour power which it was management's task to exploit in the most efficient manner possible. This was to be done by devising, through time and motion study, 'the one best way' of performing any particular task, and then by holding out financial inducements to the operative to work in this way up to the limits of his physical capacity. The individual worker, it was assumed, would always seek to avoid the 'pain' of labour by operating below his full capacity unless he was given the prospect of 'pleasure' in the form of increased earnings for increased effort. His attitudes and behaviour in the work situation would be effectively determined by the existing balance between his aversion to labour and his attraction to pay; or, put in another way, by his assessment of the terms of the 'effort bargain' which he was offered. (Goldthorpe, 1966: 2–3)

Not only did Scientific Management assume that employee behaviour would be motivated by a rather crude individualistic calculus of costs and benefits, it also sought 'the one best way' by reorganizing work according to three principles: 'the dissociation of the labor process from the skills of the workers' so that it came to depend 'entirely upon the practices of management'; 'the separation of conception from execution'; and 'the use (by management) of this monopoly over knowledge to control each step of the labor process and its mode of execution' (Braverman, 1974: 112–21). Such a strategy, it has been argued, treats the employee as 'a passive instrument of managerially planned productive activity' (Burns, 1968: 329), deprived of any opportunity to exercise skills or judgement in carrying out his or her work.

It was this 'tendency to equate men with machines' (Rose, 1975: 62) which was the point of departure for one of the earliest sources of academic criticism of the approaches of Scientific Management. The physiologists and psychologists who carried out research in Britain under the auspices of the Industrial Fatigue Research Board (and its successor the Industrial Health Research Board) and the National Institute of Industrial Psychology emphasized the importance of the 'human factor'. Workers were not to be regarded as machines but as complex organisms whose physiology and psychology needed to be understood. Though their conceptualization of the worker remained individualistic, and their methods of investigation left little or no room for considering the worker's own definition of the work situation (Goldthorpe, 1966: 4), these investigators emphasized and to some extent demonstrated the importance of taking account of the causes and occurrence of fatigue and monotony at work; and argued that the appropriate environmental conditions (lighting, rest pauses, etc.), and the careful selection of employees to suit the requirements of the job, could make work easier for the employee and less costly for the employer (Rose, 1975: 85).

'Social Man'

Mayo's critical assessment of the assumptions embodied in 'economic man' has already been noted. He was perhaps the most influential popularizer of the ideas and arguments of what came to be known as the Human Relations movement. His role in the conduct of the famous Hawthorne experiments at the Western Electric plant in Chicago between 1927 and 1931 is disputed; it has been variously claimed that he played little or no part in conducting them (Rose, 1975: 115), had overall responsibility but interpreted them idiosyncratically (Landsberger, 1958: 3), or was 'a central figure in the direction, interpretation and successful conclusion of the studies' (Smith, 1987: 118). There is no doubt, however, that the research reported in *Management and the Worker* (Roethlisberger and Dickson, 1939) as interpreted by Mayo and subsequently by many others (e.g. Brown, 1954), together with a number of derivative and supporting studies, provided the basis for an approach to work and employment which questioned the tenets of neo-classical economics and of Scientific Management and gave a major impetus to the development of the sociology of industry as a distinctive field of study.

The Human Relations approach offered alternatives to both the main assumptions embodied in the notions of 'economic man'. Employees, and by implication employers (though this was little developed by writers in the tradition), are not isolated individuals but members of social groups, who respond to the 'social norms which exist independently of particular individuals yet which prompt and constrain their conduct' (Goldthorpe, 1966: 5). Indeed, as the findings of the Bank Wiring Observation Room at the Hawthorne Works showed most clearly, such norms may lead workers to behave in ways which appear economically non-rational, like 'restricting' their output and therefore their earnings. Workers were seen as being influenced by a 'logic of sentiments' which was in marked contrast to the 'logics of cost and efficiency' which tended to dominate management (Roethlisberger and Dickson, 1939: 562–5). Social group influences were also seen as much more important for understanding employee behaviour than environmental conditions.

Further, not only was it important to acknowledge the importance of social norms, but employers and their agents, managers and supervisors, must recognize human beings' need to belong and their natural desire to co-operate in a common enterprise. 'Management has two major functions: (1) the function of securing the common economic purpose of the total enterprise; and (2) the function of maintaining the equilibrium of the social organization so that individuals through contributing their services to this common purpose obtain personal satisfactions that make them willing to co-operate' (Roethlisberger and Dickson, 1939: 569).

In principle, group influences on individuals' behaviour could be derived from outside and/or inside the plant. Mayo's belief that industrial societies had lost the 'social skills' necessary to secure stability and co-operation and were characterized by social disorganisation (Mayo, 1949: 5–10; Rose, 1975: 118–24) led him to emphasize the importance of workplace influences. Combined with a view of management and supervision as having the function of providing leadership and fostering co-operation, this focus on the workplace was reflected in the design of the many studies which followed the Hawthorne experiments: attempts to explore the consequences for attitudes and behaviour within work groups of different styles of supervision, of opportunities to 'participate', of changes in patterns of incentives and rewards, and so on. Much, though not all, research and writing in the Human Relations tradition, was thus open to the criticism of being 'plant sociology' because the analysis stopped at the plant gates; workers were considered primarily or solely in their roles as employees.

This limitation is linked to another, more serious, weakness in the interpretation of the employment relationship which is contained in the work of Mayo, his colleagues and most of his successors in the Human Relations tradition: a denial of any inherent conflict of interests between employer and employee. This stance also makes the interpretation of any evidence of conflicts in the situations they studied seriously deficient. Such conflicts were seen as pathological, to be explained away as arising either from the personal inadequacies of the individuals involved, or from deficiencies in the social skills of the managers or supervisors concerned which could be remedied by appropriate selection and training. Even though the Bank Wiring Observation Room investigation had to be brought to a conclusion because of falling demand during the Depression of the 1930s, there was inadequate recognition of the economic and social forces outside the plant which were constraining management's and workers' behaviour within it; and this remained the case for most studies using the Human Relations approach. Nor, similarly, was there much room for trade unionism and the institutions of industrial relations.

Thus the investigators in the Hawthorne experiments, Mayo, and a long list of other contributors to the Human Relations tradition (see Viteles, 1953; Tannenbaum, 1966) provided an initial basis for a sociological approach to the employment relationship, which was derived from empirical research, and clearly opposed to some of the basic assumptions of neo-classical economics and Scientific Management in its emphasis on the influence of group norms and leadership and on the social rewards from employment. It was notable, however, that the writers concerned made very few, and highly selective, references to existing contributions to social theory; and the approach was developed and the research it fostered carried out largely independently of contemporary developments in other areas of sociology. The Human Relations tradition was also characterized by a fundamental weakness: the assumption of the potential consensus of interests of employer and employed.

Thinking in Terms of Systems

The final part of *Management and the Worker* was devoted to an attempt to characterize the factory as a 'social system'. Though the formulations to be found there now seem rather unsophisticated, the use of the concept of 'system' to typify a society, or some set of social relations within a society such as an organization, has proved very attractive to many social theorists. The contributions to this tradition within sociological analysis are very diverse (Cohen, 1968). It is, however, possible to identify certain assumptions which characterize the most common uses of the concept. It implies a holistic view of social phenomena, in which the whole is seen as greater than the sum of its parts. It focuses attention on the investigation and clarification of the interrelationships and interdependencies between the elements which make up society, or some subsystem within society, elements which may variously be seen as roles, courses of action, social institutions, and so on. It encourages the identification and exploration of the unintended as well as the intended consequences of particular social processes and patterns of action. It allows the specification of a 'boundary' to a 'system' and thus the examination of relations between systems and their 'environments'. It also enables the constituent parts of any social system to be conceptualized in the same terms as the whole, as a subsystem within a larger system.

The systems concept has often been associated with 'functionalism' in sociological theory, the focus on the contribution which the parts of any social system make to the maintenance and persistence of the whole as a key to the explanation of social phenomena. This approach has frequently led to the much more controversial assumption that consensus and equilibrium are fundamental features of social systems, an assumption which can make it difficult if not impossible to provide a satisfactory account of social conflict and social change. Such implications, however, are not inherent in the use of the notion and it must remain an essential part of the conceptual language of sociology.

So far as employment relations are concerned, thinking in terms of systems offers two important, though possibly controversial, contributions. On the one hand there have been attempts, associated particularly with the work of Parsons, to conceptualize society as a social system, the economy as a subsystem within it which is engaged in various exchanges with other subsystems, and employment as one institutional form through which these exchanges are made. On the other there is a large number of writers who have regarded industrial and other work organizations as 'systems' involved in exchanges with their 'environments', one of which is the exchange of wages and salaries for the employee's contributions to achieving the goals of the enterprise.

The Economy as a Subsystem

The most ambitious attempt to analyse the social system and its constituent subsystems is probably to be found in the work of Parsons and his collaborators. Parsons developed his ideas at a very abstract level and in a way which was intended to provide a comprehensive set of categories which could be used in the analysis of all aspects of human society. His concern with employment relations was a relatively minor feature in this grand design, but some very brief and incomplete comments on this broader canvas are necessary to show how he arrived at a particular conceptualization of employment.

Parsons argued that any system of social action has to provide for four 'functional imperatives' in order to survive: adaptation to the conditions of its external environment by obtaining enough resources or facilities and distributing them within the system; goal-attainment by establishing goals, and motivating and mobilizing effort and energy towards their achievement; integration, or maintaining coherence and solidarity; and latency, or storing and distributing motivational energy to the system, involving *'pattern maintenance,* the supply of symbols, ideas, tastes and judgements from the cultural system, and *tension management,* the resolution of internal strains and tensions of actors' (Hamilton, 1983: 106–9; see also Parsons and Smelser 1956: 46–85). Within this conceptualization, as it was applied to society as a whole, the economy was seen as 'that sub-system of society which is differentiated with primary reference to the *adaptive* function of the society as a whole' (Parsons and Smelser, 1956: 20). As a system the economy has to meet the same four exigencies as the social system as a whole and this involves both its own further differentiation into primary functional bases, and interchanges across the boundaries of the economy as a subsystem with other subsystems.

One of these interchanges is institutionalized through the contract of employment between individuals in the labour force and employing organizations. 'The occupational role is thus a type of contractual relationship between an organization and an individual usually acting in a representative role as a member of a household or possibly some other collectivity' (Parsons and Smelser, 1956: 114). The interchanges between the organization or firm and the individual/household consists of more than an exchange of wages for labour services. Using the same schema of functional prerequisites, they are also seen to include, on the part of the employee, loyalty to the organization and the acceptance of authority and executive responsibility, according the firm a reputation as a good employer, and entrusting the household's security to the labour market and its constituent employing firms. In exchange, on the part of the firm, they are seen to include a basis for securing credit in expectation of certainty of income, a supportive orientation towards the worker's household, and moral approval of performance in terms of the values of economic rationality. Occupational roles can be differentiated in various ways and there would be differences in emphasis between, for example, 'labour services at a low level of technical competence and a low degree of organizational responsibility', executives, and professionals of various types (Parsons and Smelser, 1956: 146–56; Parsons, 1960: 79).

In this area of his work as elsewhere, Parsons succeeded in showing how the conceptual apparatus he had developed, of which only a glimpse has been provided here, could be applied to specific areas of interest, with some illuminating results once the somewhat impenetrable language has been mastered. His work on the professions, for example, has been particularly influential; it provided an explanation, even a defence, of the privileged status of professionals in terms of their increasingly important contribution to resolving crucial 'motivational' and other problems in advanced industrial societies (Parsons, 1960). More generally, four features of his discussion of the employment relationship can be regarded as of particular value: the emphasis on the employment contract as involving more than just an exchange of wages for labour services; the recognition that individual employees commonly enter employment as members of households towards which they have important responsibilities; the importance of the values which surround and support employment relations; and the identification of significant differences in the employment relationship for workers making different types of contribution to the organization and/or with different positions in the employment hierarchy. On the other hand, Parsons's discussion of employment relations presumes an underlying harmony of interests between employer and employee – the exchanges can be in equilibrium. For example, the relative bargaining disadvantage of the individual worker in negotiating a contract of employment is acknowledged, but trade unions are seen as providing a 'compensatory mechanism' which can, though it may not always, counterbalance this discrepancy (Parsons and Smelser, 1956: 148–9).

Organizations as Systems

Parsons's comments on organizations and employment were very much a by-product of his preoccupation with a more general theory of social systems. Most work in the sociology of organizations has had much less ambitious aims. However, for most of the period since the Second World War the dominant approach to the sociological analysis of industrial and other work organizations had been to conceptualize them as 'systems', and this is probably still the most frequent approach today. There exists a large number of variations within the systems perspective which differ considerably in terms of their assumptions, methods and substance. Central to many of them, and possibly inherent in 'systems thinking' as such, have been two main preoccupations: first, the analysis of organizations in terms of their constituent subsystems, and sub-subsystems, until particular roles in such subsystems are identified, and then exploring and clarifying the relationships between subsystems and roles: and secondly the analysis of the relationship between organizations and their environments in terms of the exchanges across the boundaries of the organization.[1]

The work of members of the Tavistock Institute of Human Relations provides clear examples of both procedures in action (e.g. Rice, 1958, 1963; Trist et al., 1963; Miller and Rice, 1967). Rice, for example, argued that any 'enterprise' has a primary task, which it must perform to survive, and then focused on the 'import-conversion-export process' by which it maintains itself in its environment. This led him to suggest that purchasing, manufacturing and sales were the three principal operating systems, with other activities providing service and control functions (Rice, 1963: 13–14, 16–25). For him, and even more so for Trist and his colleagues, the technology in use in the organization had to be seen as setting limits to the possibilities of changing the organization of work, and the definition

---

1 Emery (1969) is a useful introduction to 'systems thinking', of which Silverman (1970) provides a general account and a forceful critique. The work of the Tavistock Institute of Human Relations is discussed by Brown (1967), and can be compared with the approach offered by Katz and Kahn (1966) among many others.

of work roles and relationships, on the shop or office floor. There was still room, however, for organizational choices within such a socio-technical system; technology did not determine roles and relationships.

As is indicated by Rice's emphasis on the throughput of material commodities the employment relationship did not figure very prominently in these analyses, though there is some discussion of the cultural resources and expectations which employees bring to their employment. However, one of the areas of organizational choice could be in designing work roles to meet employees' needs 'for satisfaction and for defence against anxiety' (Miller and Rice, 1967: p.xi); roles which provided them, for example, with the opportunity to participate in the achievement of a 'whole task', to enjoy a degree of 'responsible autonomy', and, so far as possible, to belong to a 'sentient' group with which they could identify and which provided social support. These sorts of formulations indicated a clear recognition of the 'social needs' of employees, though in this case the definition of such needs was strongly influenced by psycho-analytic ideas; there was a strong presumption, too, that employees' needs, so defined, could be met by appropriate forms of work organization, at least in most cases (but see Miller and Rice, 1967: 253–4).

The employment relationship as such occupied a much more central place in the analysis offered by a former member of the Tavistock Institute, Jaques, whose work developed in a rather different direction. Working within a broadly systems perspective, however, he has sustained a highly individual approach to the analysis of employment relationships over a period of more than thirty years. In his earliest study of the Glacier Metal Company Jaques's analysis centred on relationships in 'the executive system' (Jaques, 1951), and this was contrasted with the 'representative' and 'legislative' systems in subsequent publications from the Glacier project (Brown, 1960, 1971). In exploring the nature of authority relations in organizations Jaques developed an important distinction between the 'prescribed' and 'discretionary' elements in any form of work carried out within a contract of employment.

> The *prescribed* content of a job consisted of those elements of the work about which the [staff] member was left no authorised choice . . . [They] were of two kinds: the result expected; and the limits set on the means by which the work could be done . . . The *discretionary* content . . . consisted of all those elements in which a choice of how to do a job was left to the person doing it . . . the member . . . was required, authorised, and expected to use discretion or judgement as he proceeded with his work. (Jaques, 1956: 33–4)

Jaques argued that all employment work, even the most simplified and routinized, had both prescribed and discretionary elements; that 'the essence of the effort in work is to be found in the anxiety engendered by the uncertainties which are part and parcel of the exercise of discretion' (Jaques, 1961: 89); and that the level of responsibility in any job can be 'measured in terms of the time-span of discretion in [the] job . . . the maximum period of time during which the use of discretion is authorised and expected, without review of that discretion by a superior' (Jaques, 1961: 21). Whilst the notion that employment involves the exercise of discretion within prescribed limits, both of which can be varied, has been taken up by other writers, Jaques's concentration on the level of responsibility as the only aspect of a job which needs to be assessed in relation to pay, and his argument that it can be measured, have proved much more controversial.

These ideas have been elaborated and consolidated in a more recent comprehensive statement (Jaques, 1976), where he adopted the term 'bureaucracy', which has a long and complex history as a concept (Albrow, 1970), to describe the system of roles and relations on which he wished to focus. He conceived of bureaucracies as 'secondary and dependent', set up by individual employers or an 'association' of individuals to pursue a common purpose (Jaques, 1976: 47). The employment contract and employment relations are central to the definition, and formation, of 'bureaucracies'; in contrast to the relationship to work organizations of shareholders, government ministers and officials, the officers and members of voluntary bodies, or whoever formed the 'association', the staff of 'bureaucracies' are members of the organization because they have accepted a contract of employment; one important characteristic of this is their accountability to their superiors, and ultimately to the governing body, for the quality of their work (Jaques, 1976: 55). Such organizations can still be characterized as systems, but Jaques's emphasis on the complexity of relationships which can exist in what he calls 'a hierarchically stratified managerial employment system' (1976: 55) is considerably more sophisticated than much of the writing on organizations as systems.

Nevertheless, like many writers in this tradition, he has continued to assert the possibility of creating institutions of employment which are 'requisite' in the sense that they are 'called for by the nature of things including man's nature' (Jaques, 1976: 6); ultimately there are no unresolvable conflicts or contradictions. Drawing on ideas derived from psychological and psycho-analytic theory he has argued both that the level of responsibility in a job and the level of work capacity in an individual, which will develop over a working lifetime, can be established uncontentiously; and that levels of payment can be determined, for different levels of responsibility/capacity, which will be felt to be fair. These claims must be considered at best unproven. They depend on an understanding of man's nature which is not uncontentious and assert rather than demonstrate empirically the possibility of establishing 'fair pay' and unambiguous relations of authority and responsibility in organizations. In contrast to some organizational theorists, however, Jaques has indicated that he recognizes the magnitude of the changes needed to secure 'requisite' employment relations in society; they include abundant employment, an equitable distribution of economic rewards, and safeguards for individual justice, changes which would transform the context for employment in most if not all societies. The special value in Jaques's work, however, lies in his emphasis on and exploration of the relations of super- and subordination in work organizations, his clarification of different types of role relationships within bureaucratic hierarchies, and – especially – the distinction between the prescribed and the discretionary elements in employment work.

Human Needs and Work Roles

All the approaches to employment discussed so far incorporate some notion of the human needs to be met by paid work, no matter how basic the definition of these needs might be met. A number of social psychologists, however, have developed much more complex accounts of human needs and motivation and these have been widely influential in social scientific discussions of employment. Maslow, for example, asserted that basic human needs were organized in a 'hierarchy of prepotency'; 'higher' needs only come into play as influences on behaviour when more basic needs are satisfied. The most 'prepotent' needs are physiological, to be followed as one ascends the hierarchy by the needs for safety, for 'love and affection and belongingness', for self-respect and self-esteem, and, finally, for self-actualization – 'to become everything that one is capable of becoming' (Maslow, 1943; see also Maslow, 1964). Although he expressed some reservations about the fixity of such a hierarchy in all circumstances, accepted that there were also less basic needs, and admitted that 'there are many determinants of behaviour other than needs and desires' (1943: 37), Maslow's arguments can be seen as having important implications for employment. These have been clearly put by Warr and Wall (1975: 34): 'employment in most industrialized societies caters quite well for lower-level needs. The wants which the theory predicts to be important in people are the higher-level ones to do with esteem and self-actualization . . . Can we then design jobs so that people's work engages their higher-level needs?'

Somewhat similar ideas were put forward by Herzberg (1959,1966), who argued that the factors which determine job satisfaction – achievement, recognition, the work itself, responsibility and advancement – are distinct from those which bring about job dissatisfaction – company policy and administration, supervision, salary, interpersonal relations and working conditions. The latter describe an employee's relationship to the context or environment of his or her job, and were labelled 'hygiene' factors; the former comprise the 'motivators' which can evoke superior performance and effort from the employee. No matter how satisfactory the 'hygiene factors' might be, better performance at work would only be stimulated by the appropriate motivating factors.

Subsequent research has tended to make these models of man look oversimplified, but they have made an important contribution to management theory and practice as well as within occupational psychology (Schein, 1965; Warr and Wall, 1975). The criticisms and revisions have not prevented the sort of approaches advocated by Maslow, Herzberg and others from being an important influence on the way in which the employment relationship has been conceptualized. Schein, for example, has suggested that there is a 'psychological contract' between the employee and the employing organization (1965: 64–5). Employees' effectiveness, and satisfaction with their jobs, will depend on how far their expectations are met by the organization and the organization's expectations met by employees; and how far there is agreement on what is to be exchanged; 'money . . . for time at work; social-need satisfaction and security . . . for work and loyalty; opportunities for self-actualization and challenging work . . . for high productivity, quality work, and creative effort in the service of organizational goals. . .'. Some writers on management and organizations have expressed doubts as to the possibility of meeting employees' expectations, specified in these sorts of terms, within conventionally administered work organizations (e.g. Argyris, 1957). The dominant message, however, from those who have been labelled 'neo-human relations theorists' by Goldthorpe et al. (1968: 178) and Rose (1975: 187), has been that appropriate managerial strategies *can* provide satisfactory and satisfying conditions of work and employment (e.g. Likert, 1961; McGregor, 1960).

Such assertions have raised in an acute form questions about the design of jobs in modern industry and about how far technology constrains or even determines the shape and content of work roles. In contrast to the 'neo-human relations' theorists, the so-called 'technological implications' approach offered a much less optimistic picture. Writers like Woodward (1958; 1965) and Blauner (1964) emphasized the predominant influence of technology on both the structure of work roles and the whole pattern of social relations in the organization. At least in their initial formulations, they gave little or no attention to the scope for organizational choice which has been asserted by socio-technical systems thinkers. Although it was developed from a quite different theoretical tradition, Blauner's conception of 'non-alienated' work as work which provided freedom and control, meaning and purpose, a sense of belonging and membership in society, and self-expression and self-actualization, was not incompatible with the ideas of neo-human relations theory about human needs (Blauner, 1964: 32–3). In the long view he foresaw automation solving some of the problems of the alienating jobs and working conditions which characterized much of modern industry (cf. Gallie, 1978). His and Woodward's views of contemporary industry, however, were ones which denied the possibility of an easy reorganization of work in conformity with the postulates of neo-human relations theory so as to meet employees' needs and expectations, and to provide them with 'non-alienating' employment.

The Action Frame of Reference

One of the most important lines of criticism of systems thinking came with the advocacy of an 'action frame of reference' in sociology during the 1960s. This approach gave priority to understanding the definitions of the situation of autonomous actors and the ways in which their actions constructed and maintained or changed ongoing patterns of social relations. It was given considerable popularity by the work of Goldthorpe and his colleagues on *The Affluent Worker* project, which provided a major challenge to the ideas of both neo-human relations and the technological implications approach, and stimulated a substantial body of further research within an action framework.

Drawing on the tradition of sociological theory which stems from Weber, Goldthorpe and his colleagues argued that a satisfactory explanation of workers' attitudes and behaviour involved taking account of the actors' own definitions of the situation. Rather than drawing on some supposedly universal specification of human needs, analysis should begin with the 'orientations to work' which employees actually have; 'wants and expectations are culturally determined *variables*, not psychological constants' (Goldthorpe et al., 1968: 178). Further, orientations cannot be seen as mere adaptations to the circumstances of a particular job; indeed they should be seen as influenced in important ways by employees' experiences outside and prior to employment, in family and community contexts. Nor can it be assumed that a particular work role and associated tasks will be either satisfying or 'alienating'; this will depend on the expectations the employee brings to his or her employment.

Many of these ideas can be traced in earlier writing, but Goldthorpe and his colleagues developed their own distinctive and coherent account of the employment relationship within an action frame of reference (Goldthorpe, 1966; Goldthorpe et al., 1968; also Silverman, 1970). As a reaction to notions of 'economic man', the human relations tradition, and much of the other work discussed above, had emphasized the social and psychological needs which can be met through employment. Goldthorpe and his colleagues reasserted that, especially for manual workers, employment was an *instrumental* activity, a means to an (economic) end. They suggested that differing orientations could be compared on each of four component elements, and in these terms they outlined in detail three ideal typical orientations to work: instrumental, bureaucractic and solidaristic. The four elements were:

1 the meaning of work and especially whether it is a means to an end or at least in part an end in itself;
2 the nature of involvement in the employing organization in terms of intensity (low or high) and affect (positive, neutral or negative) leading to three types of involvement: moral, calculative and alienative;[2]
3 the 'ego-involvement' of workers in work – the degree to which it is part of their 'central life interest';
4 whether workers' lives are sharply dichotomized between work and non-work (Goldthorpe et al., 1968: 38–42).

Orientations to work were seen as playing a significant part, at least in conditions of relatively full employment, in employees' choices of place of employment, leading to the formation of work-forces which

2 These terms are derived from Etzioni (1961) who developed a scheme for comparing organizations based on the mode of securing compliance from their 'lower participants'. Those in power in organizations may use coercive, remunerative or normative power to ensure compliance, and these means will tend to evoke, respectively, alienative, calculative or moral involvement from them. Etzioni argued that the 'renumerative/calculative' combination is the one which characterizes what he terms 'utilitarian' organizations (i.e. those with economic goals), though there may also be more or less successful attempts to use normative controls (paternalist or welfare oriented firms?) or coercion (forced labour).

were 'self-selected' and relatively homogeneous. The shared meanings they gave to their employment were a major influence in shaping their attitudes and behaviour at work. The sources of the specific content of orientations to work were thus to be sought outside the workplace in the employees' family, community and class situations (Goldthorpe, 1966: 10–11). In some cases typical orientations to work have been claimed to be associated with specific complexes of work and community social relations (Lockwood, 1966). Thus, for example, the 'affluent' workers studied by these investigators were described as having an 'instrumental' orientation to work (employment a means to an end; calculative involvement; work not central in their lives; work sharply separated from non-work). This had been derived from their specific backgrounds (families with dependent children; privatized life-styles; downwardly mobile), and had led them to secure relatively high paying jobs with which they were reasonably satisfied despite the low-skilled, repetitive nature of much of their work.

Almost all the steps in this explanatory framework have been subjected to keen criticism on theoretical grounds and/or in the light of further empirical research, of which Brown et al. (1983) and Watson (1987: 82–121) provide recent detailed accounts. Some of this work has led to the further differentiation of types of orientation (e.g. Ingham, 1967) or to attempts to categorize the factors ('economic', 'intrinsic', 'relational', and 'convenience') in terms of which employees' priorities regarding work can be described (e.g. Bennett, 1978). More significantly, doubts have been expressed as to the extent to which orientations are shaped solely or mainly by non-work situations and experiences; yet if they are influenced in part by workplace experiences the technology and structure of the employing organization must be granted a much greater explanatory importance than Goldthorpe and his colleagues gave them. Many employees have been shown to have multiple objectives regarding their employment, and orientations which are 'weak' (Blackburn and Mann, 1979: 239–44). In circumstances where orientations are complex, as Daniel (1969) has argued, the context in which actions are taken or attitudes expressed may be of crucial importance; quite different considerations can influence job choice, satisfaction with a job, and decisions to leave a job. The action frame of reference has also been criticized for giving inadequate acknowledgement to the constraints within which most employees have to act, for example when seeking work (something which clearly became more difficult to overlook as unemployment increased). The experience of limited or negligible choice leads many people to accommodate their expectations to what is realistically possible (Fox, 1980: 174–80), and perhaps to focus on those features of employment – such as whether to seek outdoor or indoor work (Blackburn and Mann, 1979: 109) – where there may be genuine alternative possibilities.

In the light of these criticisms and modifications it is no longer possible to utilize the framework offered by Goldthorpe and his colleagues as the main basis for a sociological account of the employment relationship. Certain features of it, however, remain of value: the emphasis on the socially constructed and socially sustained – and variable – nature of employees' expectations and priorities regarding their employment; the influence, however mediated,, which such underlying orientations to work have on attitudes and actions *vis-à-vis* the employing organization; and the need to seek the origins of the specific content of orientations to work in non-work situations and sources, as well, of course, as in the experiences of the labour market and of employment itself.

Explaining Industrial Conflict

The action frame of reference advocated by Goldthorpe and his colleagues left open the question whether or not relations between employers and employees would be characterized by conflict. 'A co-existence of conflict and cooperation' is seen 'as implicit in any economic association' (Goldthorpe et al., 1968: 196), and the preponderance of one or the other would depend on employees' definitions of how far their legitimate expectations (largely 'economic' in the case of the 'affluent' workers) were being met by their employers. With a few exceptions, which have been noted, the other approaches to the employment relationship discussed so far have included a more or less explicit understanding that such relations are potentially harmonious; though to realize this consensus it may be necessary to develop managers' social skills, to create the 'requisite' organizational structure, or to design jobs appropriately. It is now necessary to confront the question of conflict more directly and to consider the contributions to understanding of this aspect of employment relationships to be found, first, in industrial relations theory, and, secondly, in the Marxist tradition.

Frames of Reference in Industrial Relations

For the past several decades the dominant approach among industrial relations theorists in Britain has been to regard the industrial enterprise, and indeed industry as a whole, as consisting of two or more social groupings with divergent interests and objectives. Whilst such groupings may also be interdependent and have interests which can only be met by collaboration, their sectional interests will inevitably bring them into conflict. Such conflicts cannot be resolved by either asserting the prior claims of one set of interests over all the others, or declaring the conflict itself as in some sense mistaken, pathological or unreal. The two most prominent of such groupings are management and workers at the level of the employing enterprise, capital and labour in society as a whole, but a pluralist approach to industrial relations leaves space for subdivisions within these two blocks and for the identification of further interests which may be independent of either party to the conflicts, such as those of the state.

   The pluralist frame of reference has been defended as the only realistic one in comparison in particular with a unitary approach, one which suggests that the enterprise is a team, or family, with one source of authority and one focus of loyalty. Such a view has been criticized as 'ideological' in that it is at variance with the facts of industrial life yet may serve management's purposes by providing reassurance, serving as an instrument of persuasion and conferring legitimacy on the exercise of managerial authority (Fox, 1966: 3, 5). Within a unitary ideology dissent is seen as aberrant and there can be no legitimate and lasting place for representative organizations of sectional interests such as trade unions (Fox, 1973: 186–92).

In contrast to this, the dominant preoccupation within a pluralist frame of reference is with establishing structures and procedures within which legitimate conflicts of interest can be contained, and prevented from damaging the interests of all; and appropriate compromises can be worked out and agreed. Democratic political institutions are seen as providing such a framework at the level of society as a whole, and the institutionalization of industrial conflict to create an industrial relations 'system' can achieve a similar result in relation to employer-employee relations. Such institutionalization requires certain preconditions: recognition of the existence and legitimacy of conflicting interests; effective representation of those interests; an efficient system of communications between the parties; some 'flexibility of group objectives and of central direction and policy'; 'an ability and willingness to create conditions allowing the maximum realisation of sectional objectives'; and a balance of power between the parties which is not too markedly uneven (Ross, 1958: 121–32). To this list one can add that as well as the negotiation and bargaining which will characterize 'communications' between the parties there should be, and within many systems of industrial relations there is, 'a second line of institutional safeguards, a system of mediation and arbitration' (Dahrendorf, 1959: 261).

The adoption of a pluralist view, and the advocacy of the institutionalization of the industrial conflict in line with it, do have important consequences for an understanding of the employment relationship. In particular it defines trade unions and other representatives of employees as having a legitimate role not only in the labour market in securing the best possible terms for the sale of labour, but also within the employing organization in restraining, regulating or even sharing in the exercise of managerial decision-making (Fox, 1966: 7). As was the case, it can be argued, with Durkheim's conditions for a 'spontaneous' rather than a 'forced' division of labour (Durkheim 1933: 377–84) or Jaques's account of the requisite structure for a 'bureaucracy', a full working through of a pluralist approach to industrial relations could imply a much more radical restructuring of the social relations of employment than has for the most part been appreciated. Indeed it is in relation to the exercise of managerial authority that the analogy between constitutional democracy at the societal level and the pluralist model of the industrial enterprise breaks down. Representative organizations like trade unions may be seen to have a legitimate role in protecting and furthering their members' interests but, as the debates on 'industrial democracy' have emphasized, they are an 'opposition' which is never expected or allowed to become a 'government' (Brannen, 1983: 55–8).

The pluralist view of industrial relations and the industrial enterprise has come under more radical criticism, including criticism for some of those, like Fox, who initially advocated it. This has involved a challenge to the idea, explicitly recognized in statements of the pluralist position, that compromise and agreement between conflicting interests are possible in ways which are 'consistent with the general interest of the society as conceived, with the support of public opinion, by those responsible for its government' (Ross, 1958: 102). As Fox (1973: 195–6) has argued, the pluralist approach includes the 'assumption that the normative divergencies between the parties are not so fundamental or so wide as to be unbridgeable by compromises or new syntheses which enable collaboration to continue'. In a society characterized by marked inequalities of condition and opportunity, however, these assumptions merely tend to help preserve the status quo. They prevent the radical changes taking place which would reduce or eliminate altogether the inequalities of economic resources, power and status, and thus be in the real interests of subordinate groupings (Goldthorpe, 1977). Pluralists have emphasized the need for a rough balance of power in industrial relations so that bargaining does not take place under duress, and have tended to assume that such a balance in fact exists; the 'radical' critics have stressed that this assumption is unwarranted and the pluralist approach therefore flawed.

Indeed, it can be argued further that the inequalities which undermine pluralism can be seen to arise out of and to be enshrined in relations between classes which are characterized by basic and ultimately unresolvable conflicts of interest. In such a context appeals to 'the general interest' are not only mistaken but also serve to support the interests of the dominant class against the challenge from below. In so far as such domination is structured into the institutions of society, an industrial relations system which contains industrial conflict but leaves these institutional arrangements unaffected also serves the interests of the dominant class. Nor can an appeal be made to the state as an impartial arbiter: the state is a major employer, and it inevitably comes to represent and share the interests of the dominant groups in society. In Fox's later view pluralism must also be seen as an ideology, though more 'realistic' than the unitary view, which serves the interests of the propertied and more powerful class (Fox, 1973: 205–31; 1974: 248–96).

In his own detailed discussion of employment relations Fox (1974) has used Jaques's distinction between the prescribed and discretionary components of a work role to elaborate his own conception of the differences between 'high-trust' and low-trust' relationships within employment, as they can be found both vertically between superior and subordinate and laterally between colleagues. 'High-trust' relations are ones where the granting of considerable discretion to employees evokes a strong commitment to and moral involvement in the goals and values of the employing organization, whereas 'low-trust' relations comprise the opposite. This distinction enables Fox to develop an insightful account of employment relations and their dynamics and to suggest a useful typology of patterns of employer–employee relations (Fox, 1974: 297–313). It also provides the basis for a rather pessimistic account of the 'present and future problems of a low-trust society'. It does not, however, enable him to advocate any acceptable solution to these problems.

It has been claimed that the view of the employment relationship held by Fox and writers who share his position is ultimately uncertain. The radical critique of pluralism could be seen as leading to some kind of Marxist analysis, focused on class struggle and an eventual revolutionary transformation of the social order (Wood and Elliott, 1977: 110–11). Fox's concern for order and mutual survival prevents him from taking such a line and appears to leave him in a 'radical pluralist' position (Watson, 1987: 217), which involves a modification of pluralism not its rejection. It is the Marxist approach which is considered in the next section.

Marx and the Labour Process

There is little doubt that the most influential account of the employment relationship within sociology during the past decade has been that derived from the writings of Marx, an account which was popularized by Braverman in his *Labor and Monopoly Capital* (1974) and gave rise to the 'labour process debate'. Although Marx's ideas have long been influential in other areas of sociology, for example in debates about class and about the development of capitalist societies, his discussions of work and employment remained largely ignored until the publication of Braverman's book. A brief account will provide a basis for discussion of them.[3]

Marx saw the activity of production as necessary and central in any human society. One crucial characteristic of man's productive activity is that it is possible to create new value, a surplus over and above what is necessary to reproduce and maintain the workers, and the means of production, used in producing those commodities. The 'labour process' is thus also a 'valorization process'. The capitalist mode of production is distinguished by the fact that both the materials and the instruments of production are owned by capitalists whilst work on and with them is carried out by workers, who are legally free but have no rights of ownership or control over the machinery they use, nor over the products of their labour. In an objective sense they are 'alienated' from both the process and the fruits of their labour. Capitalists need workers to be able to put their capital to productive use, just as workers with no productive resources of their own need capitalists. What the capitalist employer secures through a contract of employment, however, is only the worker's *potential* ability to work, his or her 'labour power'. Control, exercised in the workplace – and sometimes outside it – by or on behalf of the employer, is necessary to ensure that the work the worker has been hired to do is in fact done, and at the required pace, to the required standards, and so on.

More contentiously, Marx argued that, in terms of a labour theory of value, workers' wages would always tend to be no more than the socially necessary costs of their own maintenance and eventual replacement by the succeeding generation. The labour they provide and the value they produce over and above these costs, which could be historically variable as customary standards of living change, form the 'surplus value' appropriated

3 This account draws particularly on Nichols (1980: 11–72), and also on Braverman (1974) and Thompson (1983). The most accessible brief statements by Marx himself are probably Marx (1958a. 1958b): for a full account see the first volume of *Capital*.

by the capitalist employer for rent, interest and profit. Within a competitive capitalist economy, with its downward pressure on the price, or exchange value, of goods and services, there is constant need to increase the productivity of labour, to reduce its cost, and thus to maintain the process of capital accumulation. This can be done in various ways: by making workers work for longer hours for the same pay; by making them work more intensively; and by cheapening the cost of labour. At different stages in the development of capitalist employment relations different means of 'subordinating labour' have had priority (Nichols, 1980: 26–7).

Braverman took as his point of departure the possibility of separating two essential characteristics of human work – conception and execution. He argued that in the conditions of monopoly capitalism which characterized the twentieth century, the production and appropriation of surplus value had been made more effective by widespread adoption of the canons of Scientific Management. Knowledge about and control over the production process became concentrated exclusively in the hands of management; mental labour was separated from manual labour; tasks were fragmented and deskilled so that cheaper labour could be employed; and close control was exercised over the activities of such workers by means such as time and motion study, machine pacing, and so on. Braverman saw such a process of 'the degradation of work' extending into all spheres of employment to include non-manual as well as manual jobs.

One of the potential strengths of a Marxist analysis of employment, which can also been seen as a source of weakness, is that, like the work of Parsons but of few if any of the others who have been discussed here, it is presented within a coherent account of (capitalist industrial) society, and links the social relations of employment to the pattern and development of social relations outside the workplace; and all within a developed and explicit conception of man, society and history. This carries with it the danger that useful ideas will be rejected because they are tainted by some unacceptable characteristics of the broader schema, and indeed raises the question of how far it is possible and legitimate to utilize the concepts and ideas separated from their overall theoretical context. The recent interest in Marx's ideas concerning the labour process, however, does appear to have had some positive consequences for the sociology of work and employment, of which three can be mentioned.

First, a Marxist analysis insists that attention should also be focused on the conditions necessary for a particular mode of production to exist and persist. In common with other approaches it is recognized that employing organizations cannot be treated as closed systems, but the interrelations between organizations and their 'environments' are treated with greater theoretical rigour in this approach than is the case in most open systems thinking. Thus it is essential for the capitalist mode of production for an adequate labour force to be reproduced on a daily and a generational basis. In most contexts the family and household, and domestic labour, provide the means for this, though in some situations the same 'need' may be largely met by the migration of workers from other societies, or from peripheral areas, often with 'pre-capitalist' peasant economies. In addition, there are certain ideological preconditions for a smooth running capitalist economy: the internalization of work obligations by employees and the acceptance of the legitimacy of managerial authority; processes of socialization and education are therefore of importance. Further, the state plays a crucial role, through its policies regarding the family, education, the labour market, industrial relations, social security and taxation, in securing the appropriate conditions for capitalist enterprises to exist and flourish.

Secondly, a fresh impetus has been given to historical studies of employment relations, to the development of forms of work organization, and to the ways in which particular patterns of social relations and associated technical developments have been socially constructed within specific historical circumstances. Thus the historical variability of employment relationships has been made the subject of investigation (e.g. Littler, 1982; Friedman, 1977; Burawoy, 1985).

Thirdly, the question of control has been rightly placed at the centre of attempts to explain the characteristics, and the dynamics, of employment relations. This issue has been one of the main sources of debate about Braverman's *Labor and Monopoly Capital* (the other is the question of deskilling discussed by Wood (1982)). Contrary to Braverman's argument, and the implications of Marx's own formulations, there is no satisfactory unilinear account of the development of control over the labour process. Both in the past and at the present time managements have had a variety of strategies available to them which give rise to rather different patterns of employer–employee relations (Hyman, 1987). Edwards (1979), for example, has identified a threefold succession of simple control through close supervision, technical control through such means as the machine pacing of work, and bureaucratic control through internal labour markets and systems of rules and procedures. Friedman (1977) has contrasted 'direct control' with the 'high trust' strategy of granting more skilled workers greater autonomy so that they will identify with the aims of the organization and act 'responsibly' with a minimum of supervision. Selection and socialization can be used to secure a compliant and committed workforce; control may be exercised indirectly through subcontractors; or some combination of these and other means could be adopted (Littler and Salaman, 1984: 49–71). Management's choice between these possibilities can be influenced by a number of factors of which one of the most important is the likely acceptance or resistance of their employees. In contrast to Braverman's account it is not possible to consider the development of the labour process without taking account of the active role played by those over whom control is exercised, but this inevitably adds to the indeterminancy of the outcome.

At the centre of the analyses of employment relations in capitalist enterprises offered by Marx and others in the Marxist tradition is the assumption that capitalist employers derive their surplus from the difference between the value created by the worker and the rewards they receive for their labour. This raises two questions which have important implications for the wider applicability of their ideas. First, is it essential to accept the labour theory of value which underlies Marx's account, and, if a critical or agnostic position is taken on that question, what if anything remains of use from the analysis? Secondly, Marx's account is explicitly focused on situations where labour is 'productive' and new value is being created. Is the analysis applicable to commercial organizations where value may be realized though not produced, to the public sector, or to employment in non-commercial organizations like voluntary bodies?

In part a negative answer to the first question makes it easier to argue the case for a positive answer to the second. Even without accepting all the elements in Marx's account, it is clear that in market economies subject to national and international competition there will be more or less constant downward pressures on labour costs leading to demands for more stringent controls over the activities of employees. Much of the remainder of the analysis should therefore still apply. Commercial and other 'unproductive' organizations are subject to the same sorts of market pressures as 'productive' ones, though there may be differences of degree. In the non-market sector employing organizations are subject to budgetary constraints which are the functional equivalent of the downward pressure on labour costs derived from the market. Thus, although some scholars (e.g. Brighton Labour Process Group, 1977) may be right to want to maintain a highly specific notion of the capitalist labour process in the context of developing a rigorous analysis within the realms of Marxist theory, the argument here is that some of the concepts and ideas developed by Marx, Braverman and others in that tradition, can contribute to a more general account of the employment relationship.

Towards a Sociology of Employment Relations

None of the bodies of research and writing discussed above provides an adequate and problem free account of the employment relationship in societies like our own. Indeed, what might seem most striking about them is that each approach focuses on certain questions and issues to the exclusion of others. Though they vary in how comprehensive they aim to be, none has provided, and few if any have attempted to provide, a framework for the analysis and understanding of employment relations which in any way offers a synthesis of existing contributions. Given the very different theoretical presuppositions of the different schools of thought this caution is almost certainly wise, and no such synthesis will be attempted here. It is possible, however, to suggest that certain themes and questions run through many of the bodies of work which have been discussed. These can be briefly stated and will provide a point of departure for considering the outline of a possible approach to the sociology of employment relationships.

Sociologists have been agreed in asserting that the relations between employers and employees cannot be understood in narrowly economic terms. Employees typically seek more than purely economic rewards from their employment; their behaviour at work is influenced by social 'factors'; indeed their entering into employment at all and their acceptance of managerial authority depend to a greater or lesser extent on the internalization of work obligations. Though the employment contract is generally seen as one involving complex, multiple exchanges, however, there is considerable disagreement as to the nature and determinants of employees' expectations regarding employment, and equally as to whether human 'needs' can be identified which employment should meet, or generally desirable conditions of work specified which would provide non-alienating employment.

Closely related to such questions is the issue of whether work can be designed and organized in ways which meet employees' expectations, whatever they may be, or needs, if such can be identified. Answers to this question vary. Some of the more optimistic demand such far-reaching concomitant changes that they may be considered unrealizable. Others more pessimistically emphasize the constraints of technology and the demands of competitive markets which severely restrict the room for maneouvre. With some limited exceptions, however, the possibility of at least some organizational choice is generally recognized.

A further issue of common concern is how to characterize the relations between employer and employee. Are they at least potentially harmonious with only inappropriate behaviour or faulty organization preventing this consensus from being realized; or is there an inherent conflict of interests between the two parties, which may coexist with common interests and mutual interdependence but can never be eliminated? Even if such inherent conflicts are recognized further questions arise as to whether they can be contained within a framework of rules and procedures or whether underlying contradictions will ultimately lead to radical change.

Not all these issues are taken up in the approach to the employment relationship outlined in the concluding sections of this chapter. The argument there, however, draws on and contributes to these debates at a number of points, and may prove to be of use for further research and theorizing.

Employment Relations

At its most basic, employment represents the exchange of pay, and possibly other rewards, for work – the buying and selling of labour power. Unlike the buying and selling of almost all other commodities, however, the exchange does not and cannot take place instantaneously. Employment, as distinct from self-employment and some other ways of providing labour services under contract, necessarily involves a continuing relationship between employer and employee. What the employer secures by employing someone is their capacity to work, and this potential can only be realized over time. In terms of Marx's categories, 'labour power' has to be turned into 'labour'.

Thus employment necessitates a continuing relationship between the buyer and the seller of labour power, and it is only within such a relationship that the terms of the exchange can really be worked out in detail. In this respect employment contracts are typically remarkably open-ended: they may specify pay-rates, hours of work, and so on, but generally leave very imprecise both what the employee will be expected to do and how hard (to use everyday language) he or she will be expected to work. This characteristic of contracts of employment has been observed by a number of writers and explained in rather different ways. Lupton and Bowey (1974: 72), for example, have argued:

> The contract of employment between an employer and an employee hardly ever specifies exactly what the employee undertakes to do during each hour or day of his employment. It is neither possible nor desirable to define every action and sequence of actions precisely, because the employer usually seeks a degree of freedom to direct the work-force to perform tasks which are appropriate to the changing demands of customers, the availability of materials, breakdown of machinery or equipment and so on. And the employee seeks a degree of freedom to respond as he thinks fit. The limits within which these freedoms may be exercised are sometimes written into a contract and sometimes 'understood', but in either case custom and practice will further elaborate what it is reasonable for the employer to demand of the employee and vice versa.

In his account of the neo-classical model of the labour market Marsden (1986: 22) comments that managerial authority is needed to play a co-ordinating role 'particularly because the labour contract is seen as one which is incompletely specified when workers are taken on, because the transaction costs of fully specifying all the tasks to be carried out *ex ante* would be too high'. Baldamus (1961: 35–6) observed that

> the formal wage contract is never precise in stipulating how much effort is expected for a given wage (and vice versa). The details of the arrangement are left to be worked out through the direct interaction between the partners of the contract. If a worker slackens his effort at one moment, the foreman's job is to remind him, as it were, that he departs from his obligations, and, in certain circumstances, it is quite possible that there may be some haggling between the two as to what is a 'fair' degree of effort in relation to the wages paid.

He then went on to argue that such a situation must be seen as unavoidable once the real nature of 'effort' is recognized.

The open-ended nature of the typical employment contract makes even more essential a characteristic of the employment relationship which also exists for other reasons: the relations between employer and employee are authority relations between superior and subordinate. In entering into employment the employee indicates a willingness to abide by the rules and regulations of the enterprise, and, more important, to accept and follow the (reasonable) instructions given by those in positions of authority. Employment relations are necessarily relations between super- and subordinates and, in Dahrendorf's terms (1959), employing organizations are imperatively co-ordinated associations.

This feature of employment is relevant for an understanding of how far relations between employers and employees are inherently consensual or conflictual. Any buying and selling relationship will tend to be ambivalent.

The parties to it are interdependent and need each other to achieve their own goals: in this case, earning an income and getting work done to produce goods or provide services. In the case of many employing organizations all parties may share an interest in the success of the enterprise in the market, or its success in whatever non-commercial arena determines the level and continuity of its resources. On the other hand the price at which the exchange of pay for 'work' takes place is a source of conflict. What is income for the employee is a cost for the employer; market or budgetary constraints will prevent the employer from meeting, or meeting fully, demands for higher pay, and may even lead to pay reductions, or to the termination of the employment contract.

In addition to these conflicting interests arising from labour market constraints, however, employer and employee have differing interests in the exercise of authority in the enterprise. Except where it is possible to establish high-trust relations on the basis of responsible autonomy for the employee, the employer has to exercise authority to make the employment contract determinate and to ensure the employee's contribution for which wages or salary are being paid. What represents control and co-ordination for the employer, however, represents restrictions on autonomy and choice for the employee. There are two sides to the exchange within the employment contract – pay and work – and each can be varied in attempts by the employer or the employee to secure an outcome which, in their view, is more satisfactory. Further, what they can regard as 'satisfactory' is more or less narrowly constrained by market forces, budgetary limits, the cost of living, and other factors beyond their control. Conflict is structured into employment relations.

It is also important to acknowledge that for most employment situations most of the time the employment relationship is asymmetrical; the power and resources of the employer typically exceed those of employees. The employees' need for a job is greater than the employer's for employees. As Beveridge (1944: 19) put it: 'A person who has difficulty in buying the labour that he wants suffers inconvenience or reduction in profits. A person who cannot sell his labour is in effect told that he is of no use. The first difficulty causes annoyance or loss. The other is a personal catastrophe.' As Beveridge also recognized the catastrophe (and asymmetry) can be greatly modified but not entirely eliminated by measures such as full employment policies or social security provision.

The Employee's Contribution

It is now necessary to look more closely at the nature of the contribution made by employees in their work in exchange for their wage or salary. An approach to this question can be made through the work of Baldamus. He argued that 'the payment of wages, salaries and other rewards' compensated workers for both the "occupational costs" connected with the acquisition of skill, experience, and occupational education', and their 'effort' (1961: 9–10). Occupational costs are described by Baldamus as being seen both to give rise to the familiar structure of income differentials through the operation of the labour market, and to justify this structure as reflecting the relative scarcity of different types of labour resources. However, Baldamus continued (1961: 29–30):

> for a very large working population, the occupational costs are *nil*, or very negligible. As far as most unskilled and semi-skilled wage-earners in factories or offices are concerned, investment in training and experience is so insignificant that it bears no relation to basic earnings. We are therefore forced to conclude that the wages of these groups are the compensation for something that has nothing to do with occupational costs. Let us call this factor the worker's input of *'effort'*, provisionally defined as the sum total of physical and mental exertion, tedium, fatigue, or any other disagreeable aspect of work. It follows, on the basis of common knowledge, that this component must also be present at all higher levels of income, although it may differ widely between different levels of the occupational hierarchy. Furthermore, as it contains many subjective elements, this component defies rigorous definition and is certainly unmeasurable.

In this account Baldamus has clearly identified two components of the contribution which an employee is expected to make in return for a wage or salary: an input of effort, and – to use the simplest term – the use of his or her skills. There are, however, two deficiencies in this initial formulation. First, the assumption is made that whereas effort 'defies rigorous definition and is certainly unmeasurable', occupational costs are strictly determinate. Secondly, there is no recognition of a further component in the contribution expected from the employee, one which Jaques argued was the central characteristic of employment work, the exercise of discretion. Indeed, in a later working paper, Baldamus himself, influenced by studies of productivity bargaining during the 1960s, introduced the idea that the degree or amount of responsibility taken by the employee is a contribution to productive activities which is also rewarded by an element in the wage or salary (Baldamus, 1967: 49).

The argument here then is that, within the employment relationship, employees are rewarded for some combination of effort, skill and discretion, which they contribute towards the achievement of their employers' purposes.[4] The implications of this position can be best set out in a series of related points.

First none of these components is measurable in an agreed and unambiguous way. This point has been put most comprehensively in the

---

4 The distinctions between effort, skill and discretion are analytical ones. They can be provisionally defined as the sum total of the physical and mental exertions involved in work as experienced by the employee (effort); the knowledge, and mental and manual abilities which have been acquired through education, training and experience (skill); and the choices and judgements which the employee is required to make, which have uncertain outcomes and therefore demand the willingness and ability to tolerate the consequent anxieties (discretion). Like all social science concepts they are terms which are widely used in less precise ways, and a good deal of further work is needed to delimit them and clarify their use in empirical investigations.

case of effort by Baldamus, who has argued that effort is an inherently subjective and unstable phenomenon; to put it in common-sense terms, only workers can know how hard they are working; only each one individually will know what their work is 'costing' them. What may seem 'hard' at one stage in the day or week, may seem much easier at another, though the 'objective' content of the task may not have changed. Attempts to measure effort from the outside, as in work study, for example, can only be 'guesstimates'. Levels of effort are made even more difficult to determine by the existence of equally variable 'relative satisfactions' associated with the deprivations which make up effort (Baldamus, 1961: 51–77). Jaques claimed to be able to measure discretion in terms of the time span index, but that assumed that responsibility is one single unilinear factor and this must at least be questioned. Studies associated with the labour process debate (e.g. Wood, 1982; Cockburn, 1983: 112–22) have emphasized the difficulties of defining, let alone measuring, skill, once one moves beyond fairly simple manual tasks. Participants in this debate, including some of the contributors to Wood's book, have added to these difficulties by failing to distinguish between skill and discretion.

Secondly, each component is to be found in virtually every job to some degree. All employment involves some physical and mental effort; no job can be regarded as completely unskilled; and, as Jaques stressed, the responsible exercise of judgement is an element, however, limited, in all employment work. The importance of employees' willing co-operation has also been emphasized by writers in the labour process debate, such as Burawoy (1979) and Thompson (1983: 153–79), and by Bendix (1963: 251):

In modern industry the cooperation needed involves the spirit in which subordinates exercise their judgement. Beyond what commands can effect and supervision can control, beyond what incentives can induce and penalties prevent, there exists an exercise of discretion important even in relatively menial jobs, which managers of economic enterprises seek to enlist for the achievement of managerial ends.

Thirdly, the indeterminancy of the components of an employee's contribution to his or her employer's activities, which is acknowledged in the notion of the employment contract as open-ended, means that what work the employee actually does – how much effort is involved in performing the job, what skills are demanded and utilized, and what judgement has to be exercised – can only be finally determined in the ongoing interaction between employee and employer (or managers and supervisors) within the employing organization. The behaviour expected of the employee is worked out in the continuing relations between managers and supervisors, and workers. With reference to the relationship between pay and effort, this has been referred to as the 'effort bargain' (Behrend, 1957). In a more general sense too, employing organizations, no matter how detailed their attempts to specify the content of jobs and the responsibilities of their holders, can always justifiably be described as representing a 'negotiated order' (Strauss et al., 1963).

Fourthly, the relative importance of the three components can vary considerably between jobs, Broadly speaking it would appear that as one ascends the conventional occupational and pay hierarchy the relative importance of effort diminishes and the levels and relative importance of skill and discretion within a work role increase. For example, to take the opposite movement, the changes associated with the introduction of the measures advocated by Scientific Management can be seen to have consisted of the removal of skills and responsibility from the roles of most production workers, whose jobs became the performance of fewer simpler fragmented tasks with much less autonomy and decision-making; their wages were lower and to a very much larger extent represented compensation for effort, at a more intensive level, rather than rewards for skill or discretion.

Fifthly, employment in different sorts of jobs with different levels and 'proportions' of effort, skill and discretion may well be associated with different sorts of packages of rewards and sanctions. Incentive payment schemes related, supposedly, to levels of effort expended by the employee, for example, are typically seen as only appropriate for certain types of manual work in certain sorts of situations (Lupton, 1961). Fox (1974: 72–9) has contrasted the 'economic exchanges' which characterize low-trust, low-discretion work roles, of which payment by results schemes would be a good example, and the 'social exchanges' with unspecified diffuse obligations – on both sides – which characterize high-trust, high-discretion work roles. Stinchcombe (1968: 183–4) has similarly argued with regard to certain forms of 'skill' that

> The system of rewards and punishments appropriate for maximising the amount of knowledge and intelligence that will be applied in a work role are likely to be quite different from those appropriate for maximising the amount of energy applied. In particular, the organisation of work roles into a *career* is much more important, and the necessity for rewarding performance from minute to minute is less important. A man's knowledge and intelligence do not vary much from one hour to the next, but vary greatly over his lifetime. Thus, the motivational devices for organising labour have to be directed toward rewarding variation over lifetimes, rather than over hours.
>
> This means that salaries are a more important form of payment than wages, and the organising of a series of salaries over a course of years – in order to encourage further learning as a qualification for future jobs – is crucial. . .

The emphasis in the above outline of the complex and indeterminate nature of the exchanges which take place within an employment relationship gives rise to a further set of questions which will allow some final points to be made. Given the considerations outlined above the occurrence of conflict between employer and employee, management and workers – though not its frequency and form – is not difficult to explain. Their interests conflict at various points and there are no objective criteria in terms of which conflicts can be settled; for example, regarding manning levels on a production line which affect the levels of effort demanded from the workers; or over the appropriate differential for a particular skill; or regarding the payment to be made for carrying a specific responsibility. What is more difficult to explain is how and why social relations in employment are so settled and free of conflicts so much of the time. There are, of course, certain objective interests in common, and these provide part of the answer, but they do not appear sufficient on their own.

Once again Baldamus can be referred to for the elements of an explanation, one worked out in his case in relation to the effort bargain and the need to account for the remarkably widespread agreement about what represents 'a fair day's pay for a fair day's work'. Baldamus (1961: 81–8) argued that there are 'social supports' for the institutions of employment. During primary socialization in the family and at school individuals internalize work obligations: the moral obligation to undertake paid work, the 'work ethic', and obligations to accept a certain degree of deprivation connected with employment and to acknowledge the legitimacy of the employer's authority derived from their ownership of property. This provides a basis for stable and co-operative relations. During the course of employment itself there develops a more precise and detailed normative understanding of the behaviour which is appropriate in the workplace:

> The interplay of these forces may readily be illustrated by the situation that faces a young person on his first entry into industrial employment. He brings with him a set of general role-expectations of what is right and wrong for him as a wage-earner. If he comes from a working-class family he will probably define work as a necessary evil and may search for an opportunity where it is relatively 'easy' to obtain a fair amount of money. This expectation acts as a social support to the institution of employment. Then he will soon have to learn the established rules of restricting output or the acceptable standards of effort, and in due course he thus incorporates into his habitual pattern of behaviour a specific set of institutional controls. In addition, his activities are minutely prescribed by the system of regulative controls that governs his particular job, the methods of production, the type of supervision, and the mode of wage-payment. The corresponding situation that faces the employer or the managerial executive in the early stages of his career is formally the same, though, of course, the content of the three factors is different. (Baldamus, 1961: 84–5)

Thus explaining the nature of the employment relationship necessarily involves considering the culture, the values and norms of the wider society and the institutional arrangements which ensure that appropriate normative obligations are internalized, and developed and reinforced by each generation. It involves, too, considering how these processes differ in their content and consequences between different classes and communities, different regions and generations. The range of variation to which this can give rise, in addition to the scope for choice available to employers and employees in structuring their relations around the employment contract, means that there can be quite considerable empirical variation in employment relationships. A focus on the employment relationship in sociology raises many questions in its own right; it is a key to understanding many of the processes which occur in organizations; and it both demands and contributes to an adequate account of the social structure and social processes of the wider society.

References

Albrow, M. 1970. *Bureaucracy*. London: Macmillan.

Argyris, C. 1957. *Personality and Organization*. New York: Harper.

Baldamus, W. 1961. *Efficiency and Effort*. London: Tavistock.

——, 1967, *Notes on Stratification Theory*. Discussion Papers, Series E, No. 5. Faculty of Commerce and Social Science, University of Birmingham.

Behrend, H. 1957. 'The Effort Bargain'. *Industrial and Labor Relations Review*, 10: 4, 503–15.

Bendix, R. 1963. *Work and Authority in Industry*. New York: Harper (first edition, Wiley, 1956).

Bennett, R. 1978. 'Orientations to Work and Organizational Analysis: A Conceptual Analysis, Integretation and Suggested Application'. *Journal of Management Studies*, 15: 2, 187–210.

Beveridge, W.H. 1944. *Full Employment in a Free Society*. London: George Allen & Unwin.

Blackburn, R.M. and Mann, M. 1979. *The Working Class in the Labour Market*. London: Macmillan.

Blauner, R. 1964. *Alienation and Freedom. The Factory Worker and His Industry*, Chicago: University of Chicago Press.

Brannen, P. 1983. *Authority and Participation in Industry*. London: Batsford.

Braverman, H. 1974. *Labor and Monopoly Capital. The Degradation of Work in the Twentieth Century*. New York: Monthly Review Press.

Brighton Labour Process Group. 1977. 'The Capitalist Labour Process'. *Capital and Class*, 1 (Spring), 3–26.

Brown, J.A.C. 1954. *The Social Psychology of Industry*. Harmondsworth: Penguin.

Brown, R.K. 1967. 'Research and Consultancy in Industrial Enterprises: A Review of the Contribution of the Tavistock Institute of Human Relations to the Development of Industrial Sociology'. *Sociology*, 1 (January), 33–60.

—— Curran, M.M. and Cousins. J.M. 1983. Changing Attitudes to Employment?. Research Paper No. 40. London: Department of Employment.

Brown, W. 1960. *Exploration in Management*. London: Heinemann.

—— 1971. *Organization*. London: Heinemann.

Burawoy, M. 1979. *Manufacturing Consent: Changes in the Labor Process under Monopoly Capitalism*. Chicago: University of Chicago Press.

—— 1985. *The Politics of Production. Factory Regimes under Capitalism and Socialism*. London: Verso.

Burns, T. (ed.) 1968. *Industrial Man. Selected Readings*. Harmondsworth: Penguin.

Cockburn, C. 1983. *Brothers: Male Dominance and Technological Change*. London: Pluto.

Cohen, P.S. 1968. *Modern Social Theory*. London: Heinemann.

Dahrendorf, R. 1959. *Class and Class Conflict in an Industrial Society*. London: Routledge & Kegan Paul.

Daniel. W.W. 1969. 'Industrial Behaviour and Orientation to Work – a Critique'. *Journal of Management Studies*, 6: 3, 366–75.

Durkheim, E. 1933. *The Division of Labor in Society*. Glencoe, Ill.: Free Press.

Edwards, R. 1979. *Contested Terrain. The Transformation of the Workplace in the Twentieth Century*. London: Heinemann.

Emery, F.E. (ed.) 1969. *Systems Thinking*. Harmondsworth: Penguin.

Etzioni, A. 1961. *A Comparative Analysis of Complex Organizations*. New York: Free Press.

Fox, A. 1966. 'Industrial Sociology and Industrial Relations'. *Research Papers*, 3, Royal Commission on Trade Unions and Employers' Associations. London: HMSO.

—— 1973. 'Industrial Relations: A Social Critique of Pluralist Ideology'. *Man and Organization*. Ed. Child, J. London: George Allen & Unwin.

—— 1980. 'The Meaning of Work'. *The Politics of Work and Occupations*. Eds Esland, G. and Salaman, G. Milton Keynes: Open University Press.

Friedman, A.L. 1977. *Industry and Labour. Class Struggle at Work and Monopoly Capitalism*. London: Macmillan.

Gallie, D. 1978. *In Search of the New Working Class. Automation and Social Integration within the Capitalist Enterprise*. Cambridge: Cambridge University Press.

Goldthorpe, J.H. 1966. 'Orientation to Work and Industrial Behaviour among Assembly-line Operatives: a Contribution towards an Action Approach in Industrial Sociology.' Unpublished paper to the Conference of University Teachers of Sociology, London.

—— 1977. 'Industrial Relations in Britain: A Critique of Reformism'. *Trade Unions under Capitalism*. Eds Clarke, T. and Clements, L. London: Fontana.

—— Lockwood, D., Bechhofer, F. and Platt, J. 1968. *The Affluent Worker: Industrial Attitudes and Behaviour*. Cambridge: Cambridge University Press.

Hamilton, P. 1983. *Talcott Parsons*. Chichester: Ellis Horwood: London: Tavistock.

Herzberg, F. 1966. *Work and the Nature of Man*. New York: World Publishing Co.

—— Mausner, B. and Snyderman, B. 1959. *The Motivation to Work*. New York: Wiley.

Hyman, R. 1978. 'Pluralism, Procedural Consensus and Collective Bargaining'. *British Journal of Industrial Relations*, 16 (March), 16–40.

—— 1987. 'Strategy of Structure? Capital, Labour and Control'. *Work, Employment and Society*, 1 (March), 25–55.

Ingham, G.K. 1967. 'Organization Size, Orientation to Work and Industrial Behaviour'. *Sociology*, 1 (September), 239–58.

Jaques, E. 1951. *The Changing Culture of a Factory*. London: Tavistock.

—— 1956. *The Measurement of Responsibility*. London: Tavistock. (References to Heinemann edition, 1972).

—— 1961. *Equitable Payment. A General Theory of Work, Differential Payment and Individual Progress*. London: Heinemann. (References to Penguin edition, 1967).

—— 1976. *A General Theory of Bureaucracy*. London: Heinemann.

Katz, D. and Kahn, R.L. 1966. *The Social Psychology of Organizations*. New York: Wiley.

Landsberger, H.A. 1958. *Hawthorne Revisited*. New York: Cornell University Press.

Likert, R. 1961. *New Patterns of Management*. New York: McGraw-Hill.

Littler, C.R. 1982. *The Development of the Labour Process in Capitalist Societies*. London: Heinemann.

—— and Salaman, G. 1984. *Class and Work. The Design, Allocation and Control of Jobs*. London: Batsford.

Lockwood, D. 1966. 'Sources of Variation in Working Class Images of Society'. *Sociological Review*, 14 (November), 249–67.

Lupton, T. 1961. *Money for Effort*. DSIR Problems of Progress in Industry, 11. London: HMSO.

—— and Bowey, A.M. 1974. *Wages and Salaries*. Harmondsworth: Penguin.

McGregor, D. 1960. *The Human Side of Enterprise*. New York: McGraw-Hill.

Marsden, D. 1986. *The End of Economic Man? Custom and Competition in Labour Markets*. Brighton: Wheatsheaf.

Marx, K. 1958a. 'Wage Labour and Capital'. *Selected Works*, Vol. 1. Marx, K. and Engels, F. Moscow: Foreign Languages Publishing House.

—— 1958b. 'Wages, Price and Profit'. *Selected Works*, Vol. 1. Marx, K. and Engels, F. Moscow: Foreign Languages Publishing House.

Maslow, A.H. 1943. 'A Theory of Human Motivation'. *Psychological Review*, 50, 370–96. (Reprinted in part in *Management and Motivation*. Eds Vroom, V.H. and Deci, E.L. 1970. Harmondsworth: Penguin, 27–41, to which page and references refer).

—— 1964. *Motivation and Personality*. New York: Harper.

Mayo, E. 1949. *The Social Problems of an Industrial Civilization*. London: Routledge & Kegan Paul.

Miller, E.J. and Rice, A.K. 1967. *Systems of Organization. The Control of Task and Sentient Boundaries*. London: Tavistock.

Nichols, T. (ed.) 1980. *Capital and Labour: Studies in the Capitalist Labour Process*. Glasgow: Fontana.

Parsons, T. 1960. *Structure and Process in Modern Society*. Glencoe, Ill.: Free Press.

—— and Smelser, N.J. 1956. *Economy and Society*. London: Routledge & Kegan Paul.

Rice, A.K. 1958. *Productivity and Social Organization. The Ahmedabad Experiment*. London: Tavistock.

Rice, A.K. 1963. *The Enterprise and its Environment*. London: Tavistock.

Roethlisberger, F.J. and Dickson, W.J. 1939. *Management and the Worker*. New York: Wiley.

Rose, M. 1975. *Industrial Behaviour. Theoretical Development since Taylor*. London: Allen Lane.

Ross, N.S. 1958. 'Organized Labour and Management. The United Kingdom'. *Human Relations and Modern Management*. Ed. Hugh-Jones, E.M. Amsterdam: North-Holland.

Schein, E.H. 1965. *Organizational Psychology*. Englewood Cliffs, NJ: Prentice-Hall.

Silverman, D. 1970. *The Theory of Organizations*. London: Heinemann.

Smith, J.H. 1987. 'Elton Mayo and the Hidden Hawthorne'. *Work, Employment and Society*, 1 (March), 107–20.

Stinchcombe, A.L. 1968. 'Social Structure and the Invention of Organizational Forms'. *Industrial Man*. Ed. Burns, T. Harmondsworth: Penguin. (First published, *Handbook of Organizations*. Ed. March, J.G. 1965. Rand McNally. 142–69).

Strauss, A., Schatzman, L., Ehrlich, D., Bucher, R. and Sanshin, M. 1963. 'The Hospital and its Negotiated Order'. *The Hospital in Modern Society*. Ed. Friedson, E. London: Macmillan. (Reprinted in *Decisions, Organizations and Society*. Eds. Castles, F.G. et al., 1971. Harmondsworth: Penguin).

Tannenbaum, A.S. 1966. *Social Psychology of the Work Organization*. London: Tavistock.

Thompson, P. 1983. *The Nature of Work. An Introduction to Debates on the Labour Process*. London: Macmillan.

Trist, E.L., Higgin, G.W., Murray, H. and Pollock, A.B. 1963. *Organizational Choice: Capabilities of Groups at the Coalface under Changing Technologies*. London: Tavistock.

Viteles, M.S. 1953. *Motivation and Morale in Industry*. New York: W.W. Norton.

Warr, P. and Wall, T. 1975. *Work and Well-Being*. Harmondsworth: Penguin.

Watson, T. 1987. *Sociology, Work and Industry*. Second edition. London: Routledge & Kegan Paul.

Wedderburn, Lord. 1986. *The Worker and the Law*. Third edition. Harmondsworth: Penguin.

Wood, S. (ed.) 1982. *The Degradation of Work? Skill, Deskilling and the Labour Process*. London: Hutchinson.

—— and Elliott, R. 1977. 'A Critical Evaluation of Fox's Radicalisation of Industrial Relations Theory'. *Sociology*, 11 (January), 105–25.

Woodward, J. 1958. *Management and Technology*. DSIR Problems of Progress in Industry, 3. London: HMSO.

—— 1965. *Industrial Organization: Theory and Practice*. Oxford: Oxford University Press.

3 New Technology and Clerical Work

Christel Lane

Introduction

The study of clerical work and workers has formed the centre of two important sociological debates. The first and longest standing debate focuses on the position of routine white-collar workers in the class structure of advanced society and on the issue whether or not there has occurred a proletarianization of either clerical positions or their occupants.[1] A central theme in this discussion has been how the work situation or, more narrowly, the labour process of office workers differs, if at all, from that of production workers. The diffusion of new technology has placed this issue once more on the sociological agenda. Another important concern of the proletarianization debate has been to establish whether or not the market position of clerical workers differs from that of manual workers. Here it has been argued that the superior mobility chances of clerical workers place them on bureaucratic career ladders and hence fundamentally distinguishes their market prospects from those of manual workers (Goldthorpe, 1980). With the exception of Crompton and Jones (1984), participants in both debates have, however, ignored the position of women who form the overwhelming majority (over 70 per cent) of clerical workers. Hence the proletarianization debate is related to a more recent and general controversy which focuses on how gender has shaped the occupational division of labour and the market capacities derived from it of both male and female workers.

A consideration of women in the context of the proletarianization thesis necessarily involves a confrontation with a second major debate, about the relation between gender and class. This has centred around the issue whether women's employment should be taken into account when examining aspects of family behaviour in relation to its class position or, more radically, when constructing a class schema from occupational categories (see, especially, Crompton and Mann, 1986). An important issue is thus whether a consideration of women's employment status and occupation would make a difference to the class schemata

---

1 Notable contributions to this debate have been the works of Klingender (1935), Lockwood (1966), Braverman (1974), Goldthorpe et al. (1969), Stewart et al. (1980) and Crompton and Jones (1984).

devised and the shifts in class boundaries identified for advanced societies. With the exception of the study by Marshall et al. (1988) arguments around these issues have, however, not been systematically linked to the earlier controversy on proletarianization.

The following account of the impact of new technology on clerical workers will confront the issues raised in these debates. It will attempt to test some of the propositions made by bringing to bear on them a wide range of new evidence on both clerical work and workers in the late 1970s and early 1980s when new technology became more widely diffused in offices. Evidence will be drawn from a large number of case studies in a variety of economic sectors and, to a lesser extent, from a recent study of technological change by Daniel (1987), based on a representative national sample of establishments (workplaces) in all economic sectors which, furthermore, compares the impact of advanced technological changes in offices on non-manual workers with the situation on the shopfloor.[2]

The main part of this chapter starts with an examination of the amount and range of new technology deployed in various sectors and of the factors which have determined a wide or limited adoption. This is followed by an investigation of the impact of new technology on the organization of clerical work and its consequences for clerks in terms of job content. This analysis is conducted separately for a sector with extensive automation – the financial services sector – and for economic sectors which have been less extensively touched by automation. The second part of the chapter studies the employment conditions of clerical workers, the social relations of clerical work and the social attributes of male and female clerks.

The Diffusion of New Technology

During the last decade, clerical work and workers have been greatly effected by the introduction into offices of 'new' technology. Although large areas of office work have been mechanized for some time, albeit to a much lesser extent than production work, a qualitatively different technology began to arrive in offices from the early 1960s onwards. The

---

2 Although the case studies are relatively narrow in scope they are often distinguished by a higher degree of methodological sophistication. Daniel's study, in contrast, employs a very basic definition of new technology which cannot convey the complexities of automation and its impact on work organization. An establishment is considered to deploy new or advanced office technology if one or more computing facilities and/or one or more word processors are utilized. The computing facility can be a mainframe or even only a connection to a mainframe. The by now widely accepted fact that the opportunities for work organization connected with the mainframe and interactive computers are fundamentally different is ignored. The results of this survey of the number of electronic devices are then aggregated to give a misleading 'average' picture in which a workplace with one mainframe computer is regarded in the same way (in relation to work organization) as an establishment with an integrated system linking interactive computers/word processors with new developments in telecommunications. Furthermore, data on changes in work organization are based only on a standardized survey of managers and, to a lesser extent, stewards, and a questioning of clerks or even workplace observation has not been attempted.

1960s saw the arrival of mainframe computers which automated only certain functions and did not fundamentally affect the whole office. The introduction, from the 1970s onwards, of interactive computers and other electronic devices, however, brought the potential of a more radical transformation of clerical work. It is only this second stage of technological development which is regarded as genuinely new in this context. The 'dialogue' facility, built into microcomputers, permits their much wider and more flexible application. A second important feature is that the developments in computerization and telecommunications now make it possible to link the performance of various office activities into an integrated system. Lastly, the great reduction in price of electronic devices, together with an increase in complexity and accuracy, have assisted their much wider diffusion. (For a more detailed account of the development and present state of the new technology, see the work of Gill, 1985: chapter 2.)

As Smith and Wield (1987a: 2) correctly observe 'little generalizable research has as yet been attempted about the differential impact of different systems (of new technology) on the vast spectrum of organizations using clerical and secretarial labour'. The differing stimulants, opportunities and constraints to automate clerical work in the various economic sectors have brought about considerable differences between them both in the degree of automation accomplished to date and in the *kind* of new technology adopted. Automation has advanced furthest in the financial services sector. In the rest of the private sector it has developed very unevenly, depending largely on size of the clerical labour force. It is least advanced in the public services sector. The differential degree of technological diffusion in different economic sectors is not the only factor which has had an impact on clerical work. Other important factors to be considered are the pace of technological change, the different types of technological devices which have been introduced, and the degree of integration of individual devices into an office system. In the following discussion of all these aspects, a distinction will be made between developments in the highly automated financial services sector (FSS), and those in the only partially automated other sectors (professional, personal and public services, manufacturing).

New Technology in Sectors with Low Levels of Automation

Although the pace of technological diffusion has accelerated in recent years even in these sectors one can still agree with Steffens (1982: 169) that 'at the present time in the UK [early 1980s] office automation is still more myth than reality', and that change has been evolutionary rather than revolutionary. In the early 1980s, new technology in offices of organizations outside the FSS consisted almost exclusively of stand-alone electronic equipment rather than those integrated systems – based on both electronic and telecommunication devices – which characterize office automation proper.[3] Fully automated office systems existed only in a

3 This is shown by the following case studies: Bird, 1980; Steffens, 1982; Bevan, 1984; Thompson, 1985; Webster, 1986.

handful of very large firms. The most widely adopted devices were the word processor (WP), 'smart' copiers (with microelectronic intelligence), mainframe, mini and microcomputers. Electronic mail facilities and VDU telex systems, linked to word processors, were found only in a few offices of even very large companies (Bevan, 1984: 11). All surveys show that the take-up of new office technology is a very recent phenomenon, having started in the late 1970s and early 1980s.

Daniel's (1987) national survey gives a picture of the uneven degree of diffusion of computers and word processors between economic sectors. These devices have been adopted more widely by establishments in the private manufacturing sector (by 47 per cent) than in the private services sector (by 37 per cent) (Daniel, 1987: 43, table 3.4). If we consider that the latter figure also includes establishments in the highly automated financial services sector, then the rest of the service sector must have a very low level of automation indeed. Private sector offices, however, have significantly more new technology than those in the public sector. Only 23 per cent of the establishments in the public services and 30 per cent in the nationalized industries deployed some advanced technology (Daniel, 1987: 43).

Nor has new technology had an appreciable impact on the work of all groups of clerical workers within these sectors. Degree of technological diffusion varies according to the size of the non-manual component within establishments and according to function. Thus while only 22 per cent of establishments in private manufacturing with less than fifty non-manual employees had word processors this figure rose to 86 per cent for establishments with more than 150 office workers (Daniel, 1987: 54, table 3.12). Similarly, while payroll and accounts departments are typically computerized, other departments providing personal or social services (e.g. social work departments in the public sector) or dealing with business partners or customers (e.g. a purchasing department) are hardly touched by computers. Daniel's (1987: 40) data for all economic sectors indicate that 61 per cent of non-manual workers are employed by establishments which have computing arrangements of word processors. It is worth pointing out, though, that these facilities may in individual cases amount to no more than one mainframe computer or word processor. Although new technology thus potentially touches upon the work of a majority of office workers only a small minority work with it for any length of time. Thus a 'local government' study established that only 4 per cent of all council staff, excluding those in the computer division, are *primarily* employed to work on new technology systems (Taylor et al., 1985). Thompson (1985: 6) aptly describes the process of office automation to date as 'a piecemeal process of trial and error for many organizations: an electronic typewriter for the director's secretary, a couple of word processors in the typing pool, perhaps a micro writer or personal computer for executives to try out, and a mainframe in the D.P. department which is looking rather out of date'.

But the speed of introduction of new technology in these sectors has greatly accelerated since the late 1970s (Bevan, 1984: 3; Smith, 1981) and is likely to continue growing. Smith (1981: 2) speaks of an increase in WP installations (for all sectors) at around 30 per cent per annum, and Barras and Swann (1984: 224) report that the value of investment in computers has been growing at over 20 per cent in the last few years, with an even higher growth rate of microcomputer systems. The picture of office automation, conveyed in this chapter, affords therefore only a snapshot of a rapidly changing process.

New Technology in a Highly Automated Sector

In the financial services sector – for instance retail banking and insurance – the rate of technological diffusion has been much faster, and new technology has been adopted in a more comprehensive and systematic way. Pressures from competition have not only accelerated the adoption of new technology to cut costs and offer better services, they have also prompted the introduction of important organizational rationalization in banks which is at least partially independent from the technological innovation (Loveridge et al., 1985: 24f: Batstone et al., 1987: 161f.) An advanced stage of automation is particularly pronounced in the banking sector, dominated by the Big Four among the London clearing banks – National Westminster, Barclays, the Midland and Lloyds. It applies with less force to the insurance sector, and there are also significant differences in development within sectors (Barras and Swann, 1983: Rajan, 1984). The prominence of this sector in recent research on new technology and clerical work may have given this sector greater centrality in our thinking about office technology than is warranted. It is important to keep the relatively high level of automation in this sector in perspective. In 1983 the banking and insurance industry employed only 3.45 per cent of the total labour force (*Annual Abstract of Statistics*, 1985).

The functions performed within the financial services sector are also distinctive. Whereas in other sectors text production amd manipulation is usually the most important function, in the financial services sector the manipulation and transmission of large amounts of standardized quantitative data are at the forefront and hence call for different work processes and electronic devices. Besides being occupied with fairly routine information-handling activities employees are at the same time engaged in the more varied and imponderable direct or indirect (telephone work) personal interaction with customers. The tension between these two very different types of activities is an important factor to be considered when examining the impact of new technology on their employment and work.

Automation in *banking* started in the 1960s when large, centrally located mainframe computers were introduced to automate consumer account records which had previously been handled manually at branch level. Also in the 1960s came automatic inter-bank cheque clearing systems involving Magnetic Ink Character Recognition (MICR) and, in 1968, the Bankers Automated Clearing Service (BACS) which introduced electronic funds transfer (EFT) between computers using magnetic tapes. This automated such transfers as salary payments, standing orders and direct debits. But only a small proportion of clearing is automated at the present time, and paper transfer is still substantial (Loveridge et al., 1985: 28).

In 1978, world-wide inter-bank electronic message transmission (SWIFT) became possible. The 1970s brought on-line computer terminals and microcomputers into the branch banks, making it possible to input data in bank networks at the point of origin as well as providing a 'dialogue' facility. There were also the beginnings of cash dispensers (CDs), Automated Teller Machines (ATMs) and counter automation.

The last two received further development during the 1980s but are, as yet, not comprehensively used. ATMs are more widely diffused than counter terminals (CTs). In the area of cheque clearing, MICR is being replaced by optical character recognition (OCR), i.e. the computer now 'reads' instructions. Home banking and electronic fund transfer at point of sale (EFT/POS) are still only incipient as integrated systems. (EFT/POS entails the substitution of electronic instructions for paper ones, such as on cheques or credit card vouchers and their transmission from the retailer (point of sale) directly to a central clearing point in the banking system.) A unified scheme of EFT/POS by the London clearing banks is contemplated to start in 1988.

The array of electronic devices and processes, automating the chief banking activities, is thus impressive but they have been introduced in a steady manner over two decades. Nevertheless, a considerable impact on the quantity and quality of employment has accompanied technological change.

In the *insurance* sector the first stage of application of computer technology came in the early 1960s and was similar to that already described for banking. The introduction of mainframe computers at head-office level automated such activities as payroll administration, accounting and premium billing. Administration became even more centralized than it had previously been, and data preparation for the computer took the form of batch processing. Only in the late 1970s and in the early 1980s did terminals and mini computers become widely installed in branch offices. An on-line locally distributed processing system became technically possible. It permits the issuing of instant quotations and of policies and has an impact on every feature of underwriting and claims. But distributed processing has not become the norm, and a large part of processing still occurs at head-office level. During the 1980s word processors, both of the stand-alone and the 'shared systems' variety, were introduced, albeit in a piecemeal manner. The integration of word processing with numerical data processing is still very underdeveloped (Barras and Swann 1983: 2). Direct computer links between field agents and central offices, cutting out branch intermediaries, are also still in their infancy.

During the early 1980s a majority of companies had reached the point where VDU terminals installed in branches gave them on-line facilities and where mini computers did a limited amount of local data processing. Any more advanced developments had occurred in only a small minority of cases (Rajan, 1984: 28). The fully automated office, linking electronic and telecommunication devices into an integrated system, is still a vision of the future in the insurance industry (Rajan, 1984: 26f.). Technological development in the insurance industry has thus lagged behind that in banking.

Change has also been more uneven within the sector. Rajan (1984: 28) sums up the process of automation as follows: 'On the evolutionary scale, the industry is now roughly at mid-point, and there is still considerable room for new applications. Even so, the sheer volume of hardware accumulated so far adds up to a formidable stock of information processing capacity.'

New Technology and Changes in Work Organization

New technology is widely presumed to have wrought fundamental changes in the nature of clerical work although the impact is not always seen to be a direct one. The advent of new technology can lead to a redesign of existing jobs and even to a change in work organization, encompassing a whole range of related jobs. An evaluation of the content of the work performed in given jobs and of changes in this content usually focuses on three major aspects: the degree of task specialization and the level of skill required; the level of discretion granted or control exerted over tasks performance or over its results, and the extent of social integration or isolation afforded by the job. A pattern of work organization assigning clerks highly specialized and fragmented tasks, requiring a low level of skill and affording little discretion, is referred to as Taylorist, after the founder of the tradition of 'Scientific Management', F.W. Taylor.

The most striking feature revealed by recent empirical studies is that, even when technological development is similar, an extreme variety in patterns of work organization exists. Hence it is difficult to generalize about outcomes across economic sectors and even organizations within sectors. The new technology facilitates certain patterns of work organization but other factors mediate its impact in significant ways. Among these, management organizational strategy or, less pointedly, practice, would appear to be particularly important. This, in turn, is shaped by various economic and social considerations.

Studies of managerial strategies in relation to new technology and clerical work have emphasized the extreme complexity in this area (Willman, 1986; Gourlay, 1987). In many cases management does not possess a systematic and consciously elaborated plan or, if such a plan exists, it changes over time as management goals are adapted to the changing economic environment. Generally speaking, management strategy becomes the more elaborated the higher the degree of automation. Many empirical studies of new technology and clerical work in sectors with low levels of automation imply the absence of a consciously articulated managerial strategy and identify only piecemeal and *ad hoc* reactions to the changed technological environment. Most surveys of developments in the FSS sector, in contrast, trace the evolvement of a more or less systematic managerial strategy on new technology. These features have obvious implications for the degree of change in clerical work associated with the introduction of new technology.

The elaboration of a managerial strategy may be influenced by a variety of considerations, connected with the overall competitive strategy of the industry or organization and with a desire to increase efficiency. The competitive position of a business organization may be maintained or enhanced by cutting costs (cutting out clerical jobs and/or raising worker productivity), or by increasing the quality of the end product. The strategy will thus vary depending on whether clerical salary costs constitute a large proportion of overall operating costs as, for example, in public administration. It will also be influenced by considerations of whether clerical labour contributes significantly to the quality of the end product, as. for example, in the professional services sector, or whether it is a relatively minor influence, as, for example, in manufacturing. The translation of this strategy into a form of work organization may, in turn, be shaped by other considerations, such as the perceived scope for rationalization, or the traditional managerial style and the pre-existing pattern of social relations between management and clerical workers. The perceived scope for rationalization depends on size of firm, available capital and, crucially, the nature of the information to be handled. Managerial style can be influenced by a variety of factors: the presence or absence of pressure from shareholders (e.g. private vs. public sector or mutual organizations); physical and social distance between top management and clerical staff (small vs. large, single vs. multi-establishment firm); and, lastly, a whole number of more imponderable features connected with the social characteristics and attitudes of individual managers.

The influence of managerial strategy, mediated by the perceived task environment, can be illustrated by contrasting developments in the financial services sector (particularly in banking) with those in other, predominantly private, sectors. Such a contrast involves, at the same time, a comparison of the work of different categories of office workers. Whereas in the financial services sector general clerical workers predominate, in other private sector studies the focus has been mainly on typists and secretaries. In the public sector both categories would be important but few studies of this sector exist. In the financial services sector, the presence of both male and female clerks, together with a relatively low degree of spatial segregation, permits a study whether advanced technology has had a different impact on the jobs of men and women. Among secretaries and typists, in contrast, who are over 90 per cent female, such as differentiated approach has no place. Lastly, clerical workers in the financial services sector have had to adjust to a wide array of electronic devices, while secretaries and typists have had to contend mainly with word processors.

The Impact of Word Processors on the Work of Secretaries and Typists

As the work of secretaries and typists had been structured differently before the advent of new technology its impact on job content, nature of control and social relations is also divergent. This is cogently expressed by Webster (1986: 120) who also carefully substantiates this point 'Generalisations about the effects of new technology are potentially misleading, since they focus upon the assumed characteristics of the technology to the exclusion of the features present in the jobs affected.'

Before the advent of the WP the job of a secretary was constituted by a variety of functions, both of a mechanical kind (shorthand, typing, filing) and of an administrative and social kind (generally servicing her boss). The range of the secretary's administrative duties has been very diverse, particularly those of the personal secretary, and the fluidity of her role must be seen as one of the determining features of secretarial job content and organizational status. The secretary alternated between functions so that her work was neither amenable to close control by her boss nor to machine-pacing. On the contrary, she enjoyed a fair degree of discretion about how to arrange her job tasks – she could even define and initiate them herself – and used machines as aids for the accomplishment of the latter. She was able to see tasks through from beginning to end so that job satisfaction and interest could develop. Her job involved a considerable amount of social contact with both superiors and other clerical staff. Frequently, senior or personal secretaries had a junior secretary or typist working for them (Vinnicombe, 1980: 65).

The introduction of the word processor, it is widely agreed, has done little to change this pattern of work organization, control and social relations (Bird, 1980: 47; NEDO, 1983: 21; Bevan, 1984: 9f.; Webster, 1986: 120f.). In none of the case studies considered were personal or departmental secretaries demoted to full-time WP operators. They merely had access to a WP which they deployed in the same way as they had once the typewriter. Bevan (1984: 9) notes that they spend no more than 50 per cent of their time in front of WPs. The introduction of WPs enables them to cope better with their previously often excessive workload and frees them from executing the more boring and repetitive work tasks. It is pointed out by several authors (Bevan, 1984; Webster, 1986; and Baldry et al. 1986) that, generally, secretaries welcome the changes the WP has made possible. In offices where more advanced information systems have been installed secretaries have acquired a number of new tasks, such as records management and information retrieval and information analysis and collation (NEDO, 1983; 21), giving them a chance to enhance their job status.

The consequence of some of the above noted developments is that secretaries' jobs, rather than being downgraded by the new technology, have often been upgraded. As word processor operators have taken over the more routine text production tasks secretaries are left with more time for administrative or even managerial tasks, or, as Bird (1980: 47) found, in some cases have become underemployed. Some organizations among her case studies were contemplating a change from personal to administrative secretary servicing several rather than one manager. But it remains to be seen whether the proprietary instincts and status strivings of managers, expressed in the 'personal secretary' syndrome, would permit this plan to come to fruition. There was no evidence in any of the studies consulted to support the claim made by Littler and Salaman (1984: 90) 'that relations between bosses and secretaries are tending to become depersonalized' due to the introduction of new technology.

The typist's job differed significantly from that of the secretary before office automation, and this different structuring has largely survived the introduction of the WP into office work. The typist is occupied with only one task: reproducing text from manuscript copy or from dictation on audio machines. More often than not the work required is simple, standardized and mundane, the more complex and interesting jobs being done by the secretary. She has therefore little scope for exercising direction over how to organize her day but is often paced by the amount of work put in front of her. If the typist is working in a typing pool she is also physically and socially separated from the rest of the office staff. Her work may be supervised by a typing pool supervisor who monitors her progress and may prevent informal socializing.

The switch from the typewriter to the WP – the latter is most likely to be of the stand-alone rather than a shared-logic' variety – has had more far-reaching changes for the typist than it has had for the secretary. But empirical studies vary about the degree and nature of such change, and very few studies arrive at unambiguous conclusions about whether overall change must be interpreted as an improvement or a deterioration in typists' work situation. This ambiguity is not only due to the diversity of management goals. It is also caused by the fact that change within individual jobs has not occurred in a unilinear direction. A typist's job may have improved along the dimension of task variety but has deteriorated in terms of work intensity, to give only one example.

Analysis of the effect of word processors on task content yields differing results in different studies. Webster (1986: 125–6) finds no change in the types of material given to operators – it has remained as standardized as it was before the advent of word processors. Wainwright and Francis (1984: 89) generally bear out the conclusion about lack of change but not the finding that all material is standardized, and they also report some cases where task variety has been increased. Buchanan and Boddy (1982), in contrast, note an increased standardization of job content, due to a decreasing variety of material. Diversity in task content and also responsibility is also created by the different ways in which the work flow of operators is regulated. In smaller firms, operators are given responsibility for all the tasks connected with word processing, whereas in some larger firms tasks have been split up and distributed among positions in a word processing hierarchy (Bird, 1980: 53, Wainwright and Francis, 1984: 134f; Bevan, 1984: 10).

Similar diversity characterizes the findings about the degree of job fragmentation of word processing operators. Although several authors report some cases where job fragmentation has increased (Baldry et al., 1986: Buchanan and Boddy, 1982: Wainwright and Francis, 1984.) this has by no means occurred in all cases. Increased fragmentation can be due to the subdivision of long documents between operators or to the physical separation between the operator and the printer. In each case the type of work organization is the result of management choice rather than being an inevitable feature of new technology.

Whether or not the introduction of word processors causes increased social isolation for operators does not receive an unequivocal answer either. Webster (1986) and Bird (1980) point out that there is no increase in social isolation if the typist worked in a pool before, but for typists in at least one study (Buchanan and Boddy, 1982: 459) the switch to the WP was utilized by management to centralize the typing service and separate typists from those who compose the material they type. On the other hand, word processor pools tend to be smaller than typing pools and are usually mere 'puddles' of around five operators (Bird, 1980: 52). There is no technical reason why they cannot be integrated into the main office.

A negative consequence of the introduction of word processors has been the incidence of health problems, such as eye strain, headaches and muscular pains (Baldry et al., 1986: 14). It is not clear at the present time whether this is largely due to the inadequate handling of new technology by inexperienced management and operators, or whether it constitutes a more serious, lasting hazard, inevitably flowing from the equipment (Thompson, 1985: 18). A more permanent increase in strain is, however, caused by the increased intensity of work connected with the use of word processors. This is reported almost universally. Baldry et al. (1986: 13) and Buchanan and Boddy (1982: 157) connect increased intensity with the facts that the 'live' screen compels the uninterrupted usage of the machine and that there are few other tasks, e.g. changing paper, to interrupt workflow.

Some authors (e.g. Downing (1980); West (1982)) claim that word processors have led to the deskilling of clerical work because word processors take over some of the skilled activities, such as working out margins or the general layout. Most case studies, however, report a shift in the kind of skills required and put the emphasis on the acquisition of new skills. Buchanan (1985: 459), for example, mentions such new skills as computer file management procedures and knowing the editing codes for the manipulation of stored text. Others speak more generally of the changeover to technical skills (Taylor et al., 1985: 278) or process skills (i.e. change from manipulative to cognitive or conceptual skills) (NEDO, 1983: 21; Wainwright and Francis, 1984: 119). Weighing up lost skills against newly acquired ones, Buchanan concludes that 'the job is therefore more skilled and demanding than conventional typing', and Taylor et al. (1985) also posit 'an increased skill content'. The NEDO study (1983: 24), which focuses on advanced information systems, goes even further and arrives at the following general conclusions. 'The evidence from this study is that advanced, interactive information systems put these trends (towards deskilling and fragmentation) into reverse. The jobs that remain, as a broad generalisation, require a greater use of discretion, initiative . . .; very few specific skills are rendered redundant . . .' There exists no firm evidence that monitoring of typists' work has significantly increased, although it is now technically possible. Wainwright and Francis (1984: 197) and Taylor et al. (1985: 70) stress that the close supervision of clerical workers comes very low on the list of benefits management expects from the new technology.

Whichever way social scientists interpret the impact of WPs on typists' job content there is little doubt in the minds of WP operators themselves. Many studies report an increase in work satisfaction among the latter, and no empirical study claims a general decrease.[4] Respondents connect an increase in work satisfaction with diverse factors: the WP allows typists to improve the quality of the finished product; it eliminates much tedium from the correction of a text; staff derive satisfaction from operating modern computing equipment; and last, but not least, most organizations have put WP operators on a higher pay grade, and their chances in the external labour market have also improved. There is some concern, however, that these satisfactions derive largely from the novelty of the jobs and thus may not endure.

Thus, secretaries' and typists' work has been quite differently affected by the arrival of the word processor, and pre-existing divergences in the task content of their jobs have largely survived. Although the work of word processor operators may have been changed along several dimensions, the extent and direction of change was found to vary significantly between cases. None of the case studies detects an unambiguous deterioration in their position in the labour process and several claim an increase in skill. This variety of outcomes has been explained mainly in terms of different management approaches to work organization. Whereas some managements use the introduction of the word processor to initiate organizational rationalization, others are quite content to perpetuate the old pattern of work organization. Among the rationalizers, some are guided only by cost considerations or regard work organizations from a purely technical point of view. Others are more inclined to reorganize the labor process bearing operators' needs in mind.

New Technology and Changes in Work Organization in the Financial Services Sector

It is widely recognized that the work of clerks in the financial services sector was already highly specialized, routinized and controlled before the advent of computerization in the 1960s (Rajan, 1984: 116). Work in the insurance sector has often been cited as representing the most extreme tendency in this direction and as an example of the industrialization of office work (Guilano, 1985: 304). The arrival of mainframe computers is said merely to have intensified this pre-existing tendency (Gourlay, 1987: 14). The introduction of on-line computers from the middle 1970s to early 1980s, however, is not portrayed as simply continuing or intensifying this development. It is generally connected with the emergence of a more complex and varied picture of work and control processes in which the new technology is seen at most as a facilitating and not as a determining factor. There exist some important differences in work organization (WO) between the two sectors as well as variation within sectors between organizations of varying size, and between head office and branches.

In the insurance industry, the lesser pervasiveness of the new technology and the less centralized form of organization adopted by some managers

---

4 Studies reporting an increase in satisfaction include: Taylor et al. (1985: 282); Buchanan and Boddy (1982: 156); Baldry et al. (1986: 12, 14); Bird (1980: 7, 49); Wainwright and Francis (1984: 195).

(distributed processing) have, at least in some companies, created forms of WO which are moving away from the Taylorist model. Integration of previously separate functions has added more variety to work (Barras and Swann, 1983: 47; Storey, 1984: 34) and has, at the least, prevented further deskilling. In some companies, which practise distributed processing, this process of integration has led to job enrichment and hence to some reskilling (Gourlay, 1987: 18, Rajan, 1984: 117). Individual staff now perform 'a further cycle of work involving customer enquiries, liaison with brokers, processing of new applications, underwriting within set limits and claims handling'. As is the case with word processor operators, there has occurred a change in the kind of skill required from apprenticeship-based clerical skills to problem-solving and diagnostic skills, not tied to the execution of specific tasks.

The investigations of work organization by Storey (1984) and Gourlay (1987) provide insights on the degree of machine-pacing and technological control associated with the new technology. Both authors stress that clerks do not work continuously with computers and that there is no possibility for machine-pacing. Several clerks share a terminal, and work on the computer is interspersed with other types of work, particularly dealing with customers. The latter fact, Storey (1984: 30) points out, makes it difficult to control work by technological means. Gourlay (1987: 14) adds that management in his case study had concluded that close monitoring of workers would not be cost effective. Both authors conclude that personal forms of control are still very prevalent and that the intensity of this control varies greatly between different supervisors. By and large both Storey (1984: 8) and Gourlay (1987: 14f.) found managerial style to be relaxed. The internalized self-control of employees, often seen to distinguish non-manual from manual workers, was still found to be extant and obviated extensive technological control. Gourlay (1987: 20) even notes an increase in the degree of job control granted to lower grade clerks, although the prestructuring of decision-making at head-office level sets limits to the scope of local autonomy. Finally, the generally positive changes in work organization, facilitated by the new technology, are also reflected in staff reactions to it which, on the whole, have been favourable (Barras and Swann, 1983: 47).

In banking, the direction of change has been more markedly towards Taylorist forms of work organisation than in insurance. This is partly due to organizational changes in several of the 'big' banks which are at least partially independent from technical change. The creation of a 'two-tier' system distinguishes between 'higher-tier' central offices – the hub, and 'lower-tier' satellite branches and entails a division of labour between the two. Satellite branches are assigned only the routine money services and are staffed with less well-trained non-career staff whereas central offices deal with the more complex and demanding banking activities which are less amenable to automation and require a more highly skilled staff. But even in banking the process of Taylorization has been only partial and inconsistent. It is necessary to distinguish between the impact of the new technology on job content and control of the work process at different organizational levels and in different functional areas. But there is also variation *within* given organizational entities, particularly at branch level. This is due to the fact, noted by Loveridge et al. (1985: 34–40), that job design is in the discretion of local management and not prescribed by technology. Thus one and the same new technological device can give rise to different forms of utilization and work organization around it. This is well illustrated by these authors with reference to counter terminals.

There is agreement in the literature that routinized detail work, dominated by the computer, is characteristic of clerks working in central data processing departments or in the machine room of branch offices. This is confirmed by clerks themselves who frequently describe their tasks as factory work (Smith and Wield, 1987b). But the latest stage of computerization has not intensified this tendency. Where clerks have known both the batch and the on-line system of data processing they generally see the latter as having brought distinct improvements in their work. It permits some discretion in arranging the workflow and thus has lessened machine-pacing (Loveridge et al., 1985: 42).

Branch work more generally, now executed increasingly by non-career staff and by part-time clerks, is also considered as having relatively low skill content and as affording little discretion and responsibility. This is particularly true for satellite branches where the specialization of clerical staff has greatly increased. But there is no strong endorsement in the literature of the claim, first advanced by Crompton and Jones (1984), that the new technology has caused further unambiguous deskilling of clerical work. Although automation has eliminated the use of some apprenticeship-based skills and has increased functional specialization, often new diagnostic skills are called for. There has also developed a growing emphasis on social skills, which are required to market the new range of services to customers (Rajan. 1984: 116; Willman, 1986: 221).

Increase in functional specialization is, to some extent, counteracted – at least in the traditional small branch – by the opportunity for clerks to execute a range of tasks, albeit all of a fairly simple nature. Job rotation can take place either on a permanent basis or at certain times of work pressure, such as lunch time, the end of the day and to cover for staff absence. Even in satellite branches where functional specialization has become pronounced, the uneven flow of work – both in terms of quantity and quality – characteristic of banking, still requires staff flexibility. Hence, despite trends towards a greater division of labour, clerks at branch level have not become detail workers, locked into *one* monotonous activity which can be paced and controlled by the new technology. Job rotation in banking, in contrast to the insurance industry, rarely provides job enrichment. At branch level it applies to both male and female clerks but it occurs in different patterns. Generally male staff are passed through the monotonous jobs, for example, work in the mech room, very quickly during training and do not return there afterwards. Women, in contrast, may spend the bulk of their time on activities like data processing, remittance work or cashiering and see very little or nothing of the more interesting and responsible work (Murray, 1986: 5; Smith and Wield, 1987b). A deterioration in the quality of their work is indicated by the fact that a significant proportion of clerks now express a general dissatisfaction with their work, stressing particularly the increased intensity and monotony of work (Murray, 1986: Smith and Wield, 1987b).

Technological control of clerical work – of both the work process and of results – is now a possibility. The capacity to increase control of clerical work by technological means is probably most developed in the banking sector, because of the combination of a highly technicized labour process and a high degree of standardization of work procedures. But there is no clear indication in the literature as to what extent this control potential of the new technology is *actually* utilized by management. The introduction of work measurement schemes is mentioned but it remains uncertain to what extent they are enforced.

This overview of changes in work organization in the financial services sector has brought out that the much more comprehensive automation of work operations has affected *all* clerical workers in these industries and has changed their work situation more decisively than in other sectors. The banking and insurance industries are characterized by a similar task environment, more pressing labour cost considerations and strong competitive pressures. Despite this similarity in constraints on management decision-making, significant differences in management approaches to work organizations have evolved.

The more decentralized organizational structure, greater preference for personal, rather than technological, control and the utilization of the new technology for job enrichment indicates a more relaxed managerial style in, at least, some insurance companies. In banking, in contrast, work reorganization has been more strongly market and technology led and, despite a paternalist management tradition, the interests and needs of clerical workers have been given no consideration in the implementation of the new strategy (Smith and Wield. 1987b).

An emphasis on diversity of work organization does not, however, deny the fact that some common patterns have emerged. These common elements in the clerical labour process are the elimination of some task-specific skills and their replacement by new diagnostic/process skills as well as a general intensification of the pace of work. These commonalities may be regarded as direct consequences of the new technology. Diversity, it has repeatedly been pointed out, is caused by the variety of managerial goals and their more or less conscious and coherent translation into practices of work organization. These strategies are to some extent shaped by the pre-existing task environment but by no means completely determined by it.

It is sometimes suggested that the degree of automation and the pattern of work organization found in the banking sector represent the situation towards which developments of clerical work in all sectors will eventually advance. While it is undoubtedly true that the diffusion of the new technology will accelerate during the coming decade and affect all sectors to a larger degree, the argument for convergence cannot be sustained. It neglects to consider the differing task environment, that is, the volume of information to be processed and the degree of standardization and subdivision to which it is amenable, as well as the differing importance clerical labour plays within management calculations on operating costs and competitive strategy. These facts will always differ and militate against the emergence of unilinear trends in the relation between advanced technology and work organization.

Given the absence of such a unilinear trend it is fair to say that new office technology, at the very least, has not led to a *further* proletarianization of clerical work. The great variety and complexity in the relation between technology and work – this applies as much to manual work on the shop floor as it does to office work – makes it hazardous to venture any general conclusions about whether or not clerical work *is* proletarianized. If, however, a more limited comparison is made of clerical work with the strongest tendency towards Taylorization (i.e. that in banking) with its equivalent on the shopfloor (i.e. assembly line work) then it becomes clear that this development has progressed much further in the latter than the former case. Alternatively, one could compare the position of clerical workers with that of manual workers who have also experienced the impact of microelectronic technology. Daniel (1987: 164) has undertaken such a comparison and concludes that, according to managers' perception, advanced technology has enriched the jobs of office workers substantially more than those of manual workers and thus gives no support to the thesis of proletarianization of clerical positions.

Conditions of Employment

A consideration of clerical work requires an examination not only of the labour process but also of the conditions under which this work is carried out. These, in turn, can be divided into economic or market conditions of work, and into social relations of work. The first comprise factors such as the size and composition of the pay packet, the number of hours worked, fringe benefits and the degree of both employment security and promotion chances. The second is concerned with the nature of relations between clerical workers on the one side and that between workers and their superiors, on the other. These aspects of clerical work, although singled out by Braverman himself (1974: 353) as indicators of the degree of proletarianization, have – with the exception of the *size* of pay packets – received little systematic coverage in empirical studies of clerical work during the 1980s.

Size and Composition of the Pay Packet

The deterioration of the size of clerical workers' pay packets in relation to that of manual workers during the last five decades is now almost a sociological commonplace in class and stratification studies of British society. It is usually cited as an important indicator of the proletarianization of routine non-manual workers. But these comparisons of income rarely disaggregate the data on pay by sex to ensure that the comparison is between like categories, nor do they always highlight the different way in which manual and clerical pay packets are generated. It will become clear later that the market conditions enjoyed by female clerks are in several ways quite different from those of their male counterparts. Any conclusions about proletarianization derived from these data depend very much on whether one compares female clerks with male manual workers or whether one makes the comparison with female manuals. From the point of view of consequences of class position for individual social consciousness, the latter would be the more appropriate, but such a comparison has rarely been made.

If one simply compares the average size of the weekly pay of clerical workers with that of the various categories of manual workers it is clear that, from the mid-1930s onwards, the differential between clerical and manual workers (particularly, semi- and unskilled ones) steadily declined and that, by the late 1970s, the level of clerical earnings had fallen below even that of semi-skilled manuals (Routh, 1980: 120, 121). By the mid-1980s this picture had not changed, and the gross weekly pay for the category 'clerical and related' of £140.80 fell well below the pay for all categories of manual workers combined – £162.20 (*New Earnings Survey*, 1986: B18–20). These aggregated figures hide important differences in earnings by sex. In 1978, women clerical workers, on average, were earning 74 per cent of the pay of their male colleagues, and for manual women the equivalent was only 60 per cent (Routh, 1980: 123, table 2.28).

The category of clerical workers is, of course, predominantly female whereas that of manual workers is largely male, and hence a comparison of aggregate pay is very misleading. If we examine the data in table 3.1 which separate out male and female earnings for both categories then the manual superiority in pay becomes much less pronounced for men and it disappears completely for women. Gross hourly earnings of women in the category 'junior office' is in fact above that of all categories of women manuals. (As the data in table 3.1, taken from Heath and

TABLE 3.1 *Gross hourly earnings (£) of economically active men and women*

Socio-economic group	Men	N	Women	N
Semi-professional	2.85	380	2.22	593
Supervisory	2.42	116	1.79	106
Junior office	1.87	578	1.50	1508
Sales	2.06	207	1.04	458
Personal service	1.26	64	1.12	735
Skilled manual	1.94	2221	1.28	202
Semi-skilled manual	1.74	975	1.29	637
Unskilled manual	1.50	285	1.11	507

Source: *General Household Survey*, 1979, quoted by Heath and Britten (1984: 478)

TABLE 3.2   *The composition of earnings in manual and clerical occupations in 1986 (full-time employees on adult rates)*

	Average gross weekly earnings in £ of which				Average weekly hours	
	Total	Overtime	PBR	Shift	Total	Overtime
Clerical and related	140.08	6.8	2.6	1.6	38.0	1.4
All manual occupations	163.2	21.8	12.4	5.3	43.6	4.7

Source: New Earnings Survey, 1986, B18–20, table X 3

Britten (1984: 477f.), show, women clerks' pay is also above that of sales and personal service workers who are often classified, together with clerical workers, as 'routine non-manual'. They suggest it would be more appropriate to lump the former together with manual women and refer to this category as 'proletarians'). Moreover, whereas the level of hourly earnings of clerical women workers rises steadily with length of service, that of manual skilled and unskilled women declines after ten and five years of service respectively (Martin and Roberts, 1984: 45).

Furthermore, as is shown in table 3.2, the overall pay of manual workers is earned during more hours of work and contains a greater fluctuating element, due to earnings from overtime, shiftwork or 'payment by results' (PBR) schemes. This makes manual pay less secure, stable and predictable. Female clerical workers also work less hours (36.4 hours) than women manuals (38.4 hours) (Martin and Roberts, 1984: 34; author's calculations from table 4.2), although the difference is less striking in the case of women workers because women manual workers do much less overtime.

One claim of the thesis of degradation of labour following automation is that a cheapening of labour occurs. There is no indication in the case studies that this has actually occurred as far as absolute or relative levels of pay are concerned. On the contrary, there are signs that the opposite trend is under way. Word processor operators, for example, receive higher hourly rates than typists, and in one industry at least – insurance – a general upgrading of staff has occurred (Batstone et al., 1987: 167). Daniel's study (1987: 249, table X.5) supports this picture. The introduction of new office technology was either found to be correlated with no change in earnings (in 74 per cent of establishments) or with increases (in 24 per cent of establishments). Cheapening of labour can, of course, be achieved in other ways, such as increasing productivity, increasing the proportion of female workers or of part-time workers. While an increased labour intensity is widely observed, a significant rise in female and part-time labour has taken place only in banking and building societies.

Turning to fringe benefits of the two categories of workers, it is undoubtedly the case that, in the post-war period, the trend has been in favour of manual workers and that the gap with routine white-collar workers has been diminished. This does *not*, however, mean that there now exists equality of employment conditions between the two. Concerning fringe benefits, such as inclusion in employers' pension and sick pay schemes and number of holidays, clerical workers still remain significantly better off than manual workers. This is true for both men and women although female clerical workers are disadvantaged in relation to their male colleagues (see data by Heath and Britten, 1984: 479, 480).

Promotion Prospects

The good chances of male clerks to achieve upward social mobility was first highlighted by Lockwood (1966). The influential study by Stewart et al. (1980) of occupational mobility patterns of male clerks during the 1960s confirmed the excellent promotion chances of male clerks in general but drew attention to the differential pattern within the larger category according to class origin. Although the authors emphasized that these promotion chances were not enjoyed by female clerks and that superior male chances were based on this inequality of opportunity, they did not provide any data on female clerks. Despite much new research on clerical work since then, the study by Crompton and Jones (1984) remains the only one providing detailed empirical data on both male *and* female promotion patterns. Their study outlines promotion profiles for the 1970s and cannot fully reflect the potential impact of new office technology which has become broadly diffused only during the 1980s. More recently, Marshall et al. (1988: chapters 4, 5) have confirmed the disproportionately low career opportunities of routine non-manual women as opposed to men, but their study does not consider the impact of new technology. Thus, in the following, a comparison will be made of promotion chances before and after the occurrence of a significant degree of automation. A picture of promotion chances during the 1980s has to be built up from scattered, incidental information, and this picture is much fuller for clerical workers in the financial services sector than for secretaries and typists in all sectors.

In banking during the 1970s, a policy of single-entry recruitment and generalist apprenticeship-type training was adhered to. At least in theory, this made every clerk a potential manager. But career opportunities were unevenly distributed between the sexes. Whereas male clerks were encouraged to acquire the qualifications necessary for promotion, female clerks either did not seek them or were actively discouraged from attending qualifying institutions (Crompton and Jones, 1984: 145). Consequently, male clerks had disproportionately good promotion chances. In the insurance and public sector the acquisition of post-entry qualifications has not been such a strict prerequisite but the advantage of male over female clerks has been the same in these latter sectors (Crompton and Jones, 1984: 84). In all three sectors, a very large minority (41 per cent) of male clerks eventually reached managerial status, and the overwhelming majority of the rest advanced to the middle levels of the hierarchy. A considerable proportion of men, however, leave their clerical jobs at a young age (between the ages of 25 and 35), thus increasing the promotion chances of those staying behind (Crompton and Jones, 1984: 90). Figures provided by Gourlay (1987: 11) shoow that in insurance a distinction between low-level exclusively female jobs and jobs concerned with more complex tasks for both men and women was already being made in recruitment in the 1970s, after the introduction of mainframe computers. Women in the financial services sector hardly ever made it to the managerial level (a mere 1 per cent) and were also grossly underrespresented in supervisory positions and even on the higher clerical grades (i.e. grades 3 and 4).[5]

The situation has always been different for secretaries and typists who never had access to managerial positions. Both have had limited promotion prospects even before the advent of new technology, although the situation for secretaries has been more varied and, in many cases, more promising than for typists.

Secretaries have always had reasonable prospects of rising internally from typist via junior secretary to senior secretary. Among the latter one can further distinguish between departmental or group secretaries and the more elevated status of personal or executive secretary. Further promotion can be achieved by moving up the organizational hierarchy with one's boss, and on the external labour market the salary of a secretary usually rises with the size of firm employing her (*Office Salaries Analysis*, 1976: 44f.). Although the formal job hierarchy is thus short, it hides a considerable range in terms of pay and degree of responsibility and status. The advancement to top secretarial positions cannot be uniformly expected. It depends, as Downing (1980: 281) points out, as much on class-specific feminine social skills as on the level of technical skill. But the secretarial structure is an inverted pyramid, and the positions for top personal secretaries far outweigh positions for junior secretaries within many private sector organizations (Vinnicombe, 1980). Thus promotion chances, albeit over a very short distance, must be excellent for well-qualified women.

The introduction of new technology has not changed this situation. Although the loss of many routine typing jobs has made it possible for secretaries to take on more management functions, none of the case study firms had developed a career structure to recognize and formalize such an increase in responsibility. For secretarial positions to become entry points into the managerial realm a far more radical (gender) ideological and organizational restructuring of office life would have to occur. But in some of the larger organizations promotion to positions in a new word processor hierarchy is occurring. Both secretaries and typists have been promoted into supervisory, training or technical support positions, connected with word processing pools (Wainwright and Francis, 1984), but such positions are not very plentiful. At the same time, the introduction of the new technology has not resulted in a deterioration of secretaries' position in the hierarchy, In none of the case studies were secretaries demoted to full-time word processor operators.

5 For details on promotion in the banking and insurance industries, see the work of Crompton and Jones, 1984: 78f., 137–8; for banking only, see the studies by Saunders and Marsden, 1981: 148–9; Povall et al., 1982: 64; *Report and Recommendations of the EOC of the BIFU*, 1981.

Typists have more limited prospects than secretaries and can rise from trainee to typist and senior typist. Some eventually become secretaries. The jobs of word processor operators have often become more divorced from those of secretaries, particularly where they were moved from their offices into a pool. Hence a move up into a secretarial position has become more difficult. But, on the other hand, word processor operators' prospects on the external labour market have improved and this fact, together with improved pay and some promotion prospects to new positions in the word processing hierarchy, has given many operators the feeling of an improved job status. This may, however, be only a transitionary phenomenon, due to the novelty of the new technology and the shortage of trained operators.

There are no systematic data available for the 1980s which could settle the question whether the wide diffusion of the new technology in the financial services sector has changed the promotion patterns in important ways. But it is generally asserted that career chances of both male and female clerks have deteriorated (e.g. Smith and Wield, 1987: Storey, 1984). The following trends are identified as having had a negative impact on promotion changes: a slower expansion of business volume or general employment; a reduction of the branch network; the tiering of branches in banking, entailing the abolition of managerial positions in the lowest tier; the automation of many control functions and the integration of previously separated functions and departments; and the greater graduate recruitment, particularly in banking. This recruitment policy has entailed a distinction between career positions, reserved for candidates with at least A-level qualifications, and non-career positions, filled by entrants with O-level qualifications or less. According to Loveridge et al. (1985: 36, 37), 'at both upper and lower ends of the career hierarchy the traditionally water-tight, single-entry bank internal labour market is becoming more permeable'.

But there is some ambiguity in the literature as to what extent the new technology has *actually* eliminated managerial positions and hence career chances. Crompton and Jones (1984: 92) and Gourlay (1987: 18) report that the new technology has led to the integration of previously separate functions and departments and hence to the elimination of managerial positions, and the latter (Gourlay, 1987: 26) also reports the abolition of some supervisory positions, previously dedicated to checking, in one large insurance company. But accounts of control processes by Wainwright and Francis (1984: 197) and Taylor et al. (1985: 70) suggest that technological monitoring of work results is used only very partially and that direct, personal control has remained the norm.

Also the abolition of specific managerial positions does not necessarily signify an overall reduction of managerial jobs. Gershuny and Miles (1983: 58–9) point out that, during the 1970s, the number of administrative, professional and technical workers per clerical worker has been rising significantly and will continue to do so during the 1980s. This is borne out for the financial services sector by Rajan's study (1984: 49, 65). Few of the firms surveyed in Rajan's large sample envisaged significant staff cuts at the managerial level. It could well be that the increased sophistication of the new technology calls for a larger managerial component which would cancel out any losses incurred by the processes just described. Daniel's data (1987: 240, table 9.23), showing an increase of 24 per cent in the middle/senior management category in establishments with new office technology, as compared with 10 per cent in those without it, provide further disconfirmation on the claim that a decline in managerial positions has reduced promotion chances.

It is pointed out by several studies of the financial services sector (e.g. Loveridge et al., 1985: Smith and Wield, 1987b) that female clerks have raised both the level of their pre- and post-entry qualifications and their career aspirations during the last decade and now stay a longer period in employment. It is likely that a similar, though less pronounced, shift has occurred in other sectors. It has thus become less easy to exclude women from promotion on grounds of deficiency in human capital. Crompton and Jones (1984: 126f.) go as far as speculating that these developments might lead to a situation where a growing proportion of women will actually gain access to managerial positions and will thus significantly diminish male career chances. The occurrence of such a development is, quite correctly, seen as seriously undermining previous conceptualizations of the class position of male clerical workers (e g those by Stewart et al. (1980) and Goldthorpe (1980)) advanced to reject the proletarianization thesis. These authors have argued that clerical positions provide access to a bureaucratic career for young men and that the occupants of those positions must, therefore, be regarded as belonging to the middle class rather than being seen as 'proletarians'. A significant reduction of career opportunities for male clerks would, of course, render this argument invalid.

But more recent studies of the financial services sector (Loveridge et al., 1985: 37; Murray, 1986: 44) see no evidence that an improvement in female career prospects has *actually* occurred or is likely to occur. Staff statistics of the Trustee Savings Bank, shown in table 3.3, reveal a stable situation between 1978 and 1983. The largest proportion of women – just under 70 per cent – are still on the three lowest grades and the proportion of women branch managers has stayed around the 1 per cent mark. Recruitment policy in at least one bank in recent years shows that among new, highly qualified staff, men outnumbered women by a proportion of 3.4: 1 (Loveridge et al., 1985).

TABLE 3.3   *Distribution of total female employees in TSB by grade 1978–83*

| Grade | Percentage of each grade which is female | | | | | |
	1978	*1979*	*1980*	*1981*	*1982*	*1983*
Clerical						
grades 1–3	69.6	70.3	69.6	69.5	69.1	69.2
grades 4–5	31.3	51.9	50.8	47.2	50.2	46.0
Assistant						
branch manager	15.5	16.6	19.7	15.7	15.9	15.7
Branch manager	0.86	1.03	1.08	0.58	0.74	0.95
Overall	55.4	56.3	56.4	55.3	54.8	54.5

Source: TSB Staff Statistics, cited by Willman, 1986: 230
Notes: Basis is full-time staff returns, new each year. Each part-timer is counted as one employee

The fact that women still interrupt their work life in order to look after their young children, albeit a little later now, continues to be a barrier, though not the only one, to promotion. Wastage figures for women on accelerated career routes in banking in the early 1980s were significantly above those for men in at least one large clearing bank (Loveridge et al., 1985: 37). Smith and Wield (1987b) found that a majority of the younger women at branch level still put marriage and child-bearing before a career.

Some evidence from the banking sector suggests that female promotion chances may have deteriorated even further. In banking, during the 1980s, there has occurred a clear shift towards recruiting (nearly exclusively female) part-time staff. Between 1979–85, nearly half the new female employment was on a part-time basis (IMS, 1986; 86). The latter are meant to fill non-career positions, designated for the execution of the increased proportion of routine, data processing functions. Changes in training courses now under discussion will serve further to intensify segmentation of career prospects along gender lines. Thus the always markedly discrepant career prospects of men and women have, at the least, been made more overt and more formalized in the banking sector. Whether or not the divergence between men's and women's prospects has also increased cannot be settled conclusively without more data. In the other sectors, in contrast, there has been no marked increase in part-time employment nor has there occurred equivalent organizational rationalization, thus obviating the same formalization and intensification of female career disqualification as in banking. But the figures for one insurance company, provided by Gourlay (1987: 11), show that, in 1984, despite a changeover to the on-line system and a general upgrading of work, women were still as underrepresented in the highest grade positions as they had been in 1975.

Men's chances of maintaining their good career prospects are not only influenced by women's labour market behaviour but also by employers' recruitment practice with regard to gender. Thus if it can be shown that there has been a significant cut back in the proportion of male recruitment the allegedly adverse impact on their career chances by new technology could be cancelled out by the reduction in competition for managerial positions. Data on job creation in banking between the 1971–8 and the 1979–85 period show that this has, indeed, been the case. Whereas the increase in male full-time employment in the first period was 36.2 per cent of the increase in total employment, in the second period it was only 27 per cent (IMS, 1986: 86). In the insurance industry, in contrast, the employment trend has not substantially changed. Men still outnumbered women in a roughly similar proportion in the second period (*Employment Gazette*, 1984; IMS, 1986: 86).

Proletarianization of women clerical workers has not only been adduced from their lack of promotion chances but also from their instability of employment and the alleged downward occupational mobility resulting from it. It has been maintained by Goldthorpe (1984) that female clerks must be considered 'proletarian' in view of the fact that, after breaks from employment, there occurs a frequent change from the clerical into the manual category and vice versa. Heath and Britten (1984: 492–5), however, refute the claim of a typical interchange between these two categories. Using data from the *National Survey of Health and Development* (1968, 1972, 1977) on the career paths of women between the ages of 22 and 32, they show that movement between the two categories is not very pronounced in either direction. They emphasize that a high proportion of women who stay in, or return to, employment have a stable commitment to a particular type of work within one of three female labour markets. The latter is also confirmed by Dex's (1987: 47f.) analysis of data from the *Women and Employment* survey. Dex (1987), sees the tenacity with which women cling to clerical occupations despite work life interruptions as an indication of a commitment to, and conscious preference for, clerical work over the semi-skilled and usually manual occupations. The degree of downward mobility out of the clerical category is the second lowest after that of 'teaching'. It remains, of course, true that the rate of withdrawal from employment is high but this is hardly a proletarian feature although it does have implications for class cohesion and behaviour.

This review of the evidence on promotion prospects of male and female clerical workers in the 1980s has yielded no support for the claim that the introduction of new technology has had a negative impact on male promotion prospects or for the thesis that an increase in female promotion prospects has diminished those of male clerks. Clerical work remains distinguished from manual work by its superior promotion chances, albeit only for men.

Employment Security

A relatively high degree of employment security of clerical workers, in contrast to manuals, has been another aspect of their employment conditions which has traditionally been marshalled against the proletarianization argument. The question, therefore, arises to what extent the introduction of new technology has undermined their employment security.

The introduction of new technology has been widely associated with a considerable loss of clerical jobs because certain clerical functions have been completely automated and worker productivity in the remaining functions has significantly increased. But new technology generates new functions and services and thus may generate new jobs. Daniel's (1987: 299) national study, for example, established that overall job loss was lower in establishments which had experienced advanced technological change in offices than in those which had not. Not all managements introduce new technology in order to save labour cost but instead pursue objectives, such as increased speed of throughput of information or enhanced service quality (Bevan, 1984: 11; Taylor et al., 1985: 71). Lastly, job reduction may merely coincide with the introduction of new technology but be due to other factors of an economic nature. For all these reasons, one can only analyse the development of clerical employment during the 1980s without, however, making strong claims about processess of causation.

National statistics reveal a picture of stagnating growth or even decline of clerical jobs. The national survey of employers, *UK Occupation and*

Employment Trends to 1990 by the IMS (1986: 170–2) shows that in the 1979–85 period there has occurred a particularly strong decline in clerical jobs in the production industries. In the service industries, a higher proportion of employers (45 per cent) include the category 'clerical and sales' among the contracting than among the expanding (31 per cent) occupational categories. But this development has been unevenly distributed among the service industries. Whereas a considerable, though reduced, employment growth took place in the financial and business services sector, a decline was recorded for the 'public administration' component of both central and local government (IMS 1986: 122). It must be remembered though, that the new office technology is a very recent phenomenon and that a more drastic impact on employment could come about in the 1990s when a more comprehensive automation is predicted to take place.

An examination of employment trends must distinguish between trends with regard to full- and part-time labour. Traditionally, part-time employment has been much less prevalent in the clerical than in the manual sector. During the 1980s, however, it has been increasing for clerical workers and this trend is likely to continue into the 1990s. The IMS Report (1986: p.xxii) points out that, whereas in the manufacturing sector both full- and part-time clerical labour will decline in the second half of the 1980s, the service sector will see an increase in part-time but a decline in full-time clerical employment by 1990. Case study data and more detailed data on employment trends in the financial services sector for the first half of the 1980s indicate that the shift to part-time employment so far has taken place only in banks and building societies whereas in all other industries there has occurred no significant change in this respect. During the 1979–85 period, part-time employment in banks amounted to over half all new female employment (IMS, 1986: 86). Although this shift does not have an effect on employment security in the current, still buoyant financial services sector, it might pose a threat during the 1990s when further advances in automation are predicted to result in job loss even in the financial services sector (Loveridge et al., 1985: 43; Shaw and Coulbeck, 1983: 6).

Case studies in sectors with a low level of automation show a highly variable pattern of employment development ranging from no job cuts at all to a cut of 50 per cent of secretarial and typing positions.[6] Different office functions have been affected to different degrees by job loss. Secretarial and typing positions – held almost exclusively by women – have been much less affected by cuts than general clerical jobs, of which only 62 per cent were held by women during the late 1970s (Bird, 1980: 1, 5). As semi- and unskilled clerical functions, such as the category 'office machine operators' have been affected particularly strongly by automation it is widely assumed that women, who are more heavily concentrated in these functions, have been more severely affected by the reduction than men. But figures on clerical employment trends are not detailed enough to substantiate this claim. The stronger overall decline of the proportion

6 This was found to be the case in the studies by Bird (1980: 33), Bevan (1984: 9), Werneke (1983), Taylor et al, (1985: 35, 147), Baldry et al. (1986: 10) and by Buchanan and Boddy (1982: 166).

of men among clerical workers between 1971–81 throws some doubt on it. According to the 1981 Population Census the proportion of men in clerical occupations fell slightly from 7.5 to 7 per cent whereas that of women rose from 30 per cent to 32 per cent (Brady, 1984: 6, figure 1.2). But the fact that the category 'clerical and related' holds the largest proportion of employed women means that any reduction in clerical employment poses a far more severe threat to female than to male employment chances.

Overall, then, there has been a moderate reduction in clerical employment. This has slightly reduced the high level of employment security enjoyed by clerks in the past. A comparison of the degree of employment security of clerks and manual workers shows, however, that clerical workers still enjoy a significant advantage in this respect (*Social Trends*, 1985: 73, table 4.26). These figures refer only to male workers but other sources (e.g. Dex, 1987: 25) indicate that they would not differ if female workers were compared. Moreover, any subjectively perceived threat to employment security for clerks must have been moderated by the fact that job cuts have been managed largely by natural wastage or jobless growth. Manual workers, in contrast, have been more likely to face compulsory redundancy. On balance, therefore, the introduction of new technology has not been accompanied by changes in employment security which can be said to have contributed to the proletarianization of either male or female clerical workers, although expected future job losses may have increased the subjective perception of insecurity. There is little discussion in the literature as to why clerical workers are at present still treated preferentially in this respect, but one is tempted to attribute this enduring advantage of clerical workers to the persistence of different social relations of work in offices.

Social Relations of Work

The character of the social relations of the office and their consequences for clerks' subjective consciousness was first analysed in Lockwood's (1958, 1966) seminal book, *The Blackcoated Worker*. He points to the trend of growing concentration of clerical workers within organizations and the ensuing bureaucratization of their conditions of employment and promotion chances, but he also emphasizes the enduring small size of the work group and the subsequent physical dispersion of clerical workers. Lockwood connects the latter fact with the close and personal work relations in offices between subordinates and superiors. He concludes that these personal forms of control and the emphasis on minute status differences make the work situation of clerical workers distinct from that of manual ones. As such, he regards it as an important influence on the development of their social consciousness, that is, on their perception of themselves as members of the capitalist enterprise and society and thus as an explanation of their lack of indentification with the working class (1966: 81).

How apposite are these observations for an understanding of the social relations of the office in the 1980s? Only a partial answer to this question is possible as this aspect of clerical work has received scant attention in recent work. There is little systematic evidence in the literature on processes of concentration and bureaucratization, but the enduring small size of work groups and its consequence for social relations has received more coverage. Information from the case studies in all sectors suggests that the small work group is still a characteristic of clerical work in the 1980s. The substitution of word processing pools for typing pools has brought about a reduction in size of those few large groups in clerical work which have been described as most akin to work groups in production. Several case studies of the financial services sector emphasize the small size of work units and the close and friendly relations between members resulting from it. Despite the advanced stage of automation in the financial services sector, direct personal control of subordinates remains widespread (Crompton and Jones, 1984; Storey, 1984; Batstone et al., 1987). But some studies of the banking (though not the insurance) sector point to the growing tension between the traditional benevolently paternalist management–worker relations and the negative impact on work organization and organizational climate of some aspects of automation, the autocractic manner of its introduction and of the new recruitment and promotion policies associated with it (Loveridge et al., 1985: Murray, 1986; Smith and Wield, 1987b).

The strongest support for the claim that social relations between management and their subordinates have remained closer and more personal in the office than on the shopfloor comes from Daniel's (1987) study. Daniel (1987: 163) found that managers were substantially more likely to report a favourable impact of new technology on clerical than on manual jobs, and they were inclined to award non-manual workers pay increases on more favourable terms. Whereas office workers generally received these increases as a personal right – their jobs were upgraded – manual workers' increases in earnings had to be secured either by collective agreements or, more frequently, by greater effort (PBR or overtime) (Daniel, 1987: 248–9). The closer relation between managers and office workers is also expressed by the fact that accounts of change, made by both management and stewards, were closer to each other in the office than on the shopfloor (Daniel, 1987 166). Lastly, managers were significantly more likely to engage in individual discussion and consultation about technical change with office than with shopfloor workers (Daniel, 1987: 133). Consequently, office workers needed union representation or collective resistance to change less than manual workers in order to be heard by management, and a virtuous circle of closer management and office labour relations was perpetuated.

Lockwood's study (1966: 78, 79), being only concerned with male clerks, merely hinted at the special quality of the relation between older male superiors and predominantly young and female subordinates. An interesting elaboration of this control relation, based on gender inequality, is provided by Downing (1980: 279f.). This relation is epitomized by that between a secretary – referred to as the 'office wife' – and her boss.[7] She

---

7 Downing, however, tends to exaggerate the degree to which personal rather than professional services are rendered by the secretary. Vinnicombe's (1980: 67) study of personal secretaries finds that the majority of such secretaries (40 per cent) spend only between 1 and 10 per cent of total work time on servicing personal needs.

points out that recruitment and promotion to certain secretarial positions depends as much on the possession of certain feminine – and also (middle) class-specific – qualities, such as poise, good dress sense, a pleasant voice, sensitivity and adaptability as on 'technical' qualifications for the job. Strong loyalty to the boss, says Downing, is built into the job. She neglects to point out, though, that, in return, the secretary receives higher status and a number of advantages in terms of work autonomy, variety and material reward. Downing sees this close relationship between secretary and boss undermined by office automation. The case studies available (Bird 1980; Webster 1986), however, do not support this part of her analysis.

Social Attributes of Clerical Workers

The study of clerical workers by Stewart et al. (1980) first emphasized the fact that it is important, in the clerical sector, to distinguish between occupational positions on the one hand and their occupants on the other. They pointed to the variety within the category of clerical workers in terms of work life mobility, social origins and educational qualifications. Male clerical workers either start their occupational life in clerical positions and move up the class hierarchy, or they start in manual jobs and clerical positions become their final destination. Female clerks, it is argued, retire from clerical employment into domestic life at an early stage. A proletarianization of clerical positions, Stewart et al., therefore conclude, cannot be translated into proletarianization of individuals who occupy these positions at various points in time. Although Stewart et al. mention gender as a worker attribute they do not empirically investigate the consequences in terms of promotion chances.

Crompton and Jones (1984) took up and developed these insights from a Marxist perspective and they accord gender, both theoretically and empirically, the centrality which it merits in a study of the feminized clerical occupations. They urge that an adequate analysis of class must integrate the empirical study of class places and of agents. Changes in the occupational structure have far-reaching implications for occupants of positions in this structure, but the characteristics of occupants also shape the nature of class places. They concluded persuasively that an adequate treatment of class in general and of proletarianization in particular must integrate the study of class places and agents and consider their reciprocal influence. Crompton and Jones partially succeed in reaching this goal in as far as they demonstrate successfully how the gender of occupants has shaped clerical places. They are, however, less successful in integrating this finding with their claim about clerical proletarianization. Male and female clerks, despite their radically different promotion chances, are both assigned to the proletariat, albeit to different strata within it. Paradoxically for a book concerned with issues of class, they also minimize the importance of individual attributes derived from class origin for an understanding of the class location of clerical workers. Their discussion of pre-entry educational qualifications and social origins takes up very little space in the book, and the implication of these attributes are very much underplayed. This general neglect of individual attributes beyond gender is characteristic of all recent studies of clerical work which, dominated by the 'labour process' debate, has completely jettisoned the investigation of individual worker attributes, underlined in the older, Weberian concern with class.

The most obvious attribute of clerical workers is that they are predominantly female. It has repeatedly been pointed out that over 70 per cent of clerical workers are women and that some clerical occupations, such as typists and word processor operators and secretaries are almost completely (over 90 per cent) feminized. The pronounced impact of gender on patterns of work organization and promotion chances, highlighted in earlier sections, has now been widely recognized by sociologists. But the implications for class analysis of women's numerical dominance of clerical occupations and of women clerks' social attributes have still not been clearly drawn out. This will be attempted in the concluding section of this chapter.

The data on the social origins of clerks, though fragmentary, point in the same direction. Stewart et al. 1980) emphasize both the diversity in class origins among male clerks according to sector of employment – the dominance of non-manual origins among insurance clerks and their underrepresentation among clerks in manufacturing enterprises – *and* the greater dominance, on average, among clerical workers of those from middle-class origins.[8] The survey of both male and female clerks' attributes by Crompton and Jones (1984: 20) indicates that only a minority – one-third – come from a working-class background.[9] The data are, unfortunately, not broken down by gender. Goldthorpe's (1980) mobility study, in contrast, shows a stronger manual origin among men in his class III, although it must be borne in mind that this category includes not only clerical workers but also sales and service workers, who tend to have more pronounced 'manual worker' origins. However, it is still less than 50 per cent who come from a manual background. Middle-class origin is more accentuated among female clerks. A recent analysis of female mobility by Goldthorpe and Payne (1986: 546, table 7) distinguished class IIIa, consisting mainly of clerical workers, from class IIIb, those in sales occupations. This shows that, due to considerable female intergenerational downward mobility in occupational terms, daughters of fathers from classes I, II, and IIIa are greatly over represented among women in class IIIa, while those from manual origins are strongly underrepresented.

A similar picture of the essentially middle-class background of clerical workers emerges if we consider educational qualifications. The data presented by Crompton and Jones (1984: 103, 141 for the years 1979–81 reveal a relatively high level of educational qualifications of both men

---

8 Class origins here means class location at the beginning of occupational life. This is likely to display a good deal of overlap with class origins, as defined by father's occupation, although this is not shown by the authors themselves.

9 The 66 per cent from non-manual origins were evenly divided between the RG's classes I and II and class III, non-manual. The authors' conclusion that 'clerks are drawn from all sectors of the population' is, therefore, misleading.

and women and the increase of that level over time. Although women are found to be less well educated than men their level was also rising steeply with decreasing age. Marshall et al. (1988: chapter 4) emphasize the large proportion of women (32 per cent) but not men (2 per cent) with high educational qualifications among those located in the routine non-manual category. Dex's (1987: 60) data from the 'Women and Employment' survey on women's highest educational qualifications on leaving school by occupational category show that the educational profile of clerical women is quite different from, and well above that of, women in any manual category. One must, therefore, conclude that the increasing automation of clerical work has not resulted in a marked shift in recruitment towards clerical workers with social attributes more akin to those of manual workers.

This short consideration of the social attributes of clerical workers has shown that, although there is some internal diversity, it is not nearly as great as Stewart et al. (1980) have claimed. There is cause for reconsidering the composition of this stratum and for revising the theoretical implications drawn from such an exercise. Stewart et al. (1980: 135) found that just over one-third of their clerks had started their working life as manual workers and that this group was particularly strongly represented in the manufacturing sector. However, given that only a minority of clerks are employed in the manufacturing sector – 4.3 per cent, according to Gershuny and Miles (1983: 80) – well-educated male clerks of non-manual origin probably form by far the predominant proportion. More importantly, given that male clerks are a mere 30 per cent of all clerks, this much vaunted diversity of social composition and occupational mobility becomes further reduced in numerical weight and hence in theoretical import. The overwhelming majority of clerks are female, and a clear majority among them come from middle-level educational groups and middle-class social origins. It can, therefore, be concluded that, in terms of social attributes, routine white-collar workers are not proletarian but lean more strongly towards the new middle class. The closer proximity of female clerks, as compared with female manuals, to other white-collar groups in both social attributes and employment conditions is also expressed in their subjective class awareness and in the social imagery they hold as shown in recent studies by Abbott (1987) and Marshall et al. (1988).

Conclusion

The preceding analysis of case studies of clerical workers from a range of industrial sectors and settings has shown that there exists a rich variety in the level and nature of automation and in its impact on work organization and, to a lesser extent, employment and promotion chances. Different groups of clerical workers – varying both in terms of function and gender – have felt the impact of these developments in different degrees.

To move beyond a mere summary of findings and relate them to the theoretical debates referred to in the introduction, some informed decisions have to be made on how to handle this internal variety and arrive at workable definitions of the social categories involved. It has already been shown that the category 'clerical workers' is not as varied in terms of social attributes as Stewart et al. (1980) have suggested and that individuals with medium high levels of education of 'middle' social (occupational) origins form the majority of this category. More crucial and problematic is the differentiation by sex and the differential market capacities possessed by the genders. Are the conditions of men and women so different that they have to be considered as separate categories in a stratification hierarchy, as is suggested by Mann (1986)? Or can the differences between them be accommodated in some way so that the methodologically much neater solution of one common class category can be retained? If we adopt Mann's solution, do we then compare clerical women with manual men or make the more plausible comparison – in terms of subjective orientations or of mobility paths – with manual women? These are clearly complex issues, and we can advance only tentative answers.

In many industrial sectors and individual firms technological development to date has been hesitant and automation has been mostly piecemeal. Consequently technological change has rarely entailed drastic organizational restructuring, and most groups of clerical workers have only been partially affected by the new technology. A work situation completely dominated by new technology and a machine-paced and/or controlled clerical worker is still an exception rather than the rule for both men and women. In this respect, as well as in terms of size of working units, general working environment and ensuing social relation of work, office work still differs from that on the shopfloor.

The relation between new technology and work organization was found to be extremely complex, and any general conclusion regarding proletarianization of male or female clerks has to be tentative. At the very least, it can be said that the movement towards more Taylorist forms of work organization, following (or, in some cases even preceding) the introduction of the mainframe computer, has been halted and, in several cases, even been slightly reversed. There is some evidence that women's position in the labour process or work situation has deteriorated more than that of their male counterparts because of their higher concentration in the lower clerical grades where the most routine operations are executed. But whether this difference between the male and female work situation – which is more a difference of degree than of kind – is big enough to justify an allocation to different class categories is debateable. Overall, then, one cannot say that the new technology has directly or indirectly led to further proletarianization of the clerical labour process.

Employment conditions and promotion prospects of clerical workers have not changed significantly during the late 1970s and early 1980s. The pattern of unequal income and, more markedly, promotion chances between male and female clerks has persisted as have the discrepancies from conditions of manual workers regardless of gender. But interpretations of such differences and commonalities from the perspective of the proletarianization thesis depend crucially on whether aggregates are compared or whether the categories on either side of the manual/non-manual divide are disaggregated by sex. The outcome of comparisons also depends on which aspect of employment conditions is selected for emphasis.

If aggregates are compared then the income of clerical workers is clearly still below that of manual workers although it is less variable and unstable and, crucially, is earned in less hours. Also fringe benefits of all clerical workers remain superior. If only male workers are compared the pay of clerical workers falls only just below that of skilled workers and, considering their still superior promotion chances, their overall market capacities must be judged superior to those of manual workers. A comparison of female clerks with women manuals reveals an even more marked overall advantage of the former in market capacities. Only when the market capacities of female clerks are compared with those of male manuals do we get a situation where the proletarianization claim carries conviction as far as the size of the pay packet is concerned, though not necessarily with respect to other aspects of market capacity. An important aspect of the proletarian condition is its insecurity in terms of employment. Although employment security has declined for both clerical and manual workers during the 1980s this decline has been significantly more serious for manual workers both in terms of its extent and in the way it is handled by employers. Hence, consideration of employment security yields no support for the proletarianization claim of either male or female clerks.

In conclusion, the foregoing analysis has attempted to consider both class places and their occupants. It has shown the complexity involved in placing clerical positions and clerical workers in the class structure of British society and has indicated that the proletarianization thesis is more difficult to sustain than is often suggested (e.g. by Crompton and Jones, 1984). The analysis has also made it clear that women must be taken into account and has shown how the outcomes of comparisons vary, depending on whether women are allocated to separate stratification categories or are considered together with men in similar occupations. Whether or not men and women routine non-manual workers should be allocated to different or the same class category will depend to a large extent on the given research problem.

References

Abbott, P. 1987. 'Women's Social Class Identification: Does Husband's Occupation make a Difference?'. *Sociology*, 1; 91–104.
Baldry, C.J., Connolly, A., Lockyer, C.J. and Ramsey, H.E. 1986. *The Introduction and Effects of Information Technology on Clerical Administrative and Technical Staff in Strathclyde Regional Authority*. Final Report to the Leverhulme Trust, University of Strathclyde. Department of Industrial Relations.

Report to the Leverhulme Trust, University of Strathclyde, Department of Industrial Relations.

Barras, R. and Swann, J. 1983. *The Adoption and Impact of Information Technology in the UK Insurance Industry.* Report No. TCCR-83-014. London.

—— and Swann, J. 1984. 'Information Technology and the Service Sector: Quality of Services and Quantity of Jobs'. *New Technology and the Future of Work and Skills.* Ed. Marstrand, P. London and Dover, NH: Francis Pinter.

Batstone, E., Gourlay, S. and Moore, H.L.R. 1987. *New Technology and the Process of Labour Regulation.* Oxford: Clarendon Press.

Bevan. S. 1984. *Secretaries and Typists: The Impact of Office Automation.* Institute of Manpower Studies, Report No. 93. Brighton: IMS.

Bird, E. 1980. *Information Technology in the Office: The Impact on Women's Jobs.* Manchester: Equal Opportunities Commission.

Bjorn-Anderson, N. 1983. 'The Changing Roles of Secretaries and Clerks'. *New Office Technology: Human and Organizational Aspects.* Eds Otway, H.J. and Peltu, M. London: Frances Pinter.

Brady, T. 1984. *New Technology and Skills in British Industry.* SPRU Report prepared for the MSC.

Braverman, H. 1974. *Labor and Monopoly Capital. The Degredation of Work in the Twentieth Century.* New York: Monthly Review Press.

Buchanan, D.A. 1985. 'Using New Technology'. *The Information Technology Revolution.* Ed. Forester, T. Cambridge, Mass.: MIT Press.

—— and Boddy, D. 1982. *Organizations in the Computer Age.* Aldershot: Gower.

Crompton, R. and Jones, G. 1984. *White-Collar Proletariat. Deskilling and Gender in Clerical Work.* London: Macmillan.

—— and Mann, M. 1986. *Gender and Stratification.* Cambridge: Polity.

Dale, A., Gilbert, G.N. and Arber, S. 1985. 'Integrating Women into Class Theory'. *Sociology,* 19: 3, 384–405.

Daniel, W.W. 1987. *Workplace Industrial Relations and Technical Change.* London: Frances Pinter.

Dex, S. 1987. *Women's Occupational Mobility.* London: Macmillan.

Downing, H. 1980. 'Word Processors and the Oppression of Women'. *The Microelectronics Revolution.* Ed. Forester, T. Oxford: Basil Blackwell.

Forester, T. (ed.) 1980. *The Microelectronics Revolution.* Oxford: Basil Blackwell.

—— 1985. *The Information Technology Revolution,* Cambridge, Mass.: MIT Press.

Garnsey, E. 1978. 'Women's Work and Theories of Class Stratification'. *Sociology,* 12: 2, 223–44.

Gershuny, J. 1983. *Social Innovation and the Division of Labour.* Oxford: Oxford University Press.

—— and Miles, I. 1983. *The New Service Economy.* London: Frances Pinter.

Gill, G. 1985. *Work, Unemployment and the New Technology.* Cambridge: Polity.

Giuliano, V.E. 1985. 'The Mechanization of Office Work'. *The Information Technology Revolution.* Ed. Forester, T. Cambridge, Mass.: MIT Press.

Goldthorpe, J.H. 1980. *Social Mobility and Class Structure in Modern Britain.* Oxford: Clarendon Press.

100   *Christel Lane*

—— 1984. 'Women and Class Analysis: A Reply to the Replies'. *Sociology*, 18: 4, 491–9.
—— Lockwood, D., Bechhofer, F. and Platt, J. 1969. *The Affluent Worker in the Class Structure*. Cambridge: Cambridge University Press.
—— and Payne, C. 1986. 'On the Class Mobility of Women: Results from Different Approaches to the Analysis of Recent British Data'. *Sociology*, 20: 4, 531–56.
Gourlay, S. 1987. *The Contradictory Process of Work Reorganisation: Trends in the Organization of Work in an Insurance Company*. Paper read at the UMIST/Aston Labour Process Conference. Manchester, April 1987.
Heath, A. and Britten, N. 1984. 'Women's Jobs Do Make a Difference'. *Sociology*, 18: 4, 475–90.
Immel, A.R. 1985. 'The Automated Office: Myth Versus Reality'. *The Information Technology Revolution*. Ed. Forester, T. Cambridge, Mass.: MIT Press.
Institute of Manpower Studies (for the Occupations Study Group). 1986. *UK Occupation and Employment Trends to 1990*. Eds Rajan, A. and Pearson, R. London: Butterworth.
Jenkins, C. and Sherman, B. 1979. *The Collapse of Work*. London: Eyre Methuen.
Klingender, F.D. 1935. *The Condition of Clerical Labour in Britain*. London: Martin Lawrence.
Littler, C.R. and Salaman, G. 1984. *Class at Work. The Design, Allocation and Control of Jobs*. London: Batsford.
Lockwood, D. 1966. *The Blackcoated Worker. A Study in Class Consciousness*. London: Unwin University Press.
Loveridge, R., Child, J. and Harvey, J. 1985. *New Technologies in Banking, Retailing and Health Services: The British Case*. Research Report Aston University: ESRC Work Organization Research Centre.
Mann, M. 1986. 'A Crisis in Stratification Theory? Persons, Households/Families/Lineages, Genders, Classes and Nations'. *Gender and Stratification*. Eds Crompton, R. and Mann, M. Cambridge: Polity Press.
Marshall, G., Newby, H. and Rose, D. 1988. *Social Class in Modern Britain*. London: Hutchinson.
Marstrand, P. (ed.) 1984. *New Technology and the Future of Work and Skills*. London and Dover, NH: Frances Pinter.
Martin, J. and Roberts, C. 1984. *Women and Employment*. London: HMSO.
Murray, F. 1986. *Banking on Clerical Skills: New Technology and the Clearing Banks in the UK*. Unpublished working paper. Sheffield City Polytechnic: Department of Computer Studies.
NEDO. 1983. *The Impact of Advanced Information Systems. The Effect on Job Content and Job Boundaries*. London: NEDO.
Office Salaries and Analysis 1976. Prepared by K.L. Scott and M.L. Deere. Beckenham, Kent: The Institute of Administrative Management.
Povall, M., de Jong, A., Chalude, A.R. and Grozelier, A.M. 1982. 'Banking on Women Managers'. *Management Today*. (February).
Rajan, A. 1984. *New Technology and Employment in Insurance, Banking and Building Societies: Recent Impact and Experience*. Institute of Manpower Series. London: Gower.

Routh, G. 1980. *Occupation and Pay in Great Britain 1906–79*. London: Macmillan.
Saunders, C. and Marsden, D. 1981. *Pay Inequalities in the European Community*. London: Butterworth.
Shaw, E.R. and Coulbeck, N.S. 1983. *UK Retail Banking Prospects in the Competitive 1980s*. London: January, Staniland Hall.
Smith, R. 1981. 'Introducing New Technology into the Office'. Work Research Unit Occasional Paper 20. London: Department of Employment.
Smith, S. and Wield, D. 1987a. 'Banking on the New Technology: Cooperation, Competition and the Clearers'. *New Perspectives on the Financial System*. Ed. Harris, L. London: Croom Helm.
——— and Wield, D. 1987b. 'New Technology and Bank Work: Banking on I. T. as an "Organisational Technology". *New Perspectives on the Financial System* Ed. Harris, L. London: Croom Helm.
Stanworth, M. 1984, 'Women and Class Analysis: A Reply to Goldthorpe', *Sociology*, 18: 2, 159–70.
Steffens, J. 1982. 'Office Automation in the UK: Some Issues and Problems'. *Policy Studies* (London), 2: 3, 169–88.
Stewart, A., Prandy, K. and Blackburn, R.M. 1980. *Social Stratification and Occupations*. London: Macmillan.
Storey, J. 1984. 'The Phoney War? New Office Technology: Organization and Control'. *Management and the Labour Process*. Eds Knights, D. and Willmott, H. London: Heinemann.
Taylor, A., Coppin, P. and Wealthy, P. 1985. *The Impact of New Technology on Local Employment (A Study of Progress and Effects on Jobs in the London Borough of Hammersmith and Fulham)*. London: Gower.
Thompson, L. 1985. 'New Office Technology: People, Work Structure and the Process of Change'. Work Research Unit Occasional Paper 34. London: Department of Employment.
Vinnicombe, S. 1980. *Secretaries, Management and Organisations*. London: Heinemann.
Wainwright, J. and Francis, A. 1984. *Office Automation, Organisation and the Nature of Work*. London: Gower.
Webster, J. 1986. 'Word Processing and the Secretarial Labour Process'. *The Changing Experience of Employment*. Eds Purcell, K., Wood, S., Waton, A. and Allen, S. London: Macmillan with BSA.
Werneke, D. 1983. *Microelectronics and Office Jobs: The Impact of the Chip on Women's Employment*. Geneva: International Labour Office.
West, J. 1982. 'New Technology and Women's Office Work' *Work, Women and the Labour Market*, Ed. West, J. London: Routledge & Kegan Paul.
Willman, P. 1986. *Technological Change, Collective Bargaining and Industrial Efficiency*. Oxford: Clarendon Press.

4 Technological Change and Manual Work

Roderick Martin

Since 1980 technological change in British industry has been extensive and rapid. The majority of such changes, especially in large enterprises, have involved the use of microelectronics. The expansion of the use of microelectronics is likely to continue and to touch almost all industries. Indeed, Freeman (1987: 16) has suggested that information technology based upon microelectronics may prove to be the foundation for a new 'techno economic paradigm' involving the transformation of 'the structure and the conditions of production and distribution for almost every branch of the economy'. The widespread use of microelectronics in industry and services, both in new production processes and in new products, raises fundamental issues about the evolution of manual work. This chapter will be concerned with the extent of its current diffusion, with management's objectives in introducing new technology, with its implications for industrial relations, with its effect on the character of work and finally with its likely consequences for employment levels.

The Diffusion of New Technology

The most common type of technological change in the 1980s has been the introduction of microelectronics. Microelectronic technology involves the use of computers to control, activate, guide and monitor the performance of electro-mechanical devices. Its distinguishing feature is the information stored in computer software, rather than any specific physical characteristic (Forester, 1985). The introduction of microelectronics differs in three major respects from technological change in the 1960s and therefore may be expected to have a different effect upon manual employment. First, it is much more pervasive. Advanced technological change has the potential to affect the whole range of what Michael Porter (1980) has termed 'value activities': infrastructure; human resource management; technology development; procurement; in-bound logistics; operations; out-bound logistics; marketing, sales and service provision. Computerization may affect particular elements in the chain, and the linkages between elements. Changes in operating systems and in human resource management have the most direct implications for manual employment, although other changes will have some impact. Secondly, the pervasiveness of microelectronic technology leads to the closer integration of each set of activities with each other, thus increasing the number of activities with direct implications for manual employment. Hence the application of information technology to in-bound logistics involves more precise scheduling of deliveries, closer monitoring of stock levels and reduction of work in progress; this increases the pressure on operations. Finally, advanced technological change also involves greater flexibility both in the technology itself and in the labour required.

One of the major reasons for its greater pervasiveness and flexibility is that it may involve the automation of a single machine or the introduction of an integrated control system. The particular type of application varies between different production systems. According to Batstone and Gourlay (1986: 167): 'in unit and small batch production technical change has largely remained at the level of the individual machine; in process production changes in both integrated control systems and in handling and storage are common, whereas in large batch and mass production integrated control systems are quite common, as also are changes in quality control and handling systems.'

Certainly, technological change has been extensive and rapid in the early 1980s. According to a survey by Northcott (1986: 103, 105), 68.2 per cent of manufacturing establishments used microelectronics at some stage of their production processes in 1985, compared with 34.2 per cent in 1981. Further, 75.7 per cent of workers in manufacturing were employed in establishments using microelectronics in 1985, compared with 43.2 per cent in 1981. Within each establishment just under a third (31.8 per cent) of production processes were controlled by microelectronics in 1985, but managers expected that usage would increase to 42.5 per cent by 1987, and ultimately to 63.5 per cent (Northcott, 1986: 197) Daniel (1987: 15, 28) presents a similar picture of extensive and rapid change; the Workplace Industrial Relations Survey in 1984 reported that the majority of manual workers were employed in establishments which used microelectronics (67 per cent) and that a smaller majority (53 per cent) worked in establishments which had experienced technological change involving microelectronics in the last three years.

Within this general picture, the pace of change has clearly varied between different types of firms and different sectors of the economy. The use of microelectronics is especially extensive in large establishments; in 1985 it was used by 96 per cent of establishments with 1000 or more employees. In contrast, it was used in only 35 per cent of firms employing 20–49, and in 44 per cent of firms employing 50–99. There are also widespread variations by type of industry. Its use has spread most rapidly in food, drink and tobacco, paper, printing and publishing, chemicals and electrical and mechanical engineering. The clothing and footwear industry makes least use of new technology, although even here over 30 per cent of establishments reported commercial applications (Northcott, 1986: 6). Foreign-owned companies were also more likely to be using microelectronics than British-owned groups, while independent British-owned companies were the least likely of all to make use of it. This was not simply the result of differences in the sectoral distribution of ownership: foreign-owned companies were more likely to use microelectronics than British companies in the same sector.

The expansion of the use of microelectronics is likely to continue, with wider application in establishments already using new technology, and usage extending from large to medium sized and smaller firms. Indeed, the NEDO IT Long Term Perspectives Group reported a predominant view amongst 'informed opinion' that by 1995 nearly 30 per cent of large enterprises (including services) would be using computer integrated manufacturing systems or fully automated offices based upon integrated computer work stations (NEDO, 1986: p.vii).

Managerial Objectives and New Technology

Technological change is not autonomous – there is no logic of technology which inevitably moulds manual work in specific directions. Intellectual, economic, political and socio-cultural factors affect the development of technology and thus the repertoire of technological solutions available to firms. Firms choose from the technologies available or under development according to their objectives and their perceptions of how different technologies will meet their objectives, taking into account the investments in plant, equipment and practices already made.

The level within the firm at which policies are formulated and crucial decisions about the introduction of technology taken can vary substantially. There might be grounds for thinking that decisions with regard to new technology would tend to be taken at a senior level because of the high level of capital expenditure involved. However, in practice, individual plant managers appear to play the major initiating role in deciding upon technological change, subject to corporate approval. Technological change is closely linked to existing production processes and the precise consequences of particular innovations are likely to vary between establishments; it would therefore be difficult for corporate level managers to make decisions affecting individual production processes. Indeed, according to the WIRS higher level survey, management's handling of technological change is more decentralized than its handling of any industrial relations issue except policies relating to the pattern of work or the number of workers employed (Martin, 1988).

The precise nature of managerial objectives in introducing technological change has been one of the central areas of debate in the literature. In his classic work Braverman placed control issues at the centre of the management strategy in introducing new technology (Braverman, 1974; Wood, 1982; Knights et al., 1985). Control issues are linked to skill: greater management control may be secured through reducing the skill level and therefore the degree of discretion granted to the operative. The incentive to increase control through deskilling is especially great where skilled workers are in short supply, given that this usually implies that they are more expensive and have enhanced bargaining power. Certainly, since Braverman's work was published in 1974, developments in computer technology have made enhanced control easier to achieve. However, Braverman underestimated the extent to which control may have a cost: in terms of supervisory personnel, expensive technology, or elaborate bureaucratic procedures. Therefore the use of new technology to increase control is likely to be limited to those circumstances where the costs of increased control are not high or where the existence of a work-force that is particularly difficult to manage makes such expenditure worth while.

Research based upon discussions with management suggests that, in practice, control is a much less significant objective for management than the reduction of production costs and improvements of product quality. The reduction in costs may be obtained through reduced consumption of raw materials or reduced energy requirements; microelectronic monitoring of process techniques frequently permits a reduction in the amount of waste raw materials or energy. More usually the objective is to reduce costs through reducing the amount or quality of labour – especially reductions in 'head-count'. In a CBI survey of collective agreements, 39 per cent of agreements referring to new technology involved reductions in employment levels, the most frequently referred to single item (Lobban, 1985). In other circumstances the same number of workers may be involved in higher levels of output, as has happened on a major scale in the banking industry, where jobless growth has occurred (Willman and Cowan. 1984: Morris, 1986). Reductions in the cost of labour may also be sought by reducing the quality of labour required, for example by replacing craftsmen by workers who have not served their time. The objective of reductions in production costs is especially prominent in mature industries, as in the motor car industry (Abernathy and Utterback, 1982). Innovations are likely to be primarily labour displacing, rather than product enhancing, when the product and the production process have become firmly established and competitive advantage can be primarily achieved through reductions in production costs and in product price. Hence technological change is primarily labour displacing in a 'mature' industry.

Although less frequently cited as an objective than cost reduction, the second major reason for the introduction of technological change is to improve product quality. For instance, in the pump industry, improved machining was introduced to produce pumps capable of serving the North Sea oil industry. Similarly, Ford management aimed to improve quality, as well as reduce labour costs, through the introduction of robots at Dagenham in the early 1980s. Overall, it is clear that – at least in management's own account of its motives – issues of labour control have a very secondary place in its calculations compared with the more fundamental objectives of improving the firm's position in the product market. Management's account of its objectives in introducing new technology may be incomplete, but empirical evidence not a a priori theorizing is required to establish this. It seems probable that to place control rather than reduced costs at the centre of managerial attention mistakes the means for the end.

New Technology and Industrial Relations

The Processes of Decision-making

One of the striking conclusions that has come out of research is the extent to which management has largely retained discretion over the introduction of new technology and has been able to implement its policies without substantial control from the trade unions. A number of earlier studies of technical change showed that in some industries – in particular, engineering – the implications of technical change for pay levels, grading, manning and work organization were subject to extensive bargaining. However, this pattern of bargaining is far from universal.

There are three strategies available to management for introducing technological change: unilateral imposition, consultation and bargaining. Firms may follow each strategy at different times, or may attempt to combine consultation and bargaining at the same time. In practice, managements have preferred a control/consultation strategy, rather than a consultation/bargaining strategy and have usually been able to follow their preferences. According to Daniel's survey, technological change was negotiated in only 8 per cent of establishments; even in large establishments, advanced technological change was negotiated in only 15 per cent of establishments employing 1,000 or more workers (Daniel, 1987: 124). Shop stewards reported negotiations a little more frequently than managers – 13 per cent compared with 8 per cent – but the overwhelming impression remains one of unilateral managerial control.

Unilateral control is justified by management on the grounds that the introduction of new technology is a standard production issue and as such an integral part of managerial prerogative. There was, however, consensus – at least at the diplomatic level - on the importance of consultation. There are difficulties in interpreting data on consultation – one person's consultation is another person's unilateral imposition. However, surveys of both management and worker representatives indicate that consultation is the norm, especially in manufacturing industry. Daniels' survey of establishment level managers and shop stewards showed a large majority (82 per cent) of establishments consulting over the most recent technological change, with consultation being especially likely in large establishments (Daniel, 1987: 116). It is notable, however, that the most common form of consultation was through informal discussion with individual workers. This occurred in 58 per cent of establishments, whereas discussions with full-time officials were held in only 16 per cent of establishments.

The extent to which the process of consultation is a formality will be influenced by the stage at which it takes place; consultation is a formality if it occurs only after the major decisions have been made. Consultation may occur early in the process of technological change, at the project planning stage, or late in the process, at the implementation stage. In practice, consultation is rare at the project planning stage, whereas it is more frequent at the implementation stage. Daniel reports that 'lack of consultation over whether to introduce the change was especially common' (Daniel, 1987: 125, 128). According to Rush and Williams's survey of consultation in the electronics industry, 32.4 per cent of firms involved workers in consultations at the planning stage, and 86.9 per cent at the implementation stage (Rush and Williams, 1984: 176).

Consultation restricted to the implementation stage makes discussion of levels of investment or technological strategy impossible. Levels of investment or the type of equipment to be purchased were rarely subjects for consultation, even in sectors with high levels of union organization. For example, the consultative committees set up at BL in the 1970s had little influence on levels of investment or on the overall approach adopted in developing the Metro, even before the Edwardes era; levels of investment were laid down in the corporate strategy, and the technological strategy was laid down in the Red Book, prepared by manufacturing engineering on a brief from marketing (Willman and Winch, 1984: 48–9). Similarly, Davies reports that 'in none of the [breweries] visited had there been any consultation concerning the initial investment decision taken at board level. In all cases decisions were finalised by management committees before they were put to employees and the unions' (Davies, 1986: 149). The most frequent subject of consultation is health and safety; Rush and Williams (1984: 176) report that health and safety issues were discussed in 69.5 per cent of cases. Other issues which were the subject of consultation were also primarily social issues, especially levels of employment. Consultation rarely concerned methods of working, although in practice methods of working are subject to *de facto* modifications by workers involved.

According to corporate level managers interviewed in connection with the WIRS higher level study, industrial relations considerations are taken into account a lot (52 per cent) or to some extent (40 per cent) in deciding upon new plant, machinery and equipment (Martin, 1988). However, managements regard labour constraints as much less important than capital constraints (Northcott, 1986: 143). Moreover, the importance really attached to industrial relations issues must be subject to doubt given that representatives of the personnel function are not usually involved in discussions on new technology (Daniel, 1987: 108). Millward and Stevens (1986: 47) comment on the limited role played by personnel departments in technical change: 'As technical change, even very unfamiliar advanced technical change was generally popular, very rarely provoked any resistance from manual workers or their representatives and was very rarely subject to collective bargaining, then little reason was seen, apparently, to call upon the personnel department.'

Management's approach to technological change might be expected to be influenced significantly by the reactions or anticipated reactions of labour. The ability to follow a unilateral strategy depends partly upon management wish and partly upon work group and union weakness. There is therefore some variation in practice between industries, reflecting differing levels of worker organization. A unilateral strategy is particularly common in retail distribution and in banking. For example, a study of the introduction of scanning equipment in a supermarket showed management pursuing a unilateral control strategy, with neither the union (USDAW) nor the workers directly involved being consulted (Bamber and Willman, 1983: 114–16).

In contrast, unilateral control strategies are less common in manufacturing, as the WIRS higher level survey indicated. On the basis of their survey of shop stewards, Batstone and Gourlay (1986: 190) conclude that new equipment was the subject of negotiation in a majority of establishments in printing, chemicals, food and drink and engineering; for example, 68 per cent of production shop stewards in the chemical industry reported that negotiations on new technology occurred at establishment level. While the omission of any questions on consultation in the Batstone and Gourlay survey may well have led to an exaggeration of the overall amount of negotiation, it supports the general picture that negotiation is more extensive in manufacturing. Negotiations also appear to have been particularly likely in public sector industries such as British Telecom and British Rail. As Daniel (1987: 113) concludes:

> If management could introduce the changes they wanted without having to take account of the views of any other group or individual, they did so. Where they consulted or negotiated, it was principally because they were required to do so, either by the industrial relations institutions at their workplace, or by resistance to the changes they wanted on the part of workers or their representatives. There was no hint of managerial commitment to worker involvement as a means of improving the form of the change or generating enthusiasm for it.

Management regarded new technology issues as an integral part of management prerogatives. Consultation was common, especially informal consultation with individual workers or with groups of workers. However, new technology was not regarded as an appropriate subject for collective bargaining, although trade-union power sometimes forced management to negotiate. Where bargaining occurred it was concerned with the price of technological change rather than with the principles underlying technological change. It is therefore hardly surprising that management has not regarded labour issues as a major barrier to introducing technological change in the 1980s.

The Trade-union Response to New Technology

The trade-union movement at national level has developed extensive policies on new technology, founded on the basic principle that technological change should only be introduced with union agreement. But trade unions have been able to exert only limited influence upon technological change, despite the development of new technology policies, partly because of the socio-economic and political context and partly because of fundamental problems which technological change poses for trade unions independently of the context in which it is introduced. Technological change poses acutely the fundamental union problem of maintaining solidarity in the face of developments which favour one group of workers over another. However, despite the failure to secure direct influence over technological change, continuing increases in the real earnings of employed manual workers, even in the context of high levels of unemployment, suggest that new technology has not undermined wider union bargaining power, at least not in the short run.

The framework for union policy on new technology is still provided by the TUC's 1979 policy statement, *Technology and Employment*. As elaborated in the Checklist for Negotiators, the TUC document has provided the constituent elements for individual union policies, brought together in different combinations by different unions. Most fundamentally, technological change should be subject to union agreement; until agreement is reached the *status quo ante* should continue. All changes should be subject to consultation. There should be no compulsory redundancies; hours should be reduced and holidays extended. Care should be taken to avoid the creation of a divided work-force in which only a minority of highly trained and highly paid workers would be employed on the new technology; training should be available to all who want it, and the rewards of increased productivity should be made available to all workers in the enterprise. Computerized systems should not be used to monitor individual worker performance. The operation of new equipment should be monitored by a joint management–union committee (Dodgson and Martin, 1987: 10). New technology should be covered by specific new technology agreements. Model new technology agreements have been published by several major unions.

In practice, unions have relied on traditional methods of exerting bargaining power rather than developing new strategies for dealing with microelectronics technology. Batstone et al. (1984) comment:

> The common tendency appears to be to treat the introduction of 'new technology' in terms of conventional trade union practice. This involves reducing its content to the conventional subject matter of collective bargaining; handling its questions and issues within the format of an arm's length, across the table negotiating procedure; and confining it to treatment within existing industrial relations machinery, institutions and relationships'.

Manual unions have been more likely than white-collar unions to rely solely upon traditional bargaining procedures, seeing new technology as no different from previous changes in production methods; for example, the AEU has negotiated few new technology agreements, despite the impact which the replacement of mechanical and electro-mechanical systems by electronic systems has had upon the work of AEU members.

The trade unions have not realized the aspirations embodied in *Technology and Employment*. On the basis of a survey of the terms of new technology agreements, Manwaring (1981: 8) concluded: 'new technology is resulting in the loss of many jobs without a reduction in hours or increase in pay and with many other negative consequences, such as an increase in shift working.' Pay settlements involving new technology have characteristically included reductions in the number employed, and the removal of restrictive practices. Following a survey of new technology agreements, Williams and Steward (1985) concluded that 'both the adoption and content of technology agreements have been limited, compared to original TUC objectives'. However, it would be misleading to see union policy as a compete failure. Most importantly, the continued rise in real earnings despite increasing unemployment (until 1985) indicates that unions have been obtaining increases in real earnings in many instances in exchange for accepting new technology and increases in flexibility. In some circumstances increases have been explicitly tied to the acceptance of changes in working practices, in others paid in the form of relatively generous annual settlements.

There are several major reasons for the failure of labour to modify management's approach to new technology significantly. Some of the reasons relate to the overall socio-economic situation of the trade unions in the 1980s, especially the high level of unemployment, the hostility of the Conservative government, and legislative changes weakening the bargaining power of trade unions and the leverage provided by industrial action (for legislation, see Wedderburn, 1985; Lewis, 1986). However, it is easy to exaggerate the significance of the socio-economic situation for the low level of union influence on new technology. Changes in the rate of unemployment are more likely to affect union bargaining power than a stable, if high, level of unemployment or slowly declining unemployment; the major rise in unemployment was in the early 1980s, and since 1985 the level has been slowly declining (Martin, 1987). The hostility of the Conservative government affects the higher levels of the trade-union movement, but does not necessarily affect the shopfloor. Similarly, the legislative changes do not necessarily affect day to day industrial relations, especially when management requires the co-operation of labour in getting new systems to operate effectively (Batstone et al., 1987). More important are issues relating directly to trade-union assumptions about new technology, and the structural problems new technology poses for trade unions.

One factor conditioning union approaches to new technology is ambivalence about whether technological change is a neutral force, developing according to its own logic, or is rather another management tool, designed to increase the rate of expropriation of surplus value. If technological change is 'neutral', an aspect of inevitable historical development, union opposition is inappropriate, involving a futile attempt to stand in the way of progress. Such opposition is especially inappropriate where competitors are introducing new technology and where new technology provides the potential for higher earnings through higher labour productivity. If technological change is not neutral, but a management device to increase exploitation, the most appropriate strategy is to respond to technological change in the same way as to other management initiatives, and to attempt to oppose or to bargain over the price for accepting change. Union ambivalence over the nature of technical change reflects the dual character of the process itself; technical change has its own logic, but it is also used by management to increase productivity.

New technology also poses major structural and tactical difficulties for trade unions, especially in reconciling the interests of different groups, whether within different unions or within the same union. Technological change is usually introduced with a guarantee of job protection for existing workers, more or less tightly defined, with reductions in employment secured by non-filling of vacancies, early retirement or voluntary redundancy. For the workers whose jobs are secured such strategies are acceptable, even if the cost may be a long-term decline in the number of jobs in the industry, and employment difficulties for new entrants to the labour force, whether young workers or married women returning to employment. New technology also has the potential to fragment workers between a high earning group using new technology and peripheral workers with lower earnings and less job security. Such divisions are easy for management to exploit, especially by appealing over the heads of workers' representatives directly to the members concerned, for example through ballots on draft agreements. Even within the strongly organized NGA the national union leadership has found it difficult to ensure that union members do not 'sell members' jobs' through accepting agreements which protect existing workers whilst reducing future jobs (Martin, 1981). Moreover, for workers concerned about job security, management investment in new technology is an indication of long-term management confidence in their future; workers may be anxious when new technology is not introduced, since it may represent a long-term run-down in their plant.

Despite the long-term importance of new technology trade unions have not invested major resources in research into new technology or into developing a 'second generation' of policies to follow the failure of the first generation. 'Few unions have a researcher responsible for new technology, and those that do spend only a fraction of their time working on new technology issues; their responsibilities are diverse and invariably include health and safety . . . unions lack the central research resources to evaluate the potential consequences of new technology, and to disseminate information on alternative ways of using technology' (Dodgson and Martin, 1987: 15). Several major unions have no official responsible for new technology, including the NGA (National Graphical Association), SOGAT 82 (Society of Graphical and Allied Trades 1982), the NUR (National Union of Railwaymen) and UCATT (Union of Construction Allied Trades and Technicians), and the only manual union with an official who spends more than half time on new technology is USDAW (Union of Shop Distributive and Allied Workers). This lack of resources partly reflects the poverty of British unions, partly their preoccupation with traditional bargaining issues, partly the difficulties of incorporating technically qualified staff in organizations which have not traditionally employed them, and partly the initial assumption that technical change is a neutral phenomenon, whose basic direction is not subject to union influence. The easiest strategy, conceptually and in terms of resources, is to regard new technology as simply another bargaining issue, with its appropriate price.

At the national level union influence on new technology has been small. However, the major negotiating arena for new technology is the company, establishment or work group. But, even at these levels the major influence has been negative, rather than positive: delaying the introduction of change, or increasing the price management had to pay, rather than redirecting change in directions preferred by union members. For example, employment generating technological change has been rare; similarly, experiments specifically to increase worker satisfaction have been rare, although some experimental schemes involving the development of manual data input in CNC machine tools have been developed (Rosenbrock, 1985; Cooley, 1987).

At a general level, the trade-union movement has supported the introduction of new technology. Indeed the trade unions have criticized management for investing too little in it, rather than too much. This orientation has survived, despite the growth in unemployment. They wished to secure an improvement in wages and working conditions in return for co-operating with new investment. In traditional bargaining terms trade unions have succeeded in securing a significant increase in real earnings for their employed members, but this has not been accompanied by direct influence on the introduction of new technology. The period of new technology agreements proved short lived, and in the majority of cases those which were negotiated fell far short of the TUC Checklist. Management often but not invariably consulted with their workers, but rarely negotiated with trade unions. From the trade-union perspective this development represented a partial success: provided that annual settlements resulted in increases in real earnings there was no significant groundswell of discontent among union members at the failure to secure negotiations specifically on new technology.

New Technology and the Nature of Work

New Technology and Skill

Braverman's study *Labor and Monopoly Capital* (1974) has provided the inspiration for several major analyses of the impact of new technology on skill. The basic thesis is succinctly summarized by Zimbalist (1979: pp.xv–xvi):

> There is a long run tendency through fragmentation, rationalization and mechanization for workers and their jobs to become deskilled, both in an absolute sense (they lose craft and traditional abilities) and in a relative one (scientific knowledge progressively accumulates in the production process). Even where the individual worker retains certain traditional skills, the degraded job he or she performs does not demand the exercise of these abilities. Thus, the workers, regardless of his or her personal talents, may be more easily and cheaply substituted for in the production process.

Manual work is subject to fragmentation, rationalization and deskilling. In sharp contrast a number of authors have argued that employers use new technology as leading to an upgrading in the skill of workers, either in the traditional sense of requiring more complex manual or, especially, intellectual operations, or in the sense of requiring increased responsibility (Blauner, 1964; Francis, 1986, Rowe, 1986). For instance, Blauner argues that responsibility replaces skill as the basis for worker satisfaction.

Both 'pessimistic' and 'optimistic' views of the impact of new technology assume a more or less determinate relation between technology and skill. The concept of skill is notoriously slippery. Three conceptions of skill coexist. The first focuses on the complexity of the task the worker performs – for instance, the manual dexterity, speed or comprehension, required. Hence machining in four axes requires greater skill than machining in three axes; electricians need to understand wiring diagrams of varying degrees of complexity. Secondly, skill may refer to the worker's capabilities, which may or may not be exercised in performing a specific task; hence the claim to skill is based on the craftsman's abilities, not upon the activities actually undertaken on the job. The claim to skilled status, and thus pay, rests on the abilities which the worker possesses, which may rarely, or never be used. Hence linotype operators in printing may be able to set by hand, but are never required to do so. Thirdly, skill may be derived from membership of a group conventionally defined as skilled, and able to maintain such definitions by control of entry into the occupation, or what Parkin has more generally described as social closure (Parkin, 1972). Hence professional associations (e.g. lawyers) may sustain professional status legitimated on the basis of skill or expertise through control of licensing practitioners even when the substantive basis for the legitimation has disappeared.

The effect of technological change upon manual skills will depend on the conception of skill adopted. If skill is defined narrowly, in terms of work performance, the effect may be direct, since technological change may involve changes in the task itself, making it simpler or more complex. Hence the number and complexity of operations performed by a machinist may be reduced with the introduction of CNC machine tools, especially if all programming is undertaken off the shopfloor and the tool is running on long cycles. If skill is defined in terms of capabilities, new technology may undermine skill in the long run, as the unused capacities become increasingly residual, but not in the short run; the survival of skill will depend upon the bargaining power of the relevant occupational group. The conception of the skilled compositor survived after the tasks of the compositor had been deskilled. If skill is defined primarily in 'political' terms, technological change may have relatively little impact, although in the long run the claim to legitimation may be undermined and the political costs of maintaining skilled status become too high. While other conceptualizations are clearly important, this section is concerned with skill as task.

The impact of technological change on skill as task depends partly on the technology itself, partly on contextual social and organizational features and partly on management choices. The emphasis of recent research is upon the malleability of technology, especially in response to management objectives or other forces. For example, Bryn Jones (1982: 198) argues that 'there is nothing "inherent" in the hardware of NC or its concept that would allow for the deskilling and control and surveillance assumed by both theorists of the labour process and publicists for the NC installation'. Hartmann et al. (1984: 317) argue that 'there was no effect of the use of CNC as such'. Similarly, there are different approaches possible to the installation of automatic machinery on motor car assembly lines, allowing different degrees of initiative to assembly line operatives. This is clear in the contrast between the approach adopted on the Metro assembly line at Longbridge in 1980, with a high degree of dedicated automation, and the more flexible approach adopted at Trollhaten in Sweden (Willman and Winch, 1984: Child, 1984). Management values and objectives, product and labour markets, organization structures and trade-union approaches influence the impact of technological change, even in the specific arena of skill as task.

Management may approach technological change with different values, either Taylorist or more human centred. Enid Mumford (1983) has demonstrated how fundamental values, for example assumptions about human nature, influence the way computer systems are developed. As writers in the labour process tradition have argued, Taylorist assumptions lead to task fragmentation, rigidity and limited discretion, although such outcomes are not inherent in the technology itself: Mumford's own ideas on computer design lead to a different approach to system design and implementation (Littler, 1985). Such values may be influenced by different national cultures, as in the contrast between Britain and West Germany (Hartmann et al., 1984: 317). Values are linked to, but not identical with, management objectives.

As argued earlier, managements have three major overall objectives in introducing new technology: reduction in costs, improvement in quality and increased control. Assessment of the impact of new technology on skill as task depends on the priority attached to each objective. At a general level, if the objective is to reduce costs new technology may be associated with either 'responsible autonomy' or 'direct control' strategies, depending upon the production system (Friedman, 1977). Responsible autonomy strategies are more likely because cheaper, and are especially necessary where the production system makes direct control difficult to achieve in practice. They involve a recognition of the limits of management direct control, but not necessarily the absence of control: control may be achieved through monitoring of performance (especially automatically) or through induction programmes. Responsible autonomy strategies do not involve an attempt to reduce skill levels. They are especially likely to be applied to maintenance workers. In short, where the management objective is to reduce costs, and the production system permits, strategies of responsible autonomy are likely to be associated with new technology. Such strategies increase skill levels, either directly or indirectly through increased responsibility.

Similar considerations apply when the management objective is to improve quality. Strategies of responsible autonomy are more likely to be associated with new technology designed to improve quality than strategies of direct control. Research has indicated the difficulties with regard to quality control derived from traditional methods of inspection and rectification, for example in the motor car industry: it is easier to maintain quality if operatives are made directly responsible for maintaining quality – the principle of right first time, which is now conventional practice at Ford, Austin Rover and Peugeot-Talbot as well as Nissan. The right first time approach involves a responsible approach by operatives, more easily developed by strategies of responsible autonomy than by strategies of direct control. Moreover, the development of the closer monitoring made possible by computers makes it possible to pinpoint sources of errors.

The product market influences the way in which technology is used by influencing the size of the batch, and the frequency of changes in machining programmes (Sorge et al., 1983). Small batch sizes involve frequent changes in program; frequent changes in program are more easily carried out on the shopfloor than by special programmers. On the other hand, large batch sizes are more easily handled by adopting a more Tayloristic approach, with special programmers. However, the major advantage of CNC machine tools, as compared with conventional machine tools, is their relative flexibility, for example, the greater ease with which edges can be changed. It is therefore likely that CNC can only be justified if there are frequent changes, and if there are frequent changes it is more likely to be adopted on an upskilling basis. The size of batch is linked to the firm's product and product market. Where demand is for small complex products, like machine tools themselves, frequent machining changes will be required and an approach based on enhancing the skills of the operative is likely to be followed.

The labour market also affects the approach adopted. Hartman and others have stressed the value of skilled craftsman operating advanced machinery, if only to minimize down-time through avoiding insensitive use of machinery (for example in continuing to machine with a worn head). However, if skilled labour is not available such preferences are irrelevant. Jones documents the effects of skill shortages on the way in which NC machine tools were used in the aeronautical engineering industry: the shortage of skilled men led to a strict division between setters and operatives (Jones, 1982: 193). On the other hand, a fear of losing skilled craftsmen through deskilling work may inhibit management from adopting a deskilling approach. Moreover, a perceived shortage of skilled labour may encourage craftsmen to oppose the adoption of a deskilling approach, recognizing that management would have difficulty in replacing them.

Organization size and structure itself may influence the extent to which a deskilling strategy is adopted. Large organizations are more likely to operate a relatively bureaucratic structure, and to adopt a deskilling approach, with programming carried out in special departments (Hartmann et al., 1984: 320). Survey evidence suggests that large establishments are more likely to have some microelectronics, but not necessarily to make the most extensive or effective use of every type of microelectronics. Computerized numerically controlled machine tools, for example, are especially suited to unit and small batch production, which may appropriately be carried out in small firms. Hence Hartmann et al. (1984: 320) comment that 'the smaller plants studied combined a strikingly higher percentage of C.N.C. machinery with personalized industrial relations, weak formal methods of organization, and traditional entrepreneurial, paternalistic style, whereas the bigger plants were sometimes prevented from large scale C.N.C. use by conventional organization and industrial relations of a more bureaucratic type' (see also Dodgson, 1985). My own case study research in machine tools indicates a similar contrast, with smaller companies making fuller and more effective use of CNC machine tools.

Part of the reason for the difficulty in using CNC machine tools in large organizations rests on the approach adopted by work groups. Where work groups have emerged that are based upon a secure division of labour, there is likely to be strong opposition to the flexibility of operations involved in the use of CNC technology – whether or not it is adopted on a deskilling basis. Hence in one large plant operating CNC the AUEW (Amalgamated Union of Engineering Workers) insisted on the manning levels and the methods of working which had been characteristic of conventional machines, until the union was defeated in a major strike in 1984, which resulted in a full flexibility agreement, including the use of semi-skilled operatives on CNC machines (Whittaker, 1988).

The evidence suggests that the effect of technological change on operator skill levels has been skill enhancing rather than the opposite. This is scarcely surprising because the major management objective has been to reduce the labour costs, especially through reducing the number of employees. The jobs lost have been primarily unskilled jobs. There has therefore been an overall increase in the skill level of the employed labour force. By reducing the number of workers it has been possible to pay higher wage rates to those who remain in exchange for higher productivity. Managements have been more interested in costs than control, and have therefore been willing to exchange the possibility of increasing control for the reality of reduced costs.

The effect of technological change upon maintenance workers may prove different: if technological change increases the skill levels of operatives, it reduces the skill levels of maintenance workers. Part of this reflects the transfer of responsibilities from maintenance to production workers, with increasing responsibility for preventative maintenance being given to production workers. At the same time managements have attempted to change the basis of allocating maintenance work, with the incorporation of maintenance workers into line responsibilities, rather than remaining in a separate maintenance department. The effect is to reduce the identification of the craftsman with the craft, and to increase identification with the company. Moreover, major maintenance work has increasingly been contracted out. In some areas, especially telecommunications, repair work has been radically simplified. With the development of electronic exchanges, instead of repairing electro-mechanical devices, printed circuit boards are simply replaced. Skill resides in diagnosis rather than in repair (Clarke et al., 1988).

Technological change has thus had divergent effects upon skill (Burgess, 1986). Some of the divergencies relate to the technology itself. However, the technology itself is rarely the primary determinant; some new technologies have little direct effect on skill levels. The effect depends upon management strategies, which in turn depend upon values and objectives, product and labour markets, political regulation, size and organization structure and the attitudes and behaviour of labour. In general, the effect of technological change is to enhance the skill level of operatives directly affected by technology, but probably to reduce the skill level of maintenance workers. The result is that the overall skill level of workers in manufacturing industry has risen with the introduction of new technology. On the other hand the jobs lost in manufacturing industry have been replaced by unskilled jobs in service industry.

The Effects of New Technology on Group Relations

When introducing technological change employers usually seek to change working practices, usually by increasing flexibility. According to Daniel's survey, workers in the majority of establishments accept such changes, whether or not they are directly associated with an increase in earnings: in general, technological change has not led directly to increases in earnings, although the extensive acceptance of increased flexibility has been accompanied by annual wage settlements in excess of the inflation rate (Daniel 1987: 167; Martin, 1987: 224–6). Such increased internal flexibility has significant implications for relations between work groups, whether in the same or different unions. One aspect of such change is its effect on traditional demarcation lines, with managements attempting to deploy labour across traditional divisions, especially in the maintenance area. For example, BL attempted to secure 'two trades maintenance' at Longbridge with the introduction of the Metro line in 1980, whereby major faults would be repaired by two engineers, one electrical, one mechanical; other separate groups were to disappear (Willman and Winch, 1984: 102; Scarborough, 1984). The increase in maintenance responsibilities of line operatives has also involved a breakdown in demarcation. In the newspaper industry the introduction of computerized photocomposition has led to the end of the traditional demarcation between journalists and the composing room, with the NUJ accepting the transfer of redundant compositors onto the editorial floor under certain conditions.

Such changes have implications for patterns of labour mobility, especially the development of labour markets internal to the firm. The extent to which internal labour markets have developed is a contentious issue. However, the requirement of technological change for increased flexibility implies the broadening of worker experience within the context of the particular firm, and perhaps increased difficulty in entering the external labour market. In the newspaper industry, for example, it would be impossible for a compositor who had transferred to the editorial floor to move to the editorial floor of another newspaper. Increased flexibility may also be associated with the closing off of recruitment possibilities above the basic entry level: workers move from less to more desirable jobs within the firm, with recruitment only at the base. Such policies are, of course, especially likely to be followed when recruitment of skilled labour from the external labour market is difficult because of a shortage of skilled workers.

Changes in technology may also affect the 'price' of labour, whether associated with a deskilling strategy or not. If the high price and scarcity of skilled labour leads to investment in new technology to reduce the need for skilled labour, the reduced demand might be expected to result in reduced price. In some instances new technology has led to a reduction in the price of labour, as in the case of linotype operators in newspapers. However, the empirical linkages between technological change and pay rates are less clear cut. The introduction of new technology is scarcely ever associated with a reduction in earnings: according to Daniel's survey (1987: 246), the introduction of microelectronic technology led to reductions in earnings in only 2 per cent of establishments (and such reductions were more likely in the public services than in the private sector). It could be argued that technological change might result in increased earnings or unchanged earnings in the short run, but cause a decline in the long run. But there is no evidence to support such a view. For example, it would not appear to be the case that industries with high rates of process innovation show a long run decline in relative earnings. If technological change leads to lower earnings, it is through a displacement effect rather than through its direct impact upon the workers involved. Indeed, the introduction of new technology may be expected to increase the price of labour directly involved, since the skill and responsibility requirements increase.

Amongst the employed, changes in technology affect the bargaining power of different groups. Hence the increase in the use of computers has created new strategic groups of workers, whose co-operation is necessary to maintain operations. In the banking industry, the staff at the central computing facilities have acquired increased bargaining power, and in at least one major clearing bank secured a very favourable pay restructuring. Similarly in newspapers, the importance of continuous computer operations has led to the need for 24 hour attendance by electricians, a coverage which was not necessary under conventional methods of production. In general the influence of the EETPU (Electrical Electronic Telecommunications and Plumbers Union) has increased and that of the AEU (Amalgamated Engineering Union) diminished.

Technological change also affects relations between workers and management. According to Braverman, technological change is a means of increasing management control; new technology introduced on Taylorist principles is associated with an increase in the division of labour, task simplification and a weakening of labour power as labour becomes more dispensable and therefore weaker. More recently, it is argued, the increased use of microelectronics enables management to monitor the performance of the individual worker more easily, leading to a further increase in management control. High levels of unemployment reinforce the disciplinary effect of new technology. However, previous sections have shown that new technology is not accompanied by an increase in the division of labour: flexibility is more important – the relevant metaphor is the cybernetic system not the ox. Increased flexibility may involve work intensification. But work intensification does not necessarily involve increased control: it may involve less control and increased earnings. In office automation new technology may involve increased control, with monitoring of key stroke counts. However, monitoring of the performance of individual workers on the shopfloor may be reduced rather than increased by new technology, especially where flexibility involves flexibility in the job rather than between jobs., The application of microelectronics to traditional assembly type operations may involve the replacement of machine-paced physical activity by the supervision of machines. A major factor is the mechanism for providing parts to automatic machinery: if part feeding remains manual, machine pacing of course continues. Trade-union policy is to oppose the use of microelectronics to monitor the performance of individual workers, and there is little evidence to suggest that managements make consistent and regular use of the capacity to use the monitoring capacity technically available to increase control over operators. The main sectors in which new technology is associated with an increase in control is repair and maintenance work, where strategies of responsible autonomy had been especially common in the past. Increased control is due partly to changes in the approach to maintenance and repair itself with increased emphasis on preventative maintenance and component replacement, and partly to changes in the organization of the maintenance areas, with reductions in the numbers organized in central workshops. However, even in maintenance and repair areas, work group power may remain undiminished because of management sensitivity to the costs of down-time. If management control has increased in general in the 1980s, the main influence on this has been the application of new technology.

In this analysis, control and power are linked, but not identical; control is structured and determinate, power contingent. Power derives from interdependence, and the ability of groups to deny resources desired by others. If new technology changes the distribution of resources it changes the pattern of interdependences and therefore the distribution of power (Martin, 1977). For instance, the development of nuclear power engineering contributed to undermining the power of coal miners and containerization contributed significantly to undermining the power of dockers. By changing the types of skill required, whether or not a deskilling strategy is followed, new technology may change existing power relations. Most fundamentally, the major resource redistributed by technological change is knowledge: groups with knowledge of the old system may lose control of knowledge under new systems (Crozier, 1964). This is especially obvious where power is based on uncertainty and on knowledge of how to cope with uncertainty. A proximate operating objective of management strategy in introducing new technology is to reduce uncertainty. Technological change which increases the reliability of production processes reduces the power of maintenance workers. The impact of such changes is obviously greater where radical technological change is involved than where technological changes is cumulative.

Technological change affects both horizontal and vertical group relations. Such changes may be an intended consequence of management strategy, designed to increase management control over labour, or to reallocate tasks between groups of workers to reduce dependence upon particular groups, especially skilled craftsmen. Alternatively, changes in the distribution of power may be the unintended consequences of new patterns of interdependence, especially resulting from changes in the control of knowledge. Management strategies designed to reduce uncertainties will undermine the position of those groups whose power had been based on the knowledge of how to cope with uncertainties. But the effect of technological change is not inevitably to increase the power of management over manual workers, since one pattern of dependence may well replace another. Where strategies have been concerned to reduce the cost of labour inputs, the result is as likely to increase as it is to reduce management's dependence upon the workers who remain.

The End of Manual Employment?

There are major problems in assessing the overall impact of new technology on manual employment, and thus the future of manual employment. The distinction between manual and non-manual employment is conceptually fuzzy, despite the traditional and extensive use of the distinction. In the present context the distinction relates to characteristics of work tasks, which have conventionally been associated with differences in physical place of work (the shopfloor not the office), in status, and in terms and conditions of employment. It is possible to discern a core of clearly manual occupations (e.g. assembly line operator), but difficult to classify a broad range of occupations, some widely found (e.g. progress chaser, warehouse operative), except in terms of common usage. Traditional differences between manual and non-manual employment, in status, and in terms and conditions of employment, are also ceasing to be relevant, with moves towards harmonization (Arthurs, 1985). There are also empirical difficulties in attempting an overall assessment, since government figures on occupational change are seriously deficient. There is no occupational equivalent to the regular assessment of industrial change in employment. It is therefore necessary to rely upon partial and irregular surveys, both official and non-official, and to infer changes in occupation from changes in industrial structure.

The future pattern of manual employment is bound up with the future of manufacturing, although the linkage is not necessarily direct. Future trends in manufacturing output will have an effect on the future of manufacturing employment, and therefore on the level of manual employment. Since 1980 manufacturing output has declined sharply, before beginning a gradual rise. Manufacturing employment dropped sharply in 1980–1, and has not risen in parallel with the revival in output, resulting in a major increase in productivity, measured per head of the employed population. Between 1979 and 1985 the number of jobs in manufacturing industry dropped by 1,838,000, or 25 per cent; by 1986 only 24 per cent of employees were employed in manufacturing industry. Approximately 300,000 jobs were probably simply transferred from 'manufacturing' to 'services' by changes in contractual arrangements, without significant changes in the jobs themselves (MSC, 1987). Jobs previously done 'in house' and therefore classed as manufacturing, were contracted out and therefore classed as 'service'. Such changes are of major significance as Fevre has shown in his discussion of contracting out in Port Talbot, but they do not indicate the end of manual employment (Fevre, 1987). The remaining jobs disappeared partly because of changes in the pattern of demand for manufactured goods, especially the decline in exports and the growth of imports, and partly because of changes in methods of production, many involving the introduction of new technology. Unfortunately, it is impossible to disentangle the effects of changes in the level of demand from the effects of new technology (Francis, 1986). Moreover, the indirect employment effects of new technology may be of major importance, but are difficult to track. As Kaplinsky (1984: 14) modestly but unhelpfully concludes, 'the extent to which automation technologies will displace labour from the manufacturing sector in the 1970s is difficult to quantify'.

Leontieff's large-scale macroeconomic research in the USA suggests that technological change is not likely to result in the disappearance of manual work. Manufacturing industry will continue to involve significant numbers of both skilled manual workers and operatives. Under three different scenarios the predicted proportion of employment made up of skilled craftsmen varies between 13.3 per cent and 14.1 per cent in 1990 and between 13.2 per cent and 15 per cent in the year 2000. The predicted proportion of employment made up of operatives (semi-skilled) varies between 16.3 per cent and 17 per cent in 1990, and between 15.6 per cent and 16.5 per cent in 2000 (Leontieff and Duchin, 1986: 14). The capital goods industry will become especially important as a source of employment. There is no similar input-output model in Britain. The Long-term Perspectives Group of the Information Technology Committee surveyed 'expert opinion' about likely long-term trends: a majority thought that employment levels would remain approximately at present levels, although a minority anticipated major decline. The majority of respondents believed that technological change was less important than economic or political factors (NEDO, 1986: 37–8). The survey did not investigate the number of jobs in manufacturing or manual employment. Northcott's survey of 1,200 establishments suggest that the introduction of micro-electronics resulted in a net decline of 87,000 jobs (both manual and non-manual) between 1983–5, or approximately 1.6 per cent of jobs in manufacturing industry (Northcott, 1986: 88). Such estimates remain highly speculative, but there is no indication of catastrophic job loss in the short term because of new technology.

However, the shape of manual employment has changed significantly since 1980, and is likely to continue changing. Large manufacturing establishments, with a heavy concentration of manual workers, are declining (Millward and Stevens, 1986: 229)., Between 1980 and 1984 22 per cent of establishments employing 2,000 or more employees experienced a decline of 20 per cent or more in employment levels, and 25 per cent a decline of 5-20 per cent. In contrast only 4 per cent reported an increase in employment. The comparable figures for establishments employing 25-49 employees were 12 per cent, 23 per cent and 13 per cent (Millward and

Stevens, 1986: 12). The Census of Employment reported a small decline in the proportion of employees in census units (usually establishments) with 2,000 or more employees from 0.5 per cent in 1980 to 0.4 per cent in 1984, and an increase in units employing 25-49 workers from 45.6 per cent to 47.6 per cent (Millward and Stevens, 1986: 331). Data on employment in small establishments are notably imprecise. However, as overall levels of employment in manufacturing industry have declined, the significance of small establishments has increased. The trend is exemplified sharply in the machine tool industry, an important sector for new technology. Between 1980 and 1985 the number of employees dropped from 96,900 in 1980 to 61,300 in 1985, a decline of 30.7 per cent. Over the same period net output per employee increased by 64 per cent from £9,490 to £15,560, while the proportion of employees in the industry employed in establishments with under 300 employees increased from 62.3 per cent in 1980 to 79.3 per cent in 1985, the number of employed in establishments of 300 or more workers dropped from 37,000 to 12,500 (Census of Production, 1980, 1985, PA 322). Overall, the average size of enterprise has also declined, although less sharply.

There is also a major change in the structure of employment in manufacturing, with a reduction in the relative size of the manual labour force. According to the Workplace Industrial Relations Survey the proportion of manual workers declined from 53 per cent to 46 per cent between 1980 and 1984 (Millward and Stevens, 1986: 13). In the engineering industry, the number of operatives declined by 40.7 per cent between 1978 and 1985, and the number of craftsmen by 33.8 per cent. During the same period the number of professional engineers, scientists and technologists increased by 46.5 per cent. In 1978, 65 per cent of employees in the engineering industry were manual workers; by 1985 the figure had fallen to 58.9 per cent – although the figures are not directly comparable, since the 1985 figure includes 60,650 foundry workers, largely manual workers, excluded in 1978 (Engineering Industry Training Board, 1986: 2). Within manual employment, the rate of decline in craft workers has been slower than the rate of decline in operatives; and according to the Long-term Perspectives Survey this trend is likely to continue.

Compared with the 1970s, manual workers are more likely to be employed in small establishments, and they are more likely to be skilled. The trend towards smaller establishments is due partly to product market changes, especially the fall in the demand for British products traditionally produced in large establishments (e.g. vehicles). Differential rates of decline in markets or market share have led to the differential mortality of establishments. It is also partly due to changes in the methods of production, with or without the introduction of new technology. Daniel reports that new technology is more likely to be labour displacing in large than in small establishments (Daniel, 1987: 217). The decline in manual employment as a proportion of manufacturing employment is both linked to differential mortality of firms and to changes in the type of labour required by new technology. In the engineering industry, the sectors traditionally employing relatively high proportions of manual workers (e.g. motor vehicles) have borne the brunt of reduced output, whilst expanding sectors (e.g. electronic data processing equipment, telecommunications equipment) employ relatively low proportions of manual workers. At the same time, according to the EITB, changes in technology have led to a reduced demand for manual workers; 'the mix of skills required by engineering employers has shifted further away from craft and semi-skilled workers towards higher level technicians and professional engineers, scientists and technologists' (EITB, 1986: 13).

The future of semi-skilled manual work is likely to be influenced by employer strategies, especially the development of internal labour markets. As argued earlier, employers may choose to operate microelectronic equipment with skilled workers, because the ability to secure maximum utilization is likely to be higher with skilled workers; skilled workers are also more likely to be able to assume responsibility for preventative and routine maintenance. However, since 1980 there has been a major drop in the number of apprenticeships, and the number of formally qualified manual workers has dropped. Skill is therefore likely to be acquired increasingly through experience, and on and off the job training provided by the employer, rather than through formal apprenticeship (Dore and Sako, 1986). Promotion from less to more skilled jobs is therefore likely to be on the basis of assessments of skill made internally rather than externally – a characteristic feature of internal labour markets.

The result of such changes in manual employment is not that technological change will lead to the end of manual employment, nor that manual workers will become powerless. However, technological change, along with other pressures, is transforming manual employment, and blurring the distinction between manual and non-manual employment. The changes are likely to reduce the significance of manual employment as a social category, but not to reduce the significance of manual employment itself.

Conclusion

This chapter has examined technological change and manual employment from a sociological perspective, viewing technology itself as a social product. The development of technology is closely linked with other features of employment, especially trends in product and labour markets, and the balance of bargaining power between management and labour. It has argued that the development of employer strategy on new technology is concerned more with profit, and at a lower level with predictability in production, than with control, although there are significant differences in approach between different groups of managers. Trade unions have exerted little influence upon the pattern of technological change, although they have secured major improvements in earnings and employment conditions, if at the cost of work intensification. The effect of new technology has not been to polarize the labour force into an elite of skilled workers and a mass of unskilled operatives, but to create a high-wage employed group separated by income differences from workers in the service sector, and from the unemployed. Technological change has not yet had a major impact upon the level of manual worker employment; in comparison with the impact of variations in the level of demand, its impact has been small, although significant. But survey evidence suggests that its impact upon employment is increasing, albeit from a low base. It is not likely to lead to the end of manual employment, but it is likely to reduce it and to provide major changes in the nature and significance of the manual work which remains.

References

Abernathy, W.J. and Utterback, J.M. 1982 'Patterns of Industrial Innovation. *Readings in the Management of Innovation.* Tushman, M. and Moore, W. Eds London: Pitman.
Arthurs, A. 1985. 'Towards Single Status?' *Journal of General Management,* 11.
Bamber, G.J. and Willman, P. 1983. 'Technological Change and Industrial Relations in Britain. *Bulletin of Comparative Labour Relations,* 12.
Batstone, E. and Gourlay, S. 1986. *Unions, Unemployment and Innovation.* Oxford: Basil Blackwell.
—— Gourlay, S., Moore, R. and Levie, H. 1984. *Workers and New Technology: Disclosure and Use of Company Information.* Oxford: Ruskin College.
—— Gourlay, S., Moore, R. and Levie, H. 1987, *New Technology and Process of Labour Regulation.* Oxford: Oxford University Press.
Blau, P.M., Falbe, C.M., Mckinley, W., and Phelps, K.T. 1976. 'Technology and Organization in Manufacturing'. *Administrative Science Quartely,* 21.
Blauner, R. 1964. *Alienation and Freedom.* Chicago: University of Chicago Press.
Braverman, H. 1974, *Labor and Monopoly Capital. The Degradation of Work in the Twentieth Century.* New York: Monthly Review Press.
Bright, J. 1956. *Automation and Management.* Cambridge, Mass: Harvard University Press.
Buchanan, D.A. and Boddy, D. 1982. *Organizations in the Computer Age.* Aldershot: Gower.
Burgess, C. 1986. *The Impact of New Technology on Skills in Manufacturing and Services.* Sheffield: Manpower Services Commission.
Child, J. 1972. 'Technology, Size and Organization Structure'. *Sociology,* 6, 369–93.
—— 1984. *Organization: A Guide to Problems and Practice.* Second edition. London: Harper & Row.
Clarke, J., McLoughlin, I., Rose, H. and King, R., 1988. *The Process of Technological Change: New Technology and Social Choice in the Work-Place.* Cambridge: Cambridge University Press.
Cooley, M. 1987. *Architect or Bee? The Hhuman Price of Technology.* London: The Hogarth Press.

Cross, M. 1964. *Towards the Flexible Craftsman*. London: Technical Change Centre.

Crozier, M. 1964. *The Bureaucratic Phenomenon*. London: Tavistock.

Daniel, W.W. 1987. *Workplace Industrial Relations and Technical Change*. London: Frances Pinter.

Dodgson, M. 1985. *Advanced Manufacturing Technology in the Small Firm*. London: Technical Change Centre.

—— and Martin, R. 1987. 'Trade Union Policies on New Technology. *New Technology, Work and Employment*, 2.

Dore. R. and Sako, M. 1986. *The Wider Labour Market Effects of the Youth Training Scheme and Young Workers Scheme*. Sheffield: Manpower Services Commission.

Engineering Industry Training Board. 1986. *Occupational Profiles*. London: EITB.

Fevre, R. 1987. 'Subcontracting in Steel'. *Work, Employment and Society*, 1, 509.

Forester, T. (ed.) 1985. *The Information Technology Revolution: The Complete Guide*. Oxford: Basil Blackwell.

Francis, A. 1986. *New Technology at Work*. Oxford: Oxford University Press.

Freeman, C. 1982. *The Economics of Industrial Innovation*. Second edition. London: Frances Pinter.

—— 1987. 'The Problem of Structural Unemployment in the 1980s in Relation to New Technology'. *Proceedings of International Conference on Labour Problems in the Advanced Technetronics Age. Tokyo: Labour Research Centre*.

Friedman, A.L. 1977. *Industry and Labour*. London: Macmillan.

Habbakuk, J.J. 1962. *American and British Technology in the Nineteenth Century*. Cambridge: Cambridge University Press.

Hartmann, G., Nicholas, I.J., Sorge, A. and Warner, M. 1984. 'Consequences of CNC Technology: A Study of British and West German Manufacturing Firms'. *Microprocessors, Manpower and Society*. Ed. Warner, M. Aldershot: Gower.

Jones, B. 1982. 'Destruction or Redistribution of Engineering Skills: The Case of Numerical Control'. *The Degradation of Work: Skill, Deskilling and the Labour Process*. Ed. Wood, S. London: Hutchinson.

Kaplinsky, R. 1984. *Automation: The Technology and Society*. London: Longman.

Kynaston-Reeves, T. and Woodward, J. 1970. 'The Study of Managerial Control'. *Industrial Organization: Behaviour and Control*. Ed. Woodward, J. Oxford: Oxford University Press.

Loentieff, W. and Duchin, F. 1986. *The Future Impact of Automation on Workers*. New York: Oxford University Press.

Lewis, R. (ed.) 1986. *Labour Law in Britain*. Oxford: Basil Blackwell.

Littler, C. 1985. 'Taylorism, Fordism and Job Design'. *Job Redesign: Critical Perspectives on the Labour Process*. Willmott, H. and Collinson, D. Aldershot: Gower.

Mackenzie, D. and Wajeman, J. 1985. *The Social Shaping of Technology: How the Refrigerator Got Its Hum*. Milton Keynes: Open University Press.

Manpower Services Commission. 1987. *Labour Market Quarterly Report* (June).

Manwaring, T. 1981. 'Trade Union Response to New Technology'. *Industrial Relations Journal*, 12: 4, 8.

Martin, R. 1977. *The Sociology of Power*. London: Routledge & Kegan Paul.

—— 1981. *New Technology and Industrial Relations in Fleet Street.* Oxford: Oxford University Press.

—— 1987. 'The Effect of Unemployment upon the Employed: A New Realism in Industrial Relations?' *Unemployment: Personal and Social Consequences*. Ed. Fineman, S. London: Tavistock Publications.

—— 1988. 'The Management of New Technology and Industrial Relations'. *Beyond the Workplace*. Eds. Marginson, P., Edwards, P., Martin, R., Purcell, J. and Sisson, K. Oxford: Basil Blackwell.

Meissner, M. 1969. *Technology and the Worker: Technical Demands and Social Processes in Industry*. San Francisco: Chandler Publishing Company.

Millward, N. and Stevens, M. 1986. *British Workplace Industrial Relations, 1980–84* Aldershot: Gower.

Morris, T. 1986. *Innovation in Banking: Business Strategies and Employee Relations*. London: Croom Helm.

Mumford, E. 1983. *Designing Human Systems*. Manchester: Manchester Business School.

NEDO Information Technology Economic Development Committee. 1986. *IT Futures Surveyed*. London: NEDO.

Noble, D.F. 1979. 'Social Choice in Machine Design: The Case of Automatically Controlled Machine Tools'. *Case Studies in the Labor Process*. Ed. Zimbalist, A. New York: Monthly Review Press.

Northcott, J. 1986. *Microelectronics in Industry: Promise and Performance*. London: Policy Studies Institute.

Parkin, F. 1972. *Class, Inequality and Political Order*. London: Paladin.

Pavitt, K. 1987. *On the Nature of Technology*. Brighton: Science Policy Research Unit, University of Sussex.

Porter, M. 1980. *Strategic Management*. Glencoe IL: The Free Press.

Rosenbrock, H.H. 1984. 'Designing Automated Systems: Need Skills be Lost?'. *New Technology and the Future of Work and Skills*. Ed. Marstrand, P. London and Dover: Frances Pinter.

Rowe, C. 1986. *People and Chips: The Human Implications of New Technology*. London: Paradigm.

Rush, H. and Williams, R. 1984. 'Constitution and Change: New Technology and Manpower in the Electronics Industry'. *Microprocessors, Manpower and Society*. Ed. Warner, M. Aldershot: Gower.

Scarborough, H. 1984. 'Maintenance Workers and New Technology'. *Industrial Relations Journal*, 15.

Sorge, A., Hartmann, G., Warner, M. and Nicholson, I.J. 1983. *Microelectronics and Manpower in Manufacturing: Application of Computer Numerical Control in Great Britain and West Germany*. Aldershot: Gower.

Wedderburn, Lord. 1985. 'The New Policies in Industrial Relations Law'. *Industrial Relations and the Law in the 1980s*. Eds. Fosh. P. and Littler, C. Aldershot: Gower.

Whittaker, H. 1988. 'Computer Numerical Control in Japan and Britain'. Ph.D. diss., University of London.

Wilkinson, B. 1983. *The Shopfloor Politics of New Technology*. London: Heinemann.

Williams, R. and Steward, S. 1985. 'Technology Agreements in Great Britain: A Survey 1977–1983. *Industrial Relations Journal*, 16.

Willman, P. 1986. *Technological Change, Collective Bargaining and Industrial Efficiency.* Oxford: Clarendon Press.

—— and Cowan, R. 1984. 'New Technology in Banking: The Impact of Autotellers on Staff Numbers. *Microprocessors, Manpower and Society.* Ed. Warner, M. Aldershot: Gower.

—— and Winch, G. 1984. *Innovation and Management Control.* Cambridge: Cambridge University Press.

Wood, S. 1982. *The Degradation of Work?* London: Hutchinson.

Woodward, J. 1965. *Industrial Organisation: Theory and Practice.* Oxford: Oxford University Press.

—— (ed.) 1970. *Industrial Organisation, Behaviour and Control.* Oxford: Oxford University Press.

5 Attachment to Work and Social Values

Michael Rose

Sociologists and psychologists, unlike economists, do not assume that people work solely for material or pecuniary reasons, nor that the quality of work performed reflects skill or training in any straightforward way . It is likely that 'economistic' wants are, overall, the most important in drawing people into employment and sustaining high levels of effort. But non-economic factors, in the wider society or in the workplace itself, can intervene significantly. Economists now pay increasing attention to them (Marsden, 1986; Dex 1985). At one time or another, investigators have picked out as the main determinant of effort a great variety of factors: the worker's level of interest in a work task, the physical environment of the workplace, the readiness to respond to leadership or psychologically skilful supervision, or strategic attitudes ('orientations') towards work (Rose, 1988).

But several developments in the 1980s raised, with increasing urgency, the question how far 'moral' factors condition work behaviour. The success of Far Eastern economies appears to be connected with a commitment to employment and effort levels that is conspicuously higher than in the West (Morishima, 1982). A growth has occurred in the range of work tasks and products calling for higher quality work, with 'discretionary effort' or 'optional ingenuity' reflecting an individual's work attachment (Yankelovitch, 1982). There has occurred a shift towards a blend of individualism and popular conventionalism in publicly expressed social and political attitudes, including calls for regeneration of traditional values (Gilder, 1982).

In the Britain of the 1980s especially, the question of attachment to work became a highly political one. Were some of the long-term unemployed 'work shy' rather than unlucky? How far could new employment legislation curb trade-union power and enable British firms to match the high productivity of Japanese firms through fostering closer employee identification with management? Could the British relearn the virtue of hard work, as their prime minister promised to make them?

International studies of work values suggested that the British might, indeed, possess a set of values about work that were distinctive. Two features of the British groups polled in these inquiries stand out. First, they appear to be motivated more highly by money rewards than other national groups. Table 5.1 seems to point this up clearly. Three times as many

Americans seemed to have an 'inner need' to work effectively. The British stood out too for their readiness to give up work if they were able to.

Of course, each group could have been strongly affected by a social norm that made respondents say what they thought they *should* say. Moreover, the way the question was put probably accounts for some of this difference. The British group filled out a questionnaire, while the other groups were given formal interviews. The British had time to consider their replies, in private, and thus, possibly, they may have given more valid replies. In fact, in other investigations, using interviewers, British people seem to answer very differently indeed: a series of carefully prepared studies (Jowell et al., 1987; Mann, 1986; Warr, 1982) show a consistently very high proportion – it is generally around two-thirds – of British respondents who claim that if they had enough money not to work they would none the less want to go on working.

But a second feature of British groups also recurs in internationally comparative studies. Trying to define the *Meaning of Work* (MOW, 1987), psychologists questioned large samples of employees in eight advanced countries. The British emerged from this inquiry as the least likely to regard work as centrally important in life (figure 5.1). The

TABLE 5.1 *State of the work ethic*

	USA	Sweden	West Germany	Japan	UK	Israel
Strong work ethic ('I have an inner need to do the very best job I can, regardless of pay')	51	45	26	50	17	57
Weak work ethic ('I find my work interesting but I wouldn't let it interfere with the rest of my life')	20	39	44	4*	32	9
Money motivated ('Work is a business transaction. The more I get paid, the more I do; the less I get paid, the less I do')	9	5	10	13	16	24
Money motivated ('Working for a living is one of life's unpleasant necessities I would not work if I didn't have to')	17	7	15	13	31	7
Don't know	3	4	5	20	4	3
%	100	100	100	100	100	100

* Incorrectly given in table printed in source.
Source: Yankelovitch et al., 1983: 398

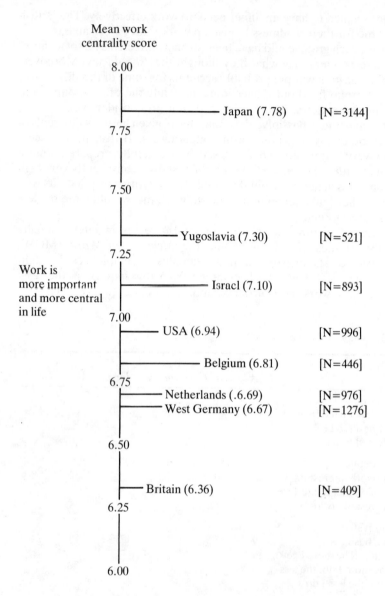

Fig. 5.1   Work centrality in eight countries

Note: Samples were composed mainly of targeted occupational groups: chemical engineers, self-employed, teachers, textile workers, tool and die makers, unemployed, 'white-collar', retired, students, 'temporary workers'. Sharp contrasts between scores for many of these groups hold up between countries. However, sample sizes, except in Japan are rather small – that for Britain is the smallest of all.

Source: MOW, 1987: chapter 5

method may, once again, in part have led to this result since many fewer British respondents were polled than any other nationality. But it seems intuitively likely that the Japanese should emerge as the most work-committed national group – however much the Japanese press may also have begun to fret about what it calls 'work-shy brats' (*The Times* 6 February, 1985), echoing more serious Japanese reports (Hayashi and Suzuki, 1984). Yet, as in the study by the Yankelovitch team (1985), the West Germans emerge as more disillusioned with work commitment than usually assumed.

How is it that such apparent inconsistencies arise? In arguments about effort and worker commitment, several distinct meanings of attachment to work are often muddled. Questions like these, however, are usually asked in the wrong way. But, in some ways worst of all, the means off answering any of them properly are lacking. These problems will be examined from several viewpoints in this chapter. Overall, the procedure is a three-stage one involving the following questions. First, what does a work ethic mean? Next, what are the main ways of characterizing changes in work values? The central argument will be that values will continue to become not more conventional – and, still less, 'Victorian' or 'bourgeois' – but more varied and less traditional.

These changes are, in part, the outcome of structural developments, especially new employment patterns and the stress upon consumption rather than production in the economy. However, they may actually reinforce the economic system, not threaten to destroy it as once was expected. But they will move society still further away from traditional middle-class modes of life and the norms and values that accompanied it.

The main theoretical issue – how economic behaviour reflects the character of a society – has always lain at the heart of sociology. While directly relevant to management theories about worker motivation (Dluglos and Weiermair, 1981), or to social policies (Freedman, 1979), it goes far beyond them. To state that attachment to work is altering involves a major claim about how advanced societies are changing *overall*.

The most vehemently expressed view about the link between social *values* and economic behaviour states that high effort levels spring from more traditional, or 'Victorian', social values. This may overstate the capacity of social values to determine social action. What are taken as values are sometimes little more than justifications, used by actors to account for behaviour actually resulting from acquisitiveness, fear, or opportunism. Other dangers of explaining behaviour by positing values will be raised in due course. Yet we cannot ignore the power of values in economic life. Max Weber's account of social change and economic growth in *The Protestant Ethic and the Spirit of Capitalism*, one of the most influential theories in the social sciences, remains a persuasive argument for the power of values (Marshall, 1982).

The Work Ethic

The work ethic notion is directly inspired by Weber's theory, but partly as a result of a misunderstanding. Many people talk about the 'Protestant work ethic'. Yet Weber himself never used this term. Weber had shown a link between business success and Protestant religion following the Reformation of the sixteenth century. He was not particularly concerned with the behaviour of ordinary employees. What counted, in Weber's eyes, was that their religious beliefs encouraged Protestant entrepreneurs to work regularly and conscientiously: but the beliefs themselves were religious values, not economic ones. Two or three centuries later, the values, largely stripped of their spiritual meaning, had diffused in a weakened form throughout society. Such 'secularized' protestantism – sobriety, truthfulness, punctuality, for example – might explain certain types of work involvement. But whether it is also called Protestant or not, the term *ethic* implies that individuals have a moral involvement in work. An inner voice constantly tells them they should work hard, and sternly forbids any slacking.

Some people do have such a moral outlook, or at least consider reluctance to work hard a sign of bad character in others and in themselves. But, rather more often, individuals work hard for reasons that are less lofty: because they respond to money incentives; because their society places high value on the possessions high earnings can buy; because they want to rise higher up a job ladder than rivals; because they need money to meet their family obligations, service their debts, or simply to survive. While subject to pressure, it is true, individuals may also possess a reverential attitude towards effort. But we cannot assume a 'hard work' pattern necessarily indicates possession of such an attitude. People who have a 'hard work' pattern may dislike working. Some psycho-therapists define extreme commitment to work as an addiction: 'workaholics' may need to work hard to camouflage failures in other areas of life.

At the same time, social actors also interpret material pressure in terms of meanings current in groups they most closely identify with. How far, and in what ways, given meanings affect economic behaviour can only be established by investigation. To ask how far people's behaviour actually is affected by a 'work ethic' can still produce highly instructive answers, provided we are ready to look at the evidence that is available and to seek out more. But in doing so, we find a different and much more complex world than the one glimpsed by politicians and press pundits.

Abandonment or Revival of Work Values?

There are two main outlooks on changes in the work ethic in recent years. The first of these can be labelled abandonment. Theories of abandonment claim that the working population once had a strong commitment to work as a moral virtue, but in recent times both business men and workers have been discarding this common economic culture. This process of general disenculturation (Rose, 1985: chapter 1) – of alleged abandonment of once accepted meanings and values about work – can be accounted for in at least two quite different ways.

A most interesting version was put forward in the 1970s by Daniel Bell (1976). Bell states that a fall in work commitment is inevitable given the move from an economy dominated by manufacturing to one based upon services, especially those which increase the number of people employed in what Bell termed the 'knowledge professions'. The work of such persons requires handling information, but also a great deal of personal contact, communication, and manipulation. The attitudes and behaviour of knowledge professionals at work centre around these 'games' between people, not around the effort of making tangible products. Loss of reverence for work as effort is both inevitable and already apparent. As the shift into a post-manufacturing economy progresses, values held by information professionals, will form the dominant pattern: 'desacralization' of the world of work will continue. For Bell, then, abandonment of the work ethic takes a chronic form. It marks the historic shift to a post-manufacturing economy. Bell calls this post-industrialism. But it is an inappropriate term because traditional industries still sustain society, and the knowledge-based new activities are organized mostly upon industrial principles.

An alternative version of abandonment sees a fall-off in commitment to work in the 1970s as a long-term effect of the three decades on prosperity following the Second World War. This golden growth era not only doubled or trebled real incomes. It also resulted in an expansion of the welfare state, permissive education, growth of workers' expectations, and relaxation of puritanical moral codes. To simplify, according to this version of the theory, prosperity undermined work involvement and work discipline through encouraging easy-going work attitudes. However, this change was not structural and permanent. Unlike post-industrial theory, this explanation sees economic values as little more than a measure of economic activity. Any 'cultural loss' may be purely temporary.

This line of thinking can lead to a quite different theory from abandonment. In its tougher versions, traditional economic values can experience revival once economic times grow hard, welfare is pruned, and individuals trim their 'unrealistic' personal expectations. If a traditional work culture was discarded during the long boom, prolonged experience of recession and high unemployment should, sooner or later, produce recommitment to a work ethic, as well as to other laudable traditional values.

Revival is constrained essentially by economic pressures. Those eager to revive the work ethic may deny that such forces can be closely controlled. In the case of Britain, this was the official view of the government which came to power in 1979. But it did not wish to moderate those pressures which had arisen, as it saw it, spontaneously, as a result of unrealistic economic behaviour. In any case, those people aged 25–45 who could not rediscover traditional values would form a squeezed radical group, trapped between blocks of more conservative-minded people (Barker, 1982).

Before these interpretations can be assessed with the care they deserve it is essential to have a clearer idea of what a work ethic can mean. According to Weber, the Protestant ethic produced a syndrome of behaviour – regular time-keeping, honesty, careful recording of accounts, saving, sobriety – that led to success for capitalist business people. Deeply held values produced behaviour which *incidentally* had economic results: the values were not explicitly concerned with economic action. The link between religion, values and work behaviour will not be examined here; it will be assumed that work behaviour may be affected significantly by values referring directly to it.

Most observers make this assumption. But work is itself a many-sided concept. Writers on the work ethic often cannot make up their minds that aspects of work behaviour and values they are dealing with. To talk of an ethic of work implies belief in the existence of a moral attitude towards work. Yet the focus of inquiry constantly shifts. The distinctions listed in the following section need to borne in mind to cope with this difficulty.

Anatomy of the Work Ethic

The work ethic cannot be investigated without a reasonably clear idea of it. Five or six distinct meanings for the work ethic are current, and several further ones occur less often. The main meanings are listed below:

1 Employment commitment. The belief that an able-bodied adult (traditionally, a man) should seek paid employment rather than live as a dependent either of the state, another individual, or a personal fortune.
2 Work centrality. Paid work activity is a more important part of life than any other single domain, such as family or politics, and as such it is the prime source of meaning and personal identity.
3 Deferment of gratification. The demands of work must always take precedence over any other claims on time, such as leisure in particular, and the enjoyment of surplus income should be put off as long as possible when it cannot be postponed indefinitely.
4 Career orientation. Work is an arena of competing individuals striving for success and achievement over the long term, and it is imperative to use talents and opportunities to the full.
5 Conscientious effort. Work tasks or responsibilities must be performed as well as they can be, even though money rewards may seem insufficient and there is no close supervision.
6 Disciplined collaboration. Readiness to accept workplace rules, industrial bureaucracy, and the legitimacy of management's right to manage, while rejecting challenges to them from (e.g.) unions.

A rather unusual form of what could possibly be called a work ethic is also widely reported in studies that are critical of traditional lower-class male attitudes towards sex roles. In such a 'machismo' definition of the work ethic, to work hard demonstrates toughness and validates male claims to the right to control and make use of women as homemakers and sex objects (Willis, 1977; Burawoy, 1979). There is insufficient space to follow this issue up here in sufficient depth.

Several of these alternatives could quite easily be found together in real life. Indeed, there is a sense in which some of them seem to imply some of the others. For a careerist, work is necessarily a central part of life. But in fact they are all logically distinct. A careerist need not have any belief in the virtue of conscientious effort. A man with 'macho' beliefs works hard because of his psychological need to prove his virility to himself and signal it to others. Some are incompatible. Striving individualism on traditional American lines conflicts with the commitment – a more 'Japanese' one – to organizational collaboration, as a classic book by W. H. Whyte pointed out thirty years ago (1957). Within others there is a serious internal tension. For example, should 'conscientious effort' be concerned with how much is produced, or with its quality?

Once the concept of the work ethic has been 'unpacked' in this way, research can estimate how far these different elements are related in any given group of people.

Testing the Hypotheses

Problem of Evidence

Social scientists may at times be too demanding in the sort of evidence they require before accepting the existence of a trend in attitudes and behaviour, or accounting for people's action in terms of changed values. To evaluate the abandonment and revival hypotheses in a way that would satisfy textbooks on research methods, an immense amount of information would be needed. Such material is not available. Attitudes and values have to be inferred from data of a very uneven quality. There is no alternative to this.

But comment on one aspect of the evidence is called for. Controversy over work values has resulted partly from over-reliance on *reports* from observers such as personnel managers or business journalists who seem well placed to know early about changes in types of attachment to work. But such evidence needs very careful assessment. From the mid-1960s, managers and business commentators began to report a fall-off in attachment to work. Between 1968–73, concern began to turn into alarm. During these years, when the advanced societies experienced a period of intense social unrest and cultural turmoil, observers perceived a growth of rebellion against the work ethic (however defined). Work commitment, some claimed, was turning into an anti-work movement, in which traditional values were being stood on their head. Social rebels, such as left-wing radicals, some union militants, and hippie drop-outs, often agreed with them (Zerzan, 1981–2).

Remarkably, reports of the spread of anti-work values continued throughout the 1970s, despite the darkening economic situation. They were still commonplace even when Margaret Thatcher began to announce the arrival of 'new realism' among the British work-force around 1980. In research being conducted by this author in 1987–8 they were often voiced by personnel and other managers in both Britain and France. It is wrong to ignore these reports. Whatever may really be happening, they show how those people making them define reality. Yet there has never been a time

when similar worries and complaints were not voiced. Nor do they eluci-
date the link between changing values and behaviour in a coherent way.

For firmer information on employee behaviour that could reflect work
values, for example their productivity, absenteeism, or strike behaviour,
there is a considerable range of material, running from official statistics
to social science monographs. Values must be inferred from actions.

Actions

Evidence on actions also suggests a rapid disaffection from work around
1970. Strike levels were low enough in the middle of the growth era
for some people to predict the imminent withering away (Ross and
Hartman, 1960) of the strike in all advanced societies. But the 1968–73
years, when protests and conflicts of all kinds reached a peak, were
marked by a world strike wave. The number and severity of strikes
increased. They occurred in countries like Sweden or West Germany
where they had seemingly disappeared. They involved white-collar, public
service or professional employees, including in some places managers,
or even the police, who were forbidden to strike by their contracts of
employment or by the law (Crouch and Pizzorno, 1978). Novel means of
industrial protest such as the work-in, or violent ones like the lock-up
of managers, became almost daily events in some countries.

Once again, although the economic down-turn after 1973 killed off the
more spectacular sorts of stoppage fairly quickly, it was only in the deep
recessionary years of the early 1980s that strikes and similar open work conflicts finally fell off dramatically (Walsh, 1983). The extraordinary industrial
relations events of these years, above all those in countries like Britain,
France and Italy, will be discussed and reinterpreted by historians. But, at
least in the case of Britain, the strike-rate was connected with the growth
of corporatist bargaining over pay levels involving the state: some unions
began using the strike as a first rather than a last resort in negotiation.

But a second feature is possibly more relevant to the work values
issue. A shift in power to the workplace level, together with a growth
in unofficial stoppages, occurred within many unions between 1960–75.
This also reflected economic circumstances and changes in the structure
of bargaining. Yet there seems to be some evidence that a further
factor was a decline in readiness to accept work discipline and the
authority of supervisors, work study specialists, and others exerting
control over individual work performance. But the strike pattern varied
so sharply between industries, and between plants in the same industry,
that such inferences must be drawn very carefully (Edwards, 1984).

Other objectively measurable patterns of action, such as time-keeping,
turn-over, absenteeism, and labour productivity, arguably are better
pointers to possible changes in work values. Unfortunately this does not
mean they are particularly good ones. Although most conflicts continued
to have clear economic aims, a growing number of the 'protest peak'
strikes included demands for less tedious work or a say for employees
in management. These types of action did seem to reflect responses

to work discipline which were heavily influenced by non-economic values. And poor time-keeping and high absenteeism might well show a fall-off in the centrality of work. Declining labour productivity seemed directly to point at lesser respect for work effort as an economic virtue.

American business and government became alarmed at what was increasingly termed a productivity crisis throughout the 1970s (Cooper et al., 1979). An international study (Kendrick, 1981) of the 1980s found that the high rates reached ten years earlier, during the protest peak period, had not been greatly reduced, despite the growing economic storm. Evidence such as this seems to count heavily against the argument for revival, provided it can be assumed that labour productivity and absenteeism mainly reflect one form or another of a work ethic.

But in fact nobody can straightforwardly assume any such thing. Labour productivity is affected by numerous material factors: management skill, age of plant and equipment, levels of training, or length of order books, for example (Nichols, 1986). It is also worth bearing in mind other problems in interpreting productivity figures. Productivity (and absenteeism) rates can vary greatly between industries, localities, and individual workplaces (Edwards, 1984). Structural change, such as rapidly declining industries, can disguise a very different underlying trend present in the dynamic new branches of production. Moreover, the argument about productivity 'decline' in the USA has really been about a decline in the rate of growth of labour productivity! In other words, Americans (and increasingly, Europeans) have been worrying not because their labour forces are becoming less productive then they were, but less productive than they *might* be, especially in comparison with those in Korea or Japan.

Similar technicalities affect absenteeism figures. Of course, it is an arresting fact that in many advanced countries absenteeism in some industries has stayed around the level it reached at the end of the growth era in 1973 (10 per cent meaning that on average each employee is away from work one whole day in each ten working days). But once again a careful look must be taken at factors external to the state of the actor's economic morale. Much justified absence from work has a medical cause. But in some countries it is relatively easy to 'medicalize' absences, either because little medical authentication is demanded or because hurried general practitioners are readier to provide it. Again, at the same time as former networks of mutual help in families and among friends have shrunk, individuals have an increasing burden of personal business; cars to get serviced, sick children to care for, houses to sell, lawyers to visit. As much of this business involves professionals who stick as closely as they can to traditional business hours, people must take off more time during their own working day to administer their private lives.

Attitudes

Attitudinal data are concerned directly with the state of mind of actors, while reports and statistics about actors' behaviour remain indirect pointers to psychological dispositions, moral standards, and images of the world. But great caution is still necessary in interpreting material. Most data were obtained by asking individuals questions in formal interviews. Answers may reflect the unreality or stress in this situation. Replies are themselves a form of behaviour too, verbal behaviour.

An attitude is not itself a value, though it may reflect a value. To give a simple example, when a worker tells a pollster that he or she finds work very unsatisfying it cannot be concluded that working itself is either valued or the reverse. The individual may value having a job, but dislike the work he or she actually does in it – either because it is, say, too demanding or, alternatively, not demanding enough. This must be remembered in approaching many of the work attitude surveys undertaken in the early 1970s, especially by some social psychologists, which claimed to show the spread of an anti-work spirit, not only among workers doing the more arduous or routine manual tasks in factories and offices, but among skilled, technical professional and managerial grades (Duncan et al., 1973). Many of these dissatisfied workers might have had a strong commitment to work that was frustrated by poor job design or indifferent management.

Later in that decade, and in the early 1980s, a number of more carefully designed studies explicitly focusing on employees' commitment to a work ethic in specific countries (Burstein, 1975) or attempting international comparisons (Yankelovitch, 1983), were undertaken. The latter study does not suggest that commitment to a work ethic had, by that date, increased with economic stress. To that extent, they count against the revival hypothesis, especially one in the form taken by post-industrial theory. These studies will be examined again later.

Work undertaken by industrial sociologists from the early 1960s to around 1980 often regarded work attitudes as aspects of broader actor orientations (Blackburn and Mann, 1979; Goldthorpe et al., 1968) or related them to images of society (Davis, 1979; Willener, 1970; Touraine, 1966; Lockwood, 1966; Popitz. 1969). The concept of work orientation as used by many of these writers overlaps that of work values as used here, especially since it was used to examine the structure of people's wants and expectations at work as a set of consciously ordered priorities. It was assumed that such priorities were systematically related to social origins and current social circumstances, and were used to plan job-seeking and job-holding strategies.

This view, especially pronounced in the early British study of highly paid industrial workers undertaken by the Lockwood team in the thriving Luton factories of the early 1960s (Goldthopre et al., 1968), was, however, subjected to increasingly severe criticism as more searching studies failed to find evidence for the widespread existence, at least among routine manual workers, of strong work orientations (Blackburn and Mann, 1979): the 'money-men of Luton', eagerly in quest of high earnings and relatively unconcerned with challenging work, solidarity with workmates, belongingness in a company, or even union loyalty, appeared increasingly exceptional in their single-mindedness. Nevertheless, Blackburn and Mann (1979: see chapters 6, 7) did agree that some work behaviour, especially labour market behaviour, could be at least partly influenced by weaker forms of work orientation. They also found a minority of individuals concerned to do a job that was 'worth while' – which they took as the product of a genuine work ethic.

The images of society literature has often been concerned mainly with people's vision of social hierarchies, especially class structures. By its nature it is often complex and extremely difficult to interpret. But it can obviously throw light on the scales of value against which economic action is measured. Davis's study (1979) is particularly interesting for its pointers to the way in which both values and imagery may relate to structural position.

It also breaks away from an apparent obsession of British industrial sociologists with semi-skilled manual workers; indeed, with semi-skilled male manual workers. The male bias of the literature on orientations has now been attacked effectively by women (Dex, 1985) and duly acknowledged by male (Brown, 1976) social scientists. Systematic analyses of the specific but altering nature of women's view of work and employment values are becoming available (Rose and Fielder, 1987; Crompton and Sanderson, 1986).

The Myth of Victorian Values

Both the abandonment and revival hypotheses assume that, in the now distant Victorian past, the majority of the work-force possessed a work ethic. No systematic demonstration of this has ever been undertaken. Where is the evidence that such a majority, or even a much higher proportion, of workers held a work ethic in the earlier years of this century, or in Victorian times? Did Victorian workers really have Victorian work values? Answers still must be partly speculative, at least for Britain, though social historians (Joyce, 1987) have recently been taking up this aspect of popular culture, and sociologists like Anthony (1986) have explored doctrines of work expounded by nineteenth-century thinkers.

Work discipline and productivity in the nineteenth century, it can be argued, did not generally depend upon a moral commitment to work among labourers or semi-skilled workers. Industrial discipline could be upheld by fear and need. Victorian employers no doubt preferred employees who were diligent and loyal, or were capable of appearing diligent and loyal. But all that many factory masters needed were employees who came to work, on time, regularly, sober, and did what they were told once they were there.

Some time ago, however, American historians began an organized search for the work ethic mong nineteenth-century workers. As it is widely accepted that Americans have generally been more closely attached to work than the British, the results of this research are worth noting. Gutman (1977) concludes that native-born white Americans lacked work discipline of any kind until late in the nineteenth century. Yankee entrepreneurs may themselves have been driven by something like the Protestant ethic, but they had to teach the appropriate habits to recalictrant employees by often brutal methods. They sponsored the propagation of a language of interpretation and evaluation of economic behaviour stressing the 'Americanness' of hard work and ambition. For each new wave of immigrants, to adopt this vocabulary was the first sign of laying serious claim to an American cultural pedigree.

Daniel Rogers (1978), however, has asserted that no sooner had American industrialists 'enculturated' the core of the labour force in a work ethic than they began to destroy it by introducing scientific management. These management techniques – time and motion study, rigidly designed tasks, tight supervision –and their associated doctrine of a sharp separation between organizers and workers, taking hold around 1900, built upon a 'low trust' model of the workplace (Fox, 1974). Workers' motivation, for scientific manager pioneers like Referick Winslow Taylor (Rose, 1988), derived from money-minded pursuit of incentives, not moral involvement in work.

Rogers may have misjudged how far scientific management amounted to an organized campaign by employers, rather than a bid for influence by professional managers; and its impact was weaker and less immediate than he asserts. Many skilled workers, and most white-collar employees, were not affected by scientific management until much later in the century. Its greatest appeal was always as a production ideology for managers. But Rogers is right to point out that work tasks and production systems designed in such a way as to compel high output, irrespective of workers' motivation, often had the unintended result of reducing whatever moral involvement in work semi skilled workers still possessed. It is also worth asking why, if most American workers possessed a work ethic, work-design devotees like Frederick Taylor gained such an audience. (Taylor testified before an American congressional inquiry that in his own experience most American industrial workers lacked a will to work (Rose, 1988: chapter 4).)

An impressive set of classic sociological studies of American workplace regimes from the 1930s to the 1960s (Rose, 1985: chapter 6), shows, first, that some American worker groups *did* continue to develop high moral involvement of a work ethic type (Dalton, 1948); secondly, that many more were committed to ambitious success striving without regarding effort as a virtue in itself (Mills, 1956); and, thirdly, that while stressing the 'patriotic' character of individual effort and striving (Warner and Low, 1947) management none the less relied upon tight work organization and tough-minded foremen ro produce results.

Most American employees maybe continued to believe that most other Americans possessed a work ethic; and those American workers who doubted whether they had a work ethic may have felt shame about what they assumed to be their deviation from the social norm (Chinoy, 1955): yet, ironically, these 'deviants' actually made up the majority of the population. It is striking, too, that by the 1950s many large employers seemed to have decided it was time to discourage the expression of any inner-driven individualism even among their managerial and professional workers, and were now trying to supplant it with a collaborative, 'other-directed' social ethic (Whyte, 1957).

Nobody has ever claimed that British employees ever possessed higher commitment to work than Americans, yet scepticism about the strength of the work ethic in the USA itself is called for. The onus of proof rests with those social scientists who accept the folk belief that the average

English Victorian worker possessed a work ethic. The best known historical examination of British economic values, Wiener's *English Culture and the Decline of the Industrial Spirit* (1981), deals with industrialists and entrepreneurs. Wiener's main theme is that many British business men have themselves lacked a strong ethic, and were from an early date actively discouraged by recessive social elites from acquiring or promoting one. Success in farming or finance was acceptable. Hard work as a pattern was considered ungentlemanly; indeed, as bourgeois, not to say petit bourgeois. *Belief* in hard work was treated by the upper class as an eccentricity. Religious minorities, such as Methodists or Quakers, whose view of economic life included something like a work ethic, were regarded as socially inferior or as cranks. Margaret Thatcher, whose own family was strongly Methodist, would undoubtedly be correct in claiming that a majority of Victorian Methodists held Victorian values: in her own contempt for the upper class there is more than a trace of vindication.

It now seems likely that historians such as Thompson (1967), or Hobsbawm (1968), have greatly overestimated the success of English entrepreneurs in implanting even such elementary rules of industrial discipline as time-keeping among the labour force. This is certainly the reading that has to be made of material relating to the Birmingham work-force – often cited as one of the more work centred towns – provided by Hopkins (1982). There is further interesting historical work waiting to be done on the topic. But the interim verdict for Victorian Britain must be that a genuine work ethic was possessed by few workers, not withstanding the high sales figures of primers like Samuel Smiles's *Self-Help* (1980 edition).

Though the historical record needs to be filled out the conclusion seems inevitable that the 'revolt against work' of the protest peak year (1968–73) must now be interpreted differently. Both the abandonment and the revival hypotheses seem much less plausible. And the implications for policy are clearer too. How can people 'rediscover' a work ethic if they, like their own parents and grandparents, never had one in the first place? People cannot be 'disenculturated' from a culture they never had. Policy can seek to implant a work ethic in the British work-force. But this is a very different problem. The starting-point must be realistic. Any new work values must be consistent with other social values and relate to the real circumstances that people meet in their lives. There is firmer ground to build on here. But a short theoretical digression is necessary at this point.

Relevant Values

Social actors are affected by strict moral codes learned in infancy, by ideas of correct behaviour current in the groups they move in, by stirring ideals that appeal to the urge to live an exemplary life, or by what those who have a religious feeling regard as the will of a higher power. All these forces are regarded as values, although they differ in the source of their justification. What they share in common, however, is an appeal to 'higher reason', by virtue of their reference to an influence beyond the needs and desires of the individual person.

At the same time, these moral resources can be regarded as a supply of instruments that enables individuals to make practical decisions on how to handle the daily problems of their lives. To note this does not mean that they must be regarded as nothing but instruments. The ultimate truth or worth of moral codes is a philosophical question beyond the scope of sociology. What matters for sociology is *what* moral language is used by *which* group of people at a particular point in time, and *how* it is used by them. Its truth value is of secondary importance to the social observer. What counts is its use value to actors. Before asking – though it remains an urgent question – whether a moral vocabulary provides valid truths, it is instructive to ask how people make use of the ideas it embodies, and why these ideas become useful to them.

People constantly interpret their experience of life. At any given time they bring to this task whatever conceptual and deontological resources (that is to say, values) they have access to. These interpretative frameworks are *normatively* ordered; they are not, at least for the sane, haphazard assemblages of meaning or arbitrarily imposed truth, but interpretations shared among members of a group through long-standing or growing agreement. People interpret life actively and purposefully. They do not, ordinarily, impose meaning on reality. Real lived experience is interpreted in order to make the sort of sense of it that would be meaningful to a respected associate. Value frameworks are applied for this purpose. Their 'truth' depends largely upon their relevance.

The view of moral culture taken here is in this respect similar to more general views of culture adopted by writers such as Pierre Bourdieu (1977) or, more particularly, Ann Swidler (1986), who suggest that culture should be considered as a set of intellectual resources utilized in devising and carrying out deliberate action and providing meaningful accounts of such action. This chapter, however, is concerned with specific changes in values, not with elaborating an abstract theory of values. Readers can judge for themselves whether it is helpful to adopt a relevance theory of values to explore alterations in work commitment. First it is important to consider the kinds of value that do seem to have been becoming more influential.

Post-Bourgeois Values

Any attempt to define what such values might be has been postponed until this point for several reasons. An examination of the abandonment and the revival hypotheses suggests that evidence for the effect of changed values on behaviour is inadequate. Structural changes may affect work behaviour and attitudes, while themselves not being the product of changed values. New values are, no doubt, closely involved in changes in attachment to work, strongly influencing the behaviour of some groups of people. Yet changes in structure sometimes accentuate and sometimes impede the expression of new value-patterns, as will be seen in the closing section. This should be remembered throughout the next few pages.

Until recently the effort to determine how new social values might be altering work attachment has been handicapped by lack of appropriate field research. Ronald Inglehart (1977), a political scientist, produced a hypothesis, based on internationally comparative research, that a 'Silent Revolution' in values had been occurring among people growing up after 1945, with a substantial minority of these younger people holding a 'post-materialist' view of the world, and other groups showing some signs of having been affected by post-material values. The political results of this value-change were visible, Inglehart claimed, especially in Western Europe, in a new kind of politics favouring single-issue campaigns (he had in mind the environmental ecological, anti-nuclear. feminist, and regionalist movements) whose main linking theme was the secondary importance of economic growth to harmonious relationships, cultural self-expression, and psychological well-being.

Inglehart's interpretation looked persuasive in the years shortly following the emergence of 'Green Politics', and the counter-cultural rebellion exemplified most colourfully by the hippies. Besides castigating profit and exploitation, the cultural rebels poured contempt on all forms of authority. More positively, they proclaimed the ideals of love, peace and togetherness, the virtue of enjoying life, and an obligation to discover and develop personal abilities. But Inglehart was unable to decide how to account for the growth of post-materialism. Post-materialism might signal the exhaustion of old political ideals, as a new political generation developed its own aims. (He was able to show that it did not simply reflect the age of respondents.) Or it might betoken a shift towards 'post-industrialism' – and the socio-cultural consequences predicted by Bell (1976). Again, it might show that higher standards of living were shifting personal expectations towards more artistic and 'spiritual' concerns, as predicted in the psychological theory of human needs (Maslow, 1970).

It seemed impossible to tell whether post-materialism was the product of a long economic boom, or of a permanent shift in socio-economic structure. It seemed to some critics of the theory (March, 1975) inappropriate to term the syndrome post-materialism when many of the rebels took for granted a high personal standard of living and eagerly consumed the products (music, travel, clothes) of which they approved. A growing number of very well-to-do people also took up some of the styles of behaviour developed by the open cultural and political rebels, without sharing their radical aims. Possibly, it seemed, all that was occurring was a shift in consumption patterns and life-styles. Complaints were also raised against the method used to distinguish and measure post-materialism.

These questions did not become urgent until around 1980. Polling studies of the economic attitudes of young adults in the mid-1970s (Yankelovitch, 1974; Duncan, 1973) seemed in line with Inglehart's results. One careful analysis of a wide range of such material (Kanter, 1978) suggested that the counter-culture rebels did provide a clue to the way work values in general might be changing, but the author added the proviso that it was important not to take them as prototypical of all significant change. As the same author pointed out (Kanter, 1978) it seemed probable that economic values were becoming more varied between social groups. Some occupations continued to hold strongly traditional achievement values. Lower income groups, notably unskilled males, were continuing to interpret work in an explicitly sexist way, (Willis, 1977). Furthermore, possibly because of the growing influence of the women's movement, and growing female participation in the labour market, women seemed to develop new interpretations of their employment behaviour and objectives.

Since then, discussion has continued to be heavily influenced by post-industrial theory (of which post-materialism is a variant). This points to the importance in economic life of a specific set of values. Six of these are worth distinguishing:

1 Self actualization. The desirability of discovering and developing the individual's talents and abilities, of finding ways of applying them usefully, even if this means sacrificing income.
2 Autonomy. Capacity for making one's own decisions free from interference, especially that of would-be authority figures.
3 Informality. Preference for face-to-face contacts and suspicion of behaviour determined by bureaucratic rules.
4 Entitlement. Insistence upon granted or presumed rights, in politics, within organizations, to welfare, etc.
5 Hedonism. Legitimacy of the wish to seek and enjoy pleasure and to avoid pain.
6 Community. Commonly shared activities are inherently more worth while provided they are undertaken voluntarily.

Some observers (Yankelovitch et al., 1983) also stress an anti-productivist dimension, with persons rejecting normal economic aims. But care needs to be taken here. Some critics of economic growth object to he 'growth at any cost' mentality, not to ecologically sound growth, or to economic efficiency on that basis. It is likewise clear that some of the above values could come into conflict in practice; hedonistic pleasure-seeking with the discipline required for realizing personal abilities, for example. All could be used to account (and justify) behaviour disruptive of normal work discipline, with the possible exception of 'community'. The author has examined these difficulties at greater length elsewhere (Rose, 1985).

Yet they might reinforce certain sorts of involvement in work. Yankelovitch (1982; 1985) believes astute managers can use them to redesign work tasks, or to build up work groups, bringing closer correspondence between values and the daily experiences of work, with an increase in attachment to the workplace. This might not, of itself, increase effort. Productivity might grow, however, through reduced turnover and absenteeism.

Serious obstacles lie in the way of such social engineering: not least, the scarcity of work design skill. Many workers would be suspicious of management's intentions. It is still a risky strategy when nobody yet knows how deeply any such new values have been implanted in different occupational or age groups. Large numbers of people, however, do answer polling questions in a way that suggests that they are affected by these values and have, to use the title of one study of them, been developing *New Rules* (Yankelovitch, 1981).

This conclusion seems at odds with the strong support for free enterprise in the 1980s. But that is partly because the label of post-materialism, conjuring up images of rebellion against the system, still clings to these values. What has been overlooked is the tension between these values and those of respectable upper middle-class life. In that sense they are 'anti-bourgeois'. But they are perfectly consistent with most norms of capitalism. Indeed, a stress on self-actualization might really be little more than a contemporary variant of go-getting individualism. As will be argued shortly, some parts of capitalist business either depend heavily on their spread or have actually tried to encourage it.

Here, post-industrial theorists like Bell (1976) surely hit the nail on the head. The capitalist economic system has ceased to be paired with a cultural system determined predominantly by the perspectives and values of a relatively cohesive upper middle class and its corresponding political elite. In this sense, the 'bourgeoisie' no longer exists. Culturally speaking, present-day capitalism is a post-bourgeois world, and will become increasingly so. As advantaged sections of other class groups have discovered new forms of consumption and leisure, they have not experienced 'embourgeoisement'. They cannot do. Bourgeois culture and society in the traditional sense have disappeared, to be replaced by a society characterized by increasing structural and cultural complexity.

The weakening of traditional bourgeois economic values is shown most graphically by the transformation of indebtedness almost into a positive virtue, and not only in house-purchase: during the British privatization bonanza in 1985–7, bank managers often encouraged clients to borrow enough to bid for large allocations of the new-issue shares, in the expectation of making a 'stag' profit. The government's intention of encouraging sober-sided people's capitalism collided with the determination of the public to make a quick killing from what Ralf Dahrendorf has called the 'casino capitalism' of the 1980s.

But structural changes will decide which of these values is most widely adopted, which groups adopt them, how strongly they hold them – or, to put things in a slightly unusual way, in line with the view of values put forward earlier, what *use* they make of them. These changes in structure also point to the breakdown of 'bourgeois' society into a culturally varied, or even fragmented, post-bourgeois world.

Structural Determinants of Work Values

The balance of employment in the advanced societies has shifted away from 'smokestack' production (e.g. steel refining and shipbuilding) and manufacturing (e.g. textiles, motor cycles) with the rise of the newly developed countries and the onset of automation. Service employment (e.g. banking, retailing, education, health and welfare) has expanded rapidly. But this does not render these economies post-industrial. An industry means any large-scale, rationally organized production. Smaller units may be supplanting gigantic 'Fordized' assembly plants. But the systems tying the smaller production units together are more carefully designed and more tightly controlled than they could be thanks in large part to cheap computerized information systems. Bell is wrong. The importance of information handling in the modern economy, as writers like Kumar (1977) long ago pointed out, renders it if anything *more* industrialized, not post-industrial. The economy of the 1930s already possessed some of the features most prominent in it fifty years later. The structural factors most affecting work commitment have changed in degree but not in kind. These important examples of the forces at work are changes in the nature of work tasks, changes in gender roles and the growth of consumerism.

The Changing Nature of Work Tasks

Service employment now provides by far the biggest block of jobs (Britain, 63 per cent; USA, 65 per cent). These range from highly responsible posts in medicine and education to more routine work in offices, sales promotion, or catering and leisure. While tasks of the latter kind are often designed narrowly, the work done by people in them cannot be checked so readily as the output of workers in a traditional mass production factory. In some, such as the servicing of many electronic devices, less skill is demanded than formerly. But, in many more, greater care or thoroughness is required as the service becomes more complex, or as consumers insist on higher quality. But increasingly, too, people doing them have more opportunity to evade supervision, to conceal bad work, or to introduce 'short cuts', though *some* unauthorized ways of doing tasks may be more effective than the official ones. It is inherently harder to check on the quality of a service task than a manufacturing operation and service tasks themselves grow more complex.

Some factories have experienced analogous changes. Much manufacturing (in engineering and clothing especially) seems to be moving towards flexible specialization (Piore and Sabel, 1984), involving short production runs of higher quality products. The production skills and work systems needed for this differ vastly from the giant 'Fordized' plants that characterized the 'fabricating' phase of industrial development in the recent past. These new manufacturing systems will allow greater discretion in how *most* workers do their tasks and how well they do them; there undoubtedly will remain a large minority of low discretion jobs (Thompson, 1983).

The discretionary effort or optional ingenuity workers exercise in doing their tasks has been growing slowly, in some cases with temporary reversals, in the last twenty years. The dominant philosophy of production engineering and work design in the twentieth century has been one of low trust (Fox, 1974), which assumes that workers are either irresponsible, unintelligent, or lazy, and usually all three. Factory tasks were designed to be 'idiot-proof' and if possible disciplined by a machine.

Workers were not expected to view their jobs as anything but a way of earning money without having to think too hard.

But the low trust philosophy began to fail conspicuously about twenty years ago. Critics argued that it was increasingly counter-productive even in the mass production factories. In service occupations, the drive to increase control through subdividing tasks to make them more repetitive collided with the higher expectations of post-war generations whose education had been aimed to increase their ability to think for themselves. Managers sometimes object that these expectations are unrealistically high. Hackman and Oldham (1980) have undertaken a careful review of the experimental evidence, concluding that redesigned work usually increases the readiness of employees to do it well.

In this context, 'doing work well' means exercising discretionary effort or optional ingenuity. Low discretion tasks are performed *less* well than in the past. A reason for this may be that rises in income and standards of living have sharpened the contrast felt by people doing such jobs between their power and discretion as consumers, and their almost infantile position as producers. While, in industrial disaster areas, higher unemployment may have increased 'realistic' readiness to tolerate low trust work – though evidence of this is lacking - there is reason to believe that, elsewhere, commitment to jobs of this kind is lower than it ever has been.

In this light, the 'anti-work' movement of the 1970s (Sheppard and Herrick, 1972) should not be read as the rejection of a work ethic by a generation 'spoiled' by welfare, prosperity and permissive education, but as an attempt to bring the dependence and low trust of the workplace closer to the growing autonomy and responsibility of private life. Wherever workers can exercise choice between low and higher discretion work they continue to do so. The implication for management is that the pressure to increase the number of higher discretion posts should not be resisted but accepted. To carry out such a change on a large scale is a daunting task. A deliberate strategy of maximizing the amount of higher discretion work would not, of itself, create closer involvement in work. But it would offer an environment in which new interpretations of work had some chance of taking hold.

The anti-work years encouraged a growth among management of a quality of work life movement (QWL) that some observers view as little more than a set of gimmicks intended to boost the prestige of professional managers (Berg et al., 1979). Some of these criticisms are cogent. Changes in work design have sometimes been superficial. Many managers have talked the language of QWL without being qualified or motivated to take serious steps towards ungrading jobs. Some have hesitated to do so, too, precisely because they feared a growth in work that they could no longer control; in other words, a growth in discretionary effort.

But their very use of the language of QWL gives certain values greater credibility and respectability. Most of these values are essentially post-bourgeois in character. The notion of self-actualization was indeed first given wide popularity through the management theorist Frederick Herzberg (1968). On the whole, then, advanced management technique may actually encourage the spread of post-bourgeois values, without managers themselves being aware of their role as social and cultural change-makers – a role many of them might view with apprehension (Rose, 1985: 107–221).

Changes in Gender Roles

Over the last few decades, but especially since the early 1960s, the formerly most common type of earner has been disappearing. This 'traditional worker', as some economists call him, was a legally married man with dependent children whose wife kept house full-time and herself had probably never been employed except temporarily or intermittently before having children. Such traditional families were once by far the most common form of domestic unit in industrial countries, accounting for upwards of 40 per cent of all households. In the USA, they now account for about 14 per cent of households (Yankelovitch, 1985). In Britain, it was possibly around 17 per cent in the mid-1980s – we lack accurate data. No other household type has yet become as common. But before long it may be overtaken by households (with children) in which lives also have current paid employment. At the same time, there has been a steady increase in other types of household – for instance, single persons, single parents, and couples in free unions. Underlying all these changes is a still more fundamental change: namely, the increasing participation of women in the labour market. As table 5.2 shows, there was by the early 1980s a great variety of household types in Britain.

The simplest measure of this is the activity or participation rate for all women. This shows the proportion of all women of legal working age who have paid employment, or who are not currently employed but are actively looking for a job. In all advanced countries this rate has been climbing since the early years of the century, rapidly during both world wars, rather slowly immediately after the Second World War, and fast again since the late 1960s.

But there are striking international differences both in the total percentages of economically active women and the rate at which they have grown, with France, West Germany and Japan coming in a 'low participation, slow increase' group – OECD estimates for 1990 put the rate at just over 50 per cent – and Britain and the USA in a 'medium growth', medium participation' group (both were already passing 60 per cent in 1980). On its own stands Sweden, where almost 90 per cent of *all* women – those with young children included – are expected to be economically active in 1990 (OECD, 1979). What is more, the Swedish rate was five points *lower* than Britain's, at only 30 per cent, as recently as 1950. In themselves, these figures give some indication of the relative spread of post-bourgeois norms between societies: not only among women themselves, but among policy makers too – public provision of child care services, or tax allowances for it, are important practical factors limiting participation by women in the labour market.

Table 5.3 shows the breakdown of women's participation in Britain by marital status. Features worth noting are the preponderance of part-time work as a whole; the particularly heavy concentration of part-timers among married women: and the low number of economically inactive single women.

TABLE 5.2   *Household and people in households: 1983*

Household type	Households (%)	People (%)
One person	24	9
Married couple	27	21
Married couple with dependent children	30	47
Married couple with independent children	8	10
Single parent with dependent children	5	5
Other type	8	8

Source: Central Statistical Office, 1985: 31, 33

TABLE 5.3   *Economic activity of women*

| Economic activity | Marital status | | | | All women |
	Married (%)	Widowed (%)	Single (%)	All (%)	Non-married (%)
Working full-time	27	40	79	64	35
Working part-time	33	23	3	11	28
Total working	60	63	82	75	6
'Unemployed'	5	7	10	9	6
Economically active total	65	70	92	84	69
Economically inactive	35	30	8	16	31

Note: Women students are excluded
Source: Martin and Roberts, 1984: 12

At the same time, there has occurred a modest decline in the activity rate for men. Once, only men who were permanently disabled or otherwise unfit for work left the labour market. In 1950, the rate was around 95 per cent. In the USA, it had fallen to a little over 75 per cent in the early 1980s (Public Opinion Quarterly, 1983). For Britain, no comparable figures are available, but the rate is probably rather higher than in the USA, though falling gently. The fall is accounted for in some degree by earlier retirements, longer periods of education or training, and return to education and training after a period in employment. But some men now take periods out of employment, or at least out of 'formal' employment, for more complex reasons. Some men can do this precisely because they have partners in well-paid employment.

This picture should not be overdrawn. In Britain, women's participation is still significantly lower than men's. Women are far more likely to be working in jobs that are part-time. The official hour-limit for part-time work is set rather high, it is true; but part-timers lack the same rights as full-timers and their status is generally lower. In recruitment and promotion women continue to suffer discrimination. Employers find ways of evading equal employment and equal pay legislation. Women often continue to be partronized or sexually harassed by men in many workplaces. But the spread of women's employment, and a slow movement towards greater equality of treatment, continues.

Growth in female employment has affected the work values debate in two decisive ways. First, there is the question whether women have different work values than men. Polling evidence, for example, shows twice as many women as men saying that they work for expressive reasons (e.g. interest in the work, enjoyment of company rather than the money reward); while two thirds of men say they would continue working even if they had enough money to live on, rather fewer women say so (Rose, 1985: 98). Secondly, women make demands on work organizations – time off to care for sick children, for example – that some managers interpret as the reflection of 'un-commercial' values, or an unacceptable attack on organizational 'culture': the right to wear trousers is treated in such a way in some British companies.

What such 'values' reflect is the different situation of women in the labour market. Many married women employees, or women who expect soon to be married, still tend to think of themselves as an ancillary wage-earner, paying for 'extras' such as holidays or helping finance a mortgage on a larger house. An increasing number drive to work in a second car, itself an 'extra' that enables the wife to earn the income to pay for it. Many lack the longer perspective on employment most men have. But more women are acquiring a career outlook on work. This must be seen partly as a result of opportunities, which have expanded steadily in some occupations. But some change in perspectives, at least among some women, is unboubtedly occurring (Crompton and Sanderson, 1986; Rose and Fielder, 1987).

The growth of demands on employers – what has been called the organizational civil rights movement (Kanter, 1978) – to introduce systematic variations in work rules or established practices to facilitate women's employment, need not be seen as an expression of specific 'female' work values. But the pressure behind the movement is clearly more than instrumental.

One of the most important structural effects of growing women's employment may well be upon the employment values of *men*. The majority of men remain in terms of income and job prospects 'the breadwinners' – or, rather the *main* breadwinners – in dual earner couples. But an increasing minority of people (Rose and Fielder, 1987) question whether men should automatically be regarded as the breadwinners. Households where a man supports a high-flying wife's career, especially by giving up work entirely, remain very rare and subject to severe strains (Hochschild, 1988). There is a more common pattern in which a working woman supports a husband in full-time higher education or retraining (Lichter, 1984). Husbands disillusioned with their own careers or 'workaholism' sometimes abandon them for something they regard as more worthwhile only because they have a wife with a career.

Dual earning households have been produced partly by growing consumer expectations and the increase in people's financial obligations. In this sense, women's growing employment follows the need for income. But in another sense, and especially where couples have more or less similar incomes and prospects, dual earning can be viewed as a shield from the pressure to which a single-earner houshold is exposed. Men in such partnerships need not view their own jobs in quite the way they would have done fifty years ago. Thus, there may be a sense in which women are being constrained by various pressures to adopt new interpretations of their economic role, with the result that they begin searching for normative ideas that will be relevant to their new circumstances. But for the USA certainly, firm data point towards the acquisition of some important new work values among younger women in particular (Lindsay and Knox, 1984).

The Growth of Consumerism

Deferment of gratification – the postponement of enjoyment – is perhaps the keystone of what we think of as Victorian values. In the work domain, the sterner kind of Victorian employer sought to minimize the distraction of employees from the serious business of work. Indulgence of the pleasure principle would reduce capacity to work hard, both mentally and physically. Profit depended above all on the ability of workers to produce. But as growing numbers of workers themselves enjoyed higher real income, logic began to point in a different direction. Henry Ford did not originate twentieth-century consumerist theory completely alone, but he became its most celebrated exponent. Ford recognized that workers themselves were becoming a vast new market for goods. They should be encouraged to consume as well as to produce. The economic history of the last seventy years could be interpreted in terms of the resulting shift. The ideal economic citizen ceased to be a thrifty producer and became an avid consumer.

Good consumers are shaped by three main factors: research to ascertain what demands are unfulfilled; advertising to announce that a product to fulfil them is available; and easy credit to reduce the perceived problem of paying for newly desired goods and services. This effort is highly professional and generally successful. It has sides that have always horrified puritans. When workers began to acquire white goods (e.g. freezers, washing-machines) in large quantity, for the first time some observers condemned them for 'seeking status' as middle-class people by buying 'unnecessary' goods purely for conspicuous consumption.

Washing machines serve a useful purpose as well as giving a sense of participation in 'the consumer community'. The utility of other goods and services purchased in increasingly large volume may be more debatable. That is not a relevant matter here. The point is that a vast effort goes into persuading people to adopt a pleasure-hunting approach to life. It seeks to alter their perception of indebtedness, their entitlement to consume, and their readiness to wait for enjoyment. Sometimes, in an inspired slogan such as 'Take the waiting out of wanting', the advertising industry combines all three value messages.

The full effect on work-related behaviour of this constant pressure to consume freely is not well known. A common view is that people contract so much debt as consumers that they have no alternative but to work hard as producers. This interpretation confuses 'working hard' with working so as to earn a higher income: the two are not the same. Pressures to increase earnings could impel workers to *reduce* their effort, in order to earn more overtime pay to make up lost production: such crises are not unknown in some workplaces in the months leading up to Christmas. But to stress immediate gratification creates a conflict with normal work discipline.

Conclusion

This chapter has stressed an idea of social values which has to do with planning, accounting for, and justifying action. This does not mean that social actors are to be seen as coldly rational, scheming beings, though some social actors are. People always need an appropriate language in which to account for and appraise their own behaviour and that of others. This language may not be fully shared by other actors, or well understood by all who make use of it. In times of rapid social and economic change, imprecision and incomprehension are higher. The task of accounting for a person's own and for other people's behaviour grows harder. This makes the job of the social investigator more exciting, but also more frustrating. Dependable information is harder to find and more difficult to interpret.

The examination of contemporary economic values is an urgent task. In Britain, the area has become additionally interesting because of the political stakes that have been placed upon changing people's economic perspectives and values. It has been pointed out that the objective of reverting to Victorian values is unrealistic: it is impossible to put the clock back, especially in a democracy, even when the past that is invoked really occurrred; it is altogether impossible when the past is a myth.

Indeed, in examining the data that are available on changes in the recent past in values relevant to economic life, it is striking that those values that are repeatedly ascribed especially to younger generations, are, in a number of ways, increasingly dissimilar to those cherished by more traditionally minded upper middle-class people. In a word, these values are post-bourgeois. There are no good grounds for believing that the trend towards their wider adoption will be reversed. However, different social groups will make use of them to a varying degree.

This process is connected, in ways that remain insufficiently understood, with structural changes in economic and social life. While it is wrong to view value-change merely as the product of these structural forces, they would be unlikely to occur in isolation. Structural change offers people new opportunities, which may not be taken if old values are retained. It likewise confronts them with new challenges that have to be handled competently: sometimes this too involves the sacrifice of formerly secure values. People need to explain to themselves and others what they are doing in these circumstances, in a language that carries conviction as a morality.

The relevance theory of values underlying this view does not deny the independent power of values to affect behaviour. Structural opportunities or pressures do not cause people to shop around casually for new values. People will accept comforting fictions about the world at large or about their own actions, in order not to sacrifice their former value commitments. The process of change is gradual and incremental, not dramatic and abrupt. Justifications must *justify*. Values must themselves be *valued*. But the content of value systems, however falteringly at times, will alter with the real world of social relations.

More research on the character of contemporary work values, and their distribution between groups (and societies) needs to be undertaken. But these are likely to be more productive if inquiries assume that such values have been influenced, more or less strongly, by post-bourgeois ideology and the growing structural variety of personal circumstances in the post-manufacturing economy.

References

Anthony, P. 1983; 1986. *The Ideology of Work* London: Heinemann.

Baker, P. 1982. 'Radicals in a Generation Gap'. *New Society* (25 November).

Bell, D. 1976. *The Cultural Contradictions of Capitalism.* London: Heinemann.

Berg, I. et al., 1979. *Managers and Work Reform: A Limited Engagement.* New York: Free Press.

Blackburn, R.M. and Mann, M. 1979 *The Working Class in the Labour Market.* London: Macmillan.

Bourdieu, P. 1977. *Reproduction in Education, Society and Culture.* London: Sage.

Brown, R.K. 1976. 'Women as Employees: Some Comments on Research in Industrial Sociology'. *Dependence and Exploitation in Work and Marriage.* Eds. Barker, D.L. and Allen, S. London: Longman.

Burawoy, M. 1979. *Manufacturing Consent.* Chicago: The University of Chicago Press.

Burstein, M. et al., 1975. *Canadian Work Values,* Ottawa, Ont.: Information Canada.

Chinoy, E. 1955. *Automobile Workers and the American Dream.* New York: Doubleday.

Cooper, M.R. et al. 1979. 'Changing Employee Values: Deepening Discontent?' *Harvard Business Review,* 57 (January–February), 117–25.

Crompton, R. and Sanderson, K. 1986. 'Credentials and Careers: Some Implications of the Increase in Professional Qualifications Amongst Women'. *Sociology,* 20 (February), 25–42.

Crouch, C. and Pizzorno, A. 1978. *The Resurgence of Class Conflict in Western Europe.* 2 volumes, London: Macmillan.

Dalton, M. 1948. 'The Industrial Rate-buster:: A Characterization'. *Applied Anthropology*, 7, 1–14.

Davis, H.H. 1979. *Beyond Class Images: Explorations in the Structure of Social Consciousness.* London: Croom Helm.

Dex, S. 1985. *The Sexual Division of Work.* Brighton: Wheatsheaf.

Dluglos, G. and Weiermaier, K. 1981. *Management under Differing Value Systems.* West Berlin: de Fruyter.

Duncan, O.D. 1973. *Social Change in a Metropolitan Community.* New York: Russel Sage Foundation.

Edwards, P.K. 1983. 'The Pattern of Collective Industrial Action'. *Industrial Relations in Britain.* Ed. Bain, G.S. Oxford: Basil Blackwell.

Fox, A. 1974. *Beyond Contract: Work, Power and Trust Relations.* London: Faber.

Freedman, D.H. (ed.) 1979. *Employment: Outlook and Insights.* Geneva: International Labour Office.

Gilder, G. 1982. *Wealth and Poverty.* London: Buchan and Enright.

Goldthorpe, J., Lockwood, D., Bechhofer, F. and Platt, J. 1968. *The Affluent Worker: Industrial Attitudes and Behaviour.* Cambridge: Cambridge University Press.

Gutman, H.G. 1977. *Work, Society and Culture in Industrialising America.* Oxford: Basil Blackwell.

Hackman, R.S. and Oldham, G.R. 1980. *Work Redesign.* London: Addison-Wesley.

Hayashi, C. and Suzuki, T. 1984. 'Changes in Belief Systems, Quality of Life Issues and Social Conditions over 25 Years in Post-war Japan'. *Annals of the Institute of Statistical Mathematics.* 36: 1, 135–61.

Herzberg, F. 1968. *Work and the Nature of Man.* London: Staples Press.

Hobsbawm, E. 1968. *Labouring Men.* London: Weidenfield and Nicholson.

Hochschild, A.R. 1988. 'The Economy of Gratitude'. *The Sociology of the Emotions.* Eds Frenke, D. and McCarthy, D. Greenwich, NJ: JAI Press.

Hopkins, K. 1982. 'Working Hours and Conditions during the Industrial Revolution: A Reappraisal'., *Economic History Review*, 1: 1, 52–6.

Inglehart, R. 1977. *The Silent Revolution,* Princeton: Princetown University Press.

International Social Security Associationd 1981. *Absenteeism and Social Security.* Studies and Research Series Report 16. Geneva: ISSA.

Jowell, R. et al. 1987. *British Social Attitudes: The 1987 Report.* Aldershot: Gower.

Joyce, P. (ed.) 1987. *The Historical Meanings of Work.* Cambridge: Cambridge University Press.

Kanter, R. 1978. 'Work in a New America'. *Daedalus*, 107, 47–78.

Kendrick, J.W. 1981. 'International Comparisons of Recent Productivity Trends'. *Contemporary Economic Problems.* Ed. Fellner, W. Washington DC.: American Enterprise Institute.

Kumar, K. 1977. *Prophacy and Progress.* Harmondsworth: Penguin.

Lichter, D.T. 1984. 'Socio-economic Returns to Migration Amongst Married Women'. *Social Forces*, 62: 2, 487–503.

Lindsay, P. and Knox, W.E. 1984. 'Continuity and Change in Work Values Among Young Adults: A Longitudinal Study'. *American Journal of Sociology*, 89: 4, 918–31.

Lockwood, D. 1966. 'Sources of Variation in Working Class Images of Society'. *Sociological Review*, 14: 3: (Reprinted in Bulmer, M. (ed.) 1975. *Working Class Images of Society*. London: Routledge & Kegan Pual).

Mann, M. 1986. 'Work and the Work Ethic' *British Social Attitudes: The 1986 Report*. Eds. Jowell, R. et al. Aldershot: Gower.

March, A. 1975. 'The Silent Revolution, Value Priorities, and Quality of Life in Britain'. *American Political Science Review*, 69: 1, 21–30.

Marsden, D. 1986. *The End of Economic Man? Custom and Competition in Labour Markets*. Brighton: Wheatsheaf.

Marshall, G. 1982. *In Search of the Spirit of Capitalism*. London: Hutchinson.

Martin, J. and Roberts, C. 1984. *Women and Employment: A Lifetime Perspective*. London: HMSO.

Maslow, A. 1970. 'A Theory of Human Motivation'. *Management and Motivation*. Eds Vroom, V.H. and Deci, E.L. Harmondsworth: Penguin.

Meaning of Work (MOW) International Research Team. 1987. *The Meaning of Working*, London: Academic Press. 1987.

Mills, C.W. 1956. *White Collar*. Oxford: Oxford University Press.

Moorhouse, H.F. 1987. 'The "Work Ethic" and "Leisure" Activity: The Hot Rod in Post-War America'.

Morishima, M. 1982. *Why Has Japan 'Succeeded'?* Cambridge: Cambridge University Press. *The Historical Meaning of Work*. Ed. Joyce, P. Cambridge: Cambridge University Press.

Nichols, W.A.T. 1986. *The British Worker Question: A New Look at Workers and Productivity in Manufacturing*. London: Routledge & Kegan Paul.

OECD. 1979. *Demorgraphic Trends*. Paris: OECD.

Piore, M. and Sabel, C.F. 1984. *The Second Industrial Divide: Possibilities for Prosperity*. New York: Basic Books.

Popitz, H. 1969. 'The Worker's Image of Society'. *Industrial Man*. Ed. Burns, T. Harmondsworth: Penguin.

Public Opinion Quarterly. 1983. 'American at Work;. *Public Opinion Quarterly*, 4: 4, 21-39.

Rogers, D.T. 1978. *The Work Ethic in Industrial America, 1850–1920*. Chicago: University of Chicago Press.

Rose, M. 1985. *Reworking the Work Ethic*. London: Batsford.

—— 1988. *Industrial Behaviour: Research and Control*. Harmondsworth: Penguin.

—— and Fielder, S. 1987. 'The Principle of Equity and the Labour Market Behaviour of Dual Earner Couples'. SCELI Working paper series. Oxford: Nuffield College.

Ross, A.M. and Hartman, P.T. 1960. *Changing Patterns of Industrial Conflict*. New York: Wiley.

Sheppard, H.L. and Herrick, N.Q. 1972. *Where Have All the Robots Gone? Workers' Dissatisfaction in the 70s*. New York: Free Press.

Smiles, S. 1980. *Self-Help*. London: John Murray. (First published 1859).

Swidler, A. 1986. 'Culture in Action: Symbols and Strategies'. *American Sociological Review*, 51: 2, 273)86.

Thompson, E.P. 1967. 'Time, Work Discipline, and Industrial Capitalism' *Past and Present*, 38: 1, 56–97.

Thompson, P. 1983. *The Nature of Work*. London: Macmillan.

Touraine, A. 1966. *La Conscience ouvrière*. Paris: Seuil.

Walsh, K. 1983. *Strikes in Europe and the United States: Measurement and Incidence*. London: Frances Pinter.

Warner, W.L. and LOW, J.O. 1947. *The Social System of the Modern Factory*. New Haven, Conn.: Yale University Press.

Warr, O. 1982. 'A National Study of Non-financial Employment Commitment'. *Journal of Occupational Psychology*, 55, 297–312.

Whyte, W.H. 1957. *The Organization Man*. Harmondsworth: Penguin.

Weiner, M. 1981. *English Culture and the Decline of the Industrial Spirit, 1850–1980*. Cambridge: Cambridge University Press.

Willener, A. 1970. *The Action Image of Society*. London: Tavistock.

Willis, P. 1977. *Learning to Labour*. Farnborough: Saxon House.

Yankelovitch, D. 1974. 'The Meaning of Work'. *The Worker and the Job: Coping with Change*. Ed. Rosow, J.M. Englewood Cliffs, NJ: Prentice-Hall.

—— 1981. *New Rules: Searching for Self-Fulfilment in a World Turned Upside Down*. New York: Random House.

—— 1982. 'The Work Ethic is Underemployed'. *Psychology Today*. (May), 187–93.

—— 1985. *A World at Work*. New York: Basic Books.

—— et al. 1983. *Work and Human Values: An International Report on Jobs in the 1980s and 1990s*. New York: Aspen Institute for Humanistic Studies.

Zerzan, J. 1981–2. 'Anti-work and the Struggle for Control'. *Telos* 50, 187–93.

6 Gender and the Experience of Employment

Kate Purcell

Gender is an attribute which indviduals of both sexes bring to the workplace as a component of their identity, which influences the sort of work they do, where and with whom they work and how they are treated by their workmates, supervisors, managers and others with whom they interact in the course of their employment.[1] As such, gender is a central component of experience at work, as of most social interaction, both implicitly and explicitly, but gender is not *simply* an extrinsic attribute which is a component of the supply characteristics of employees and employers. Precisely because employment relationships are concerned with the distribution of task and authority and these are most often segregated according to sex, the workplace, as the site of tertiary socialization for most people, is the main arena where they learn to play adult gender roles, to develop and modify their performance and interpret the significance of gender in the structure and interaction of the organization and its wider setting (Purcell, forthcoming). Perhaps the most important aspect of this tertiary socialization is learning the conventions and limits of 'normal' adult gender, including sex-appropriate occupations, tasks and performances.

Brown (1976) has made the point that, prior to the 1970s, most industrial and occupational sociology studies failed to recognize that gender and gender relationships are important dimensions of both the way in which employment is structured and the way in which work is experienced. The majority of writers and researchers have tended either to assume that all 'workers' are male or their gender is not a relevant variable. Some have gone to the other extreme and seen gender as a primary variable which divides workers into the binary division of 'workers' and 'women workers', taking it as axiomatic that most women in paid work have orientations to work and extrinsic constraints which are different to those of most men.

In this chapter, the evidence for differences in male and female attitudes to work will be reviewed, the sexual division of labour and explanations of why gendered occupational segregation has evolved and is sustained

1 I am indebted to Peter Elias, without whose practical suggestions, encouragement and diplomacy this chapter would be considerably less coherent or even unpublished, and to John Purcell, without whose willingness to bear a ridiculously asymmetrical domestic workload over an unreasonably long period it would never have been written at all.

will be considered, as will the extent to which established patterns have been changing. Using recent research findings, the chapter concludes by focusing on the gender process, arguing that it is a key aspect of workplace interaction, industrial relations and, thus, the experience of work.

Gender and Attitude to Work

The gender stereotypes and domestic divisions of labour between the sexes which implicitly define the parameters of debates about women's employment and occupational segregation have more often been assumed than investigated. Furthermore, the underlying assumptions made about *men's* orientations to paid work, domestic work and childrearing are even more questionable. Certainly, male gender has been subjected to less research scrutiny and, where male employees' orientations to work have been investigated, it has been with reference to a different scale of values and range of options to those against which women's motivations are assessed. The finding that certain groups of male manual workers have had extrinsic orientations to work and derived their main sense of identity from their patterns of consumption and privatized home lives (Goldthorpe et al., 1968) or attach more importance to work connected with their leisure interests (Moorhouse, 1984) is not analogous to the often unsubstantiated assumption that women's 'central life interests' are invested in their family roles and domestic responsibilities. The former relate primarily to individual satisfactions whereas the latter concerns other-directed activity. Sociologists have asked male workers why they choose to work on a conveyor belt rather than in a craft workshop, or invited them to evaluate the relative job satisfaction or skills involved in different jobs they have experienced. They have rarely asked *why* men have a job, whether they would prefer to work part-time, requested that they rank parenthood and employment in terms of importance to their identity or, most importantly, inquired whether they feel that being a man affects either their ability to do their job or the attitudes of workmates, bosses and clients towards them.

To some extent, it is obvious why this is the case. Women are perceived to have a career option which men do not have: marriage and motherhood. This reflects Wadel's (1979) observation that folk concepts and economists' concepts of what constitutes work vary and vary systematically with gender. For women, the family provides an alternative *work* role identity in a way that is less the case for men (Purcell, 1978). However, the evidence cited in Dex's chapter conclusively demonstrates that these aspects of identity and the workload which they generate are no longer experienced by the majority of women as alternatives to employment, but as complements to it. But like all successful ideological constructs, the notion of women's choice has just enough truth in it to remain a powerful influence on gender stereotypes and, through stereotypes, on people's expectations and behaviour.

The debates on the extent to which work is experienced as a 'central life interest' (Dubin, 1956) have tended to juxtapose real situations where work roles manifestly lack scope for intrinsic satisfaction with a somewhat idealized notion of craftworking fulfilment. British research evidence concerning work attitudes and orientations to work has been evaluated and summarized by Brown et al. (1983), who concluded that while most employees' attachment to work is primarily calculative and may be more so during a period of recession, men as well as women cite the social aspects of work – working conditions, work environment and the social relations encountered there – as major considerations in determining their degree of satisfaction. As Daniel (1969: 373) pointed out, most surveys show that nearly all workers are comparatively satisfied with their jobs. The more interesting question is whether they are satisfied *in* the job or *with* the job.

Goldthorpe et al. (1968: 178) recognized that 'wants and expectations are culturally determined variables, not psychological constructs'. Responses to questions about satisfaction with employment have to be evaluated in relation to the alternatives available. For most women, the choice is between the boredom and domestic isolation of housework or boring paid work which provides some opportunities for social interaction and companionship. Research findings frequently appear to show that social relations and convenience factors are more important for females than for males and that most females give lower priority to opportunities for promotion and training than most men (Brown et al., 1983; Ballard, 1984; Martin and Roberts, 1984). Previous studies (e.g. Dubin et al., 1976) have found women to be more satisfied with less objectively satisfactory employment, which may well reflect their realistically lower expectations of fulfilment, interest and good wages. To put it bluntly, if employees working in low skilled repetitive jobs are asked what they like about their work, it should not be surprising if the answer is given in terms of earnings, as in *The Affluent Worker* studies (Goldthorpe et al., 1968). The remuneration of the majority of women in employment does not put them, relatively speaking, in the 'affluent' category, so that their only *possible* sources of satisfaction are going to be in relationships with workmates or variables such as convenience in terms of proximity to home or hours which fit in with other responsibilities. Similarly, men in badly paid unfulfilling work and men who work part-time have been found to cite 'social' reasons and convenience as the main sources of satisfaction at work (Nichols and Armstrong, 1976).

For those women with formal occupational qualifications, the choice they are faced with tends to be limited to either such routine jobs or to higher-status, generally more pleasant jobs at the lower levels of career structures. This is particularly the case if they require part-time employment. The fact that many women, particularly after a career break, are overqualified for the jobs they are doing, makes it unlikely that they will *expect* a high level of satisfaction. In addition, the finding that women less often invest in post-experience training and career development (Crompton and Jones, 1984) and more often experience downward occupational mobility when they return to work after periods of childrearing (Elias and Main, 1982; Martin and Roberts, 1984) is consistent with women's different *structural* relationship to the family and to employment. Elias (1988a) found the career profiles of highly qualified women and women who do not have children most closely approximate to those of similarly qualified men. Conversely, part-time women employees' prioritizing of convenient hours and proximity to home, along with their lack of concern with promotion prospects and training (Ballard, 1984; Brown et al., 1983) is indicative both of the fact that paid work is a less substantial component of their lives, which is undertaken as additional to, and required to accommodate, other responsibilities, and realistically recognizes that part-time employees are virtually never given the opportunity to develop their human capital at work (Ballard, 1984).

Part-time employment in Britain is normally undertaken by people (overwhelmingly married women) who are primarily economically dependent on someone else. While alleviating married women's financial dependency, it arguably ultimately reinforces unequal roles and economic power in the family and in employment. It has been recognized (Diamond, 1980) that women's earnings are vital in raising many family incomes above the poverty line and are an increasingly significant determinant of living standards. Polarization between two-earner and no-earner families is encouraged by occupational segregation – particularly in the concentration of women in part-time jobs – and by social policy, particularly relating to unemployment and social security benefit payments (Pahl, 1984; Morris, 1985). Research among women employees in the early 1970s indicated that they regarded redundancy with a certain degree of impunity, in the belief that they would be able to find alternative employment without difficulty (Wood, 1981; Pollert, 1981). More recent work on redundant manual working women suggests that they approach impending loss of jobs with considerably more pessimism (Coyle, 1984; Martin and Wallace, 1984), realistically assessing their chances of immediate re-employment as slight. Both these studies found that the majority of employed women's attachment to paid work was similar to men's, in so far as they defined employment as a necessary and natural component of their lives, whether their employment was full-time or part-time.

Sources of Gender Segregation

As the data cited by Dex indicate, the overall pattern or gender segregation in British employment has remained surprisingly stable, despite the increase in female economic activity rates, the introduction of equal opportunities legislation, occupational diversification and industrial restructuring. Explanations for the existing pattern of gender segregation in employment can be superficially divided into two basic categories: those which derive from the sexual division of labour in the family and those which derive from the organization of employment itself (Stacey, 1981). These tend in practice to be mutually reinforcing.

The model of households headed by a complementary partnership of man-the-breadwinner and woman-the-homemaker continues to provide the template for family law, fiscal policy and social policy legislation, whose combined effect is to reinforce women's dependence (Beechey and Whitelegg, 1986). Substantially different rates of pay for 'men's jobs' and 'women's jobs' reinforce both occupational segregation and women's dependency in the family and thus, as well as domestic roles constraining employment, gender roles in the household have been reinforced by opportunities in the labour market (Garnsey, 1978).

The range and content of work carried out in both the public sphere of employment and the private sphere of the household have an important impact on women's economic activity, most importantly in the extent to which labour-intensive tasks have become automated and work previously undertaken on an unpaid basis in the home has been transformed by mass production. Changes such as the decline in domestic service and the expansion of public and personal services may not be exactly two sides of the same coin but they are intimately related. Similarly, the reduction of commodities and services produced in the home, such as food and clothing, and the expansion in completed goods and market services brought into the household as alternatives has meant that the range of tasks carried out in the household has diminished while the demand for labour in manufacturing and the collective provision of services has increased. Despite an increased interest in do-it-yourself home development and maintenance and, for some sections of society at least, in self-provisioning and the rediscovery of traditional crafts and domestic skills (Gershuny, 1978), most households have been moving away from, rather than towards, self-sufficiency. As Pahl's (1984) research on the Isle of Sheppey illustrated, engaging in such domestic 'reskilling' is a luxury which is only easily available to people with a comfortably high household income from the formal economy, predominantly those in dual-earner households.

In addition, although most research on the domestic division of labour in households where the 'breadwinner' is unemployed reveal that, if anything, gender roles and males' lack of participation in household tasks are reinforced rather than challenged (McKee and Bell, 1985; Pahl and Wallace, 1985; Morris, 1985), there is evidence that women's employment in two-earner households does tend to facilitate, if not a more egalitarian sexual division of labour, at least a proportionately higher level of male participation in childcare and housework (Martin and Roberts, 1984: 100–2; Pahl, 1984: 110). Data from time budget studies suggest that, in general, men's participation in these activities has steadily increased over the last two decades (Gershuny, 1987). But both those and detailed studies of housework, childcare and domestic divisions of labour (Pahl, 1984; Oakley, 1974; Derow, 1982; Hertz, 1986) reveal that even in households where both partners are in full-time employment, the domestic division of labour is more likely to be asymmetrical than symmetrical and that such symmetries as exist are more likely to be balanced upon a traditional gendered than androgynous basis. As a reflection of the fact that full-time employment, parenting and domestic efficiency are incompatible without third-party support (Delphy, 1976: 161), two-earner households most often survive by co-opting paid or unpaid helpers to carry out these latter, traditionally 'female' tasks; and these helpers are almost invariably women (Yeandle, 1984: 156; Martin and Roberts, 1984; Rapoport and Rapoport, 1976; Hertz, 1986: 162 ff.).

The asymmetry in the distribution of 'caring' responsibilities which has evolved in the patriarchal sexual division of labour in the household and the wider community (Finch and Groves, 1983; Cunnison, 1986) is also symptomatic of the power differential which arises from women's economic dependency and has promoted the institutionalization of a 'deferential dialectic' as part of 'normal' gender interaction (Bell and Newby, 1976). The fact that gender adds a particular dimension to relations of authority and subordination is illustrated by male reluctance to work of female supervisors (Kanter, 1977: 197–205) and the belief that men make 'better' bosses (Wacjman, 1983: 173). The classic example of such institutionalized deference in employment is the personal secretary–boss relationship, where deference and 'femininity' are an important part of the job training of aspiring secretaries (McNally, 1979: 57–9; Valli, 1986) and where the workload of such women is frequently assumed to have boundaries encompassing tasks which have more 'caring' than clerical content (Benet, 1972; McNally, 1979: 70).

The Gendering of Jobs

Gender differentiation is implicit in the segmentation of occupations, which have been revealed at workplace level to be more segregated by sex than aggregate figures suggest, both at the level of job and tasks allocated (Martin and Roberts, 1984; Craig et al., 1984; Bielby and Baron, 1986; Crompton and Sanderson, 1986). In the 1981 Women and Employment Survey, only 42 per cent of full-time and 30 per cent of part-time female employees did similar jobs to male workmates. Women working in segregated occupations or environments, particularly those who worked part-time, were more likely to see their work as 'women's work' than those who were employed in workplaces where men did similar work. A parallel tendency for men employed in workplaces where women did similar work to be less likely to see their work as 'men's work' than men in sex-segregated occupations was revealed by the responses of husbands interviewed for the survey. But there was an important difference in the types of reasons men and women gave for regarding their own work as more appropriate for their own sex. The men believed on the whole that women *could not* do their work for practical reasons; physical limitations, lack of skills or training, working conditions, whereas women more often saw men as not so much incapable as unlikely to do their jobs for social or economic reasons – the fact that such jobs were widely regarded as being 'women's work' and, accordingly, low paid (Martin and Roberts, 1984: 30–1). These responses highlight the different labour market conditions under which, by and large, men and women sell their labour.

Women's labour has been used in a very much wider range of occupations than those in which they are currently employed. It has been argued that the separation of home and work effected by the industrial revolution narrowed the range of opportunities available to women, particularly married women, to participate both formally and informally in production and civic activities (Clark, 1919; Thirsk, 1985), so that gender segregation in employment crystallized and progressively increased throughout the eighteenth and nineteenth centuries. In jobs where they might generally be expected to perform less efficiently than men due to physiological differences, such as coalmining and heavy industry, women's participation, like children's, was ultimately precluded in Britain on moral rather than utilitarian or economic grounds (Hewitt, 1958; Johns, 1984; Pinchbeck, 1981), reflecting the presumed desirability of women's confinement to the private sphere. The participation and survival of women in 'traditionally male' jobs during and after the two world wars in Britain (Braybon, 1981; Summerfield, 1984; Riley, 1984) were explicitly restrained by patriarchal views about 'women's place' and the presumed interests of 'the family'. Contrary to the belief that gendered barriers were overthrown in the interests of wartime expediency, employers and government were slow to introduce shifts and childcare arrangements to facilitate women's participation in employment, even when faced with acute labour shortages in the wake of male conscription.

However, beliefs about women's 'proper sphere' and the attributes which are presumed to equip them for it, have also been seen by employers as positive incentives to recruit female labour for certain types of jobs. Ideas about 'natural' differences between the aptitudes, roles and orientations to work of women and men permeate the sexual divisions of labour in employment. Women are often credited with the possession of skills which are assumed to derive directly from female physiological and psychological characteristics – manual dexterity, gentleness, caring and acquiescence – and, because their 'central life interest' is assumed to be the family rather than employment, a greater tolerance of boredom and repetition at work, less ambition and less willingness to take responsibility and exert authority. An excellent example of the way in which ideology, management strategies and specific cultural variables interact is provided by Dunning (1986: 160–1) who cited a Japanese manager's experience of attempting to replicate Japanese recruitment strategies in a British subsidiary:

> We started off by recruiting female school leavers but found them undisciplined, bad timekeepers and lacking motivation. In Japan, they would have been trained to be housekeepers. Nowadays we prefer to employ 20–25 aged married women. They often need the money, have learned to manage their own house, and have a greater sense of responsibility . . .

Pearson's (1986) analysis of multinational export-manufacturing firms indicates that, like the company discussed by Dunning, their recruitment practices demonstrate a marked preference for 'green' female labour for most production and assembly work, even where there is a surplus of male labour, but they are prepared to modify their selection criteria in the light of local and cultural variables. Different cultures have different constraints: patriarchal, religious, in terms of family-building norms and fecundity; which affect the supply of labour, particularly female labour. Thus, in Malaysia, the preferred female operative appears to be young and childless, whereas in Barbados she is an older, post-childbearing mother. Pearson cites research indicating systematic differences in recruitment patterns of different industries in the same locality and similar industries in different localities, concluding that although it is possible to identify common objectives pursued by employers through gendered occupational segregation policies, the tactics they use in the recruitment and deployment of labour will ultimately depend on the pool of labour available and the cultural, political and technical environment in which they are operating.

Studies of the link between technology and the type of labour used go some way towards explaining the process involved in gendered occupational segregation. A fascinating analysis by Glucksmann (1986) of the 'new' manufacturing industries which developed in Britain in the inter-war years (electrical engineering, the car and aircraft industries, chemicals, synthetic fibres, food processing, etc.) suggests that the availability of young women, eager to reject the constraints, humiliations and low wages of domestic service in favour of employment in the new factories, was a factor in determining the work-force recruited. She concludes, however, that their main attractions to employers were their youth, which endowed 'suppleness of fingers' and the aptitude and energy to do repetitive, precise assembly work efficiently, quickly and cheaply; and their sex, which, given demographic norms and the sexual division of labor in marriage and the family, ensured a conveniently high turnover of those whose youth and efficiency were running out, encouraged by the formal or informal operation of a marriage bar in most sectors of employment. She sees the demand for new types of employee – fewer craftsmen and more semi-skilled process workers – as being a far more important determinant of women's employment patterns than any inherent characteristics or preferences of women themselves. Thus employer's *beliefs* about gender and the relative cheapness of female labour, rather than technology, are the primary causal variables in the allocation of such work to women rather than men.

Custom and practice may go some way towards explaining current patterns of occupational segregation, given that sex stereotyping tends to be self-perpetuating for social as well as economic reasons, but only detailed historical analysis at cultural, occupational, industrial and organizational levels can reveal how particular jobs originally came to be seen as the prerogative of one sex or the other (Crompton, 1987, forthcoming). The most illuminating studies carried out recently have attempted to analyse the evolution and interrelationships of occupational and organizational hierarchies and divisions of labour. At a comparative level, Crompton's (1988) analysis of the age and gender distribution of clerks across different industries enabled her to identify the extent to which such occupations have become increasingly feminized and indicates that some industries and organizations have been more impervious to change in the sexual division of labour than others. Focusing on one particular industry, Siltanen's (1986) analysis of the gendered occupational distribution of postal delivery workers and telephonists indicates a complex interaction of supply and demand factors. Her research revealed that insufficient male applicants for delivery work and female applicants able and willing to work 'unsocial hours' as telephonists led to the dilution of previously rigidly gendered occupational groups. She records the Union of Post Office Workers' (UPW) temporarily successful resistance to the recruitment of women for delivery work in defence of it as a breadwinner (or what she calls a 'full wage' as opposed to 'component wage') occupation, and assesses the reasons why equal opportunities legislation has had less impact on recruitment ot these jobs than might have been expected. She argues that concentrating on gender divisions in employment reifies 'gender' as part of the construction of occupational categories and task allocation in a way that may obscure how such categories have evolved and how they are maintained. It deflects attention from underlying variables which are correlated, but not synonymous with, sex and gender; for example, financial need, alternative responsibilities or opportunities and the earnings potential of specific jobs.

The implication of this is that focusing exclusively on gender or on the part-time/full-time distribution may confuse rather than clarify why jobs come to be allocated to different categories of employee. Once jobs have come to be seen as 'female' rather than 'male' or ungendered they are more likely to be seen by employers as amenable to part-time organization. Thus the initial conditions which generate gender segmentation may be shortage or availability of male or female labour, but once the job becomes identified with one sex, perception of it as a potential job for members of the other sex is less likely and its gendered character is consolidated by custom. Beechey and Perkins (1987: 37) make the point that where 'male' jobs have characteristics which might, in terms of economic rationality, lead employers to organize employment on a part-time basis, the required flexibility and accommodation of uneven workloads over the working day or week tends to be achieved by other means; for example, by overtime or complex shiftworking arrangements.

Changes in Patterns of Gender Segregation

At the level of particular organizations, there is some evidence that gendered occupational and task segregation may have been increasing in manual work (Westergaard and Restler, 1975: 103; Craig et al., 1984; TUC, 1983: 7). Cockburn (1986) carried out case studies in three types of employment: pattern-making and cloth-cutting in the clothing industry, warehousing in mail order firms and X-ray departments in hospitals. She wanted to investigate the extent to which technology which substantially alters the skill and task range of previously gendered jobs might lead to the breaking down of occupational demarcations and gender barriers, thus redistributing employment between the sexes, and o explore the criteria applied in allocating completely new jobs with no ndered custom and practice. In all three of the selected sectors, she und an element of deskilling and, in the case of clothing and mail ler, loss of 'female' jobs, but her main finding was the extent to which gender permeated the organization of employment and the division of labour in the workplaces she studied. She concluded that the ideological context in which labour is supplied, demanded and deployed reinforces and perpetuates gender segregation, erecting and sustaining 'invisible barriers' between male and female jobs and skills which derive momentum from the expectations and prejudices of the participants: men and women, employers and employees. The predominant direction of influence she identifies, in what is intrinsically a reflexive relationship between policy and practice, is of custom and practice upon policy; thus, her conclusion that 'opportunity is not enough' (Cockburn, 1986: 187).

Game and Pringle (1983) have suggested that, as traditional bases of skill distinctions are being eroded by changing technology and other organizational innovations, gender has frequently become a scarcely disguised basis for differentiating job grades. After studying gender at work in a variety of very different industries – banking, 'white goods' manufacturing, retailing, computing, health care, and housework – they concluded that the sexual division of labour is remarkably flexible in terms of the tasks which men and women actually perform in the course of employment. The only invariable aspect of all the employment situations they investigated was that there *were* distinctions between work regarded as primarily or exclusively appropriate for either men or women. Where existing distinctions had been eroded by changes in technology or work organization, new distinctions were found to have been made to distinguish 'men's' and 'women's' jobs, or one or other sex had been allocated different tasks. They argue that slight differences between job content are used to rationalize different job grading and to reassure men of their superiority by distinguishing what they do from 'women's work'. 'The distinction lies not in the inherent quality of the work but almost entirely on the meaning given to it in particular contexts' (Game and Pringle, 1983: 31). This endorses Crompton and Jones's (1984) finding that the non-manual labour force is systematically divided by gender. While acknowledging the greater overall investment in training and career development of males, they observed that many women carried out comparatively high level, responsible tasks, of which they concluded that 'if a *man* had been occupying these positions, he would be in a "promoted" grade' (Crompton and Jones, 1984: 244).

Thus the structure of the labour force, from national and industrial to establishment and workshop level, is systematically gendered. Despite the exhortations of the Equal Opportunities Commission and other interested parties to break down gender segregation in employment and career choice, the recruitment and distribution of males and females throughout the labour force suggests that most employers, employees and careers advisory staff continue to regard most occupations as either exclusively or predominantly male or female and occupational segregation patterns are perpetuated by recruitment and promotion practices. Service sector employment growth has included a tiny but growing minority of women acquiring professional qualifications and entering professions and occupations previously overwhelmingly dominated by men. There have been successive initiatives at a national level to encourage girls to consider training and occupations in which they have been underrepresented in the past, particularly engineering, technical and scientific areas of employment (Engineering Council, 1985; Kelly, 1987). A number of women have thus been enabled to train as engineers (Newton, 1987) but this was clearly despite being handicapped by the prejudices of employers, superiors and male colleagues (Breakwell and Weinberger, 1987: 17–18), who regarded 'token women' as liable both to experience and cause problems. This compares interestingly with the experiences of men who work in environments where they are in a minority, who appear to derive occupational and psychological benefit from being 'token men'. Even men in gender atypical jobs, such as male nurses, have been found to be in an advantageous position to their female colleagues: more likely to be promoted and to be taken seriously by doctors and other superordinates (Wharton and Baron, 1987: 576).

As entry to 'service class' careers – including the management of industry – becomes increasingly dependent upon possession of formal credentials (Goldthorpe, 1982: 18; Abercrombie and Urry, 1983: 150), discriminatory recruitment and employment policies become more difficult to maintain. However, even in occupations where there are no formal barriers to sex equality, such as teaching and banking, vertical gender imbalances exist to a degree that suggests segregation mechanisms operate more or less explicitly, although vertical barriers may be more permeable than the barriers to horizontal integration. For example, Llewellyn (1981) described how her research in banking uncovered the different criteria applied, and career development envisaged, for male and female school leavers who were ostensibly recruited to the same trainee grade. Crompton and Jones (1984: 145) found that management in the finance sector often actively discouraged women from acquiring post-entry qualifications which would have equipped them for promotion. Crompton and Sanderson (1986), discussing the career patterns of women with professional occupational qualifications, suggest that current trends in such employment indicate both the possibility of increasing convergence between male and female career paths and some evidence of the development of gendered 'niches' within professions.

Legge (1987) provides an illuminating discussion of one such area of relatively high female employment in a predominantly 'male' career; the personnel specialism within management in Britain. She discusses how the personnel function developed from 'employee welfare' concerns in the nineteenth century: the 'caring' aspect of management which was, perhaps unsurprisingly, predominantly allocated to women. In 1927, membership of the professional association of personnel specialists was 420, of whom less than twenty were men, but she argues that, as the personnel function came to be regarded as more important and closely related to productive efficiency, the proportion of male personnel specialists increased, to 40 per cent by 1939, and to over 80 per cent by 1970 (Legge, 1987: 34–42). In addition, there is evidence that women in the profession were more likely to be in subordinate positions and confined to the welfare and administrative rather than industrial relations and policy-making functions (Long, 1984); a pattern which is reflected throughout management (Hunt, 1975; Kanter, 1977; Hennig and Jardim, 1978) and the professions generally (Crompton and Mann, 1986; Spencer and Podmore, 1987). Legge reflects that, as the personnel function is seen as increasingly peripheral in the context of 1980s managerial 'strategic realism', women may be expected to form an increasing proportion of the occupational membership, since she takes personnel management to be a paradigmatic example of the inverse relationship between the perceived power of an occupational group and the proportion of women employed. However, there are significant differences among organizations in terms of their attitudes to equal opportunities and job segregation. Crompton and Jones (1984: 189–92) found that the organizations which they studied were characterized by distinctive 'organizational cultures' which were more or less conducive to equal opportunities. Clearly, women stood less chance of recruitment and career development in the organization where the manager tended to think in terms of recruiting 'a good left back' rather than simply an underwriting clerk (Crompton and Jones, 1984: 190).

It is unlikely that women's experience in the late 1980s will be characterized by greater equality of opportunity, although in the short term there are likely to be more new jobs for women than men, particularly in personal and miscellaneous services (IER, 1987; Elias and Purcell, 1988). Many of these jobs, however, are likely to be insecure, low-paid and part-time. In manufacturing, where women's share of skilled work has been decreasing throughout this century in Britain, semi-skilled and unskilled jobs are disproportionately vulnerable to displacement by technology, as is also the case in low-skilled clerical occupations. Recent work on the trends in part-time and full-time working (Elias, 1988b), covering the period 1971–86, shows that there has been a steady and significant decline in the proportion of part-time employees in most of the manufacturing sector, particularly in areas which have traditionally used female part-time employees for manual assembly or packing work (e.g. electronic engineering). Increased productivity in manufacturing has been pursued by 'hard' changes in production technologies, but also by 'soft' changes in the organization of work (Massey and Meegan, 1982). It has been argued that one of the more important changes in the latter category has been the shift from the formal to informal economy in the last ten years (Murray, 1983) and that this has particularly been true of the clothing industry, an important sector of women's employment with implications for the measurement of femal economic activity rates (Mitter, 1986: 44). Although there is disagreement about the dimensions of the 'hidden work-force', it is widely recognized that officially recorded female activity rates considerably underestimate women's paid work, particularly in the provision of personal services such as childcare, domestic service and in the clothing industry, which is largely comprised of small units of production which often rely on networks of outworkers and homeworkers. Official estimates suggest that, while the manufacturing sector has been diminishing overall, the use of outworkers – whose work is done solely or mainly away from their employer's premises (Hakim, 1985: 66) – has been increasing.

Both the decline in manufacturing homeworking (Rubery and Wilkinson, 1981; Allen and Wolkowitz, 1987) and the utility to employees of 'hi-tech' homeworking (Huws, 1984; Bisset and Huws, 1984) have been questioned, suggesting that trends in neither area of employment are likely to lead to an improvement in women's employment prospects or conditions of employment, or to change in the sexual division of labour. Hakim (1987: 93) estimates that one-quarter of males and half of all females currently in the labour force are employed in relatively insecure or temporary work and that there has been a parallel substantial growth in self-employment without employees, particularly among women (Creigh et al., 1986) which is more a reflection of lack of employment opportunities than spontaneous entrepreneurial growth.

As long as the occupational structure remains segmented along gendered lines and social policies reinforce rather than challenge a segregated sexual division of labour in the family, gender is likely to remain an important determinant and restraint in workplaces. Neither women's nor men's experience of employment can be understood without reference to gender relations outside work, but much can be learned about gender divisions in society as a whole by considering, as well as the evolution of gendered employment structures, the process of gender relations in employment.

Gender and Social Interaction at Work

Ethnographic research (Purcell, 1982, forthcoming) carried out among semi-skilled manual workers in an engineering firm (NICO) in the north of England in the early 1980s, illustrates the significance of gender in workplace organization and interaction. Earlier research on manual workers' attitudes and experience with regard to the sexual division of labour at work had led to the finding that gender was apparently a less important variable in influencing employees' political attitudes and behaviour than factors such as plant size, industry and occupation (Purcell, 1984), although it had been observed that, quite apart from the gendered allocation of task and status within workplaces, a great deal of work-related and other forms of social interaction at work were defined, restricted and expressed in terms of gender.

In examining the relevance of gender at work it is useful to distinguish between two broad categories of actions, interactions and events: those which exhibit formally organized, taken-for-granted differences between men and women, as exemplified by the sexual segregation of occupations (which is not intrinsically related to sex although defined by gender) and can be termed *implicit* gender; and actions, interactions and events which are specifically related to, or draw attention to, sex differences – such as real or mock flirtation – which constitute *explicit* gender. The two are, of course, situated on the same continuum, but it may be useful to separate them analytically. Cockburn's research drew attention to the barriers which implicit gender maintain and her interviews elicited statements from employers which revealed these implicit assumptions. Participant observation research enables researchers to analyse explicit gender interaction and its relationship to the implicit structures which underlie the process of gender at work which, because of its subjective and sensitive nature, is less amenable to more structured methods of research and analysis.

Gender is suffused with beliefs about sex differences and sexuality, and is defined by what are believed to be sex-related characteristics and potentials. It is, like colour, age and physiological attributes, part of the immediately visible presentation of self and a primary identifying characteristic. This is so much the case that it is difficult for men and women to have relationships with each other, from the most casual, transitory public encounters to the most intimate friendship, without awareness of their gender being part of the relationship. Simmel (1950) claimed that consciousness of gender is a constant aspect of female experience to a greater extent than is the case for men, which may be an accurate observation of experience in patriarchal cultures where women tend to be objectified in popular culture (Berger, 1972; Goffman, 1976). In fact, the observations at NICO suggest that a major reinforcement of women's perpetual gender consciousness is the fact that, in the factory at least, they were rarely allowed to forget that they were women. They were addressed, responded to and handled, both literally and metaphorically, as women rather than as people or as workers.

Thus implicit gender was an attribute which defined people's place in the structure and their roles in the processes of work. Clearly, gender is an important attribute which employees bring to the workplace, which often determines their type of employment and rate of pay. Explicit gender determined that awareness of gender identity and sex differences were an integral dimension of work experience. Throughout the course of the working day, the women's gender was frequently referred to, acknowledged or implied, mediated by flirtation, exaggerated chivalry and teasing. The men's gender was less often explicitly drawn attention to by the women and was more often implicitly or explicitly revealed by male-initiated gendered interaction. This is not to argue that gender is a less important dimension of work experience for men than for women: indeed, the reverse may be the case. The point is that for most men, gender interaction and the reinforcement of male identity at work is generally a positive experience, promoting social and personal integration rather than drawing attention to role conflict and status ambiguity. Pollert (1981: 79) perceptively noted that women who are employed in factory work are deviating from 'appropriate' gender roles. Men in repetitive, unfulfilling factory work can at least derive satisfaction from the knowledge that they are doing 'men's work' (Willis, 1977: 99) but women in factories cannot derive analogous satisfaction; factory work is not a 'feminine' occupation.

It is instructive to consider the collective identities of male and female factory workers. Men may be referred to as 'the lads', but the endowment of such membership is more an accolade than – as is usually the case with 'the girls' – a diminution (Westwood, 1984: 24–5) and is less imbued with notions of sex and gender. A woman may be referred to as 'one of the lads' with approval, whereas to regard a man as 'one of the girls' would definitely diminish him and cast doubts on his virility The 'old boys' network' and similar male cameraderie reinforces male bonding in higher status employment and has a similar effect of excluding and marginalizing women (Kanter, 1977). Given the extent to which people experience and respond to one another according to the categories to which their attributes appear to assign them, allied to the fact that in essentially patriarchal societies, sex is not only a binary distinction but also hierarchical, this is not surprising. What is, perhaps, surprising, is the extent to which the dynamics of gender relations have been virtually overlooked as a variable in workplace interaction, organizations and the labour process itself in the development of industrial and organizational sociology.

Gouldner (1957: 285), discussing the complexities of social roles, observed that 'many sociologists give little indication of the fact that the people they study in offices, factories, schools or hospitals are also males and females'. To some extent, a significant proportion of more recent sociology, while taking account of gender, continues to underestimate its importance. The way in which gender defines and restricts women's experience as factory workers has recently received incisive exploration (Pollert, 1981; Cavendish, 1982; Westwood, 1984) but even in these feminist analyses, the *process* of gender (cf. Thompson, 1965: 357 on the process of class), while recognized to be a crucial dimension of work experience, is rarely scrutinized in its own right. In particular, the importance of the sexual aspect of gender has been subsumed within a consideration of power differences, without detailed analysis of how sex, as a component of gender, is mobilized in the exercise and deflection of power.

Freudian psychology sees sex as a central preoccupation of humanity and sexuality as perhaps the most important dimension of the self, yet industrial psychology has had little to say about gender and sex in workplace interaction. This is not to argue that sex is literally the lowest common denominator of life or of work experience, but sex and its cultural interpretation, gender, are such overwhelming and inescapable aspects of experience and identity that it is difficult to see how an adequate account of social action can be given without reference to the gender of the participants and the implications for that of their interaction (cf. Morgan, 1986). These implications have more often been assumed with reference to gender stereotypes than observed. The significance of gender within the context of what actually happens at work is so much part of the implicit experience of employment that dramatized depictions of workplace interaction are full of gendered ritual, social exchange and relationships.

Paradoxically, women's assumptions of roles and statuses traditionally filled by men makes the gendered content of work roles and relationships more visible, in so far as the significance of *women's* sex on both how she operates and how she is responded to, tends to be subjected to scrutiny in a way that 'normal' gendered hierarchical relations are not. The most vivid illustrative example is perhaps Mrs Thatcher, whose sex is seen to be a relevant consideration for political analysts to take account of when assessing her performance and, indeed, has been alleged to be an important aspect of her leadership tactics: 'Her sex has helped shape her style of government. In the early days, according to John Hoskyns, she used the fact that she was a woman very powerfully to get her own way. She was deliberately unreasonable, emotional, excitable, instead of being calm and consensus-seeking' (Harris, 1988: 18). Such stereotype-laden comment illustrates the extent to which professional behaviour and interaction are observed and interpreted as gendered; perhaps particularly in a context where the gender of the actor concerned is regarded as marginally inappropriate. Mrs Thatcher's professional and political identity is intimately bound up with her identity as a woman. She has been praised, criticized, parodied and manipulated for propaganda purposes as alternatively 'tough' (and therefore atypical of women in that she appears not to be inhibited by 'normal' female 'weaknesses') and 'caring' (the good housekeeper and mother who understands the really important things in life and whose gender therefore equips her particularly well for humane and thrifty leadership).

Where the gender dimension of work relationships has been examined by sociologists, it has usually been in the context of discussion of the informal systems which operate in work environments. Banter about sex and the objectification of women have frequently been recorded as being among the main topics of everyday conversation in male work groups (Brown et al., 1973; Roy, 1974; Burawoy, 1979; Cockburn, 1983; Morgan, 1987) and equivalent ribaldry has been observed among female workers (Wilson, 1963; Morgan, 1969; Pollert, 1981; Cavendish, 1982; Cunnison, 1983; Westwood, 1984). Mock flirtation and gendered joking behaviour have been noted by all the above authors and subjected to detailed ethnographic analysis in a Glasgow printworks by Sykes (1966), who concluded that such exaggerated role playing and symbolic behaviour serves the function of controlling sexuality in mixed sex workplaces; an objective, according to Burrell (1984) which is also a major formal preoccupation of bureaucracy. Sykes's analysis, however, assumes that the formal and informal systems of the factory are separate and that 'joking behaviour' and 'real' relationships between people are also distinct and unambiguous, which is questionable. Perhaps the clearest exposure of the ambiguities involved has been provided by those who have studied gender interaction in offices, particularly between bosses and secretaries (Benet, 1972; McNally, 1979; Crompton and Jones, 1984). Their studies have revealed not only how sex-typed interaction ritual and the gender hierarchy structure work relationships; but also how the place of employment is seen by the participants to provide opportunities for 'real' romantic and sexual partnerships and encounters.

Roy (1974) has carried the analysis forward both by considering the wider spectrum of sexual and gender interaction and monitoring the impact of gender relations on work group behaviour and productivity. He argues that the formal and informal systems in the workplace are spatially and temporally interlocked and are effectively part of the same system. This leads him to incorporate aspects of workplace interaction not normally taken account of in industrial sociological analysis. He observed that:

When a situation is one of men and women working side by side or sharing a task that calls for team work, Eros may infiltrate the production line to evoke attachments of various qualities and dura-

tions of affection, ranging from the protracted attentions of true love
to ephemeral ardencies of the opportune moment. (Roy, 1974: 46)

Quinn (1977) indicates that such infiltration is not confined to the
production line, citing examples from commercial and medical work
institutions. Such British evidence as there is suggests that a substantial
minority of people first meet their marriage partner in the course of training
or employment and that the workplace may be the most common place
for love affairs, illicit or otherwise, to begin (Hearn and Parkin, 1987: 14).
   Roy's observations and discussions with his workmates, however,
indicate that the workplace is not simply a recruitment source for leisure
or domestic partnerships; the very fact that such liasons are negotiated and
carried out both during work and outside it means that they are also part
of work situations, with implications not only for those directly involved
but for the whole work group and the conduct of work. This leads him to
postulate, in the light of cases he observed, that the sexual dynamics of an
attachment between two people who work together may have a cyclical
effect on productivity. During the initial stage of courtship, productivity
and congenial relations throughout the group appeared to be enhanced;
once relationships became established, there was some evidence of wider
harmony being threatened by the exclusiveness of the romantic dyad –
particularly since the 'factory wife' like the 'office wife' (Benet, 1972)
tended to be of subordinate status to her 'spouse' and her intimacy
with him was observed to cause, or be assumed to cause, favouritism and
consequent jealousies; and not surprisingly, the decline of relationships
tended to cause disruption, tensions, absenteeism and a variety of problems
which disrupted the flow and efficiency of production. Quinn (1977) also
documented positive and negative impacts of romantic attachments in
organizations, but concluded that such relationships are potentially more
dangerous for women than for men in the long run, since problems arising
from them were more likely to result in the woman's employment being
terminated than the (usually higher status and therefore more occupationally secure) man's. Roy's findings among manual workers confirm this.
   Sexual harassment, ranging from mild verbal innuendo to sexual
molestation and rape, has been more often alluded to than systematically
researched in Britain, but surveys indicate that cases brought to industrial
tribunals represent a very small proportion of women for whom it has
been a problem (Leeds TUCRIC, 1983; Sedley and Benn, 1982). McKinnon
(1979) cites numerous examples of women's sexuality being assessed as part
of job specifications, of favours being offered and threats being made
by men, often in superordinate positions, to women at work. Roy's
(1974) research leads to the bleak conclusion that, although the myth
of 'true love' may have had some currency among the population he
studied, his 'factory wives' were largely used and abused by the men
in a calculative way which degraded both parties, with the women
almost always regarded as sex objects rather than people.
   Sykes (1966) concluded that the most gendered teasing in the printworks
where he conducted his research took place between 'old' men (defined as

over 25 and/or married) and 'young' women (under 25 and/or unmarried) and thus, he hypothesized that it served to control sexuality at work by ritualizing interaction between potential but taboo sex partners. Observations at NICO, where most of the interaction was among 'old' women and 'old' men according to Sykes's definitions, led to the conclusion that it was not sexuality that was thus controlled, but women, whose gender was constantly drawn attention to. Thus, participant observation revealed that the distinction between the sexist 'joking behaviour' directed largely at women by men, described by Sykes, and sexual harassment, is very slim.

Burrell (1984) suggests that sexual relations at work represent a major frontier of control and resistance in organizations. It is in the interests of the formal organization to minimize the impact of variables which are extrinsic to its objectives. Burrell argues that the survival of sexuality as an important variable in the workplace represents resistance to such bureaucratic control. While it is clearly true that the full range of heterosexual attachments identified earlier in this chapter by Roy are found in work organizations, ethnographic studies suggest that Burrell's analysis may be somewhat optimistic, particularly from women's point of view. Although most of the males and some of the females involved may be resisting tedium and the depersonalizing straitjacket of bureaucratic control, on the whole, the expression of and reference to sexuality and gender differences in the workplace more often indicate male attempts to control and restrict women (Pollert, 1981; Cavendish, 1982; Westwood, 1984; Purcell, forthcoming). Whether gender interaction at work is characterized by hostility and harassment or by chivalry and flirtation, the net effect is to remind women of their subordinate gender and, usually, occupational status and, in the case of women in 'male' environments or occupations, of their essential marginality and vulnerability in 'male' territory. In a recent survey (Leeds TUCRIC, 1983) it was found that women who worked in gender-atypical work environments were twice as likely to report having experienced sexual harassment at work than women who worked in traditionally 'female' areas of employment.

Although women are far from being passive victims and, collectively and individually, have been observed to exhibit a wide variety of protective responses and counter-assaults to exert countervailing control, they are generally coerced into responding in terms defined by men (Webb, 1984). Observational research at the NICO engineering firm revealed that even in amicable intergender exchanges such as real or mock flirtation, the interaction was invariably initiated by the man, whether verbal or tactile, with the woman forced to respond according to a prescribed pattern. Thus an arm would be thrown proprietorially around a women's shoulder or a hand would grasp her knee or thigh as she worked at her bench and she would be expected to respond with warmth or at least wit; or, walking through a 'male' work area, she would be wolf-whistled at or subjected to a running commentary about her possession, or lack, of physical charms. The only successful defence observed was humorous counter-attack which played along with the initiated ritual, but even in this there tended to be tension, as is characteristic of joking behaviour (Radcliff-Brown, 1952).

Women who responded coldly by attempting to ignore the 'game' or refusing to play along with it were subjected to increasingly hostile teasing and personal criticism. Women who responded warmly tended to be 'led on' and ultimately ridiculed. There appeared, to be no 'correct' response which would guarantee immunity from such joking or harassment, but it was observed that the older women tended to be better at deflecting attention from themselves and that they often came to the defence of their younger colleagues.

The other conclusion reached with regard to gendered joking behaviour was that, far from suppressing or repressing sexuality on the shopfloor, such interaction enflamed and encouraged the development of both public and clandestine relationships. Marriages, long-term extramarital affairs and 'ardencies of the opportune moment' were observed or alleged to have been initiated on the NICO shopfloor. As is characteristic of research on socio-sexual behaviour, direct observational data were limited and subjects' reports have to be treated with caution, although the fact that allegations were made about illicit relationships indicates at least the symbolic significance of sexuality and its importance as an item of conversational currency in the workplace. The problem for sociologists wishing to understand the labour process, and for employers and employees, is that such concerns and activities are a central component of employment experience and cannot be regarded as extrinsic factors which can be excluded from organizational analysis.

Gender, Power and Industrial Relations

An important implication of the gendered structure and processes of employment for organizational sociologists is that not only have women been socially inhibited and discouraged from deviating from their appropriately gendered tasks and role playing; they have also been discouraged from exercising full citizenship rights (Marshall, 1950) in the workplace, particularly in the sphere of industrial relations. As is discussed in chapter 17, trade union membership in Britain has been declining in recent years and the only substantial area of expansion of both employment and union recruitment has been among female non-manual employees. Consequently, it might be expected that trade unions would be increasingly concerned with equal opportunities and other issues relating to women's employment, particularly the terms and conditions of employment of part-time workers. The Donovan Commission (1968: 91–2) drew attention to the underutilization of women's potential as employees and the failure of the trade unions to promote their interests. This coincided with the new wave of feminist consciousness in the late 1960s and increasing economic activity and recruitment to trade unions of married women, all of which, allied to international developments, combined to generate conditions conducive to the introduction of equal opportunities and sex discrimination legislation. Since then the TUC and individual unions, particularly those with a high proportion of female members, have become increasingly concerned with equal opportunities and 'women's issues' but this has often been a formal rather than enthusiastic concern, particularly at local and shopfloor level, tempered by ambivalence about the relative virtues, and incompatibility of, support for 'the family wage' and equal pay (Barrett and McIntosh, 1980; Campbell, 1982) and underlying beliefs about the sexual division of labour in the private and the public spheres.

In 1979, the TUC published a ten-point charter to promote *Equality for Women Within Trade Unions* in affiliated unions, but it was found to have had what was euphemistically referred to as 'a mixed response' among unions (EOC. 1983; Coote and Kellner, 1980) with little evidence of change in ratios of women and men appointed to union posts. Many unions continued to discriminate against women within their own ranks and those unions which did take significant action to promote the interests of their female members were almost exclusively confined to white-collar unions with large numbers of women members: the National Association of Teachers in Further and Higher Education, the National Union of Teachers (NUT), National Association of local Government Officers (NALGO), National Union of Journalists (NUJ), Banking Insurance and Finance Union (BIFU), National Union of Public Employees (NUPE) and the Administrative Clerical and Technical Section of the Transport and General Workers Union (ACTS) (Boston, 1987: 329 ff.; Cockburn, 1987: 12–14).

It should also be noted that part-time employees are less likely than full-timers to have access to, or belong to, trade unions. Sixty-nine per cent of full-time employees, but only 50 per cent of part-time employees interviewed in the Women and Employment Survey had access to union membership in their employment and 51 per cent of full-time, but only 28 per cent of part-time employees, were union members. The proportion of women who were union members was inversely related to the number of hours per week worked, with only 17 per cent of those who worked less than 16 hours per week belonging to a union (Martin and Roberts, 1984: 56–59). Differences in union membership between male and female employees have often been assumed to illustrate women's lesser commitment to paid work and greater political conservatism, but an examination of the distribution of male and female union membership and political attitudes reveals that the organization and market situation of the industry, plant size and hours of work are more reliable correlates of union membership and political attitudes than gender itself (Purcell, 1984; Elias and Bain, 1988).

Furthermore, Cockburn (1987) points out that while it is true that women in employment have less often been shop stewards, voted in union elections, been to union meetings or taken industrial action and that their attitudes towards both political parties and trade unions tend to be more suspicious, their political orientation in terms of response to particular issues and moral absolutes is often to the left of their male colleagues (Cockburn, 1987: 20). She argues that the majority of women may refuse to engage with, or identify with, organized politics at national and workplace levels because of the preponderance of men within such organizations and what she alleges to be the 'male' adversarial approach

to internal procedure and political action which tends to predominate.
Research in work organizations suggests that Cockburn may be correct
in her diagnosis that many women in employment effectively boycott
trade-union activities because of its apparent irrelevance to their day-
to-day experience at work. None of the women at NICO were active
in the union, although all were union members and Labour voters, who
belonged to the union because they believed in workers' representation
and their own responsibility to be members; but most of them also
agreed with the statement that 'the unions have too much power in
this country' and all of them were cynical about the motives and
work capacities of those who *were* active in the union locally. These
contradictions are not an unusual finding (Beynon and Blackburn, 1972;
Pollert, 1981; Cavendish, 1982; Westwood, 1984) and are not confined
to women in employment. Cavendish (1982: 136) commented on the
union at UMEC, the factory where she worked as a participant-observer:

> The women on the line were pretty negative about the union's
> activities in the factory. They said they were never told what
> was going on, and only learnt about decisions after they affected the
> wage packet. They were kept in the dark, their views weren't
> properly represented, and the dues of 30p a week were too high for
> the service they got.

Only a minority of employees tend to be active union members and both
Burawoy (1979) and Palm (1977) make the explicit point that most employees
refer to 'the union' as if it is something separate from them. Conversely,
Cavendish notes that while women were negative about union *activities*
they were strongly committed to the union in principle 'and often said
that they, the women on the line, were the union' (Cavendish, 1982: 137).
This illustrates Cockburn's point that disenchantment with union practice
and politics is not synonymous with lack of radicalism. It is only when a
particular conflict arises that trade union members tend to become aware
of their collective interests and, in instances of industrial action involving
women, there is plenty of evidence that women have been as committed
to defence of their jobs, the redressal of grievances and support for fellow
workers, as men (Purcell, 1984; Wacjman, 1983). Women's support groups
during the miners strike of 1984–6 were acknowledged to be a radicalizing
and pivotal force which had a major impact upon solidarity within most of
the mining communities (Loach, 1985). The extent to which women tend
to be more passive and exploitable as employees than men reflects their
concentration in low-skilled, low-paid, part-time and expendable jobs
rather than their gender, since men in similar jobs exhibit similar orientations to work and attitudes to trade unions (Lupton, 1963; Purcell, 1984).

In their study of a food factory employing full-time and part-time
workers of both sexes, Beynon and Blackburn (1972: 122), while labelling
women as having 'lower commitment, to work and trade-union membership, observed that the full-time women were the most vociferous group in
terms of raising grievances with supervisors and management. They noted
that 'grievances which may analytically be defined as "individual" – such

as being moved from one job to another – became defined within the work group as collective' (1972: 113). Such solidarity is at odds with the more usual picture of individualistic, privatized, apolitical women which, in fact, Beynon and Blackburn anticipated in their initial classification of the expected orientations to work of men and women (1972: 9).

Nevertheless, if Cockburn is correct that women have a more consensual, albeit radical approach to politics and industrial relations, as has been argued by feminist psychologists to be a feature of gender difference in contemporary Western cultures (Miller, 1976; Gilligan, 1982), it may be that they have different ways of handling conflict at work. Raising a grievance collectively, without recourse to union intervention, may be a politically more astute, diplomatic and effective way of exerting control. Observations at NICO revealed several instances of work group negotiation and resolution of conflict between employees and management involving both male and female employees' grievances, all of which were initiated and led by women (Purcell, forthcoming). Perhaps the more important observation, particularly in the light of such action, was the way in which the women's union representatives and management did not *expect* the women to be involved or interested in formal industrial relations events or issues. During the participant observation period at NICO, instances were observed of a Pension Fund election being presented to the women as something they were unlikely to be interested in; of them being told after the event, rather than consulted before, about an overtime ban and other industrial action; of them invariably having to ask the (male) shop steward in their workshop about what had happened at major meetings concerning pay negotiations and the disbanding of the joint negotiating committee; and ambiguity on their own, the union and the management's parts about who exactly *was* their union representative – 'the lady shop steward' in another workshop or the male one in their own. Pollert (1981) describes similar ambiguities and 'oversights' at the tobacco factory where she carried out her research.

At NICO, the 'lady shop steward' complained when interviewed that she was often not consulted, not told about meetings and not taken seriously by fellow union officers and management, an accusation which was substantiated during interviews with managers and other union activists. Imray and Middleton (1983: 17–18) cite a classic example of a female shop steward being chivalrously marginalized by her male colleagues despite her concern to become fully involved in her union. Other union women have reported similar lack of encouragement (Coote and Kellner, 1980) and such evidence demonstrates that an important reason for women's generally low profile and lack of activism in trade unions is clearly overt and more subtle male exclusionary tactics, even in the case of women who have been manifestly prepared to participate in traditional 'adversarial' industrial relations politics.

Conclusion

Research on gender and the experience of employment suggests that it is impossible to understand the gendered structure of employment or the processes in workplaces which sustain it, without reference to the sexual division of labour in British society as a whole; its historical evolution and the social and economic policies which currently underpin it. Theoretical analysis of the interrelationships between patriarchy and capitalism (for example, Hartmann 1979; Beechey, 1987; Walby, 1986) has stimulated much debate and research, but, in itself, is limited to the construction of hypotheses about why men and women do the jobs they do and share domestic responsibilities and childcare to a more or less egalitarian degree. Empirical research, examining both employment trends and practice in particular industries, occupations and organizations, is increasingly clarifying the hidden structures and dynamics of gender relationships in employment and other social institutions (Cockburn, 1986; Siltanen, 1986; Beechey and Perkins, 1987; Crompton, 1987). In the same way as the relative advantages and disadvantages to girls and boys of single-sex and coeducational schooling have been observed and debated (Deem, 1978; Kelly, 1987; Arnot, 1986; Stanworth, 1981) it would be illuminating to observe the positive and negative effects for employers and employees of mixed and single-sex work groups, same and different sex supervision and the presence or absence of occupationally successful women in organizations as role models to motivate ambition and achievement in women lower down the career structure. Where change, particularly the encouragement of women to achieve occupationally higher status and more skills, is being initiated, it is very often handicapped by the failure to recognize the extent and pervasiveness of gender inequalities both in the workplace and the home. The unequivocal evidence of the twelve years following the enactment of equal opportunities legislation is that the provision of formal equality of opportunity in training and employment makes an impact on, but does not radically alter, gender segregation and occupational inequalities. A clearer understanding is required of the links between gender stereotyping, group behaviour and the dynamics of organizations – particularly the significance of sexuality, which can have a major stabilizing or destabilizing influence on work relationships.

References

Abercrombie, N. and Urry, J. 1983. *Capital, Labour and the Middle Classes.* London: George Allen & Unwin.

Allen, S. and Wolkowitz, C. 1987. *Homeworking: Myths and Realities*. London: Macmillan.

Argyris, C. 1957, *Personality and Organisation*. New York: Harper & Row.

Arnott, M. 1986. 'State Education Policy and Girls' Educational Experiences'. *Women in Britain Today*. Eds V. Beechey and E. Whitelegg. Milton Keynes: Open University Press.

Ballard, B. 1984. *Employment Gazette*, 92 (September), 409–16. London: Department of Employment.

Barrett, M. and McIntosh, M. 1980. 'The Family Wage: Some Problems for Socialists and Feminists'. *Capital and Class*, 11 (Summer), 51–72.

Beechey, V. 1987. *Unequal Work*. London: Verso.

—— and Whitelegg, E. 1986. *Women in Britain Today*. Milton Keynes: Open University Press.

—— and Perkins, T. 1987. *A Matter of Hours*. Cambridge: Polity.

Bell, C. and Newby, H. 1976. 'Husbands and Wives: The Dynamics of the Deferential Dialectic'. *Dependence and Exploitation in Work and Marriage*. Eds Barker, D.L. and Allen S. London: Longman.

Benet, M.K. 1972. *Secretary*. London: Sidgwick and Jackson.

Berger, J. 1972. *Ways of Seeing*. Harmondsworth. Penguin.

Beynon, H. and Blackburn, R.M. 1972. *Perceptions or Work*. Cambridge: Cambridge University Press.

Bielby, W.T. and Baron, J.N. 1986. 'Men and Women at Work: Sex Segregation and Statistical Discrimination'. *American Journal of Sociology*, 91, 759–99.

Bisset, L. and Huws, U. 1984. *Sweated Labour: Homeworking in Britain Today*. London: Low Pay Unit.

Blackburn, R.M. and Mann, M. 1979. *The Working Class in the Labour Market*. London: Macmillan.

Boston, S. 1987. *Women Workers and the Trade Unions*. London: Lawrence and Wishart.

Braybon, G. 1981. *Women Workers in the First World War: The British Experience*. London: Croom Helm.

Breakwell, G. and Weinberger, B. 1987. 'Young Women in 'Gender-atypical' Jobs'. Research Paper No. 49. London: Department of Employment.

Brown, R.K. 1976. 'Women as Employees: Some Comments on Research in Industrial Sociology' *Dependence and Exploitation in Work and Marriage*. Eds Barker, D.L. and Allen, S. London: Longman.

——, Brannen, P., Cousins, J. and Samphier, M. 1973. 'Leisure in Work: The "Occupational Culture" of Shipbuilding Workers'. *Leisure and Society in Britain*. Eds Smith M.A., Parker, S. and Smith, C. London: Allen Lane.

—— Curran, M. and Cousins, J. 1983. 'Changing Attitudes to Employment?' Research Paper No. 40. London: Department of Employment.

Burawoy, M. 1979. *Manufacturing Consent*. Chicago: University of Chicago Press.

Burrell, G. 1984. 'Sex and Organisational Analysis' *Organisation Studies*, 5: 2, 97–118.

Campbell, B. 1982. 'Not What They Bargained For' *Marxism Today* (March).

Cavendish, R. 1982. *Women on the Line*. London: Routledge & Kegan Paul.

Clark, A. 1919. *Working Women of the 17th Century*. London: G. Routledge and Sons Ltd.

Cockburn, C. 1983. *Brothers: Male Dominance and Technological Change.* London: Pluto Press.

—— 1985. *Machinery of Male Dominance.* London: Pluto.

—— 1986. 'Opportunity is Not Enough'. *The Changing Experience of Employment.* Eds Purcell, K., Wood, S., Waton, A. and Allen, S. London: Macmillan.

—— 1987. *Women, Trade Unions and Political Parties.* London: Fabian Society.

Coote, A. and Kellner, P. 1980. *Hear This Brother: Women Workers and Union Power.* London: New Statesman Report 1.

Coyle, A. 1984. *Redundant Women.* London: The Women's Press.

Craig, E., Garnsey, E. and Rubery, J. 1984. 'Payment Structures and Smaller Firms: Women's Employment in Segmented Labour Markets'. Research Paper No. 48. London: Department of Employment.

Creigh, S. et al. 1986. 'Self-employment in Britain: Results from the Labour Force Survey 1981–84'. *Employment Gazette,* 94 (June), 183–94. London: Department of Employment.

Crompton, R. 1987. 'Gender, Status and Professionalism'. *Sociology, 21 (August), 413–28.*

—— 1988. 'The Feminisation of the Clerical Labour Force Since the Second World War'. *The Feminisation of Office Work.* Ed. G. Anderson. Manchester: Manchester University Press.

—— (forthcoming). *Gendered Jobs and Social Change.*

—— and Jones, G. 1984. *White-Collar Proletariat.* London: Macmillan.

—— and Mann, M. 1986. 'Women and the Service Class'. *Gender and Stratification.* Cambridge: Polity Press.

—— and Sanderson, K. 1986. 'Credentials and Careers: Some Implications of the Increase in Professional Qualifications Amongst Women', *Sociology,* 20 (February), 25–42.

Cunnison, S. 1983. 'Participation in Local Union Organisation: School Meals Staff: A Case Study' *Gender, Class, and Work.* Eds Gamarnikow, E., Morgan, D., Purvis, J. and Taylorson, D. London: Heinemann.

—— 1986. 'Gender, Consent and Exploitation Among Sheltered Housing Wardens' *The Changing Experience of Employment.* Eds Purcell, K., Wood, S., Waton, A. and Allen, S. London: Macmillan.

Daniel, W.W. 1969. 'Industrial Behaviour and Orientation to Work'. *Journal of Management Studies,* 6: 3, 366–75.

Deem, R. 1978. *Women and Education.* London: Routledge & Kegan Paul.

Delphy, C. 1976. 'Continuities and Discontinuities in Marriage and Divorce' *Dependence and Exploitation in Work and Marriage.* Eds D.L. Barker and S. Allen. London: Longman.

Derow, E. 1982. 'Childcare and Employment: Mothers' Perspective' *Strategies for Integrating Women into the Labour Market.* Eds Hvidtfeldt, K., Jorgensen, J. and Nielsen, R. Denmark: Women's Research Centre in Social Sciences.

Diamond. 1980. Royal Commission on the Distribution of Income and Wealth. *Report.* London: HMSO.

Donovan 1968. Royal Commission on Trade Unions and Employers' Associations 1965–8 *Report.* Cmnd 3623. London: HMSO.

Dubin, R. 1956. 'Industrial Workers' Worlds: A Study of the "Central Life Interest" of Industrial Workers' *Social Problems*, 3, 131–42.

—— Hedley, R.A. and Taveggia, T.C. 1976. 'Attachment to Work'. *Handbook of Work, Organisation and Society*. Ed. Dubin, R. Chicago: Rand-McNally College.

Dunning, J. 1986. *Japanese Participation in British Industry*. London: Croom Helm.

Elias, P. 1988a. 'Family Formation, Occupational Mobility and Part-time Work' *Women and Paid Work*. Ed. Hunt, A. London: Macmillan.

—— 1988b. 'Sectoral Trends in Full-time and Part-time Employment'. Project Report to the Department of Employment. Coventry: Institute for Employment Research, University of Warwick (unpublished).

—— and Main, B. 1982. *Women's Working Lives*. Coventry: Institute for Employment Research, University of Warwick.

—— and Bain, G. 1988. 'The Dynamics of Trade Union Membership'. Coventry: Institute for Employment Research, University of Warwick.

—— and Purcell, K. 1988. 'Women and Paid Work: Prospects for Equality'. *Women and Paid Work*. Ed. Hunt, A. London: Macmillan.

Ellis, V. 1981. *The Role of Trade Unions in the Promotion of Equal Opportunities*. Manchester: Equal Opportunities Commission and Social Science Research Council.

Engineering Council 1985. *Career Breaks for Women*. London: Engineering Council.

Equal Opportunities Commission 1983. *Women and Trade Unions: A Survey*. Manchester: EOC.

Finch, J. and Groves, D. (eds) 1983. *A Labour of Love: Women, Work and Caring*. London: Routledge & Kegan Paul.

Gamarnikow, E., Morgan, D., Purvis, J. and Taylorson, D. (eds) 1983. *Gender, Class and Work*. London: Heinemann.

Game, A. and Pringle, R. 1983. *Gender at Work*. Sydney: Allen & Unwin.

Garnsey, E. 1978. 'Women's Work and Theories of Class and Stratification' *Sociology*, 12: 2.

Gershuny, J. 1978. *After Industrial Society? The Emerging Self-service Economy*. London: Macmillan.

—— 1987. 'Daily Life, Economic Structure and Technical Change'. *International Social Science Journal*, 11 (August), 337–42.

Gilligan, C. 1982. *In A Different Voice*. Cambridge, Mass.: Harvard University Press.

Glucksmann, M. 1986. 'In a Class of Their Own? Women in the New Industries in Inter-war Britain' *Feminist Review*, 24 (Autumn), 7–37.

Goffman, E. 1976. *Gender Advertisements*. London: Macmillan.

Goldthorpe, J.H. 1982. 'On the Service Class, its Formation and Future' *Social Class and the Division of Labour*. Eds Giddens, A. and McKenzie, G. Cambridge: Cambridge University Press.

—— Lockwood, D., Bechhofer, F. and Platt, J. 1968. *The Affluent Worker: Industrial Attitudes and Behaviour*. Cambridge: Cambridge University Press.

Gouldner, A. 1957. 'Cosmopolitans and Locals: Towards an Analysis of Latent Social Roles' *Administrative Science Quarterly*, 2, 218–306.

Hakim 1985. 'Employers' Use of Outwork: A Study Using the 1980 Workplace Industrial Relations Survey and the 1981 National Survey of Homeworking. Research Paper No. 44. London: Department of Employment.

——— 1987. 'Homeworking in Britain', *Employment Gazette*, 95 (February), 99–104. London: Department of Employment.

Harris, R. 1988. 'Prima Donna Inter Pares' *The Observer (3 January)*, 18–9.

Hartmann, H. 1979. 'Capitalism, Patriarchy and Job Segregation by Sex'. *Capitalist Patriarchy and the Case for Socialist Feminism*. Ed. Eisenstein, Z. New York: Monthly Review Press.

Hearn, J. and Parkin, W. 1987. *'Sex' at 'Work'*. Brighton: Wheatsheaf.

Hennig, M. and Jardim, A. 1978. *The Managerial Woman*. London: Marion Boyars.

Hertz, R. 1986. *More Equal Than Others: Women and Men in Dual Career Marriages*. Berkeley and Los Angeles: The University of California Press.

Hewitt, M. 1958. *Wives and Mothers in Victorian England*. London: Rockliff.

Humphries, J. 1977. 'Class Struggle and the Persistence of the Working Class Family' *Cambridge Journal of Economics* (September).

Hunt, A. 1975. *Management Attitudes and Practice Towards Women at Work*. London: HMSO.

Huws. U. 1984. 'The New Homeworkers'. *New Society*. (March).

Imray, L. and Middleton, A. 1983. 'Public and Private: Marking the Boundaries' *The Public and the Private*. Eds Gamarnikow, E., Morgan, D., Purvis, J. and Taylorson, D. London: Heinemann.

Institute for Employment Research 1987. *Review of the Economy and Employment*. Coventry: IER, University of Warwick.

Johns, A. 1984. *Coalmining Women: Victorian Lives and Campaigns*. Cambridge: Cambridge University Press.

Kanter, R. 1977. *Men and Women of the Corporation*. New York: Basic Books.

Kelly, A. (ed.) 1987. *Science for Girls?* Milton Keynes: Open University Press.

Leeds TUCRIC, 1983. *Sexual Harassment of Women at Work*. Leeds: Leeds TUCRIC.

Legge, K. 1987. 'Women in Personnel Management: Uphill Climb or Downhill Slide?' *In A Man's World*. Eds Spencer, A. and Podmore, D. London: Tavistock.

Llewellyn, C. 1981. 'Occupational Mobility and the Use of the Comparative Method' *Doing Feminist Research*. Ed. Roberts, H. London: Routledge & Kegan Paul.

Loach, L. 1985. 'We'll be Here Right to the End . . . And After: Women in the Miners' Strike' *Digging Deeper*. Ed. Beynon, H. London: Verso.

Long, P. 1984. *The Personnel Specialists: A Comparative Study of Male and Female Careers*. London: IPM.

Lupton, T. 1963. *On the Shopfloor*. London: Pergamon.

McKee, L. and Bell, C. 1985. 'Marital and Family Relations in Times of Male Unemployment'. *New Approaches to Economic Life*. Eds Finnegan, R., Gallie, D. and Roberts B., Manchester: Manchester University Press.

McKinnon, C. 1979. *Sexual Harassment of Working Women*. New Haven and London: Yale University Press.

McNally, F. 1979. *Women For Hire: A Study of the Female Office Worker.* London: Macmillan.

Marshall, T.H. 1950. *Citizenship and Social Class.* Cambridge: Cambridge University Press.

Martin, J. and Roberts, C. 1984. *Women and Employment: A Lifetime Perspective.* London: HMSO.

Martin, R. and Wallace, J. 1984. *Working Women in Recession.* Oxford: Oxford University Press.

Massey, D. and Meegan, R. 1982. *The Anatomy of Job Loss.* London: Methuen.

Miller, J.B. 1976. *Towards a New Psychology of Women.* Boston: Beacon Press.

Mitter, S. 1986. 'Industrial Restructuring and Manufacturing Homework: Immigrant Women in the UK Clothing Industry' *Capital and Class,* 27 (Winter), 37–80.

Moorhouse, H.F., 1984. 'The Work Ethic and Hot Rods'. Paper given at the British Sociological Association Conference at Bradford University, April.

Morgan, D. 1986. 'Gender'. *Key Variables in Social Investigation.* Ed. Burgess, R. London: Routledge & Kegan Paul.

Morgan, D.H.J. 1969. 'Theoretical and Conceptual Problems in the Study of Social Relations at Work: An Analysis of Differing Definitions of Women's Roles in a Northern Factory'. Ph.D thesis, University of Manchester.

—— 1987. '"It Will Make a Man of You": Notes on National Service, Masculinity and Autobiography'. Studies in Sexual Politics No. 17. Manchester: Department of Sociology, University of Manchester.

Morris, L.D. 1985. 'Renegotiation of the Domestic Division of Labour in the Contest of Male Redundancy' *Restructuring Capital.* Eds. Newby, H. et al. London: Macmillan.

Murray, F. 1983. 'The Decentralisation of Production – the Decline of the Mass-collective Worker' *Capital and Class.* (Spring).

Newton, D. 1987. 'Women in Engineering'. *In A Man's World.* Eds Spencer, A. and Podmore, D. London: Tavistock.

Nichols, T. and Armstrong, P. 1976. *Workers Divided.* London: Fontana.

Novarra, V. 1981. *Mens Work, Women's Work.* London: Marion Boyars.

Oakley, A. 1974. *The Sociology of Housework.* Oxford: Martin Robertson.

Pahl, R.E. 1984. *Divisions of Labour.* Oxford: Basil Blackwell.

—— and Wallace, C.D. 1985. 'Household Work Strategies in an Economic Recession'. *Beyond Employment.* Eds Redclift, N.D. and Miginone, E. Oxford: Basil Blackwell.

Palm, G. 1977. *The Flight From Work.* Cambridge: Cambridge University Press.

Pearson, R. 1986. 'Female Workers in the First and Third Worlds: The "Greening" of Women' Labour'. *The Changing Experience of Employment.* Eds Purcell, K., Wood, S., Waton, A. and Allen, S. London: Macmillan.

Pinchbeck, I. 1981. *Women Workers and the Industrial Revolution.* London: Virago.

Pollert, A. 1981. *Girls, Wives, Factory Lives.* London: Macmillan.

Purcell, K. 1978, 'Working Women, Women's Work and the Occupation of Being a Woman'. *Women's Studies International Quarterly,* 1 (Summer).

—— 1982. 'Female Manual, Workers, Fatalism and the Reinforcement of Inequalities'. *Rethinking Inequality*. Eds Robbins, D. et al. Farnborough: Gower.

—— 1984. 'Militancy and Acquiescence Amongst Women Workers'. *Women in the Public Sphere*. Eds Siltanen, J. and Stanworth, M. London: Hutchinson.

—— (forthcoming). *Gender at Work*. Oxford: Oxford University Press.

Quinn, R.E. 1977. 'Coping with Cupid: The Formation, Impact and Management of Romantic Relationships in Organisations'. *Administrative Science Quarterly*, 22 (March), 30–45.

Radcliff-Brown, A.K. 1952. *Structure and Function in Primitive Society*. London: Cohen and West.

Rapoport, R. and Rapoport, R. 1976. *Dual Career Families Re-examined*. London: Martin Robertson.

Riley, D. 1984. *War in the Nursery*. London: Virago.

Roy, D.F. 1974. 'Sex in the Factory. Informal Heterosexual Relations between Supervisors and Work Groups'. *Deviant Behaviour*. Ed. Bryant, C.D. Chicago: Rand McNally.

Rubery, J. and Wilkinson, F. 1981. 'Outwork and Segmented Labour Markets'. *The Dynamics of Labour Market Segmentation*. Ed. Wilkinson, F. London: Academic Press.

Sedley, A. and Benn, M. 1982. *Sexual Harassment at Work*. London: National Council for Civil Liberties (NCCL).

Siltanen, J. 1986. 'Domestic Responsibilities and the Structuring of Employment'. Eds. Crompton, R. and Mann, M. *Gender and Stratification*. Cambridge: Polity Press.

Simmel, G. 1950. *The Sociology of George Simmel*. Trans., ed. and introduced by Wolff, K.H. Glencoe, Ill.: The Free Press.

Spencer, A. and Podmore, D. (eds) 1987. *In a Man's World: Essays on Women in Male-dominated Professions*. London: Tavistock.

Stacey, M. 1981. 'The Division of Labour Revisited Or Overcoming the Two Adams'. *Practice and Progress: British Sociology 150–80*. Eds Abrams, P., Deem, R., Finch, J. and Rock. P. London: George Allen & Unwin.

Stageman, J. 1980. 'Women in Trade Unions'. Occasional Paper No. 6. Hull: Industrial Studies Unit, Adult Education Department, University of Hull.

Stanworth, M. 1981. *Gender and Schooling*. London: Hutchinson.

Summerfield, P. 1984. *Women Workers in the Second World War: Production and Patriarchy in Conflict*. London: Croom Helm.

Sykes, A.G.M. 1966. 'Joking Relationships in an Industrial Setting'. *American Anthropologist*, 68, 188–93.

Thirsk, J. 1985. Foreword. *Women in English Society 1500–1800*. Ed. Prior, M. London: Methuen.

Thompson, E.P. 1965. 'The Peculiarities of the English'. *The Socialist Register*. Eds Miliband, R. and Saville, J. London: The Merlin Press.

Trades Union Congress (TUC). 1979. *Equality For Women Within Trade Unions*. London: TUC.

—— 1983. *Women in the Labour Market*. London: TUC.

Valli, L. 1986. *Becoming Clerical Workers*. Boston and London: Routledge & Kegan Paul.

Wacjman, J. 1983. *Women in Control.* Milton Keynes: Open University Press.

Wadel, C. 1979. 'The Hidden Work of Everyday Life'. *Social Anthropology of Work.* Ed. Wallman, S. London: Academic Press.

Walby, S. 1986. *Patriarchy at Work.* Cambridge: Polity.

Webb, S. 1984. 'Gender and Authority in the Workplace'. *Looking Back: Some Papers From The BSA 'Gender and Society Conference'.* Studies in Sexual Politics No. 1. Manchester: Department of Sociology. University of Manchester.

Westergaard, J. 1970. 'The Rediscovery of the Cash Nexus' *The Socialist Register.* Eds Miliband, R. and Saville, J. London: The Merlin Press.

—— and Restler, H. 1975. *Class in a Capitalist Society.* London: Heinemann.

Westwood, S. 1984. *All Day, Every Day.* London: Pluto.

Wharton, A.S. and Baron, J. 1987. 'So Happy Together? The Impact of Gender Segregation on Men at Work' *American Sociological Review,* 52 (October), 574–87.

Willis, P. 1977. *Learning to Labour.* London: Saxon House.

Wilson, C.S. 1963. 'Social Factors Influencing Industrial Output. A Sociological Study of a Factory in North West Lancashire'. PhD. thesis, University of Manchester.

Wood, S. 1981. 'Redundancy and Female Unemployment'. *Sociological Review,* 29: 4.

Yeandle, S. 1984. *Women's Working Lives.* London: Tavistock.

7 Patterns of Conflict and Accommodation

P.K. Edwards

This chapter focuses on forms of accommodation and adaptation that workers develop as part of their day-to-day workplace existence. It looks at behaviour which appears under headings such as output restriction, sabotage and pilfering, and it tries to outline a sociological perspective on these things. To look at such mundane matters might seem to be less important than a consideration of grand questions such as management strategy or class consciousness. But they are significant for several reasons. They have been less intensively debated than the grand questions. They relate directly to workers' daily lives and comprise a more central aspect of the social relations of work than do issues of strategy and consciousness. And they underlie many of these issues. When analysts of strategy refer to workers' resistence against a system of control, or when students of class consciousness and action discuss what Miliband (1978) calls a growing desubordination of the working class, they presuppose a capacity of workers to exert some form of control of their own work lives. This capacity, together with the conditions affecting its use and its contradictory dynamics, is the central concern here.

The need for such a focus is illustrated by current tendencies in the sociology of work relations. These have been dominated by the work of Braverman (1974), with his interest in the long-term degradation of labour. As Stark (1980: 93) notes, Braverman gave no attention to the informal ways in which workers could resist or modify capitalists' control. Even studies which try to take account of 'resistance' can posit a bleak contrast between the deliberate control strategies of employers and the negative resistance of workers (Gordon et al., 1982; for criticism see Nolan and Edwards, 1984). As Salaman (1986: 21) argues, the view of workers as 'passively accepting and being duped by management strategies' is unsatisfactory; it is necessary to see all employees as 'engaged in active efforts to make sense of, and to a degree achieve control over, their work destinies and experience'. This represents a conscious return to some of the traditional concerns of industrial sociology, as exemplified by Gouldner's (1954) study of informal relations.

There is a danger in this reaction to Braverman. The rejection of structural determinism can lead to a return to an approach which stresses self-activity and the negotiation of order to the neglect of the structural conditions which shape behaviour (Eldridge, 1973). In particular, the argument that patterns of conflict cannot be reduced to managerial control strategies can imply that there is no logic or dynamic of control and that workers and managers are not divided by any fundamental conflict of interest. There is a body of literature which accepts criticisms of Braverman without retreating into eclecticism or interactionism (Burawoy, 1984; Edwards, 1986, 1987a; Friedman, 1987a, 1987b; Hyman, 1987). It argues that workplace relations are underlain by a basic antagonism between capital and labour over the ways in which workers' capacity to work is translated into actual effort. But there are elements of co-operation, for employers need to secure workers' continued willingness to work while workers rely on firms for their livelihoods (Cressey and MacInnes, 1980). The basic antagonism does not determine actual events but has to be interpreted in practice: there is a negotiation of order, but it takes place in a definite material context.

The idea of contradictions is central here. As Hyman (1987: 30) argues, it is not a matter of strategy or the negotiation of order occurring where structural influences are weak; 'action' does not simply fill the spaces left over after structural forces have had an effect. These forces exert contradictory demands which have to be managed, and it is out of this process of day to day relations that patterns of workplace order are generated. They express the contradictions of the capital–labour relation and they have a dynamic of their own which cannot be reduced to models of deliberate, planned strategy. As Hyman (1984: 185) puts it, 'the contradictory position of management – co-ordinator of a complex and often baffling productive operation, yet at the same time a vehicle of discipline, control, and often disruptive pressure – evokes contradictory responses'.

This chapter uses this perspective to examine the social relations of work. First, it asks why and how informal practices develop, arguing that these have a contradictory character: they simultaneously reflect workers' efforts to exert their control and an accommodation with, and indeed often an active pursuit of, organizational rules. But informal practices are not the same everywhere. 'Pilfering' for example is not a standard phenomenon but has widely varying forms and meanings. Secondly, therefore, different types of workplace relations are identified and some reasons for the differences are suggested. A conclusion to emerge is that patterns of relations are not just the product of external forces but have logics of their own. This point is illustrated and developed in the third section, which takes one very conflict-prone industry, the docks, and explore the evolution of workplace relations by workers and managers themselves. In the course of this examination a perspective on the most obvious manifestation of industrial conflict, the strike, is outlined. In contrast to conventional explanations, which rely on factors such as 'community isolation' or technology, it is argued that an understanding of the nature of conflict must focus on the logic of struggles at the point of production.

Informality, Fiddles and Work Groups

It is a commonplace that organizations do not operate as they are supposed to do, and that fiddles and short cuts subvert or amend official expectations. This has led to the conventional distinction between formal and informal rules, or between official and unofficial norms. But these contrasts are not very helpful (Hill, 1974). They assume a complete and unambiguous set of formal or official rules against which informal practices can be measured. But the employment contract cannot be specified so precisely, for its essential characteristic is that workers' creative capacities are being deployed: it is impossible to specify a complete set of formal rules (Baldamus, 1961). 'Informality' is not, moreover, the exclusive property of workers, for managements can equally well draw on customs and understandings (Armstrong et al., 1981). And workers' actions do not just undermine formal rules: as shown below, many 'unofficial' practices can, by interpreting formal expectations, contribute to managerial goals.

A useful way round these problems has been offered by Goffman (1961: 172). Although based on a study of mental hospitals, it can be applied directly to work organizations; and although Goffman is strongly identified with the interactionist perspective criticized above, his analysis can readily be incorporated in a more complete approach. Goffman introduces the term secondary adjustment, defined as 'any habitual arrangement by which a member of an organization employs unauthorized means, or obtains unauthorized ends, or both, thus getting around the organization's assumptions as to what he should do and get and hence what he should be'. The emphasis is on organizational assumptions, and not just formal rules, so that the problem of silences in formal expectations is avoided. The purpose of the idea of secondary adjustments is not to make a sharp distinction between normal co-operation and adjustments that challenge this co-operation. On the contrary, it is to point to the interplay between normality and conflict. Adjustments do not start to work after formal rules have been specified in exact detail. They can promote customs that subvert managerial expectations, but they can also be ways of living with these expectations. As means of asserting workers' individuality and, as Goffman stresses, of sustaining a self-identity, they may help workers to create spaces for themselves and may thus reflect an accommodation with a system of control. A specific practice can contain several contradictory elements.

Fiddles

'Output restriction' is a good example. The practice of putting ceilings on the amount of work done per day has been noted from early craft societies onwards. It has been carried out by unorganized workers as well as members of trade unions (Mathewson, 1969). As Burawoy (1979: p.x) notes, it has been attributed by conservatives to 'the natural indolence of workers, poor communication between workers and managers, inadequate attention to the human side of the worker, or the "false consciousness" of workers in not appreciating that their interests are identical with those of management'. Radicals have romanticized it by seeing it as 'an expression of class consciousness'. An adequate analysis avoids these one-sided views by getting beneath the label of 'restriction' to examine the nature and consequences of the behaviour that it identifies.

The benefits to workers of output restriction, and of 'restrictive practices' generally, have been well documented (Roy, 1952; Hickson, 1961; Aldridge, 1976). These include protecting a piecework rate from managerial attempts to cut it, stabilizing earnings, allowing workers to gain some leisure once their stint has been completed, and promoting work group solidarity. But is restriction a useful analytical category? Lupton (1963: 182) studied a factory with very clear output ceilings, but argued that to sustain a claim that a group of workers was restricting output it would be necessary to have a neutral measure of a proper day's work and techniques to measure actual against potential output so that deliberate restriction could be isolated: in most situations, these will be absent, and to speak of restriction 'is merely to express an opinion that workers ought to do more'. Lupton also showed that many workers' activities did not directly lead to limiting output. He used the workers' own term, 'fiddles', to describe secondary adjustments around the effort bargain, defining them as means of 'systematic manipulation of the incentive system' (1963: 182).

A list of fiddles noted by Lupton and other writers (for example Brown, 1973; Klein, 1964) includes being booked onto one job while in fact working on another (thus making earnings on the higher-paying jobs); being booked as 'waiting', that is off piecework, while getting ahead on a job, thus minimizing the time recorded as being on piecework and hence raising earnings; limiting production to protect rates; holding back the booking of some output so as to regularize earnings from week to week; working with deliberate slowness when under work study to try to secure a loose rate; and running machines faster than is officially prescribed. Such fiddles are embedded in a workplace culture and they are not simply restrictive. Some of them, for example altering the time of booking of output, do not affect total production and are largely neutral as far as managerial interests are concerned. Others, most significantly increasing machine speeds, directly contribute to output. It is well established that workers have detailed practical knowledge of the idiosyncracies of particular machines, of whether quality is acceptable, and how to keep machines going (Kusterer, 1978; Manwaring and Wood, 1984). In deploying this knowledge they are likely to bend or break formal rules. Indeed, they have to do so, because these rules cannot cover every eventuality and have to take for granted the willing application of workers' skills. The fiddle is a form of 'secondary adjustment', containing elements of co-operation with production as well as 'restriction'.

Fiddles are not limited to pieceworkers in factories. Harper and Emmert (1963) studied American postal workers, and discovered a range of secondary adjustments such as the illicit use of private cars to deliver mail and holding back letters from one day to another to reduce the number of deliveries. Ditton (1979) worked among baker workers paid by time and analysed a large number of ways of manipulating time, including having most of the work group go home early at the end of a shift, with one staying behind to clock the others out. Blau (1963) has described illicit practices among white-collar office workers. And Mars (1982) has drawn together a wide range of studies of occupational crime to show that fiddles are endemic in most jobs although their nature varies considerably. Like Lupton, Mars uses the concept of fiddling in place of more emotive terms such as crime. These terms conceal more than they reveal, for they assume that there is a clear distinction between criminality and normality and that crimes are restricted to an aberrant minority. Mars shows how many 'crimes' emerge out of workers' day-to-day practices and how these practices are taken for granted features of the occupations concerned. They are seen as criminal neither by workers nor, in general, by managers.

Role of the Work Group

Accompanying a focus on output norms has been attention to the work group. There has been a tendency to assume that attempts to control effort are universal and that all workers tend to form groups for this purpose. This goes back to the famous Hawthorne researches (Roethlisberger and Dickson, 1939), which argued that all workers tended to form work groups for the cohesion and social satisfactions that they could provide. A good deal of American research followed this lead. Seashore's (1954: 36) questionnaire, for example, started its questioning on the cohesiveness of work groups by asking, 'do you feel that you are really a part of your work group?' The possibility that groups, in the sense of stable entities with their own standards and the means to enforce them, might not even exist was not considered. Lupton's study, cited above, was based on a comparison of two workplaces, and in one of these collective output norms were absent. Many other studies have shown not only that such norms are far from universal but also that the conditions to sustain them, such as willingness to discuss earnings with fellow workers and to restrict effort when under work study, may well not exist (Armstrong et al., 1981; Edwards and Scullion, 1982).

Whether work groups form, and if so how strong the norms governing behaviour are, cannot be assumed in advance. Neither should effort bargaining or fiddles be assumed to depend on a group for their operation. Cunnison (1966) has shown how workers in a garment factory bargained vigorously as individuals, coining the term 'militant individualism' to analyse the behaviour. And Mars (1982) classifies fiddles on two dimensions, one of which is the strength of group ties. Some fiddles, for example the collection of scrap metal and the sharing of the proceeds by crews of dustmen, are collectively organized. Others, such as short-changing by supermarket employees, depend more on individual initiative. Other cases seem to fall between these extremes.

Group fiddles can be more developed than individual ones. Crucially, they can sustain rules and customs that institutionalize a system of secondary adjustments. Studies of workplaces with little collective worker organization show that management can discipline fiddlers relatively easily: the fiddle is illicit (albeit often taken as a fact of life by all concerned), and there is no collective support for anyone penalized. A sharp contrast is provided by strong work groups, for whom an injury to one is an injury to all. But more important than the ability to resist managerial punishment is the growth of fiddles into understood ways of organizing work. Management may cede to gangs of workers the right to allocate workers to tasks and other aspects of internal organization. Fiddles develop a degree of respectability and can become part of a complex web of 'custom and practice' (Brown, 1972). The key point is that the 'same' activity, such as clocking another worker out, can vary in its meaning from being a totally illicit activity, through being tolerated as a way of giving workers some satisfactions, to being an established and accepted custom which workers are willing and able to defend.

Fiddles do not, then, depend on work groups, although the extent of group formation will powerfully shape their character. This is not to say that non-group fiddles depend on individual fancy. Any occupation has its traditions and understood ways of doing things; workers entering them have to 'learn the ropes' (Geer et al., 1968), which includes learning informal understandings as well as formal instructions. As Mars argues, fiddle-proneness is a characteristic of occupations. Someone starting work as a bread roundsman not only faces different structural conditions from a factory worker but also comes to define work in a way shaped by occupational socialization. Fiddles grow out of, and in turn help to reinforce, traditions of specific occupations.

The Role of Management

Why do managements tolerate them? There is plenty of evidence that first-line supervisors do not just tolerate fiddles as constraints that they are forced to accept but also take them for granted as ways of getting work done. This is shown most clearly in studies of custom and practice, which have demonstrated that customary rules are often jointly produced by workers and supervisors. In some cases, foremen go further and directly instruct workers in fiddles. Mathewson (1969: 30–1) suggested that this was quite common; Ditton (1977a) has shown how trainee bread roundsmen are educated in fiddles by supervisors; and, perhaps most famously of all, Bensman and Gerver (1963) have documented how foremen in the aircraft industry instructed workers in the use of the 'tap', an illicit device that forced bolts into position, whose use could seriously weaken an airframe. Supervisors find fiddles useful because they give workers some interest in the job and thus make the task of supervision easier.

Other benefits accrue to management more generally. Lupton argued that fiddles helped to reduce other, and potentially more costly, adaptations such as absenteeism and quitting: tolerating a few fiddles can be a relatively cheap way of getting workers to keep working. The industrial relations literature on job controls, which can be seen as developed forms of group fiddles, points to several benefits for management such as a reduction in the level of supervision necessary if work organization is left to work groups; it has also been argued that the costs, in terms of limitations on managerial prerogative, have often been quite small

(Hyman and Elger, 1981). The actual operation of fiddles also helps management as workers learn to do jobs more quickly than work study times dictate. Bending the rules is, in any event, necessary. As already noted, no rules can lay down exactly what workers shall do, and in using their own skills and knowledge workers can assist in managerial aims, even though in doing so they subvert the formal rules.

Fiddles can also involve workers in ignoring safety standards as they chase higher earnings. Piecework is associated with higher rates of serious accidents than daywork, and there also seems to be tendency for pieceworkers not to report minor accidents because of the time lost by going for treatment (Wrench, 1978; Wrench and Lee, 1978). In situations of intense managerial pressure, as in the Hungarian factory described by Haraszti (1977), workers can in effect be forced to adopt dangerous practices if they are to attain an acceptable level of earnings. It would be too simple to say that managements have an interest in unsafe working practices. But, as Nichols and Armstrong (1973) stress, even sophisticated employers who do not use piecework can generate strong pressures to get the job done. Workers feel the need to cut corners. Accidents are the result. Employers do not 'want' accidents, but accidents are the result of the organization of production. In so far as accidents can be blamed on workers' carelessness or neglect of safety rules, moreover, responsibility can be shuffled off onto the victims.

In some industries, notably hotels and catering, fiddles serve another role. They help to sustain a system of low wages and arbitrary managerial power: low wages because fiddles provide alternative sources of income; and arbitrary power because workers who fiddle lay themselves open to dismissal if they are found out (Ditton, 1977b). As Mars (1982: 149–52) notes, in many such occupations, the cost of such standard fiddles as short-changing and over-changing falls on the customer and not the employer.

The most fundamental managerial benefits of fiddles have been highlighted by Burawoy (1979) in his study of an American engineering factory. The effort bargain becomes a game, with workers feeling that they have won if they can earn some time to themselves or raise their earnings a little. But games 'are played within limits defined by minimum wages and acceptable profit margins', for if profits are threatened managements will act to stamp out fiddles, and 'the very activity of playing a game generates consent with respect to its rules (1979: 89, 81).

This argument should not be seen as a straightforward incorporation thesis to the effect that management grants concessions the better to enforce acceptance of its own authority. It is, first, not a matter of deliberate intention. The benefits that accrue to management may emerge in an unplanned way and to identify the benefits that derive from a system is not to argue that these benefits are the reason why the system was instituted in the first place. A good example is the rule on seniority which operated in Burawoy's plant and which was characteristic of unionized manufacturing establishments. It ensured that promotion and lay-off in the event of a lack of orders were determined by a worker's seniority in the plant. It thus protected workers from favouritism and managerial whims, but also contributed to a reliance on seniority rights and thus undermined collective challenges to management. Studies of the origins of seniority show that it was the product of major struggles by workers, with any managerial benefits arising only subsequently (Schatz, 1983: 105–19; Gersuny and Kaufman, 1985).

Incorporation arguments tend, moreover, to assume that capitalist authority can be unambiguously buttressed. It is true that Burawoy exaggerates the extent and permanence of workers' acquiescence (Edwards, 1986: 50–2), but there is no need to follow him in this. Workplace relations are in a state of tension and movement. They involve a blend of conflict and accommodation, and specific arrangement represent a compromise in the class struggle, and one, moreover, which contains concrete benefits for workers. The compromise cannot be reduced to incorporation.

Managements play a key role not only within the workplace but also as mediators of external conditions. Many fiddles are covert and fragile, and managerial toleration may disappear when conditions change. Thompson and Bannon (1985), for example, show how the powerful job controls developed by one group of workers in an electronics factory were wiped out when competition and rationalization led to the closure of the plant. More generally, workers, although capable of exerting considerable influence on the conduct of work, enter a terrain whose contours have already been shaped by managerial decisions on plant layout and payment systems.

Patterns of workplace relations, and the behaviour that arises from them, cannot, then, be seen in terms of contrasts between control and resistance or normality and conflict. Conflict and consent are interwoven within the same phenomena, and to apply labels such as output restriction or sabotage can be highly misleading. Having explained the basic nature of secondary adjustments in the workplace, two issues arise. First, the social meaning of behaviour that is labelled as, say, sabotage or pilfering varies greatly between different occupations. Secondly, some of the causes of these differences must be considered. These two issues are tackled in the following section.

Meanings and Causes of Modes of Adjustment

Types of Fiddle and Effort Bargaining

Various classifications of work groups have been proposed, one of the best known being that of Sayles (1958). As argued above, however, fiddles can exist without groups, and not all groups engage in fiddles. What is suggested below is not a way of analysing the sociability and social cohesion of work groups but a classification of different sorts of bargaining with employers.

Four types can be distinguished, with the first of these having two subtypes (Edwards, 1986: 226–36). Non-militant workers do not have any developed sense of opposition to management. The first subgroup includes workers who are subject to tight managerial control in the form of strict discipline and close supervision. Examples include the workers in three factories studied by Armstrong et al. (1981) and the supermarket workers described by Mars (1982: 66–75). In such cases, workers are generally powerless and lack the resources to bargain openly with management.

This does not mean that fiddles are absent. Even under slavery, workers can develop means of making the system of domination tolerable and can establish some tacit understandings as to normal levels of effort (Genovese, 1976: 587–621). Studies of workplaces under capitalism have documented a range of practices. These include the short-changing and pilfering of goods described by Mars, and high levels of absenteeism and labour turnover (Edwards and Scullion, 1982). Managerial policy is also more complex than a simple imposition of control. Managers often depend on key groups of skilled workers, to whom they grant concessions; discipline can be tempered by a concern to be seen to be 'fair', for example in the allocation of work; and 'control' involves a complex interplay of strict discipline, paternalism, and concern for workers as individuals. Employers generally can often create loyalty by being 'understanding' in terms of workers' personal interests, even though this is in the context of an overarching domination; this approach has been analysed with particular reference to the control of women workers (Freeman, 1982: 143–9). But modes of accommodation tend to be individualized. Workers do not seem to see their behaviour in terms of 'resistance' or 'getting back at management': there is no direct connection between, say, going absent frequently and resentment against management. There is an indirect connection in that the outside observer can explain absenteeism in terms of a need to escape intense control. But the behaviour does not alter the nature of that control. Indeed, by acting as an escape valve for discontents, quitting, in particular, can help to reproduce the pattern as discontented workers find leaving to be the easiest option.

The second type of non-militant approach occurs where workers are controlled less directly and are given autonomy but where they do not use their freedom to pursue aims that conflict with those of management. Situations with quality of work life experiments or autonomous teams are examples: unlike the direct control case, discipline is not overt and absenteeism and quitting are rare forms of escape, for wages and work conditions are very good. Workers are persuaded to co-operate. A case close to this model is the 'ChemCo' works studied by Nichols and Beynon (1977). There was a sophisticated regime, and workers were generally individualized and lacked collective attitudes. This does not mean that conflict was absent. There were minor instances of sabotage. More importantly, the organization of work, in particular the demands of shift work, put great strains on workers and led to considerable resentment. But there was little way for this resentment to be made manifest, and it was balanced by wages and other extrinsic benefits. Since conflict is structured into any employment relationship, a pattern of workplace relations cannot dissolve this conflict. But it can manage it in different ways. Under sophisticated control, the co-operative aspects of work are emphasized, and the space for fiddles is reduced; indeed, managements would claim, the need for them is also eliminated, since workers are treated as responsible adults.

These two subtypes are not 'ideal types', for examples of them can be found in the real world. But neither are they the only possible forms of non-militant response. Direct control, for example, can vary in intensity. As suggested above, where employers rely on workers' skills it can become a system of mutual obligations. But the types indicate two of the main ways in which the social relations of work can prevent the emergence of open struggles to control the effort bargain. Again, the presence of such struggles is a matter of degree, and the direct control pattern merges with the second main type.

This may be termed militant individualism, to use the term coined by Cunnison (1966). In her study of garment workers, there was 'an individual struggle between worker and manager over the fixing of the weekly wage, and over matters affecting it, such as piece rate prices and the allocation of work' (1966: 89). Workers were as individualized as in non-militant cases, but they had an awareness of a conflict of interest over the effort bargain, and they pursued their own interests actively. Their controls over how and when they worked were more established than practices bearing on similar matters would be in non-militant cases because workers had some recognized rights which management had come to accept. Sykes (1969a, 1969b) describes a different form of the same pattern in his study of navvies: they had a self-image of tough independence, and expressed this in a willingness to quit a job at a moment's notice. They did not operate as work groups but there was a shared tradition of independence from management.

The third pattern involves more of a collective approach. It embraces the well-known cases studied by Roy, Lupton and Burawoy. Workers here tend to have group norms governing effort standards and to engage in a wide range of fiddles. These have, moreover, attained the status of customary rules. The sabotage practised by Bensman and Gerver's aircraft workers would fit into this category, for it had a collective basis and was recognized by supervisors as an accepted activity. The job controls deployed by these workers are, however, limited in scope. They concentrate on the immediate effort bargain. Lupton's workers, for example, bargained to obtain a good price on jobs introduced in their shop but they apparently had few links with other groups of workers and they did not influence the wider parameters of the effort bargain such as manning levels, the allocation of work, and the amount and allocation of overtime. The role of shopfloor union organization in influencing the shape of the effort bargain was very limited, as was also the case in Burawoy's factory.

The final type, the organizational pattern, involves a wider approach. In significant parts of the engineering and printing industries, and also among dockers and coal miners, workers' workplace organizations have been able to influence such things as the division of tasks between workers, the allocation of overtime, and the application of discipline. Examples from engineering include groups of toolmakers who forbade the movement of workers between types of machine and who refused to allow managers to offer overtime to whomever they chose, insisting instead that if overtime was to be worked anyone in the shop should have access to it (Edwards and Scullion, 1982: 207–8); and gangs of workers in the car industry, who were paid as teams and who organized their own work with minimal involvement from management (Friedman, 1977). The power of printers' chapels is legendary; the case of the docks, together with some comments on coal, is considered below.

The precise types of job control practised under the organizational pattern will vary according to the exigencies of the work task: printers and car workers operate differently because of differences in work organization. But the common feature is the ability to regulate work through controls of manning levels and the mobility of workers between tasks: managers cannot decide on these things, and in practice shop stewards can have a veto over proposed changes. There is still a negotiation of order, but workers' customs have become accepted as part of the structure of the situation. Workers have an established shopfloor organization instead of only the solidarity of the work group.

The limitations of this type of organization need to be borne in mind. Even in the car industry, developed steward organizations have been limited to the Midlands firms, and in an industry as allegedly militant as coal cases of employer domination and weak unionism have been documented (Waller, 1983). The gang system could also be divisive since each gang wanted to maximize earnings and was led to intensify effort, to try to rid itself of its weaker members, and to compete with other gangs for the best work (Tolliday, 1986: 211). Because job controls depended on action at the point of production they could lead to a sectional consciousness and be vulnerable to managerial counter-attack (Hyman and Elger, 1981). Divisions between work teams and their leaders could also arise. The docks, for example, certainly had some dock-wide practices and traditions that went beyond the 'collective' approach. But these rested on the autonomy of gangs of dockers. There was a relation of support and tension between gangs' job controls and wider solidarity. Such qualifications notwithstanding, the organizational approach is important in showing that effort controls are not just work group phenomena as the older American studies suggested and as even Burawoy (1985) is prone to imply.

The meaning of a phenomenon going under the same label varies dramatically between the types of bargaining. Consider sabotage. The sabotage of the strictly controlled non-militant worker is likely to be a spontaneous expression of frustration against intense work pressures. In the case studied by Cunnison (1966: 117–8), by contrast, workers had developed the practice of 'dabbing' the adhesive which held pieces of cloth together instead of spreading it thoroughly. This was sabotage not in the sense of deliberate destruction but of a reduction in quality which emerged out of the control of effort. Managers tried to prevent the practice but failed to do so. Workers' bargaining awareness, together with the power that they had created, enabled it to remain as an acknowledged, if illegitimate, aspect of the work. This case is an example of what Taylor and Walton (1971) term utilitarian sabotage, that is, the result of attempts to make the job easier. Such sabotage is perhaps more developed where there is a collective approach. Taylor and Walton cite the study by Bensman and

Gerver (1963) mentioned above. Here, destruction of the product is not the aim; this is the incidental result of efforts to 'make out' under distinct technical conditions (the nature of the product) and social organization (a pay system that encouraged speed, and workers with the group solidarity to sustain the practice). Finally, the organizational pattern is likely to mean that sabotage as a means of making out is rare because workers have many other means of controlling the effort bargain. Certainly, the alleged restrictive practices of groups such a printers do not include sabotage.

As shown elsewhere, this argument can be applied to other 'forms' of conflict (Edwards, 1986: 236–61). Since 'output restriction' was discussed above, variations in its use may be briefly summarized. Far from it being universal, it appears to be largely absent in non-militant workplaces because workers lack the awareness of interests opposed to management to pursue effort bargaining. Militant individualism tends to involve the worker as an individual bargaining over piece rates and work allocation, but no group controls of effort. The collective approach is the home of traditional output quotas as described by Roy and others. But even here such practices are not universal: in one of the factories studied by Edwards and Scullion (1982), which they called the Components Factory, there was the usual array of piecework fiddles but these did not comprise formal output quotas, whose absence could be attributed to lack of fear of rate-cutting and a fairly stable institutional environment. All workers in a given type do not practise controls identically. Sabotage seems to have been rare in the plants studied by Roy and Lupton, for example, presumably because fiddles did not have fateful consequences for product quality. In the Components Factory, utilitarian sabotage occurred, but output ceilings were absent. Finally, under the organizational pattern output restriction ceases to be a purely work group activity and becomes part of a developed set of job controls which are likely to embrace demarcation lines between trades and the joint determination of work allocation (whereas under the other types the allocation of work tends to be a managerial prerogative). 'Output restriction', like sabotage, is a variable phenomenon.

The foregoing discussion has concentrated on manual workers in factories to draw out the very different work relations that characterize even this reasonably homogeneous group. The types should not be seen as exclusive categories but as ways of approaching a given workplace. It is, for example, possible for elements of direct control and collective orientations to coexist, for example in a firm trying to modernize a traditional paternalist order.

The types may not, moreover, translate exactly into other settings. Consider clerical workers. As noted above, Blau has shown that some such workers employ informal output ceilings and sanctions against 'rate busters' that are similar to practices under the collective pattern. But he considers these to be 'vague and ineffective' when contrasted with the activities of blue-collar workers. 'The effort of these white-collar workers to standardize productivity was half-hearted, at best, because they were conflicted about it. Remaining true to type as middle-class individuals, they believed that superior ability, ambition, and efficient performance should be rewarded' (Blau, 1963: 184–5). Crozier (1971: 132) adds the interesting comment that unlike manual workers, who are 'separated and protected as much as oppressed by the class barrier, white-collar employees do not resist by means of solidarity but rather by indifference and apathy'.

These authors probably exaggerate the significance of the manual/non-manual divide: manual workers can display indifference and individualism as well as solidarity. And it is not clear whether embracing a particular set of values about individual achievement is the product of being 'middle class' or is part of an ideology that is reproduced in the workplace. There may be features of clerical work which distinguish it from manual jobs. These include the importance of promotion, at least for some categories of worker, and the greater discretion which (again, some) white-collar workers enjoy, which means that the distinction between using discretion to advance organizational aims and exploiting it to create space for oneself may be particularly hard to draw. Such features are likely to promote particular complexes of co-operation and conflict.

The categories offered above are not designed to make rigid distinctions between occupations. They are intended to provide some benchmarks which can then be used to study other groups. Workplace relations are complexes of many different elements and the connections between conflict and co-operation need to be teased out. But the benchmarks help to identify how overt and developed the struggle to control effort has become. Some reasons why workplaces have one pattern of relations and not another may now be considered.

Sources of Variation in Effort Bargaining

Among the most obvious possible determinants of bargaining behaviour are structural conditions such as technology. Kuhn (1961) studied a tyre and an electrical engineering factory and argued that the technology of the former, being based on team working, encouraged work group formation, while the greater division between workers in the latter promoted isolation. This in turn meant that the tyre plant had more effort bargaining. But the technical organization of work does not stem from the hardware of the technology alone. Hill (1974: 217) argues that the 'best documented' influence on group formation is 'the lay-out of the production system which results both from the nature of the technology used and from the division of labour imposed by management (which is not necessarily constrained by the technology)'. Within one technology, management can vary the social organization of work. A famous example of this is Trist and Bamforth's (1951) study of coal mining. A new system of mining, the longwall method, had replaced a traditional system in which workers worked as teams. The result was poor co-ordination between workers and hostility between the shifts responsible for different phases of the operation. Trist and Bamforth recommended altering the cycle of production to bring the technical and social systems into line. Although the larger claims of this 'socio-technical' school are open to serious criticism (Kelly, 1978), this example shows that the hardware does not bring with it a particular organization of work, for the allocation of tasks between shifts could be changed.

Even with these qualifications, the causal influence of the technical division of labour has been widely questioned. The more or less uniform technical systems of car firms in Britain have been associated with very different patterns of shopfloor relations (Turner et al., 1967). Virtually identical oil refineries in Britain and France had markedly different patterns of bargaining (Gallie, 1978).

A second structural factor is the nature of the product market. This is not seen as exerting direct effects in the way in which technology promotes or hinders interaction between workers. Its effects are related to employer strategy. For Burawoy (1979), for example, a competitive market leads to a coercive management regime, which can be seen as, in turn, leading to the individuation of the work-force. The examples of non-militant direct control cited above came from highly competitive industries such as clothing and footwear. Firms enjoying more stable market conditions may be able to afford some effort bargaining and fiddles.

Counter-examples can readily be given. For the competitive case, the standard one is the building industry, where competition between many small firms has not prevented developed job controls, which have on occasions reached the organizational level (see Price, 1980). And not all monopolistic firms have experienced effort bargaining. Most obviously, several of them have moved towards sophisticated personnel policies in an effort to generate a 'high trust' individualized commitment to the firm, non-union firms such as IBM being prominent examples (Peach, 1983). But the fact that they have the resources and will to do so is not separate from their market or technical conditions: their market power gives them the ability to afford expensive personnel policies, their interrelated production systems are vulnerable to stoppages, and so on.

The conditions considered so far relate to the general promotion of group awareness and a willingness to bargain with the employer. As noted in discussing sabotage, several other features of the nature of work facilitate the development of particular responses. Why, for example, is pilferage common in retailing and the docks? Mars (1982: 138–57) outlines some of the factors. In situations where the exact quantity or quality of an item is hard to specify, there is room for fiddling. It is, for example, hard to establish the precise number of of bricks delivered to a building site or how much drink was consumed at a wedding: portions can be diverted to illicit uses. This process is assisted if it is difficult or expensive to employ monitoring or surveillance equipment. Fiddling is also promoted by such factors as an arrangement's being a 'passing trade', that is, there is no continued relationship between fiddler and the victim, and the possession of real or imagined expertise by the fiddler, Mars's example being garages which charge for repairs that they have not done or which skimp on work and materials.

Some of these factors were used by Lupton (1963) to explain why fiddles and a collective approach existed at 'Jay's Engineering' but were absent in the 'Wye' garment factory. He listed sets of internal and external factors such as the size of the firms, the policy of the trade unions and the payment system, but gave most weight to technology and the product market. For example, stable conditions and monopoly control encouraged Jay's management to tolerate fiddles whereas in the garment industry intense competition and rapidly changing styles led to a more coercive approach. But, as Lupton himself has pointed out (Lupton and Cunnison, 1964: 124), causal influences do not vary independently of each other but tend to come in clusters. Competitive markets, small firms, and simple systems of piecework tend to go together, so that it is impossible to unravel their separate effects. Moreover, as Cunnison (1966: p.xxiv) points out, internal and external factors are not separate. Lupton took union policy, namely the support for shopfloor organization in the engineering union and the dislike of it by the garment union, as an external factor. But it was also internal in the sense that the engineering union's policy was the product of its members' own defence of shopfloor custom, as even a cursory glance at the history of shop steward organization will show, while the garment union's *raison d'être* was to 'take wages out of competition' and to stabilize the industry, a strategy which would be undermined if bargaining at shopfloor level was tolerated. These policies were intimately connected with the nature of workplace relations in the two industries.

To explain the pattern of relations in a given workplace thus requires attention to a cluster of influences and to their interaction. In some comparisons the role of a given factor may stand out clearly. Consider, for example, why 'Wye' had a non-militant pattern while, as noted above, the 'Dee' plant studied by Cunnison was characterized by militant individualism even though it was in the same locality and industry and was of a similar size. The technical organization of work may have had an effect. 'Dee' retained the system traditional in the industry, known as 'working through', wherein the division of labour was minimal and workers performed a whole series of tasks; management depended on them, and bargaining awareness grew. At 'Wye' a more fragmented, assembly-line type of operation had been introduced which, it may be suggested, broke down workers' job controls. In this particular context, technical relations had distinct effects.

These conditions should be seen not as exerting determinate effects on workplace relations but as influences which put certain pressures on managements and workers. These pressures have to be interpreted at the workplace. The work of Armstrong et al. (1981) in particular shows how the effects of competitive conditions were interpreted: management, for example, could use legitimatory arguments about the need to remain competitive in order to have its definition of shopfloor practice, such as the need to change working arrangements or the impossibility of increasing bonus payments, accepted. The arguments had to be made, and a system of order had to be produced and reproduced. There was nothing inevitable in the process. But the legitimatory resources provided by product market conditions made some outcomes more likely than others. Many other studies (e.g. Burawoy, 1979; Cockburn, 1985) stress that ideology is produced within work and not just imported from outside. As workers and managers try to make sense of their worlds, they generate systems of meaning which reflect and reinforce a pattern of relationships. The workers studied by Armstrong et al. had limited means to control the effort bargain not just because of external forces, or even because of the power of management to impose sanctions, but also because they accepted, and indeed helped to reproduce, the existing structure of control. The power of management was not exercised overtly, for the pattern of relations had its own logics which were taken for granted. For most of the time, workers and managers are not engaged in active struggles but try to accommodate to the world as they find it. In doing so, they produce workplace cultures as well as goods and services.

Workplace relations involve a continuous negotiation of order wherein understandings and accommodations are generated. They are influenced by clusters of characteristics including the nature of the technology and the shape of the product market. But they also have histories and dynamics of their own, with the parties coming to take for granted particular ways of doing things. These dynamics do not just pass on structural effects but develop logics of their own. Customs of trades are social products, but these are just as 'real' as a technology. The dynamics and dialectics of shopfloor relations may be considered by looking in more detail at the particular case of the docks.

Strike-proneness and Workplace Relations: The Case of the Docks

To understand the nature of workplace conflict it is necessary to address the dialectics of workplace relations: the ways in which the interaction of workers and employers mediates structural conditions and generates distinct combinations of co-operation and resistance. The docks illustrate this in a particularly clear way. In doing so, they throw light on several standard theories of industrial conflict, for dockers have behaved in ways which these theories cannot grasp. The theories are first reviewed with reference to the docks before a more adequate analysis is summarized.

Theories of Strike-proneness

Theories of strikes need be examined only briefly. Hyman (1984) has already surveyed many standard explanations such as technology and 'poor communications', and his demonstration of the faults with each does not need repetition. There are, moreover, surprisingly few theories which try to explain why some occupations are more strike-prone than others, as distinct from those which consider differences between countries, variations over time, or the general reasons for industrial conflict. Even Hyman looks at theories only for their general validity, and he does not try to show how the various factors he considers might be brought together to explain why some groups have been more strike-prone than others.

Perhaps the most famous theory is that of Kerr and Siegel (1954): dockers, along with groups such as miners and workers in logging camps, form 'isolated masses'. They are separated from other social groups and have a high degree of internal cohesion and class identity. There are no institutions to mediate between employers and workers, and industrial relations are characterized by bitter conflicts. Kerr and Siegel add a second argument, namely, that physically demanding and dangerous jobs will attract tough, combative workers who are more likely to strike than are more passive workers. Data on strike rates in eleven countries were used to support this argument.

The picture of tough workers with strong bonds of solidarity certainly appears to fit groups such as dockers and miners, and they have featured in similar guise in other writers' characterizations of the 'traditional proletarian' (Lockwood, 1966). The evidence suggests a more complex picture, however. Miners in different countries have had very different strike rates, and solidarity has been far from universal; even where present, solidarity can promote self-discipline and co-operation as much as militancy, and it can sometimes collapse into individualism (Rimlinger, 1959). Strike activity in mining has also varied dramatically over time in ways which the isolated mass thesis cannot explain. Some groups in dangerous jobs and forming isolated masses have not been particularly strike-prone, steel workers being a good example (Edwards, 1977). Similarly, some strike-prone groups have not been in isolated masses, with British car workers being an obvious case in point. And studies of workers who are in isolated masses and who do strike a good deal have argued that the explanation of strike behaviour does not lie in massness. Meat freezing works in New Zealand are a case in point, for workers here are often far from centres of population, do dangerous jobs, and have been strike-prone. Yet Geare (1972, 1973) shows that the use of strikes can be explained by the nature of the work, which is monotonous, noisy and unpleasant, and by the bargaining opportunities presented by it: there was a fixed amount of work to be done, determined by the number of sheep killed in a season, and workers were thus in a strong bargaining position. The account is consistent with Kerr and Siegel's auxiliary hypothesis about tough workers but not with their emphasis on mass isolation.

Such points assume the coherence of the idea of 'massness'. It contains two strands, that workers are entirely separated from employers and that occupational communities are divorced from other social influences. Both are questionable. As we have seen, all workplace relations involve the negotiation of conflict and consent, and to reduce any pattern to total antagonism is to oversimplify, and probably seriously distort, the picture. An image of insulation from the outside world is misleading. Studies of miners (e.g. Moore, 1974; Waller, 1983) suggest a more complex picture with bonds of deference and dependence tying workers to employers and with politics and religion linking miners to the outside world. Such studies show not only that the particular groups studied did not conform to the mass model but also that any such model is liable to caricature the negotiation of order.

More fundamentally still, the isolated mass hypothesis has a very undifferentiated view of workplace relations: workers and managers are mere cyphers responding to their condition, and relations are simply antagonistic. As we have seen, the effects of conditions such as 'massness' are mediated by actors' behaviour, and this behaviour is more complex than the idea of the isolated mass can allow. As shown below in the case of dockers, the development of a tradition of workplace relations is a process about which the static model of massness can say little.

This is not to say that everything mentioned by Kerr and Siegel is incorrect. It is true that groups such as miners have displayed remarkable solidarity. The British strike of 1984–5 is widely seen as a key example. Even the fact that miners in Nottinghamshire and other parts of the country did not join the strike need not contradict the point, for all that need be argued is that there is something about the communities of miners which promotes solidarity once a particular decision has been taken. There is room to argue about the depth of solidarity and about how it is sustained. But the basic point that occupational communities vary in their cohesion should not be neglected.

Bulmer (1975) elaborates on the idea of the occupational community. Such a community exists where the social relations of work carry over into non-work lives, where people spend their leisure time with people from the same industry, and where the community is insulated from outside pressures. In coal, he argues, the danger of the work and dependence on others, together with the physical isolation of mining communities, promote a sense of community. On the docks, the solidary nature of work groups and their freedom from supervision have a similar consequence. This idea is important in suggesting that 'community' is variable, that it has different causes, and that its consequences for workplace relations can differ. Dockers and miners may both have occupational communities but this need not mean that such communities have identical characteristics. It is also useful in suggesting how a particular type of community can sustain a pattern of industrial relations. The dockers' community tradition promotes work group loyalty. That in the mines does this but can also produce a wider allegiance to the whole of a pit. By contrast, lorry drivers also have an occupational community, according to Bulmer, by virtue of being cut off from their places of residence, but this identification with the occupation is not associated with strong work group identity. Lorry drivers work as individuals and their group solidarity is likely to be limited (Hollowell, 1968).

The concept of community is not intended directly to explain strike activity. A strong occupational community need not imply a high strike rate, and strike-prone occupations do not necessarily have strong communities (as car workers again show most clearly). What it can do is to help to understand the character of workplace relations and the connections between work and non-work factors without following the errors of the 'isolated mass' view. Thus the solidarity of mining villages reflects the nature of the work and their physical isolation. This in turn helps to understand the processes involved in strikes, notably how strikes can be sustained by traditions of solidarity or undermined by their absence.

An occupational community can affect workers' self-identity. But it does not provide the immediate reason for striking. Clegg (1979: 273–7) has provided one of the few attempts to identify common conditions that have promoted strikes in Britain. He identifies two that have characterized the main strike-prone industries of docks, coal, cars, and shipbuilding. These are uncertain and fluctuating earnings, and fragmented collective bargaining. The uncertainty of earnings generates discontent, while fragmented bargaining creates the opportunity for frequent bargaining pressure. As Eldridge (1973) points out in discussing one of the studies on which Clegg draws, namely the book on the car industry by Turner et al. (1967), this type of explanation is useful in linking structural factors with actors' own meanings and perceptions. The conditions of earnings and bargaining structure can be seen as causes for differences between these and other industries; and evidence from strikes shows that workers did experience fluctuating earnings as a source of discontent. Workers are not presented as the passive recipients of their condition. The account is also able to embrace the car industry, which, as seen above, does not fit explanations based on technology or occupational communities.

As argued elsewhere (Edwards, 1983: 223–6), however, there are problems with this account. The two conditions mentioned are not sufficient for a high strike rate: other industries such as footwear have had fluctuating earnings and fragmented bargaining but a low strike rate. Cases where one or both conditions have been changed have also proved a problem. On the docks, the reform of industrial relations associated with 'decasualization' was designed to deal with both, but as Clegg admits strike rates have stayed high. His explanation is that 'striking can become something of a habit' (1979: 280), which is hardly satisfactory unless the reasons why dockers clung to the habit are identified, a task undertaken (in outline form) below.

The implication is that to try to find one or more factors which increase strike-proneness is misguided. Conter-examples to single-factor theories can readily be advanced. More importantly, a given factor may require others in order to operate. It is, for example, obvious that one of the characteristics of Britain's most strike-affected industries is a developed workplace trade-union organization. Such organization has been necessary to sustain the ability to strike regularly by turning generalized discontents into grievances that can be pursued. But the law-like statement, 'union organization is necessary for a high level of strikes' faces numerous problems: in countries, notably those in the developing world, where striking is more associated with national politics than with collective bargaining, the point may not hold; the conditions promoting a particular type of organization have to be specified; and, once such precision is attempted, the point may become a tautology.

As writers such as Bulmer and Eldridge also stress, attention has to be paid to action as well as to the structural conditions of behaviour. Occupational communities have to be created and sustained, and the 'habit' of striking has to be inculcated in new generations of workers. Theories of strikes which neglect this point can soon sink into determinism. As noted at the start of this chapter, moreover, action does not just fill in the gaps left over by structural forces. It interprets and gives meaning to them. Recent studies of the docks provide a valuable illustration of how an adequate perspective on strikes can be produced.

Work Relations and Job Controls on the Docks

In the last twenty years dock work has been revolutionized with the introduction of container ships and mechanized cargo handling. Since the concern here is with historical developments, attention will concentrate on the traditional system as described by writers such as Hill (1976) and Wilson (1972). Some comments on the significance of recent changes are made at the end of the chapter.

Under the non-mechanized system, work was highly irregular, due to seasonal fluctuations in traffic and daily and even hourly changes in the demand for labour: a ship in port is idle, and its owners want to minimize the time taken to load and unload it. When a ship was in dock, labour was in great demand, but as soon as the job was finished there was no work. Although the work was heavy and unpleasant, the image of dockers as unskilled and undifferentiated is a myth, for there was traditionally specialization between cargoes and a clear skill hierarchy within each part of the trade (Lovell, 1969: 37–57). This system exacerbated fluctuations in labour demand, for a ship needed not just a given number of dockers but a particular combination of trades, and delay was costly. It was in the interests of shipowners to have an excess supply of labour so that the workers they needed were available at short notice.

In most countries, the result has been a casual system of employment: workers were hired for each job as they were needed. This might be expected to lead to complete anarchy but in fact a complex system of regulation has developed. The differentiation of workers by skill and type was one key factor. The other was the organization of workers into gangs. Loading a cargo needs a team including workers on the quayside, crane operators, slingers, and the most skilled men who packed goods in the hold. Employers preferred to hire gangs who could work together, and the gang became the basic unit of work organization. The obvious payment system to use was piecework: so much per cargo handled. All these factors tended to make the gang an autonomous unit. There was none of the machine-pacing of work that characterized factory labour, and neither was there a major role for the foreman in the direction of the work process: work tasks were not standardized and workers decided among themselves how to carry them out.

By far the best account of the operation of the casual system is that of Phillips and Whiteside (1985; see also Whiteside, 1985). They show how the parties to it developed interests in its operation which defied successive efforts to rationalize the industry. There were two main benefits of casualism for the workers: it meant that there was no need to work a continuous six- (or later five-) day week, for wages were high when workers were actually working, so that it was possible to maintain work rhythms that were in sharp contrast to the regularized, routinized and disciplined labour of factory operatives; and workers were not tied to any one employer but could see themselves as free and autonomous workmen (Phillips and Whiteside, 1985: 33–6). The resulting work habits became deeply ingrained.

It is not surprising to find a whole series of work practices that other writers have described. Mars (1982) has shown how the gang system encouraged highly organized means of pilfering cargo: goods were readily available, there was little managerial presence, and the gang provided social support for the pilferer. Mellish and Collis-Squires (1976) have described how discipline and time-keeping were handled through norms developed by the gangs themselves and not through formal disciplinary procedures: gangs decided when and how to work, and it was not for management to intervene. Wilson (1972) has pointed to the common practice, known in Liverpool as welting, whereby a gang would have half its members working while the other half rested, and sometimes even left the workplace entirely. There was thus a complex set of controls of how and when work was carried out which emerged out of customs of the job.

An interesting example is the 'continuity rule', for this shows how a practice initiated by employers can be turned to workers' advantage (Wilson 1972: 216–18). It was introduced in 1944 and required that the movement of a given cargo should be completed by the gang which started the job. It was intended to force men to stay on unattractive jobs instead of switching to better ones. But it was slowly turned from a guarantee that the employer would have labour to a restriction on mobility, with the 'job' being defined more and more strictly so that workers could not be moved from one hatch of a ship to another. It was not, however, simply restrictive, for it also helped to protect workers from favouritism, 'since by preventing transfers in mid-turn it ensured that blue-eyed boys did not get all the good work' (Wilson, 1972: 217). And its restrictive character was not simply imposed on employers but grew out of a particular organization of work.

Why, then, did employers tolerate this system? They had their own interests in casual employment. Phillips and Whiteside (1985: 55–6) give three: it was feared that permanent labour would be less productive because it would remove the disciplines of insecurity; a permanent labour force would not contain all the skills needed for each cargo; and casualism weakened the unions. These authors also show how various efforts to end the casual system foundered not only because of opposition from the workers but also because employers lacked the determination, unity and organization to push it through. There were many small employers who could live with the system, and managerial control techniques were primitive or non-existent. Firms relied on workers' self-organization and were in no position to assert their own control.

Various periods of strike militancy on the docks, notably those following the Second World War and during the late 1960s and early 1970s, can thus be placed in context. On the former, Phillips and Whiteside (1985: 237–53) note institutionalist explanations, such as that offered by the Devlin committee of inquiry (1965), which see the casual system as causing rootlessness and disorderly industrial relations. Workers' motives are here viewed as a secondary consequence of the system and not as an integral part of it.

Militancy in fact reflected workers' resistance to efforts at decasualization. Workers were strongly committed to the traditional system. A drive for efficiency led to the increasing use of disciplinary sanctions as managements tried to force workers to behave in regular ways. Absenteeism, for example, was so high that numbers of dockers equivalent to 18 per cent of the workforce were appearing annually before disciplinary committees. Workers used strikes to resist efforts to control their behaviour.

On the 1960s and 1970s, attention has concentrated on the recommendations of the Devlin committee, namely that the casual system should be ended. Durcan et al. (1983: 281–311) provide the most thorough analysis. The details of this cannot be considered here, but some implications for the 'institutionalist' account of ,strikes offered by Clegg may be pursued. The most obvious point is that decasualization did not lead to a decline in strike activity, which suggests some error or omission in the Devlin solution and also in Clegg's theory of strikes. Durcan et al. suggest three explanations. First, the process of trying to introduce major change in an industry as traditionally strike-prone as the docks was almost bound to lead to conflict. Secondly, there were features of the economic environment to which the committee should have given attention. Containerization and the changing distribution of traffic between the ports reduced the demand for labour from the late 1960s; this encouraged a return to the high levels of conflict which had marked the late 1940s as dockers reacted to increased insecurity. Thirdly, rapid technological change, to which the committee gave no attention, further intensified conflict.

This revised institutionalist account has several strengths. It relates strike activity to changing labour market circumstances and to technological change. It thus goes beyond the identification of factors internal to the industrial relations system such as the pay structure. In analysing the immediate influences on strikes it makes a crucial contribution to the explanation of a particular pattern of activity. But it does not pretend to explain the origins of dockers' traditions or to go deeper into the nature of workplace relations.

Phillips and Whiteside offer many insights on these things. Consider, for example, their account of a highly publicized strike over a 'dirty' cargo in 1948. When a gang was suspended for refusing to work at the specified rate,

> a major strike started. Sympathetic action did not spring from a common conviction that the gang was right in its claim that the cargo was dirty, but from a collective rejection of the right of the local [docks] board to punish dockers who had been following traditional procedures by refusing to touch a cargo [until a rate had been agreed]. (Phillips and Whiteside, 1985: 251)

It was not so much the particular incidents sparking off strikes that were important but the changing nature of managerial discipline and workers' reactions to this.

It is the kind of explanation involved in this account which is most important here. It is not limited to the minutiae of the strike in the manner characteristic of journalistic and some historical accounts. Neither does it explain dockers' behaviour as the product of their being an isolated mass or of other structural conditions. Instead, it shows how structural forces interacted with long-standing traditions to produce a distinctive set of expectations among dockers. When these expectations were violated, a strike was the natural result. More generally, the analysis shows how the social relations that coalesced into a tradition mediated influences stemming from the technology and the labour market. When deciding whether or not to strike, workers will not generally give explicit attention to such influences (although in developing their tactics they may consider such things as the state of demand for their firm's products). They will, rather, respond in terms of their understandings of how the world works and ought to work. An adequate account needs to reveal the operation of these understandings and to explain how they are generated and sustained. Structural conditions are certainly important here, but they have effects only because of the ways in which they are mediated by experience.

Conclusions: Consciousness and Action

Three other points are illustrated by this example. First, an account stressing the social mediation of structural forces should not be taken to the extreme of arguing that the situation is entirely open and that dockers can define the situation in any way they choose. Their occupational community helped them preserve the casual system, but mechanization has eventually led to the decline of traditional dock work. As Phillips and Whiteside (1985: 272) stress, however, there was no inevitable trend to rationalization, for dock employers had shown little interest in replacing the casual system. An external threat, namely the wish of the Labour government of 1964–70 to promote planned growth and reform, was necessary before the casual system was eliminated. And this was achieved only at the cost of very large financial inducements to dockers, inducements that would arguably have been unnecessary had the dockers' traditions been less resilient.

Secondly, it should not be assumed that dockers' defence of their traditions was a simple matter of their asserting their interests as against those of employers. A critic of their behaviour could well point to its consequences: high labour costs in ports covered by the decasualization programme and the growth of independent docks such as Felixstowe; the loss of jobs; and so on. The disadvantages of the casual system, notably its insecurity, were also clear. Dockers were attached to it not because it was ideal but because it offered known benefits. They might well have preferred something else, and could also have acknowledged its consequences. But they were certainly not the authors of the casual system. They turned some aspects of it to their own advantage, but its results were not intended by anyone.

Thirdly, there is no reason to suppose that dockers had a distinctive class consciousness. From the debate about different types of working-class orientations to work and images of society (especially Lockwood, 1966), it might be expected that dockers would exhibit a traditional proletarian perspective based on an occupational community, a strong intra-class solidarity, and a two-class, conflict-based image of society. Hill (1976: 108–15) shows that dock workers do not differ much from other workers in their general social imagery or orientations to work, a conclusion echoed by Allen (1984), who also shows that there was no difference between dockers at Southampton who had worked under the traditional pre-mechanized production system, and who should be particularly 'proletarian' in outlook, and those without this experience. As for the idea of an occupational community, dockers do not seem to have been particularly tied to their occupation. Their job controls reflected some specific and historically grounded struggles around the effort bargain. 'Voluntaristic' considerations can be blended with structural ones to produce nuanced explanations (see also Edwards, 1987a, for elaboration of this point).

This is not to deny that groups such as dockers exhibit distinctive patterns of workplace behaviour. Quite the reverse. The problem in a long line of sociological theorizing is the view that a group's militancy should be explained in terms of its class imagery and solidarity or its community integration. But in terms of general social attitudes the traditional proletarian does not stand out from other workers. And community integration has to be created and reproduced. Such factors should not be neglected, and neither should the sorts of influence considered by more institutionally oriented studies, such as changing market and technical conditions, be ignored.

But a sociological perspective on strikes tries to do at least three things. First, it does not treat factors such as technical change as asocial forces but considers them in the light of the strategies and policies of employers. The docks provide a negative example of this, since the apparent logic of modernization and decasualization was long delayed by the preference for the old system among employers and workers. Secondly, structural conditions are not seen as exerting determinate effects: a given condition such as a tighter labour market can have varying consequences depending on other circumstances and on how managers and workers interpret the ambiguous signals that they receive. Thirdly, it examines the logics and assumptions that develop within a particular workplace order. It is this focus on the contradictory politics of workplace relations, together with the customs to which they give rise, which explains 'habits' and 'traditions' of striking and which is essential to a sociological understanding of the nature of strike action.

Conclusions

The foregoing discussion has tried to give some feel for the day-to-day generation and maintenance of order in the workplace, for the dialectics of the relationships which emerge, and for the place of 'conflict' or 'resistance' in these relationships. Particular weight has been placed on the internal dynamics of patterns of job regulation: customs and understandings are not the automatic result of structural conditions but have to be developed and sustained. Such conditions can certainly constrain the freedom of people to create collective norms for the control of effort, but even in such cases modes of adaptation are available. These can, as with pilferage and related fiddles, give workers some power: workers are active creators of the world in which they live, as they try to infuse their jobs with meaning and to make them tolerable.

Although the possibility of workers' shaping the effort bargain is ever present, because the labour contract cannot be exactly specified, the ways in which this possibility is actualized vary dramatically. Differences between workplaces have been addressed above, but variations over time are also important. Many of the studies discussed were conducted long ago, Roy's for example in 1945, Blau's in 1949, and Lupton's and Cunnison's in the late 1950s. It should not be assumed that the fiddles practised then have survived intact. Changes in pay systems away from piecework have reduced the opportunity for certain types of fiddle connected with the booking of output. And massive technical changes have affected the organization of work. Coyle (1984: 51), for example, notes that in the clothing industry the skills of working through analysed by Cunnison, which were very important in sustaining militant individualism, are used only very rarely. Although Burawoy's study was conducted as recently as 1974/5, massive changes in the American industrial relations system have undermined the bases of 'game playing'. Firms have sought wage concession in the face of foreign competition, and the old forms of consent, in which individual rights protected by a grievance procedure were balanced against the employer's control of the organization of work, has been challenged as firms have set up non-union plants or tried to institute new forms of commitment based on flexibility, participation and wider job responsibilities (Kochan et al., 1986). Burawoy (1985) himself has described these changes as replacing the old hegemonic order with a hegemonic despotism. Similar tendencies towards the acceptance of new working practices and the goals of production have been at work in Britain (Edwards, 1987b). The implication is that the space for fiddles has been eroded, with workers' creative capacities being harnessed directly to the goals of production and with the room for informality being restricted.

New technologies are widely seen as reducing workers' discretion over the organization of work. In some industries, change has had profound effects. On the docks, for example, container systems and the bulk transport of goods such as grain have reduced the need to handle individual cargoes. It seems likely that dockers' traditional skills have been undermined, and more likely that opportunities for pilferage have been tightly constrained. Such changes within occupations have to be placed in the context of wider changes in the labour market. Employment on the docks has fallen dramatically (from 80,000 in 1956 to 25,000 in 1980 and a mere 12,000 in 1985), and there have also been marked declines in employment in other sectors where 'restrictive practices' have been most common. The docker's pilferage and the engineering pieceworker's fiddle are now less representative of workplace behaviour than they were in the past.

It would, however, be a mistake to assume that conflict around the effort bargain has been eliminated. Many areas of employment continue to be characterized by direct controls of work. Here, such convert practices as individual fiddles, together with quitting and going absent, are likely to remain important forms of reaction, although possibly more difficult to use as unemployment makes it easier for employers to use the threat of dismissal as a sanction. The growing areas of employment, namely the personal service sectors, are also ones where fiddles have thrived in the past, hotels and catering being good examples. The much-vaunted growth of self-employment may also encourage fiddles. One of the more aggressive types of fiddler identified by Mars (1982) is the individual on the look out for personal advantage, salesmen being prominent cases. Tax fiddles and fiddles against the customer are well-known elements of some occupations dominated by the self-employed. These things do not bear directly on the employment relationship, of course. But they suggest that the illicit practices, of which fiddles around an effort bargain between an employer and an employee are special cases, may well take on a new significance. To the extent that changes in the nature of employment point to an individualization of ties between worker and employee, forms of secondary adjustment are likely to move towards the individual, and perhaps even non-militant, types identified above, and away from collective and organized types.

This may be counteracted in part, however, by collective resentment at the loss of space provided by secondary adjustments. Mars (1982: 189–91) gives an interesting discussion of a strike by firemen in 1977. Firemen had no record of militancy and yet they were willing to strike, even in the face of condemnation for endangering lives. Part of the explanation, Mars argues, is that new forms of rota system were reducing the opportunity to 'moonlight': on night shifts, firemen had been able to sleep when not out on a call, and several of them took second jobs during the day. Attacking a fiddle provoked discontent which contributed to a strike. Similar processes can be discerned among other hiterto quiescent groups such as teachers, civil servants and nurses. Not all of them have enjoyed fiddles, of course, but they have had space to define their own tasks and to determine, within limits, how hard they should work. Cutbacks on manpower and increased work loads have intensified the pressure of work, and this can be seen as a major element in militancy. Many workers in these sectors appear to have an ambivalent attitude, on the one hand disliking militancy and clinging to ideas of duty to the pupil, client or patient, but on the other feeling threatened by their employers and wanting to assert their own interests.

The consequences of trying to reduce fiddles thus warrant attention: as in Gouldner's (1954) study, where relatively minor indulgencies were attacked and this sparked off a strike that was arguably more damaging to the firm, it may not be in a firm's long-term interests to try to eliminate all fiddles. To the extent, moreover, that firms seek the active commitment of workers, they become increasingly dependent on tacit skills and on informal adjustments. And the uncertainties of the managerial task as analysed by Streeck (1987) suggest that schemes of commitment may be less thoroughgoing than they appear. Fiddles and informality may change their form but the dialectics of conflict and consent will continue to characterize workplace relations.

References

Aldridge, A. 1976. *Power, Authority and Restrictive Practices: A Sociological Essay on Industrial Relations*. Oxford: Basil Blackwell.

Allen, P.T. 1984. 'The Class Imagery of "Traditional Proletarians".' *British Journal of Sociology*, 35 (March), 93–111.

Armstrong, P.J., Goodman, J.F.B. and Hyman, J.D. 1981. *Ideology and Shop Floor Industrial Relations*. London: Croom Helm.

Baldamus, W. 1961. *Efficiency and Effort*. London: Tavistock.

Bensman, J. and Gerver, I. 1963. 'Crime and Punishment in the Factory: The Function of Deviancy in Maintaining the Social System'. *American Sociological Review*, 28 (August), 588–98.

Blau, P. M. 1963. *The Dynamics of Bureaucracy: A Study of Interpersonal Relations in Two Government Agencies*. Revised edition. Chicago: University of Chicago Press.

Braverman, H. 1974. *Labor and Monopoly Capital: The Degradation of Work in the Twentieth Century*. New York: Monthly Review Press.

Brown, W. 1972. 'A Consideration of "Custom and Practice".' *British Journal of Industrial Relations*. 10 (March), 42–61.

—— 1973. *Piecework Bargaining*. London: Heinemann.

Bulmer, M.I.A. 1975. 'Sociological Models of the Mining Community'. *Sociological Review*. 23 (February), 61–92.

Burawoy, M. 1979. *Manufacturing Consent: Changes in the Labor Process under Monopoly Capitalism*. Chicago: University of Chicago Press.

—— 1985. *The Politics of Production*. London: Verso.

Clegg, H.A. 1979. *The Changing System of Industrial Relations in Great Britain*. Oxford: Basil Blackwell.

Cockburn, C. 1985. *Machinery of Dominance: Women, Men and Technical Know-How*. London: Pluto Press.

Coyle, A. 1984. *Redundant Women*. London: The Women's Press.

Cressey, P. and MacInnes, J. 1980. 'Voting for Ford: Indstrial Democracy and the Control of Labour'. *Capital and Class*, 11, 5–53.

Crozier, M. 1971. *The World of the Office Worker*. Trans. David Landau. Chicago: University of Chicago Press.

Cunnison, S. 1966. *Wages and Work Allocation: A Study of Social Relations in a Garment Workshop*. London: Tavistock.

214   *P.K. Edwards*

Devlin. 1965. Committee of Inquiry into Certain Matters Concerning the Port Transport Industry. *Final Report.* Cmnd 2523. London: HMSO.

Ditton, J. 1977a. *Part-Time Crime: An Ethnography of Fiddling and Pilferage.* London: Macmillan.

—— 1977b. 'Perks, Pilferage and the Fiddle: The Historical Structure of Invisible Wages'. *Theory and Society,* 4 (Spring), 39–71.

—— 1979. 'Baking Time'. *Sociological Review,* 217 (February), 157–67.

Durcan, J.W., McCarthy, W.E.J. and Redman, G.P. 1983. *Strikes in Post-War Britain: A Study of Stoppages of Work due to Industrial Disputes, 1946–73.* London: Allen & Unwin.

Edwards, P.K. 1977. 'The Kerr-Siegel Hypothesis of Strikes and the Isolated Mass: A Study of the Falsification of Sociological Knowledge'. *Sociological Review,* 25 (August), 551–74.

—— 1983. 'The Pattern of Collective Industrial Action.' *Industrial Relations in Britain.* Ed. Bain, G.S. Oxford: Basil Blackwell.

—— 1986. *Conflict at Work: a Materialist Analysis of Workplace Relations.* Oxford: Basil Blackwell.

—— 1987a. 'Understanding Conflict in the Labour Process: The Logic and Autonomy of Struggle'. *Labour Process Theory.* Eds Knights, D. and Willmott, H. London: Macmillan.

—— 1987b. *Managing the Factory: A Survey of General Managers.* Oxford: Basil Blackwell.

—— and Scullion, H. 1982. *The Social Organization of Industrial Conflict: Control and Resistance in the Workplace.* Oxford: Basil Blackwell.

Eldridge, J.E.T. 1973. 'Industrial Conflict: Some Problems of Theory and Method'. *Man and Organization.* Ed. Child, J. London: Allen & Unwin.

Freeman, 1982. 'The "Understanding" Employer'. *Work, Women and the Labour Market.* Ed. West, J. London: Routledge & Kegan Paul.

Friedman, A. L. 1977. *Industry and Labour: Class Struggle at Work and Monopoly Capitalism.* London: Macmillan.

—— 1987a. 'The Means of Management Control and Labour Process Theory: A Critical Note on Storey'. *Sociology,* 21 (May), 287–94.

—— 1987b. 'Managerial Strategies, Activities, Techniques and Technology: Towards a Complex Theory of the Labour Process. *Labour Process Theory.* Eds Knights, D. and Willmott, H. London: Macmillan.

Gallie, D. 1978. *In Search of the New Working Class.* Cambridge: Cambridge University Press.

Geare, A.J. 1972. 'The Problem of Labour Unrest: Theories into the Causes of Local Strikes in a New Zealand Freezing Works'. *Journal of Industrial Relations,* 14 (April), 13–22.

—— 1973. 'The Conflict over Strike Causes in Otago and Southland Meat Freezing Works'. *Journal of Industrial Relations,* 15 (April), 89–97.

Geer, B., Vivona, C., Haas, J., Woods, C., Miller, S. and Becker, H. 1968. 'Learning the Ropes'. *Among the People.* Eds Deutscher, I. and Thompson, E.M. New York: Basic Books.

Genovese, E.D. 1976. *Roll, Jordan, Roll: The World the Slaves Made.* New York: Vintage.

Gersuny, D. and Kaufman, G. 1985. 'Seniority and the Moral Economy of US Automobile Workers, 1934–46'. *Journal of Social History,* 18 (Spring), 463–75.

Goffman, E. 1961. *Asylums: Essays on the Social Situation of Mental Patients and Other Inmates*. Harmondsworth: Penguin.

Gordon, D., Edwards, R. and Reich, M. 1982. *Segmented Work, Divided Workers: The Historical Transformation of Labor in the United States*. Cambridge: Cambridge University Press.

Gouldner, A. W. 1954. *Patterns of Industrial Bureaucracy*. New York: Free Press.

Haraszti, M. 1977. *A Worker in a Worker's State: Piece-Rates in Hungary* Trans. M. Wright. Harmondsworth: Penguin.

Harper, D. and Emmert, F. 1963. 'Work Behavior in a Service Industry'. *Social Forces*, 42 (December), 216–25.

Hickson, D.J. 1961. 'Motives of Workpeople who Restrict Their Output'. *Occupational Psychology*, 35 (July), 111–21.

Hill, S. 1974. 'Norms, Groups and Power: The Sociology of Workplace Industrial Relations'. *British Journal of Industrial Relations*, 12 (July), 213–35.

—— 1976. *The Dockers: Class and Tradition in London*. London: Heinemann.

Hollowell, P.G. 1968. *The Lorry Driver*. London: Routledge & Kegan Paul.

Hyman, R. 1984. *Strikes*. Third edition. London: Fontana-Collins.

—— 1987. 'Strategy or Structure: Capital, Labour, and Control'. *Work Employment and Society*, 1 (March), 25–55.

—— and Elger, T. 1981. 'Job Controls, the Employers' Offensive and Alternative Strategies'. *Capital and Class*, 15 (Autumn), 115–49.

Kelly, J.E. 1978. 'A Reappraisal of Sociotechnical Systems Theory'. *Human Relations*, 31 (December), 1069–99.

Kerr, C. and Siegel, A. 1954. 'The Interindustry Propensity to Strike'. *Industrial Conflict*. Eds Kornhauser, A., Dubin, R. and Ross, A. M. New York: McGraw-Hill.

Klein, L. 1964. *'Multiproducts Ltd': A Case Study on the Social Effects of Rationalized Production*. London: HMSO.

Kochan, T. A., Katz, H. C. and McKersie, R. B. 1986. *The Transformation of American Industrial Relations*. New York: Basic Books.

Kuhn, J.W. 1961. *Bargaining in Grievance Settlement: The Power of Industrial Work Groups*. New York: Columbia University Press.

Kusterer, K. 1978. *Know How on the Job*. Boulder, Col.: Westview.

Lockwood, D. 1966. 'Sources of Variation in Working Class Images of Society'. *Sociological Review*, 14 (November), 249–67.

Lovell, J. 1969. *Stevedores and Dockers: A Study of Trade Unionism in the Port of London, 1870–1914*. London: Macmillan.

Lupton, T. 1963. *On the Shop Floor: Two Studies of Workshop Organization and Output*. Oxford: Pergamon.

—— and Cunnison, S. 1964. 'Workshop Behaviour'. *Closed Systems and Open Minds*. Ed. Gluckman, M. Chicago: Aldine.

Manwaring, T. and Wood, S. 1984. 'The Ghost in the Machine: Tacit Skills in the Labor Process'. *Socialist Review*, 74, 57–86.

Mars, G. 1982. *Cheats at Work: An Anthropology of Workplace Crime*. London: Counterpoint.

Mathewson, S.B. 1969. *Restriction of Output among Unorganized Workers*. Carbondale: Southern Illinois Univesity Press. (Originally published 1931).

Mellish, M. and Collis-Squires, N. 1976. 'Legal and Social Norms in Discipline and Dismissal'. *Industrial Law Journal*, 5 (September), 164–77.

Miliband, R. 1978. 'A State of Desubordination'. *British Journal of Sociology*, 29 (December), 399–409.

Moore, R. 1974. *Pitmen, Preachers and Politics: The Effects of Methodism in a Durham Mining Community*. Cambridge: Cambridge University Press.

Nichols, T. and Armstrong, P. 1973. *Safety or Profit: Industrial Accidents and the Conventional Wisdom*. Bristol: Falling Wall Press.

—— and Beynon, H. 1977. *Living with Capitalism: Class Relations and the Modern Factory*. London: Routledge & Kegan Paul.

Nolan, P. and Edwards, P.K. 1984. 'Homogenise, Divide and Rule: An Essay on *Segmented Work, Divided Workers'*. *Cambridge Journal of Economics* 8 (June), 197–215.

Peach, L.H. 1983. 'Employee Relations in IBM'. *Employee Relations*, 5:3, 17–20.

Phillips, G. and Whiteside, N. 1985. *Casual Labour: The Unemployment Question in the Port Transport Industry, 1880–1970*. Oxford: Clarendon Press.

Price, R. 1980. *Masters, Unions and Men: Work Control in Building and the Rise of Labour, 1830–1914*. Cambridge: Cambridge University Press.

Rimlinger, G. V. 1959. 'International Differences in the Strike Propensity of Coal Miners: Experience in Four Countries'. *Industrial and Labor Relations Review*, 12 (April), 389–405.

Roethlisberger,W.J. and Dickson, W.J. 1939. *Management and the Worker: An Account of the Research Program Conducted by the Western Electric Company, Hawthorne Works, Chicago*. Cambridge, Mass.: Havard Unviersity Press.

Roy, D. 1952. 'Quota Restriction and Goldbricking in a Machine Shop'. *American Journal of Sociology*, 57 (March), 427–42.

Salaman, G. 1986. *Working*. Chichester: Ellis Horwood.

Sayles, L.R. 1958. *The Behavior of Industrial Work Groups: Prediction and Control*. New York: Wiley.

Schatz, R. 1983. *The Electrical Workers: A History of Labor at General Electric and Westinghouse, 1923–60*. Urbana: University of Illinois Press.

Seashore, S.E. 1954. *Group Cohesiveness in the Industrial Work Group*. Ann Arbor: Survey Researcher Center, University of Michigan.

Stark, D. 1980. 'Class Struggle and the Transformation of the Labor Process: A Relational Approach'. *Theory and Society*, 9 (January), 89–130.

Streeck, W. 1987. 'The Uncertainties of Management in the Management of Uncertainty: Employers, Labour Relations and Industrial Adjustment in the 1980s'. *Work, Employment and Society*, 1 (September), 281–308.

Sykes, A.J.M. 1969a. 'Navvies: Their Work Attitudes'. *Sociology*, 3 (January), 21–35.

—— 1969b. 'Navvies: Their Social Relations'. *Sociology*, 3 (May), 157–72.

Taylor, L. and Walton, P. 1971. 'Industrial Sabotage: Motives and Meanings'. *Images of Deviance*. Ed. Cohen, S. Harmondsworth: Penguin.

Thompson, P. and Bannon, E. 1985. *Working the System: The Shop Floor and New Technology*. London: Pluto.

Tolliday, S. 1986. 'High Tide and After: Coventry Engineering Workers and Shopfloor Bargaining, 1945–80'. *Life and Labour in a Twentieth*

Century City: The Experience of Coventry. Eds Lancaster, B. and Mason, T. Coventry: Cryfield Press.

Trist, E.L. and Bamforth, K.W. 1951. 'Some Social and Psychological Consequences of the Longwall Method of Coal-getting'. *Human Relations*, 4 (February), 3–38.

Turner, H.A., Clack, G. and Roberts, G. 1967. *Labour Relations in the Motor Industry*. London: Allen & Unwin.

Waller, R. J. 1983. *The Dukeries Transformed: The Social and Political Development of a Twentieth Century Coalfield*. Oxford: Clarendon Press.

Whiteside, N. 1985. 'Public Policy and Port Labour Reform: The Dock Decasualization Issue, 1910–50' *Shop Floor Bargaining and the State: Historical and Comparative Perspectives*. Eds Tolliday, S. and Zeitlin, J. Cambridge: Cambridge University Press.

Wilson, D. 1972. *Dockers: The Impact of Industrial Change*. London: Fontana-Collins.

Wrench, J. 1978. 'The "Piecework Effect"': Payment by Results and Industrial Safety'. Occasional Paper 3. Birmingham: University of Aston Sociology Group.

—— and Lee, G. 1978. 'Piecework and Industrial Accidents: Two Case Studies in Birmingham'. Occasional Paper 5. Birmingham: University of Aston Sociology Group.

8   The Frontier of Control

Eric Batstone

The frontier of control may be defined for the purposes of this chapter as referring to the range of issues over which workers have some degree of collective influence, primarily, but not exclusively, through trade unions. This definition differs somewhat from Goodrich's (1920) classic use of the term in that it is not principally concerned with regulation at the workplace and places greater emphasis upon more formal collective regulation than upon the role of the work group.

While the question of union control figures importantly in a variety of debates, assessments of its range and significance vary widely. On the one hand it is claimed that worker – and more specifically union – control has been excessive, being a factor in Britain's poor economic record in the past (Hayek, 1980; Minford, 1982). On the other hand, a more radical tradition sees the degree of collective worker control as being relatively marginal and indicative of a failure on the part of trade unions and the labour movement adequately to protect and promote the interests of the working class (Fox, 1973; Hyman, 1978).

These sharply contrasting interpretations are in large part to be explained by the perspectives of the commentators themselves. Where it is believed that the general welfare is best served by the freeworking of the market and the maintenance of employer prerogative, then even a fairly limited degree of worker control may be seen as harmful. The same degree of influence, however, is likely to be interpreted as marginal if it is believed that the transformation of society is an essential precondition for any significant improvement in the life chances of the working class.

It is not the intention of this chapter to enter into this debate, but rather to seek to assess the range of collective influence and to examine a number of arguments which have attempted to explain it. This, however, is far from a simple task, not least because of the data available. Two principal kinds of data are available, both with their own particular weaknesses. The first are case studies, primarily of individual workplaces and, to a lesser extent, of industries. While these frequently contain important insights, it is often difficult to build up a general picture from them because the cases are

Editorial Note: Eric Batstone left a lengthy first draft of this chapter. I have exercised considerable editorial discretion in arriving at the final text. We had discussed the chapter in detail, however, and I am confident that it accurately reflects his views at the time. I am very grateful to Bill Cox for his help with the references and for his comments and suggestions on the text.

atypical, because not all areas of (potential) control are covered and because definitions of what constitutes control are rarely made explicit and are likely to vary between studies. The second source of data is a number of surveys, which have investigated, among other topics, the range of bargaining. While it is easier to assess the typicality of their findings, the surveys frequently leave the definition of bargaining to respondents and, relatedly, fail to investigate the degree of influence which is achieved through the bargaining process. In this chapter both kinds of data will be employed, although particular emphasis will be placed upon survey data which permit a more systematic testing of relevant theories and hypotheses.

The first task of this chapter, therefore, is to provide a broad outline of the pattern of control – or more strictly of the range of bargaining – in Britain and to assess how this compares with the pattern in other countries.

The Pattern of Control

Just as there are differences of view concerning the significance of union or collective control, so there are also differences of view concerning trends in that control. For some there has been a more or less steady reduction attributable to the decline of craft control and the institutionalization of relations between capital and labour (see, e.g., Price, 1980 for a qualified statement of this view). For others, the spread of union organization and associated institutions of joint regulation suggests a trend in the opposite direction (see, e.g., Marshall, 1950 for an influential statement of this view).

While any thorough assessment of these views is very difficult given the nature and limitations of the available data, it seems plausible to suggest that the former view is in danger of exaggerating the significance of collective control in the past (if only because many workers were not craftsmen and many craftsmen were not unionized in the nineteenth century) and of drawing too close a link between job content and collective control. Such arguments may therefore pay insufficient attention to the rise of trade unionism among other work groups and to the influence which these work groups have achieved over time. For example, even if we take the limited index of union influence over pay – as indicated by the coverage of collective agreements – it has been estimated that the number of workers covered trebled from around 2.4 million in 1910 to over 7 million in 1933 and then doubled to around 15 million by the mid-1960s (Clegg, 1985: 548-9: Donovan. 1968: 10).

While over the longer term, it seems likely that there has been a trend towards greater union influence, there have clearly been considerable fluctuations around the trend. For example, there seems little doubt that the range of union influence tended to increase from the late nineteenth century to around 1920 and declined substantially thereafter until the late 1930s. Subsequently, union influence tended to increase and this trend accelerated until the late 1970s, since when it has declined – although, as will be discussed later, not to the extent sometimes

TABLE 8.1　*Range of bargaining over specified non-pay issues in 1980 and 1984*

| | Manual workers | | Non-manual workers | |
	1980 %	1984 %	1980 %	1984 %
Physical working conditions	92	78	88	76
Redevelopment within establishment	79	62	78	61
Staffing/manning levels	76	55	74	55
Recruitment	69	38	69	39
Redundancy	88	–	84	–
Size of redundancy payments	–	46	–	49
Holiday entitlement	96	–	94	–
Length of working week	95	–	92	–
Major changes in production methods	65	–	56	–
Capital investment	39	–	36	–
Pensions	76	–	84	–

Base: establishments where appropriate unions were recognized
Note: indicates non-coverage of issue in survey
Source: Daniel and Millward, 1983: 197; Millward and Stevens, 1986: 248–53

suggested.

　The most systematic evidence about trends in union influence over the last two decades comes from survey data on the range of bargaining. By taking the range of bargaining as a crude indicator of the range of union influence, we can develop a general picture of developments since the 1960s. Though the surveys are not strictly comparable, it is possible to make allowances for these variations in coverage. A more serious problem in taking the range of bargaining as an indicator of the extent of union influence lies in the fact that the range of bargaining may not be a clear guide to the degree of influence or control exerted by trade unions. For example, a situation in which a union makes major concessions over manning levels cannot be distinguished from one in which a union successfully resists job reductions. This is a significant weakness, but possibly not as substantial as might at first be supposed. Given that unilateral union control is extremely limited, it is probable that the degree of union control is greater where some form of bargaining occurs than where it does not. Even if a union makes major concessions in negotiations, it does not follow that it has exerted no control: the concessions may well have been even greater if there had been no bargaining.

　The survey data on bargaining suggest that the range of bargaining increased from the mid-1960s and throughout most of the 1970s. This picture is broadly supported by data concerning the range of issues negotiated in various industries and across plants of different size, and also by respondents' views concerning trends in bargaining (for a detailed discussion of the evidence, see Batstone, 1984: 128–36). The

TABLE 8.2   *Cross–national comparisons of collective influence*

	A *Influence of representative bodies*	B *Scope of collective bargaining*
Belgium	2.4	1.0
Denmark	1.9	0.9
Finland	1.5	1.0
France	2.1	0.5
West Germany	2.6	0.6
Italy	2.5	0.6
Netherlands	2.1	0.8
Norway	2.1	1.0
Sweden	2.8	1.0
Austria	–	1.0
Canada	–	0.4
USA	–	0.5
Japan	–	0.2
UK	2.2	0.6

Note: In column A 1=low, 5=high: in column B 0=low, 1=high
Sources: A: IDEa, 1981: 153; B: Cameron, 1984: 165

most systematic recent data on the subject derive from the 1980 and 1984 Workplace Industrial Relations Surveys (WIRS), which covered establishments employing more than twenty-five people and obtained information on the extent of joint regulation over a number of specific non-pay issues (Daniel and Millward, 1983; Millward and Stevens, 1986). The findings of the surveys are set out in table 8.1. As the range of issues covered in the 1980 survey was wider than that in the 1984 survey and as other changes in question format were made, caution is required in drawing comparisons between the results.

The implications of the decline in bargaining range between 1980 and 1984 are discussed in a later section of this paper. At this point a number of more general features of the data are worthy of note. While the range of subjects investigated in the surveys was strongly biased towards work organization issues, the data indicates a striking pattern. Bargaining is most common on issues which most directly and immediately touch upon the wage–effort bargain. Hence, issues such as holiday entitlement, length of the working week and physical working conditions were reported to be the subject of negotiation for manual workers in over 90 per cent of cases in 1980. Other issues which bear more directly upon management's use of labour – such as redeployment and manning levels – were less often the subject of bargaining. More strategic issues, notably capital investment, were said to be bargained over in only a minority of cases in 1980. The evidence here suggests, therefore, that union control tends to be greater the more directly issues impinge upon the wage–effort bargain and the less they can be defined as bearing upon strategic issues.

Another way of looking at the data is to see how many of the ten issues investigated in 1980 were the subject of negotiation in different establishments.[1] Five or less of the issues were the subject of negotiations in just 13 per cent of establishments where manual unions were recognized, but only in a third of cases were all issues said to be the subject of negotiation. In other words, the range of bargaining varied considerably, although, where manual unions were recognized, there was generally a significant range of bargaining. It should be remembered, however, that the data relate only to establishments employing more than twenty-five people in which an appropriate union was recognized.

It is useful to place the British pattern of union influence in context by comparing it with the range of collective influence in other countries. In a cross-national study undertaken in the 1970s, a systematic attempt was made to assess the influence wielded by representative worker bodies – unions or works councils – at the workplace level (for details of the method of construction of the measure, see IDE, 1981a: 46–82). As can be seen from column A of table 8.2, the level of collective influence in Britain was towards the middle of the range: representative bodies in a number of countries have somewhat more influence and others have rather less.

However, unions may achieve influence not only at the workplace but also through discussion and bargaining with the state. In a study focusing upon the period 1965–82, Cameron (1984) attempted to construct a measure of the scope of collective bargaining which focused on this dimension. His findings are shown in column B of table 8.2. At this level, it can be seen that the scope of union influence in Britain is relatively modest compared with many of the other societies investigated, notably the Scandinavian countries, Austria, Belgium and the Netherlands. In other words, the tendency for union influence to be concentrated upon the more immediate aspects of the wage–effort bargain is not one which is typical of all countries, or, to put the point more cautiously, is less pronounced in some other countries than it is in Britain. Furthermore, it would seem that there is little relationship between the influence of works-based representative bodies and the scope of collective bargaining more generally.

In sum, while the data need to be treated with considerable caution, a number of points appear worthy of note. First, in Britain union influence tends to be concentrated upon the more immediate aspects of the wage–effort bargain, whereas this is less the case in some other societies. Secondly, it is clear that the range of collective worker influence differs considerably between establishments in Britain and across societies. Thirdly, the range of collective worker influence in Britain has varied significantly over time. The task of the remainder of this chapter is to assess different

1 This analysis is based on the survey data from the Workplace Industrial Relations Surveys of 1980 and 1984 and was carried out by the author as part of the 'Labour Regulation and Economic Performance' project with J. Muellbaeur, K. Denny and K.I. McDonald (Nuffield College, July 1986 to Sept. 1987) and funded by the Economic and Social Research Council. Further use is made of findings from this project on pages 228, 233, 236, 239 and 240 of this chapter.

explanations of these findings. It is useful to begin with a consideration of the general factors which are likely to shape the frontier of control. This will be followed by a discussion of a number of more specific arguments.

The Basic Model

The frontier of control is essentially an issue of power relations: management agreement to conceding some degree of control to worker collectivities is ultimately a reflection of the costs and sanctions which workers might otherwise impose upon management. However, an analysis of power relations needs to take account of three interrelated elements: the power resources of the parties, the goals to which they aspire, and a series of strategic considerations relating to their chances of success (Korpi, 1978: 31–44, Korpi, 1986).

The power resources of a trade union can be seen as consisting of two basic elements: the first of these are the resources possessed by individual workers and members, the second the unions' ability to combine and mobilize these resources and, thereby, to build up their own organization. The importance of power resources lies in the ability they provide to impose sanctions, directly or indirectly, upon the employer. Classically, emphasis has been placed upon the ability of trade unions to hit the profits of the capitalist. But not all employers are capitalists – indeed, in Britain in 1986, over a quarter of the employed labour force was employed in the public sector (Central Statistics Office, 1987: 201). Moreover, according to data from the 1983 British Election Survey, just over 60 per cent of the trade-union members among the employed were in the public sector.[2] In other words, to understand the pattern of union control it is necessary to take much more account of the public sector than has traditionally been the case. For the logic of action in the public sector is very different from that in the private sector: the primary goal of the employer is to maintain political legitimacy and, therefore, the power resources of a union have ultimately to be assessed in terms of its ability to endanger this legitimacy.

The resources of the membership can take a wide variety of forms but three elements are particularly worthy of note. The first concerns the ability to disrupt the production of the goods and services which the employer provides – that is, the position of workers in the production process. The second concerns the scarcity value of the characteristics which the worker brings to the employer; this clearly relates to the state of the labour market. The third factor of relevance, particularly in the public sector but also in the private sector, is the political influence that workers can wield, most notably through the electoral process.

The second component of union power resources concerns the unions' ability to tap and combine the resources which workers individually

---

2 This finding derives from data compiled as part of the 1983 British General Election Study conducted by A. Heath (Oxford). R. Jowell (Social and Community Planning Research), J. Curtice (Liverpool) and J. Field (Social and Community Planning Research).

possess. Not only do they have to be able to draw workers into membership (or association with the union) but they have also to be able to induce workers to mobilize the resources they possess. In addition, the union may be able to 'save' the power resources of its members in a variety of ways: through union dues it can build up an organizational structure which permits the more efficient use of resources; it can build up a variety of services which may alleviate some of the costs for members associated with mobilization; and it may also be able to 'bank' resources through inducing the employer to recognize the role of the union in the determination of a range of issues – that is, through institutionalization.

The primary resources of the employer lie in the fact that he recruits labour and, typically, has greater financial resources, making it possible to survive a stoppage of work more easily than can workers. The degree of solidarity between employers – for example, through employers' associations – may be significant. Offe and Wiesenthal (1980) have argued that the problems of combination. encountered by capital are far less than those encountered by labour since inanimate capital can be merged in a way in which human labour cannot and because the goals of the employer are favoured by the mobilization of bias in the structure of society. It is arguable, however, that they underestimate the problems which employers confront in determining their strategies, particularly in the face of union challenge. Moreover, in their discussion of the problem of combination, they use the terms capital, shareholder and employer with some casualness. While inanimate capital may be combined with ease, it does not follow that those who possess the capital and determine its use can so easily be fused. The interests of different companies, shareholders and managers may often conflict and, as Schmitter and Streeck (1981) and Bowan (1982, 1985) have argued, there may be strong free-rider incentives, particularly in competitive markets.

Finally, in discussing relative power resources, it is often insufficient to look at the resources of the employer and union alone. For conflicts within the industrial sphere will often have wider ramifications. Hence, the state – even beyond its own role as an employer – may seek to influence the way in which industrial relations are conducted. This is not the place in which to engage in a discussion of the role of the state. But what is important is the growing recognition of the fact that arguments which simply stress the way in which the state is necessarily subordinated to the aims of capitalism are grossly oversimplified (Crouch, 1979; Zeitlin, 1985). The state has its own particular interests: it may have to mediate between conflicting industrial interests, it may be concerned with the welfare of the economy as a whole. But, most crucially, a government has to be concerned with its own continuation in office. Accordingly the precise form that intervention takes can vary considerably depending upon the objectives of the government and the structural conditions it confronts. Where there are strong ties between the party in power and the union movement, or where trade unions are especially strong, its intervention may lead not to a reinforcement of the power of employers but to an extension of the range of union influence into areas relating to economic and social policy.

Whatever the particular balance of the power resources of unions and employers, it is clear that the development of such resources will be crucially affected by the goals or objectives of the parties. The extent to which the employer is prepared to commit power resources to a fight with trade unions will depend upon both the centrality of winning the conflict and the costs and risks incurred in the conflict itself. Here there is an important contrast to the problems which a trade union faces. For while trade unions are solely concerned with factors relating to the employment relationship, the employer is not primarily interested in the employment and control of labour. A great deal of the debate on the labour process has failed to take sufficient account of this, but it is important in that the employer continually has to assess the way in which his other priorities will be affected if he commits resources to a confrontation with a trade union. Hence while, given their resources, one might expect large firms to be better able to resist trade-union attempts to achieve control, in fact the range of control tends to be significantly higher in large rather than in small firms.

Similarly the implications of a union's ability to mobilize power resources will be affected by the goals that guide union action. The nature of trade-union goals has long been the subject of debate. However, much of the literature has been of an essentially prescriptive kind. In contrast, the position adopted here is that the character of union goals does not derive from some inherent nature of trade unionism, but is the product of specific social and cultural conditions and as such must be determined empirically. Potentially such goals may range from a concern with class war and the transition to socialism to a narrow concern to maximize workers' immediate economic interests. There appears to be considerable continuity in the nature of union goals in particular societies across time. This indicates the need to investigate the social origins of the goals which trade unions pursue. Important issues here concern the effects of institutionalization, the structure of the trade union and its internal distribution of power.

Finally, it is essential to take account of strategic considerations. This point cannot be overemphasized, for it highlights that trade unions and employers may not, in fact, seek to realize their 'major' goals if these are not seen to be feasible in the face of a particular set of contingencies. This type of argument has recently been stressed by writers adopting a rational choice approach. Przeworski and Wallerstein (1982; Przeworski, 1985) and Lange (1984), for example, have used prisoner's dilemma games to show that, at least under particular conditions, it may be rational for trade unions to co-operate in wage regulation even when the primary goal is assumed to be the maximization of worker incomes (see also Crouch, 1982). One may know that one's preferred goal is strongly opposed by the other party, who is therefore prepared to mobilize his superior power resources, whereas a lower order option will have a better chance of success. In these circumstances, it might be expected that the union would pursue the lower order goal.

This argument has a more general significance. Many writers have suggested that trade unions have frequently moderated their goals because they have become incorporated as a result of the institutionalization of bargaining procedures. The rational choice arguments highlight the possibility – and at a general level one can say no more than this – that more conventional liberal pluralist arguments may well be more plausible, namely that any such presumed moderation reflects the fact that through these procedures and by the moderation of the demands which they put forward, unions can in fact achieve more for their members than they can through more radical demands.

Even in the absence of formal procedures, unions may fail to pursue their primary goals. However, if each party comes to believe that a policy of eradicating the other is not viable and if they also come to share a relatively accurate assessment of the balance of power and the pattern of their respective 'priorities-in-action', then neither party may see much value in engaging in conflicts which are costly to both sides and whose typical outcomes can be predicted with a certain degree of confidence. There is therefore an incentive to develop procedures for reaching agreement without the expenditure of power resources.

Outcomes cannot, of course, be predicted with total confidence on all occasions and the exceptions may prove extremely costly to one party or the other – both in terms of the concessions extracted by the other party and in terms of its own ability to mobilize in the future. These uncertainties may further induce the parties to seek 'safer' methods. This may mean that in specific instances, for example, the gains won by a union are less than they might have been, but equally, there may be other occasions when procedural routes achieve gains (or minimize losses) where outright conflict would have meant resounding defeat, with drastic implications not only immediately but also in the longer term.

While it is possible to outline in these terms a model of the general factors that determine the frontier of control, it is clearly essential to move on from there to explain the specific form that these factors take and hence the empirical variations in the frontier of control. However, despite the centrality of this question to a wide range of debates, relatively few attempts have been made to develop such theories in a systematic manner. A number of arguments relate to particular dimensions of the basic model. The following section will consider explanations relating to production systems, markets, institutionalization and the role of the state, before looking at the influence of the structure and strategies of employers and trade unions.

The Significance of Production Systems

One factor which has received a good deal of emphasis in many explanations of the frontier of control has been the nature of production systems and, in particular, technology. The details and conclusions of these arguments often differ significantly. However, one of the clearest examples of such an evolutionary model – which draws strongly upon the somewhat more confusing arguments of writers such as Mallet – is that of Posner (1970). He identifies three broad stages of technological development in capitalist societies. The first of these is craft-based systems of mass production under which craft unions, building upon the autonomy of the craftsman, exert a significant degree of control over both the job and the labour market, and may also aspire to an extension of autonomy through the removal of the capitalist. The second phase of technological development – mass production – removes or significantly weakens the role of the crafts. An associated loss of intrinsic job interest and discretion shifts worker interests in an economistic direction. This requires a more bureaucratic structure of trade unions which become national in character, and political involvement of a social democratic, rather than radical, nature in order to protect workers from the vicissitudes of the market. The range and depth of union control therefore declines. However, this trend is reversed with the introduction of automated production systems. Under these conditions the knowledge and autonomy of the worker increases and he becomes concerned with the uses to which his skills are put. The result is the development of a new form of unionism which aspires once more to an extension of the range of control and is committed to a socialist transformation of society.

This type of argument has much to recommend it in terms of its neatness. Unfortunately, there are many reasons for doubting its credibility. One major problem is that it pays scant attention to the partially independent role of trade unions, employers and the state. Even if workers do generate new sets of demands due to new types of work experience, these are likely to be mediated by unions whose characteristics derive from an earlier phase of production. Variations in the structure of trade unionism between different countries are marked and can in part be explained by the time at which industrialization occurred and, relatedly, the extent to which craft unionism had become firmly established. As Turner (1962: 14) notes, 'the character of organisations is very much a product of their ancestry and the circumstances of their early growth' (see also Fox (1985) and Kahn-Freund (1979) on the importance of history and heritage in explaining the pattern of control sought by British trade unions). If technology were crucial, one would expect similar patterns of control in different countries where identical technologies were employed – but cross-cultural research by Gallie (1978), Batstone (1978) and Lash (1984) casts doubt upon this contention. Similarly, it would be very difficult to explain the variation in the scope of bargaining across countries noted above in terms of the influence of technology.

There are very serious difficulties in classifying technology and in establishing the relationship between the dominant technology in an establishment and the nature of the typical worker-machine interface (see e.g. Woodward, 1965, 1970; Meissner, 1969; Davis and Taylor, 1972; Nichols and Beynon, 1977; Batstone et al., 1987), and this provides a further reason for treating arguments about the centrality of technology with caution. A number of surveys in recent years in Britain have included questions which endeavour to categorize technology in a variety of ways. Batstone and Gourlay (1986) used the traditional classification of unit, batch, mass and continuous process production as well as seeking to classify new technology where it had been introduced; the 1980 Workplace

Industrial Relations Survey investigated the degree of integration of the production process (Daniel and Millward, 1983; 230), while the 1984 WIRS provided data on the nature of new technology and the use of machines of varying degrees of sophistication and automation (Daniel, 1987). However, attempts to explain the range of bargaining in terms of the various measures of technology contained in these surveys meet with little success. Indeed, the survey data suggest that rather than technology shaping the role of the union, the characteristics of the industrial system, including union organization, have significant effect upon the way in which new technology impinges upon workers (Batstone and Gourlay, 1986; Batstone et al., 1987).

Despite the weaknesses of these more ambitious theories, one can nevertheless expect the nature of the production system to have some impact upon the frontier of control. In particular, it has been widely argued that it influences the power resources of workers (see Batstone et al., 1978: 27–32 for a discussion of relevant arguments). It affects the possession of skills which necessarily impose limits upon the extent to which methods and performance can be minutely determined by the employer. Skill is often associated with a second widely noted factor – occupancy of a crucial position in the overall production system (Sayles, 1958). A further factor of importance is the speed or immediacy with which sanctions by key workers impinge upon the broader production system. For example, integrated production systems are generally seen to be more susceptible to disruption than more fragmented ones where buffer stocks can be employed.

It is clear, then, that features of the production system can affect the power resources of individual workers. However, the power resources of a union depend not only upon the position of individual workers within the production process, but also on the ability of the union to mobilize and co-ordinate those individual resources.

The Role of Markets

The main significance of market forces is generally seen to lie in their effects upon the distribution of power resources between the parties, although such effects may be amplified by associated changes in goals and strategy. Two types of market force are relevant – one relating to the product market (or its equivalent in political terms), and the other to the labour market. The two are of course closely interrelated. The traditional argument is markedly simple: the power of workers increases when product and hence labour demand is high so that the range of collective control might be expected to increase. Conversely, when product and labour demand fall, then the employer has less need of production and can find alternative labour more easily, so that worker sanctions are likely to have less influence. Accordingly the range of union control might be expected to decline.

However, market forces may also be expected to have additional effects. Classically, for example, it has been argued that union membership is likely to decline in slack labour markets since the gains relative to the costs of membership decline. A vicious cycle of declining control and membership may therefore result. Further, as union influence declines, expectations may change to accommodate to the new realities of the balance of power and this may lead to a moderation of goals. In this sense, market forces might be seen to affect all three aspects of the frontier of control.

There are, however, a number of potential weaknesses to this argument. First, while the employer may not require the normal level of production in a period of slack demand, he might be expected – with certain exceptions – to be keen to ensure that he can meet market demand or attempt to increase market share. The implication of this is that he will want to ensure a continuation of supplies, and hence will be concerned not to induce the union to impose sanctions. At the same time, of course, the union might be expected to become increasingly concerned with the survival of the company (no matter what its particular preferences as between wages and employment) and so may adopt a more co-operative stance. While, therefore, the degree of oppositional union control may decrease, it is far from evident that the pattern of control will be fundamentally altered.

This assumes that the employer, even in a period of mass unemployment, will not seek to overcome any worker resistance by resort to alternative labour or labour forms. A good deal has been made recently of claims that many employers are resorting to a variety of forms of peripheral labour and this would seem to cast doubt upon the earlier argument (Rubery et al., 1984). But the best available data suggest that such trends have been greatly exaggerated, at least as far as larger establishments are concerned. Hence, for example, comparison of the 1980 and 1984 Workplace Industrial Relations Surveys (Millward and Stevens, 1986: 209–12) suggests that the proportion of establishments (with more than twenty-five employees) using temporary, freelance, outworking and short-term contract labour actually fell between the two periods (although again changes in question format call for caution in making comparisons and the use of peripheral labour through increased subcontracting was not investigated). More generally, there are serious doubts as to how far large employers in particular could economically make frequent or widespread resort to alternative labour: there would be severe problems in finding adequate numbers with the skills and experience required, and in addition the transaction costs involved in hiring and firing, training and familiarization would often be extremely high (Williamson, 1975; Batstone and Gourlay, 1986: 6–7). A number of studies have pointed to the growing importance of plant-specific skills that can be acquired only through substantial experience with the firm concerned (Doeringer and Piore, 1971; Berger and Piore, 1980). While the trend may have been exaggerated, it is likely to have limited the substitutability of labour even in slack labour market conditions.

We noted earlier that employers and unions often have an incentive to stabilize their relationships and hence the broad pattern of control. This derives from the adoption of a long-term perspective associated with iterative games. This argument suggests that, unless employers believe that by 'punching their weight' in slack markets they can remove the union once and for all or that the reduced level of demand and availability of alternative labour are permanent, they have an interest in not seeking dramatically to reduce the degree of union control. This would be so since otherwise they might then reasonably expect the unions to maximize their advantage if and when market forces turn in their favour (the 'tit for tat' argument in game theory). It is not surprising, therefore, to find that employer strategy in the USA has recently taken two main forms: 'union-busting' in weakly organized sectors and a somewhat closer, more integrative approach where union organization is strong (Kochan et al., 1986). In Britain attempts to remove trade unions have been remarkably few.

The impact of labour market conditions on trade-union power is clearly an issue of major relevance given the sharp rise in unemployment in Britain in the early 1980s. It is clear that trade-union membership has indeed been substantially affected. In their analysis of changes in union representation between 1980 and 1984, Millward and Stevens (1986: 52) report that 'If stability characterised the public sector, change was more characteristic of the private sector. In private manufacturing there was a quite striking decline in the proportion of workplaces with trade union members, particularly manual trade union members for whom the proportion declined from 76 to 66 per cent'. However, when they came to analyse the causes of this decline, they found that their panel data suggested that there was little sign among firms that had survived throughout the period of a decline in union presence. This strongly suggested that the major cause of the fall in the proportion of unionized firms was the disproportionate closure of larger manufacturing firms that had been particularly likely to be unionized.

Moreover, workplace organization would appear to have survived the difficult labour market conditions of the early 1980s surprisingly well. Overall, between 1980 and 1984, the number of workplace representatives is estimated by Millward and Stevens (1986: 84–8) to have risen from about 317,000 to around 335,000, with particularly marked rises in the public sector and private services offsetting a decline in manufacturing. Even among manual workers, there appears to have been an increase in the number of shop stewards relative to the number of workers they represent (Batstone and Gourlay, 1986: 77, 137; Millward and Stevens, 1986: 85, 88.) Similarly, formal industrial relations procedures with regard to issues such as discipline and dismissal, the handling of disputes over pay and conditions of employment and the resolution of individual grievances would appear to have become even more widespread in British industry in the early 1980s (Millward and Stevens, 1986: 169–76).

The evidence about the effective levels of influence exercised by unions is rather more difficult to interpret. Overall, between 1980 and 1984, there was an increase in the proportion of workplaces where rates of pay were determined by collective bargaining. This was largely attributable, however, to the growth of the proportion of workplaces in the public services sector. Within private manufacturing industry, the coverage of pay bargaining declined in the early 1980s and this decline could not be accounted for simply by the decline of large establishments. Whereas in 1980 the most recent pay increase had been determined by collective bargaining in 65 per cent of establishments in private manufacturing, by 1984 the proportion had fallen to 55 per cent (Millward and Stevens, 1986: 225–7).

In addition, though the data must be treated with some caution because of changes in question format, there would appear to have been a significant decline in the joint regulation of non-pay issues over the same period (see table 8.1 above; Millward and Stevens, 1986: 249–53). This is the clearest evidence that the unfavourable labour market conditions of the early 1980s had a definite effect in weakening union controls. There was, however, considerable variation between different sectors of the economy. A survey of a number of industries in 1984 by Batstone and Gourlay (1986: 139) showed that union controls over work practices and effort levels were more likely to have increased than decreased between 1979 and 1984 in sectors such as finance and the civil service, whereas in British Telecom and in engineering the reverse was the case. Similarly, the Workplace Industrial Relations Surveys suggest that while there was a very marked decline in the joint regulation of non-pay issues in private services and manufacturing, the nationalized industries had been relatively protected (Millward and Stevens, 1986: 248–51).

More generally, one of the more striking historical trends has been the way in which the frontier of control appears to have become less susceptible to market forces. This is suggested – and one can put it no more strongly than that – by a variety of data. For example, while union density fell by less than a fifth between 1979 and 1984, it fell by approximately a third in the first half of the 1920s.[3] In the nineteenth century, though reliable data are obviously not available and differences in social and political conditions and in legal provisions must also be taken into account, the evidence suggests that the effects of the business cycle on trade unions were far more severe. In the earlier part of the century, the combined impact of economic depression and employer opposition appears to have been capable of extensively eliminating union organization. The development of trade unionism on a more organizationally and financially secure basis from the mid-century onwards, mainly but not exclusively among craft workers, helped ensure that those unions which the Webbs (1911: 335) termed the backbone of the movement could survive subsequent economic down-turns organizationally intact if severely weakened. This was not true of more recently established and more precariously positioned unions which organized workers without the market advantages offered by the possession of a skill. These unions disappeared in very large numbers during the depression of the latter half of the 1870s (Webb and Webb, 1911: 334–9). There was no comparable decimation of trade-union organization in the early 1980s.

A second indicator concerns the presence of workplace representatives. Though there is a lack of systematic evidence, it appears that with high

---

3 The fall in trade-union density for the first half of the 1920s has been estimated on the basis of data from Bain and Price (1980: 37). The fall in density between 1979 and 1984 has been estimated on the basis of trade-union membership figures from the Employment Gazette (Feb., 1987: 84–6) and the Annual Reports of the Certification Officer for 1979 and 1986 and figures for national employment and unemployment from the Central Statistics Office's Economic Trends (Annual Supplement 1986 Edition: 99). The figure for the fall in density between 1979 and 1984 is not based on a full analysis of density and should be taken as an approximate estimate.

unemployment in the inter-war period, shop steward organization was seriously, if variably, weakened – and in some cases eliminated – in sectors where it had been previously well established (Clegg, 1985: 310–11, 437–41; Hyman, 1987: 132–9). As we have seen, this has not occurred in the 1980s, though there have been significant shifts in shop steward distribution. Thirdly, though bargaining range has declined since the late 1970s, it would still appear to have been higher in 1984 than it was in the late 1960s and early 1970s, despite the very large increase in unemployment in the intervening period.

One factor which might help to explain this declining susceptibility to market forces is the development of the welfare state, so that the personal costs of unemployment are less now than they were in the past. According to such arguments, the unemployed are less likely than they were to be prepared to undercut any union monopoly. But two factors give reason to doubt the importance of this argument – first, there is not a neat relationship of the kind which might be expected between the timing and scale of public support for the unemployed and the admittedly crude indicators of union influence. Secondly, the extent to which the availability of benefit payments explain unemployment appears to be relatively small (Atkinson et al., 1984; Micklewright, 1985; Narendranathan et al., 1985).

Three types of factor are probably of significance in any long-term reduction in union susceptibility to adverse market conditions. The first is the development of a long-term perspective on the part of both unions and employers associated with the institutionalization of a degree of union influence. The second is the extent to which employers have developed patterns of labour regulation in which the union figures significantly, thereby making dramatic changes in employer–union relations uncertain and potentially costly. The third concerns the changing distribution of union influence: of particular significance here is the fact that union membership is becoming more concentrated in areas where market forces have, at least to date, been relatively less challenging to union control, notably the public sector and non-manual services.

In sum, it appears to be the case that a slack labour market weakens union control. But the arguments advanced in support of this view frequently underestimate the constraints which employers face in seeking to exploit short-term market advantage and the way in which unions may be able to moderate the impact of market forces. In addition, the long-term perspective implicit in institutionalization and the way in which union presence becomes built into forms of labour regulation appear to have reduced – although certainly not eradicated – the susceptibility of the frontier of control to market forces.

Institutionalization and the Role of the State

A third type of factor which has received considerable emphasis in attempts to explain the frontier of control is institutionalization. The origins of institutionalization have already been touched upon. In this section, therefore, attention is turned to the broader effects of the development of institutional arrangements. In particular, two broad sorts of argument require consideration. The first of these concerns the way in which the establishment of procedures affects the goals of actors. The second concerns the effects of different forms of institutional arrangement.

It is often argued that the establishment of formal industrial relations procedures leads to a moderation of union demands and an isolation of industrial relations from the political sphere. At the extreme, for example, it is sometimes claimed that trade unions under these conditions focus upon economistic demands which are deemed to be more capable of compromise and effectively drop any demands for a significant extension of control. It has already been pointed out that a moderation of demands might come about for reasons other than a change in goals, such as a rational estimate of the chances of success of different demands. But there are also a number of other considerations which are worthy of note in this context. In the first place, such an argument is mistaken, not only in assuming that compromise is inherently easier on financial than on control issues, but also because it underplays the control implications which may be associated with payment systems.

It is also worthy of note that the presumed economism associated with institutionalization pays scant attention to the non-pay controls which trade unions continue to enjoy. Indeed, far from there being an inverse relationship between the degree of institutionalization and the range of collective influence, there is a positive relationship. Hence, for example, the IDE study (1981a: 168–72) concluded that the key factor explaining the degree of effective influence which workers exerted collectively at the workplace was the extent to which there were formal participative arrangements (IDE, 1981a: 168–72). A similar picture is suggested by survey data in Britain; here also the range of bargaining tends to be greater the higher the degree of formalization. Furthermore, it would appear that, far from formal agreements constraining bargaining, they tend to provide a basis for supplementary bargaining (Batstone, 1984; Batstone and Gourlay, 1986).

One of the major arguments that tends to be advanced as to why institutionalization should weaken workers' power is that through such procedures union leaders become dominated by institutional as against member interests. There is certainly this possibility. But two points need to be remembered. First, there is a risk of exaggerating the extent to which institutional and member interests conflict. If formal union organization were not preserved, it is open to question how far unions, depending solely upon mass mobilization, would be able to maintain the degree of influence and control which they now exercise. Secondly, if trade unions are encapsulated by a liberal rhetoric through institutionalization, it seems reasonable to expect that a similar process occurs amongst employers. In other words, if one espouses this type of argument, there is a need to take into account not only any shift in priorities on the part of unions, but also shifts in the attitudes of employers.

However, the precise nature of institutional arrangements may significantly affect priorities and strategies and hence the pattern of union influence through the way in which it shifts the distribution of power within unions and employers. Two somewhat conflicting views can be identified. Cross-national comparative research stresses the way in which centralized bargaining facilitates a class rather than a sectional approach and leads to a broader range of union control. On the other hand, in the British debate, it is often argued that more centralized bargaining may weaken union control since bargaining tends to be more isolated from the shopfloor and since the views of workers in more militant plants may be overruled by those in more moderate ones.

There is probably some truth in the contention that centralization weakens direct job controls and workplace militancy. But two points need to be noted. First, in strongly organized plants the union is likely to achieve some degree of control no matter what the formal level of bargaining. Indeed, the available evidence suggests such a pattern both in Britain and in other countries – for example, the degree of control exerted by works councils in West Germany varies considerably and frequently goes beyond that indicated by the relevant legislation (Streeck, 1984: 25, 35). Often this will occur because a more centralized formal bargaining pattern facilitates multi-level bargaining, although this will also depend upon how tightly the central agreements are made (Clegg, 1976: 90–1). Secondly, under more decentralized arrangements, it may be true that some workplace unions achieve a very significant degree of control, but there will be many others where the degree of control is very marginal.

A central question arises, however, of how we are to explain variations in the level at which bargaining occurs. Clegg (1976: 10) has argued that this is mainly to be explained by the strategies of employers and the state. Others have placed much greater emphasis upon the role that trade unions themselves can play in determining the bargaining level (e.g. Korpi, 1983). It seems probable that the relative importance of these factors has differed between societies and has depended upon the particular historical conditions under which the pattern of collective bargaining became established.

Certainly, however, the role of the state has been significant in many countries, not only in shaping the pattern of collective bargaining in terms of levels and units, but also in terms of the scope of union influence. As Clegg (1976: 112) has argued, 'It is easier for the law to mould collective bargaining when it is immature and unformed than when it has grown up and taken shape'. He notes, moreover, that while the law may have an important impact, its precise significance may not be foreseen by its architects. The role of the state is not confined to legislation; it may also play a major role in creating expectations about legitimate worker influence more directly through its powers as an employer. Different legal traditions are of considerable significance; for example, they can impose informal pressures upon employers to recognize and deal with trade unions, as was the case in Britain from the late nineteenth century onwards (Fox, 1985).

The actual role which the state plays in affecting the scope of union influence is shaped by many factors, including its political complexion, the extent to which unions and employers seek to employ political means and its own internal structure. What is striking, however, is that the scope of collective bargaining tends to be greater where social-democratic parties have been in power for a considerable period of time. This reflects not only the legislative activities of the state, but also the tendency for corporatist arrangements, which significantly extend the scope of union influence, to be more common in such countries. This highlights the way in which the labour movement can seek to achieve its goals both politically and through more conventional forms of collective bargaining. The important thing to note is that political influence may be used not only to shape economic and social policy, but also to shift the balance of power more directly within the workplace through legislation.

In conclusion, much of the discussion of institutionalization has extended beyond a simple model and has focused upon the way in which institutional arrangements may shape the priorities of negotiators and shift the balance of power within the parties themselves. The latter may then lead to changes in the strategies pursued and to changes in the ease with which resources can be mobilized. In short, it is widely held that institutionalization affects all three of the key factors identified above as being important in explaining the pattern of union influence.

The Structure and Strategy of Employers

As has been already stressed, the primary goal of the employer is not the control of labour, but rather – in the case of the private employer at least – the achievement of profits. His interest in labour is therefore derivative and secondary. It follows that on many issues the employer will not mobilize his full resources since this may incur heavy costs in relation to his primary goal. However, it also follows from this argument that if a union poses a fundamental challenge to the employers' interests, then more resources will be mobilized by the employers. This is an important explanation of the limited range of bargaining: the differential mobilization of resources means that unions have a greater chance of achieving control in areas where employers' fundamental interests are not challenged. Often it will be the case that a more radical attempt to achieve control will mean that the union risks losing such control as it currently has.

The specific character of employer organization also has major implications for the influence exercised by trade unions. The extent to which employers act cohesively varies significantly. It is not the case that employers in Britain, for example, act as a cohesive unit and, indeed, there are strong free-rider incentives. Employer combination is, however, far more significant in many other countries. Overall, there is a striking pattern: the cohesiveness of employers' associations is closely associated with the pattern of trade-union organization and the level at which collective bargaining occurs. Given the tendency for the scope of bargaining to be greater the more centralized the pattern of industrial relations, employer unity is often associated with a greater range of influence among trade unions (although it should also be noted that the pattern of industrial relations tends to be more peaceful).

Even within societies where the key formal level of bargaining is above the plant or company, the internal organization of management is also significant in affecting the pattern of union control and its implications for management. While the available evidence is less than ideal, it would appear that the sophistication of management organization varies significantly between countries (Horovitz, 1980; Jamieson, 1980; Child and Kieser, 1979; Maitland, 1983). Two factors are of particular importance. First, where management is unable to plan and organize production efficiently, it becomes even more dependent upon worker co-operation than would normally be the case. As a result, the potential sanctions available to workers increase and hence, in terms of work organization, their control is likely to be deeper (although patchy, depending upon their position in the production process). This does not necessarily mean that the range of union influence increases; indeed to the extent that such control is associated with a fairly decentralized pattern of industrial relations it is often narrower – but it does mean that relations are likely to be more conflictual and harmful to the goals of the employer. Secondly, companies vary in their sophistication concerning labour relations and this is likely to influence their ability to maintain control of the shopfloor. This may be an important factor in Britain. Case study evidence suggests that British companies are not only less sophisticated in technical terms, but also in their labour relations policies. As the Donovan Commission noted, for example, industrial relations issues were often left in effect to lower levels of management and labour considerations rarely figured in strategic decision-making (Donovan, 1968; 25, 41–4). The consequence is that the pattern of union control in Britain may cover a narrower range, but it imposes more constraints upon employers (although this is not to say that poor productivity is primarily due to union controls).

The range of union influence varies significantly by type of employer. Most notably in Britain, the range of union influence is greatest in the public sector. This is still true even though Conservative governments of recent years have attempted to reduce the role of public sector unions. Analysis of the 1984 WIRS survey, for example, shows that the mean number of issues bargained over in the public sector was 3.1 for both manual and non-manual workers. The corresponding figures in the private sector were 2.4 for manual workers and 2.3 for non-manual workers. The reasons for this can be seen to lie in the fact that the state's main priority – political legitimacy – is often more susceptible to worker pressure, both directly through ballot box and indirectly through their ability to obstruct the provision of goods and services on which wider public support for the government depends. The range of bargaining also tends to be greater in multi- than in single-plant companies. This may well reflect a greater 'professionalization' of management in this type of company, Such managers are less likely to – and indeed are less able to – lay claim to the 'prerogatives of ownership' to which many owner-managers are deeply wedded.

However, what is perhaps most striking is the extent to which employers' willingness to accept union influence has changed over time. In the nineteenth century, for example, many employers were not prepared even to recognize unions, whereas now the range of control in many unionized companies is considerable. Why has this change come about?

Kerr et al. (1973: 158–60) point to six factors which encourage employers to deal with trade unions – social values stressing the freedom of the individual, individual worker pressure from more informed and educated workers, government pressure, union pressure, pressure from other managements and competitive pressure. In general terms it seems that employers adjust to permitting some role for unions in large part through the pressures imposed upon them – this derives both from workers directly and also indirectly through the state. However, an important factor may also be changes in the nature of employers themselves. One common argument has focused on a presumed divorce between ownership and control. The thrust of this thesis is that professional managers, rather than capitalists, have come increasingly to determine corporate policy. Such managers, it is argued, are less likely to be dominated by concern with the maximization of profits or with the rights of ownership and are more ready to accept a wider social responsibility. Such tendencies will be further encouraged by the fact that their own legitimacy cannot rest upon the direct rights of ownership. Claims such as competence and the mediation of competing interests have instead often been held to underlie managerial 'rights' and can be seen as more favourable to union influence.

In recent years, increasing doubt has been cast upon this presumed divorce between ownership and control and hence, at first sight, upon the importance of the rise of professional manager. But this still appears to be an important factor. The criticisms that have been developed of the general thesis have stressed important continuities in the links between ownership and control through the existence of interlocking networks and the preservation of important forms of 'ultimate' control. However, for the organization of labour relations in the firm, it is more immediate forms of control that are critical and changes in the relationship between private owners of capital and executive management appear to be of significance here. Relations with the unions within companies are handled by professional managers and many British boards concern themselves very little with industrial relations issues (Jacobs et al., 1978; Marsh, 1982). This suggests that the ideologies of professional managers may be of relevance to understanding management's readiness to accept a degree of union control.

This seems to have been a particularly important factor in the increased acceptance of union influence in the later 1960s and the 1970s. This period saw a variety of initiatives by employers and the state which were aimed at transforming the pattern of industrial relations. One of the most important of these – which within academic circles is generally associated with the Donovan Commission – aimed at shifting bargaining away from its sectional shopfloor pattern to a more coherent and systematic form at the level of the workplace. For this to occur it was stressed that management had to think more coherently about industrial relations,while shop stewards had to develop a form of organization which would permit them to act in a more co-ordinated manner. Such a structure of bargaining it was claimed, would permit the negotiation of necessary changes in working practices. The precise implications of such reforms for the degree of union control have been a matter of some disagreement. While many radicals argued that such reforms would eradicate union control, the proponents of reform argued the reverse. They stressed the way in which the pattern and orientation of union control would change and argued that unions would, in effect, trade off their detailed shopfloor control for an influence in more general and strategic issues.

The reform strategy was widely adopted in the late 1960s and early 1970s, with the formalization of industrial relations at the workplace and, in particular, the adoption of productivity bargaining. Workplace union organization spread into new sectors and companies and at the same time the sophistication of shop steward organization increased. However, while the Donovan Commission promoted the idea of reform from a liberal pluralist philosophy, its influence was in practice somewhat limited. More important, it seems, were broader changes within companies associated with the merger and takeover boom (Batstone, 1984: 68–9). The new, enlarged companies confronted general problems of management structure: in an attempt to overcome this, multi-divisional structures were widely adopted and there was an increase in the management division of labour. As part of this, there was a significant growth of personnel management, which was associated with a formalization of procedures and greater institutional support for trade unions within the workplace. A second set of factors encouraging these developments was government action; for example, the 1971 Industrial Relations Act, whose logic was quite different from that of the Donovan Commission, encouraged the further development of the personnel function as a means of protecting companies from the law. In addition, income policies – which often permitted above the norm pay increases if they were associated with increased productivity – encouraged workplace bargaining over productivity.

A second employer strategy developed from the mid-1970s – namely, the introduction of participative techniques (Beaumont and Deaton, 1981; Hawes and Smith, 1981; Brown, 1981; Daniel and Millward, 1983: 132–3). This development can be seen as reflecting in part the limited gains derived from workplace reform. While this had led to an expansion of the range of union control, it was far from clear that union control had changed – as had been hoped – to a more co-operative form. However, the new policies were also encouraged at the time by the political threat to introduce legislation permitting unions to place representatives on the board of directors. In fact, such possibilities rapidly fizzled out, given the lack of enthusiasm of many unions and shifts of influence within the Labour Party. Employer interest in participative techniques continued, however, albeit in a changed form as the political atmosphere shifted from one of a high degree of support for unionism to the reverse.

In the latter part of the 1970s, the primary participative initiative was in the area of union-based joint consultation. The range of issues over which consultation occurred was typically relatively wide, touching upon – if only rather superficially – issues relating to management strategy. This development was widely seen as threatening union control in two ways. First, it was argued that employers were shifting issues away from collective bargaining and into consultation, with the result that union views were merely taken into account by management rather than issues being, as with collective bargaining, subject to mutual agreement. Secondly, it was argued that the introduction of consultation would lead to a change of attitude on the part of shop stewards such that, even where they had some degree of formal control, they would in practice fail to challenge management. There is little support for the first argument: analysis of the 1984 WIRS data shows that the wider the range of issues which are discussed, or on which information is provided, in joint consultative committees, the wider tends to be the range of bargaining.

Other forms of participation or involvement have also been fairly widely adopted since the late 1970s (Batstone and Gourlay, 1986: 117-20; Millward and Stevens, 1986: 163-7). Initially, a significant minority of companies introduced semi-autonomous work groups and similar schemes of job enrichment or enlargement. More recently, greater stress has been placed upon various forms of communication system, such as briefing groups and quality circles. Again, it has been argued that such individualistic strategies will tend to reduce the degree of union control, first by bypassing the channels of collective bargaining and, secondly, by affecting the attitudes and perspectives of union members. Again, however, analysis of the available survey evidence provides little support for these views.

A further corporate strategy which, it is believed, might similarly weaken union control or at least alter the ways in which it is exercised relates to a variety of schemes of financial reward which aim to foster identification between the worker and the company. These include profit-sharing and shareholding schemes and a variety of value-added bonuses. Again, the available evidence suggests that, at least to date, these have had little impact upon the range of bargaining. It may, moreover, not be too implausible to suggest that such schemes could serve to expand the range of union influence. This might happen in two ways. First, if such schemes are negotiated, then it is likely that unions will demand to have the right to inspect accounting data in order to be able to ensure, for example, that bonuses are valid. Secondly, to the extent that such schemes mean that management performance can significantly and directly affect workers' earnings, it might be expected that unions would become increasingly concerned about broader aspects of corporate policy. There is no a priori reason to believe that such union involvement will necessarily be of a more co-operative nature – this will depend, among other things, upon management competence.

In sum, the available evidence provides little support for many recent arguments concerning the effects of participative techniques upon the nature and extent of union control. The interesting question is clearly why these techniques appear to have had such limited impact to date. One possible explanation is that the implications of involvement strategies have not fed through to the more general structure of management. These techniques are frequently tacked on to existing forms of labour administration, key aspects of which may be quite contradictory to the principles informing involvement strategies. A second explanation relates to a more general weakness of British management. If management is to operate effectively, it is necessary for it to have an organization structure which permits the representation and integration of various specialisms and areas of activity (Chandler and Daems, 1980). A characteristic of British management has been the failure to integrate different functions and an overemphasis on issues of finance; the result is that production issues and labour relations receive insufficient attention (Williams et al., 1981; Fidler, 1981). As a consequence, work organization is often poorly planned. Despite the existence of a personnel function, work organization issues are left to lower levels of management with different sets of priorities from those of higher management.

Trade Union Structure and Strategy

Three broad sets of factors relating to union organization can be seen as affecting the extent of union influence. These are the degrees of mobilization, scope and sophistication respectively.

Taking first the issue of mobilization, it is clearly necessary that membership density should be relatively high if the union is to have any significant degree of influence. Hence, for example, if we take various European countries, we find that at workplace level the basic unit of collective representation tends to be union-based where density is high but not – at least formally – where union density is lower (see, for example, the country studies in IDE, 1981b). However, density is not the only factor in mobilization; the level of commitment and involvement is also of central importance. It has generally been the case that particular types of worker have been more union-oriented than others. Traditionally, skilled workers have been more union-oriented than non-skilled; men have also been seen traditionally as more active than women – although these differences appear to be declining (Bain and Elsheikh, 1979; Elsheikh and Bain, 1983; Bain and Elias, 1985). Full-time workers have been more active than part-timers. The analysis of survey evidence on the range of bargaining indicates that the proportion of part-time workers is of particular importance in explaining variations in bargaining range. The higher the proportion of part-time workers, the lower the range of bargaining even when allowance is made for other characteristics of union organization. In addition, there are marked regional and industrial variations in the mobilization of workers. Historical and community factors appear to be of considerable significance in accounting for this; for example, the existence of occupational communities has traditionally been seen to strengthen union orientation.

The scope of a trade union refers to the range of workers it has in membership, although, where there is a multiplicity of unions, various forms of co-operation between them can have the effect of making them act as if they were a more all-encompassing organization. At the most general level, it is perhaps useful to refer to Olson's (1982:

17–24) theory of interest groups: he argues that the broader the scope of a union's membership, the broader the perspective which the union will adopt. While this relationship would appear to be generally plausible, two points should be noted. First, the scope of a union may in part shape its strategy, but equally union scope will tend to reflect the strategy of its activists. For example, a union devoted to the protection and promotion of the interests of a craft group is likely to restrict membership to workers engaged in the relevant craft. The second point concerns Olson's more general theories; he suggests that all-encompassing organizations will tend to be more oriented to the common interest so that, for example, they will be less obstructive to measures aimed at increasing economic growth. This is because the broader the scope of a union, the larger the area of overlap between its members and the society at large: hence the union will receive not only the gains from its actions but can also expect to incur the general costs of its actions. By contrast, a more sectional organization may receive all of the gains, but few of the costs.

However, it does not follow that an all-encompassing union will necessarily be more co-operative in its stance towards management; this will depend, among other things, on the extent to which it considers that management actions are in its interest. It is possible, therefore, that all-encompassing organizations may alternatively be the most co-operative towards the employer or the most strongly opposed. However, the crucial factor is that there is likely to be a relationship between the range of union influence and the scope of the trade union. It does not follow from this that the depth of union influence will follow the same pattern. For example, craft unions – typically representing a relatively small proportion of a workforce and often with a membership spread across a range of industries – may demonstrate little concern with the general business strategies of employers but will seek to maintain a very high degree of control over immediate work issues such as demarcation, training and manning levels.

Finally, as with management, organizational sophistication is also of significance. For a union to act in a manner consistent with its scope, it requires a particular organizational form. For example, an all-encompassing organization will in reality act as a series of sectional groupings unless it has some effective means of overall co-ordination. It requires – in addition to a high level of mobilization – an organizational structure which permits the representation of sectional interests and their co-ordination, and also the resources to plan strategy at this co-ordinated level. Hence, for example, for a shop steward organization to act effectively it needs an adequate distribution of shop steward constituencies and a structure which permits their co-ordination – shop steward committees, senior shop stewards and, where the membership is large, full-time stewards. Similar models can be developed at other levels of union organization; for example, if a union confederation is to act as an effective voice for the union movement, it not only needs to have the bulk of unions affiliated to it, but it also requires the right and the resources to co-ordinate action. Hence, the British TUC has a structure which imposes serious limits upon its ability to act as the representative of the union movement – it has very limited resources and few powers to impose sanctions or to control the actions of member unions. This is in marked contrast, for example, to the Swedish trade-union confederation, LO.

Co-ordination need not necessarily mean oligarchy, although in some cases it may do so. What the above argument suggests, however, is that what is often interpreted as oligarchy or the expression of the institutional and self-interests of a powerful union leadership may in fact reflect other considerations. That is, such structures – oligarchical or not – may permit coherent policy formulation which takes into fuller account the interests of the membership as a whole and facilitates a more critical assessment of the union's relative power and the formulation of the most cost-effective strategies.

Certainly, there is now considerable evidence to support the importance of the factors of scope and sophistication. Indeed, if we compare the overall range or scope of collective bargaining at national level between countries, a strikingly simple pattern emerges: namely, the broader the scope and the greater the sophistication of union movements, the greater the scope of bargaining. Clearly, this raises further major explanatory problems of why trade-union movements should take particular forms in different countries. Different explanations lay stress on historical factors, union characteristics or the strategies of employers and the state. However, all that is important for our present purposes is that there is a close relationship between the characteristics of trade unions, employers associations and the level of bargaining.

Research in Britain has also revealed the importance of union sophistication at workplace level for patterns of bargaining. For example, Batstone and Gourlay (1986) examined trade-union organization in a number of industries and developed an index of workplace sophistication that took account of union density, the number of shop stewards, the presence of senior and full-time stewards, the frequency of steward meetings and the extent of inter-union meetings. This revealed significant differences between sectors in the degree of union sophistication. More sophisticated workplace organizations tended to have closer links with the external union and were more centralized, but there was no evidence that this implied a loss of membership influence. What was clear was that the level of sophistication had an important influence on the level of trade union influence. In the private sector, it was the key factor that affected the range of bargaining. In the public sector where negotiations were centralized above the level of the workplace, the sophistication of workplace organization did not affect the range of issues bargained over but it did influence the extent to which these issues were bargained over at establishments or shopfloor level (Batstone and Gourlay, 1986: 90–105, 134–5).

More detailed case study evidence also supports this contention. For example, Batstone et al. (1987) showed in some detail the relationship between the sophistication of shop steward organization and the range of union control, both in general terms and in relation to the introduction of new technology. A further case study looked at the importance of shop steward organization from a more processual perspective (Batstone et al., 1977). These case studies emphasized that there was an important interaction between steward sophistication, membership consciousness and the degree of union control. While membership consciousness may be a critical factor in the development of steward sophistication and both may be important for the degree of union control achieved, the case study evidence suggests that it is equally true that a significant degree of union control is important in maintaining membership consciousness – for it means that members 'think union' whenever they confront problems in the workplace and are aware in day-to-day terms of the role which the unions plays.

Conclusions

Early in his book, Goodrich (1920: 18) notes as follows: 'Nor is control so simple and definite a thing. The word is a slogan and a convenient general term. But in reference to the facts of industry it breaks up into a bewildering variety of rights and claims.' Almost seventy years later, this cautionary note remains valid. Not only is the frontier of control in industry more fluid and variable than other more fixed 'frontiers' but, as noted at the beginning of this chapter, what is seen by some as an advanced frontier may appear to others to be a decidedly modest one. While empirical research must be our main source of guidance in attempting to assess the nature and extent of worker control, it will not, for this reason, eliminate important areas of disagreement about what is, and will remain, one of the central questions in the study of industrial relations. The aim of this chapter has been consequently to explore some of the wider theoretical issues that necessarily arise when control and its frontier are investigated. This involved primarily the consideration of both general (power relations) and specific (production systems, markets, institutionalization and the role of the state) factors which, together with the structures and strategies of the parties, have been widely held to be critical for the shaping of the frontier of control.

References

Atkinson, A.B., Gomulka, J., Micklewright, J. and Rau, N. 1984. 'Unemployment Benefit, Duration and Incentives in Britain: How Robust is the Evidence?' *Journal of Public Economics*, 23 (February/March), 3–26.

Bain, G.S. and Elsheikh, F. 1979. 'An Inter-Industry Analysis of Unionisation in Britain'. *Britain Journal of Industrial Relations*, 17 9 (July), 137–57.

—— and Price, R. 1980. *Profiles of Union Growth: A Comparative Statistical Analysis of Eight Countries*. Oxford: Basil Blackwell.

—— and Elias, P. 1985. 'Trade Union Membership in Great Britain: An Individual-Level Analysis'. *British Journal of Industrial Relations*, 23 (March), 71–92.

Batstone, E. 1978. *Arm's Length Bargaining: Workplace Industrial Relations in France*. Mimeo.

—— 1984. *Working Order: Workplace Industrial Relations over Two Decades*. Oxford: Basil Blackwell.

—— Boraston, I. and Frenkel, S. 1977. *Shop Stewards in Action: The Organization of Workplace Conflict and Accommodation*. Oxford: Basil Blackwell.

—— Boraston, I and Frenkel, S. 1978. *The Social Organization of Strikes*. Oxford: Basil Blackwell.

—— and Gourlay, S. 1986. *Unions, Unemployment and Innovation*. Oxford: Basil Blackwell.

—— Gourlay, S., Levie, H. and Moore, R. 1987. *New Technology and the Process of Labour Regulation*. Oxford: Oxford University Press.

Beaumont, P. and Deaton, D. 1981. 'The Extent and Determinants of Joint Consultative Arrangements in Britain'. *Journal of Management Studies*, 18 (January), 49-71.

Berger, S. and Piore. M.J. 1980. *Dualism and Discontinuity in Industrial Societies*. Cambridge: Cambridge University Press.

Bowman, J. 1982. 'The Logic of Capitalist Collective Action'. *Social Science Information*, 21 (August/October), 571–604.

—— 1985. 'The Politics of the Market: Economic Competition and the Organization of Capitalists'. *Political Power and Social Theory*, 5, 35–88.

Brown, W.A. (ed.) 1981. *The Changing Contours of British Industrial Relations*. Oxford: Basil Blackwell.

Cameron, D.R. 1984. 'Social Democracy, Corporatism, Labour Quiescence and the Representation of Economic Interest in Advanced Capitalist Societies'. *Order and Conflict in Contemporary Capitalism: Studies in the Political Economy of Western European Nations*. Ed. Goldthorpe, J.H. Oxford: Clarendon Press.

Central Statistics Office. 1986. *Economic Trends: Annual Supplement*. London: HMSO.

—— 1987. *Economic Trends: Annual Supplement*. London: HMSO.

Certification Office for Trade Unions and Employers Associations. *Annual Report for 1979*.

—— *Annual Report for 1986*.

Chandler, A.D. and Daems, H. (eds) 1980. *Managerial Hierarchies: Comparative Perspectives on the Rise of the Modern Industrial Enterprise*. Cambridge, Mass.: Harvard University Press.

Child, J. and Keiser, A. 1979. 'Organization and Managerial Roles in British and West German Companies'. *Organizations Alike and Unlike: International and Inter-Institutional Perspectives on the Sociology of Organisations*. Eds. Lammers, C.J. and Hickson, D.J. London: Routledge & Kegan Paul.

Clegg, H.A. 1976. *Trade Unionism under Collective Bargaining: A Theory Based on Comparisons of Six Countries*. Oxford: Basil Blackwell.

—— 1985. *A History of British Trade Unions Since 1889: Volume II 1911–1933*. Oxford: Clarendon Press.

Crouch, C. 1979. 'The State, Capital and Liberal Democracy'. *State and Economy in Contemporary Capitalism*. Ed. Crouch, C. London: Croom Helm.

—— 1982. *Trade Unions: The Logic of Collective Action*. London: Fontana.

Daniel, W.W. 1987. *Workplace Industrial Relations and Technical Change*. London: Frances Pinter.

—— and Millward, N. 1983. *Workplace Industrial Relations in Britain*. London: Heinemann.

Davis, L.E. and Taylor, J.C. (eds) 1972. *Design of Jobs*. Harmondsworth: Penguin.

Department of Employment. 1987. 'Trade Union Membership in 1985'. *Employment Gazette*, 95 (February), 84–6.

Doeringer, P.B. and Piore, M.J. 1971. *Internal Labour Markets and Manpower Analysis*. Lexington, Mass: D.C. Heath.

Donovan. 1968. Royal Commission on Trade Unions and Employers' Associations 1965–1968. *Report*. Cmnd 3623. London: HMSO.

Elsheikh, F. and Bain, G.S. 1983. 'Unionisation in Britain: An Inter-Establishment Analysis Based on Survey Data'. *British Journal of Industrial Relations*, 18 (July) 169–78.

Fidler, J. 1981. *The British Business Elite*. London: Routledge & Kegan Paul.

Fox, A. 1973. 'Industrial Relations: A Social Critique of Pluralist Ideology'. *Man and Organisation*. Ed. Child, J. London: Allen & Unwin.

—— 1985. *History and Heritage: The Social Origins of the British Industrial Relations System*. London: Allen & Unwin.

Gallie, D. 1978 *In Search of the New Working Class*. Cambridge: Cambridge University Press.

Goodrich, C. 1920 (reprinted 1975). *The Frontier of Control: A Study in British Workshop Politics*. London: G. Bell.

Hawes, W. and Smith, D. 1981. 'Employee Involvement outside Manufacturing'. *Employment Gazette*, 89 (June), 265–71.

Hayek, F.A. 1980. *Unemployment and the Unions 1980s: The Distortion of Relative Wages by Monopoly in the Labour Market*. London: Institute of Economic Affairs.

Hyman, R. 1978. 'Pluralism, Procedural Consensus and Collective Bargaining'. *British Journal of Industrial Relations*, 16 (March), 16–40.

—— 1987. 'Rank-and-File Movements and Workplace Organisation, 1914–1939'. *A History of British Industrial Relations: Volume II 1914–1939*. Ed. Wrigley, C.J. Brighton: Harvester Press.

Horovitz, J.H. 1980. *Top Management Control in Europe*. London: Macmillan.

Industrial Democracy in Europe (IDE) International Research Group. 1981a. *Industrial Democracy in Europe*. Oxford: Clarendon Press.

—— 1981b. *European Industrial Relations*. Oxford: Clarendon Press.

Jacobs, E., Orwell, S., Paterson, P. and Weltz, F. 1978. *The Approach to Industrial Change*. London: Anglo-German Foundation for the Study of Industrial Society.

Jamieson, I. 1980. *Capitalism and Culture: A Comparative Analysis of British and American Manufacturing Organisations*. Farnborough: Gower.

Kahn-Freund, O. 1979. *Labour Relations: Heritage and Adjustment.* Oxford: Oxford University Press.

Kerr, C., Dunlop, J.T., Harbison, F.H. and Myers, C.A. 1973. *Industrialism and Industrial Man.* Harmondsworth: Penguin.

Kochan, T.A., Katz, H.C and McKersie, R.B. 1986. *The Transformation of American Industrial Relations.* New York: Basic Books.

Korpi, W. 1978. *The Working Class in Welfare Capitalism: Work, Unions and Politics in Sweden.* London: Routledge & Kegan Paul.

—— 1983. *The Democratic Class Struggle.* London: Routledge & Kegan Paul.

—— 1986. *Power Resources Approach versus Action and Conflict: On Causal and Intentional Explanation in the Study of Power.* Stockholm: Swedish Institute for Social Research.

Lange, P. 1984. 'Unions, Workers and Wage Regulation: The Rational Bases of Wage consent'. *Order and Conflict in Contemporary Capitalism: Studies in the Political Economy of Western European Nations.* Ed. Goldthorpe, J.H. Oxford: Clarendon Press.

Lash, S. 1984. *The Militant Worker: Class and Radicalism in France and America.* London: Heinemann.

Maitland, I. 1983. *The Causes of Industrial Disorder: A Comparison of a British and a German Factory.* London: Routledge & Kegan Paul.

Marsh, A.I. 1982. *Employee Relations Policy and Decision-Making.* Aldershot: Gower.

Marshall, T.H. 1950. *Citizenship and Social Class.* Cambridge: Cambridge University Press.

Meissner, M. 1969. *Technology and the Worker.* San Francisco: Chandler.

Micklewright, J. 1985. 'Fiction versus Fact: Unemployment Benefit in Britain'. *National Westminster Bank Quarterly Review* (May), 52–62.

Millward, N. and Stevens, M. 1986. *British Workplace Industrial Relations 1980–1984.* Aldershot: Gower.

Minford, P. 1982. 'Trade Unions Destroy a Million Jobs'. *Journal of Economic Affairs,* 2 (January), 73–9.

Narendranathan, W., Nickell, S. and Stern, J. 1985. 'Unemployment Benefit Revisited'. *Economic Journal,* 95 (June), 307–29.

Nichols, T. and Beynon, H. 1977. *Living with Capitalism Class Relations and the Modern Factory.* London: Routledge & Kegan Paul.

Offe, C. and Wiesenthal, H. 1980. 'Two Logics of Collective Action: Theoretical Notes on Social Class and Organisational Form'. *Political Power and Social Theory,* 1, 67–115.

Olson, M. 1982. *The Rise and Decline of Nations: Economic Growth, Stagflation and Social Rigidities.* New Haven: Yale University Press.

Posner, C. 1970. 'Introduction'. *Reflections on the Revolution in France: 1968.* Ed. Posner, C. Harmondsworth: Penguin.

Price, R. 1980. *Masters, Unions and Men: Work Control in Building and the Rise of Labour, 1830–1914.* Cambridge: Cambridge University Press.

Przeworski, A. 1985. *Capitalism and Social Democracy.* Cambridge: Cambridge University Press.

—— and Wallerstein, M. 1982. 'The Structure of Class Conflict in Democratic Capitalist Societies'. *American Political Science Review,* 76 (June), 215–38.

Rubery, J., Tarling, R. and Wilkinson, F. 1984. 'Industrial Relations Issues in the 1980s: An Economic Analysis'. *Industrial Relations in the Future*. Eds. Poole, M., Brown, W., Rubery, J., Sisson, K., Tarling, R. and Wilkinson, F. London: Routledge & Kegan Paul, 95–137.

Sayles, L.R. 1958. *The Behavior of Industrial Work Groups: Predictions and Control*. New York: Wiley.

Schmitter, P.C. and Streeck, W. 1981. *The Organisation of Business Interests*. Berlin: International Institute of Management.

Streeck, W. 1984. *Industrial Relations in West Germany*. London: Policy Studies Institute.

Turner, H.A. 1962. *Trade Union Growth, Structure and Policy: A Comparative Study of the Cotton Unions in England*. London: Allen & Unwin.

Webb, S. and Webb, B. 1911 (first published 1894). *The History of Trade Unionism*. London: Longman.

Williams, J., Williams, K. and Thomas. D. 1981. *Why Are The British So Bad At Manufacturing?* London: Routledge & Kegan Paul.

Williamson, O.E. 1975. *Markets and Hierarchies*. New York: Free Press.

Woodward, J. 1965. *Industrial Organization: Theory and Practice*. Oxford: Oxford University Press.

Woodward, J. (ed.) 1970. *Industrial Organization; Behaviour and Control*. Oxford: Oxford University Press.

Zeitlin, J. 1985. 'Shop Floor Bargaining and the State: A Contradictory Relationship'. *Shop Floor Bargaining and the State*. Eds Tolliday, S. and Zeitlin, J. Cambridge: Cambridge University Press, 1–45.

PART II
The Social Organization
of the Labour Market

9 Employers and the Labour Market

Jill Rubery

Introduction

The key distinguishing feature of recent contributions to the analysis of labour markets has been an increasing focus on the role of the firm in structuring employment. Firms are no longer considered to be passive agents. Instead of responding mechanistically to economic or social forces they are identified as exercising discretion in their employment policies. This focus on employer policy represents a major break with traditional approaches to labour market analysis (Baron, 1984): within economics the human-capital explanation of labour market inequality concentrated almost exclusively on the characteristics of the individual workers (Mincer, 1970) and within sociology the status attainment approach emphasized the role of societal needs and societal structures. Little attention was paid to the characteristics or the needs of the actual organizations which created and shaped the jobs which the individuals held. Firms or organizations have now been recognized as requiring study in their own right and analyses of the labour market or social stratification which abstract from the institutional structures through which the pattern of employment is determined have increasingly been recognized as unsatisfactory.

The first section of this chapter provides a brief summary of the re-emergence of theoretical interest in the role of employers in the labour market. This interest became evident in the 1970s but was sustained and developed in the 1980s by the increasing interest in policies to make employment and labour costs more flexible. The second section explores the empirical evidence for the proposition that there is an independent role for employer policy in structuring pay and employment, and the third examines whether there has been a move towards more flexible employment forms in response to the recession. The final section reviews the current state of theoretical and empirical debate and makes some suggestions for further extension and development of this approach.

The Rediscovery of the Employer as an Active Agent in the Labour Market

Several different theoretical developments and debates led to the redis-covery in the 1970s of the firm or the employer as an active agent in the labour market. The neo-classical economists' investigation of the economics of information ran parallel to the labour process and labour market segmentation debates in the 1970s. In the late 1970s and through the 1980s, the emphasis of these debates switched from the explanation of stable structures of inequality to investigations of the changing boundaries of labour market segments within the 'labour market flexibility' debate.

Neo-classical Theory and Employer Strategy

For a neo-classical economist the factors that give rise to long-term differences in earnings derive from the characteristics of the individual employees. Pay differentials are explained in terms of the relative quality or productivity of the workers, measured primarily by their human capital acquisition; deviations which are not explicable in these terms are held to derive either from unmeasurable differences in the perceived benefits of jobs, (for example, workers are paid less in small firms because they are deemed to value the better quality of the work environment), or from temporary disequilibria in the labour market. Thus firms in the short run may pay wages that deviate from the market rate for that quality of labour, but in the long run labour mobility between firms and product market pressures will ensure that the wage payments are brought into line. The proposition that employer strategy may have a permanent impact on the job structure requires a departure from the fundamental proposition that markets will in the long term lead to equalization of returns for factors of similar productivities.

The theoretical problems of ascribing any positive role for the firm in determining employment structures within neo-classical theory increasingly came to be recognized as a factor which reduced the usefulness of the theory in explaining labour market patterns and processes. This impasse has been 'solved' for neo-classical economists by two theoretical developments which enable them to ascribe a role for firms or organizational structures in determining economic outcomes. The first is the recognition of the specificity of investments, and in particular the specificity of human capital investments (Oi, 1962; Becker, 1964). If there is no market in which workers can sell their human capital because it is specific to only one firm, then there is no determinate market solution to how the costs of investment are distributed or what the returns to investment will be; all neo-classical economics can do is posit that there will be a sharing of both the costs and the returns to investment between the workers and the employer, but the division implicitly depends on employer strategy on the one hand and worker bargaining power on the other.

The second 'solution' has been to recognize the existence of information costs, in particular the costs associated with the labour contract. In order to avoid hiring costs and to reap the benefits of firm-specific investments in human capital, labour contracts tend to be continuous and open-ended. This characteristic of the labour market was seen to open up a role for the firm in structuring employment. On the one hand, these kinds of costs were seen as the explanation for the development of internal markets or hierarchies (Williamson, 1975) in order to minimize transaction costs associated with the continual renegotiation of long-term contracts. On the other hand, the open-endedness of the labour contract and, in particular, that of the wage-effort bargain led to the development of models of employer strategy to minimize total wage costs over the long term taking into account the impact of these strategies on labour effort and productivity.[1]

These two developments taken together can be used to explain why labour markets tend not to work as predicted by simple models of competition. Firms in practice are not indifferent between their own workers and workers with similar qualifications but outside the firm. Indeed, they positively prefer to continue to employ their existing workforce because of their firm-specific skills and the knowledge the firm has acquired about their capacity and willingness to work. Under these conditions the market can no longer be relied upon to ensure that firms offer similar terms and conditions for the same 'grade' of labour. The potential divergence in payment systems increases further if firms face costs in measuring and maintaining labour effort; for example, some firms may then use pay instead of supervision to maintain output standards, and also concern themselves with the impact of their employment policies on morale and motivation as well as total wage costs (see Lindbeck and Snower, 1985: 46–7). However, while these developments allow neo-classical theory to escape from the problems of empirical verification, at the same time they pose a dilemma for neo-classical theory (Maurice et al., 1986: 204). The so-called strengths of neo-classical theory have been its generality and its ability to predict equilibrium outcomes. The development of models of multiple equilibria based on information costs, bargaining strategies, and non-transferability of factors detract from these characteristics and pull it in the opposite direction towards historical, institutional and contingent explanations of market outcomes.

Employers and Labour Market Segmentation

Neo-classical theory, even in its modern forms, stops far short of studying collective structures, including firms 'in and for themselves as independent theoretical objects' (Maurice et al., 1986: 204). It is the recognition of the firm as an independent agency in the labour market that has been one of the main outcomes of the labour process and labour market segmentation debates.

This theoretical approach applies specifically to the outcomes, and not the starting-points for the debates. There were two opposed starting-points for the development of segmentation theory associated with two different sets of authors: the institutional and micro-based theory of dual labour markets associated with Doeringer and Piore (1971) and the radical segmentation school which took the analysis of class conflict as its theoretical focus.

1   For critical assessments of these approaches see Brown and Nolan, 1988; Lindbeck and Snower, 1985; Green, 1988.

For Doeringer and Piore (1971) the labour market was segmented into a primary sector with good jobs, offering high pay and promotion prospects and the secondary sector where pay was low and employment casual. Subsequent critiques of this work have shown the model to have essentially neo-classical underpinnings. Labour market dualism emerged because of the need for firm-specific human-capital investment in some firms and industries and not in others. This specificity restricted labour market mobility and competitive forces acting both between primary and secondary segments and within the primary segment itself. Thus the introduction of a more specific role for the firm than is allowed for in neo-classical theory arises from factors that are explicable within that theoretical framework (Rubery, 1978; Cain, 1976). Moreover, the admittance of some role for employer strategies was made more acceptable by the proposition that those firms offering primary employment to maximize long-term returns on their investments in skills were able to adopt this policy because of imperfections or oligopoly in their product markets.

Thus, in many ways, the dual labour market theory is an extension of prior developments within neo-classical theory, namely the existence of firm-specific skills, restricted labour mobility and the prevalence of imperfect competition. The main differences were that the previous *ad hoc* descriptions of the effects of firm-specific investments on employment patterns in particular firms of for particular categories of labour (Lester, 1952; Oi, 1962) were developed into a theory of labour market structure and inequality and that the consequences of opportunities for employer discretion and employment stability were explored and developed to their logical limits. Non-competitive employment structures were seen not to be transient deviations from market equilibria but capable of long-term survival as they became protected by the twin forces of custom and practice and employer intertia.

The conclusion that arose from this analysis of internal labour markets was that 'present market structures will often reflect the influences of earlier economic and technological conditions' (Doeringer and Piore, 1971: 63). It was this recognition of a role for institutional structure which provided a catalyst for the emergence of a labour market segmentation literature which did not take neo-classical theory as its starting-point (Wilkinson, 1981; Nolan, 1983; Osterman, 1984; Tarling, 1987). Within this non-neoclassical approach the historical development of the firm is seen as a central determinant of current structure.

The hypothesis that reduced competition in the product market facilitated the development of structured labour markets was taken to much further extremes by the radical segmentation and labour process theorists. In these theories firms were assumed to be able to pursue policies and strategies that were designed to further the interests of capital as a class. Inter-class competition was thus held to dominate over intra-class competition. For the labour process theorists such as Braverman (1974) capital was seen to be pursuing a strategy of increasing its control over the labour process by reducing the scope for individuals to use judgement and skill (see chapter

4). The radical theorists noted the same tendencies towards deskilling in the development of technology but drew different conclusions as to where the interests of capital lay. Homogenized and deskilled labour might be more likely to develop collective opposition towards capital and thus capital needed to create 'artificial' divisions among the workforce through the creation of job ladders and pay hierarchies (Gordon, 1972; Edwards et al., 1975; Gordon et al., 1982). These very different perspectives, however, embody similar views on the relative insignificance of the firm. The Braverman concern with individual skill is analogous to neo-classical theory where the productivity of a firm is determined by the productivity of individual units of factors of production. Collective action and consciousness in the radical theory was considered from a class or societal perspective. Both perspectives thus abstract from social organization at the point of production.

Critiques of both the labour process and radical segmentation hypotheses have singled out the problems of sustaining the proposition that inter-class competition dominated over intra-class struggles. Unless product market competition is restricted, however, the theories fail to provide an adequate theory of behaviour of individual firms. The radicals had gone so far as to suggest that firms would act against their own short-term interests, sacrificing quantitative for qualitative efficiency (Gordon, 1976). But this hypothesis appeared incompatible with a world in which increasing market share could still be the dominant motivation for individual capital. Moreover, explanations of the existence of segmented markets needed to take into account the interests of trade unions in creating sheltered and higher paid sectors, so that neither the actions of capital nor labour could be said to be explicable solely by the interests of the class as a whole (Elbaum and Wilkinson, 1979; Rubery, 1978; Nolan and Edwards, 1984). Braverman's hypothesis of deskilling at first sight appeared to escape these criticisms, as the reduction in skilled workers was expected to benefit individual firms as well as collective capital through a reduction in the wage bill. However, this hypothesis relied on an essentially human-capital view of wage determination. If workers have collective and not simply individual bargaining power, moves to deskill an activity through the application of new technology can lead to increases in pay for the workers concerned if the enhanced productivity and greater interdependencies in production are used to enhance bargaining power (Rubery, 1978).

These empirical and theoretical critiques called not for a simple rejection of segmentation theory but for a reformulation. While this work has argued for much more attention to be paid to the characteristics of the specific historical conjuncture and the diversity of interests of capital and labour, it has retained the initial hypotheses of non-neutral development of technology and forms of work organization.[2] Essentially what has been

2   For examples of this type of approach applied to specific studies in Britain and other advanced countries see Wilkinson, 1981; Villa, 1986; Lorenz, 1983; Craig et al., 1982, 1985; Tarling, 1987.

discarded are the simplistic assumptions of unidimensional motivations for employers and workers, and the pre-eminence of inter-class over intra-class strategies and competition. The need to re-establish a role for inter-capitalist competition at the centre of the theoretical approach became increasingly apparent as the world moved from the comparatively stable production systems of the 1960s to the recession and intensified competition of the 1970s and 1980s.

From Segmentation and Deskilling to Flexibility

These economic developments overtook the labour market segmentation debates in the 1970s. While the precise definitions and classification systems for labour markets segments were still being debated (Reich, 1984) the industrial and employment systems were being rapidly restructured (Bluestone and Harrison, 1982; Massey and Meegan, 1982) The issue became not the explanation of the persistence of stable differences in employment rewards between sectors and organizations, but the analysis of how boundaries between primary-type and secondary-type employment were being redrawn as employers responded to changing product and labour market conditions by developing new employment strategies. The main economic explanations of restructuring of employment were expressed in terms of employers' search for greater flexibility in employment. This search for flexibility was attributed to two factors: the changes in the overall product market conditions, in which the share of stable and predictable demand sectors was decreasing and the increase in the fixed costs of employment for core workers as a result of social and political developments which had led to improvements in their employment conditions (Berger and Piore, 1980).

Evidence of the increased importance attached to firms' production and market requirements is found in the framework adopted for the flexibility debate itself. Traditional analyses might have sought to explain the decline of primary-type employment in terms of a slackening labour market reducing the need for firms to offer advantageous working conditions for workers with scarce or firm-specific skills. In contrast, the flexibility debate has seen the main incentive to come from the changing productive system. This approach has been adopted at both a macro and a micro level. Piore looked at the implications of the search for flexibility for the structure of industry and employment as a whole; two examples of these effects were the growth of the small firm sector in Italy and the growth of the temporary work sector in France.

Within Britain the flexibility debate has been located mainly at the micro level. This focus arose because of the development of the influential Atkinson (1985) model of the flexible firm. This model argues that increasing uncertainty in product markets has led firms to seek to reduce the size of their core workforces; the peripheral workforces including part-timers, subcontractors, temporary workers and the like provide firms with both numerical flexibility and a flexible reserve of specialist skills. At the same time the core workforce is further reduced in size and made more adaptable to increasingly variant production demands through the development of functional flexibility among core workers. This micro model, based on small numbers of case studies of firms, has been widely taken up and used as a means of predicting or explaining changes at the labour market level such as the growth in part-time working. Industrial relations specialists have also taken up the issue of the trend towards functional flexibility, particularly within the core craft manufacturing workforce (Willman and Winch, 1985; Daniel, 1987). Job demarcations and control over the labour process have been seen to be central to the power of the trade-union movement in Britain. Thus the debate over flexibility in the labour market has not been confined simply to the structure of jobs and rewards but has extended to issues of broader class relations, thereby paralleling the different concerns we identified in the segmentation debate.

Empirical Evidence on the Role of Employers in the Labour Market

The first proposition that we need to examine in the light of empirical evidence is that employers have a relatively independent role in structuring pay and employment. This task is made more complex by the existence of legal, social and institutional pressures to enforce common employment and labour standards on firms. The segmentation hypothesis rests on the assumption that market forces alone will not be sufficient to bring about standardization and only active labour market regulation is likely to achieve harmonization. As Britain has traditionally had very weak forms of regulation at the labour market level, and even these have been largely removed under recent employment legislation (Rubery, 1986; Rubery et al., forthcoming), we could reasonably expect to find evidence of considerable employer diversity if these hypotheses are to be supported.

Detailed surveys of earnings carried out at the plant level have tended to support the hypothesis of non-equalization of rewards for similar workers even in the same industry or location. To summarize the findings of one particularly intensive study of earnings in engineering plants in Birmingham and Glasgow in the 1950s and 1960s:

> If plants are arranged in descending order according to their wage levels in different periods, then the ranking which emerges shows considerable stability in all periods examined . . . The behaviour of the inter-plant wage structure is only partly explicable in terms of competitive forces. Non-wage conditions did not seem to be particularly favourable in low-wage plants. The limits to wage differentials are not, then, very narrow. This is because the work force of a plant is differentiated from non-employees by acquired experience and skill and, probably more important, because wages are high in those plants where profits are high or where higher wages can be passed on through higher prices due to favourable product market

TABLE 9.1 *Pay levels by size of organization*

	Manufacturing		Non-manufacturing		All sectors	
	Manual	Non-manual	Manual	Non-manual	Manual	Non-manual
	(average weekly earnings)					
Males and females						
Size of organization:						
< 10 employees	141.3	200.8	119.1	161.3	123.7	167.8
10–24	150.2	209.5	137.4	174.7	142.5	182.7
25–49	154.9	215.1	143.6	184.4	149.2	193.4
50–199	155.1	213.0	153.6	198.9	154.6	203.9
200+	179.0	226.8	167.9	199.9	172.8	204.5
All	169.6	221.6	158.0	195.9	163.2	200.9
Males						
Size of organization:						
< 10 employees	147.0	223.2	125.4	195.0	130.0	200.9
10–24	160.4	239.0	144.2	216.2	150.5	222.7
25–49	169.2	252.4	151.1	233.8	159.7	240.2
50–199	170.8	254.9	162.6	253.0	167.5	253.8
200+	193.0	260.1	178.8	245.8	184.8	249.0
All	183.4	255.7	167.5	241.2	174.4	244.9
Females						
Size of organization:						
< 10 employees	92.1	–	79.7	114.7	81.7	115.1
10–24	94.4	124.1	88.2	123.5	91.1	123.6
25–49	93.8	124.1	89.8	124.3	92.2	124.3
50–199	102.5	128.7	94.2	132.1	100.3	131.1
200+	118.9	142.3	109.4	152.6	114.0	151.5
All	111.6	136.7	103.1	147.0	107.5	145.7

Source: New Earnings Survey, 1986

conditions. The circumstances of the individual plant are, therefore, an important determinant of wage levels, a possibility which is excluded in the competitive model. (Mackay et al., 1971: 97–8)

These conclusions are quoted at length partly because they are the findings of sceptics in the segmentation debate; the overall conclusion of the authors is that 'our general impression would be that the economist's model of labour market behaviour gets pass marks' (Mackay et al., 1971: 388). The authors came to this conclusion because they found little support for the labour market segmentation models based on internal labour markets and internal mobility. However, despite high levels of labour mobility between firms and industries it was found that 'an employee's increase in earnings over any substantial period of time will depend more on the plant in which he is employed than on the external employment conditions for the particular skill be possesses' (1971: 400). This result in fact implies an even stronger independent role for employer strategy than that suggested by neo-classical theory as even labour mobility is not sufficient to ensure competitive outcomes.

Many other studies have confirmed these patterns of plant-based wage structures. The industrial relations literature has increasingly emphasized the importance of plant-based wage systems in most of manufacturing (Brown and Nolan, 1987), and as the national agreements in key areas such as the engineering industry began to be given less emphasis by the trade-union movement, the wage policy of the particular plant became an even more important determinant of relative pay than skill category (Nolan and Brown, 1983). In the same vein, studies of the effects of abolishing wages councils (which set legal minimum wages in certain industries in Britain) revealed both wide wage differentials between plants and a tendency towards greater dispersion in the absence of industry-based minimum controls, supporting again the hypothesis that without systems of regulation of minimum standards the diversity of employment conditions offered by employing organizations would not be eliminated by market forces (Craig et al., 1982; Rubery, 1987).

One of the problems of directly testing for the effects of industry or organization on pay has been the absence of national data sets which take the firm or plant as the unit of analysis rather than the individual. Although the consistency and size of the dispersions within each occupation and industry provided a priori support for the existence of wage differences between employing organizations (Craig et al., 1982: chapter 7), only in 1986 was the New Earnings Survey data analysed by size of plant. These data, presented in table 9.1, show a strong linear trend in average earnings by size of plant for both male and female manual workers and female non-manual workers. Only male non-manual workers tend to fare relatively well in medium-sized plants. These effects could be even more pronounced within industries as there is clearly both an industry and a size of firm effect on wage structures. Moreover, our own research has shown that size of firm is primarily related to higher pay because of the greater likelihood of union organization; in industries that are non-union, size of firm is no guarantee of high pay. However, this does not imply that large non-union firms do not have an independent influence on pay and are governed by market forces; those that anticipate potential unionization may indeed adopt employment policies similar to the internal labour market model, whereas those which consider the threat of unionization to be weak may be in a position to impose lower wages and less secure employment conditions than even some small non-union firms (Rubery, 1987).

A further major finding of empirical research comparing pay structures between plants is that not only are there wide differentials for comparable workers but even wider differentials for comparable jobs defined by job content. One of the main ways in which employers are able to pay very different wages for similar jobs is by recruiting workers from different labour force segments. Workers in a disadvantaged position in the labour market because of their social or demographic characteristics (e.g. age, gender and racial group) or because of other characteristics that are taken as indicators of work quality (work experience, unemployment history, education) may be employed on low-paid jobs which require similar levels of skill and commitment as jobs held by more primary-type workers. Often these low-paid jobs are categorized as lower skilled and of lower status than any systematic assessment of job content would support (Craig et al., 1982, 1985; Armstrong, 1982, Crompton and Jones, 1984; Blackburn and Mann, 1979). Firms often require equal degrees of responsibility, stability, on the job experience and levels of manual skill from low-paid as from high-paid workers. These findings contrast with the original hypotheses of dual labour market theory where firm-specific skills would be confined to the primary sector and where secondary sector workers, although not rewarded necessarily 'fairly' for their labour, would nevertheless tend to be relatively unstable and unproductive workers. This structuring of the labour supply emerges not simply from inequalities in the system of social reproduction but also as a consequence of employers' selective recruitment strategies. These confine groups of workers to a limited range of jobs while at the same time providing the scope for employers to offer wages to these groups which do not reflect their relative worth to the firm.

This interdependency between employer strategy and workforce divisions is recognized primarily in relation to the impact of internal labour market systems on those included and those excluded. In Britain this type of labour market division exists but does not apply across all occupations or industrial sectors; in some industries access to better paid jobs is conditional on experience within the internal market but in others there is considerable mobility between firms for workers seeking promotion (Mackay et al., 1971; Ashton et al., 1982). In fact there is little evidence of the existence of widespread opportunities for semi- or unskilled workers to obtain promotion out of these job ranks through internal labour markets. Recent findings of the Workplace Industrial Relations Survey (WIRS) confirm this general pattern and indicate the greater importance of internal promotion for supervisory than for skilled or professional jobs (see table 9.2). Moreover nationalized industries make much greater use of internal promotion than manufacturing or services in the private sector.

The recruitment practices of firms, however, still have important

TABLE 9.2a *Level of jobs filled by external recruitment, 1984*

	Unskilled manual %	Semi-skilled manual %	Skilled manual %	Clerical, secretarial, administrative %	Supervisors or foremen %	Junior technical or professional %	Senior technical or professional %	Middle or senior management %
All establishments	46	42	37	46	15	49	30	21
Base: establishments with any of types of employees specified in column heads								
Unweighted	*1667*	*1347*	*1472*	*1960*	*1611*	*1443*	*1472*	*1906*
Weighted	*1494*	*1117*	*1220*	*1876*	*1298*	*1153*	*1225*	*1794*
Private manufacturing[1]	50	50	45	43	17	48	26	24
Private services	50	40	41	51	12	49	30	19
Nationalized industries	33	60	29	41	8	30	11	20
Public services	42	31	22	42	19	51	33	21

[1] Bases for the subcategories in the variable were calculated in the same way as for the total but have been excluded from the table for presentational reasons

TABLE 9.2b *Level of jobs filled by internal transfers or promotions, 1984*

	Unskilled manual %	Semi-skilled manual %	Skilled manual %	Clerical, secretarial, administrative %	Supervisors or foremen %	Junior technical or professional %	Senior technical or professional %	Middle or senior management %
All establishments	5	14	12	19	31	18	20	17
Base: establishments with any of types of employees specified in column heads								
Unweighted	*1667*	*1347*	*1472*	*1960*	*1611*	*1443*	*1472*	*1906*
Weighted	*1491*	*1117*	*1220*	*1876*	*1298*	*1153*	*1225*	*1794*
Private manufacturing[1]	6	23	13	12	35	20	13	18
Private services	5	10	11	20	35	20	20	14
Nationalized industries	7	20	29	26	30	32	30	33
Public services	4	7	10	20	22	14	25	20

[1] Bases for the subcategories in the variable were calculated in the same way for the total but have been excluded from the table for presentational reasons

Source: Millward and Stevens, 1986: tables 8.1, 8.4

effects on an individual's life chances as it is employers who ultimately decide on access to jobs. In Britain internal promotion opportunities for the semi-skilled may be limited but so are the *external* opportunities for advancement as a result of general policies of employers and, indeed, trade unions to use restrictive entry systems for access to skilled jobs. However, pay differs for similar work between firms so that it still matters where a job is held even if the chances for further advancement within the firm are limited. Moreover, such limited promotion opportunities as do exist are more likely to be given to internal semi-skilled workers than external semi-skilled workers.

All entry criteria adopted by firms necessarily restrict the employment opportunities of some parts of the workforce and enhance those of others. For example, Ashton et al. have pointed to the severe effects of the use of age restrictions on entry for young adults who were disadvantaged by first entering the labour force at a time of recession. They have failed to gain the experience considered necessary for an adult job but are not eligible because of their age for entry to training jobs. In other countries these same restrictions do not apply with the same force either because age discrimination is less prevalent in general or because it is accepted by employers that young adults may still be queuing to gain entry to permanent employment for the first time. The impact of recruitment policies are generally not given much weight in the non-classical literature; career progression is seen as a function of individual characteristics and not employer recruitment and promotion policy. Women who face interrupted careers are argued to face lower wages because of depreciated human capital, lack of work experience (Zabalza and Arrufat, 1985) or wage discrimination (Main, 1987) and not because of the obstacles to regaining entry to primary or internal labour markets emerging from employers' policy on age restrictions.

Even though employers' influence on employment opportunities extends beyond that of the internal promotion system there is some evidence suggesting that the importance of enterprise-specific labour markets may be increasing in Britain. There has been a decline in the extent to which individuals see themselves as having an *occupational* identity and an increase in identity with an *enterprise* (Brown et al., 1983). Recent changes to the system of training in Britain have effectively broken down the apprenticeship system which was based on the concept of general and occupational skills and paved the way for more firm-specific systems of training, based on multiple skills for specific technologies (Marsden and Silvestre, 1986). Data on new job starts from the General Household Survey also point to an increase in the number of people starting new jobs without a change of employer, and a decrease in those starting new jobs involving a change of employer. To what extent these trends are the result of the recession and rationalization of employment or more permanent changes towards greater reliance on the internal labour market is not yet clear. There is also evidence that in the recession workers have had to rely increasingly on having personal contacts with firms, either through employers or existing employees to gain access to employment at all. This system has been labelled the extended internal labour market as employers have defined their labour market segment to include its existing employees and their contacts outside in order to minimize recruitment problems and ensure social control over new recruits (Manwaring, 1984). Firms' influence extends into the external market also through the use of casual workers who form pools of labour that can be called on by the firm when required but who are not offered permanent jobs within the firm.

Employers are thus found to have a significant influence on both pay and employment access. The third main proposition of the labour market segmentation and the labour process literature is that employer strategy should have an independent influence on systems of work organization and control. Empirical work on this topic, which is necessarily primarily case study based, has found no evidence to support deterministic explanations of work organization, whether technological or market based. How firms implement new technologies or organize their system of work varies between industries and between firms within the same industry (see chapter 4). Moreover, within Britain the system of trade-union organization and its responses to technological development have been found to have a major influence on work organization (Elbaum and Wilkinson, 1979; Lorenz, 1983). This work on the labour process and systems of organization and control found more scope for the use of a wide range of systems of work organization, including subcontracting and homeworking (Rubery and Wilkinson, 1981), which previously had been associated with declining or backward firms and industries than was allowed for either by neo-classical theory or the labour process theorists (Marglin, 1978). The later concern with flexibility rekindled interest in the opportunities for the spread of these supposedly outdated forms of work organization, together with the more 'modern' forms of flexible working such as part-time and flexi-time, and it is the empirical evidence on the spread and significance of flexibility in the labour market that must be considered next.

Labour Flexibility and Employer Policy

Flexibility is often defined as referring to numerical, functional and financial flexibility; the ability to vary the quantity of labour, the skills deployed and the cost of labour (Atkinson, 1985). These categories can not be used directly in discussing the empirical evidence as the same categories of labour or employment forms may serve more than one of these purposes dependent on the specific industrial and institutional context. For example, part-time working may be used as it may be easier to adjust the quantity of labour to demand (numerical flexibility), but it also provides opportunities to lower hourly wage costs, intensify the pace of work and avoid national insurance contributions, all of which contribute to financial flexibility. To examine the evidence on flexibility we will thus look at the evidence for the spread of different labour market phenomena that have come to be associated with flexibility. These

FIGURE 9.1 *Employment trends 1971–1986 (1971=100)*

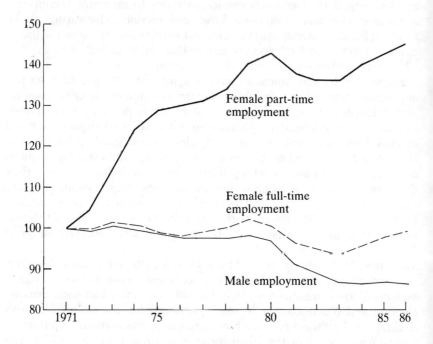

Source: 'Employees in Employment'. *Employment Gazette* (January 1987) and
   Employment Gazette Historical Abstracts, 1–2 (August 1984, April 1985)

include non-standard employment, pay flexibility, intensification of work
effort and flexibility in skills and job demarcations.

Non-standard Employment

One of the main focuses of the flexibility debate has been on the growth
of non-standard employment, including in this category part-time work,
temporary work, self-employment and homework. In countries outside
Britain these employment forms have been seen to offer considerable
advantages in numerical flexibility; for example, in France non-standard
employment contracts are used to avoid the protection provided by the
common law system against dismissal to employees with standard contracts
(Michon, 1981); in Italy self-employment and homeworking have grown
in part because of restrictions on dismissals by trade unions within the
formal sector of the economy (Brusco, 1982). In Britain the protection
provided by common law and even by trade unions against dismissal
is relatively weak so that their use to increase flexibility to hire and
fire is likely to be limited. The opportunities they offer to lower
hourly wage costs or to purchase labour in more flexible amounts
take on much greater importance in the British context. Given this,

TABLE 9.3 *Proportion of establishments using non-core workers by broad sector, 1984*

	All establishments	Private manufacturing	Private services	Nationalized industries	Public services
					Percentages
Any non-core workers used	45	52	43	22	47
Types of non-core workers used					
Short, fixed-term contract	19	11	11	13	39
Temps	18	22	23	10	9
Freelancers	14	20	18	2	6
Homeworkers, outworkers	4	12	3	*	*
					Numbers
Numbers of non-core workers used					
Short, fixed-term contract	174,000	23,000	43,000	5,000	102,000
Temps	161,000	51,000	75,000	4,000	32,000
Freelancers	208,000	31,000	108,000	–	69,000
Homeworkers, outworkers	23,000	17,000	7,000	–	–
Base: all establishments					
Unweighted	*2019*	*595*	*597*	*196*	*634*
Weighted	*2000*	*424*	*843*	*106*	*627*

Source: Millward and Stevens, 1986: 208

it is questionable whether it is appropriate to compare the extent of flexible working over time or across countries by adding together these different forms of flexibility; they will, therefore, be treated separately.[3]

Part time working is the most pervasive form of non-standard employment in Britain and now accounts for over 40 per cent of women's jobs, and close to 20 per cent of total employment. Figure 9.1 shows that part-time work is the only type of employment to have grown consistently during the 1970s and 1980s. Its relatively high incidence has recently been shown in a comparative study with West Germany to be explicable by the favourable tax treatment of part-time work in Britain which effectively provides employers of part-timers with a legal subsidy compared with the employers of full-timers (Schoer, 1987).[4] However, perhaps even more significant than the evidence that employers do take advantage of the clear tax benefits is that the extent to which they do so varies by industry and occupational group. Employer policy appears not to be simply determined by labour cost. Product markets, technology, labour supply, and co-ordination of the internal system of work organization all influence the extent to which these tax subsidies are taken up. Part-time working increased in manufacturing in the late 1960s and early 1970s but its relative share of employment has stabilized and even reduced. In contrast part-time working in services has increased absolutely and relatively. This use, however, is related to differences in the labour process; services often have to be produced directly in response to customer orders and it is in these production conditions that part-time work is seen as particularly valuable (see Robinson and Wallace, 1984; Mallier and Rosser, 1979; Beechey and Perkins, 1985; Craig et al., 1985, for case study evidence on the use of part-timers). Where work scheduling is not so directly determined by customer demand and where continuity and social interaction of employees in the production process is valued, part-time working is not considered by employers to be so desirable. Thus there are limits to the expansion of part-time working set by employers' policies other than minimization of wage costs. These limits derive in part from the lack of an extensive pool of male labour for part-time work. Indeed, the cost and other advantages of part-time work have not been such as to lead to any major change in the sexual division of labour. Part-time work has not been extensively used as a direct substitute for either male or even full-time female labour, and the main explanation of its growth lies in sectoral change combined with new forms of work organization in expanding industries (Rubery and Tarling, 1988).

Temporary work can take the form of agency work, casual work or fixed term contracting. The 1984 Workplace Industrial Relations Survey found that 18 per cent of establishments with over twenty five-employees made some use of agency workers, with the percentage higher in the

3 See Hakim (1987b) for a recent example of the alternative approach. She places great stress on the similarities in the share of flexible employment, defined as non-full-time permanent employment, within EEC countries but then goes on to show the great disparities between the countries in forms of flexible employment and shares of male and female involvement.
4 In Britain both employers and employees are exempted from payment of national insurance contributions if earnings are below £41 per week (May 1988).

private than the public sector (see table 9.3). Fixed term contracting was much higher in the public than the private sector, possibly because of stronger expectations in the public sector of 'jobs for life', particularly for professionals unless a non-standard contract is used. A survey by the Institute for Manpower Studies found evidence of growing use of temporary work particularly among larger establishments, as firms were unwilling to commit themselves to permanent recruitment under uncertain demand conditions (Meager, 1986). However, they also found that the use of temporary workers was confined to mainly low-skilled occupations and they were not considered suitable for jobs requiring any significant level of firm-specific skills. Looking at the incidence of temporary working from the labour force side, the Labour Force Sample Survey found that in 1985 4 per cent of men and 8 per cent of women were in temporary work, a slight decrease for men and a slight increase for women since 1983 (*Social Trends*, 1986). Most of the increase came in part-time work which accounted for 60 per cent of all temporary jobs. Moreover, Hakim (1987b) shows that even though temporary work has increased somewhat in the 1980s it is still at a comparable level to that found in 1975. The main conclusion must be then that temporary work accounts for a relatively low proportion of all jobs in Britain and that its use is unlikely to show rapid growth at a time when the protection provided by a standard employment contract is being continuously eroded. It is used most widely in circumstances where firms wish to avoid difficulties with their existing staff, and particularly to avoid disturbing 'good' industrial relations by declaring redundancies for permanent staff.

There is much stronger evidence of a growth in self-employment, which grew by 48 per cent between 1979 and 1984 and accounted for over 11 per cent of employment in 1984 (Spilsbury et al., 1986; Creigh et al., 1986). It is less clear, however, if the cause of the expansion of self-employment is to be found in a rebirth of entrepreneurial spirit, a response to unemployment or a change in employer policy. The last explanation has been the one primarily favoured by the flexibility debate; employers concerned to reduce overheads have encouraged their staff to become self-employed. These people then continue to carry out the same type of work as before but under a different employment contract. Such data as are available do not, however, tend to support this explanation as the prime cause of the increase in self-employment; among the 17 per cent of 'new' self-employed in 1984 almost all had changed occupation or the firm they worked for on becoming self-employed (Creigh et al., 1986). Thus while case study evidence suggests that these practices are found in particular firms it is not sufficiently widespread to explain the increases at the macro level. It may be more plausible to explain the growth in self-employment by unemployment. Spilsbury et al. (1986) point out that the major spurt in self-employment coincided with the rapid rise in unemployment between 1979 and 1981. These supply-side responses to unemployment may in turn lead to a change in employer policy if the availability of a self-employed sector encourages firms to make increased use of subcontracting. Most of the self-employed work long hours (20 per cent over 60 hours per week) so that if effort and rewards are taken into account together self-employment may be associated with an explanation of secondary work through self-exploitation.

Some of the self-employed may be more properly described as homeworkers, because in Britain, unlike in some advanced countries, there is no clear cut legal or tax definition separating self-employment from homeworking (Varesi and Villa, 1986; Deakin and Rubery, 1986). Recent surveys have pointed to the difficulties of defining homeworking (Hakim, 1985); indeed, one of the interesting facets of recent research on homeworking has been the overlap between self-employment, homeworking, freelancing and small businesses, both with respect to the place of work and their relationships to the market. Homeworking is associated with a subordinate market position, analagous to that of wage labour, but many self-employed also find themselves in a subordinated position dependent on a small number of clients. Because of definitional difficulties it is not possible to be certain of the directions of trends. Most surveys point to an expansion apart from the recent WIRS which showed a significant decrease between 1981 and 1984; but this survey excluded establishments with under twenty-five employees where most of the homeworking may be concentrated. From the somewhat confusing evidence certain points remain clear: homeworking is found in 'modern' as well as traditional industries (Huws, 1984) and its use for non-manual work may now be higher than for manual work (Hakim, 1985, 1987a); its use is concentrated in particular industries and sectors, and more recently it has been found to be prevalent among ethnic communities in inner city areas (Mitter, 1986). there is no general or common strategy by firms to use homeworking to meet current economic conditions and its use remains relatively specific to certain technological, economic and social conditions; nor, however, is homeworking an anachronistic or outdated form of work (Rubery and Wilkinson, 1981) as its growth in computer-based work clearly demonstrates. Moreover, many firms use homeworkers as a means of expanding their pool of *skilled* labour at relatively low cost and not as a form of casual or unskilled employment. It is probably the latter types of homeworking that are in general most subject to displacement by technical change.

The evidence for a major transformation of the employment system based on more flexible employment forms is thus weak; part-time working is by far the most important form of non-standard employment but its recent relative growth owes as much to the continued expansion of the industries in which part-time work has long been used as to recent changes in employer strategy. Moreover the benefits of part-time working to employers and its costs to employees arise as much from the opportunities it offers to reduce the wage bill on a permanent basis as from opportunities to adjust continuously the number of labour hours purchased to take account of fluctuations in demand.

Pay Flexibility

Empirical work has found no evidence of the pay flexibility expected by neo-classical economists in response to high levels of unemployment; real and money wages have continued to rise in Britain despite unemployment levels of over 3 million (Knight and Mayhew, 1987). Both neo-classical and labour market segmentation theorists have explained the absence of pay flexibility in the face of unemployment by models which allow employers to have some scope or discretion to fix pay at non-market clearing rates (Lindbeck and Snower, 1985; Brown and Nolan, 1988). However, while there is no general downward movement there is evidence of increasing dispersion of pay rates, both between firms and between categories of employees. The overall dispersion of earnings has widened considerably in the 1980s and the relative share of low-paid workers increased (Rubery, 1986; Low Pay Unit, 1987). The fragmentation of collective bargaining and the weakening controls over wages at the industry and national level through the government's employment legislation has left ever increasing segments of the labour market exposed to relative and real wage erosion;[5] and at the same time there has been an expansion of industries where low pay predominates. Some of the types of employment that have been growing fast, such as part-time work, are also associated with low pay.

The changes in the labour market and in labour legislation have thus provided firms with more scope to pursue low-wage employment strategies but again it is not perhaps the high incidence of these strategies that is notable but the fact that they are confined to a relatively narrow range of firms and sectors. For example, even the use of the Youth Training Scheme as a means of providing cheap labour has been confined to a limited range of industries, primarily retailing and catering, while other industries have not taken much advantage of the opportunities to substitute effectively free youth labour for adult labour (Ashton et al., 1987).

Public sector employers have been under particular pressure to cut wage costs because of government policy on public expenditure. Public services have been contracted out as this avoids the problems of imposing wage cuts on existing employees and preserves the public sector's image as a 'good' employer (Moore, 1985; Walker, 1985). Moreover, contracting out has been used most where there was clearly scope for private sector employers to offer lower wages and conditions than in the public sector. These services employed the lowest paid workers, mainly part-time women, but some improvement in their conditions had been achieved because of the efforts of public sector unions and public sector employers who fostered a 'good employer' image by providing pro rata pay and benefits for part-timers. It is in these employment sectors where the labour market sets no effective floor to wages and leaves non-union private employers free to pay very low wages (Craig et al., 1985; Rubery, 1987).

5 The main ways in which the government's legislation has weakened controls over pay at the national level have been through restricting sympathy strikes and secondary picketing, abolishing the fair wages, resolution which ensured that firms contracting to the government paid fair wages abolishing provisions for applying industry agreements to non-union firms, reducing the powers of wages councils which set legal minimum wages in sectors such as retailing and clothing (particularly by taking the under-21s out of scope) and by forbidding clauses in contracts stipulating minimum pay rates or unionization as a condition of receiving the contract.

Flexibility of Work Effort and Access to Multi-skilled Labour

Changes in the intensity of work effort is an alternative method of reducing labour costs to lowering pay levels. In the public sector workers ward off privatization threats by promising increases in productivity for the same pay. Private contractors have cut costs by reducing labour hours, thereby intensifying work effort as well as reducing quality standards. The nationalized industries have also experienced the most dramatic decreases in manning levels and changes in work organization; this increased intensity of work effort has been associated with new working time arrangements in some industries, for example, flexible rostering in the railways (see Ferner, 1985) or new working arrangements brought in with new technology as in the coal industry (see Burns et al., 1985), or simply by decreases in manning levels prior to privatization, for example, baggage handling at British Airways. The major employment reductions in the private sector since 1979 and the associated changes in work organization have also led to widespread increased pressure on the pace of work for those in employment. Manning levels and the pace of work have become less subject to trade-union bargaining in the 1980s, indicating a change in employer strategy towards more independent determination of work organization and the speed of work.[6] These changes in the scope and effectiveness of collective bargaining have occurred without the actual dismantling of collective bargaining institutions within establishments.

Increasing the range of tasks on which workers can be employed may also intensify the pace of work as this facilitates full utilization of labour during its employed hours. These issues of multi-skilling take on even greater importance for labour where the change in particular job boundaries have implications for trade-union demarcations and control. Much of the flexibility debate in Britain has thus been centred on the implications for trade unions of employer strategies to introduce multi-skilling among craftsmen; moreover, the 1984 WIRS survey found that action on breaking down craft demarcations was the factor that distinguished most clearly between managers who were actively increasing flexibility of working conditions and those who were not making major changes (Daniel, 1987). It is also notable that in the majority of plants in the survey some move towards flexible craftworking had been made.

Flexibility: An Assessment of the Evidence

Considering all the currently available evidence the flexibility hypothesis appears to be poorly supported. There is fairly clear cut evidence of a relatively fast rate of change in work organization and an increase in

---

6 See Willman and Winch (1985) on the car industry; Millward and Stevens (1986) and Daniel (1987) for national survey statistics and Batstone (1984) and Edwards (1987) for manufacturing industry data.

independent managerial determination of working practices. But there is much less evidence to support the hypothesis that these changes are following the stereotype of the Atkinson model; while there is evidence of a growth of some kinds of 'flexible' employment, and in particular part-time work, these changes are as much associated with sectoral change as with changes in strategy at the firm level. Where there is evidence of a change in employment practices, for example of the use of youth labour as a cheap labour substitute, it is the change in government labour market policy that has provided the main impetus to such change and not autonomous changes in employer strategy. Data at the macro level might underestimate changes at the micro level as some firms might be rapidly increasing their use of flexible labour while others have moved in the opposite direction. However, even surveys of individual firms revealed mixed evidence of the extent of change: Atkinson and Meager (1986: 26) themselves conclude on the basis of a recent survey that they have undertaken of seventy firms in four industries: 'Although the observed changes (towards greater flexibility) were widespread, they did not cut very deeply in most of the firms, and therefore the outcome was more likely to be marginal, ad hoc and tentative, rather than a purposeful and strategic thrust to achieve flexibility'.

Further Developments in the Analysis of Employer Strategy and the Labour Force

The survey of the theoretical and empirical literature on employer policy and employment has been found to support the hypothesis of a relatively independent or autonomous role for the firm in determining the structure of jobs and rewards. Nevertheless, various problems and inadequacies have emerged in the way the literature has conceptualized the role and motivations of the firm. These problems require further theoretical work in two main areas: the relationships between the firm and the production system and the relationships between the firm and the social system.

The Firm and the Production System

There are two main areas in which most of the existing work on employer policy and employment can be criticized: first, in the way the determinants of policy at the level of the individual firm are conceptualized, and, secondly in the way in which the relationship between change at the micro level of the economy and change at the macro level are analysed.

The main problem with the specification of motivation at the level of the firm is the overemphasis on the 'labour problem', whether it is the problem of labour costs or the problem of labour resistance that is seen to exercise the minds of management. This focus can be contrasted with that adopted by organization theorists, notably the contingency school theorists such as Woodward (1965) who through empirical studies in the

1960s found that the efficient forms of organization were related to the size of the organization and also to its external 'contingent' conditions including market and technological opportunities. This work was largely ignored by the labour market segmentation and labour process schools, partly because organization theorists did not pay particular attention to the 'labour problem', but also because these findings were used only to explain micro-level behaviour and were not generalized into a framework for analysing the development of the employment system. However, the consequence of this neglect was an overemphasis on the role of labour and a dismissal of technological, market and organizational considerations except in so far as they impinged directly on labour.[7]

The narrowness of the approach has been revealed by empirical research undertaken by the Labour Studies Group:

> The extent of the adjustment to changes in the level and structure of demand varied widely between firms . . . But whatever the degree of changes they were seldom confined to labour costs in ways suggested by the flexible firm analysis. Design, the sourcing of finished products and components, the techniques and organisation of production were all affected to varying degrees. Moreover, generally speaking, changes in employment, skill structure and the conditions of employment were derived from technical, organisational and other developments. (Rubery et al., 1987: 149)

The emphasis on labour arises from inadequate treatment of the nature of competition. The initial contributions to the labour market segmentation debate, as noted above, in practice argued that segmentation derived from the decline of product market competition. Oligopolistic markets were seen to provide firms with the opportunities for exercising discretion in employment and in some more extreme versions intra-class competition had almost entirely given way to inter-class competition. In the flexibility hypothesis product market factors were given greater prominence, but the strategies of firms were restricted to choosing between stable and variable segments of product market demand. Firms' strategies did not extend to changing the structure or variability of market demand (for example, through more active marketing or distribution policies), nor to competing through the bundle of factors that have come to be known as non-price competition (e.g. product development, product design, product quality, delivery dates, after sales service). This more complex picture of competition allows for the development of competitive strengths along several dimensions, all of which have consequences for labour organization which may be conflicting or complementary. Price factors, or the stability of demand for a given product, are not

---

7 It is notable that both Woodward from the contingency school and Edwards from the labour process, labour market segmentation school set out to explain the transition from direct to bureaucratic forms of control within organizations but from completely different perspectives. Edwards in adopting a labour process hypothesis failed to reference the technological and market explanations of Woodward of the same process.

sufficiently broad conceptualizations of firms' competitive strategies or objectives on which to base a theory of employers' labour force policies.

A move towards a more complex treatment of competition is already evident in the further development of Piore's work. Piore and Sabel have moved away from the simple flexibility hypothesis and developed a concept of flexible specialization. Saturated product markets and the expanded opportunities for small batch production provided by micro-processor technology have led to increasing emphasis on design and variety in competition. These developments in competition have in turn been used to explain the relative growth of the small firm sector and the apparent re-emergence of a demand for craft-type skills among the labour force. While the move to a less unidimensional theory of competition is welcome, problems arise with the particular predictions of the model. In the first place, large firms have shown themselves to be more adaptable to market patterns of flexible specialization than was anticipated. Secondly, the re-emergence of craft skills is only likely to affect a small minority and, if these jobs are concentrated in small and often non-union firms, the gains to labour are less than evident.

A more sophisticated approach to the determinants of employer competitive strategy at the level of the firm also has implications for other levels of analysis. The system of competition cannot be considered independent of firms' strategies but is shaped by the collective efforts of firms to maintain or improve competitiveness; in other words, markets are social constructs as much as organizations. This perspective again widens the scope for different forms of labour organization which are compatible with competitiveness or efficiency.

This dispersion of forms of organization, however, complicates the movement from micro to macro levels of analysis and vice versa (Tarling, 1981). It cannot be considered appropriate to use the essential neo-classical methodology and generalize to the macro level from the behaviour of a single representative firm. In practice this has often been the approach adopted, particularly in the recent flexibility debate. Changes have been explained solely with respect to intra-firm changes and not inter-firm behaviour and compositional change. Changes in the aggregate number of secondary and primary-type jobs in the economy, even measured along only one dimension such as wages, could arise from changes in each or any of the following dimensions of the structure of pay: the width of intra-firm wage differentials, the range of firms' average pay levels, the share of low-paying firms within an industry and low-paying industries within the economy, and the overall size of the economy, determined by changes in effective demand. It becomes even more essential to identify these components of employment change, if, as segmentation theory suggests, change along one dimension may not be independent of change along another. For example, decreases in aggregate demand may not only have differential effects on different types of firms and industries but may also lead to changes in firms' individual strategies, leading, perhaps, to more subcontracting or wider internal differentials which in turn will affect the distribution of pay generated by the employment system.

The Firm and the Social System

The dominant message of the labour market segmentation literature has been that the structure of jobs and employment is determined within specific firms and organizations and not in the labour market. However, this perspective should also allow for the system of social organization, and, in particular, the structure of the labour supply and the social and legal framework that underpins the employment contract to have a major influence on the employment policies pursued within those organizations.

Indeed, one of the major modifications that has been made to labour market segmentation theory is the recognition of a role for the structure of labour supply in shaping employment. The classification of particular jobs as low skilled or low paid has been found not to be determined by either technical job content or the market characteristics of the firm in which the jobs are located. The characteristics of the employees who carry out these jobs also have a major influence; for example, jobs will be low paid or considered unskilled because they are performed by female labour or by unqualified labour. The structuring of labour supply into advantaged or disadvantaged groups provides employers with a wider range of potential employment strategies than technical or market differences in jobs would provide. From the perspective of the individual employer these divisions are already determined so that he or she is able to employ women on low wages on relatively skilled jobs because they have already been categorized in the social and the economic sphere as relatively disadvantaged workers. However, at the aggregate level these divisions are not independent of employer strategy: the social divisions affect employers' own perceptions of which characteristics in jobs or workers require rewards and the divisions themselves are created or reinforced by inequalities in access to employment and rewards within firms and organizations.

This interdependency between supply-side structures and employer strategy is still not always recognized, even by those using a segmentation approach. Thus the explanation of increasing employment flexibility in terms of employers facing new technical and market needs may have exaggerated the importance of demand over supply-side factors. Much of the switch towards more flexible or low-paid employment may prove to be a product of unemployment (Standing, 1986) and government's deregulation policies which have created conditions in the labour market that employers are happy to take advantage of, justifying their policies by changing market or technological needs.

The relationship between organizational structures and societal structures has been developed into a theoretical framework by the Laboratoire d'economie et sociologie du travail in Aix-en-Provence, known as the LEST school. They undertook a comparative analysis of organization-al and employment structure in plants with similar technological and market characteristics in France and Germany. Wide differences in the employment structure were found that could be related to the different systems of education and training in the two countries, and which, in turn, had become embedded in systems of industrial and organizational behaviour. LEST used these facilities to argue for a 'societal approach' which is capable of 'bringing to light different forms of societal coherence' (Maurice et al., 1984; 232). Firms still have an active role in shaping labour markets but there will be no convergence in forms of organization between countries simply because of similar technical or market characteristics. Other comparative work on employment systems has supported the need for a societal approach, whether in explaining the different roles of women in the labour market system (Rubery, 1988), or the differences in the incidence and nature of unemployment (Ashton, 1986).

There are also similarities between the societal approach suggested by the LEST school and the productive systems approach proposed by Wilkinson (1983). Productive systems include not only labour power and the means of production but also the system of financial and organizational control and the social and political framework in which the productive system operates. The ways in which these elements may combine to define a productive system are many and various; it is the efficiency of the productive system as a whole which will determine relative strength in the national and international product market and not the organization of the individual elements such as labour. This analysis allows for variations in systems of organization between industries and countries as well as between firms and suggests that simplistic universal models of good employer strategies or good systems of labour market regulation are inappropriate for understanding the relationship between labour organization and economic efficiency.

Conclusion

The widespread interest in employer policy and its role in structuring employment since the early 1970s has done much to rescue labour market analysis from its previous concerns with individuals and to focus attention on the more central and useful questions of what determines the structure of jobs and rewards that are open to individuals. Much still needs to be done to integrate the analysis of employer policy and the labour force within a more general framework of forms of competition and systems of social organization. One of the obstacles to the development of such an integrated framework has been the fragmentation of social science disciplines. Segmentation theory and the role of employer policy has been one of the few areas of debate to attract interest and contributions across disciplines but more needs to be done to break down the distinctions between labour economics, organization theory, industrial relations or the sociology of work. If jobs and rewards are structured within firms then labour market analysis which abstracts from firms and ignores the issues of work organization and industrial relations becomes increasingly irrelevant. At the same time, if the organization of labour within firms is to be effectively analysed, employer policies towards labour must be situated within an overall analysis of their competitive strategies. The prime need is, therefore, for further progress in the development of an integrated analysis of the organization and structure of employment.

References

Armstrong, P. 1982. 'If It's Only Women it Doesn't Matter so Much'. *Work, Women and the Labour Market.* Ed. West, J. London: Routledge & Kegan Paul.

Ashton, D. 1986. *Unemployment under Capitalism: The Sociology of British and American Labour Markets.* Brighton: Harvester.

—— Maguire, M. and Garland, V. 1982. 'Youth in the Labour Market'. Research Paper No. 34. London: Department of Employment.

—— and Maguire, M. 1986. 'Young Adults in the Labour Market'. Research Paper No. 55. London: Department of Employment.

—— Maguire, M. and Spilsbury, M. 1987. 'Re-structuring the youth labour market'. Paper prepared for the IXth Conference of the International Working Party on Labour Market Segmentation, Turin.

Atkinson J. 1985. 'Flexibility: Planning for an Uncertain Future'. *Manpower Policy and Practice,* 1 (Summer), London: 26–9.

—— and Meager, N. 1985. *Changing Working Patterns.* London: NEDO.

—— and Meager, N. 1986. 'Is Flexibility Just a Flash in the Pan?' *Personnel Management* (September). 26–9.

Baron, B. 1984. 'Organizational Perspectives on Stratification'. *Annual Review of Sociology,* 10, 37–69.

Batstone, E. 1984. *Working Order: Workplace Industrial Relations over Two Decades.* Oxford: Basil Blackwell.

Becker, G. 1964. *Human Capital: A Theoretical And Empirical Analysis with Special Reference to Education.* New York: National Bureau of Economic Research.

Beechey, V. and Perkins, T. 1985. 'Conceptualising Part-time Work'. *New Approaches to Economic Life.* Eds Roberts, B., Finnegan, R. and Gallie, D. Manchester: Manchester University Press.

Berger, S. and Piore, M.J. 1980. *Dualism and Discontinuity in Industrial Societies.* Cambridge: Cambridge University Press.

Blackburn R.M. and Mann M. 1979. *The Working Class in the Labour Market.* London: Macmillan.

Bluestone, B. and Harrison, B. 1982. *The Deindustrialisation of America.* New York: Basic Books.

Braverman, H. 1974. *Labor and Monopoly Capital: The Degradation of Work in the Twentieth Century.* New York: Monthly Review.

Brown, R.K., Curran, M.M. and Cousins, J.M. 1983. 'Changing Attitudes to Employment?' Research Paper No. 40. London: Department of Employment.

Brown, W. and Nolan, P. 1988. 'Wages and Labour Productivity'. *British Journal of Industrial Relations*, forthcoming.

Brusco, S. 1982. 'The Emilian Model: Productive Decentralisation and Social Integration'. *Cambridge Journal of Economics*, 6 (June), 167–84.

Burns, A., Newby, M. and Winterton, J. 1985. 'The Restructuring of the British Coal Industry'. *Cambridge Journal of Economics*, 9 (March), 93–110.

Cain, G. 1976. 'The Challenge of Segmented Labour Market Theories to Orthodox Theory: A Survey'. *Journal of Economic Literature*, 14, 1215–1257.

Craig, C., Rubery, J., Tarling, R. and Wilkinson, F. 1982. *Labour Market Structure, Industrial Organization and Low Pay*. Cambridge: Cambridge University Press.

—— Rubery, J., Tarling, R. and Wilkinson, F. 1985. 'Economic, Social and Political Factors in the Operation of the Labour Market'. *New Approaches to Economic Life*. Eds Roberts, B., Finnegan, R. and Gallie, D. Manchester: Manchester University Press.

—— Garnsey, E. and Rubery, J. 12985. 'Payment Structures and Smaller Firms: Women's Employment in Segmented Labour Markets'. Research Paper No. 48. London: Department of Employment.

Creigh, S., Roberts, C., Gorman, A. and Sawyer, P. 1986. 'Self-employment in Britain: Results from the Labour Force Surveys, 1981–1984' *Employment Gazette* 94 (June), 183–94.

Crompton, R. and Jones, G. 1984. *White-Collar Proletariat* London: Macmillan.

Cross, M. 1986. *Towards the Flexible Craftsman*. London: Technical Change Centre.

Daniel, W.W. 1987. *Workplace Industrial Relations and Technical Change*. London: Frances Pinter.

—— and Millward, N. 1983. *Workplace Industrial Relations in Britain*. London: Heinemann.

Deakin, S. 1986. 'Labour Law and the Developing Employment Relationship in the UK'. *Cambridge Journal of Economics*, 10 (December), 225–46.

—— and Rubery, J. 1986. 'Typology, Dimensions and Regulation of Homework in the UK'. *Homeworking in Italy, France and the United Kingdom: Final Report*. Eds Varesi, P. and Villa, P. Brussels: Commission of the European Community.

Doeringer P. B. and Piore M. J. 1971. *Internal Labor Markets and Manpower Analysis*. Lexington, Mass.: D.C. Heath.

Edwards, P. 1987. *Managing the Factory: A Survey of General Managers*. Oxford: Basil Blackwell.

Edwards, R. 1979. *Contested Terrain: The Transformation of the Workplace in the Twentieth Century*. London: Heinemann.

—— Reich, M. and Gordon, D. (eds) 1975. *Labor Market Segmentation*. Lexington, Mass.: D.C. Heath.

Elbaum, B. and Wilkinson, F. 1979. 'Industrial Relations and Uneven Development: A Comparative Study of the American and British Steel Industries. *Cambridge Journal of Economics*, 3 (September), 275–303.

Ferner, A. 1985. 'Political Constraints and Management Strategies: The Case of Working Practices in British Rail'. *British Journal of Industrial Relations*, 23 (March), 47–70.

278   *Jill Rubery*

Gordon, D.M. 1972. *Theories of Poverty and Underemployment* Lexington, Mass.: D.C. Heath.

—— 1976. 'Capital Efficiency and Socialist Efficiency'. *Monthly Review,* 28 (July–August), 19–39.

—— Edwards, R. and Reich, M. 1982. *Segmented Work, Divided Workers.* Cambridge: Cambridge University Press.

Green, F. 1988. 'Neoclassical and Marxian Conceptions of Production. *Cambridge Journal of Economics,* forthcoming.

Hakim, C. 1985. 'Employers' Use of Outwork'. Research Paper No. 44. London: Department of Employment.

—— 1987a. 'Home-based Work in Britain'. Research Paper No. 60. London: Department of Employment.

—— 1987b. 'Trends in the Flexible Workforce'. *Employment Gazette,* 95 (November), 549–60.

Huws U. 1984. 'New Technology Homeworkers'. *Employment Gazette,* 92 (January), 13–17.

Knight, J. and Mayhew, K. 1987. 'Introduction to Special Issue, Wage Determination and Labour Market Inflexibility'. *Oxford Bulletin of Economics and Statistics,* 49 (February), 1–9.

Lester, R.A. 1952. 'A Range Theory of Wage Differentials'. *Industrial and Labor Relations Review,* 5 (July), 483–501.

Lindbeck, A. and Snower, D.J. 1985. 'Explanations of Unemployment'. *Oxford Review of Economic Policy',* (Summer), 34–59.

Lorenz, N. 1983. 'The Labour Process and Industrial Relations in the British and French Shipbuilding Industries, from 1880 to 1970: Two Patterns of Development'. Ph.D. thesis, University of Cambridge.

Low Pay Unit. 1987. *Cheap Labour: Britain's False Economy,* Pamphlet no. 45. Eds Brosnan, P. and Wilkinson, F. London: Low Pay Unit.

Mackay, D., Boddy, D., Brack, J., Diack, J. and Jones, N. 1971. *Labour Markets under Different Employment Conditions.* London: George Allen & Unwin.

Main, B. 1987. 'Hourly Earnings of Female Part-time Versus Full-time employees'. London: Centre For Economic Policy Research Workshop on Male–Female Differences in the British Labour Market.

Mallier, T. and Rosser, M. 1979. 'The Changing Role of Women in the British Economy', *National Westminster Bank Quarterly Review* (November), 54–65.

Manwaring, T. 1984. 'The Extended Internal Labour Market'. *Cambridge Journal of Economics,* 8 (March), 161–87.

Marglin, S. 1978. 'What Do Bosses Do?' *The Division of Labour: the Labour Process and Class Struggle in Modern Capitalism.* Ed. Gorz, A. Brighton: Harvester Press.

Marsden, D. and Silvestre, J.-J. 1986. 'The Economic Crisis and Labour Market Regulation in France and Great Britain. Is There Convergence to a New Pattern of Regulation?' Paper presented to the VIIIth conference of the International Working Party on Labour Market Segmentation, Cambridge.

Massey D. and Meegan, R. 1982. *The Anatomy of Job Loss: the How, Why and Where of Employment Decline.* London: Methuen.

Maurice, M., Sellier, F. and Silvester, J.-J. 1984. 'The Search for a Societal Effect in the Production of Company Hierarchy: A Comparision

of France and Germany'. *Internal Labor Markets*. Ed. Osterman, P. Cambridge, Mass.: MIT Press.
—— et al. 1986. *The Social Foundations of Industrial Power*. Cambridge, Mass.: MIT Press.
Meager, N. 1986. 'Temporary Work in Britain'. *Employment Gazette*, 94 (January), 7–15.
Michon, F. 1981. 'Dualism and the French Labour Market: 'Business Strategy, Non-standard Job-forms and Secondary Jobs'. *The Dynamics of Labour Market Segmentation* Ed. Wilkinson, F. London: Academic Press.
Millward, N. and Stevens, M. 1986. *British Workplace Industrial Relations 1980–84*. Aldershot: Gower.
Mincer, J. 1970. 'The Distribution of Incomes: A Survey with Special Reference to the Human Capital Approach'. *Journal of Economic Literature*, 8 (March), 1–26.
Mitter, S. 1986. 'Industrial Restructuring and Manufacturing Homework: Immigrant Women in the UK Clothing Industry'. *Capital and Class*. 27 (Winter), 37–80.
Moore, R. 1985. 'Free to Fall: Employment and Health and Safety'. Paper prepared for the VIIth Conference of the International Working Party on Labour Market Segmentation, Santiago de Compostela.
Nolan, P. 1983. 'The Firm and Labour Market Behaviour'. *Industrial Relations in Britain*. Ed. Bain, G. Oxford: Basil Blackwell.
—— and Brown, W. 1983. 'Competition and Workplace Wage Determination'. *Oxford Bulletin of Economics and Statistics*, 45 (August), 269–87.
—— and Edwards, P. 1984. 'Homogenise, Divide and Rule: An Essay on *Segmented Work, Divided Workers*'. *Cambridge Journal of Economics*, 8 (June), 197–215.
Oi, W. 1962. 'Labor as a Quasi-fixed Factor'. *Journal of Political Economy*, 52 (December), 53–55.
Osterman, P. (ed.) 1984. *Internal Labor Markets*. Cambridge, Mass.: MIT Press.
Piore, M. and Sabel, C. 1984. *The Second Industrial Divide*. New York: Basic Books.
Reich, M. 1984. 'Segmented Labour: Time Series Hypothesis and Evidence'. *Cambridge Journal of Economics*, 8 (March), 63–8.
Robinson, O. and Wallace, J. 1984. 'Part-time Employment and Sex Discrimination Legislation in Great Britain'. Research Paper No. 43. London: Department of Employment.
Rubery J. 1978. 'Structured Labour Markets, Worker Organisation and Low Pay'. *Cambridge Journal of Economics*, 2 (March), 17–36.
—— 1986. 'Trade Unions in the 1980s: The Case of the United Kingdom'. in R. Edwards et al. (eds.) *Unions in Crisis and Beyond: Perspectives from Six Countries*. Eds Edwards, R., Garonna, P. and Todtling, F. Dover, Mass.: Auburn House.
—— 1987. 'Flexibility of Labour Costs in Non-union Firms'. *Flexibility in Labour Markets*. Ed. Tarling, R. London: Academic Press.
—— (ed.) 1988 *Women and Recession*. London: Routledge & Kegan Paul.
—— and Wilkinson, F. 1981. 'Outwork and Segmented Labour Markets'.

The Dynamics of Labour Market Segmentation. Ed. Wilkinson, F. London: Academic Press.

—— Tarling, R. and Wilkinson, F. 1987, 'Flexibility, Marketing and the Organisation of Production'. *Labour and Society,* 12 (January), 131–51.

—— and Tarling, R. 1988. 'Womens' Employment in Declining Britain'. *Women and Recession.* Ed. Rubery, J.

—— Tarling, R. and Wilkinson, F. (forthcoming). 'Government Policy and the Labor Market: The Case of the UK. *The State and the Labour Market: Employment Policy, Collective Bargaining and Economic Crisis.* Ed. Rosenberg, S. New York: Plenum Publishing.

Schoer, K. 1987. 'Part-time Employment: Britain and West Germany'. *Cambridge Journal of Economics,* 11 (March), 83–94.

Spilsbury, M. et al. 1986. 'The Distribution and Growth of the Self-employed using Data from the Labour Force Surveys 1979–1984'. Labour Market Studies Group mimeo, University of Leicester.

Standing, G. 1986. *Unemployment and Labour Market Flexibility: The United Kingdom.* Geneva: International Labour Organization.

Tarling, R. 1981. 'The Relationship between Employment and Output: Where Does Segmentation Theory Lead Us?' *The Dynamics of Labour Market Segmentation.* Ed. Wilkinson, F. London: Academic Press.

—— (ed.) 1987. *Flexibility in Labour Markets.* London: Academic Press.

Varesi, P. and Villa, P. 1986. *Homeworking in Italy, France and the United Kingdom: Final Report.* Brussels: Commission of the European Communities, Employment, Social Affairs and Education.

Villa, P. 1986. *The Structuring of Labour Markets: A Comparative Analysis of the Steel and Construction Industries in Italy.* Oxford: Oxford University Press.

Walker, J. 1985. 'Central Government Policy and the Local Authority Labour Market in England and Wales 1979–84'. Ph.D. thesis, University of Cambridge.

Wilkinson, B. 1983. *The Shopfloor Politics of New Technology,* London: Heinemann.

Wilkinson, F. (ed.) 1981. *The Dynamics of Labour Market Segmentation.* London: Academic Press.

—— 1983. 'Productive Systems'. *Cambridge Journal of Economics,* 7 (September–December), 413–29.

Williamson, O. 1975. *Markets and Hierarchies.* New York: Free Press.

Willman, P. and Winch, G. 1985. *Innovation and Management Control: Labour Relations at BL Cars.* Cambridge: Cambridge University Press.

Wood, S. (ed.) 1982. *The Degradation of Work?* London: Hutchinson.

Woodward, J. 1965. *Industrial Organisation: Theory and Practice.* Oxford: Oxford University Press.

Zabalza, A. and Arrufat, J.L. 1985. 'The Extent of Sex Discrimination in Great Britain'. *Women and Equal Pay: The Effects of Legislation on Female Employment and Wages in Britain.* Eds Zabalza, A. and Tzannatos, Z. Cambridge: Cambridge University Press.

10 Gender and the Labour Market

Shirley Dex

The traditional topics of interest in the sociology of labour markets are shared with economists and include the determination of pay and income distribution, the matching of people to jobs, and the structure of employment and unemployment. The economist's concept of a market, bounded by demand and supply considerations and viewed through the decision-making of unisex individuals has had much influence on the study of labour markets. Sociologists interested in labour markets have had to compete for a hearing and much of their work has taken the form of criticizing the economic paradigm and its unwarranted status; in particular, there are criticisms of the abstract theorizing, the individualistic assumptions and the lack of interest in structure.

A consideration of gender in labour markets is another of the more recent ways sociologists, feminists and some radical and institutionalist American economists have joined forces to criticize further economic models of labour markets. In particular, the examination of women's position in labour markets shows up the limitations of a narrowly focused economic framework and challenges the suitability of traditional concepts of analysis. Reconceptualizations in the approach to labour market analysis have been in progress therefore, and they are reviewed in this article. For example, the conventional divisions between paid employment and unpaid work and between market production and non-market production have been challenged; links have been made between sexual divisions in the market and within the household; the meaning of unemployment and the notion of individualistic supply decision-making have been questioned; and the structures and processes of occupational segregation and segmentation are being documented.

This article will review the background to these changes and the way in which conceptualizations have changed in each of these conventional topic areas. The investigation of gender divisions has proved to be an important vehicle via which we are gaining a richer and better understanding of labour markets and their operation. Gender divisions have not always been found to be the most important labour market divisions, but their examination has certainly been the means by which many exciting new conceptualizations have come to light.

Pay Determination

The average earnings of women are well below those of men in all major industrialized countries. In Britain in 1983, the ratio of women's to men's full-time hourly earnings was 73 per cent. In the USA and in France similar figures apply. In France in 1980 the ratio was 72.4 and in the USA it was 60.2 for the ratios of annual earnings of full-time employees. In Britain the earnings differentials exist even when examined at a highly disaggregated occupation by industry level (Sloane, 1987). Some changes have occurred to the differential and the ratio is higher in the 1980s than it was in the 1950s and 1960s, but as a differential it has a long history, as Edgeworth's (1922) consideration of this topic reveals. Even since the Equal Pay Act was introduced into Britain in 1970 for operation in 1975, the differential remains, as it does in other countries with similar legislation (O'Neill, 1984). The persistence of these differentials raises a number of questions about the workings of labour markets. Can women's lower pay be explained by their lower labour market participation? Has increased women's labour force participation made any difference to their relative earnings? Is it women's occupational distributions which determine their lower pay, or are women discriminated against in pay in a way that is now illegal? Have legislative changes made any difference to these ratios? These theoretical and policy issues are closely linked since one needs to understand why gender differentials in pay arise and how they can change in order to assess whether policy initiatives or legislation have influenced them. Economists and sociologists have addressed themselves to these issues. Some of the analysis of these issues is highly quantitative, which perhaps explains why relatively few British sociologists have examined this issue. American sociologists, however, are thoroughly involved in debates about the causes of pay inequalities and as the debate has moved to consider how much women's occupations are responsible for their relatively low pay, more British sociologists have made a contribution to this area of research.

The Orthodox Tradition

The orthodox tradition of economic analysis, which has the longest standing analysis of pay, suggests that the pay of individuals is determined in a labour market. The forces of supply and demand for labour meet in this conceptual market-place and are equated by allowing the price to vary, which, in this case, is the wage rate. There will be one wage rate at which the supply and demand for labour will be in equilibrium, and at that wage rate the market will be cleared; there will be no involuntary unemployment since everyone who wants to work at the going wage rate will be able to work. There can be excess supply or demand if the wage rate is not at equilibrium level. Also, restrictions can be imposed on markets to stop them operating effectively; for example, minimum wage laws, trade unions restricting the supply of labour, people not having perfect information about vacancies or wage rates, or people being unwilling to move to the job vacancies. Within this framework, if the components of demand and supply can be specified, then wage rates will be predictable.

On the demand side, employers are thought to have a unisex outlook and to be concerned wholly with the worker's level of productivity. Earnings differentials between workers of the same level of productivity would be expected to be eliminated over time through the forces of competition; employers' preferences for cheaper labour power would bid up wages through their extra demand for these cheaper workers. Within the orthodox theory, therefore, persistent wage differentials between groups of workers could be the result of three factors: either workers may have differing productivities and be unequal in the employer's eyes, or workers may have differing supply preferences and choose lower or higher paid jobs as their preference, or the market may have some monopoly elements which prevent wages being equalized. Orthodox economists have tended to think that the differentials between men's and women's pay are too great to be explained by monopoly elements, and the trend has been to look to supply-side differences in men's and women's job preferences and in their productive potential; in the latter case human-capital theory has developed to analyse differences in individuals' productive potential. Sociologists have been critical of human-capital theory explanations. Feminist sociologists and some American radical economists have been drawing attention to the important part played historically by male dominated trade unions who have excluded women from certain occupations and who have contributed thereby to the formation of segmented labour markets. More of the details of these explanations and their critics are outlined below.

Human-capital Theory

Human-capital theory, elaborated largely by American economist Gary Becker (1964) is a theory about individual decision-making in which an individual can make an investment in his or herself by devoting time to studying, gaining additional educational qualifications or by acquiring skills and work experience. Such activities do not provide much immediate benefit, but they do provide a return in the future so that they can be thought of as an investment in one's own human capital. The activities which contribute to human capital are those the market is willing to reward. The decision about whether to make a particular investment should be made, along with all decisions, by comparing the present costs with the future stream of benefits. The idea, then, is that an individual's earnings can be explained in terms of their level of human capital; that is, their education, training and experience. Differences in earnings are to be explained by differences in human capital. Some writers take the extreme view that human-capital theory is sufficient to explain all of differences between men's and women's earnings. Other economists admit that part of the gap may be due to discrimination against women.

  Whilst the predictions of this theory overlap with the way education and experience are accumulated over the life cycle, the earnings differences between individuals and groups are usually far greater than the theory would suggest. Initially, it seemed that human-capital theory explained only part of earnings differentials. Over time, the theory's advocates have made stronger claims for it. At the extreme, it is argued that if only we had better measures of work experience, both in its amount and quality, better measures of quality differences in education, and measures of other unobservable differences in the productive potential of men and women (or whites and blacks) then these productivity differences would turn out to explain the whole of the earnings differentials between genders. Not all would agree. Explaining differences in earnings by this theory relies upon having accurate information about work experiences; such information was not available when these theories were being proposed, although it did become available in the 1970s in the USA. The lack of accurate information is a problem particularly for groups, like women, who are known to have interruptions in their work experience.

The application of human-capital theory to the problem of women's earnings was undertaken first by Mincer and Polachek (1974) and Polachek (1975). They argued that women have different expectations from men about their lifetime labour force participation, so women therefore make different investments and accumulate less human capital which gives them lower lifetime earnings; the main difference is that women are expected to plan to interrupt their work experience for childbirth. Women were predicted to have slower wage growth prior to their interruptions if they anticipated interruptions. Using data from the US National Longitudinal Survey which gives more accurate work experience measures for women, the gross earnings ratio between white married women and married men was increased from 66 per cent to 80 per cent. The initial studies of British women by Greenhalgh (1980) and Zabalza and Arrufat (1985) found that it was possible to explain some but not all of the earnings gap between men and women. These studies suffered from the lack of accurate work history data for the women, thus they did not accurately control for the differences in work experiences of men and women.

Main (1984) has replicated Mincer and Polachek's work using British data which have far more accurate work history information for women. On average, in 1980, the Women and Employment Survey found that women were working 65 per cent of their potential working lives; the proportion appears to be increasing. Main found that women's wages would be 20 per cent higher were it not for the interruptions in work experience over childbirth. Siebert and Sloane (1981) found that simple male and female earnings in the workplace were fairly similar after controlling for productivity differences. A study by Sloane at an establishment level found that human capital differences explained between 50 and 90 per cent of the variation in earnings of gender groups.

Even though we now have better measures of the amounts of women's employment experiences, its quality can still vary. In Britain where many women are known to work part-time, one could argue that this should be recognized in the calculations, otherwise the amount of women's work experiences will be being overestimated, the returns to that experience underestimated, and part of the gap between men's and women's earnings will remain unexplained when it could potentially be explained. Main (1987) has now shown that a substantial part of the earnings differences between men and women can be attributed to differences in part-time or full-time status of jobs. Main estimated that it is possible to close two-thirds of the gap in earnings between women in part-time employment, who are much more likely to have interrupted work histories than those who are in full-time employment, and males in full-time employment, by giving them a continuous record of employment. However, a continuous work history would only contribute to closing one-third of the gap between women's and men's earnings. What is always assumed in these studies is that men have uninterrupted work experiences since leaving school. This may or may not be true, especially if the samples include a sizeable proportion of younger workers. It is such an accepted view that it has not until recently been thought worth collecting men's work history data, although a considerable amount of men's data are now in the process of being collected.

Joshi and Newall (1986) have analysed a cohort of men and women born in 1946 who had pay data at age 26 and at 32. Work experience does not have the same effect on men's and women's earnings in their results; men's pay increased faster than women's pay for each year worked. Like Main, they found that working part-time reduced earnings after controlling for other differences, by about 10 per cent. Women with low-status employment and no qualifications experienced the greatest differential in comparison with men with respect to how their earnings were affected by employment experience.

A gap still remains to be explained in all studies. Differences in work experience are undoubtedly important in understanding women's relative earnings. However, part-time working also appears to be in part responsible for women's lower earnings in Britain. It is possible to calculate the cost to women's lifetime earnings of their time out of the labour market, their propensity to return to part-time jobs and the consequent downward occupational mobility which ensues. Joshi (1985) has put the estimate at twelve to fourteen years worth of annual average earnings. Since there is much less part-time work in most other industrialized economies than in Britain, this part of the explanation of earnings differentials may not be cross-culturally valid. It is also worth noting that in countries where women work full-time and with relatively uninterrupted work experience, as in France, the earnings gap between genders still exists even though it is smaller. Whilst human capital differences are relevant to an explanation of earnings differences between men and women in competitive market economies, they are only a part of the explanation. There is a notable lack of consideration of demand-side factors and unionization in this theory which has provoked critics.

Human-capital theory has been criticized in a number of ways. Bowles and Gintis (1975) were critical of the omission of social class as an explanatory variable. Social class has been thought to be an important determinant in individuals' decisions to gain additional qualifications or years of education; the middle classes have been thought to be more prepared to sacrifice current earnings in order to acquire education. Human-capital theory has not recognized these distinctions. Empirical studies of the wage growth after childbirth of American women have been at odds with the human-capital predictions. If, as appears to be the case, women can quickly recoup earnings losses from time out of employment for childbirth, why should they take childbirth into account when making occupational choices, as human-capital theory assumes they do? Mincer and Ofek (1982) attempted but did not succeed in reformulating human-capital theory to be consistent with the new data. Stewart et al. (1985) are critical of the human capital models. They take a different approach to earnings determination, based on a survey which asked people about the characteristics of their occupations. This included a question on which sex more typically did each of the jobs or whether both did. They found that the gender composition of occupations makes a substantial contribution to the determination of income, after 'market' factors have been taken into account. They interpret their results to mean that market factors are not a good explanation of the differences.

Another difficulty with human-capital theory is a causality problem about whether women's earnings opportunities cause them to make lower investments in human capital, or whether their lower earnings are caused by their lower investment levels. At at more fundamental level, it is possible to criticize the notion of productivity embedded in human-capital theory. It only counts as productive those skills which the market rewards. It does not recognize what the French have called tacit skills which both women and men can have. However, this lack of recognition is more of a problem for women. Many of the skills women have go unrewarded and unrecognized. Even at the level of so-called justifiable market productivity characteristics, women get penalized if criteria like length of service are used for promotion or recruitment to certain jobs. It is not clear that length of service enhances one's productivity in many jobs, so the idea that one's human capital depreciates when women are not employed, thus justifying their lower pay, clearly is not true. One might reasonably argue that human capital depreciated whilst workers are at work if they have to do monotonous or stressful jobs.

Segmented Labour Market Theories

A set of theories have emerged as a criticism of orthodox economists' approaches to the issue of earnings differentials. They link together pay differentials with occupational segregation, poverty, and race and sex discrimination. They began to be popular in the 1960s and 1970s amongst American radical and institutionalist economists, for example, Edwards, Reich and Gordon (1975). Gradually these theories crossed the Atlantic and they have been taken up in Britain by sociologists.

Piore's (1975) model of labour market segments is the best known and essentially divides the labour market into two segments, although one of the segments has a subdivision. His description (1975: 126) captures the main elements of the model:

> The basic hypothesis of the dual labour market was that the labour market is divided into two essentially distinct sectors, termed primary and secondary sectors. The former offers jobs with relatively high wages, good working conditions, chances of advancement, equity

and the due process in the administration of work rules and above all, employment stability. Jobs in the secondary sector, by contrast, tend to be low paying with poor working conditions, little chance of advancement, a highly personalized relationship between workers and supervisors which leads to wide latitude for favoritism and is conducive to hard and capricious work discipline and with considerable instability in jobs and high turnover among the labour force.

Writers tend to diverge in their views on the number of segments and on the causes of segmentation in labour markets. There are now a wide variety of segmented labour market models, as Loveridge and Mok (1979) illustrate. They vary mainly in the number of segments they describe and in the criteria which characterize and identify the different segments. In all, women are thought to be a part of the poorer secondary sector. Doeringer and Piore (1971) described the process of segmentation by introducing the concept of the 'internal labour market' which was suggested to be a feature of the primary sector. Internal labour markets are those in which the competition for jobs is restricted to internal candidates within the organization. Their development has been thought to benefit both workers and management in the context of changing industrial structure and technology. Since the majority of women were thought to be part of the secondary sector workforce in these models, they would be excluded from the internal labour market career structures.

Segmented labour market theories were imported into Britain largely through two papers, one by Doeringer and Bosanquet (1973), the other by Barron and Norris (1976); the latter specifically examined the place of women. Barron and Norris suggested that British women workers fitted the description of the secondary work-force since they had lower pay, they were concentrated in unskilled and insecure jobs, they were more likely to be made redundant than men and less likely to be upwardly mobile. Moreover, women were thought to have the necessary attributes which made them a suitable secondary work-force; namely, they are meant to be easily dispensible, they do not value economic rewards highly, they are easily identifiable as a group, they are not ambitious to acquire training or work experience and they are relatively ununionized and unlikely to develop solidaristic links with their fellow workers.

This view of women workers and their place in the labour market has been thought to be unsatisfactory for a number of reasons. Labour market theories which see women as a homogeneous mass of workers located in a single segment cannot hope to gain an accurate picture of the dynamic relationships within labour markets. Beechey (1978) criticized segmented labour market theories since they were not specific enough about women's position in the industrial and occupational structure; nor did they explain the post-war expansion in Britain of large numbers of women's jobs in the public sector, because they concentrated on manufacturing industry. Rubery (1978) criticized these theories for paying insufficient attention to the role of trade-union and workers' organization. This latter criticism has been taken up in the work of an American author, Edwards (1979).

Edwards has argued for introducing the negotiation process between labour and capital into accounts of segmentation in order to prevent them being overly deterministic. In his view, workers and capitalists are thought to be struggling over issues of control in the workplace, and the outcome of the struggle is not determined beforehand. Edwards links the development of segmented labour markets to a description of a set of historical changes in the systems of control that have operated in industry. Women are brought into this schema during the monopoly-capitalist phase as wage labour and part of the secondary labour force; patriarchal relations are also seen to have played a role in determining women's position. Edwards's theory still has its weaknesses and critics. Matthaei (1983) has criticized Edwards for failing to pay sufficient attention to the differences between women's jobs in his theory, the consequence of which is that his choice of labour market segments are not relevant to women. He places secretaries, nurses and craftsmen in the same category as managers and doctors.

Studies sympathetic to the notion that labour markets are segmented now appear to have moved away from making the grander theoretical and sweeping overviews. They have begun to focus more on small-scale and highly detailed case studies. The aim has been to use such case studies to find out more about the processes whereby earnings and earnings differentials come into being and are maintained within workplaces or industries. The Applied Economics Department at Cambridge has played an important role in this (Labour Studies Group, 1985; Wilkinson, 1981; Craig et al., 1982, 1985), and there are a growing number of sociological studies, for example, by Coyle (1982) and Armstrong (1982). These studies are charting the institutional mechanisms of pay negotiations and they are showing the enormous complexity of such arrangements, the mixture of formal pay negotiating mechanisms, informal arrangements and social conventions, all of which play a part in keeping women and low-paid workers in a weak bargaining position. Women who take up part-time work are particularly vulnerable to these effects. The concept of 'skill' which conventionally carries greater rewards has been shown to be socially constructed and the subject of bargaining procedures. This work is described in more detail below. The pay implications of this sort of labelling are not difficult to predict. Bargaining processes in which male dominated trade unions are at the forefront have not helped women to break down these divisions and in many cases have instigated them in the first place.

As well as the demand-side studies described above, there have been more detailed examinations of women's occupational histories. Dex (1987) has shown that women's lifetime occupational histories can be used to chart a series of labour market segments which are appropriate for women's employment; they include, 'the primary non-manual sector' (professionals, teachers), 'the women's primary sector' which is subdivided into two parts, manual (skilled manual) and non-manual (clerical), and 'the women's secondary sector' (semi-skilled and unskilled) which is also divided into two, full-time and part-time. There is movement between some of these, in particular directions. The common route of taking a part-time job after childbirth is often associated with downward occupational mobility since part-time jobs in Britain are mostly very low skilled and low paid. Taking a part-time job after childbirth has been estimated to increase the likelihood of the woman experiencing downward occupational mobility by around 30 per cent. These segments have only been described for women; clearly there is a need to get an overall picture of men's and women's positions and relationships. However, the picture is not static and the part-time sector has been expanding rapidly in Britain.

In the USA the debate between human-capital theorists and institutional approaches has taken place through quantitative regression studies which have set out to test the hypotheses of the alternatives. American researchers Bibb and Form (1977) and Beck et al. (1978) found evidence supporting the need for a structural view of the labour market to supplement a supply-side human-capital view. Borooah and Lee (1986) have done similar work in Britain. However, Kalleberg and Sorenson's (1983) review of the American work suggests that the results of such studies are not unambiguous because they contain methodological problems. On the whole, these studies have not paid particular attention to gender divisions so that they do not take our understanding of the place of gender in labour markets any further.

The question of how far women's earnings are a product of their occupational position has been considered. The latest calculations by Sloane (1987) suggest that reallocating women between occupations in the same proportions as men would not improve their earnings as much as giving them the average earnings men are paid whilst leaving women in the occupations they are already in. Chiplin and Sloane (1974) found the same result in an earlier and less disaggregated analysis, so little has changed since the Equal Pay Act came in.

Skill

One of the factors which earnings differentials are accepted to rest upon is that different jobs involve different levels of skill, and that skill should be rewarded. This concept has been seen to form the basis of occupational classifications and occupational rankings. Research has suggested that the concept of skill cannot be regarded as unproblematic, as it has tended to be. This area of research is leading to radical criticisms of the work on women's position in labour markets. Empirical work has revealed that the meaning of skill is socially constructed. The study by Craig et al. (1982) study of the process of producing paper boxes in Britain found that women who worked on hand-fed machines were considered, classified and paid as unskilled workers. Men who produced cartons on a more automated process which required less individual concentration were classified as semi-skilled, a higher level of skill. There is a sense in which 'unskilled' comes to be defined as anything women do.

Other studies reviewed by Phillips and Taylor (1980), Game and Pringle (1983) and Coyle (1982) have reached similar conclusions. They have added the dimension to the picture that many skill divisions between men and women in the clothing industry, for example, have emerged through the struggle of unionized men, often in craft-based unions, attempting to maintain their skilled title and the associated pay differential over women, despite the decline in technical skill content of their jobs. There are also cases of sewing done by men being labelled 'skilled' and sewing done by women being labelled 'semi-skilled'. The dubious nature of these skill divisions can be seen most vividly through the introduction of new technology. One study of the clothing industry found that men who were forced to take on machinery work usually done by women and labelled semi-skilled fought to have the work redefined as skilled. It would appear to be the case that for a woman to become skilled in the clothing industry, she would have to change her sex. Other examples of the importance of male dominated trade unions and their important part in creating and maintaining skill divisions along gender line comes from Armstrong (1982). He also points out that skill divisions can overlap with the degree of capital intensity in a production process, in which case 'women's work' is the labour intensive kind.

The process takes on a slightly different form outside manufacturing industry, where craft-based unions are absent. On the whole, the services sector has been the one which has grown and offered the growing women's work-force new (part-time) jobs. Crompton, Jones and Reid (1982) and Davies (1975) have documented these distinctions in clerical occupations. The idea that women's work is unskilled or semi-skilled can be built in from the start, and paid at suitably low-skilled rates. The expansion of public sector jobs has taken place on this basis. The caring occupations, childcare, nursery nurses and the whole array of social service jobs done by women (e.g. home helps) are all thought to be generally unskilled. What this means is that the skills involved are not recognized as skills by either employers or by society. Also part-time work appears to be being defined as inherently low skilled. The cost advantages to employers are obvious. The ultimate area of women's low-skilled work is in the home in unwaged childrearing and domestic responsibilities.

It is worth considering how the different valuations of work have arisen and why they persist. Part of the reason for the hierarchy between men's and women's work is undoubtedly related to the fact that men's work is paid and that women have often gone unpaid for their contribution. Since our economic system measures its wealth and value by adding up the paid work done, it is not surprising that being paid takes on a particular value of its own. There will, of course, be scarcity value for some abilities, and this in part explains why housework is not valued highly, since, as Richards (1980) suggests, anyone can do it. The scarcity value of so-called men's skills does not explain divisions between paid jobs. Neither is it clear that childrearing is unskilled or something which anyone can do efficiently.

Women and men have accepted these status distinctions to some extent. However, Martin and Roberts (1984) found that women's views about what is women's work depended to some extent on whether or not they worked with men. These women realized that men were not doing 'women's jobs' because they were not prepared to do women's work with the low pay it entails. Husbands, on the other hand, who were in more sex-segregated workplaces than the women, were more likely to think that women could not do their work, rather than think that they would not be prepared to do it. When faced with redundances, as Coyle (1984) illustrated, women felt protective towards their jobs and appear to be less likely then to give men's jobs any priority over their own. The men may become more entrenched in traditional views under this sort of pressure. Armstrong (1982; 27) found the attitude of the men to women's redundancies was 'Oh well, if its only women it doesn't matter so much'.

There appear to be a series of factors which have helped to construct and now maintain the gendered divisions of skill. These include the societal valuation of paid work, union-negotiated labels of skill for certain men's jobs and the attitudes and acceptance by men and women of gender divisions. These factors underly pay differentials based on skill divisions and need to be incorporated into theorizing about labour market relationships, rather than treated as unproblematic.

Conclusions

We can now begin to evaluate this area of research on pay determination and assess the progress made. The dissatisfaction with orthodox economics led to segmented labour markets being suggested; the latter can be seen as a response to orthodox economics which stresses the importance of the demand side to labour markets, especially for explaining gendered divisions. Since arriving in Britain, there has been a maturing process; empirical studies have replaced speculative theorizing, particularly about the place of women in the labour market, and more grounded theories are emerging. However, the processes are complex and changing. As well as gaining increases in their work experience, women are fast gaining marketable credentials, as Crompton and Sanderson (1986) show. To the extent that human capital is important, we would expect to see women's earnings rising in the future. Whether a sufficient rise occurs will, in part, be a test of this theory. This is a different development than has been taking place in the USA where, as described earlier, the trend has been to test the alternative explanations of earnings differentials between genders in quantitative studies using secondary data sources on the whole. They have failed to resolve this debate since there is supportive evidence for each view.

A recognition of the importance of both human-capital differences and structural divisions for explaining earnings differentials has grown amongst many researchers. Human capital is by no means a sufficient explanation of earnings differences, however, as the segmented labour market theorists and others have shown. Differences of view can still be found over the emphasis given to the importance of these supply and demand aspects. One can see here how the economists' paradigm of a labour market has set the context and dominated the concerns of these debates, if not all the substantive content of research. However, changes are on the way. It is being recognized that there are other aspects to the problem to be taken into consideration. The nature of skill and the way it is socially constructed has been seen to be an important aspect of gendered pay differentials. The role of ideology and state policies, alongside the supply and demand considerations, and the way both supply and demand factors can be formed

FIGURE 10.1 *Women as a percentage of occupational labour force.
Great Britain 1975 and 1983*

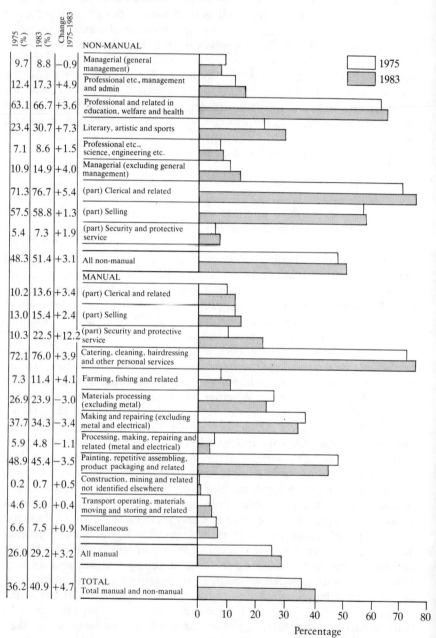

Source: Equal Opportunities Commission, *Eighth Annual Report*, 1983, 1984

interactively with state policies are also important. It has long been recognized that institutional factors play an important part in earnings determinations at the workplace, alongside supply and demand factors. Further consideration to some of these concerns will be given below. Studies of earnings and labour force participation within a broader framework have shown that employment takes place within the context of a certain division of labour within the home, where women take primary responsibility for childcare. One cannot examine labour market relations, therefore, without at the same time understanding the division of labour within the household.

The Structure of Employment

Interest has grown in describing and explaining how the structure of employment is divided along gendered lines. Women are concentrated in a small number of occupations and industries, and concepts like 'women's work' and 'men's work' are offered, usually in conversation, for this division. The occupational division is not unrelated to pay differentials, as we saw in the previous section, and as will be considered further below. However, there are other issues than the pay implications to consider why women (and men) are located in these occupations, as outlined below. The concept of occupational segregation is one which is important in this subject area.

Occupational Segregation

The concept of occupational segregation is one which owes its origin wholly to the growing interest in women's employment, and, in particular, to the way women are distributed through occupational categories in comparison with men. Measures have been devised specifically to register the extent of the divisions and whether they have changed in size over time. It has also become a central concept in debates which are occurring in both the USA and in Britain over whether equal opportunities and civil rights legislation in the 1960s and 1970s have had any effects on women's occupational and pay distributions.

As well as being primarily in clerical, semi-skilled factory and semi-skilled domestic work (e.g. waitresses, barmaids, school meals), women constitute a high proportion of certain occupational categories. The concentration in certain occupations can be seen in figure 10.1. In 1983, for example, women constituted 67 per cent of the professional and related (education, welfare and health), 77 per cent of clerical (non-manual), 59 per cent of selling (non-manual), 76 per cent of catering, cleaning, etc. and 45 per cent of painting and repetitive assembling occupational categories. There is some evidence that British black women are more concentrated in a few occupations than women in general, as Parman (1982) shows. Women's occupational distribution in other industrialized economies is very similar to that in Britain, with some minor variations. Many of the British women's jobs are part-time; 45 per cent of the total of women's jobs in 1984.

A number of measures have been used to capture this concentration, and they are reviewed by Hakim (1979). Hakim also discusses the important distinction between horizontal and vertical occupational segregation; horizontal segregation occurs if women and men are working in different types of occupations, whereas vertical occupational segregation exists if men are mostly in higher grade occupations and women in lower grade ones. Blau (1975) has a further distinction between inter-occupational segregation, that is, between occupational categories, and intra-occupational segregation, within an occupational category. Research initially tended to concentrate on horizontal and inter-occupational segregation since it is much more difficult to obtain data which would indicate the extents of the other types of segregation. However, through the legislative interest in sex discrimination, and new surveys, more detailed data on women's and men's position within organizations which can be used to monitor vertical occupational segregation over time is becoming available.

Hakim's calculations of occupational segregation measures illustrated that the extent of segregation depends upon the measure used. Nevertheless, the measures do still provide a reasonable guide to the way segregation has changed over time. Over the period 1900–70, occupational segregation has declined slightly in Britain but more in the USA. The proportion of women in professional work (lower and higher grades) declined in both countries between 1940 and 1970. Part of the explanation for the changes is that men made inroads into women's occupations, but the reverse did not take place. More recent studies by Hakim (1981) for Britain, and Beller (1982a, 1982b) and England (1982) for the USA, show that between 1967 and 1977 occupational segregation has declined more substantially in Britain and the USA. Women were found to have an increased likelihood of working in a typically 'male' occupation, particularly professional and managerial jobs and especially in the USA. Recession in the late 1970s is thought, however, to have worsened women's position. The improvements in the USA are attributed to equal opportunities legislation, although this is debated. Despite the improvements, occupational segregation remains widespread.

The Women and Employment Survey of 1980 provided evidence that intra-occupational segregation was widespread (Martin and Roberts, 1984), and the General Household Survey confirms these results. They found that 63 per cent of women were in jobs done only by women and the equivalent figure for men was 80 per cent. Higher level occupations were less likely to find women working only with women, and women who worked part-time in any occupation were much more likely to work only with women. Whilst the extent of occupational segregation appears to increase because of part-time work, the major determinant of the extent of the segregation is that women are in certain occupations, rather than that they are in part-time jobs. Sloane's work on the New Earnings Survey suggests that vertical occupational segregation is far more important that horizontal segregation in explaining women's lower earnings than men. Thus women are disadvantaged in promotion within occupations in comparison with men.

The introduction of the concept of occupational segregation has provided us with a much clearer and a more accurate description of gender-divided labour markets. We can see the extent of these divisions and the relative lack of change over a century. There have of course been changes in women's jobs over this century, most notably a movement out of domestic service, although it is debatable just what sort of change this is. It could be argued that it is not women's jobs or occupations which have changed, so much as their organization. When in domestic service, women did the same jobs within a house, food preparation, cleaning, sewing, etc. as they now do in factories or workplaces. Specialization in one particular task has of course increased, probably to the detriment of the intrinsic interest in the job.

Explanations of Occupational Segregation

There are a variety of explanations why it is that women are doing these jobs. One argument put forward by some economists is that women choose certain occupations, namely women's occupations, in preference to others. We will examine this view in more detail below. Hartmann (1979) has argued that the concept of patriarchy is important to the explanation; that is, the domination of women by men which is argued to predate capitalist class domination. The argument put forward is that excluding women from certain occupations is one of the new ways, under capitalism, that men have devised to keep women dependent on men since it keeps women in low paid-jobs, thus encouraging them to marry and be dependent on men's wages within marriage. Matthaei (1983), Beechey (1986) and Walby (1986) show through case studies that a single explanation is not sufficient. Women can be seen to have pressed for entry into some occupations, in the health occupations for example; in others more active resistance from male trade unions has kept them out. There are also ideological factors which have influenced why women are in some occupations and not in others; in Britain, women's occupations are also divided according to whether they are part-time or full-time. The risk of sexual harassment and 'hanky-panky' have been used by employers as a justification for not allowing men and women to work together, as Game and Pringle (1983) show. Such behaviour whether actual or imagined undoubtedly suits men well in their efforts to guard their privileged labour market positions. In the following subsections, a number of contributory elements to women's occupational segregation in Britain are examined; women's occupational choice, the role of part-time employment, and the role of changing technology.

Occupational Choice

Research into the subject of occupational choice has been concerned with how individuals end up in certain occupations. There is some debate about how far it is a conscious choice. Much of the emphasis has been on young people and their transition from school to work, and early studies as reviewed in Dex (1985) tended to assume that an occupation is what one is paid for, and that young women were not interested in their jobs since they were just filling in time before getting married. Work on this topic in the 1950s began to see occupational choice as a development process instead of an event, and Ginzberg (1951) charted a series of phases through which young men's choices were thought to develop; these became the framework for much research in the USA until Blau and Duncan (1967) set off a trend of quantitative investigations into the factors affecting the first occupations and subsequent statuses of young men. Women came to be included in time (Dex, 1985). In Britain theoretical debates took the centre of the stage and these are reviewed below.

Roberts (1968, 1973) suggested that young people have very little sense of choice and that, instead, the process whereby they come to be matched to jobs is best conceived as being one of allocation. The empirical evidence that working-class children get working-class jobs, and middle-class children get middle-class jobs etc. was used to support the idea of an allocation process. Willis's (1977) study of working-class boys revealed that the allocation process was a complex one which included the active role and choices of the boys themselves. Gendered choices were given little consideration.

Empirical studies of young women did start to take place in the 1970s, encouraged by feminist researchers, and much more is now known about how young women choose their occupations and make the transition from school to work from McRobbie (1978), McRobbie and Garber (1975), Sherratt (1983) Coyle (1984), Griffin (1985) and Breakwell and Weinberger (1986), for example. The results overlap with those from quantitative studies; home background, ethnic origin and education are important influences on choices. The fact that mothers (and fathers) are in certain occupations obviously sets a framework for daughters' (and sons') choices. Factors like intelligence, ability, personality, interests, values and occupational knowledge also play a part. Young women have not been found to have a domestic orientation when they have been studied; they seem to give priority to getting a paid job, although they do have concepts like 'glamour' influencing their choices.

A completely different line of interest in occupational choice has come from economists seeking to apply human-capital theory to this subject. They want to argue that it is women's preferences for different occupations which are responsible for their choices. Individuals are assumed to choose their occupation with a view to maximizing lifetime earnings, given their level of investment in education and training. Polachek (1976) has suggested that women choose to enter occupations for which earnings losses when one is absent are the smallest. Women are thought to find occupations attractive, therefore, if their skills deteriorate least whilst they are absent from the labour force during childbearing. Polachek is implying that so-called 'women's occupations' are those which penalize labour force absence the least, and that is why there are so many women in them. He claimed to provide some empirical support for this view.

There have been critics of Polachek's reasoning and his empirical work. England (1982) has pointed out that this theory fails to explain why women would choose occupations with low levels of rewards for experience. If women only plan to have intermittent employment, greater lifetime earnings will accrue in an occupation which rewards what little experience one does accumulate. It is more rational, therefore, for women to choose an occupation where the appreciation rate which rewards experience is greater than the depreciation rate which affects time out of employment. England concludes that women do not maximize lifetime earnings by choosing traditional female occupations. Beller (1982a) criticized Polachek's empirical work on which the claim rests. These authors have continued to debate the empirical basis for the human-capital view in Polachek (1985) and England (1985). It is worth noting that the inconsistent rationality implied by the human-capital view remains unresolved by these debates. Thus a major weakness remains in orthodox economists' explanation of women's occupational choices and women's occupational segregation. However, there is a sense in which these authors and others would agree. They would all accept that women's labour market decisions and their domestic life are interrelated.

The empirical studies which touch upon this issue, limited as they are, have found that large proportions of each gender exhibit similar attitudes towards work. These similarities have often been neglected in favour of stressing the differences; for example, Johnson and Townsend (1976), Brown et al. (1983), and Agassi (1982). Also, women's attitudes towards work have been found to be more positive than is often supposed, as Martin and Roberts (1984) and Dex (1988) show.

Part-time Work

Any explanation of women's occupational segregation in Britain has to address the fact that so much of women's employment is part-time. Also, occupational segregation increases when part-time employment is considered. Part-time work has been increasing in Britain since the 1960s and 88 per cent of all part-time employees were women in 1984, according to the Labour Force Survey. Approximately 45 per cent of employed women are in part-time work. There is a pattern of returning after childbirth to a part-time job, as described earlier. Much part-time work is in service industries and is low paid and thought to be low skilled. The growth of part-time work in Britain has raised questions about why this has occurred, which occupations and industries are using part-timers and why, and how part-time work fits into the overall employment relations.

A major theoretical argument has been advanced by Walby (1987) and Pollert (1987) that the growth in women's part-time employment has arisen predominantly because of employers' desires for flexibility, and that part-time work is the latest expression of long-standing patriarchal relationships which have operated in the workplace and the home. That women have chosen these part-time jobs is of secondary importance in explaining their growth, although there are clear benefits to women from doing part-time work, if they accept the primary responsibility for childcare. Beechey and Perkins (1987) and Robinson and Wallace (1984) have shown some of the reasons employers give for taking on part-timers. It can be to meet fluctuations in demand or be suited to the nature of the work. Also, it clearly fits in with many women's preferences, given that they want to work *and* accept responsibility for childcare at home. The fact that Britain has far more part-time workers than other countries has led to a search for the causes. Dex and Shaw's (1986) comparison of Britain and the USA has shown how employers' insurance payments for employees, taxation structures, taxation's treatment of childcare expenses, equal opportunities policies and supply and demand considerations all come together to help explain Britain's much higher incidence of part-time work. The availability of childcare facilities, at a reasonable price, is undoubtedly another consideration which affects women's labour force decisions. The demand-pull of employers who see the benefits has probably been the strongest influence encouraging this growth. However, one cannot explain why it is that women and not some other group fill these jobs without recourse to ideological factors about women's views of their roles and employer's views about what is appropriately 'women's work'.

Changing Technology

Some important insights into gender relations and occupational segregation are being gained from studies of how new jobs are created, and how they get allocated between men and women. Braverman's (1974) neo-Marxist work has set the framework for this analysis. His account of the labour process is one in which technological change breaks down jobs into progressively less skilled tasks. The term 'deskilling' has been used to describe this process. Braverman's analysis drew in the sexual division of labour by pointing to the deskilling of clerical tasks into simpler components like copy-typing and filing. Also, women are seen to be part of the redistribution of jobs away from manufacturing towards services.

Feminists have criticized the concept of deskilling because it accepts a notion of skill which is romanticized, based on a male artisan, and which is not clearly defined; also, it is premised on an uncritical acceptance that women's work is always of low skill and status. There is a need to clarify the various meanings of skill to make any further progress; that is, whether it is the technical content, the control over the production process, the conventional definitions, or the scarcity element which is meant. The discussion of skill earlier in this chapter found that whilst occupations can involve genuine technical competence, and women have not pursued training and apprenticeships to the same extent as have men, skill can also be unrelated to technical competence, and be a negotiated title to justify a pay differential at women's expense. MacKenzie and Wajcman's (1985) study of technology concluded that 'skill' is set up by one or more competing groups to close off some market positions to others. The process of deskilling, to the extent that it has occurred, has been criticized because it has affected men's so-called skills, not women's, and has posed a threat to their masculinity.

Case studies of individual industries by Harvey (1987) and Game and Pringle (1983) conclude that the division of labour is not determined by biological or technological factors, but rests on the power and choice rooted in capital and gender relations. Biological reasons are often given for why women do or do not do certain jobs which are claimed to be heavier, more boring and repetitive, or need scientific or mechanical skills. Cockburn's (1985) and Harvey's (1987) studies of the gender relations in workplaces show that sexual symbolism attaches to objects and it is important in the job allocation process between gender groups. Examples are given of young men who will not mop the floor because that is women's work although they will sweep it with a long brush. Cockburn's (1986) study of girls in atypical jobs on YTS shows that the environment of work is important; that is, a male culture can be sufficient to dissuade women from pursuing atypical careers. Lee and Wrench's (1987) study of the effects of YTS found that the greater availability and variety of training schemes for young people had the effect of merely translating an earlier gender division into a new context so that gender continued to structure young people's life chances. It would appear, therefore, that new jobs and new technologies only modify the gendered distribution of jobs, and that when new jobs are created, old symbolism is drawn on to decide whose jobs they are.

Employment, Work and Unemployment

Waged and Unwaged Work

Some of the recent developments have been questioning the conventional divide between waged employment and unwaged work. Feminist research in particular has wanted to argue that this distinction is not clear cut; the boundary is shifting and the two types of work are intimately interrelated often to the extent that labour market theories which ignore unwaged labour will be weakened by so doing.

One way in which the waged–unwaged division is broken down is to see housework and motherhood as occupations on a par with others. Oakley has written about the experiences of housework (1974) and motherhood and childbearing (1979) in a way that shows that these activities are work, in the same sense as any paid occupations and that many of the experiences of working are common across all types of work. Barker and Allen (1976) argued similarly that there are more things in common across the wage–unwaged divide than there are differences. One implication of this view is that research on work can just as well take place in the home as it can in organizations. The Domestic Labour Debate between Marxist-feminist writers has been an attempt by one group to formalize the role of women's domestic labour and recognize its value and necessity in the process of production. These debates are reviewed in Dex (1985). Other writers have documented the interrelationships between public and private spheres of life, and the gender divisions on which such distinctions rest; for example, Siltanen and Stanworth (1984) and Finch (1983). Finch shows the relationships between waged and unwaged work by describing the way certain men's jobs rely on a wife's servicing activities.

The boundary between waged and unwaged work is seen to be unclear when informal economies are examined, and researchers are documenting the complexity of definitions of work and relationships between the various types. Informal working arrangements clearly form a vital part of the whole set of labour market relationships. The black economy is one aspect, although relatively little is known about it because of the difficulties of undertaking research on this topic. There are a growing number of studies of homework, outwork and freelancing, for example, by Hakim (1984a, 1984b) and Cragg and Dawson (1981). These workers are in varied occupations and have varied experiences, although they are more predominantly in services. In 1981 there were estimated to be approximately 658,250 of them, 2.8 per cent of the labour force; this may be an underestimate since homeworkers are difficult to track down. Approximately 45 per cent of homeworkers are thought to be women. On average, homeworkers have lower pay and worse contracts of employment, if they have contracts at all.

These relatively newly identified sectors of labour markets await a theoretical integration with the rest. There is a framework, linked to the segmented labour market literature which uses the concepts of core and periphery to divide up different types of employment, but it is not well formulated as it stands, and is somewhat oversimplified for the complex set of relationships which are being documented in labour market research, as Redclift and Mingione (1985) point out. Pahl (1984) has argued that the notion of 'the informal economy' should be discarded. He argues that because employers are not declaring their full income, or fulfilling their obligations under employment legislation, essentially does not change the social relations between employees and employers enough to put them in a separate economy. However, the social relations of work are modified by this behaviour and it clearly is important to chart the implications of these differences in workers' position, especially when the majority of them are women. The labels used to classify these differences is a less important issue.

Unemployment

An important counterpart to considerations of how employment is structured along gendered lines is to consider how unemployment is structured. Much of the sociological interest in unemployment has been concerned with the experience of unemployment by individuals, most often men in the past. More recently this focus on the experience of unemployment has extended to examining the effects on the household members and relationships; also women's experiences of unemployment have been receiving attention. It is not the intention to consider all aspects of gender and unemployment here. However, it is necessary to consider some aspects of the meanings and definitions of unemployment in order to consider how they play a role in the structure of labour markets overall. With the rise in interest in women's role in labour markets, sociologists and feminists have given more consideration to the issues of who is affected by unemployment and why. Sinfield (1981) reviews the general material in this field. This chapter will limit itself to the questions how gender groups are affected and whether women are a reserve army of labour.

The idea of a reserve army of labour comes from Marx, although he did not define the concept very precisely. At the most general level the reserve army consists of 'every labourer . . . when he is only partially employed or wholly unemployed' (Marx, quoted in Anthias, 1980: 51). It is a relative surplus population therefore. Some concrete categories of this reserve are 'the floating category' in which labourers are sometimes attracted and other times repelled into modern industry; 'the stagnant category', the labourers who are irregularly employed; and 'the latent category' which is mainly the agricultural population displaced by the capitalist penetration of modern industry. Women have been argued to be part of the reserve army in the post-war economy for a number of reasons. They have been increasingly drawn into the wage labour force, and often into jobs with poor conditions and little security in terms of their contracts of employment; thus women would be expected to be more disposable and more vulnerable than men to cyclical fluctuations.Beechey (1977) argued therefore that women were part of the reserve because of their experiences, even if they did not fall neatly into one of the existing categories of reserve. Power (1983) argued that women fit into the latent reserve category because of changes in the nature of housework over the twentieth century. Since housework no longer involves production, but merely reproduction and maintenance, women and the family are now more dependent on capitalist production which has taken over home-based production and releases women to join the labour force.

Anthias (1980) has been critical of applying the reserve army notion to women. She argued that the concept can only apply to a labour force that is made unemployed and then used as a reserve. These may or may not be more likely to be women or other minority groups. Anthias is critical also of the marginalization of women's employment which is implicit in the concept of the reserve, and she suggests a framework which seeks to integrate women and take their employment seriously.

The debate between Marxist-feminists over this issue is instructive of the struggles women are having in breaking new ground in their theorizing about women's work. The same issues can be seen in the domestic labour debate, and in other fields of industrial sociology. There is a desire to avoid the theoretical domination of and subordination to earlier male or abstractly formulated theories, without wanting to dismiss old concepts for the sake of having something new. The application of earlier concepts, whether they be Marxist or other, leaves obvious cracks in the analysis. It is clearer to see what is not acceptable than to provide the necessary integration. A framework which links women's position in the home and their position in the labour force to men's positions in both of these spheres, and which explains the changes which have been occurring, is far from being fully outlined.

In seeking to examine the incidence of unemployment by gender a number of problems arise. Who is counted as unemployed rests on the definition of what counts as unemployment. From the earliest days of unemployment records in Britain, the measure and definition has been linked to the eligibility for national insurance benefits, though the precise relationship has changed. What has been common is that the eligibility criteria have discriminated against women, as Garside (1980) describes. Thus women have had a disincentive to register as unemployed or to think of themselves as unemployed. (Cragg and Dawson (1984) document the variety of ways women who are not employed view their situation.) The unemployment figures underestimate, by large proportions therefore, the number of women who have been unemployed. One estimate by Roberts (1981) suggests it is as much as 60 per cent underestimated. (It is interesting to note that in the USA where the collection of unemployment statistics rests on a survey, rather than on voluntary registration as in Britain, women's unemployment is consistently above that of men's.) There is little serious analysis of women's unemployment which can be done with the British series on women's unemployment therefore. Researchers have had to find ways round this problem.

Bruegel (1979) used the yearly British employment changes from 1950 to 1978 to examine the issue whether women were a more disposable work-force than men. She concluded that where women and men work together, as in manufacturing industries, women seem more susceptible than men to unemployment. In the service sector, however, where women predominate, they were shielded from the impact of recession because of the growth of this sector. Rubery and Tarling (1983) confirmed that women have amplified cyclical fluctuations in manufacturing, but not in all sectors. Dex and Perry (1984) who conducted a more disaggregate analysis than Bruegel, also extending the data from 1978 to 1981, found that women did not unequivocally suffer in recession more than men, even in manufacturing industries; the conclusions were found to vary according to which manufacturing industry was examined, and according to whether absolute or percentage, or part-time or full-time jobs were compared for men and women. Part-time jobs in manufacturing underwent greater proportionate fluctuations than full-time jobs, but this applied to both men's and women's jobs. As the recession deepened, the service sector remained buoyant, largely through the continued growth of part-time women's employment. Women appear to have been sheltered from the effects of recession to a large extent by being in part-time jobs in the expanding sector of the economy. These results do not fit in very well with the notion that women are part of a reserve army of labour.

Joshi (1982) used insurance card records to examine fluctuations in women's unemployment in comparisons with men's. She found that there was a greater tendency for women to drop out of the labour force, but the cyclical elasticities of men and women, that is, their sensitivity to fluctuations in the economy, were not significantly different.

Older married women were found to be a particularly stable work-force. Joshi's results support the idea that women are not a marginal work-force, and that they are not a homogeneous lump, all behaving in the same way. Life cycle variations in women's labour force participation are clearly important to the understanding of their position.

Empirical work on the structure of unemployment and the question of whether women are a reserve army of labour or a disposable work-force buffeted by economic fluctuations suggest they are not. One could argue that these are the wrong questions to have been asking about gendered divisions, questions which have been directed too much by existing male centred theorizing. Of course, it has been a valuable and necessary exercise to put these questions to rest, but it leaves the task of formulating and answering more specific gender-related questions about the fluctuations in women's and men's employment and unemployment still to be done.

Conclusions

Since the 1960s, there has been a considerable amount of research into women's position in labour markets. Initially, the effort was directed towards finding out about women since they had been neglected by many of the then existing traditions of sociological research. Gradually the emphasis has moved away from focusing on women to a considera-tion of gender relations as researchers have recognized the importance of the interrelationships between women's and men's labour market experiences. Much has been learned about women and about gender relations over the past two decades. Also, many conceptual changes have been injected into sociological research as a result of these developments.

Gender divisions have been shown to be pervasive across a range of social institutions, labour markets included. In the labour market, the role that gender plays is complex. As Game and Pringle (1983) have described, gender is fundamental to the way work is organized and work is central to the social construction of gender. The new developments have involved both negative and positive aspects. The conventional dichotomies of work/home, production/consumption, formal/informal, public sphere/private sphere have been found to be misleading ways of conceptualizing gender relations, although they may have ideological uses. Research has tended to break down these conceptual divisions. The new developments have also involved a recognition of the importance of life-cycle variations in women's and men's work activities and relations. Women's and men's position in labour markets are not homogeneous, and they can be seen to rest on a number of factors; on ideological views about what is women's (and men's) work; on ideological views about women's place and role within the household; on how the labour market has evolved through the interaction of state policies, trade-union and employers' behaviour, and women's behaviour; also some discrimination takes place against women, both within and prior to entry into labour markets. The changes which have occurred are wide-ranging in their impact and the implications are not yet fully understood or embraced.

References

Agassi, J.B. 1982. *Comparing the Work Attitudes of Women and Men*, Lexington, Mass.: D.C.Heath.

Anthias, F. 1980. 'Women and the Reserve Army of Labour: A Critique of Veronica Beechey'. *Capital and Class*, 10 (1980).

Armstrong, P. 1982. 'If It's Only Women it Doesn't Matter So Much. *Work, Women and the Labour Market*. West, J. Ed. London: Routledge & Kegan Paul.

Barker, J. and Downing, H. 1980. 'Word Processing and the Transformation of the Patriarchal Relations of Control in the Office.' *Capital and Class*, 10, 64–99.

Barron, R.D. and Norris, G.M. 1976. 'Sexual Divisions and the Dual Labour Market'. in D.L. Barker and S. Allen eds. *Dependence and Exploitation in Work and Marriage*. Eds. Barker, D.L. and Allen, S. London: Longman.

Beck, E.M., Horan, M. and Tolbert, C.M. 1978. 'Stratification in a Dual Economy: A Sectoral Model of Earnings Determination'. *American Sociological Review*, 43, 704–20.

Becker, G.S. 1975. *Human Capital*. Second edition. Washington, DC: National Bureau of Economic Research.

Beechey, V. 1977. 'Some Notes on Female Wage Labour in Capitalist Production'. *Capital and Class*, 3, 45–66.

—— 1978. 'Women and Production: A Critical Analysis of Some Sociological Theories of Women's Work'. *Feminism and Materialism*. Eds. Kuhn, A. and Wolpe, A.M. London: Routledge & Kegan Paul.

—— 1979. 'On Patriarchy'. *Feminist Review*, 3, 66–82.

—— 1986. 'Women's Employment in Contemporary Britain'. *Women in Britain Today*. Eds. Beechey, V. and Whitelegg, E. Milton Keynes: Open University Press.

—— and Perkins, T. 1987. 'A Matter of Hours: Part-time Employment in Coventry. Cambridge: Polity.

Beller, A. 1982a. 'Occupational Segregation by Sex: Determinants and Changes'. *Journal of Human Resources*, 17:3, 371–92.

—— 1982b. 'Trends in Occupational Segregation by Sex'. Working Papers in Population Studies No. PS 8203. School of Social Sciences. Urbana-Champaign: University of Illinois.

Bibb, R. and Form, W.H. 1977. 'The Effects of Industrial Occupational and Sex Stratification on Wages in Blue-collar Markets'. *Social Forces*, 55, 974–96.

Blau, F. 1975. 'Sex Segregation of Workers by Enterprise in Clerical Occupations'. *Labour Market Segmentation*. Eds. Edwards, R., Reich, M. and Gordon, D. Lexington, Mass.: D.C. Heath.

Blau, P.M. and Duncan, O.D. 1967. *The American Occupational Structure.* New York: Wiley.

Borooah, V.K. and Lee, K.C. 1986. 'The Effects of Changes in Britain's Industrial Structure on Female Relative Pay and Employment, 1960–1980'. Discussion Paper No. 4. Cambridge: Cambridge Growth Project, Department of Applied Economics.

Bowles, S. and Gintis, H. 1975. 'The Problem with Human Capital Theory: A Marxian Critique'. *American Economic Review* (May).

Braverman, H. 1974. *Labor and Monopoly Capital. The Degradation of Work in The Twentieth Century.* New York: Monthly Review Press.

Breakwell, G.M. and Weinberger, B. 1986. 'Young Women in "Gender-Atypical" jobs: The Case of Trainee Technicians in the Engineering Industry'. Research Paper No. 49. London: Department of Employment.

Brown, R.K., Curran, M. and Cousins, J. 1983. 'Changing Attitudes to Employment'. Research Paper No. 40. London: Department of Employment.

Bruegel, I. 1979. 'Women as a Reserve Army: A Note on Recent British Experience'. *Feminist Review*, 3.

Chiplin, B. and Sloane, P.J. 1974. 'Sexual Discrimination in the Labour Market'. *British Journal of Industrial Relations* (November).

Cockburn, C. 1985. 'The Gender of the Job: Workplace Relations and the Reproduction of Sex Segregation'. Paper given to the ESRC Symposium on Segregation in Employment, University of Lancaster.

—— 1986. 'Training for "Her" Job and for "His"'. Report to the Equal Opportunities Commission.

Coyle, A. 1982. 'Sex and Skill in the Organisation of the Clothing Industry'. *Work, Women and the Labour Market.* Ed. West, J. London: Routledge & Kegan Paul.

—— 1984. *Redundant Women.* London: The Women's Press.

Cragg, A. and Dawson, T. 1981. 'Qualitative Research among Homeworkers'. Research Paper No. 21, London: Department of Employment.

—— and Dawson, T. 1984, 'Unemployment Women: A Study of Attitudes and Experiences'. Research Paper No. 47. London: Department of Employment.

Craig, C., Rubery, J., Tarling, R. and Wilkinson, F. 1982. *Labour Market Structure, Industrial Organisation and Low Pay.* Cambridge: Cambridge University Press.

—— Garnsey, E. and Rubery, J. 1985. 'Pay in Small Firms: Women and Informal Payment Systems'. Research Paper No. 48. London: Department of Employment.

—— and Wilkinson, F. 1985 'Pay and Employment in Four Retail Trades. Research Paper No. 51. London: Department of Employment.

Crompton, R., Jones, G. and Reid, S. 1982. 'Contemporary Clerical Work: A Case Study of Local Government'. *Work, Women and the Labour Market.* Ed. West, J. London: Routledge & Kegan Paul.

—— and Sanderson, K. 1986. Credentials and Careers: Some Implications of the Increase in Professional Qualifications Amongst Women'. *Sociology*, 20 (February), 25–42.

Davies, M. 1975. 'Women's Place is at the Typewriter: The Feminization of the Clerical Labor Force'. *Labour Market Segmentation.* Eds. Edwards, R., Reich, M. and Gordon, D. Lexington, Mass.: D.C. Heath.

Dex, S. 1984. 'Women's work histories: An Analysis of the Women and Employment Survey'. Research Paper No. 46. London: Department of Employment.

—— 1985 *The Sexual Division of Work*. Brighton: Wheatsheaf.

—— 1987. *Women's Occupational Mobility: A Lifetime Perspective*. London: Macmillan.

—— 1988. *Women's Attitudes Towards Work*. London: Macmillan.

—— and Perry, S.M. 1984. 'Women's Employment Changes in the 1970s'. *Employment Gazette*, 92: 4, 151–64.

—— and Shaw, L. 1986. *A Comparison of British and American Women's Work Histories*. London: Macmillan.

Doeringer, P.B. and Piore, M.J. 1971. *Internal Labor Markets and Manpower Analysis*. Lexington, Mass.: D.C. Heath.

—— and Bosanquet, N. 1973. 'Is There a Dual Labour Market in Great Britain?' *Economic Journal* (June).

Edgeworth, F.Y. 1922. 'Equal Pay to Men and Women for Equal Work'. *Economic Journal*, 32.

Edwards, R., Reich, M. and Gordon, D. 1975. *Labor Market Segmentation*. Lexington, Mass.: D.C. Heath.

—— 1979. *Contested Terrain*. New York: Basic Books.

England, P. 1982 'The Failure of Human Capital Theory to Explain Occupational Sex Segregation'. *Journal of Human Resources*, 17:3, 358–70.

—— 1985. 'Occupational Segregation: Rejoiner to Polachek'. *Journal of Human Resources*, 20:3, 441–2.

Finch, J. 1983. *Married to the Job: Wives Incorporation in Men's Work*. London: Allen & Unwin.

Game, R. and Pringle, A. 1983. *Gender at Work*. Sydney and London: Allen & Unwin.

Garside, W.R. 1980. *The Measurement of Unemployment: Methods and Sources in Great Britain 1950–1979*. Oxford: Basil Blackwell.

Gershuny, J. 1983. *Social Innovation and the Division of Labour*. Oxford: Oxford University Press.

Ginzberg, G.E. et al. 1951. *Occupational Choice*. New York: Columbia University Press.

Greenhaugh, C. 1980. 'Male-Female Wage Differentials in Great Britain: Is Marriage an Equal Opportunity'. *Economic Journal*, 90; 360.

Griffin, C. 1985. *Typical Girls: Young Women from School to the Job Market*. London: Routledge and Kegan Paul.

Hakim, C. 1979. 'Occupational Segregation'. Research Paper No. 9. London: Department of Employment.

—— 1981. 'Job Segregation: Trends in the 1970s'. *Employment Gazette* (December), 521–9.

—— 1984a. 'Homework and Outwork: National Estimates from Two Surveys'. *Employment Gazette*, 92: 1, 7–12.

—— 1984b. 'Employers' use of Homework, Outwork and Freelancers'. *Employment Gazette*, 92: 4, 144–50.

Hartmann, H. 1976. 'Capitalism, Patriarchy, and Job Segregation by Sex'. *Signs*, 1:3 137–68.

—— 1979. 'The Unhappy Marriage of Marxism and Feminism: Towards a More Progressive Union'. *Capital and Class*, 8, 1–33.

Harvey, J. 1987. 'New Technology and Gender Divisions of Labour'. *The Manufacture of Disadvantage*. Eds. Lee, G. and Loveridge, R. Milton Keynes: Open University Press.

Johnson, M.R.D. and Townsend, A.R. 1976. 'The Field of Recruitment to New Manufacturing Establishments in the North East'. North East Area Study Working Paper. No. 40. University of Durham.

Joshi, H.E. 1982. 'Secondary Workers in the Cycle'. *Economica*, 48, 29–44.

—— 1984. 'Women's Participation in Paid Work'. Research Paper No. 45 London: Department of Employment.

—— 1985. 'Gender Inequality in the Labour Market and the Domestic Division of Labour'. *Rethinking Socialist Economics*. Eds. Nolan, P. and Paine, S. Cambridge: Polity.

—— Layard, R. and Owen, S. 1985. 'Why are More Women Working in Britain?' *Journal of Labor Economics*, 3:1, 5147–76.

—— and Newall, M.L. 1986. 'Pay Differences between Men and Women: Longitudinal Evidence from the 1946 Birth Cohort'. Discussion Paper No. 156. Centre for Economic Policy Research.

Kalleberg, A.L. and Sorenson, A.B. 1983. 'Sociology of Labor Markets'. *Annual Review of Sociology*, 5, 351–79.

Labour Studies Group. 1985. 'Economic, Social and Political Factors in the Operation of the Labour Market'. *New Approaches to Economic Life*. Eds. Roberts, B., Finnegan, R. and Gallie, D. Manchester: Manchester University Press.

Lee, G. and Wrench, J. 1987. 'Race and Gender Dimensions of the Youth Labour Market: From Apprenticeship to YTS'. *The Manufacture of Disadvantage*. Eds. Lee, G. and Loveridge, R. Milton Keynes: Open University Press.

Loveridge, R. and Mok, A. 1979. *Theories of Labour Market Segmentation*. The Hague: Martinus Nijhoff.

Mackenzie, D. and Wajcman, J. (eds) 1985. *The Social Shaping of Technology*. Milton Keynes: Open University Press.

McRobbie, A. 1978. 'Working Class Girls and the Culture of Feminimity'. *Women Take Issue*. Ed. Women's Studies Group. London: Hutchinson.

—— and Garber, J. 1975. 'Girls and Subcultures'. *Working Papers in Cultural Studies*, 7:8.

Main, B. 1984. 'Women's Earnings: The Influence of Work Histories on Rates of Pay'. University of Edinburgh, mimeo.

—— 1987. 'Hourly Earnings of Female Part-time Versus Full-time employees'. Discussion Paper. University of Edinburgh.

Marsden, D. 1986. *The End of Economic Man: Custom and Competition in Labour Markets*. Brighton: Wheatsheaf.

Martin, J. and Roberts, C. 1984. *Women and Employment: A Lifetime Perspective*. London: HMSO.

Matthaei, J.A. 1983. *An Economic History of Women in America: Women's Work, the Sexual Division of Labour, and the Development of Capitalism*. Brighton: Harvester Press.

Mincer, J. and Polachek, S. 1974. 'Family Investment in Human Capital: Earnings of Women'. *Journal of Political Economy*, 82:2.

—— and Ofek, H. 1982. 'Interrupted Work Careers'. *Journal of Human Resources*, 17, 3–24.

Oakley, A. 1974. *The Sociology of Housework*. Oxford: Martin Robertson.
—— 1979. *From Here to Maternity: Becoming a Mother*. Harmondsworth: Penguin.
—— 1980. *Women Confined: Towards a Sociology of Childbirth*. Oxford: Martin Robertson.
O'Neill, J. 1984. 'Earnings Differentials: Empirical Evidence and Causes'. *Sex Discrimination and Equal Opportunity*. Eds. Schmid, G. and Weitzel, R. Aldershot: Gower.
Pahl, R.E. 1984. *Divisions of Labour*. Oxford: Basil Blackwell.
—— and Wallace, C. 'Household Work Strategies in Economic Recession'. *Beyond Employment: Household, Gender and Subsistence*. Eds. Redclift, N. and Mingione, E. Oxford: Basil Blackwell.
Parman, P. 1982. 'Gender, Race and Class'. *The Empire Strikes Back*. London: Hutchinson.
Phillips, A. and Taylor, B. 1980. 'Sex and Skill: Notes towards a Feminist Economics'. *Feminist Review*, 6, 79–88.
Piore, M.J. 1975. 'Notes for a Theory of Labor Market Stratification'. *Labour Market Segmentation*. Eds. Edwards, R., Reich, M. and Gordon, D. Lexington, Mass.: D.C. Heath.
Polachek, S. 1975. 'Discontinuities in Labor Force Participation and its Effects on Women's Market Earnings'. *Sex, Discrimination and the Division of Labor*. Ed. Lloyd, C.B. New York: Columbia University Press.
—— 1976. 'Occupational Segregation: An Alternative Hypothesis'. *Journal of Contemporary Business*, 5, 1–12.
—— 1985. 'Occupational Segregation: A Defence of Human Capital Predictions'. *Journal of Human Resources*, 20:3, 437–40.
Pollert, A. 1987. 'Flexible Patterns of Work and Ideology'. Paper presented at conference, Part-time Work: Whose Flexibility? September. University of Bradford.
Power, M. 1983. 'From Home Production to Wage Labour: Women as a Reserve Army of Labor'. *Review of Radical Political Economics*, 15:1, 71–91.
Redclift, N. and Mingione, E. (eds) 1985. *Beyond Employment: Household, Gender and Subsistence*. Oxford: Basil Blackwell.
Richards, J.R. 1980. *The Sceptical Feminist*. Harmondsworth: Penguin.
Roberts, B. Finnegan, R. and Gallie, D. (eds) 1985. *New Approaches to Economic Life*. Manchester: Manchester University Press.
Roberts, C. 1981. 'Women's Unemployment'. Paper presented to SSRC workshop on Employment and Unemployment, mimeo. October.
Roberts, K. 1968. 'The Entry into Employment: An Approach Towards a General Theory'. *The Sociological Review*, 16, 165–84.
—— 1973. 'An Alternative Theory of Occupational Choice'. *Education and Training*, 15, 310–11.
Robinson, O. 1979. 'Part-time Employment in the European Community'. *International Labour Review*, 118:3.
—— and Wallace, J. 1984. 'Part-time Employment and Sex Discrimination Legislation in Great Britain'. Research Paper No. 47. London: Department of Employment.
Rubery, J. 1978. 'Structured Labour Markets, Worker Organization and Low Pay'. *Cambridge Journal of Economics*, 2:1, 17–36.

—— and Wilkinson F. 1979. 'Notes on the Nature of the Labour Process in the Secondary Sector'. *Low Pay and Labour Markets Segmentation*. Conference papers. Cambridge.

—— and Tarling, R.J. 1983. 'Women in the Recession'. Economic Reprint No. 68. Cambridge: Department of Applied Economics.

Sherratt, N. 1983. 'Girls, Jobs and Glamour'. *Feminist Review*, 15, 47–61.

Siebert, W.S. and Sloane, P.J. 1981. 'The Measurement of Sex and Marital Status Discrimination at the Workplace'. *Economica*, 48.

Siltanen, J. and Stanworth, M. 1984. 'The Politics of Private Woman and Public Man'. *Theory and Society*, 13:1, 91–118.

Sinfield, A. 1981. *What Unemployment Means*. Oxford: Martin Robertson.

Sloane, P.J. (ed.) 1980. *Women and Low Pay*. London: Macmillan.

—— 1987. 'Male-female Earnings Differences Revisited: A Disaggregated Analysis of the New Earnings Survey Data Tapes'. Discussion Paper 87–03. Aberdeen: Department of Economics.

Stewart, A., Blackburn, R.M. and Prandy, K. 1985. 'Gender Earnings: The Failure of Market Explanations'. *New Approaches to Economic Life*. Eds. Roberts, B., Finnegan, R. and Gallie, D. Manchester: Manchester University Press.

Walby, S. 1985. 'Approaches to the Study of Gender Relations in Unemployment and Employment'. *New Approaches to Economic Life*. Eds. Roberts, B., Finnegan, R. and Gallie, D. Manchester: Manchester University Press.

—— 1986. *Patriarchy at Work*. Cambridge: Polity Press.

—— 1987. 'Flexibility and the Sexual Division of Labour'. Paper presented to conference, Part-time Work: Whose flexibility? September. University of Bradford.

Wilkinson, F. (ed.) 1981. *The Dynamics of Labour Market Segmentation*. London: Academic Press.

Willis, P.E. 1977. *Learning to Labour: How Working Class Kids get Working Class Jobs*. London: Saxon House.

Zabalza, A. and Arrufat, J.L. 1985. 'The Extent of Sex Discrimination in Great Britain'. *Women and Equal Pay*. Eds. Zabalza, A. and Tzannatos, Z. Cambridge: Cambridge University Press.

11 Discrimination and Equal Opportunity in Employment: Ethnicity and 'Race' in the United Kingdom

Richard Jenkins

This chapter focuses upon the manner in which forms of social identification concerned with ethnicity and 'race' figure in labour recruitment and employment in the United Kingdom.[1] There are three central themes: first, the nature of ethnic and 'racial' discrimination; secondly, the relationship between labour-market disadvantage and formal educational or skill qualifications, and thirdly, strategies and problems in the pursuit of greater equality of opportunity. First, however, it is necessary to clarify the definitions of a number of basic concepts which will be used throughout.

What, for example, is meant by 'ethnicity'? In the most basic definition, drawing on the work of social anthropologists such as Barth (1969) and Cohen (1978), ethnicity is simply the social organization of cultural diversity. In this approach, which can legitimately trace its roots back to the classic formulations of Weber (1978: 385–99), ethnic identity and the boundaries of ethnic groups are situationally defined by the actors concerned, subject to negotiation and redefinition within the constraints of history and present circumstances. Among the elements of culture which make up ethnicity are language, religion, kinship, patterns of residence and the mundane routines of everyday life and subsistence. In the United Kingdom, the ethnicity approach has informed a number of empirical studies of work and employment (see, e.g., the essays collected in Wallman, 1979).

The ethnicity paradigm has come in for criticism from a number of directions. Rex, for example, has argued that it is important to distinguish 'race' – social identity based upon folk or common-sense 'racial' categories – from ethnicity, because of the more restricted set of situations which are characterized by 'race relations' and the higher levels of conflict which they engender (1973: 184). Authors working within an ethnicity framework, many of them coming from the structural-functionalist tradition of British social anthropology, have tended to stress 'ethnicity as a social

1 Bob Cormack, Duncan Gallie, Bob Osborne and John Wrench all made useful comments on an earlier draft of this chapter. I did not always choose to incorporate their suggestions, however, and the responsibility for any imperfections is all my own.

resource' at the expense of an analysis of inter-ethnic conflict. Nor have anthropological analyses of ethnicity paid much attention to relationships of power and domination. In addition, as Bourne and Sivanandan have argued (1980: 35), too strong an emphasis upon the culture, values and orientations of ethnic minorities themselves can appear to be 'blaming the victims' for their own disadvantage.

Despite such criticisms, however, a recognition of the role of ethnicity in inter-group relations remains important. In stressing social processes, the approach discourages overly deterministic analyses. The intrusion of irrelevant biological models of 'race' is also discouraged by the stress placed upon the social construction of ethnic and 'racial' categories by those working within a theoretical framework concerned with ethnicity. Finally, the emphasis upon actors' own definitions of the situation is a healthy safeguard against ethnocentrism.

The concept of 'race' is equally problematic. Throughout this chapter the word will remain within inverted commas in order to signify its contested status. In particular, it must be stressed that no biological reference is denoted by its use. It simply refers to popular models of 'racial' differentiation. There are no grounds for suggesting that 'real' differences between 'races' are the cause of 'racial' differentiation (Rex, 1986: 15–17; Stone, 1985: 9–33). There are, however, good grounds for insisting upon a clear definition of racism. An historically specific facet of ethnicity characterizing situations of ethnic subordination and domination, racism is typically the categorization of 'them', as opposed to the ethnic identification of 'us' (Banton, 1983: 10). Two other aspects of racism are important in the definition proposed here. First, racism categorizes the 'other' as inherently different and typically inferior (whether culturally or biologically), and denies the possibility of egalitarian coexistence. Secondly, racism involves the disadvantageous treatment of the 'other', whether intentionally or not (Jenkins, 1986: 4–6). This definition is in broad agreement with writers such as Barker (1981) in insisting that neither prejudice nor intentionality are necessary aspects of racism.

The final concept which must be defined at this stage is 'discrimination'. Put at its simplest, this is no more than telling the difference (or *a* difference) between people or things; a less general definition would imply an element of choice or evaluation. Looked at in this way, discrimination is basic to the 'freedom' of the capitalist labour market: workers choose which jobs to apply for, recruiters adjudicate between competitive job candidates in order to choose one and reject the others. In much popular usage, however, the word has acquired a more pejorative meaning. Discrimination is largely taken to mean a choice between people on the basis of criteria which are inadmissable, either *tout court* or in a specific context. Discrimination has come to mean *unfair* discrimination. Unless otherwise indicated, this is the sense in which the word will be used in the discussion which follows.

In looking at ethnic discrimination in employment in the United Kingdom, there is a range of possibilities from which to select topics and data. In the main, this chapter will concentrate upon two subjects: black workers in Great Britain and the distinction between Catholic and Prot-

estant workers in Northern Ireland. There is a considerable amount of
argument as to whether or not it is appropriate to use the category
'black' to include both people whose origins lie in the Caribbean region
and those with antecedents in the Indian subcontinent. Inasmuch as
both sets of people, in addition to the important cultural and historical
factors which serve to differentiate them, share a similar experience of
racist discrimination in the British context, and in the absence of any
better nomenclature, this inclusive usage will be maintained here. Where
appropriate, of course, specific black ethnic minorities will be identified
and discussed as such. The reader should, however, remember that the
term 'black' is a personal choice of the author, and not without its critics.

Black and White Workers in Great Britain

As recent historical scholarship has demonstrated, a small population of
black people has been present in the British Isles for centuries (Fryer, 1984;
Ramdin, 1986; Visram, 1985; Walvin, 1984). It was only in the post-war period, however, that black migrant workers arrived in large numbers, settling
as permanent communities in most of Britain's industrial areas. The legal
and political framework within which this movement of population occured
was the British Nationality Act 1948, which established the right of people
from British colonies and the Commonwealth countries to settle and work
in Britain. Between the arrival of the SS *Empire Windrush* from the West
Indies in 1948 and the introduction of the Commonwealth Immigration Act
in 1962, which heralded the end of mass New Commonwealth immigration,
something of the order of half a million black people arrived in Britain
(Deakin, 1970: 44–55; Jones and Smith, 1970: 5–17). Since then most of the
expansion in the black population has reflected either natural increase or
family reunification. By 1985, according to the Labour Force Survey, the
black population of Great Britain was 2.4 million (approximately 4.4 per
cent of the total population), made up of just over a million Asians,
just over half a million Afro-Caribbeans and over half a million people
from other ethnic minorities (Department of Employment, 1987: 19).

By and large, the motivation for this migration was largely economic
(Watson, 1977: 6–7). To simplify the matter considerably, perhaps to
oversimplify it, the 'push' factors were underemployment and poverty in
the countries of origin, the 'pull' factor, labour shortages in Britain. A
major exception to this broad generalization was the movement of Asian
families from East Africa in the late 1960s and early 1970s as a result
of political developments in Kenya and Uganda. The jobs which most
migrants entered were typically unskilled or semi-skilled, comparatively
low paid, disproportionately likely to involve shift working and were mainly in the manufacturing sector (Daniel, 1968: 57–62; Deakin, 1970: 72–82).

To characterize these migrations as primarily economic is not, however,
to exhaust the explanatory possibilities. There is, for example, some debate
as to how the employment of the early generations of black workers in
post-war Britain should be understood in the context of the development

of the national economy. Peach, for example, writing about migration from the Caribbean, conceptualizes black workers as 'replacement labour', drawn in to fill the labour-market niches deserted as undesirable by local workers during a period of economic growth (Peach, 1968). Duffield, however, in his study of Punjabi labour in the foundry industry argues that black labour, particularly in situations where trade unions were weak, moved into new (and unskilled) occupational niches created by the technological restructuring of the labour process (Duffield, 1985, 1988).

The two explanations are, of course, not necessarily contradictory. Both processes are likely to have been at work in different contexts. The merit of Duffield's analysis, however, is that it draws our attention to the importance of the resistance offered by white workers, both informally and formally through their unions, as a factor limiting the access of black migrant workers to 'better' jobs and occupations (Phizacklea and Miles, 1987; Wrench, 1987). Racist discrimination is not the prerogative of employers. Whatever the precise nature of the discrimination, however – and this will be discussed in more detail later – there is little doubt that black workers in the 1950s and 1960s did not end up located in the bottom reaches of the labour market because of *their* occupational goals or social aspirations (Jenkins, 1986: 8–13).

During this period, continental Europe, particularly France, Germany, Switzerland and the Benelux countries, was also experiencing labour immigration. Some of the new arrivals were from colonies or ex-colonies; others, the larger proportion, were drawn as 'guest workers' (*gastarbeiters*) from the underdeveloped margins of the Mediterranean – Southern Italy, Yugoslavia, Turkey, Greece, North Africa and the Iberian peninsula (Berger and Mohr, 1975; Castles, Booth and Wallace, 1984; Castles and Kosack, 1985; Edye, 1987; Paine, 1974). While there are some similarities between the British and European cases, the comparison should not be overdrawn. First, the European countries differ substantially from each other in law and policy. Secondly, the swingeing – although, in time, moderated – legal constraints upon *gastarbeiters*, and the political goal of maintaining them as strictly temporary sojourners, renders their position very different to ex-colonial migrants in Britain with partial or full rights of citizenship and settlement.

The most comprehensive recent information about the labour-market position of black workers in Britain comes from the 1985 Labour Force Survey (Department of Employment, 1987). Looking at the employment status of those in work, the most obvious difference relates to self-employment: 14.0 per cent of white male workers were self-employed, as compared to 8.5 per cent of West Indians, 23.7 per cent of Indians, 21.4 per cent of Pakistani or Bangladeshis and 22.9 per cent of East African Asians. For women workers, the figures are white workers 6.6 per cent, West Indians 0.9 per cent, Indians 9.4 per cent and East African Asians 11.9 per cent. The Labour Force Survey figures for Pakistani or Bangladeshi women are – for all categories of economic activity – too small to be reliable.

There are also differences with respect to industrial distribution: 23.5 per cent of white males who are in paid employment or on government schemes work in manufacturing, compared to 30.4 per cent of ethnic minority males. For construction, the percentages are 11.7 and 5.2 respectively; for distribution, hotels, catering and repairs, 15.8 and 25.1; and for transport and communications, 8.0 and 12.4. The pattern for women workers is different: women ethnic minority workers are disproportionately represented in manufacturing (21.9 per cent, as compared to 14.9 per cent of white women workers) and the health service (16.8 per cent, as against 10.5 per cent). They are *under*represented in education (6.0 per cent compared to 11.4 per cent). The overrepresentation of black workers in manufacturing has rendered them particularly sensitive to changes in the economic climate and more vulnerable to redundancy and lay-offs than white workers.

Perhaps the most striking difference between black and white workers revealed by the Labour Force Survey is, in fact, their propensity to suffer unemployment. Taking the overall view, the unemployment rate for white workers (10 per cent) is half that for ethnic minorities. The situation of young workers is most severe: 16 per cent of economically active white young people between 16 and 24 years were unemployed, compared to 33 per cent of ethnic minorities. The minority groups worst affected were Pakistanis and Bangladeshis (31 per cent), followed by West Indians (21 per cent) and then Indians (17 per cent).

A largely similar picture is painted by the other major source of data, the Policy Studies Institute's *Black and White Britain* survey (Brown, 1984). The successor to the famous PEP surveys (Daniel, 1968; Smith, 1974, 1977), the PSI study provides clearer information than the Labour Force Survey concerning certain aspects of the labour-market disadvantage experienced by black workers. For example, there are clear ethnic differences with respect to occupational level. Whereas 23 per cent of white men in the PSI survey were in non-professional or non-managerial white-collar jobs, this was true for only 10 per cent of West Indians and 13 per cent of Asians. In semi-skilled manual jobs, however, the figures are 13 per cent of white men, 26 per cent of West Indian men and 34 per cent of Asian men. In the unskilled manual category, the percentages are 3 per cent, 9 per cent and 6 per cent respectively. For women workers, the results for semi-skilled manual jobs are white women 21 per cent, West Indians 36 per cent and Asians 44 per cent. In non-manual jobs the figures are broadly comparable for white and West Indian women (55 and 52 per cent) with Asian women at 44 per cent.

The PSI findings also reveal the extent of important ethnic differences with respect to conditions of employment. For instance, Asians and West Indians (both men and women) are appreciably more likely than white workers to work shifts. Despite this, however, ethnic minority men, in particular, earned on average approximately twenty pounds a week less than white workers at the time of the survey (1982). In some regions and at some job levels, the earnings differential was much greater than this; at *all* occupational levels the average wage for black workers was below that for white workers.

The 1982 PSI survey provides a useful point of comparison with the earlier PEP surveys. Such a comparison throws light on the extent and nature of the impact of the recession upon black workers (Brown, 1984:

173–83). At the risk of oversimplifying, the position can be summarized thus: while there has been no convergence of the labour-market situations of black and white workers with respect to industrial or occupational concentration, job levels, pay or working patterns, the marked gap between them with respect to unemployment has widened.

Among the reasons for this deteriorating situation are the following. First, because of the manner of their incorporation into the labour force in the 1950s and 1960s – something which will be discussed in more detail later – black workers are disproportionately more likely to be in industries (manufacturing and the health service, for example), occupations (unskilled and semi-skilled manual jobs) and locations (inner-city areas and the declining industrial areas of the West Midlands and the North) which are particularly severely affected by unemployment (Massey and Meegan, 1982). Factors such as these are probably the most influential in determining the disproportionate distribution of unemployment between white and black workers (Rhodes and Braham, 1987). Secondly, there is some evidence to suggest that, just as there is discrimination *against* black people in recruitment, so there may also be discrimination in doubtful *favour* of them when it comes to choosing workers for redundancy or other kinds of involuntary severance (Smith, 1981: 67–93). Racism, it seems, operates at ports of entry *and* exit. Once unemployed, black workers are, as a consequence, likely to experience particular problems in the job search. Thirdly, deliberate discrimination aside, employers are likely to discriminate unfavourably against workers with interrupted labour-market careers. For the reasons which have just been discussed, black workers are more likely to experience such an employment pattern. Thus a vicious cycle of insecure employment and unemployment is created. Finally, some research has suggested that recession-related changes in recruitment procedures, in particular an increased propensity to use internal recruitment and 'word of mouth' networks (Ford et al., 1984; Jenkins et al., 1983; Manwaring, 1984), are particularly disadvantageous for black workers (Jenkins, 1984). More recent research, however, has cast some doubt on the general thesis about the impact of the recession upon recruitment practices (Ford et al., 1986). 'Word of mouth' recruitment and the internal labour market will be discussed further below.

Although black workers in general are disproportionately vulnerable to unemployment, it is clear that young black people are most severely affected. So much so, in fact, that some commentators have talked about 'black youth in crisis' (Cashmore and Troyna, 1982). This topic will be considered further in the discussion of education and its relationship to employment. Suffice it to make two points here. First, the evidence that young black people are systematically and seriously disadvantaged within the Youth Training Scheme and other government schemes is overwhelming (Cross, 1987; Cross and Smith, 1987; Lee and Wrench, 1987; Pollert, 1985). Among the most important reasons for this are racist discrimination and unchallenged commonsensical assumptions about the goals and training needs of black young people. Secondly, while accepting the central importance of policing practices and policies as the seeds of disorder, there can be little doubt that black youth unemployment was one factor underlying the disorders ('the riots') of 1981 and 1985 in British cities (Benyon and Solomos, 1987; Solomos, 1985, 1986). Despite subsequent public commitments by various state and other agencies to addressing the problem of black youth unemployment, the situation does not seem to have changed much for the better.

The connection between violent conflict and unemployment is often mooted. It should, however, only be made with caution and in the context of other factors and relationships. This is particularly the case with respect to inter-ethnic relations in Northern Ireland, the next topic to be discussed.

Catholic and Protestant Workers in Northern Ireland

In the opening discussion, reference was made to Rex's remark that one reason for distinguishing conceptually between ethnicity and 'race' was that 'race relations' give rise to more serious conflict than do ethnic relations. Northern Ireland is an interesting exception to this generalization, although there has been some academic controversy relating to whether the situation there can be conceptualized as a situation of 'racial' conflict (Moore, 1972). Following the line of argument put forward by Sarah Nelson (1975), the current social science consensus is that it is not appropriate to analyse Northern Ireland within a 'race relations' framework. This is the view adopted in this discussion.

While there is no space here for an extensive discussion of the Northern Ireland situation, such as those available in the volumes edited by Boal and Douglas (1982) or Darby (1983), for example, some background material may be useful. Two ethnicities in conflict – Protestant and Catholic – were established by the sixteenth-century plantation of the north of Ireland by English and Scottish (Protestant) settlers and the consequent economic dispossession and political exclusion of the Irish (Catholic) population. The resulting ethnic hierarchy of advantage and disadvantage was consolidated during the nineteenth-century industrial revolution, when the north-eastern end of the island developed into an urban industrial centre on a par with Clydeside and Merseyside. Catholics migrated from rural areas to undertake unskilled work in the cities and towns of Ulster. Sectarian ethnicity was manipulated as an industrial relations strategy by local employers, and turned to advantage by the Protestant work-force. The twentieth century has been marked by political conflict, as a consequence of the partition of Ireland in 1921 and the creation, within the United Kingdom, of a six-county state – Northern Ireland – dominated by Protestant interests. The current 'troubles' began in the late 1960s, arising out of Catholic civil rights agitation and the violent Protestant response to those demands, and have coincided with a period of marked economic decline, part of the wider national and international recession. In 1972 direct political control of Northern Ireland was assumed by the United Kingdom government, although the province remains legally and administratively distinct from Great Britain.

One of the most recent sources of information relating to ethnic dis-advantage in employment in Northern Ireland is the 1983–4 Continuous Household Survey (Department of Finance and Personnel, 1985). Looking at employment status, the difference between Catholics and Protestants surveyed is striking: 35 per cent of Catholic men and 17 per cent of Catholic women were unemployed, by comparison with 15 per cent of Protestant men and 11 per cent of Protestant women. Looking at those in the sample who were unemployed, it is clear that long-term unemployment is more prevalent in the Catholic community: 44 per cent of unemployed Catholics had been out of work for more than two years, compared to 33 per cent of unemployed Protestants. Of those interviewed who had been unemployed for less than a year, 54 per cent of Protestants had suffered only one or two spells of unemployment in the previous two years, as compared to 43 per cent of Catholics. In summary, Catholics are more likely to be unemployed and they are more likely to be unemployed in the long term (see also Osborne and Cormack, 1986).

This sorry situation is, given the well-attested relationship between occupation and vulnerability to unemployment, at least in part a reflection of the occupational structure of the two communities. The relationship between education and labour-market disadvantage will be examined in a later section. The Continuous Household Survey reveals that while 38 per cent of Protestants were in professional, managerial or other non-manual occupations, this was true of only 27 per cent of Catholics. At the other end of the spectrum, 37 per cent of Catholics were in unskilled or semi-skilled manual occupations, by comparison with 31 per cent of the Protestants interviewed. Bearing in mind this relatively small differential between the two populations with respect to unskilled and semi-skilled employment, an obvious implication is that occupational factors can only account for a small part of their difference with respect to unemployment. Looking at the situation of young workers, research suggests not only that, as elsewhere in the United Kingdom, young people are most severely affected by unemployment, but that Catholic young people are particularly vulnerable (Cormack and Osborne, 1983; Murray and Darby, 1983). This is, at least in part, a consequence of demographic factors. The Catholic community, in reflection of differential fertility rates, is a younger population than the Protestant community, although the significance of this is offset to some extent by higher levels of emigration among Catholics (Compton, 1982: 99–102).

A further useful source of information is the official consultative paper on equal opportunity in Northern Ireland (Department of Economic Development, 1986). Drawing on a variety of data sources, and discussing gender and disability as well as ethnicity, this report supplies some extra detail not available elsewhere. Looking at increases in unemployment with the recession, while the overall Protestant unemployment rate rose from 6 per cent at the 1971 Census to 10 per cent in 1981, the equivalent figures for the Catholic population are 14 per cent and 25 per cent. Although the degree of differential unemployment between the two communities varies from place to place, its existence is widespread throughout the province.

This situation of Catholic disadvantage in employment has persisted since the nineteenth century (Hepburn, 1983). Similar patterns are revealed in analyses of data deriving from the 1971 Census and the Irish Mobility Study (Aunger, 1983; Miller, 1983, 1986). As we have seen, there is little indication that the gap between the two populations in this respect is closing, despite the fact that Protestant workers have, with the deepening of recession since the late 1970s, become more likely to suffer unemployment (Cormack and Osborne, 1987; Miller and Osborne, 1983). Employment has always, even during periods of comparative prosperity such as the 1960s, been a scarce resource. Sectarian ethnicity has served to maintain the relative economic advantage experienced by Protestants, although there is evidence of improving Catholic employment profiles in the public sector (Osborne, 1987).

To round out the picture further, it must be noted that while Northern Irish welfare benefits are in line with British scales, average wages in the province are lower and the cost of living higher. The result, particularly for the long-term unemployed in Norther Ireland – who are, it should be remembered, disproportionately Catholic – is family poverty at a level markedly higher than that found on the other side of the Irish Sea (Black et al., 1980; Evason, 1985). Such a conclusion is supported by the 1983–4 Continuous Household Survey: 29 per cent of Catholic households 'frequently' or 'always' experienced difficulty in paying the rent, as opposed to 21 per cent of Protestant households (and the latter is, itself a high enough proportion to cause concern). Similarly, the Survey reveals significantly lower ownership levels of telephones, fridges, freezers and cars among Catholic households.

There has been a fair amount of lively academic controversy about whether Catholic disadvantage in employment is due to discrimination or other factors. This controversy should be viewed in the context of a wider debate relating to the 'troubles': to what degree can the conflict be related to the economic and other grievances of Northern Irish Catholics – caused, so much conventional wisdom would have it, largely by discrimination – and to what degree is it the result of Irish nationalism?[2] Doherty, for example, has suggested (1982) that higher levels of unemployment among Catholics can *in part* be explained by their greater concentration in rural areas west of the River Bann, away from centres of industrial employment. More controversially, Compton (1982, 1986) argues that higher Catholic fertility rates and larger families may account in large part for Catholic unemployment and lower-class status. Broadly similar arguments have been put forward by Hewitt (1981) and Kelley and McAllister (1984), who, along with Whyte (1983), have also reviewed the evidence for the presence of discrimination against Catholics prior to the 'troubles' and suggested that it was less prevalent than has been often supposed.

This, by now considerable, body of revisionist scholarship is impressive. It is, however, subject to a number of important criticisms. First, and

---

2 Contributions to this debate other than those cited in the text include those of Hewitt (1983, 1985, 1987), Kovalchek (1987), O'Hearn (1983, 1985, 1987) and Simpson (1983: 100–7).

probably most important, even when factors such as geographical location, class status and family size are controlled for, there is a significant ethnic factor apparently working to the economic advantage of Protestants (Miller, 1986: 226). In Belfast, for example, 27 per cent of the variation in unemployment rates may be attributed to ethnicity (Doherty, 1982: 242). Secondly, in explaining away Catholic disadvantage as due to family size or father's occupational status, for example, these factors are treated as independent variables. In fact, they are themselves likely to be dependent upon past or present discrimination (Kennedy, 1973). Thirdly, much of the revisionist argument relies for its force on a crude model of blatant discrimination, ignoring the subtleties of 'indirect' forms of discrimination, as discussed in the next section. Finally, and this will also be discussed later, there is, in fact, good evidence of sectarian discrimination before the introduction of direct rule from Westminster in 1972, and some evidence for its subsequent persistence.

The research reviewed above suggests that, while the Northern Ireland situation is one of 'ethnic' not 'race relations', it has much in common with the state of affairs in Great Britain described in the previous section. Catholic disadvantage in employment is an interrelated compound of – among other things – the following ingredients: the history of their incorporation into the labour market, locational factors, demography, the occupational structure of the Catholic labour force and discrimination. This latter, perhaps the most important single factor in many people's eyes, is the subject of the next section.

The Nature of Discrimination

Discrimination has already been defined in such a way as to stress a process of unfair differentiation between people. At this point it is important to reiterate that, in the word's non-perjorative sense, recruitment into employment is of necessity discriminatory: applicants are either accepted or rejected. On what basis does this decision-making process operate? What are employers doing in the recruitment process?

Research in both Northern Ireland and Britain has suggested that employers routinely use two different kinds of selection criteria: *suitability* and *acceptability* (Jenkins, 1983: 101–13; 1986: 46–70). Both types of criteria are related to the efficient functioning of the worker and the workplace, as perceived by management. Suitability is functionally specific, inasmuch as it is concerned with the individual's ability to perform the tasks required by the job. Criteria of suitability might include physique, particular experience or formal educational, trade or professional qualifications. Acceptability is functionally non-specific, concerned with the general control and management of the organization: will the recruit 'fit in' to the context in question, is he or she 'dependable', 'reliable' and hard working, will the new worker leave after a short time? Criteria of acceptability, highly subjective and dependent upon managerial perceptions, include appearance, 'manner and attitude', 'maturity', gender, labour-market history and age and marital status. The basic distinction between acceptability and suitability – and in practice it is not always clear cut – has been taken up by other researchers concerned with discrimination (e.g. Curran, 1985: 30–1; Lee and Wrench, 1987: 88). In one of the most sophisticated discussions of the issue, Jewson and Mason have further suggested that to criteria of suitability and acceptability should be added *collectivist* and *individualist* principles of recruitment, to produce four modes of discrimination: determinism, rational-legality, particularism and patronage (1986a: 44–8). Which versions of suitability (determinism or rational-legality) or acceptability (particularism or patronage) are of most importance in a particular context may, according to their argument, have implications for the promotion of equal opportunity policies.

Criteria of suitability are undoubtedly influential in recruitment, particularly during the early stages, in shortlisting, for example. Acceptability is, however, important in determining final selection outcomes, particularly – although by no means exclusively, – in manual and routine non-manual occupations (Ashton, Maguire and Garland, 1982; Blackburn and Mann, 1979; Silverman and Jones, 1976). The issue of suitability will be discussed in the following section.

To look at acceptability here, there is a considerable amount of evidence to suggest that black workers are systematically disadvantaged by selection criteria of this kind. First, managerial concern with the capacity to 'fit-in', for example, may be racist in a fairly straightforward fashion: 'the lads won't like it' has been frequent justification for refusing employment to black applicants (Commission for Racial Equality, 1981). It should also be recognized, of course, that there is considerable truth in this: the lads *don't* like it. Trade unions have been, and are, a major brake – as democratic organizations representing the interests of the majority of their members – upon the pursuit of ethnic equality in employment (Phizacklea and Miles, 1987; Rolston, 1980; Wrench, 1987). Secondly, the implicit nature of many criteria of acceptability, their informality and taken-for-grantedness, allows racism to slip unremarked upon into the recruitment process. To digress for a moment, it is clear that direct racist discrimination remains a problem for black workers. This has been amply demonstrated in recent 'discrimination tests' or 'situation tests', which document the responses of employers offering job vacancies when contacted by candidates of differing ethnic identities. In Nottingham in the late 1970s, 48 per cent of the employers tested discriminated against West Indian and Asian applicants (Hubbuck and Carter, 1980). In tests in London, Birmingham and Manchester in 1984 and 1985, the equivalent figure was 37 per cent (Brown and Gay, 1985). The difference between the two studies may, in part, reflect the wider range of occupations surveyed in the more recent study.

Other aspects of the notion of acceptability may also systematically disadvantage black job-seekers, albeit without any necessarily prejudicial intent on the part of the recruiter (Jenkins, 1986: 80–115). Stereotypes of the acceptable worker interact with widely held ethnic stereotypes to the detriment of black candidates. Given the demographic structure of the black population, biased, as a recently migrant population, towards the youthful end of the spectrum (Department of Employment, 1987: 19), criteria such as 'maturity' or male age and marital status – 'a married man with two kids, a mortgage and a car' – will, at the present time, exclude disproportionately more black than white candidates. More generally, the routine ethnocentrism of notions of acceptability and the diagnostic cues upon which they rest is likely subtly to load the dice in favour of applicants whose verbal and non-verbal cultural repertoires harmonize with those of recruiters (Akinnaso and Seabrook Ajirotutu, 1982; Gumperz, 1982). Since most recruiters are white and British, this means applicants who are also white and British.

One of the original contexts within which the distinction between suitability and acceptability was formulated was research into young people and the labour market in Belfast (Jenkins, 1983; 101–13). With respect to selection criteria of acceptability and ethnic discrimination in Northern Ireland, there is little in the way of directly comparable research evidence. Common sense and everyday experience suggests that many Protestant employers regard Catholics as less acceptable, as lazy, disloyal or 'shifty', for example. Such is the nature of Northern Irish ethnic stereotypes (O'Donnell, 1977). There is, however, evidence of past sectarian discrimination of a more straightforward kind (e.g. Barritt and Carter, 1972: 93–108; Fair Employment Agency, 1983b: pp. i–xi). The persistence of such discrimination at the present time is less easy to document directly, in the absence of situation testing or investigative qualitative research. Such research and evidence as there is, however, points, by strong implication, towards its continued significance (Fair Employment Agency, 1983a: 7–10; 1984: 25–31; Miller, 1986: 227–30; Osborne, 1982).

There is one important dimension of recruitment – directly related to notions of acceptability and ethnic discrimination – where comparable material does exist. 'Word of mouth' recruitment through informal social networks has been documented in Britain (Brooks and Singh, 1979; Jenkins, 1986: 135–50; Lee and Wrench, 1983) and Northern Ireland (Cormack and Osborne 1983; Jenkins, 1983: 114–28; Maguire, 1986). This, and other evidence,[3] demonstrates the importance to employers of personal recommendations and informal recruitment channels, both because of their relative cheapness and convenience, but also as a source, in managers' eyes, of more acceptable recruits. As a form of closure and channel of participation, they also frequently attract the support of trade unions. Recruitment procedures of this kind are often disadvantageous to black workers in Britain and Catholics in Northern Ireland, for a number of reasons. Their informality, for example, provides for the operation of nepotism, sectarianism and racism. Less obviously, the flow of vacancy information is generally restricted within the networks of the existing work-force of a given establishment. If this work-force is overwhelmingly

---

3 Other important studies of 'word of mouth' recruitment are by Granovetter (1974), Grieco (1987), Manwaring and Wood (1984), Manwaring (1984), Wood (1986), Rees (1966), Sheppard and Belitsky (1966) and Windolf (1986).

of a particular ethnicity or 'race', it is likely to remain so (Commission for Racial Equality, 1982). This is an important mechanism serving, whether by force of inertia or exclusionary intent, to maintain ethnic employment hierarchies and differentials and produce labour-market closure (Kreckel, 1980). The undoubted importance of 'word of mouth' recruitment is a barrier to equality of opportunity in Britain and Northern Ireland.

Banton, in the course of developing a rational choice model of ethnic relations, has distinguished between *categorical* and *statistical* discrimination (1983: 274). Categorical discrimination entails treating someone in a particular way simply because they are, for example, black (or a member of any specified category). Statistical discrimination, however, involves treating someone in a particular fashion because it is believed that, as members of a socially specified category, they are more or less likely to possess a valued or stigmatized attribute.

Categorical discrimination, therefore, includes the straightforward racist discrimination discussed above. A leading American economist has described this as a 'taste for discrimination'; in the conventional neo-classical model of the labour market, their taste for discrimination is something which employers seek to indulge to the maximum (Becker, 1971: 13–17). Fevre, in his study of the Yorkshire wool textiles industry, offers a broadly similar argument when he says that white employers have an *absolute* belief in the total inferiority of black workers in *all* jobs, only employing them when there is no other choice (1984: 106–25, 147–56). Although there is no need to review them in detail here, there are a number of criticisms, both empirical and conceptual, to which the 'taste for discrimination' model is vulnerable (Joll et al., 1983: 131–53; Sloane, 1985).

Statistical discrimination corresponds to the discrimination resulting from the use of criteria of acceptability. Black workers, for example, are less likely to be recruited because – for whatever reasons – they are believed to be less likely than whites to prove reliable, manageable, or whatever. If black workers or Catholics are believed to be less likely than whites or Protestants to be suitable in particular contexts, because a greater proportion lack the required training or experience perhaps, this is also an example of statistical discrimination. The point is that statistical discrimination does not mean that the recruiter views *all* blacks or *all* Catholics as less suitable or acceptable than whites or Protestants. It is simply that a greater proportion of the stigmatized than the non-stigmatized group is believed to be deficient in these respects. It is, therefore, rational behaviour on the part of the employer, albeit based upon faulty information or stereotypes, to discriminate against them as a collectivity.

From the discussion so far, it should be clear that statistical and categorical discrimination interact in the recruitment process to the systematic disadvantage of black workers in Britain and Catholics in Northern Ireland. They are complementary explanations rather than alternatives. The distinction is important inasmuch as the notion of statistical discrimination lays bare the situational logic of the 'some of my best friends are black, but . . .' rationalization for ethnic discrimination. This is a useful contribution to an understanding of the way in which individuals can vehemently deny being racist or sectarian, but continue to discriminate knowingly against black people or Catholics. It is also an explanation of the recruitment of token – and highly visible – members of ethnic minorities: 'so-and-so's all right, but . . .' Whatever else ethnic discrimination may be, it is rarely just straightforward, i.e. categorical racism or sectarianism. The notion of statistical discrimination takes the discussion beyond simple models of prejudice and relates employment discrimination to the rational goals of managers and recruiters.

Another way of conceptualizing discrimination is the legal distinction between *direct* and *indirect* discrimination created by the 1975 Sex Discrimination Act and the 1976 Race Relations Act (section 1(i)(b)). Drawing directly upon American experience, this categorization has no equivalent in Northern Irish fair employment law, so the discussion will be confined to Great Britain. Direct discrimination is quite straightforward; it involves the intent to discriminate on ethnic or 'racial' grounds.[4] Indirect discrimination, a concept which is in some respects similar to the idea of institutional racism (Dummett, 1973: 131–53), occurs when practices which are nominally equivalent in their effects upon different groups of people create conditions or requirements which can be less easily satisfied by a certain group, as a consequence of which members of that group suffer a detriment (Lustgarten, 1980: 43–64; McCrudden, 1982a). The practices concerned must not, for indirect discrimination to be proved, be justifiable on the grounds of business necessity. Examples of practices which have fallen foul of the law in this respect are inappropriate English language requirements, 'word of mouth' recruitment (in certain settings) and dress regulations (such as those requiring female shop assistants to wear uniform skirts – an obstacle for Muslim women).

The introduction of the notion of indirect discrimination into English law was an attempt to tackle routine (and frequently thoughtless) ethnocentrism and the everyday practices, incrementally formed during the historical establishment of custom and practice, which serve to produce and maintain ethnic inequalities. It was also a recognition of the inherent difficulties in attempting to prove intentionality in discrimination. As such, it has had only a limited success, due to weaknesses in the defi- nitions of 'justifiability' and 'condition or requirement' (Commission for Racial Equality, 1983: 11–12; Jenkins, 1986: 249–52), the inability of English common law to accommodate the kind of social scientific or statistical evidence upon which the American law relies (McCrudden, 1983: 66–7) and the pro-management bias of Industrial Tribunals (Hepple, 1983: 83).

Analytically speaking, the distinction between indirect and direct dis- crimination, while it focuses our attention upon the subtleties of ethnic disadvantage, is of only limited and imprecise utility. It is, in fact, more an aspect of the situation being studied than an analytical tool of any

---

4 In fact, it is a little less clear than this. The Commission for Racial Equality has argued (1983: 11) that, as legally defined, direct discrimination need not be intentional. It is, however, difficult to imagine how treating someone unfavourably on racial grounds, to paraphrase section 1(i)(a) of the Race Relations Act 1976, can be anything other than intentional.

exactitude. The next important aspect of that situation to be discussed here is the relationship between ethnic disadvantage in employment and educational achievement.

Education, Skill and Disadvantage

The relationship between educational attainment and labour market outcomes has been the object of much research, both at the macro level of statistics and surveys (Bowles and Gintis, 1976; Goldthorpe, 1980; Jencks, 1973; Sewell and Hauser, 1975) and the micro level of ethnography and participant observation (Coffield et al., 1986; Griffin, 1985; Jenkins, 1983; Willis, 1977). The topic has also engendered a considerable amount of more or less heated argument, both political and academic (Hurn, 1978: 85–107; Karabel and Halsey, 1977: 307–65; Oxenham, 1984). The flavour of some of this discussion is accurately captured in phrases such as 'the great training robbery' (Berg, 1970) and 'the diploma disease' (Dore, 1976). The debate within labour market economics about 'human capital' remains lively and of relevance (Siebert, 1985). Regardless of which view is adopted, it seems safe to conclude that whatever the relationship between education and labour-market outcomes might be, it is neither straightforward nor self-evident.

To look at the situation of black young people, the great majority of whom have received all their education in Britain, it may be summarized thus: while most British-born Asian children (Bengali speakers apart) do well in school, their Afro-Caribbean peers achieve less, in formal educational terms, than white children (Jeffcoate, 1984; Parekh, 1983). The reasons for this state of affairs are controversial and there is not space to discuss them here (see Rampton, 1981; Stone, 1981; Swann, 1985). What, however, are its implications for labour-market outcomes?

The nature and extent of the labour-market disadvantage of black workers in Britain has already been outlined. Young black workers are particularly disadvantaged. To what degree is their labour-market position related to their levels of formal educational achievement? Lee and Wrench, in their study of apprenticeships (1983), found that although the Asian, West Indian and white youngsters they studied had similar aspirations and levels of educational achievement, the white sample was more successful in obtaining apprenticeships. The gulf between career goals and outcomes was most marked for the black samples.

Other research has produced similar findings. The Afro-Caribbean youngsters in one study were markedly less successful than their white equivalents in obtaining the kind of jobs they wanted. This difference could not be explained by the educational differences between the two groups (Commission for Racial Equality, 1978). Subsequent research has confirmed this pattern (Anwar, 1982). Further, while most young Asians achieve *at least* as much as young white people with respect to formal educational qualifications, this does not appear to translate into comparable employment outcomes. Although Asian young people suffer from unemployment to a lesser extent than Afro-Caribbean youth, they are consistently and significantly more likely to be unemployed than young white people (Brown, 1984: 190).

Longitudinal studies of a cohort of white and West Indian school leavers in the 1970s point in the same direction (Dex, 1982; Sillitoe and Meltzer, 1986). Black youngsters, both male and female, are more likely to fail in pursuing their goals, and their employment careers are more subject to interruption by 'involuntary events' (dismissal, redundancy or personal circumstances external to the workplace). As a result, they are more vulnerable to unemployment. These contrasting employment profiles cannot be related to educational differences. This research, and that of others (Brown, 1984: 135–6; Roberts et al., 1981), also demonstrates that black young people are more interested, and have higher participation rates, in further education, than the white population.

To emphasize the point further, Cross's analysis of the accessibility of vocational training for black young people in Britain demonstrates that the unemployed black youngster is typically better qualified than his or her white equivalent (1982a). He has also shown that the *ratio* of black to white unemployment is higher for young people in non-manual or skilled manual occupations requiring formal educational qualifications, even though the unskilled suffer higher *levels* of unemployment (Cross, 1982b: 47–8). What is more, despite the fact that black people are, for the purposes of this particular comparison, similarly qualified to white people, they have been disproportionately placed on state employment schemes 'with a tenous or non-existent connection with the labour market' (Cross, 1987: 86). Finally, although formal qualifications are for white people a buffer, to some extent, against unemployment, the same does not appear to be the case for black people (Smith, 1981: 16–17).

Research in Northern Ireland has shown that much of the long-standing educational differential between the Catholic and Protestant populations had been eroded by the late 1970s. There was, however, still an appreciable under-representation of Catholics in the group of schoolchildren obtaining five or more O-levels or A-levels (Osborne and Murray, 1978). The gap between the two populations has continued to decrease, but more slowly. Important factors influencing this process are social class, the experience of unemployment and the provision of grammar school places (the Northern Ireland secondary education system remains selective and is, effectively, ethnically segregated). Nor is it simply a matter of level of qualifications: there remains a tendency for Catholic pupils to be overrepresented in arts and humanities subjects by comparison with mathematics and the sciences (Osborne, 1985). A similar concentration is apparent in higher education, where the expansion of Catholic participation has largely taken place towards the low end of the spectrum (Osborne et al., 1983).

What is, however, clear is that the major employment differentials between the two populations are not attributable to educational differences: 'protestant and catholic pupils with the same level of academic attainment do not have the same success in obtaining employment' (Department of Economic Development, 1986; 10). Nor are these differentials easily attributable to ethnic differences with respect to 'attitudes to work'

326   *Richard Jenkins*

(Miller, 1978). These conclusions are supported by research concerned with the post-school transition of working-class youth in Belfast and Derry (Cormack and Osborne, 1983; Murray and Darby, 1983).

There is a clear conclusion to be drawn from the evidence summarized above: while there are differences between blacks and whites or Catholics and Protestants as collectivities, with respect to educational achievement, these are only in very small part, if at all, the 'cause' of the current employment differentials which exist between them. Nor is this causal relationship, such as it may be, immediately obvious or straightforward. This is not to say, however, that education is irrelevant to labour-market outcomes. Rather, the suggestion is that educational attainment is influential in the context of other factors, having a different 'trade-in' or market value for members of different ethnic groups.

Formal educational qualifications are one aspect of suitability, as discussed in the previous section on the nature of discrimination. Another important facet of suitability is formally recognized or accredited skill. It has already been demonstrated that British black people and Northern Irish Catholics are disproportionately represented in unskilled and semi-skilled jobs. Bearing in mind the socially constructed and situationally defined nature of 'skill' (Lee, 1981), it is reasonable to ask how this situation has developed.

Looking at black workers, there are a number of factors to take into account. In the first place, the original wave of post-war migrants were specifically recruited to fill jobs at the bottom end of the market. Most of them have remained there, trapped by a combination of stigmatization, language barriers (for some) and their own eventual acquiescence. Secondly, the skills possessed by many migrants were rejected by British employers and trade unions. For many, the move to Britain resulted in deskilling and occupational downgrading (Daniel, 1968: 57–82; Phizacklea and Miles, 1980: 78–89; Ratcliffe, 1980: 19–21). Thirdly, for subsequent generations of British-born black people access to skill training such as apprenticeships has been systematically frustrated by a combination of direct and indirect discrimination (Lee and Wrench, 1983). There is a wide body of research which demonstrates that black people, regardless of educational suitability, find it more difficult to obtain training, particularly at higher levels or in vocationally relevant areas (Cross, 1987; Lee, 1987). Finally, with respect to those dimensions of skill which are informally constituted in experience, the acquisition of such experience depends on 'getting in' in the first place. This is likely to be more difficult for black workers than for white workers.

The situation for Catholics in Northern Ireland is, in some respects, broadly comparable. Historically speaking, Catholics were incorporated into the labour market in Northern Ireland as ex-agricultural workers regarded as, at best, semi-skilled. This process was dependent upon their systematic and organized exclusion from skilled work by an alliance of organized (Protestant) labour and Unionist employers. Patterns of recruitment into training and skilled positions were set up which, combined with the sectarian geography of residence and employment in places like Belfast and violent intimidation during times of tension, ensured the virtual monopoly of skilled work by Protestants. The pattern persists to this day: such evidence as is available suggests that Protestant school leavers are more likely to obtain 'proper' apprenticeships, for example, than their Catholic counterparts who end up, at best, in government Training Centres, with less expectation of a job at the end of their training (Cormack and Osborne, 1983; Murray and Darby, 1983). Finally, as in the case of British black workers, higher levels of unemployment among Catholics, and their concentration in certain kinds of employment, renders them disproportionately less likely to have access to the important informal dimensions of skill acquisition.

Skill requirements and even the definition of 'skill', change with economic circumstances. In the last fifteen years a number of important changes have occurred, in Britain and Northern Ireland, which are relevant to this discussion. There has been a massive increase in unemployment, a shift away from employer-based training towards government training schemes, a decline in manufacturing and an expansion of service-sector employment, an expansion of part-time employment (often taken by women) and a revolution in information technology. In theory, this might present an opportunity for ethnically disadvantaged men – and women – to improve their relative labour-market position. Inasmuch as the attributes which are likely to be required of workers in the future are *generic capacities* rather than *specific skills* their exclusion from skill training may be less of a disadvantage.

This does not, however, appear to be the case, as the material on ethnic disadvantage testifies. The continued importance of criteria of acceptability, combined with trends in industrial location away from inner-city areas (where the majority of black people live) and heightened competition for the scarce resource of employment, seems likely to ensure that any changes with respect to relative ethnic disadvantage in employment are likely to be for the worse, not for the better. This issue will be discussed in greater detail in the next section.

The arguments advanced in this section concerning the relationship between educational qualifications and labour-market outcomes should not be interpreted as suggesting that the pursuit of more and better education by ethnic minorities is futile. This is emphatically not the case (Troyna and Smith, 1983). What is important, however, is that education should not be held out as offering, in and of itself, social mobility or enhanced labour-market position.

Towards Greater Equality

In interpreting the facts of ethnic disadvantage in employment in the United Kingdom, a number of factors have been highlighted as contributing to the situation: prejudice or ethnic antipathy, more subtle forms of discrimination (both intentional or otherwise), the – possibly unintended – consequences of informal recruitment procedures, the history of any specific group's incorporation into the occupational and industrial structure, demographic factors, geographical location and – something about which more will be said below – the recession. Although first-generation migrants may have been educationally and, for some at least, linguistically at a disadvantage, these factors are not a convincing explanation for the labour-market experience of their children.

As Marx said, having interpreted the world in various ways, the point is to change it. It is possible to distinguish four strategies for, or approaches to, the amelioration of ethnic disadvantage: the legal, the administrative, the voluntaristic and that associated with struggle or community action. Before discussing each of these, it is necessary to clarify what the goals of such strategies might be.

Essentially, there are two different kinds of goal: 'fair shares' and 'equality of opportunity' (Mayhew, 1968). The first is the more radical, depending upon mechanisms of reverse or positive discrimination to redistribute resources more equitably within society. This is a collectivist social philosophy of group entitlements. The second, resting upon an individualistic philosophy with its roots in the freedom of the market, aims to remove discriminatory barriers on the demand side and encourage thereby the participation of members of disadvantaged groups in the 'normal' processes of social mobility. Equal opportunity is the less controversial objective; positive discrimination – and the manner in which it has been pursued in the USA – has generated at least as much heat as light in academic and political debate.[5] As the law and state policy presently stand in the United Kingdom, the emphasis is almost exclusively on equality of opportunity. This is the main focus, therefore, of the discussion which follows.

The law is one of the main mechanisms which has been used to try to improve the lot of black Britons and Northern Irish Catholics with respect to employment. The 1968 Race Relations Act expanded the scope of the 1965 Act to prohibit discrimination in employment. The 1976 Race Relations Act drew the novel distinction between direct and indirect discrimination, in the process broadening the theoretical reach of the law considerably, established the Commission for Racial Equality (CRE) by the amalgamation of the Race Relations Board and the Community Relations Commission, permitted direct access for complainants to the Industrial and Employment Appeal Tribunals and defined certain narrow conditions under which 'positive action' – not, it should be noted, 'positive discrimination' – is permissible (Lustgarten, 1980; McCrudden, 1981).

Despite these legal provisions, there is a consensus that the actual impact of the 1976 Act has, at best, been minimal (Lustgarten, 1987: 14–15; Sanders, 1983: 75). The evidence summarized earlier in this chapter is clear in this respect. There are a number of reasons for this unhappy situation, some of which have already been touched upon: the nature of British common law, the increasing complexity of the

5 The debate on positive discrimination has generated a large literature; see e.g. the contributions by Banton (1984, 1985), Cohen et al., (1977), Eastland and Bennett (1979), Edwards (1987), Liebman (1983), Lustgarten (1980), McCrudden (1983), McKean (1983) and Young (1987). This is only a very small selection.

discrimination case law, specific weaknesses in the framing of the 1976 Act, lack of political support for the principles informing the Act and resistance on the part of employers to state or legal intervention in their affairs (Jenkins and Solomos, 1987: 210–12).

In Northern Ireland, following the van Straubenzee report, the 1976 Fair Employment Act (Northern Ireland) prohibited discrimination on the grounds of political or religious affiliation. It established the Fair Employment Agency (FEA), with the twin duties of eliminating discrimination and promoting equality of opportunity. In the first of these objectives the Act and the Agency have not been particularly successful (McCrudden, 1981, 1982b; Rolston, 1983). The reasons for this failure include caution and lack of enforcement experience within the FEA, lack of confidence in the Agency's ability to effect change on the part of the Catholic community, the inadequacies of the Act – particularly the absence of any explicit concept of indirect discrimination, confusion about the Agency's semi-autonomous role within the Northern Ireland state and resistance by Protestant employers and workers. In addition, the Act suffers some of the same problems with the common law as the 1976 Race Relations Act in Britain.

Many of these criticisms are summarized in the Standing Advisory Commission on Human Rights report (1987) on discrimination in Northern Ireland. This document was accompanied by a comprehensive – and locally controversial – three-volume research report (Smith and Chambers, 1987). Among the proposals announced in February 1988 by the Northern Ireland Department of Economic Development (DED) in the wake of these reports are the prohibition of indirect discrimination, the introduction of statutory requirements that all firms with more than twenty-five employees monitor their work-forces and that *all* employers provide equality of opportunity and the replacement of the FEA by a newer, more powerful, organization. All these will be enshrined in new legislation.

Moving on to the administrative approach, as advocated by Lustgarten (1987), this suggests that the state, using its power as an employer, contractor and consumer, should intervene directly to ameliorate ethnic disadvantage, changing its own employment practices and those of the organizations with which it does business. Since 1982 the Northern Ireland government has, for example, refused to accept contract tenders from firms not holding an Equal Opportunity Certificate issued (and removable) by the FEA. As yet, however, there is little evidence of this power being used to any great effect. The DED's proposals of February 1988 include a strengthening of this sanction.

If one accepts Miller's analysis of the resistance of government in Northern Ireland to the investigation of its own employment policies and procedures by the FEA (1986: 227–30), then the prospects seem less than bright. Where such, admittedly external, administrative pressure has been felt, however – from the United States Air Force in its dealings with Short Brothers and Harland – some changes have resulted (Darby, 1987: 68–9). There is, what is more, some evidence, in the shape of the Northern Ireland Civil Service's Equal Opportunities Unit, that government is beginning to take the issue of putting its own house in order more seriously than it has done in the past (Cormack and Osborne, 1987). The Secretary of State has also increasingly been publicly supporting the pursuit of equal opportunity. External political influences – in the shape of Dublin and the Anglo-Irish agreement – are also important here.

In Britain, there is less enthusiasm on the part of central government for an administrative approach, in large part at least because of the political tenor of the post-1979 Conservative administrations with respect to 'race', equal opportunity and state intervention (Solomos, 1987). Some local authorities, both as employers and – in pursuit of their perceived duties to promote equal opportunity under Section 71 of the Race Relations Act – with respect to 'contract compliance' (the insistence that contractors for authority business are equal opportunity employers), have enthusiastically adopted such an orientation. During 1987 these contract compliance approaches were threatened by the new Local Government Bill, which aimed to outlaw the use of non-financial criteria in local authority contractual decision-making. In the light of its conflict with Section 71 of the 1976 Act, this clause in the Bill was, however, modified. State intervention with respect to inner-city programmes and training also fall within the administrative approach. In the area of training, for both young people and adults, there is evidence that black people are systematically disadvantaged (Cross, 1987; Lancashire Industrial Language Training Unit, 1983). With respect to the inner city, in the absence of any attempt either to reverse industrial locational shifts (Fothergill and Gudgin, 1982; Massey and Meegan, 1982) or take seriously the 'racial' dimension of the inner-city problem (Rex, 1981), little seems likely to change. The contrast between the Conservative government's different positions in Belfast and at Westminster with respect to equality of opportunity is an instructive example of the expedient contextuality of policy-making.

Administrative pressure and the threat of legal sanctions are, of course, designed to evoke 'voluntary' responses from employers. The promotional work of the CRE (Ollerearnshaw, 1983) and the FEA (Darby, 1987) is also directly aimed at this goal. The major voluntarist response is the organizationally specific equal opportunity policy, a package of employment policies and procedures designed to ensure equality of opportunity within an organization. Such a package might include ethnic monitoring, more formal recruitment procedures, compensatory training and changes to the organization's channels of recruitment. The changes which have been introduced by Short Brothers and Harland in Belfast, as mentioned above, are an example of such a policy, as is the approach adopted by the Ford Motor Company (House of Commons, 1981: 850–73). Reviewing the recent literature (Hitner et al., 1982; Jenkins, 1986: 189–219; 1987; Jewson and Mason, 1986b, 1987; Torrington et al., 1982; Young, 1987; Young and Connelly, 1981) there are a number of broad conclusions which may be offered concerning the limitations of equal opportunity policies.

First, the introduction of such policies is subject to all the general constraints, to do with things such as habit, inertia, communication problems and personnel performance, which are attendant upon any process of change or innovation within bureaucratic organizations. Secondly, and more specifically, considerable resistance may be encountered from white, male work-forces – from management to shopfloor – to the notion of equal opportunity. The employment procedures of the organization, thirdly, may require considerable modification in order to improve accountability and allow for a monitored recruitment and promotion process. Without systematic monitoring, it is impossible to enforce an equal opportunity policy. Fourthly, there is a considerable amount of confusion about what 'equal opportunity' actually means, and how it relates to notions such as 'positive discrimination' and 'positive action'. The lack of clear guidance from the law and other authoritative policy sources in certain areas is a problem. Fifthly, the weakness of the personnel function within many organizations serves to limit the effectiveness of employment policies for which they are responsible. Equal opportunity is generally an issue which is handled by personnel (Jenkins and Parker, 1987). Finally, the importance of training as an integral part of equal opportunity initiatives, in terms of equalizing access to all training opportunities, specific training for equal opportunity and the provision of compensatory training, is often overlooked (Lee, 1987). Taken as a whole, these must be considered major barriers to the effectiveness of equal opportunity policies. They are not, however, insuperable and progress is being made in places to overcome them.

Finally there is the role of struggle or community action in ameliorating labour-market disadvantage. In the USA for example, black political pressure, both constitutional and 'on the streets', has been a major factor producing change (Burstein, 1985). The scope for such action in Britain seems limited, however, largely because, given the numerical size of the black vote and the continued significance of popular racism,[6] there is little or no political mileage to be had, on either the left or the right, from such an issue. Central government, despite the importance of the 'inner cities' issue in the period following the 1987 General Election, has yet to recognize the role of the unemployment of young black people in the 'riots' of the early 1980s. In municipal local government, where the black vote may be more important, there has been more enthusiasm for the promotion of equal opportunity (Ben-Tovim et al., 1986). In the light of central government's limitation of the powers and responsibilities of local authorities in Great Britain, however, the future of such initiatives seems to be in doubt.

With respect to Northern Ireland, there can be little disagreement that the political violence of the last eighteen years or so has had an enormous impact upon the economy: employment has been lost and inward investment deterred. It is difficult to imagine any sense in which the minority population can have benefited *economically* from such a situation. The gap between the two populations remains, although employment profiles for Catholics employed in the public sector are improving (Osborne, 1987: 274–7). It is, of course, true that the struggle in which the Catholic community, or

---

6 On the continued vitality of popular racism, see the evidence provided by Cashmore (1987), Jenkins (1986: 80–115), Jowell and Airey (1984: 122–30) and Jowell et al. (1986: 149–50).

sections of it, is involved is a *political* struggle. The removal of discrimination or the promotion of greater equality are pursued only as secondary consequences of the overall goal, the unification of Ireland.

Community action of another kind includes self-help. One form of self-help which has frequently been proposed as an avenue of escape from disadvantage for minorities is self-employment and business (Sowell, 1981). For a number of ethnic communities in the USA this has, indeed, proved to be the case (Bonacich and Modell, 1980; Light, 1972), as too for the Jewish community in Britain (Aris, 1970; Pollins, 1982). In Britain the field of 'ethnic business' has been a growing area of research activity (Waldinger et al., 1985; Ward, 1987; Ward and Jenkins, 1984). One of the clearest conclusions to be drawn from this research is that, in the present situation, business activity offers ethnic minorities in Britain only the most limited mobility opportunities, and this for only some minorities. Nor is ethnic business likely to be able to fill the role in inner-city regeneration which some politicians have claimed for it, if only because of the small numbers of entrepreneurs involved and the precarious marginality of their enterprises (Aldrich et al., 1984; Auster and Aldrich, 1984). This is not, of course, to suggest that ethnic business activity is undesirable. It is simply that one should be sceptical of claims that self-employment and entrepreneurship are solutions to ethnic disadvantage in the labour market. The number of black people to whom such solutions are open is likely to be small.

In both Britain and Northern Ireland, the strongest barrier to greater equality of opportunity is neither legal, administrative, organizational nor political. The deteriorating United Kingdom economic situation since the early 1970s – the recession – is probably the single most important obstacle, although it is inextricably bound up with the four factors mentioned above (O'Dowd, 1986; Rhodes and Braham, 1987). There are a number of reasons why this is so, some of which have already been discussed.

The historical pattern of labour-force participation of black people and Catholics has rendered them vulnerable to unemployment, in a situation where 'traditional' unskilled and semi-skilled manual work and manufacturing employment are in decline. Similarly, particularly in Britain, the migration of industry away from the inner city has left many ethnic minority communities marooned in terms of employment. In Northern Ireland, although some attempt has been made to use government-assisted employment policies to rectify the situation (Bradley et al., 1986), the bulk of employment has always been sited in Protestant areas, and there is evidence that the differential in this respect is widening (Doherty, 1982; Hoare, 1982). The demographic profile of the two minority communities, weighted towards the younger end of the spectrum in each case, further renders them more vulnerable to youth unemployment.

At the time of increased competition for the scarce resource of employment, it is likely that, for a variety of reasons, exclusionary strategies will be employed by majority workers. Ethnic sentiment is unlikely to decrease in salience – and it must be recognized that the 'troubles' in Northern Ireland further exacerbate the situation – and greater labour-market closure may be a result. If it is the case that employers are, for a variety of 'non-ethnic' reasons, increasingly likely to turn to informal recruitment channels (and, it should be remembered, there is conflicting research evidence in this respect), processes of labour-market closure and segmentation are given further momentum. Black workers and Catholics are likely to be even more firmly shut out of employment.[7] For employers, having to manage and survive in an economically hostile environment, equal opportunity is likely to be regarded as a low priority, particularly given, in the absence of strong legal or administrative pressure, the low cost of ignoring the issue. Finally, in a labour market which has become a buyer's market, and an associated political climate which stresses market freedom and minimum regulation or state intervention with respect to capital, many employers are likely to be impatient with attempts to promote or enforce equal opportunity.

Looked at in the light of the above, the most pressing question, perhaps, is not what can be done to improve the labour-market position of minority workers? It is, rather, how can their position be prevented from deteriorating further? It is a question for which there appear to be few likely answers.

Conclusions

To sum up this review of ethnic disadvantage in employment in the United Kingdom there are a number of points which require emphasis. First, in looking at the situation of black workers in Britain and Catholics in Northern Ireland, it is necessary to recognize the historical importance of colonialism in creating the present state of affairs. It is precisely in the contrasts between the two cases in this respect – in the nature of the original colonial situations, subsequent economic developments, patterns of migration and the contemporary state and political contexts – that their major lines of differentiation lie. In Northern Ireland, the primary principle of social cleavage, for the purposes of our discussion, is political ethnicity; in Britain, it is a case of racism and economic exploitation.

Beyond this, however, there are many similarities: in the nature of labour-market disadvantage, processes of discrimination, the role of education, strategies for the pursuit of greater equality of opportunity and the gloomy prospects for the reduction of ethnic differentials in employment. Little has so far been done, however, with respect to systematic comparative research into ethnic disadvantage in employment in Great Britain and Northern Ireland. This chapter has done little more than scratch the surface of the problem. Therein lies a worthwhile avenue for further investigation.

7 Such a conclusion could seem to imply an increasing degree of dualism in the UK labour market. Writing in the early 1970s, Bosanquet and Doeringer (1973) suggested that the dual labour-market model (Doeringer and Piore, 1971) might apply to the UK, a view that was subsequently strongly criticized by, among others, Blackburn and Mann (1979: 23). The dualist model, albeit in developed forms, has continued to be applied to the USA (Edwards, 1979; Gordon et al., 1982; Piore, 1979) and Europe (Berger and Piore, 1980). Without wishing to advocate the use of the dual labour-market model as such, it may be time to reconsider whether, in fact, the situation has changed at all since Blackburn and Mann's critique, and, if so, in what ways.

334   *Richard Jenkins*

References

Akinnaso, F.N. and Seabrook Ajirotutu, C. 1982. 'Performance and Ethnic Style in Job Interviews'. *Language and Social Identity*. Ed. Gumperz, J.J. Cambridge University Press.

Aldrich, H., Jones, T.P. and McEvoy, D. 1984. 'Ethnic Advantage and Minority Business Development' *Ethnic Communities in Business*. Eds Ward, R. and Jenkins, R. Cambridge: Cambridge University Press.

Anwar, M. 1982. *Young People and the Job Market – A Survey*. London: Commission for Racial Equality.

Aris, S. 1970. *The Jews in Business*. London: Cape.

Ashton, D.N., Maguire, M.J. and Garland, V. 1982. 'Youth in the Labour-Market'. Research Paper No. 34. London: Department of Employment.

Aunger, E.A. 1983. 'Religion and Class: An Analysis of 1971 Census Data'. *Religion, Education and Employment*. Eds Cormack, R.J. and Osborne, R.D. Belfast: Appletree Press.

Auster, E. and Aldrich, H. 1984. 'Small Business Vulnerability, Ethnic Enclaves and Ethnic Enterprise'. *Ethnic Communities in Business*, Eds Ward, R. and Jenkins, R. Cambridge: Cambridge University Press.

Banton, M. 1983. *Racial and Ethnic Competition*. Cambridge: Cambridge University Press.

—— 1984. 'Transatlantic Perspectives on Public Policy Concerning Racial Disadvantage'. *New Community*, 11 (Spring), 325–36.

—— 1985. *Promoting Racial Harmony*. Cambridge: Cambridge University Press.

Barker, M. 1981. *The New Racism: Conservatives and the Ideology of the Tribe*. London: Junction Books.

Barritt, D.P. and Carter, C.F. 1972. *The Northern Ireland Problem: A Study in Group Relations*. London: Oxford University Press.

Barth, F. (ed.) 1969. *Ethnic Groups and Boundaries*. Bergen: Universitetsforlaget.

Becker, G.S. 1971. *The Economics of Discrimination*. Second edition. Chicago: University of Chicago Press.

Berg, I. 1970. *Education and Jobs: The Great Training Robbery*. Harmondsworth: Penguin.

Berger, J. and Mohr, J. 1975. *A Seventh Man*. Harmondsworth: Pelican.

Berger, S. and Piore, M.J. 1980. *Duality and Discontinuity in Industrial Societies*. Cambridge: Cambridge University Press.

Ben-Tovim, G., Gabriel, J., Law, I. and Stredder, K. 1986. *The Local Politics of Race*. London: Macmillan.

Benyon, J. and Solomos, J. (eds) 1987. *The Roots of Urban Unrest*. Oxford: Pergamon.

Black, B., Ditch, J., Morrisey, M. and Steele, R. 1980. *Low Pay in Northern Ireland*. London: Low Pay Unit.

Blackburn, R.M. and Mann, M. 1979. *The Working Class in the Labour Market*. London: Macmillan.

Boal, F.W. and Douglas, J.N.H. (eds) 1982. *Integration and Division: Geographical Perspectives on the Northern Ireland Problem*. London: Academic Press.

Bonacich, E. and Modell, J. 1980. *The Economic Basis of Ethnic Solidarity: Small Business in the Japanese American Community*. Berkeley: University of California Press.

Bosanquet, N. and Doeringer, P.B. 1973. 'Is There a Dual Labour Market in Great Britain?'. *Economic Journal*, 83 (June), 421–35.

Bourne, J. and Sivanandan, A. 1980. 'Cheerleaders and Ombudsmen: The Sociology of Race Relations in Britain'. *Race and Class*, 21 (Spring), 331–52.

Bowles, S. and Gintis, H. 1976. *Schooling in Capitalist America*. London: Routledge & Kegan Paul.

Bradley, J.F., Hewitt, V.N. and Jefferson, C.W. 1986. 'Industrial Location Policy and Equality of Opportunity in Assisted Employment in Northern Ireland 1949–1981'. Research Paper 10. Belfast: Fair Employment Agency.

Brooks, D. and Singh, K. 1979. 'Pivots and Presents: Asian Brokers in British Foundries'. *Ethnicity at Work*. Ed. Wallman, S. London: Macmillan.

Brown, C. 1984. *Black and White Britain: The Third PSI Survey*. London: Heinemann.

—— and Gay, P. 1985. *Racial Discrimination: 17 Years After the Act*, London: Policy Studies Institute.

Burstein, P. 1985. *Discrimination, Jobs and Politics: The Struggle for Equal Employment Opportunity in the United States since the New Deal*. Chicago: University of Chicago Press.

Cashmore, E.E. 1987. *The Logic of Racism*. London: Allen & Unwin.

—— and Troyna, B. (eds) 1982. *Black Youth in Crisis*. London: Allen & Unwin.

Castles, S., Booth, H. and Wallace, T. 1984. *Here for Good: Western Europe's New Ethnic Minorities*. London: Pluto.

—— and Kosack, G. 1985. *Immigrant Workers and Class Structure in Western Europe*. Second editon. Oxford: Oxford University Press.

Coffield, F., Borrill, C., and Marshall, S. 1986. *Growing Up at the Margins*. Milton Keynes: Open University Press.

Cohen, M., Nagel, T. and Scanlon, T. (eds) 1977. *Equality and Preferential Treatment*. Princeton: Princeton University Press.

Cohen, R. 1978. 'Ethnicity: Problem and Focus in Anthropology'. *Annual Review of Anthropology*, 7, 379–403.

Commission for Racial Equality. 1978. *Looking for Work: Black and White School Leavers in Lewisham*. London: CRE.

—— 1981. *BL Cars Ltd . . . Report of a Formal Investigation*. London: CRE. CRE.

—— 1982. *Massey Ferguson Perkins Ltd . . . Report of a Formal Investigation*. London CRE.

—— 1983. *A Consultative Paper. The Race Relations Act 1976 – Time for a Change?*. London: CRE.

Compton, P.A. 1982. 'The Demographic Dimension of Integration and Division in Northern Ireland'. *Integration and Division*. Eds Boal F.W. and Douglas, J.N.H. London: Academic Press.

—— 1986. *Demographic Trends in Northern Ireland*. Report 57. Belfast: Northern Ireland Economic Council.

Cormack, R.J. and Osborne, R.D. 1983. 'The Belfast Study: Into Work in Belfast'. *Religion, Education and Employment*. Eds Cormack, R.J. and Osborne, R.D. Belfast: Appletree Press.

—— and Osborne, R. D. 1987. 'Fair Shares, Fair Employment: Northern Ireland Today'. *Studies* (Autumn), 273–85.

Cross, M. 1982a. *Transformation Through Training?* Berlin: CEDEFOP.

—— 1982b. 'The Manufacture of Marginality'. *Black Youth in Crisis*. Eds Cashmore, E. and Troyna, B. London: Allen & Unwin.

—— 1987. '"Equality of Opportunity" and Inequality of Outcome: the MSC, Ethnic Minorities and Training Policy'. *Racism and Equal Opportunity policies in the 1980s*. Eds Jenkins, R. and Solomos, J. Cambridge: Cambridge University Press.

—— and Smith, D.I. (eds) 1987. *Black Youth and YTS: Opportunity or Inequality?* Leicester: National Youth Bureau.

Curran, M.M. 1985. *Stereotypes and Selection: Gender and Family in the Recruitment Process*. London: HMSO.

Daniel, W.W. 1968. *Racial Discrimination in England*. Harmondsworth: Pelican.

Darby, J. (ed.) 1983. *Northern Ireland: The Background to the Conflict*. Belfast: Appletree Press.

—— 1987. 'Religious Discrimination and Differentiation in Northern Ireland: The Case of the Fair Employment Agency'. *Racism and Equal Opportunity Policies in the 1980s*. Eds Jenkins, R. and Solomos, J. Cambridge: Cambridge University Press.

Deakin, N. 1970. *Colour, Citizenship and British Society*. London: Panther.

Department of Economic Development. 1986. *Equality of Opportunity in Employment in Northern Ireland. Future Strategy Options. A consultative Paper*. Belfast: HMSO.

Department of Employment. 1987. 'Ethnic Origins and Economic Status'. *Employment Gazette*, 95 (January), 18–29.

Department of Finance and Personnel. 1985. *Continuous Household Survey: Religion*. PPRU Monitor No. 2/85. Belfast: Department of Finance and Personnel.

Dex, S. 1982. 'Black and White School-leavers: The First Five Years of Work'. Research Paper No. 33. London: Department of Employment.

Doeringer, P.B. and Piore, M.J. 1971. *Internal Labor Markets and Manpower Analysis*. Lexington, Mass.: D.C. Heath.

Doherty, P. 1982. 'The Geography of Unemployment'. *Integration and Division*. Eds Boal, F.W. and Douglas, J.N.H. London: Academic Press.

Dore, R.P. 1976. *The Diploma Disease*. London: Allen & Unwin.

Duffield, M. 1985. 'Rationalisation and the Politics of Segregation: Indian Workers in Britain's Foundry Industry, 1945–62'. *Race and Labour in Twentieth Century Britain*. Ed. Lunn, K. London: Frank Cass.

—— 1988. *Black Radicalism and the Politics of De-Industrialisation: The Hidden History of Indian Foundry Workers*. Aldershot: Avebury.

Dummett, A. 1973. *A Portrait of English Racism*. Harmondsworth: Pelican.

Eastland, T. and Bennett, W.J. 1979. *Counting by Race*. New York: Basic Books.

Edwards, J. 1987. *Positive Discrimination, Social Justice and Social Policy: Moral Scrutiny of a Policy Practice*. London: Tavistock.

Edwards, R. 1979. *Contested Terrain: The Transformation of the Workplace in the Twentieth Century*. New York: Basic Books.

Edye, D. 1987. *Immigrant Labour and Government Policy*. Aldershot: Gower.

Evason, E. 1985. *On the Edge: A Study of Poverty and Long-term Unemployment in Northern Ireland*. London: Child Poverty Action Group.

Fair Employment Agency. 1983a. *Report on Employment Patterns in the Londonderry Area*. Belfast: FEA.

—— 1983b. *Report of an Investigation by the Fair Employment Agency . . . Into the Non-Industrial for Northern Ireland Civil Service*. Belfast: FEA.

—— 1984. *Report of an Investigation by the Fair Employment Agency . . . Into the Fire Authority for Northern Ireland*. Belfast: FEA.

Fevre, R. 1984. *Cheap Labour and Racial Discrimination*. Aldershot: Gower.

Ford, J., Keil, T., Jenkins, R., Bryman, A. and Beardsworth, A. 1984. 'Internal Labour Market Processes'. *Industrial Relations Journal*, 15 (Summer), 41–50.

—— Bryman, A., Beardsworth, A.D., Bresnen, M., Keil, E.T. and Jenkins, R. 1986. 'Changing Patterns of Labour Recruitment'. *Personnel Review*, 15:2, 14–18.

Fothergill, S. and Gudgin, G. 1982. *Unequal Growth: Urban and Regional Employment Change in the UK*. London: Heinemann.

Fryer, P. 1984. *Staying Power: The History of Black People in Britain*. London: Pluto.

Goldthorpe, J.H. 1980. *Social Mobility and Class Structure in Modern Britain*. Oxford: Clarendon Press.

Gordon, D.M., Edwards, R. and Reich, M. 1982. *Segmented Work, Divided Workers*. Cambridge: Cambridge University Press.

Granovetter, M.S. 1974. *Getting A Job: A Study of Contracts and Careers*. Cambridge, Mass.: Harvard University Press.

Grieco, M. 1987. 'Family Networks and the Closure of Employment'. *The Manufacture of Disadvantage*. Eds Lee, G. and Loveridge, R. Milton Keynes: Open University Press.

Griffin, C. 1985. *Typical Girls? – Young Women from School to the Job Market*. London: Routledge & Kegan Paul.

Gumperz, J.J. 1982. *Discourse Strategies*. Cambridge: Cambridge University Press.

Hepburn, A.C. 1983. 'Employment and Religion in Belfast, 1901–1951'. *Religion, Education and Employment*. Eds Cormack, R.J. and Osborne, R.D. Belfast: Appletree Press.

Hepple, B.A. 1983. 'Judging Equal Rights'. *Current Legal Problems*, 36, 71–90.

Hewitt, C. 1981. 'Catholic Grievances, Catholic Nationalism and Violence in Northern Ireland during the Civil Rights Period'. *British Journal of Sociology*, 32 (September), 362–80.

—— 1983. 'Discrimination in Northern Ireland: A Rejoinder', *British Journal of Sociology*, 34 (September), 446–51.

—— 1985. 'Catholic Grievances and Violence in Northern Ireland'. *British Journal of Sociology*, 38 (March), 102–5.

—— 1987. 'Explaining Violence in Northern Ireland'. *British Journal of Sociology*, 38 (March), 88–93.

Hitner, T., Knights, D., Green, E. and Torrington, D. 1982. 'Racial Minority Employment: Equal Opportunity Policy and Practice'. Research Paper No. 35. London: Department of Employment.

Hoare, A.G. 1982. 'Problem Region and Regional Problem'. *Integration and Division*. Eds Boal, F.W. and Douglas, J.N.H. London: Academic Press.

House of Commons, 1981. *Fifth Report from the Home Affairs Committee, Session 1980–1981, Racial Disadvantage*. 4 vols. HC424-i to HC424-iv. London: HMSO.

Hubbuck, J. and Carter, S. 1980. *Half a Chance? A Report on Job Discrimination against Young Blacks in Nottingham*. London: Commission for Racial Equality.

Hurn, C.J. 1978. *The Limits and Possibilities of Schooling*. Boston: Allyn and Bacon.

Jeffcoate, R. 1984. *Ethnic Minorities and Education*. London: Harper & Row.

Jencks, C. 1973. *Inequality: A Reassessment of the Effect of Family and Schooling in America*. Harmondsworth: Peregrine.

Jenkins, R. 1983. *Lads, Citizens and Ordinary Kids: Working-class Youth Lifestyles in Belfast*. London: Routledge & Kegan Paul.

—— 1984. 'Black Workers in the Labour Market: The Price of Recession'. *New Approaches to Economic Life*. Eds Roberts, B., Finnegan, R. and Gallie, D. Manchester: Manchester University Press.

—— 1986. *Racism and Recruitment: Managers, Organisations and Equal Opportunity in the Labour Market*. Cambridge: Cambridge University Press.

—— 1987. 'Equal Opportunity in the Private Sector: The Limits of Voluntarism'. *Racism and Equal Opportunity Policies in the 1980s*. Eds Jenkins, R. and Solomos, J. Cambridge: Cambridge University Press.

—— Bryman, A., Ford, J., Keil, E.T. and Beardsworth, A. 1983. 'Information in the Labour Market: The Impact of Recession'. *Sociology*, 17 (May), 260–7.

—— and Parker, G. 1987. 'Organisational Politics and the Recruitment of Black Workers'. *The Manufacture of Disadvantage*. Eds Lee, G. and Loveridge, R. Milton Keynes: Open University Press.

—— and Solomos, J. 1987. 'Equal Opportunity and the Limits of the Law: Some Themes'. *Racism and Equal Opportunity Policies in the 1980s*. Eds Jenkins, R. and Solomos, J. Cambridge: Cambridge University Press.

Jewson, N. and Mason, D. 1986a. 'Modes of Discrimination in the Recruitment Process: Formalisation, Fairness and Efficiency'. *Sociology*, 20 (February), 43–63.

—— and Mason, D. 1986b. 'The Theory and Practice of Equal Opportunities Policies: Liberal and Radical Approaches'. *Sociological Review*, 34 (May), 307–34.

—— and Mason, D. 1987. 'Monitoring Equal Opportunities Policies: Principles and Practice'. *Racism and Equal Opportunity Policies in the 1980s*. Eds Jenkins, R. and Solomos, J. Cambridge: Cambridge University Press.

Joll, C., McKenna, C., McNabb, R. and Shorey, J. 1983. *Developments in Labour Market Analysis*. London: Allen & Unwin.

Jones, K. and Smith, A.D. 1970. *The Economic Impact of Commonwealth Immigration*. Cambridge: Cambridge University Press.

Jowell, R. and Airey, C. (eds) 1984. *British Social Attitudes: The 1984 Report*. Aldershot: Gower.

—— Witherspoon, S. and Brook, L. (eds) 1986. *British Social Attitudes: The 1986 Report*. Aldershot: Gower.

Karabel, J. and Halsey, A.H. (eds) 1977. *Power and Ideology in Education*. New York: Oxford University Press.

Kelley, J. and McAllister, I. 1984. 'The Genesis of Conflict: Religion and Status Attainment in Ulster, 1968'. *Sociology*, 18 (May), 171–90.

Kennedy, R.E. 1973. 'Minority Group Status and Fertility: The Irish'. *American Sociological Review*, 38 (February), 85–96.

Kovalcheck, K.A. 1987. 'Catholic Grievances in Northern Ireland: Appraisal and judgement'. *British Journal of Sociology*, 38 (March), 77–87.

Kreckel, R. 1980. 'Unequal Opportunity Structure and Labour Market Segmentation'. *Sociology*, 14 (November), 525–50.

Lancashire Industrial Language Training Unit. 1983. *In Search of Employment and Training*. London: Commission for Racial Equality.

Lee, D.J. 1981. 'Skill, Craft and Class: A Theoretical Critique and a Critical Case'. *Sociology*, 15 (February), 56–78.

Lee, G. 1987. 'Training and Organisational Change: The Target Racism'. *Racism and Equal Opportunity Policies in the 1980s*. Eds Jenkins, R. and Solomos, J. Cambridge: Cambridge University Press.

—— and Wrench, J. 1983. *Skill Seekers – Black Youth, Apprenticeships and Disadvantage*. Leicester: National Youth Bureau.

—— and Wrench, J. 1987. 'Race and Gender Dimensions of the Youth Labour Market: From Apprenticeship to YTS'. *The Manufacture of Disadvantage*. Eds Lee, G. and Loveridge, R. Milton Keynes: Open University Press.

Liebman, L. 1983. 'Anti-discrimination Law: Groups and the Modern State'. *Ethnic Pluralism and Public Policy*. Eds Glazer, N. and Young, K. London: Heinemann.

Light, I. 1972. *Ethnic Enterprise in America: Business and Welfare among Chinese, Japanese and Blacks*. Berkeley: University of California Press.

Lustgarten, L. 1980. *Legal Control of Racial Discrimination*. London: Macmillan.

—— 1987. 'Racial Inequality and the Limits of Law'. *Racism and Equal Opportunity Policies in the 1980s*. Eds Jenkins, R. and Solomos, J. Cambridge: Cambridge University Press.

McCrudden, C. 1981. 'Legal Remedies for Discrimination in Employment'. *Current Legal Problems*, 34, 211–33.

—— 1982a. 'Institutional Discrimination'. *Oxford Journal of Legal Studies*, 2 (Winter), 303–67.

—— 1982b. 'Law Enforcement by Regulatory Agency: The Case of Employment Discrimination in Northern Ireland'. *Modern Law Review*. 45:6, 617–36. 45: 6, 617–36.

—— 1983: 'Anti-discrimination Goals and the Legal Process'. *Ethnic Pluralism and Public Policy*. Eds Glazer, N. and Young, K. London: Heinemann.

McKean, W. 1983. *Equality and Discrimination under International Law*. Oxford: Clarendon Press.

Maguire, M. 1986. 'Recruitment as a Means of Control'. *The Changing Experience of Employment*. Eds Purcell, K., Wood, S., Waton, A. and Allen, S. London: Macmillan.

Manwaring, T. 1984. 'The Extended Internal Labour Market'. *Cambridge Journal of Economics*, 8 (June), 161–87.

—— and Wood, S. 1984. 'Recruitment and the Recession'. *International Journal of Social Economics*, 11; 7, 49–63.

Massey, D. and Meegan, R. 1982. *The Anatomy of Job Loss*. London: Methuen.

Mayhew, L. 1968. *Law and Equal Opportunity*. Cambridge, Mass.: Harvard University Press.

Miller, R. 1978. 'Attitudes to Work in Northern Ireland'. Research Paper 2. Belfast: Fair Employment Agency.

—— 1983. 'Religion and Occupational Mobility'. *Religion, Education and Employment*. Eds Cormack, R.J. and Osborne, R.D. Belfast: Appletree Press.

—— 1986. 'Social Stratification and Mobility'. *Ireland: A Sociological Profile*. Eds Clancy, P., Drudy, S., Lynch, K. and O'Dowd, L. Dublin: Institute of Public Administration.

—— and Osborne, R.D. 1983. 'Religion and Unemployment: Evidence from a Cohort Survey'. *Religion, Education and Employment*. Eds Cormack, R.J. and Osborne, R.D. Belfast: Appletree Press.

Moore, R. 1972. 'Race Relations in the Six Counties: Colonialism, Industrialisation and Stratification in Ireland'. *Race*, 14 (July), 21–42.

Murray, R. and Darby, J. 1983. 'The Londonderry and Strabane Study: Out and Down in Derry and Strabane'. *Religion, Education and Employment*. Eds Cormack, R.J. and Osborne, R.D. Belfast: Appletree Press.

Nelson, S. 1975. 'Protestant "Ideology" Reconsidered: The Case of "Discrimination"'. *British Political Sociology Yearbook*, 2, 155–87.

O'Donnell, E.E. 1977. *Northern Irish Stereotypes*. Dublin: College of Industrial Relations.

O'Dowd, L. 1986. 'Beyond Industrial Society'. *Ireland: A Sociological Profile*. Eds Clancy, P., Drudy, S., Lynch, K. and O'Dowd, L. Dublin: Institute of Public Administration.

O'Hearn, D. 1983. 'Catholic Grievances, Catholic Nationalism: A Comment'. *British Journal of Sociology*, 34 (September), 438–45.

—— 1985. 'Again on Discrimination in the North of Ireland: A Reply to the Rejoinder'. *British Journal of Sociology*, 36 (March), 94–101.

—— 1987. 'Catholic Grievances: Comments'. *British Journal of Sociology*, 38 (March), 94–100.

Ollerearnshaw, S. 1983. 'The Promotion of Employment Equality in Britain'. *Ethnic Pluralism and Public Policy*. Eds Glazer, N. and Young, K. London: Heinemann.

Osborne, R.D. 1982. 'Fair Employment in Cookstown? A Note on Anti-Discrimination Policy in Northern Ireland'. *Journal of Social Policy*, 11 (October), 519–30.

—— 1985. 'Religion and Educational Qualifications in Northern Ireland'. Research Paper 8. Belfast: Fair Employment Agency.

—— 1987. 'Religion and Employment', *Province, City and People: Belfast and its Region*. Eds Buchanan. R.H. and Walker, B.M. Antrim: Greystone

Books/British Association for the Advancement of Science.

—— and Murray, R.C. 1978. 'Educational Qualifications and Religious Affiliation in Northern Ireland'. Research Paper 3. Belfast: Fair Employment Agency.

—— and Cormack, R.J. 1986. 'Unemployment and Religion in Northern Ireland'. *Economic and Social Review*, 17 (April), 215–225.

—— and Cormack, R.J. 1987. 'Religion, Occupations and Employment, 1971–1981'. Research Paper 11. Belfast: Fair Employment Agency.

—— Cormack, R.J., Reid, N.G. and Williamson, A.P. 1983. 'Political Arithmetic, Higher Education and Religion in Northern Ireland'. *Religion, Education and Employment*. Eds Cormack, R.J. and Osborne, R.D. Belfast: Appletree Press.

Oxenham, J. (ed.) 1984. *Education Versus Qualifications?* London Allen & Unwin.

Paine, S. 1974. *Exporting Workers: The Turkish Case*. Cambridge: Cambridge University Press.

Parekh, B. 1983. 'Educational Opportunity in Multi-Ethnic Britain'. *Ethnic Pluralism and Public Policy*. Eds Glazer, N. and Young, K. London: Heinemann.

Peach, C. 1968. *West Indian Migration to Britain*. London: Oxford University Press.

Phizacklea, A. and Miles, R. 1980. *Labour and Racism*. London: Routledge & Kegan Paul.

—— and Miles, R. 1987. 'The British Trade Union Movement and Racism'. *The Manufacture of Disadvantage*. Eds Lee, G. and Loveridge, R. Milton Keynes: Open University Press.

Piore, M.J. 1979. *Birds of Passage: Migrant Labour and Industrial Societies*. Cambridge: Cambridge University Press.

Pollert, A. 1985. *Unequal Opportunities: Racial Discrimination and the Youth Training Scheme*. Birmingham: Trade Union Resource Centre.

Pollins, H. 1982. *Economic History of the Jews in England*. Toronto: Associated University Presses.

Ramdin, R. 1986. *The Making of the Black Working Class in Britain*. Aldershot: Gower.

Rampton, A. 1981. *West Indian Children in our Schools*. Cmnd. 8273. London: HMSO.

Ratcliffe, P. 1980. *Race Relations at Work: An Investigation into the Extent and Sources of Inequality in the Treatment of Ethnic and Racial Minorities*. Leamington Spa: Warwick District Community Relations Council.

Rees, A. 1966. 'Information Networks in Labour Markets'. *American Economic Review*, 56 (May), 559–66.

Rex, J. 1973. *Race, Colonialism and the City*. London: Routledge & Kegan Paul.

—— 1981. 'Urban Segregation and Inner City Policy in Great Britain'. *Ethnic Segregation in Cities*. Eds Peach, C., Robinson, V. and Smith, S. London: Croom Helm.

—— 1986. *Race and Ethnicity*. Milton Keynes: Open University Press.

Rhodes, E. and Braham, P. 1987. 'Equal Opportunity in the Context of High Levels of Unemployment'. *Racism and Equal Opportunity Policies in the 1980s*. Eds Jenkins, R. and Solomos, J. Cambridge: Cambridge University Press.

Roberts, K., Duggan, J. and Noble, N. 1981. 'Unregistered Youth Unemployment and Outreach Careers Work. Final Report, Part One: Nonregistration'. Research Report No. 31. London: Department of Employment.

Rolston, B. 1980. 'The Limits of Trade Unionism'. *Northern Ireland: Between Civil Rights and Civil War*. Eds O'Dowd, L., Rolston, B. and Tomlinson, M. London: CSE Books.

—— 1983. 'Reformism and Sectarianism: The State of the Union after Civil Rights'. *Northern Ireland: The Background to the Conflict*. Ed. Darby, J. Belfast: Appletree Press.

Sanders, P. 1983. 'Anti-discrimination Law Enforcement in Great Britain'. *Ethnic Pluralism and Public Policy*. Eds Glazer, N. and Young, K. London: Heinemann.

Sewell, W. and Hauser, R. 1975. *Education, Occupation and Earnings*. New York: Academic Press.

Sheppard, H.L. and Belitsky, A.H. 1966. *The Job Hunt*. Baltimore: Johns Hopkins University Press.

Siebert, W.S. 1985. 'Developments in the Economics of Human Capital'. *Labour Economics*. Carline, D., Pissarides, C.A., Siebert, W.S. and Sloane, P.J. London: Longman.

Sillitoe, K. and Meltzer, H. 1986. *The West Indian School-Leaver*. London: HMSO.

Silverman, D. and Jones, J. 1976. *Organisational Work: The Language of Grading/The Grading of Language*. London: Collier-Macmillan.

Simpson, J. 1983. 'Economic Development: Cause or Effect in the Northern Ireland Conflict'. *Northern Ireland: The Background to the Conflict*. Ed. Darby, J. Belfast: Appletree Press.

Sloane, P.J. 1985. 'Discrimination in the Labour Market'. *Labour Economics*. Eds Carline, D., Pissarides, C.A., Siebert, W.S. and Sloane, P.J. London: Longman.

Smith, D.J. 1974. *Racial Disadvantage in Employment*. London: Political and Economic Planning.

—— 1977. *Racial Disadvantage in Britain*. Harmondsworth: Pelican.

—— 1981. *Unemployment and Racial Minorities*. London: Policy Studies Institute.

—— and Chambers, G. 1987. *Equality and Inequality in Northern Ireland*. London: Policy Studies Institute.

Solomos, J. 1985. 'Problems but Whose Problems: The Social Construction of Black Youth Unemployment and State Policies'. *Journal of Social Policy*, 14 (October), 527–54.

—— 1986. 'Political Language and Violent Protest: Ideological and Policy Responses to the 1981 and 1985 Riots'. *Youth and Policy*, 18 (Autumn), 12–24.

—— 1987. 'The Politics of Anti-discrimination Legislation: Planned Social Reform or Symbolic Politics?'. *Racism and Equal Opportunity Policies in the 1980s*. Eds Jenkins, R. and Solomos, J. Cambridge: Cambridge University Press.

Sowell, T. 1981. *Markets and Minorities*. Oxford: Basil Blackwell.

Standing Advisory Commission on Human Rights. 1987. *Religious and Political Discrimination in Northern Ireland: Report on Fair Employment*. Cmnd 237. Belfast: HMSO.

Stone, J. 1985. *Racial Conflict in Contemporary Society*. London: Fontana.

Stone, M. 1981. *The Education of the Black Child in Britain*. London: Fontana.

Swann. 1985. *Education for All*. Cmnd. 9453. London: HMSO.

Torrington, D., Hitner, T. and Knights, D. 1982. *Management and the Multi-Racial Work Force*. Aldershot: Gower.

Troyna, B. and Smith, D.I. (eds) 1983. *Racism, School and the Labour Market*. Leicester: National Youth Bureau.

Visram, R. 1985. *Ayahs, Lascars and Princes: The Story of Indians in Britain 1700–1947*. London: Pluto.

Waldinger, R., Ward, R. and Aldrich, H. 1985. 'Ethnic Business and Occupational Mobility in Advanced Societies'. *Sociology*, 19 (November), 586–97.

Wallman, S. (ed.) 1979. *Ethnicity at Work*. London: Macmillan.

Walvin, J. 1984. *Passage to Britain*. Harmondsworth: Pelican.

Ward, R. 1987. 'Resistance, Accommodation and Advantage: Strategic Development in Ethnic Business'. *The Manufacture of Disadvantage*. Eds Lee, G. and Loveridge, R. Milton Keynes: Open University Press.

—— and Jenkins, R. (eds) 1984. *Ethnic Communities in Business: Strategies for Economic Survival*. Cambridge: Cambridge University Press.

Watson, J.L. 1977. 'Introduction: Immigration, Ethnicity, and Class in Britain'. *Between Two Cultures*, Ed. Watson, J.L. Oxford: Basil Blackwell.

Weber, M. 1978. *Economy and Society*. Berkeley: University of California Press.

Whyte, J. 1983. 'How Much Discrimination Was There Under the Unionist Regime, 1921–68?' *Contemporary Irish Studies*. Eds Connell, J. and Gallagher, T. Manchester: Manchester University Press.

Willis, P. 1977. *Learning to Labour*. Farnborough: Saxon House.

Windolf, P. 1986. 'Recruitment, Selection and Internal Labour Markets in Britain and Germany'. *Organization Studies*, 7: 3, 235–54.

Wood, S. 1986. 'Recruitment Systems and the Recession'. *British Journal of Industrial Relations*, 24 (March), 103–20.

Wrench, J. 1987. 'Unequal Comrades: Trade Unions, Equal Opportunity and Racism'. *Racism and Equal Opportunity Policies in the 1980s*. Eds Jenkins, R. and Solomos, J. Cambridge: Cambridge University Press.

Young, K. 1987. 'The Space between Words: Local Authorities and the Concept of Equal Opportunities'. *Racism and Equal Opportunity Policies in the 1980s*. Eds Jenkins, R. and Solomos, J. Cambridge: Cambridge University Press.

—— and Connelly, N. 1981. *Policy and Practice in the Multi-Racial City*. London: Policy Studies Institute.

12 Unemployment in Britain

Catherine Marsh

This chapter will explore some of the definitional problems of the concept of unemployment, and describe the numbers deemed unemployed by various definitions, with international and historical comparisons.[1] It will then look at a variety of explanations for the level of and rise in the unemployment figures. Finally, the social consequences of unemployment for the individuals unemployed and for society as a whole will be considered. How many? Why? So what? Three deceptively simple questions that prove surprisingly hard to answer clearly.

Numbers

Definitions

Unemployment invites contrast with employment rather than work. The employment contract has become the predominant social relationship under which people work in Western industrialized countries; the proportion of work that is performed under this contractual relationship is still increasing all over the world, and is sometimes taken as an indicator of the level of economic development of a country. Unemployed people, when they fail to be able to strike such a contract with an employer, lack access to the predominant mode of work itself. It is still unclear whether the problems faced by the unemployed strictly stem from lack of work or lack of employment. However, since employment and work are synonymous for so many, working and having a job are treated as functionally equivalent in this chapter.

The unemployed are not just people without work but people who would participate in the formal economy if they could find work to do. They are considered to be part of the labour force, and are distinguished conceptually from the economically inactive who would not want to work even if a job was offered to them. One of the consequences of economic change, however, is that it is increasingly hard to make clean distinctions between different economic categories. Other contributors to this volume

1 The author is grateful to José Luis Alvaro, George Bain, Brendan Burchell, John Devereux, Colin Fraser, Duncan Gallie, Bob Rowthorn, Jill Rubery and Dave Taylor who gave her many useful thoughts on an earlier draft of this paper.

have shown how difficult it is to distinguish the self-employed and employed (Rubery), for example, or formal and informal employment (Harris). The line between the unemployed and the inactive is also a particularly hard one to draw, since it depends on making assumptions about hypothetical situations.

There are broadly two approaches to identifying the unemployed. One is an institutional approach: to count the number of people whom the social security system recognizes as officially unemployed. The other involves trying to establish in an interview if the person would accept a job if it was offered. Neither approach can claim to yield the absolute 'truth' about the number of unemployed, because no one objective definition of unemployment can be given.

Official statistics. Until October 1982, monthly counts were made of unemployed persons in Britain who were registered as seeking employment. People had two motivations for registering: to try to find work and to gain entitlement to unemployment benefit. Staff at employment offices accepted them on the register if they were capable of and available for work, whether they were entitled to unemployment benefit or not; they denied registration to those who refused an offer of suitable employment without good cause. Aggregate tallies of those registered were published monthly by the Department of Employment.

As a result of a review of these procedures, however, registration became voluntary in October 1982, and the count of those registered became incomplete as an estimate of the numbers unemployed. The basis of the statistics therefore changed to those receiving at least one of three types of benefit available to the unemployed: unemployment benefit to which everyone with relevant insurance contributions is entitled, supplementary benefit which unemployed people may be entitled to claim if they can show they need it, and credits of National Insurance contributions. (A small group who claim benefit are not included when unemployed claimants are counted – the temporarily stopped and adult students seeking temporary work.)

The claimant count, probably more so than the registration count which preceded it, therefore reflects not just changes in the underlying level of labour surplus, but also changes in entitlement under the benefit system. After over thirty years of relative stability in the method of counting the unemployed, nineteen changes were made between the summer of 1979 and the winter of 1986 to the method of counting the unemployed, almost all of which, critics claim, kept the official monthly statistics down (Unemployment Unit, 1986a: 14); the government's response is that many of the older procedures for counting the unemployed yielded overestimates, since they included many who had effectively withdrawn from the labour force.

The effect of the largest change – the move from registrants to claimants – can be quantified, as the Department of Employment has produced a consistent series of the claimant count back to 1971 standardized on the definitions and procedures operating in the summer

TABLE 12.1   *Claimant count of unemployed in Britain in March – May 1986*

	Unemployed school leavers	Other unemployed ('000s)	Total
Male	57.7	2,130.3	2,188.0
Female	42.8	950.7	993.5
All	100.5	3,081.0	3,181.5

of 1986 (Department of Employment, 1985, 1986a: 422). Although one can estimate the effect of the other individual changes at the time they were implemented, it is hard to know what the cumulative effect over time has been, since many of them would have affected the same people. The Unemployment Unit, a research and campaigning organization for the unemployed, produces a monthly unemployment index (Unemployment Unit, 1984: 3) which estimates the unemployment rate in the United Kingdom on the definition of unemployment in use before the major changes were made in 1982; in May 1986, for example, when the official count was 3,271,000, the UU Index stood at 3,716,000.

For the rest of this chapter we shall consider unemployment in the spring of 1986 in Great Britain; the exclusion of Northern Ireland is regrettable, but comparable alternative estimates of unemployment are not available for Northern Ireland. The claimant count shown in table 12.1 suggests that unemployment was a much more severe problem for men than for women in 1986, a conclusion that needs some modification as will be shown shortly. School-leaver unemployed claimants accounted for 3 per cent of the total, but many more of them were on schemes of various kinds; there has been a dramatic change in job opportunities for young people in the last decade: whereas, in 1978, 85 per cent of 16 year old school leavers entered employment, by 1985 this had fallen to 30 per cent, with 49 per cent on the Youth Training scheme and 21 per cent unemployed (Ashton and Maguire, 1988).

Survey-based approaches to unemployment.   An alternative to the official statistics is to consider the survey evidence of the number of people who would have been in work if jobs had been available. The best source for this is the Labour Force Survey, a large annual survey, involving one in every 350 households in the United Kingdom. All household members without jobs are asked whether they would like a job, whether they are currently available for work, and whether they have looked for work in the last week and the last month. Those who have not looked for work are asked why not.

The International Labour Organization issues broad guidelines for constructing an internationally comparable measure of unemployment from survey data: those who are available for work and have looked for work in the last four weeks. This is quite a stringent indicator of labour surplus. As interpreted in Britain, it excludes those who did not look because they thought there were no jobs, and those who in better times might have made themselves available for work; the ILO acknowledges that the

TABLE 12.2   *Alternative definitions of the unemployed in Britain: estimates from Labour Force Survey in spring 1986*

	All	Men ('000s)	Women
'Unemployed' by survey criteria* of whom:	2,976	1,791	1,186
claiming benefits	2,103	1,573	530
not claiming benefits	873	217	656
Claimant count of whom:	3,167	2,178	989
'unemployed' by survey criteria	2,102	1,573	530
worked during last week	206	117	88
not 'unemployed' by survey criteria	859	488	371

* Unemployed by survey criteria are those who were available for work in the following fortnight and who had sought work in previous four weeks
Source: Department of Employment, 1987: 209

criterion of looking for work in times and areas of acute job shortage may be relaxed, but the British interpretation does not relax it (Taylor, 1988).

The ILO estimate of unemployment in Britain is not very different from the official statistics in aggregate, although many of the individuals counted by the two methods are different; the ILO estimate of unemployment picks up many more women, for example. Table 12.2 compares estimates of the number who would be counted as unemployed by the ILO definition with the claimant count in the spring of 1986.

The number of people who were not picked up in the claimant count in spring 1986 but who were available for and had sought work in the last month is 873,000, three-quarters of whom were women. However, this cannot simply be added to the count of claimants, since there were claimants who on these survey criteria were not unemployed; 206,000 claimants had done some work during the reference week and 859,000 either said they had not looked for work in the last four weeks or had looked but were not available for work.

The Department of Employment excludes those 206,000 who had done any work in the previous week from its ILO measure of the unemployed. However, only a very limited amount of work can be done while benefit is being claimed; some of the 206,000 will have been doing as little as one hour per week. Moreover, all these people are claimants and have satisfied increasingly stringent requirements at the Jobcentre that they want work and are available for it. This group should probably also be deemed unemployed. If we make this assumption, the count would seem to have 873,000 false exclusions and 859,000 false inclusions, a net undercount of 14,000 in the official statistics.

However, neither official nor ILO procedures use a very generous definition of unemployment. The same survey evidence allows one to explore other indicators of the potential size of labour surplus in Britain. Such explorations suggest that both definitions provide underestimates.

TABLE 12.3   *Other potential workers in Britain in spring 1985: reasons for not looking for work in previous week among non-claimants who would like work and are available for work, but have not looked in last four weeks*

	All	Men ('000s)*	Women
Looking after family/home	490	10	490
Retired from paid work	130	80	50
Believes no jobs available	90	30	60
Long-term sick	70	40	30
Students	60	30	30
Other	80	20	60
All	916	204	712

* These figures are estimated to nearest 10,000, and totals will therefore not always tally
Source: Estimates based on spring 1985 Labour Force Survey; kindly supplied by the Department of Employment

There are people who are not claimants and who are not in the ILO unemployment count because they have not looked for work, but who nonetheless say they would like a job and are available for work. Unfortunately, the latest year for which full figures are available is 1985; they probably provide reasonable estimates for 1986, however, as the 1985 and 1986 LFS estimates are very similar in other respects.[2] In the spring of 1985, there were an estimated 916,000 such people. Their reason for not looking for work in the last week is shown in table 12.3.

There is, of course, no way of knowing how many of these people would actually take a job if one were offered to them. Many economists are prepared to include those whose sole reason for not looking for work was that they believed there were no jobs available; such people are gracefully termed 'discouraged workers'. However, the question which solicits reasons asks 'why not?', a type of question which is notoriously unreliable; as a result, the particular category chosen in reply may be somewhat arbitrary. Cross-cultural comparisons suggest that many of the other groups could be drawn into the formal economy under the right conditions; in France or Sweden, where good childcare arrangements are possible and good maternity benefit is paid, full-time participation rates are much higher than in Britain, and in the USA, where workers cannot be compulsorily retired at a set age, the participation rates of the elderly are also higher. The point is that all these people without work said they would like a job and were available to start within the next two weeks.

Neither the claimant count nor the survey estimates of the labour surplus take account of people's preferences for full-time or part-time jobs. A more

2 In an article in Jan. 1988 *Employment Gazette*, data are presented from the 1986 LFS, including a cross-tabulation of reasons for not looking for work by availability and desire for work; unfortunately, it is only given for claimants.

refined measure of unemployment might convert the unemployment count into estimates of demand for full-time equivalent jobs, and then add to these calculations an estimate of how many full-time jobs would be needed to fill the demand of employed people who say they would like to be working more hours per week than they are at present. Comprehensive data to make this sort of calculation are not readily available, unfortunately.

Finally, it is necessary to consider how to treat the increasing number of people on special government training or employment schemes; there were 615,000 such people in the spring of 1986. Estimates of youth unemployment vary widely depending on whether young people on schemes are included or omitted from either the numerator or denominator of the unemployment rate (Raffe, 1985). The official rates in the *Employment Gazette* include them in the denominator only, thus giving the most favourable impression.

Ostensibly people on government schemes should be treated like others receiving full-time education or training, and thus excluded altogether from the labour force. However, many in these schemes are parking there while they continue their job search; young people on the Youth Training Scheme, for example, have low expectations for their training and tend to leave the minute they are offered a job (Raffe, 1988). The Department of Employment itself estimates that the 'register effect' of the 615,000 workers on these schemes is 465,000: that is the number who would be on the unemployment figures if the schemes did not exist.

A different justification for excluding them from the unemployment count is that such trainees should be counted as employees; a common criticism that has been made of government training and employment schemes is that they are providing cheap replacement for more expensive labour. It is harder to estimate the employment effect of the schemes; employers, when asked, estimate that well under half the trainees would have been taken on without such schemes (Deakin and Pratten, 1987).

However, it would be wrong to depict training schemes as 'mere' disguises for the true extent of unemployment; their psychological advantages over unemployment are well documented (Breakwell, 1985). Perhaps the solution is to say that a new category of activity status has emerged in most industrial societies: incumbents of government schemes. The critical question to raise about such schemes is whether they are likely to succeed in promoting the skills necessary for economic recovery.

In summary, we can see from the list below a picture of the size of the various estimates of the labour surplus:

Claimant count	3,167,000
Net undercount compared with ILO definition	14,000
ILO inactive non-claimants who would like work and are available for work	916,000
Estimated register effect of government schemes	465,000
Total	4,562,000

Only the top two lines carry the social definition of 'unemployed'. The rest are in theory inactive in the formal economy, but, under suitable conditions, they might be expected to enter it if jobs were to become available. However, the distinction is in practice very blurred; during the same episode of claiming, for example, people drift in and out of the ILO definition of unemployed as their motivation for job search waxes and wanes (White, 1983).

How Many Experience Unemployment? Stock Versus Flow

The world is not neatly divided into the employed and the unemployed; moreover, jobs, employment statuses and activity statuses do not remain tattooed for life on people's forearms. Large numbers of people suffer casual, irregular employment, interspersed with spells of unemployment (Townsend, 1979; Norris, 1978; Daniel, 1981b). People follow patterned trajectories through both the occupational structure and through the activity structure of society, though not always on the professional model of an upwardly progressing 'career' (Stewart et al., 1980).

One of the most important advances in the study of unemployment in the late 1970s and 1980s has been the recognition of the importance of a dynamic approach. The characteristics of those who are unemployed at any one point in time cannot be generalized to all those who experience unemployment over a period of time. Many more important questions can be addressed by considering incidence rather than prevalence: how many new cases occur over a fixed period of time, how many old cases are cured, and how many seemingly cured cases endure further bouts (Daniel, 1981a)?

The Department of Employment's monthly count of the unemployed represents the stock of those claiming benefit when the records are summarized on the second Thursday of each month, a snapshot of the number unemployed at one point in time. The monthly net change in the count is not great; during 1986, for example, the median monthly change was around 50,000. However, this can disguise the fact that there are huge flows on and off the cumulated total of claimants each month. Typically, during 1986, 400,000 people entered or left the claimant count each month. As a result, while the unemployment rate at any one point in time in this year was around 12 per cent, many more experienced unemployment at some point during the year.

The stock statistics in the *Employment Gazette* of November 1987 (1987: S38) indicate that the median duration of completed spells of unemployment in spring 1986 was 14.5 months. The duration statistics tend to underestimate the length of a spell of unemployment; if a person claiming benefit has a period of illness while unemployed, for example, he or she leaves the claimant count while claiming supplementary benefit on grounds of sickness. However, even 14.5 months is not the typical experience of anyone entering the count. In fact, in spring 1986, of those becoming unemployed, a quarter left unemployment within four weeks, half left within three months, and two-thirds left within six months (*Employment Gazette* 1987: S40).

The degree of movement on and off the register in some particular

TABLE 12.4   *Probability of remaining unemployed for the following three months: Greater London, July 1987*

Probability calculated at	Male	Female
Entry to the register	0.21	0.20
1 month after registering	0.43	0.42
2 months after registering	0.65	0.64
3 months after registering	0.87	0.86

Source: Devereux, 1987

areas makes it essential to consider the flows on and off the register rather than just the typical durations in the stock. In Greater London, for example, probabilities of leaving the register decline sharply with duration of unemployment. As table 12.4 shows, a new claimant in Greater London in July 1987 only had a 20 per cent chance of staying unemployed for three months. However, having been on the register three months, the probability of staying unemployed for the next three months is up to around 86 per cent. It is almost as if there are two distinct subpopulations moving through the London register: a large number of short-term unemployed whose unemployment turnover is very fast, and a much smaller number of long-term unemployed (Devereux, 1987).

Unfortunately, the regularly published DE flow statistics do not reveal how many of the flow statistics represent the same people moving on and off the register. For this evidence, once again we must turn to the survey-based estimates. National data from the Social Attitudes Survey in 1986, when around 3.1 million people or 13 per cent of the labour force were out of work at any one point in time, suggest that three in ten of all men and women in the labour force had been unemployed at some time during the previous five years (table 12.5).

Many studies of unemployment, including most of those mentioned in later sections, are based on samples of the stock rather than of the flow. As a result, these studies are not representative of the people who typically experience unemployment, but only of those who are typically found on the register at any point in time. While the long-term problem is undoubtedly severe and increasing in the 1980s recession, the modal experience of unemployment is relatively short; stock samples tend to hide this fact, and are thus biased against the young, the skilled and the mobile. Moreover, having drawn a stock sample, many researchers proceed to cross-tabulate their results by duration of unemployment, as if this enabled them to capture dynamic experiences of unemployment; it does not: such cross-tabulations compare radically different groups of people rather than the same people at different points of a bout of unemployment.

The fact that the number of people who flow through the unemployed register over a period of time is much greater than the stock at one point in time has been interpreted in different ways. If re-employment is on the cards for so many, perhaps this takes the sting out of the unemployment experience (Daniel, 1981b) and militates against either the political or recreational mobilization of the unemployed (Roberts et al., 1987). However,

TABLE 12.5   *Recent experience of unemployment in Britain, 1986*

Question: During the last 5 years (that is, since March 1981) have you been unemployed and seeking work for any period? If YES: For how many months in total during the last 5 years?

	Men				Women			
	emp. (%)	s/e (%)	un. (%)	all (%)	emp. (%)	s/e (%)	un. (%)	all (%)
Never unemployed	79	82		70	80	90	–	71
Unemployed 1–3 months	9	5	7	8	7	3	17	8
Unemployed 4–12 months	8	8	25	10	9	7	32	12
Unemployed 12+ months	4	5	68	12	4	–	51	9
	100	100	100	100	100	100	100	100
N	817	142	129	1088	668	29	96	793

Base: All those in the labour force in 1986
emp. – currently employed
s/e – currently self-employed
un. – currently unemployed
Source: Social Attitudes Survey, 1986

the argument can be turned on its head: it also means that unemployment, with all its painful consequences whatever the duration, has an effect on a much wider range of individuals that might at first appear.

Historical and International Comparisons

Much of our understanding about unemployment, its causes and consequences, is still formed from the depression of the 1930s, not that of the 1980s; similarities and contrasts between the two experiences are constantly being drawn, and most tend to assume that the levels of unemployment in Britain in the 'great' depression were much higher than levels now. There are two important ways in which the crisis of the 1980s is not as bad as that of the 1930s. First, as will be seen later, the real earnings of those in employment have not fallen. And, secondly, total output has not yet fallen much or in a sustained manner in any of the OECD countries (although the story with respect to manufacturing industry is different).

However, when we come to ask how much worse unemployment in the 1930s was compared with today, the comparison does not unambiguously favour today. Of course, the problems of definition are compounded before the era of either comprehensive insurance or large-scale survey research; the numbers unemployed before 1920 have to be estimated by finding out the unemployment rate among trade unions who kept records and extrapolating with adjustments to a less well-organized and less secure sector, for example. Feinstein, who used the entire civilian labour force as the denominator in his historical series (1972), suggests that unemployment reached a maximum of 15.6 per cent of the work-force in 1932, a figure reached once more in 1981, and on a much bigger base. So, in terms

TABLE 12.6   *Ranking of employment performance in OECD countries*

| | | Level in 1985 | | Growth rate 1973–85 | |
		unemployment rate	employment rate	unemployment rate	employment rate
Best:	Switzerland	1	5	3	16
	Norway	2	2	2	1
	Japan	3	6	4	7
	Sweden	4	1	1	2
	Austria	5	11	7	12
	New Zealand	6	12	9	9
	Finland	7	4	6	6
	USA	8	7	5	3
	Denmark	9	3	12	5
	Australia	10	10	11	10
	West Germany	11	13	13	17
	Italy	12	16	8	8
	France	13	14	14	15
	Canada	14	8	10	4
	UK	15	9	15	13
	Belgium	16	15	16	14
	Netherlands	17	17	17	11
	Ireland	18	18	18	18
Worst:	Spain	19	19	19	19

Unemployment rate is unemployment (national definitions) as a percentage of the labour force
Employment rate is civil employment as a percentage of population aged 15–64 years
Source: Rowthorn and Glyn, 1987

of sheer numbers affected, the unemployment problem is as great in the crises of the 1980s as it was in the 1930s. Moreover, while welfare benefits for the unemployed today are in absolute terms an improvement on the situation in the 1930s and their position relative to earnings has improved, they are still insufficient to keep many of the unemployed out of poverty (as we shall see in the final part of this chapter).

Several lessons can be drawn from putting current unemployment rates in Britain in comparison with other OECD countries in their experience of unemployment, as is done in table 12.6. Britain had one of the highest unemployment rates in 1985 and one of the highest rates of growth of unemployment between 1973 and 1985 in the OECD. However, if one considers how well countries have performed in terms of proportion of the total adult population in employment, Britain seems more typical, especially over this long time period; the activity rate of married women has risen strongly, although the tempo has been slowed by the recession.

The seemingly star performers of Switzerland and Austria have only kept their unemployment so low by repatriation of a large number of *gastarbeiters*: they rank favourably in the unemployment league, but any measure which considers the change in the size of their domestic population over a longer period of time reveals how they have achieved their 'employment miracle'. Table 12.6 also gives the lie to the idea that technical change is the most important cause of unemployment: Japan, with the fastest rate of technological innovation in the OECD, still has a very low unemployment rate. The all round real star performers are Sweden and Norway. Norway, as Nicholas Kaldor regularly reminded the House of Lords, showed how a country could use oil revenues as an opportunity to restructure and modernize (e.g. Kaldor, 1982). Sweden, in the eyes of many commentators (Rowthorn and Glynn, 1987; Therborn, 1986; Therborn et al., 1986) shows what a political commitment to full employment at both a state level and in trade unions and society can achieve. However, this leads into the explanations that have been advanced for different levels of unemployment, which will be considered in the next section.

Explanations

Neo-classical economics, working as it so often does with idealized views of the market-place for both products and labour, has had a difficult time explaining how unemployment occurs at all. In theory, although exogenous changes in trade, in tastes or in technology might cause workers in one branch of industry to be made redundant, supply and demand should eventually balance out, and new work should be found for the displaced workers, albeit at lower wages than previously: wages should find their natural level. In fact, nobody has believed quite this version of the orthodoxy for fifty years; the arguments are about where the account goes wrong.

The Traditional Theories

Modern explanations of the genesis of unemployment mostly stem from three traditional theories: Marxist, Keynsian and classical. It will be useful to begin by restating each very briefly.

Marx saw nothing stable and self-regulating about markets. He saw two complementary processes generating unemployment, one long run and the other shorter term. He foresaw a long-run tendency in capitalist societies for the ratio of capital to labour (the 'organic composition of capital') to rise because of firms' drive for technological innovation in order to remain competitive; this brought about a general tendency for labour to be displaced by machinery. Since profits were only made on the labour that was newly added to the product, there would be a tendency for the rate of profit to decline. Declining profitability, instead of proceeding at a stable rate, would occur in short-run crises – periods when capital lost its value, when wages reduced and when bankruptcies and unemployment accelerated (Marx, 1870).

Keynes (1936) also disbelieved the claims that the market-place would adjust to imbalances of supply and demand. He focused on aggregate demand in the economy as a whole; demand for products determined demand for labour. He argued that economies can get into self-fuelling upward and downward spirals. In good times, demand for goods leads to investment, paying workers in the investment industries who would then demand more consumption goods, thus fuelling the upwardly spiralling demand; this could lead to price inflation and wage increases as firms poached other firms' workers. In bad times, demand for goods decreases, firms lay workers off, and unemployment depresses aggregate demand even further.

A major difference between the Marxist and the Keynsian account is in the macroeconomic solutions proposed. The state, Keynes believed, could short-cut this spiral by engaging in a programme of public works, paid for by increased taxation or by borrowing, and thus generate demand which would in turn stimulate private industry. Marxists, on the other hand, argue that the state must plan a broader range of investments directly, as it is the only body capable of taking a perspective which is sufficiently comprehensive and long range to permit very different rates of profit to flourish in different sectors of the economy and over time.

By contrast, the classical economists from Adam Smith and Jean Baptiste Say onward have been deeply hostile to government interference of all kinds except to ensure the operation of an unfettered market. Problems such as unemployment arise, they argue, when obstacles prevent the surpluses of goods or labour from finding their true price level and thus being absorbed; left to its own devices, the labour market would eventually clear as people's wage and price expectations were brought into line with reality. If unemployment persists, the classical economist looks first to the pricing of labour and at mechanisms which produce 'rigidities' in the wage system. Such rigidities are almost universally viewed as problems on the supply side of the equation – the workers' fault – either through faulty perceptions of wages and prices, or through political and institutional obstacles such as trade unions, protective legislation and the level of social security benefit.

Neo-Marxist and Neo-Keynesian Theories

Many modern Marxists accord to the state a 'relatively autonomous' power to influence important features of social structure. Marxists writing about unemployment have suggested that the policies of the state are important in explaining variations in the aggregate amount of unemployment. Therborn (1986) and Rowthorn and Glynn (1987) have argued that the international differences in unemployment, noted in table 12.6, are the result not of blind market forces but of states and governments taking very different policy stances. Sweden and Norway, for example, have kept unemployment low because the ruling parties and the trade unions in those societies have shown a commitment to full employment: politicians and public alike are prepared to meet the costs of redistributing work and income to a potentially disadvantaged minority. The recent rapid growth of unemployment in Britain, on the other hand, is the result of policies carried out by a different balance of state forces. In the last analysis, Marxists believe that moves have to be made away from a fully market economy if the problem of unemployment is to be avoided.

There has also been a move, in modern Marxist accounts, beyond national confines to consideration of a world economic system in which transnational corporations are the key actors (e.g. Glyn et al., 1987; Ashton, 1986). During the 'Golden Age' immediately after the Second World War, rising real wages for workers and those supported by the state were matched by rising investment and productivity in expansion that was predominantly domestically based. However, from the beginning of the 1970s investment and productivity declined, while organized labour was able to continue to extract real wage increases, thus producing a severe profits squeeze in the industrialized world.

The response of international corporations, which pursue profit rather than national interest, was to locate what new investment there was in those countries that provide the best conditions for profitability. Thus, what for the advanced industrialized countries is a 'world recession' may in actual fact represent a transfer of much manufacturing from expensive labour in the profit-squeezed advanced economies to much cheaper and more docile labour in the Third World; Korea and Taiwan have not been so affected by the 'world' recession (Jordan, 1982), at least during the 1970s (Glyn et al., 1987).

Explanations of unemployment which focus on aggregate demand faced growing difficulties in the 1970s and 1980s, as the economic policies which were informed by this perspective failed to deliver the goods; both unemployment and inflation unaccountably rose together. The Cambridge Keynsians have argued that the problems stemmed from inadequate management of structural shifts in the economy. The special problems faced by Britain, they argue, stem from her decline as a manufacturing power (Kaldor, 1978). Since the end of the nineteenth century, Britain's share of world trade has been diminishing at a geometric rate, and her ability to pay for imported food and raw materials with manufactured goods has been declining as other nations have grown in industrial stature. Imported goods constituted 5 per cent of domestic demand in 1953 but one-third in 1983. What has been a long-run decline relative to other countries has turned into an absolute decline in manufacturing in recent years as British goods, made on old machinery, have not proved competitive in markets that are increasingly demanding in terms of quality. Without the fortunate coincidence of North Sea oil and gas, Britain's economic situation would be catastrophic. Lesser deviations from an unbridled market economy are proposed as solutions to this problem: a period of restructuring, during which import controls are tightly applied, would be required to turn the situation round, as the Cambridge Economic Policy Group argued with respect to the 1970s and early 1980s (Cambridge Economic Policy Group, 1971–84).

This view of unemployment is certainly supported by the statistics on the last employment of the unemployed, who come overwhelmingly from the manufacturing industries, and on overall trends in the labour force, which reveal that the manufacturing labour force has declined by about one-third in the last ten years. As a corollary, the job loss has been highly geographically concentrated in those regions of the country which are dependent on manufacturing.

In trying to provide a microeconomic foundation for their views, other reappraisals of Keynes have proposed a theory of rationing: wages do not adjust immediately to market conditions but are fixed, at least for the time it takes employers and workers to react to them (e.g. Muellbauer and Portes, 1978); the intellectual task is then to state the conditions under which such self-imposed rations are 'consistent' with each other: that perceptions of the amount of work there is gives rise to a given amount of demand for and supply of labour which in turn produces the original perceived amount of work. But, as Lindbeck and Snower (1985) have argued, they have not explained why wages are impervious to supply and demand during this critical period.

Neo-classical Theories

The neo-classical economists have been grappling with a very different set of issues. For them, the debate has centred round deviations from an idealized state of nature, 'the natural rate of unemployment'; the unemployment that occurs when people have correct expectations of wages and prices. It is voluntary by definition: it is the rate of unemployment people choose to tolerate rather than drop their wages to the point where they would gain employment. Deviations from this natural rate have traditionally been explained by looking at how faulty expectations of wages (and prices, in order to assess the real value of wages) develop.

Several different mechanisms have been proposed for the failure of expectations to match reality (a clear account of these is given in Lindbeck and Snower, 1985). Some believe that the workers are a fault. Milton Friedman (1976), for example, believes that inflation has led workers to expect price increases greater than actually occur, and therefore to refuse certain jobs on the grounds that the real wages are not high enough. Another suggestion is that workers misperceive the wage distribution and remain unemployed while they search for jobs with higher wages than are on offer.

Others consider the mechanisms whereby employers set the wage for a job. Firms, Phelps (1967) argues, set their wages relative to their perception of average wages outside the firm; the natural rate of unemployment occurs when each firm sets its wage equal to its perceived average market wage. When inflation exists, firms may in the short run trade on the fact that workers have imperfect information about real wage levels and set their rates lower than this, but workers' expectations soon adapt to this and there is a return to the natural rate.

But if these mismatches between expectations and reality are patterned, why do they not become part of public knowledge, and discussed in the press? Why should economic agents not adjust their behaviour to take them into account? This is the line of argument developed by the 'rational expectations' school (Muth, 1961). In trying to save the importance of perceptions in the face of the very obvious empirical fact that economic actors do not respond in the predicted manner, these economists argue that there is forecasting error, that the mismatches are not patterned, that unemployment is a random and therefore unpredictable event, or, only slightly more realistically, that expectations about real wages undergo cyclical swings.

What is so striking about all these explanations based on perceptions and expectations is that they are rarely if ever based on empirical research into the perceptions and expectations of the economic actors involved, either firms demanding labour or workers supplying it.

More recently, alternative explanations based on institutional practices have been adduced. Some see the problem in the nature of the employment contract: workers, disliking risk-taking more than firms, make implicit contracts with employers that bind them to that firm and stop labour contracts from being renegotiated regularly (Azariadis, 1975). As a result, fluctuations in supply and demand lead to some workers being laid off for periods, rather than the wages of all workers rising and falling.

Others have laid the fault at the door of the unions, which have prevented wages sinking to a point where it becomes profitable for employers to take more workers on. In the Thatcherite version of this explanation (e.g. Minford, 1983), unions pursue not the general welfare of all the work-force, employed and unemployed, but solely the interests of those in employment. The remedy proposed is to attack the power bases of the trade unions. In the social-democratic version, Layard and Nickell (1985) argue that buyers in any market-place have significantly less power than sellers; the latter determine prices whereas the former only determine quantity. As a result, workers and their unions (i.e. the sellers of labour) determine a price at which they will sell their labour, which produces unemployment; some form of incomes policy is required to prevent this happening.

Finally, the old spectre of social security benefits acting as a general disincentive to work appears in several accounts. When replacement ratios (of benefits to incomes while at work) become too high, the incentive to work is reduced (Minford, 1983). The psychological mechanism is as follows. Workers approach the labour market with a 'reservation wage' in mind like the reservation price at an auction: a price below which the commodity will not be offered for sale. These reservation wages are formed by comparison with the major alternative to earning a wage, namely state benefits. Unrealistically high reservation wages are then held to account for the continuing high levels of unemployment. (This argument has strong affinity with the job search theories mentioned above.) Such reservation wages, it should be noted, are not usually obtained by asking workers the sort of wage they are looking for; they are inferred from workers' behaviour.

This theory fails the empirical test once these reservation wages are sought directly. It is simply not the case that workers with high expectations of their wage on returning to work stay out of the labour market longer than those who expect to earn less (Moylan et al., 1984). Furthermore, the idea that people are well informed about benefits is crucial to this argument; in fact, people know very little about their entitlement to benefit (Wallace, 1987), even among those claiming benefit – under-claiming is a significant problem.

Technological Change

The theoretical debate in economics may seem rather arid in that its empirical basis is so slender. But it does act as an important counter to some of the more lurid accounts heralding the end of work and the imminent arrival of automated society.

It is hard to sustain empirically an argument that there is a general trend away from human labour power. For the past 200 years, the rate at which human capital has been replaced with inanimate capital has been unprecedentedly strong. Workers feared innovations from mules and spinning jennies to steam power, and usually quite rationally, for their introduction was used to depress wages and increase the employers' control over the production process. In time, however, workers displaced in one branch are absorbed in another, and society creates new demands for labour.

One particularly paradoxical pattern to the change is that while the demand for services relative to material goods probably does increase as societies grow wealthier (Bell, 1974), services can just as well be provided by capital goods (Gershuny and Miles, 1983): we demand that our clothes be cleaner now than previously, but we may achieve this by purchase of automatic washing machines. No one has shown that microchips have speeded the basic process of technical innovation, or altered long-run changes in product mix or the occupational skills required to produce them, changes which can be traced through the boom years of the 1950s and 1960s as well as through the recessions of the 1970s and 1980s.

One version of the end of work thesis suggests that we are witnessing at least the demise of the employment contract; small businesses, groups of self-employed contractors, are politically popular (e.g. Leadbeater and Lloyd, 1987). Indeed, for some neo-classical economists it is a recurring puzzle that the unemployed, when unable to find work from employers, should not undercut the existing work-force by setting up in business on their own (Lindbeck and Snower, 1985). Such a view overlooks the economies of scale which large enterprises can effect, the need for capital investment in most lines of business, and, probably most importantly, the psychological conditions of the unemployed, which will be discussed in the next section. The growth of self-employment is linked more to a country's politics and policies; Britain's rise of self-employment during the past decade is not common practice in other OECD countries; it is probably best viewed as a concomitant to casualization and the growth of the flexible work-force (Rubery, this volume).

Changes in the Size of the Work-force

There have also been important changes in the quantity of labour to be supplied as the second column of table 12.6 indicates; unemployment may have risen but employment has also risen throughout OECD countries.

Demographic change has a part to play in the explanation of unemployment levels (Rowthorn and Glynn, 1987). The second generation of the post-war baby boom has been entering the labour market for the first time since the beginning of the 1970s, causing acute competition for entrance jobs in the labour market and creating particular employment difficulties for young people, over and above the problems faced by new entrants to a declining job market (Raffe, 1986). In the EEC as a whole, the working age population increased 2.4 million between 1975–80 and 6.5 million from 1980–5 (Leadbeater and Lloyd, 1987: 27). However, the increase in Britain was less marked than elsewhere, which makes Britain's unemployment performance even more dismal. Another important factor is that female participation rates have continued to rise – both in employment and education – come boom or recession. Although jobs (primarily in the service sector) have also increased, this has not been fast enough to prevent some growth in female unemployment (Coyle, 1984).

These various explanations are extremely hard to summarize. It is one thing to list them, but quite another to integrate them, to say which are incompatible with which others, let alone to try to provide quantitative estimates of the relative contribution each makes to understanding the total problem. Some of the explanations, such as the Keynsian ones, are better at providing answers to the question of why there are not more jobs, while others, such as the neo-classical descriptions of problems with the labour supply, are better at explaining why particular types of individual have greater difficulty than others in getting jobs. The task of integrating the various explanations is probably not possible with our current understanding (Standing, 1983,1984).

To those who want to see objective proof of various theories of causation of unemployment, the strongest empirical fact must surely be that the problem is primarily a problem of market societies. While there are all sorts of other economic problems besetting state socialist countries (underemployment included), unemployment is not one of them (Hutchings, 1967). The Soviet Union's unemployment rate is so small it probably represents between job movement; Gregory and Collier (1987) estimate on the basis of interviews with emigrés that the Soviet Union's unemployment rate in the late 1970s was around 1 per cent. East Germany has a chronic labour shortage. While many criticize and will continue to criticize the behaviour of governments and trade unions, it is clear that Adam Smith's market-place has proved incapable of solving the problem spontaneously (Eatwell, 1982).

Consequences

A paradox appears in much of the literature about the consequences of unemployment. On the one hand, the burden is held to fall on the shoulders of a few, exacerbating existing inequalities and polarizing society (e.g. Pahl, 1984) and increasingly dividing the work-force into a secure, primary sector and a casualized secondary sector (Garnsey et al., 1985). On the other hand, unemployment is thought to permeate through the whole of society, having a depressing, policing effect on the wider work-force (e.g. Grunberg, 1986) and attacking the bases of the well-organized and previously secure (e.g. Harris, 1987). Indeed, both ideas are often presented simultaneously with no comment being offered on the contradiction (e.g. Allen et al. 1986).

In this section, attention will be restricted to the two most direct consequences of unemployment: on psychological well-being and on income. A very wide range of other consequences is documented in the literature, but space precludes their consideration (for an excellent, if now somewhat dated review, see Hakim, 1982).

Effect on Psychological Well-being

There are very many studies which document the distressed psychological condition of the unemployed – too many to cite separately; good general reviews of the literature are to be found in Warr (1987), Kelvin and Jarrett (1985) and Fryer and Payne (1986). A sufficient number of these studies are based on longitudinal evidence to make it possible to conclude that the relationship is causal and that unemployment damages mental health rather than that people with poor mental health are more likely to be unemployed.

In literature stemming back to the 1930s (e.g. Eisenberg and Lazarsfeld, 1938), unemployment is sometimes portrayed as a process with a series of fixed stages through which all pass. The evidence for such staged responses is, however, not very firm. Most of it, as Kelvin and Jarrett (1985) point out, is based on unsystematic research, colourful autobiographies, memoirs, or intensive unstructured interviews with the unemployed. Stage accounts tend to describe the experience of the long-term unemployed, thus often missing the experience of the casually employed who may have qualitatively different psychological experiences. Most of the evidence is derived from samples of the unemployed stock by cross-tabulating a psychological variable by duration of unemployment. As was argued earlier, this is an extremely risky procedure.

And there is little basic agreement on what the stages are (Fryer, 1986); even the same authors on different occasions see only two – despair to apathy (Jahoda et al., 1933) – or six – injury, numbness, adaptation, growing hopelessness, evaporation of resources and eventually acquiescence and apathy (Eisenberg and Lazarsfeld, 1938). Most such accounts follow some variant on optimism–pessimism–fatalism; depressingly, the most basic point of agreement is that the endpoint is not adaptation in terms of a creative response to unemployment (Breakwell, 1985), but resignation, apathy and despair (Miles, 1983; Kelvin and Jarrett 1985).

If the studies are not in agreement at the descriptive level, the explanation of the mechanisms of distress are even less in accord. Several different (but not necessarily mutually exclusive) theories can be identified.

Loss.   The first set of ideas is broadly Freudian in orientation. People are driven by the work principle – a basic human need to use their intellectual and manual skills. The process of coming to terms with the loss of work is considered similar to the process of grieving, and coming to terms with the loss of any other dearly valued person or symbolic object (Parkes, 1971). Archer and Rhodes (1987) point to many similarities in response to unemployment and bereavement: pre-occupation, feelings of anger and guilt, loss of self-identity, the need to work hard psychologically to bring the subjective, assumptive world into line with the new reality, and greater stress the more the job is loved. (They also note that many of the problems of bereavement research are being replicated with work on unemployment: longitudinal studies are rare, the wider family is neglected, and refuge is sought in stage models rather than the preferred 'episodic' models.)

Such Freudian ideas have influenced writers such as Fagin and Little (1984) as they grappled with explanations of the psychological distress of the families they studied. In many important respects, however, unemployment is *not* like being bereaved. It is not final in the same way, and is certainly not experienced as final; even the long-term unemployed, the old and workers in areas where the objective chances of finding jobs are the smallest, sustain hopes that they themselves will find work, even if only temporary or casual, and that there will be an economic upturn. Moreover, the actual object lost, the particular job, is not the stimulus for grief as it is in bereavement; people hope to find another job, but not the one they actually lost.

Self-concept.   Another explanation of the psychological damage wreaked by unemployment is proposed by Kelvin and Jarrett (1985), who see the mechanism as operating principally through the self-concept. In a society that uses work as the principal mechanism for awarding esteem, the unemployed suffer in two ways. First, their very identity as unemployed is negative, and draws attention to their lack of a place in society's distribution of rewards. And, secondly, by referring to someone as 'an unemployed lorry driver', one is implying that the situation is transitory and, by implication, that the explanation is frictional rather than structural. The unemployed constantly face difficulties with self-definition that causes them acute distress.

Deprivation.   A somewhat more social account of the distress experienced by the unemployed has been proposed by Marie Jahoda, whose professional and political concern with the issue of unemployment spans fifty years; she was one of the team who conducted the famous study of unemployment in Marienthal, a small Austrian village which was devastated by unemployment in the 1930s (Jahoda et al., 1933). Employment, Jahoda (1982) argues in Mertonian fashion, has both manifest functions (making a living) and latent functions which can be identified by examining the deprivations experienced by the unemployed. The unemployed lose:

1 activity;
2 a time structure for the day;

3 the social contacts which work brings;
4 social status, personal and group identity;
5 participation in collective social endeavours, and thus a sense of wider purposes and goals in life.

While many of the aspects of unemployment as economic deprivation have changed since the 1930s, she argues, it still robs people of these latent consequences of work, and is therefore still extremely painful.

The theory has been criticized (Fryer, 1986) as being hard to operationalize, hard to separate empirically from evidence of other distressing consequences of unemployment, and hard to separate from consequences of loss of latent functions of work which are not distressing. Jahoda's theory, Fryer argues, confuses symptom (felt deprivation) and cause (objective deprivation from latent functions of work). It is true that the empirical validation of the theory has been rather thin. Jahoda herself (1982) relies upon reinterpretation of evidence from other studies which did not set out directly to test the ideas. These studies, moreover, are uniquely of the unemployed; a theory about the latent functions of employment does require some comparable data on the employed.

The most direct and comprehensive validation has been conducted by Miles and his colleagues at the University of Sussex. They systematically compared the five latent functions (which they more neutrally refer to as 'categories of experience') across employed, unemployed and non-employed groups (Miles, 1983; Miles and Howard, 1984). The results seem to validate the importance of four of the five latent functions, but cast doubt on the importance of time structuring; they find, for example, that housewives' well-being is *negatively* associated with the extent to which the day is structured. These studies, however, use volunteer samples for the non-employed and some of the employed, which probably makes them above averagely well motivated and active (Rosenthal and Rosnow, 1975). Kilpatrick and Trew (1985) have provided further validation for the importance of activity *per se*; they studied the life-styles of a stock sample of claimants in Northern Ireland; cluster analysis identified four different types on the basis of their daily activities; the more active groups had much better mental health than others.

Agency. Fryer (1986) proposes an alternative 'agency theory' to explain why being unemployed is such a negative experience. Criticizing Jahoda as implicitly viewing human beings as passive, he proposes instead a model of people as rational, active, and calculating. The problem is not that work deprivation *causes* a psychological response behind the back of the economic actor; the problem experienced by the unemployed is that they have their strategies and plans rudely interrupted, and this explains their distress.

However, if Jahoda's theory is not well validated, this agency theory is hardly validated at all. The evidence of eleven people that Fryer and Payne (1984) managed to track down who unusually had no adverse reactions to unemployment hardly counts. Somewhat more persuasive is Fryer and McKenna's (1987) demonstration that a group of workers who were temporarily laid-off had fewer psychological problems than a group who had been permanently declared redundant. Since both groups were being denied the latent functions of work, one explanation might be that the laid-off were able to plan the future better, but many other alternatives for the same findings could be presented.

Freedom, as Engels would put it, is the recognition of necessity. Access to these categories of experience is probably best viewed as a causal *precondition* for agency. The best studies into the relationship between economic experience and subjective reality have moved beyond a false opposition between agency and causality; Gambetta (1987), for example, in trying to explain the educational decisions of Italian youth faced with the possibility of unemployment, undertakes a sophisticated comparison of the extent to which there are factors pushing them into further education from 'behind their backs' and the extent to which they consciously and intentionally 'jump' into further education.

The theories considered so far might be termed 'person-centred' models: the starting-point is the experience and needs of the individual, although Jahoda's theory constantly stresses the social and institutional location of the individual. More recently, two theories have been put forward which focus more on the situation in which an individual operates. These theories have been particularly useful in providing a framework whereby unemployment research can be integrated with other occupational psychology.

Stress.   Payne and Hartley (1987) have focused on the stresses in a person's environment that give rise to negative experiences. Their useful study also demonstrates the importance of basic elements of security: money and health. Stress, they argue, is generated by the balance between the problems facing the unemployed and the degree of supports, constraints and opportunities that exist in their environment. The impact of the environment can be modified by the financial situation and by personality variables such as the person's repertoire of coping tactics. Interviews with a stock sample of unemployed male claimants suggested that the primary causes of poor psychological functioning are money worries and ill-health; but even after their effect had been taken into account, the more opportunities the unemployed received in their environment and the fewer the constraints, the better off they were.

Vitamins.   Peter Warr has proposed the most comprehensive 'situation-centred' theory to account for the distressing impact of unemployment (1987). His starting-point is different aspects of the environment which people face; he has proposed a 'vitamin model' to explain how these environmental influences affect the mental health of individuals. Vitamins, he argues by analogy, influence physical health up to a certain point beyond which there is either no increased effect or the effect is positively poisonous. However, Warr also believes individuals have some scope to change this environment, and thus mitigate some of the worst effects of unemployment.

A great strength of this theory is that it has grown as much out of studies of the psychology of work as it has out of studying the psychology of non-work. He identifies nine categories of the work environment which are the foundations of mental health, some of which are like vitamins A and D (and damage beyond a certain point), and others which are like vitamins C and E (and produce diminishing returns):

1 opportunity for control (AD);
2 opportunity for skill use (AD);
3 externally generated goals (AD);
4 variety (AD);
5 environmental clarity (AD);
6 availability of money (CE);
7 physical security (CE);
8 opportunity for interpersonal contact (AD);
9 valued social position (CE).

These nine features of the environment facilitate or constrain personally important processes and activities. The unemployed usually face environments that are lacking in most of these vitamins. The model incorporates most of Jahoda's five functions, (mostly in 3,6,8 and 9), but also adds additional dimensions of importance. And Warr's masterly summary of *Work, Unemployment and Mental Health* (1987) provides better validation for this typology than has ever been provided for Jahoda's. However, the causal relationship between the different components awaits elaboration; it could well be that lack of money, for example, gives rise to all the other elements.

This discussion has concentrated on general explanations for the distress of unemployment. A striking feature about this psychological literature is that the effects do seem to have their effect across the board. However, it should be noted that there are some subgroups for whom the experience is not quite as terrible as it is for others. The interesting hallmark of all such groups is that they experience *lower* rates of unemployment than their comparators: women suffer more keenly than men, at least when they are single (Warr and Parry, 1982), white people suffer more than black people (Warr et al., 1985), the old suffer more than the young (Roberts et al., 1982; Warr, 1987: 226), the British suffer more than the Spanish.[3]

Warr himself argues that the most important explanation for this differential impact is varying work commitment (Warr, 1987: 226). However, work commitment is not very variable; the Protestant work ethic, whose demise has been regretted by politicians and pundits alike, seems alive, well and surprisingly unvarying even in conditions of mass unemployment (Furnham (1982), although Kelvin and Jarrett (1985) have some reservations). In a study of 16–19 year olds, for example, Breakwell (1985) found work commitment was already so high that it could not explain variations in distress.

---

3 Indicative evidence from secondary analysis of *Eurobarometer* surveys conducted by the European Commission in all EEC countries suggests that the employed in Spain are significantly lower in psychological well-being than their counterparts in Britain, but the unemployed in Britain have worse psychological health than the Spanish unemployed.

A further interesting possibility remains that these subgroup differences arise from relative deprivation: people make their comparisons within subgroups and therefore feel less aggrieved when they are part of a group where many are suffering the same conditions as themselves. One important area for future research must be to pin down precisely the comparative reference groups of the unemployed (Merton, 1957).

Effect on Income

In the previous section of this chapter, the views of economists who argued that the level of real incomes caused unemployment were propounded. In this section, the opposite view will be argued: that unemployment is an important cause of low income.

The incomes of the vast majority decline on unemployment, a fact whose social significance is deepened when one remembers that the unemployed are drawn from very low-earning sectors; half the unemployed studied in the 1978 DHSS longitudinal flow sample (Moylan et al., 1984), for example, had incomes in the bottom fifth of the earnings distribution immediately prior to unemployment. One reason for the low starting-point of the unemployed is that many of them have already been subject to some casualization from a previous unemployment experience; it is not just a corollary of their low skills as individuals, since so many of them have done a skilled job at some previous point in their past (White, 1983).

On average, the income of the household containing the unemployed person declines to around one-half to two-thirds of what it had been previously (Moylan et al., 1984). Only a small proportion are better off on benefit than they were previously; estimates of the exact proportion vary from around 6 per cent (Moylan et al., 1984) to around 10 per cent (Hawkins, 1984).

There are many criteria one could adopt to define poverty, and they are the subject of much dispute, especially those which relate to the state supplementary benefit levels. The definition which can be given the best theoretical defence (e.g. Sen, 1987) is being unable to afford goods and services which are consensually viewed by the general public as being basic necessities. Mack and Lansley (1985) conducted a survey in 1984 in which they established a list of twelve things that over two-thirds of the population viewed as necessities: enough money for public transport, a warm waterproof coat, three meals a day for children and so on. The poor are people who lack several of these necessities.

On such a definition, unemployment brings the majority of households it affects into the ranks of the poor. In 1984 fully 58 per cent of people living in households where the head was unemployed were poor, and nearly one-third were intensely poor – they lacked a very large number of basic necessities of life. Unemployment also accounts for an increasing proportion of those in poverty; by 1984, of the 1.7 million adults who were calculated as being intensely poor, 45 per cent lived in households with unemployed heads, and of the 0.9 million intensely poor children, fully two-thirds lived in households with an unemployed head (Mack and Lansley, 1985: 186, 303). As a result, while it is important conceptually to distinguish the consequences of unemployment from those of poverty, it is important to realize that the two are for very many people the same thing.

Nor does the black economy mitigate the worst effects. It has become the sociologist's version of the cannibalism myth and researched in much the same way – through hearsay from natives slightly more civilized than those in the deep jungle (Arens, 1979); for example, an estimate that unemployed people in Liverpool may be getting £30 more per week than official figures suggest (Matthews and Stoney, 1987) is derived by asking unemployed what they think other unemployed people get on the side, a methodology which panders to the moral panic of the welfare scrounger (Golding and Middleton, 1979). Much lower estimates have been obtained by Pahl (1984) from the Isle of Sheppey; he points out that black economy activity requires tools and resources such as transport which are much more likely to be held by the employed than the unemployed. The unemployed even have difficulty getting on their bikes to find black market work, since they are less likely than the employed to own one (Miles, 1983)! However, although the black economy may be small as a supplementary factor to an unemployed person's budget, it may have other important consequences for the relationships of power between employers and employees.

While it is clear that the unemployed are desperately poor, it is harder to assess the polarizing or permeating effect of unemployment on the total distribution of incomes. Overall inequality in British personal incomes has increased since the mid-1970s, but no one has yet apportioned the growth to different effects. It would be a hard task, as it would also involve studying changes in household structure, but Piachaud (1987) has suggested that research into the distribution of incomes and the resulting discussion of issues of equity and efficiency cannot proceed further until the interaction between the distribution of income and the distribution of work has been clarified.

One fact about the household structure of unemployment is clear: the unemployed tend to live together more than would be expected by chance. The General Household Survey repeatedly shows that employed heads of households are twice as likely as unemployed heads to have working wives; the DHSS cohort study of the unemployed flow found that 17 per cent of wives of the unemployed were themselves unemployed, compared with 4 per cent for all wives (Moylan et al., 1984); unemployed sons are more likely than others to have unemployed fathers (Nabarro, 1980); unemployed 16–19 year olds are three times as likely to live in households where someone else is unemployed than their employed counterparts (Payne, 1987); overall, 30 per cent of White's (1983) long-term unemployed sample had another family member also unemployed. This clustering will tend to increase inequality in the distribution of incomes except to the extent that the unemployed are younger than average and therefore they are more likely than average to live in multi-earner families.

The explanations for the clustering are harder to provide (for a good review see Cooke, 1987). The explanation given for husband–wife

TABLE 12.7   *Male and female earnings 1970–87*

| | Gross earnings for full-time workers whose pay was not affected by absence | | | | | | | | | | | |
| | Male earnings | | | | | | Female earnings | | | | | |
	MED £	D_L	Q_L	MED	Q_u	D_u	MED £	D_L	Q_L	MED	Q_u	D_u
1970	143	65	80	100	127	161	77	66	80	100	129	170
1971	143	66	80	100	126	161	80	67	80	100	127	166
1972	148	65	82	100	127	161	85	66	79	100	126	167
1973	156	66	82	100	126	158	86	67	81	100	129	165
1974	155	67	79	100	125	157	88	68	80	100	124	159
1975	157	67	80	100	125	158	95	67	82	100	126	164
1976	163	68	80	100	126	159	103	66	81	100	126	166
1977	151	68	82	100	125	158	99	69	83	100	123	162
1978	160	67	80	100	126	158	102	69	83	100	125	161
1979	165	66	80	100	124	157	102	69	83	100	126	159
1980	164	66	81	100	127	162	104	68	82	100	126	161
1981	165	66	80	100	130	168	107	68	80	100	130	173
1982	166	65	79	100	129	168	107	67	80	100	129	169
1983 (old)	173	64	79	100	130	170	114	66	80	100	129	168
1983 (new)	171	63	78	100	130	170	114	66	81	100	130	167
1984	177	62	77	100	130	171	117	66	79	100	130	166
1985	177	61	77	100	131	171	118	66	79	100	131	164
1986	185	60	77	100	132	173	123	65	77	100	133	170
1987	198	59	76	100	132	176	133	64	78	100	133	172

Key: MED = median; Q_L = lower quartile; D_U = upper decile, etc.
Source: New Earnings Survey, 1974, Part A: table 15; 1987, Part B: 28–29. From 1983 the new series is based on adult earnings; median incomes are expressed in 1986 pounds

clustering is usually the 'earnings disregard' of supplementary benefit (e.g. Minford, 1983). Analysis of women's work histories (Joshi, 1984) suggests that 14 per cent of wives withdraw from the labour force when their husbands lose their jobs while 3 per cent of inactives enter it, but women deny that this has anything to do with benefits; they cite instead the increased need to provide care for the family, perhaps an indicator of the poor state of health of many unemployed people. Other possible explanations are the contaminating effects of other household members' demoralization or low motivation (Payne, 1987), loss of the resources necessary for work such as a car (Pahl, 1984) and, most importantly, demand-side factors which mean that all members of the same household may be competing in a labour market which is similarly depressed.

   Classical economists also predict another income consequence of unemployment: a decline of the earnings of those in work, particularly those with whom the unemployed are competing. This has not happened. The explanations for the failure of wages to 'downward adjust' during the recession were discussed earlier. There are two significant points to note from table 12.7. First, since 1980 there has been a reversal of the longer run trend towards greater equality in the earnings distribution. Secondly, however, this has not produced a reduction in the absolute earnings of any group while in employment; even the lowest decile has managed to retain its real value. The brunt of the income problems felt during the recession has been borne by the unemployed.

Some Final Comments

In the last part of this chapter, the focus has been restricted to direct measures of satisfaction and psychological well-being, or that substitute which economists feel much happier dealing with, namely money. Unemployment seems to have polarized the distributions significantly. It has achieved this not by its effect on the employed work-force, but by the direct deleterious effect of unemployment *per se*.

Many other consequences could also have been documented. The correlations which have been evident for some time between unemployment and many different forms of individual pathology have been given a causal interpretation because of recent longitudinal research. Unemployment affects physical health (Smith, 1987) and increases risk of death (Brenner, 1979), and this is not just a selection effect of ill workers losing their jobs (Moser et al., 1986). While the evidence of the effect of unemployment on alcohol and tobacco consumption is somewhat contradictory (Brenner, 1979; Smart, 1979), a longitudinal study in Edinburgh suggests that unemployment greatly increases the use of cheaper, illicit drugs (Peck and Plant, 1986). Tarling (1982), in a review of the relationship between crime and unemployment, argued that only individual level data could clinch a causal interpretation of the well-established correlation between unemployment and crime; Farrington et al., (1986) report the results of a longitudinal survey which provides precisely the kind of evidence sought.

Its impact reaches beyond the unemployed individual. Strains are imposed on the whole family (Allatt and Yeandle, 1986; Fagin and Little, 1984) and the difficulties created for relations between husband and wife has been a subject of comment from the 1930s to the present (Jahoda et al., 1933; McKee and Bell, 1985); this is presumably the major explanation behind the robust finding in almost any study of the unemployed that many fewer unemployed have stable partners than one would expect for people of that age group (e.g. White, 1983; Moylan et al., 1984). Child abuse of all kinds is much more common among families where the head of household is out of work (Browne and Saqi, 1987).

Nor has there been time even to touch upon the effects of unemployment on the wider political culture; the growing political alienation of the unemployed; the effect on the organizations of the employed and on the morale of trade unions and the new version of the withering away of the strike; the reversion to pre-industrial forms of protest among the unemployed with the riots in the inner city; on the devastating hollowness of a social culture based on material acquisition when the bottom line

– the money – is withdrawn; and the emergent youth cultures which reflect uncertainty and permanence of job insecurity. There has only been limited research into these broader political consequences; they urgently need attention.

References

Allatt, P. and Yeandle, S. 1986. 'Its Not Fair, Is It?: Youth Unemployment, Family Relations and the Social Contract'. *The Experience of Unemployment*. Eds Allen, S. et al. London: Macmillan.

Allen, S., Waton, A., Purcell, K. and Wood, S. 1986. *The Experience of Unemployment*, London: Macmillan.

Archer, J. and Rhodes, V. 1987. 'Bereavement and Reactions to Job Loss: A Comparative Review'. *British Journal of Social Psychology*, 26; 3, 211–24.

Arens, W. 1979. *The Man-Eating Myth*. Oxford: Oxford University Press.

Ashton, D.N. 1986. *Unemployment under Capitalism: The Sociology of British and American Labour Markets*. Brighton: Wheatsheaf.

—— and Maguire, M.J. 1988. 'Re-structuring the Labour Market: The Implications for Education and Training'. International Centre for Management and Labour Market Studies, University of Leicester, mimeo.

Azariadis, C. 1975. 'Implicit Contracts and Underemployment Equilibria'. *Journal of Political Economy*, 83, 1183–202.

Banks, M.H., Ullah, P. and Warr, P. 1984. 'Unemployment and Less Qualified Urban Young People'. *Employment Gazette*, 92, 343–6.

Bell, D. 1974. *The Coming of Post-Industrial Society*, London: Heinemann.

Breakwell, G. 1985. 'Young People In and Out of Work'. *New Directions in Economic Life*. Eds Roberts, B., Finnegan, R. and Gallie, D. Manchester: Manchester University Press.

Brenner, H. 1979. 'Mortality and the National Economy'. *The Lancet*, 568 (September) 15.

Browne, K. and Saqi, S. 1987. 'Parent-Child Interaction in Abusing Families: Its Possible Causes and Consequences'. *Child Abuse: An Educational Perspective*. Ed. Maher, P. Oxford: Basil Blackwell.

Cambridge Economic Policy Group. 1971–84. *Cambridge Economic Policy Review*. Aldershot: Gower.

Cooke, K. 1987. 'The Withdrawal from Paid Work of the Wives of Unemployed Men: A Review of Research'. *Journal of Social Policy*, 16; 3, 371–82.

Coyle, A. 1984. *Redundant Women*. London: Women's Press.

Daniel, W.W. 1981a. *The Unemployed Flow: Stage 1: An Interim Report*. London: Policy Studies Institute.

—— 1981b. 'Why is High Unemployment Still Somehow Acceptable?'. *New Society*, 55, 495–7.

Deakin, B.M. and Pratten, C.F. 1987. 'Economic Effects of YTS'. *Employment Gazette* (October), 491–7.

Department of Employment. 1983. 'Unemployment Flows: New Statistics'. *Employment Gazette* (August).

—— 1985. 'Unemployment Adjusted for Discontinuities and Seasonality' *Employment Gazette* (July).

—— 1986a. 'Classification of Economic Activity'. *Employment Gazette* (January).

—— 1986b. 'Unemployment Figures: The Claimant Count and the Labour Force Survey'. *Employment Gazette* (October).

—— 1987. '1986 Labour Force Survey and Revised Employment Estimates'. *Employment Gazette* (April), 201–10.

Devereux, J. 1987. 'Calculating Sample Size from Response Rates and Unemployment Outflow Estimates'. Working paper 1. Cambridge: Social and Political Sciences Committee.

Eatwell, J. 1982. *Whatever Happened to Britain?* London: BBC and Duckworth.

Eisenberg, P. and Lazarsfeld, P. 1938. 'The Psychological Effects of Unemployment'. *Psychological Bulletin*, 35, 358–90.

Fagin, L. and Little, M. 1984. *The Forsaken Families: The Effects of Unemployment on Family Life*. Harmondsworth: Penguin.

Farrington, D.P. et al. 1986. 'Unemployment, School Leaving and Crime'. *British Journal of Criminology* (October), 26: 4, 335–56.

Feinstein, C.H. 1972. *Statistical Tables of National Income, Expenditure and Output of the UK, 1855–1965*. Cambridge: Cambridge University Press.

Friedman, M. 1976. *Price Theory*. Chicago: Aldine.

Fryer, D.M. 1986. 'Employment Deprivation and Personal Agency during Unemployment: A Critical Discussion of Jahoda's Explanation of the Psychological Effects of Unemployment'. *Social Behaviour*, 1: 1, 3–24.

—— and McKenna, S. 1987. 'The Laying Off of Hands'. *Unemployment: Personal and Social Consequences*. Ed. Fineman, S. London: Tavistock.

—— and Payne, R.L. 1984. 'Proactivity in Unemployment: Findings and Implications'. *Leisure Studies*, 3, 273–95.

—— and —— 1986. 'Being Unemployed: A Review of the Literature on the Psychological Experience of Unemployment'. *Review of Industrial and Organizational Psychology*. Eds Cooper, C.L. and Robertson, I. Chichester: Wiley.

Furnham, A. 1982. 'The Protestant Work Ethic and Attitudes towards Unemployment'. *Journal of Occupational Psychology*, 55, 277–85.

Gambetta, D. 1987. *Were They Pushed or Did They Jump?* Cambridge: Cambridge University Press.

Garnsey, E., Rubery, J. and Wilkinson, F. 1985. 'Labour Market Structure and Workforce Divisions'. *Work, Culture and Society*. Eds Salaman, G. and Deem, R. Milton Keynes: Open University Press.

Gershuny, J.I. and Miles, I.D. 1983. *The New Service Economy*. London: Frances Pinter.

Glyn, A., Hughes, A., Lipietz, A. and Singh, A. 1987. 'The Rise and Fall of the Golden Age'. Paper produced as part of the research programme on Global Macroeconomic Policies of the World Institute of Development Economic Research, Helsinki.

Golding, P. and Middleton, S. 1979. *Images of Welfare*. London: Macmillan.

Gregory, P.R. and Collier, I.L. Jr. 1987. 'Unemployment in the Soviet Union: Evidence from the Soviet Interview Project'. Working Paper No. 35. Urbana-Champaign, IL.: Soviet Interview Project.

Grunberg, L. 1986. 'Workplace Relations in the Economic Crisis: A Comparison of a British and a French Automobile Plant'. *Sociology*, 20: 4, 503–29.

Hakim, C. 1982. 'The Social Consequences of High Unemployment'. *Journal of Social Policy*, 11: 4, 433–67.

Harris, C. 1987. *Redundancy and Recession in South Wales*. Oxford: Basil Blackwell.

Hawkins, K. 1984. *Unemployment*. Harmondsworth: Penguin.

Hutchings, R. 1967. 'The Ending of Unemployment in the USSR'. *Soviet Studies*, 19, 29–52.

Jahoda, M. 1982. *Employment and Unemployment: A Social-Psychological Analysis*. Cambridge: Cambridge University Press.

—— Lazarsfeld, P.F. and Zeisel, H. 1933. *Marienthal: The Sociography of an Unemployed Community*. English translation, 1972. London: Tavistock.

Jordan, B. 1982. *Mass Unemployment and the Future of Britain*. Oxford: Basil Blackwell.

Joshi, H. 1984. 'Women's Part in Paid Work. Further Analysis of the Women in Employment Survey'. Research Paper No. 45. London: Department of Employment.

Kaldor, N. 1978. *Further Essays on Economic Theory*. London: Duckworth.

—— 1982. Speech to the House of Lords. 3 February, Reprinted as Chapter 16 of *The Economic Consequences of Mrs Thatcher*, Ed. Butler, N. London: Duckworth.

Kasl, S.V., Gore, S. and Cobb, S. 1975. 'The Experience of Losing a Job: Reported Changes in Health, Symptoms and Illness Behaviour'. *Psychosomatic Medicine*, 37: 2, 106–22.

Kelvin, P. and Jarrett, J.E. 1985. *Unemployment: Its Social Psychological Effects*. Cambridge: Cambridge University Press.

Keynes, J.M. 1936. *The General Theory of Employment, Interest and Money*. London: Macmillan.

Kilpatrick, R. and Trew, K. 1985. 'Lifestyles and Psychological Well-being Among Unemployed Men in Northern Ireland'. *Journal of Occupational Psychology*, 58, 207–16.

Layard, R. and Nickell, S. 1985. 'The Causes of British Unemployment'. Discussion Paper No. 209. London: Centre for Labour Economics.

Leadbeater, C. and Lloyd, J. 1987. *In Search of Work*. Harmondsworth: Penguin.

Lindbeck, A. and Snower, D.J. 1985. 'Explanations of Unemployment'. *Oxford Review of Economic Policy*, 1: 2, 34–59.

Mack, J. and Lansley, S. 1985. *Poor Britain*. London: George Allen & Unwin.

McKee, L. and Bell, C. 1985. 'Marital and Family Relations in Times of Male Unemployment'. *New Approaches to Economic Life*. Eds Roberts, B., Finnegan, R. and Gallie, D. Manchester: Manchester University Press.

Marx, K. 1970. *Capital: A Critique of Political Economy*. Volume I. London: Lawrence and Wishart.

Matthews, K.G.P. and Stoney, P. 1987. 'The Black Economy: The Evidence from Merseyside'. *Quarterly Economic Bulletin*, 8: 2, 26–36.

Merton, R.K. 1957. *Social Theory and Social Structure*. New York: The Free Press.

Miles, I. 1983. 'Adaptation to Unemployment?'. Occasional Paper No. 20. Brighton: University of Sussex, Science Policy Research Unit.

—— and Howard, J. 1984. 'Categories of Experience in Different Social Groups'. Brighton: University of Sussex, Science Policy Research Unit, mimeo.

Minford, P. 1983. *Unemployment: Cause and Cure*. Oxford: Martin Robertson.

Moser, K.A., Goldblatt, P.O., Fox, A.J. and Jones, D.R. 1986. 'Unemployment and Mortality 1981–83: Follow up of the 1981 LS Census Sample'. Working paper No. 43. London: Social Statistics Research Unit.

Moylan, S., Miller, J. and Davies, R. 1984. 'For Richer, for Poorer? DHSS Cohort Study of Unemployed Men'. DHSS Social Research Branch research report No. 11. London: HMSO.

Muellbauer, J. and Portes, R. 1978. 'Macroeconomic Models with Quantity Rationing'. *Economic Journal*, 88, 788–821.

Muth, J.F. 1961. 'Rational Expectations and the Theory of Price Movement'. *Econometrica*, 29, 315–350.

Nabarro, R. 1980. 'The Impact of Workers from the Inner City of Liverpool's Economic Decline'. *The Inner City*. Eds Evans, A. and Evans, D. London: Heinemann.

Norris, P. 1978. 'Unemployment, Subemployment and Personal Characteristics'. *Sociological Review*, 26, 89–108, 327–47.

Pahl, R. 1984. *Divisions of Labour*. Oxford: Basil Blackwell.

Parkes, C.M. 1971. 'Psycho-social Transitions: A Field for Study'. *Social Science and Medicine*, 5, 101–15.

Payne, J. 1987. 'Does Unemployment Run in Families? Some Findings from the General Household Survey'. *Sociology*, 21 (May), 199–214.

—— and Hartley, J. 1987. 'A Test of a Model for Explaining the Affective Experience of Unemployed Men'. *Journal of Occupational Psychology*, 60, 31–47.

Peck, D.F. and Plant, M.A. 1986. 'Unemployment and Illegal Drug Abuse: Concordant Evidence from a Prospective Study and National Trends'. *British Medical Journal*, 293 (October), 929–32.

Phelps, E. 1967. 'Phillips Curves, Expectations of Inflation and Optimal Unemployment over Time'. *Economica*, 34, 254–81.

Piachaud, D. 1987. 'The Distribution of Income and Work'. *Oxford Review of Economic Policy*, 3: 3.

Raffe, D. 1985. 'Youth Unemployment in the UK 1979–1984'. Paper commissioned by International Labour Office, Centre for Educational Sociology, University of Edinburgh.

—— 1986. 'Change and Continuity in the Youth Labour Market. A Critical Review of Structural Explanations of Youth Unemployment'. *The Experience of Unemployment*. Eds. Allen, S., Waton, A., Purcell, K. and Wood, S. London: Macmillan.

—— 1988. 'The Status of Vocational Education and Training 2: The Case of YTS'. Paper presented to the ESRC/DE workshop on Research on Employment and Unemployment (29 January). London.

Roberts, K., Duggan, J. and Noble, M. 1982. 'Out-of-school Youth in High Unemployment Areas: An Empirical Investigation'. *British Journal of Guidance and Counselling*, 10, 1–11.

—— Brodie, D. and Dench, S. 1987 'Youth Unemployment and Out-of-home Recreation'. University of Liverpool, mimeo.

Rosenthal, R. and Rosnow, R. 1975. *The Volunteer Subject*. New York: Wiley.

Rowthorn, B. and Glyn, A. 1987. 'The Diversity of Unemployment Experience since 1973'. Paper prepared for the research programme on Global Macro Economic Policies of the World Institute of Development Economic Research, Helsinki. University of Cambridge, mimeo.

Sen, A. 1987. *The Standard of Living*. Ed. Hawthorn, G.P. Cambridge: Cambridge University Press.

Smart, R.G. 1979. 'Drinking Problems among Employed, Unemployed and Shift Workers'. *Journal of Occupational Medicine*, 11, 731–6.

Smith, R. 1987. *Unemployment and Health*. Oxford: Oxford University Press.

Standing, G. 1983. 'The Notion of Structural Unemployment'. *International Labour Review*, 122 (March–April).

—— 1984. 'The Notion of Technical Unemployment'. *International Labour Review*, 123 (March–April).

Stewart, A., Prandy, K. and Blackburn, R.M. 1980. *Social Stratification and Occupations*. London: Macmillan.

Tarling, R. 1982. 'Unemployment and Crime'. Research Bulletin No. 14. London: Home Office Research and Planning Unit.

Taylor, D. 1988. 'Employment Changes since 1979'. *Unemployment Bulletin*, 26 (February).

Therborn, G. 1986. *Why Some Peoples are More Unemployed than Others*. London: Verso.

—— Visser, W. and Wijnhoven, R. 1986. 'Unemployment: Its Political Determination, Definition, Structuring and Ambiguous Importance'. Paper presented to the ECPR workshop on the Politics of Unemployment, Goteborg. Nijmegen: Catholic University, mimeo.

Townsend, P. 1979. *Poverty in the United Kingdom*. Harmondsworth: Penguin.

Unemployment Unit. 1984. *Unemployment Bulletin*, 11, (January). London: Unemployment Unit.

—— 1986a. *Unemployment Bulletin*, 22, (Winter). London: Unemployment Unit.

—— 1986b. *Unemployment Bulletin*, 20 (Summer). London: Unemployment Unit.

Wallace, C. 1987. 'Between the Family and the State: Young People in Transition'. *The Social World of the Young Unemployed*. Ed. White, M. London: Policy Studies Institute.

Warr, P.B. 1987. *Work, Unemployment and Mental Health*. Oxford: Clarendon Press.

—— and Parry, G. 1982. 'Paid Employment and Women's Psychological Well-being'. *Psychological Bulletin*, 91, 498–516.

—— Banks, M. and Ullah, P. 1985. 'The Experience of Unemployment among Black and White Urban Teenagers'. *British Journal of Psychology*, 76, 75–87.

White, M. 1983. *Long-term Unemployment and Labour Markets*. London: Policy Studies Institute.

13 Employment, the Household and Social Networks

Lydia Morris

Introduction

Throughout the 1980s we have seen a growing interest in the household as a focus for research, an approach exemplified by Ray Pahl's *Divisions of Labour* (1984), and featuring prominently in the work of Harris et al. (1987). The household perspective also figures in large-scale research projects currently being funded under two ESRC initiatives,[1] and has clearly influenced work on a smaller-scale being carried out by postgraduates and individual research workers throughout the country. What are the reasons behind the fashion for the 'household strategy' study, and what promise does it hold that proves so strong in its appeal to social scientists?

One overriding concern of sociologists in recent years has been the challenge of documenting and interpreting the effects of far-reaching change in some of the most basic foundations of social life. Over the last twenty years this country has experienced dramatic economic decline and major restructuring of industry and employment. Although the consequent shrinkage of jobs in heavy industry throughout the 1960s and 1970s was to some extent balanced by an expansion of service-sector employment, the result was nevertheless a rise in male unemployment to a peak of 13.3 per cent in March 1987, while in specific areas the rate was as high as 30 per cent. The unemployed have also been subject to increases in the duration of periods without work, and among the young there are sections of the population that have never been employed.

The loss of employment for large numbers of people has raised doubts about the utility of models of social structure based on employment relations, and has led some writers, notably Pahl and Gershuny (1979, 1980), to try to think in new ways about work. This endeavour, in turn, prompted inquiry into self-provisioning, communal exchange, and the organization of social and domestic life, and thus began to establish connections between areas of study previously treated separately. Attempts to forge these connections made it increasingly apparent that a number of the central questions to be posed as a result of changes in the economy could best be addressed at the level of the household.

1 The Social Change and Economic Life Initiative, and the Changing Urban and Regional System Initiative.

Economic change over the last two decades has meant not only rising numbers of workers experiencing unemployment, but has also produced critical changes in the composition of the work-force. Employment for women, largely concentrated in the growing service sector, was increasing just as male employment was in decline. Although this service-sector growth has by now abated, and women have increasingly come to be represented (and in fact underrepresented) in unemployment statistics, the effects of the shift in employment patterns or 'restructuring' have persisted.

The number of women employees in Britain has grown from 6.7 millions in 1948 to 9.2 millions in 1980. By 1984 they made up 43 per cent of the total labour force. Much of this increase in women's employment has been in part-time work, however, and there has been a further associated change. In 1951 30 per cent of the women's work-force were married; by 1971 the figure has risen to 63 per cent and by 1984 had reached 69 per cent.[2] To many these employment changes, especially when set against rising male unemployment, suggested the inevitability of a significant challenge to the basis of established gender relations within the household.

In the light of the changes documented above it is possible to begin to identify those research questions which make the household an important locus of investigation. High levels of unemployment made paid work an unsatisfactory basis for conceptualizing social structure, and research into unpaid work assumed correspondingly greater significance. Attention has accordingly been turned towards the household; the site of much of the work – domestic labour, self-provisioning, childcare – carried out beyond the confines of the workplace.

In addition to these specifically work-related interests are topics more directly concerned with the nature of life and relationships within the household, that is, with domestic organization, which is, however, inextricably linked to gender relations and the sexual division of labour. The household, seen as the theatre of many aspects of the relationship between men and women, is the obvious place in which to investigate the effects of male unemployment, and the impact of changing labour force patterns, especially the increased employment of married women.

A concern with the household has also emerged in a rather different context: from the province of 'family sociology'. Anthropological work has for some time been at pains to emphasize the conceptual difference between the family and the household,[3] while in our own society the residential arrangements commonly associated with the nuclear family have often blinded us to this distinction. Nevertheless, it is both possible and advisable to differentiate between, on the one hand, types of household composition or patterns of residence, and, on the other, nuclear and extended family relations, from which no residential pattern *necessarily* follows.

2 Figures from Dex (1985) and from the General Household Survey (1984: table 6.12 for increases in part-time working, table 6.24 for composition of the female labour force).
3 An example of an anthropological discussion of their distinction in a research context is to be found in Solien (1960). For a discussion of the domestic group see Goody (1972), and for a conceptual discussion of family and household see Harris (1983: 41).-

This move becomes particularly significant in the light of recent enthusiasm for 'household' research since it means, at least potentially, that household composition and formation will not be taken as given and can themselves become topics of investigation. As a result, the residential unit will the more easily be placed in its social, economic and kinship setting, and, as shall be seen, this development is of crucial importance in attempts to research into 'household responses' to economic change.

There are, of course, a number of difficulties which arise when researchers attempt to realize the promise of the household approach, not least of which is that of identifying a relevant literature. The potential field is so broad that it is rare to find all possible aspects of the perspective combined in one study. Rather there exists a collection of non-comparable studies which tend to focus on specific areas of interest within the household – domestic labour, household finance, power and decision-making, self-provisioning and labour market position – but are in no way cumulative, or even mutually informing. The result is not 'a literature' on the relationship between the household, employment and social networks, but rather distinctive pockets of material. The work required to bind them together has only relatively recently begun.

Changing Patterns of Work

Reconceptualizing Work

One source of the current wave of household studies seems to have been an attempt to rethink 'work', and a critical move here was made by Gershuny (1977, 1979). His early writing made a connection between jobs lost in 'formal' employment as a result of world recession, improved manufacturing productivity and high-cost services; and a reclamation of areas of work by the household in the form of 'self-provisioning'.

However, while Gershuny was attempting to understand aggregate data by speculating on related patterns of household production and consumption, Pahl was embarking upon a study which approached the same questions from the opposite end. He started out by asking what was happening *inside* different households, and how one might begin to understand the domestic organization of time and labour in terms similar to those proposed by Gershuny, that is, by an examination of changing work patterns.

Gershuny and Pahl together (1979, 1980) began to speculate about the way in which changes in employment patterns and in the organization of labour within the household could best be conceptualized. They developed a perspective which emphasized that work was not confined to employment in the formal economy and, borrowing from a feminist literature which stresses the role of domestic labour in production (see Molyneux, 1979), argued that it was necessary to enlarge our notion of what constituted work.

The *informal* economy, or, more correctly, the informal sector, was to be central to this endeavour and was broken down by Gershuny and Pahl (1980) into the following spheres:

1 the household – where goods or services are produced by members of the household for their own consumption;
2 the underground (or hidden) – where production is wholly or partly for sale or barter which is concealed from the relevant authority;
3 the communal – where goods and services are produced *not* for sale or barter, but neither for consumption by the producer.

The 'household' and 'communal' spheres were later considered together as one corner of the triangular relationship depicted below:

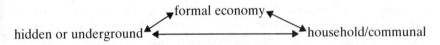

It was then proposed that changes in the nature of work could be analysed in terms of shifts between three 'economies': the formal, the communal and the underground (Gershuny and Pahl, 1980). This development, intended to facilitate a conceptual linkage between macro and micro analysis, also encouraged speculation about the future. Pahl and Gershuny seemed convinced (Gershuny and Pahl, 1980; Pahl, 1980) that as opportunities for 'formal' employment dwindled, people would be freed from the 'realm of necessity' (Pahl, 1980: 17) to realize their individual, social and financial potential in an 'autonomous mix' which would lead to higher levels of personal satisfaction. Thus, argued Pahl, work identity could be maintained in the face of formal unemployment in a way which might well prove to be more rewarding: 'When the conditions of work are bad in the formal economy and the opportunities for informal work are good, unemployment could, under certain specified conditions, be a positive benefit' (1980: 5). And so the scene was set for speculation and research about precisely how the organization of life at household level was changing, or, to use Pahl's terminology, how households were developing 'new ways of getting work done': new work strategies. The relationship between different categories of work was felt to be shifting, to the advantage of the informal sector of the economy; households, it was argued, were increasingly performing their own services and engaging in reciprocal exchange with other households. In other words, people were reclaiming the right to define and organize their work.

A number of loosely formulated ideas and assumptions sprang forth. It was suggested, for example, that in the workings of the informal economy the poor may be advantaged because of previously constructed support systems and experience of hardship, and the possibility was floated that those least incorporated into the formal sector might be best placed in the informal (Pahl, 1980), provided they had available the appropriate skills and a network of contacts through which to exploit them.

These early ideas were soon to be questioned by Pahl himself, and by work being carried out in a number of related areas. In his final account of his research findings in Sheppey (1984) Pahl in fact laid to rest the suggestion that informal activities of self-provisioning, communal labour exchange, or even illicit earnings were the answer to decline in 'formal' economic activity, and instead furnished evidence of an increasing polarization between working and workless households. Opportunities for work, both formal and informal, were concentrated in some homes and absent from others and the good side of unemployment was not so easy to find.

Household Strategies

Despite this substantial revision of his earlier more speculative work, Pahl's book *Divisions of Labour* established a pioneering approach to the study of the household from which much subsequent research has benefited. His central concern was to investigate the nature and sources of labour harnessed by different households in their efforts to maintain a given standard of living. It is in this context that he introduced the notion of a household work strategy: 'the best use of resources for getting by under given social and economic conditions' (1984: 20), to be defined later in the book as 'how households allocate their collective effort to getting all the work that they define has, or they feel needs, to be done' (1984: 113). The emergent 'strategy' was then to be understood against the background of a local market for labour, in Pahl's study of the Isle of Sheppey. His early attempts to formulate the way in which a strategy was constituted posed the questions: 'which work in which (sector of the) economy, for which member of the household, for how long?' (1984:119), and the strategy was therefore to be understood as 'involving different household members in different spheres of work using different sources of labour in a particular milieu as they move through the domestic cycle' (1984: 139). Pahl's research objective was to document the varied outcomes of these factors, that is, the strategies arrived at by different households on Sheppey, and perhaps his most surprising finding was that the range of diversity was rather narrow – role reversal, for example, is relatively uncommon and instead of diversity we find polarization. This result invites some examination of the processes by which strategies are arrived at and the constraints under which they are constructed, and here the voluntarism implied by the term, as well as the implicit assumption of consensual decision-making, is somewhat misleading.

Pahl was not himself blind to such flaws in his perspective (Pahl and Wallace 1984: 329) but the closest he comes to isolating the means by which a strategy emerges is in his observation that type of work done is to be understood 'by exposing the pattern of relations in which it is embedded' (1984:126). Such an analysis is not entirely achieved in the book, however, and indeed would have required the consideration of a number of topics not actually addressed in the research design.

Components in the Work 'Strategy'

Thus, pioneering though Pahl's work was, his research was essentially concerned to document types of strategy, and hence neglected their emergence or construction, and the identification of constraining factors. Any further progress in this direction would depend upon research into the internal dynamic of the household and its relation to the employment position or work prospects of various household members, as well as a close examination of the links which connect these individuals to different kinds of work opportunities.

Inside the household the critical areas of concern are the organization of domestic labour, where Ray Pahl (1984) did make considerable advances, and the management and control of household finance, an area of research developed by Jan Pahl (e.g. 1980, 1983). Both of these aspects of domestic life may be related to the labour market activities and prospects of different household members, as will be shown, but in focusing attention on the *internal* characteristics of the household it is important not to neglect to take account of *external* influences (cf. Harris et al., 1987: 140). The nature of opportunities available to household members, for example, will vary by virtue of the characteristics of the local market for labour, and the individuals' strengths and weaknesses within that market.

It is essential therefore, to examine the position of the household and its members in the local labour market, and to uncover the way in which that position is influenced by relationships within the home, and access to opportunities through networks of contact which may extend beyond household boundaries. In addition, the constraints imposed by the nature of the social, economic and statutory environment in which the household is located must be identified. Nowhere are these constraints more apparent than in the case of married women. An examination of their distinctive labour market position, especially when considered alongside the effect of benefit regulations, provides the key to why role reversal is not more common, and why in only a minority of cases does it constitute a viable 'strategy'.

Changing Household Employment Structure

In the early stages of industrialization paid employment became available to men on increasingly preferential terms,[4] and men's superior position in the labour market both fostered, and was in turn reinforced by, the notion of a male breadwinner. It was in this context that the concept of the family wage evolved, and the TUC came to struggle, on behalf of its members, 'to bring about a condition where their wives would be in their proper sphere – at home – instead of being dragged into competition for livelihood against the great and strong men of the world'.[5]

The basis of this position was a claim for payment which would enable a man to maintain a wife and children. Its economic logic is that the wage should provide sufficient income to sustain a wife whose domestic services

---

4 See Brenner and Ramas (1984), and Walby (1987) for a discussion of the process by which men consolidated their position as employees, in some cases at the cost of women. Siltanen and Stanworth (1984) include discussion of women's workers and trade-union organizations.
5 Quoted in Land (1976).

transform the wage into the means of subsistence, whilst also guaranteeing the social and biological reproduction of the labour force. The demand for a family wage thus carried with it the assumption that married women would not need (or wish) to seek employment. It was backed both by male trade-union pressure and an associated ideology concerning gender roles.

The restructuring of employment, which has been slowly underway since the 1960s and has accelerated noticeably through the 1980s, seemed, at first, set to overthrow traditional patterns. The reorganization of work, both paid and unpaid, was assumed to be occurring not simply between sectors and between households but *within* the home. Household members were, according to early speculation, assessing their situation, their prospects and their needs, and working out an appropriate strategy: 'no longer do we have . . . a universal, sex-linked division between the male "chief earner" in the formal economy and his unpaid and dependent wife engaged in unremunerated housework. Nor is there such a rigidly sex-linked division of labour between men and women in the practice of domestic work' (Gershuny and Pahl, 1981: 86). Among early popular reaction to changes in the composition of the labour force was the assumption that women were taking over from men as principal earners. The notion of a family wage implying a *sole* earner for the whole domestic unit held so firm that aggregate figures of employment were taken to correspond to household arrangements, and the increasing participation of married women in the labour force prompted popular speculation about role reversal.

Households experiencing male unemployment provide an interesting test case of how far a change in household gender roles has really gone. Data are available at national level which give cause to doubt the assumption that the rise in married women's employment has meant that wives are ousting husband's as breadwinners. The General Household Survey (1984: table 6.18) shows that in 61 per cent of married couples where the man was employed the wife was also in paid work, whilst in homes experiencing male unemployment only 27 per cent had wives who were earning. This pattern reflects one aspect of what Pahl (1984) has termed a process of social polarization, which produces a concentration of work in some homes and unemployment in others. The distinction seems to be on the increase nationally for between 1973 and 1984 the number of two earner couples rose by 6 per cent while non-earners also rose by 7 per cent (GHS, 1984: table 6.18).

Various studies, often qualitative and small in scale, have documented this trend. Bell and McKee (1985), for example, in a study of male unemployment in Kidderminster, interviewed forty-five couples and noted:

> Only two wives could be said to have entered permanent (but part-time) employment as a consequence of their husband's job loss. Three other wives maintained their jobs despite their husband's unemployment and were characterised by either having well-paid or longer established jobs. The remaining wives either engaged in temporary casual or informal work, withdrew from work, postponed or rejected totally the return to work. (1985: 393)

A similar study of forty redundant steelworkers in South Wales (Morris, 1985a: 404) found that cases of women taking on employment in response to their husband's job loss were rare, and indeed many women themselves experienced redundancy shortly after their husbands. The study states that any likelihood of a woman taking on the role of main wage-earner has been reduced by the impact of the recession on the availability of employment for women.

The value of such small-scale research is that it can provide some insight into the financial calculations made by women in examining the incentive to take on employment. Thus, a number of wives commented that it would not financially be worth their while to work, since their earnings would be deducted from their husband's claim for supplementary benefit. This number is likely to increase as more households move from dependence on unemployment benefit with its more generous disregards of earnings, to sole reliance on supplementary benefit.

The Disincentive Effect

Large-scale studies have provided statistical data concerning the influence of the disincentive effect on the emergence of the by now familiar 'polarization' of households, highlighting the significance of the move from unemployment benefit (contributory) to supplementary benefit (means tested).

Daniel and Stilgoe (1977), in a longitudinal analysis of a DHSS cohort study, found that where married men in the 24–44 age group had full-time working wives they had themselves been employed for a majority of the three year period covered (1976–9), while in cases where the wife had no paid job the men had been out of work most of the time. Over the period of the study 10 per cent of employed wives left employment and 5 per cent took up jobs, in contrast to 20 per cent and 6 per cent respectively for a later study (1978–9) reported by Moylan et al. (1984).

Although Daniel (1981) found only 2 per cent of wives moved from being economically active to being inactive within a *month* of their husband's registering as unemployed, a shift might be expected to occur when eligibility for unemployment benefit runs out, or when the man's unemployment starts to look long-term. Moylan et al., for example, report that the wives of men receiving unemployment benefit with its more generous disregards, were less likely to give up paid work than the wives of men receiving supplementary benefit. Although they note a number of other factors which operate independently of this effect, including a weaker tendency to be employed *before* the husband's job loss, they nevertheless conclude that 'Some of the changes in the wives' employment status seem to be systematically related to the type of benefit the family was receiving in respect of the man's unemployment. The main result is the high proportion of wives in the families receiving Supplementary Allowance who left employment' (1984: 131–2). Joshi (1984: 25) helpfully runs through a number of reasons for an association of unemployment between husband and wife, which for women may include an increased domestic load as a result of the husband's presence at home, a wish to share time together, or a reluctance to usurp the breadwinner role. Like other writers, she also notes the disincentive created by benefit rules, and particularly supplementary benefit.

Morris (1987b: 10) has speculated on the potential for change, since from April 1988, for couples who have been unemployed for two years or more there is a flat-rate disregard of part-time earnings at a higher level of £15 per week, as opposed to the previous £4 disregard. This may of course result in competition between spouses over who has the right to earn (and hence dispose of) such additional income.

The Labour Market Position of Married Women

A full understanding of the disincentive effect requires an examination not just of benefit rulings but of their interaction with married women's position in the labour market. Unless a woman can earn substantially more than the household can claim in benefit, she will be deterred from earning at all. It is therefore the disadvantaged position and poor prospects of the majority of married women, as much as the disincentive effect, which will mean that a wife is unlikely to become a sole earner. The growing concentration of part-time employment among married women makes such an outcome even less probable, though it remains to identify the reasons for this concentration.

In considering the question of role reversal and the significance of increased labour market participation for married women, it is important to note recent developments in a literature concerned with the relationship between domestic responsibilities and the structuring of employment. This approach has been criticized for taking the woman's domestic role as given and failing to examine the processes by which traditional sexual divisions emerged (see Beechey and Perkins, 1987), and important criticisms have also been levelled against the assumption of homogeneity within gender categories (Redclift, 1985).

Nevertheless, it remains possible to identify particular *categories* of a population, notably married women with children, and seek to explore the relationship between their domestic circumstances and their experience in employment. Thus the DE/OPCS Women and Employment Survey (Martin and Roberts, 1984: 13) finds age of the youngest child to be a key factor in whether or not women are employed, and in the kind of employment they hold. Employed women with dependent children are overwhelmingly concentrated in part-time work. The same survey, however, reports high levels of satisfaction among part-timers with their hours of work, a result explained by the importance for many married women of finding employment which accommodates domestic and childcare obligations. Harris and Morris (1986) report women actively seeking out such employment, and in this context it is also interesting to note

Hakim's (1987: 240) findings on homeworkers, who are disproportionately married women with dependent children. Such data certainly discourage speculation about significant change in gender roles within the home.

This should not, however, distract our attention from the fact that employment opportunities are structured by employers. It is the availability of particular kinds of jobs which will make it possible for those with pressing domestic and childcare responsibilities to slot into positions which accommodate these needs; and it may be to the employer's advantage to construct jobs of a particular kind – for example, workers earning less than £35 a week, who will usually be employed part-time, require no national insurance contribution (Townsend, 1986), and offer flexibility and disposability (Beechey and Perkins, 1987).

Research in this area all points to the conclusion that some attention must be paid to the relationship between the supply of, and demand for, particular kinds of labour (cf. Dex, 1985). A number of studies have attempted to show that women's search for employment will be based not simply on their *own* availability or commitments, but will also take account of the kinds of *jobs* they know to be available. Conversely, employers will have notions about what is appropriate work for women, and research-ers have accordingly begun to investigate the creation of 'gendered' employment opportunities (e.g. Curran, 1984; Beechey and Perkins, 1987).

Research in Hartlepool (Morris, 1987b: 95–6) has taken up this point in connection with the 'disincentive effect' of benefit rulings. With recession it has been increasingly important for employers to keep costs low, and the creation of part-time work is one way of doing so. This will mean that women have a decreased chance of finding full-time employment just at a time when their husbands are most likely to be unemployed. Employers are in a position to create and recruit to gendered part-time employment because there are women whose domestic circumstances, together with established ideas about gender roles, will mean that part-time work is their preferred option. The result is a level of earnings which cannot equal, much less better, the income provided by benefit; hence the two earner/no earner household pattern, created by an interaction between the effects of supplementary benefit rulings, women's domestic and childcare obligations and the nature of the market for married women's labour.

Inside the Household

The Division of Domestic Labour

While there is still considerable debate and speculation about the his-torical developments which led to the consignment of women to the domestic sphere (e.g. Brenner and Ramas, 1984), sociologists have seen in current circumstances of falling male employment and expanded female employment a new opportunity to study the mechanisms of interaction between the public and private sphere, domestic labour and wage labour, and sexual divisions within marriage. As a result, responsibilities for, and participation in, domestic labour have begun to receive serious attention.

By 1969 the accepted wisdom among family sociologists was that a 'great transformation' had occurred (Young and Willmott, 1957); the lives of husband and wife were becoming increasingly shared in terms of both companionship and involvement in domestic labour. A review of developments in the literature at this time can be found in Harris (1983) and will be mentioned only briefly here. Harris identifies the work of Elizabeth Bott (1957) as the point of departure for debate about changing marital relations in contemporary Britain. She attempted to investigate variations in degrees of 'jointness' and 'segregation' between husband and wife's domestic and leisure activities, whilst accepting as given the traditional division of labour between the sexes.

Wilmott and Young (1957) gave the *differences* identified by Bott a *temporal* dimension by arguing that there was emerging 'a new kind of companionship among men and women'. They developed their position more fully in *The Symmetrical Family* (1973), suggesting that the middle classes were at the forefront of a move towards symmetricality in marriage, by which they meant that husband and wife were increasingly sharing in the complementary and hitherto largely segregated tasks of wage-earning and domestic labour.

Doubt is cast on this 'optimistic' interpretation of their data by a number of other studies. The Pahls (1971) discuss the stress involved for middle-class wives when the *ideal* of sharing in marriage is contradicted by the primacy attached to the husband's paid work, which encourages a marked sexual division of labour, while the Rapoports (1971, 1976) highlight the difficulties experiences by dual career couples, and the resultant role conflict for the women. Other evidence, at around the same time, seemed to point to the continuing primacy of the woman's domestic role. Ann Oakley (1974), in her pioneering study of housework in a small sample of middle- and working-class homes, produced considerable detail on domestic responsibilities summed up in her statement that 'In only a small number of marriages is the husband notably domesticated . . . home and children are the woman's primary responsibility'. Her findings are confirmed in a subsequent work by Stephen Edgell (1980) who does note, however, that there is some indication of a change in the way men and women *think* about their respective roles. He reports evidence of a growing flexibility in attitudes and behaviour, which has nevertheless left the established sexual division so far free from serious challenge. More recent data seem to confirm this conclusion. Reporting on findings from an inner-city survey, and from BBC time budget data Gershuny (1982) identifies a gender specialization in domestic tasks which is also reported in analyses of the ESRC time budget data (Gershuny et al., 1986). This research identifies a core of routine domestic tasks which are principally the responsibility of women, with men more likely to perform non-routine tasks. In the mid-1970s husbands performed less than one-quarter of all domestic work and less than 10 per cent of routine domestic work (Gershuny 1982).

Gershuny and Jones (1987), using data from a total of seven surveys,[6] do, however, note a doubling of male routine domestic work between 1974–5 and 1983–4, albeit from a low base, during which period female involvement in non-routine tasks also increased. This is not to say that gender specialization does not persist, but rather that there has been a blurring of boundaries in the sexual division of domestic labour.

In his analysis of this division Harris (1983) focuses on the relationship between the two spheres of public and private life around which traditional gender roles have crystallized. He interprets these roles as 'an adaptation to the demands made upon the domestic group by the occupational system' (1983: 230), although, like many other writers, he also notes that the historical conditions which produced a primarily domestic role for women require further investigation. This point aside, the recent growth in married women's employment, and the release of many men from the rigours of the occupational system by unemployment, raise the question whether a gendered distribution of responsibility for domestic labour will endure.

Domestic Labour and Married Women's Employment

We have already noted that married women in employment tend to have husbands who also have a job, and the concentration of part-time employment among women suggests they they may be accommodating a 'traditional' division of domestic labour – though of course full-time jobs may simply be unavailable. Martin and Roberts (1984: 64) report some findings on the competing demands of home and jobs for women. Of full-time workers, 34 per cent scored high on difficulty in coping with these demands, and only 22 per cent scored low, whereas for part-time workers the figures were 21 per cent and 39 per cent respectively. Among both full- and part-time workers the childless women generally found it easier to cope, and among full-time workers those with dependent children had greater difficulties than those with grown-up children, especially the non-married.

These findings do suggest that employed women continue to carry their traditional responsibilities in the home, although the problem with the research is that it gives no direct data on men. The use of both male and female respondents is, however, a considerable strength of Pahl's work in Sheppey (1984). Pahl presents a complex account of the organization of domestic work, and finds the key explanatory variables to be stage in the domestic cycle and employment status.

The main argument is straightforward enough, and supports Edgell's notion of growing flexibility within the context of established gender roles. Although Pahl finds no evidence to suggest the complete overthrow of 'traditional' divisions, he does report (1984: 275–6) that the more hours the female partner is in employment then the *less* conventional is the organization of domestic labour. The same effect is found the fewer hours

6 The 7 surveys referred to are the 1983 Mass Observation collection, the 1961 BBC survey, the 1971 Symmetrical Family Survey, the 1974/5 BBC survey, the 1981 Scottish Sample and the 1983/4 ESRC and BBC surveys.

the male partner is employed, except in cases of male *un*employment, where the association is reversed. This is an issue to which we will return.

Pahl also makes the point that the woman's domestic burden is particularly high when she is not in gainful employment and there are young children in the home. This is interpreted as a life-cycle effect. When women in such circumstances take on employment it will usually be part-time and though their domestic duties remain high Pahl argues that the *generally* high level of domestic work to be done will necessitate male participation.

It may be in these terms that findings by Laite and Halfpenny (1987: 220) are to be understood. They note, in a study of households in Macclesfield and Blackburn that women in part-time employment perform more of the core 'female' tasks than either full-time or non-employed women (though it is not clear whether they are referring to proportion or amount). Their findings appear to be consistent with the conclusion of Gershuny et al. (1986: 33) that a disproportionate domestic burden on women employed part-time is likely to stem from childcare and child-related domestic work, since women with young children usually opt for part-time work.

Gershuny's earlier research (1982) which also addressed the question of household divisions of labour, reports that in general the unpaid work of employed wives does not decline in proportion to their increase in paid work, and that 'even in the most liberated, young, two-job household' the husband averages only 15 per cent of routine domestic work.

The ESRC time budget data is helpful here. For couples with children and two full-time jobs, mens' routine domestic work was found to be higher than in other couples (Gershuny et al., 1986: 33) but this was only true for homes with very small children. In other two earner homes women were found to bear a heavier 'dual burden' of paid and unpaid work. This result corresponds to Pahl's argument that the more adults there are in the home the more likely it is that the woman will perform a traditional female (i.e. domestic) role; the converse of the effect of the presence of young children on male involvement. The total amount of domestic work to be done is reduced and hence male participation is reckoned to be less necessary.

Gershuny (1982) interprets a tendency for work to cumulate on employed wives not as a complete absence of adaptation to their employment but as a result of insufficient compensation. This view is consistent with Laite and Halfpenny's finding (1987: 229) that where men and women share the same employment status men do more of the domestic tasks than in other households. Indeed over the period 1961–84 Gershuny and Jones (1987: 48) report that a 10 per cent reduction in men's paid work has been largely offset by an increase in unpaid domestic work, while both full-time and part-time employed women have experienced a 10 per cent decrease in domestic work.

It is interesting to counter this statistical data with a more qualitative piece of research on sixty-two married women in employment (Yeandle, 1984). One-third of the women acknowledged an important contribution by husbands to domestic work, but male readiness to co-operate was seen to depend on how significant the woman's earnings were judged to be for the household's standard of living.[7] Such findings inevitably encourage speculation about the man's domestic role when he is no longer an earner himself.

Male Unemployment and Domestic Labour

As noted earlier, Pahl found that in cases of male unemployment the correlation between increased domestic work with reduced hours of paid work was broken. Where the man was unemployed the woman was more likely to perform a traditional female (domestic) role than when he was not. Of unemployed men whose wives were not working, 89 per cent fell into the most conventional category of low participation in domestic work.

This topic has been the subject of considerable investigation and a number of small-scale studies have given detailed attention to the effect of male unemployment on participation in domestic labour. Marsden (1982: 119) reports findings from research into unemployment among the skilled and unskilled working class noting resistance from men to assuming domestic tasks, as well as defensiveness from women reluctant to relinquish their role. Marsden also notes the effect of male presence in generating tension and creating more work, a point confirmed by Bell and McKee (1985: 397) and by Morris (1985a).

Research in South Wales (Morris, 1985a) revealed that while some men began their period out of work by assuming more domestic tasks, enthusiasm soon waned. Others confined their work in the home to areas which have traditionally fallen to men – such as decorating, maintenance and gardening. The general impression was that within working-class culture there are strong feelings against male involvement in tasks commonly regarded to be essentially female.

This should not obsure the presence of some faint indications of change, and the research reports variations on a 'traditional' model of domestic labour in terms of rigidity and flexibility (Morris, 1985a: 414). Thus, although there is some evidence of a blurring of the boundaries which segregate male and female labour, there is no evidence of a fundamental shift away from the traditional pattern. Whether such slight indications of flexibility represent the first step in some more far-reaching reorganization of domestic labour is not yet clear.

Further progress has been made, however, with data from the 1983/84 ESRC time budget (Gershuny et al., 1986). Unemployed men were found to carry out three times as much routine domestic work as men in employment, but *less* than the non-employed women they were living with. Reporting on the same data Thomas et al. (1985) note that the contribution of unemployed men to domestic work fell below that of non-employed and part-time employed women, but above that of full-time women.

The findings seem at variance with Pahl's data, which suggest that the division of domestic labour is more marked with male unemployment. Definitive conclusions would, however, require longitudinal data

---

7 The notion of a uniform *household* standard of living is itself problematic, as a subsequent section of the present work makes clear.

on *change* in individual households, not just a static measurement. Certainly Morris's work suggests that there can be slight shifts which are perceived by the man as highly significant but which still leave fairly rigid gender divisions of labour. We should also bear in mind the possibility of regional cultural variations according to the class composition, work-force characteristics and gender-related traditions in particular areas. Massey (1984) has argued that the contrasts are considerable.

Other recent research has focused on the very specific case of role reversal households, and Laite and Halfpenny (1987: 229) report 'a substantial redistribution of all household tasks from wives to husbands in reverse role households, but . . . even here, women still do more than men'. An important contribution to research in this area has been completed by Wheelock (1986). Her analysis uses a typology similar to that proposed by Morris, but applies it to a very particular sample: forty working-class couples in which the woman is employed – though with hours varying from five to thirty per week – and in which the man is unemployed. She summarizes her findings as follows: 'It is . . . very striking that half the couples have distinctly non-traditional forms of organisation for family work, while only a quarter of the sample fall into the traditional – rigid category'. What is also striking is that the degree of change seems to be closely related to the number of hours worked by the woman (cf. Pahl, 1984; Morris, 1985a) which suggests that *male* (un)employment status is not the only significant factor in changed behaviour. Indeed, what may also be said of Wheelock's evidence is that *despite* the traditional reversal of roles in paid employment, only *half* the sample showed a change in domestic arrangements. This brings us back to Morris's conclusion (1985a: 414) that there are powerful social forces at work which will tend to preserve the status quo.

There is clearly some relationship between the availability for paid employment and domestic and childcare obligations, as illustrated by married women's concentration in part-time work but this relationship is not a straightforward one, for, as we have seen, male *availability* for domestic work by virtue of job loss will not necessarily transform into full male *responsibility*. Even when considerable shifts have occurred, the traditional divisions are still detectable. To understand the source and nature of constraining influences, however, it is essential to look beyond the confines of the home and place the household in its social context.

Household Finance

A second important aspect of relationships inside the household is the control and management of household finance. Our understanding of the implications of different systems of management hinges on the distinction between household income and domestic income (Morris, 1984: 494): Household income refers to the total income of all household members from whatever source. Domestic income refers to the total income available for spending on the collective needs of the household (i.e. food, fuel and accommodation). Domestic income may thus be significantly lower than household income.

The distinction is illuminated by Gray's discussion (1979) of 'collective expenditure', that is, that made on behalf of the household, and 'personal expenditure', made on behalf of individuals. The designation of money from household income to serve as domestic income or for personal spending would be a function of *control* of that income.

There is some evidence to suggest that systems of organizing household finances will be influenced by, and act upon, behaviour and experience in the labour market. Morris with Ruane (1988) has reviewed the evidence of such a relationship in a Department of Employment research project. The earners of income are likely to exert most influence over its spending and this may translate into power within the household (cf. Pahl, 1983). But, it is also the case that attitudes towards work, and behaviour in the labour market can be better understood with reference to access to, uses of, and benefit from earned income.

These issues raise obvious questions about the motivation for earning, the balance between concern for self, as against the household as a collectivity, the ways in which an individual's concerns are reflected in, or shaped by, spending obligations within the home, and the influence of social conventions such as those embodied in gender roles and kinship obligations.

There are four basic models for the organization of household finances (cf. Pahl, 1983) which may be briefly characterized as follows:

1 The whole wage system. In this system one partner is responsible for managing all household finances, and responsible for all expenditure.
2 The allowance system. Here the main earner hands over a set amount for housekeeping and uses the remainder for his or her own designated areas of expenditure.
3 Shared management system. Both partners have access to all household income, and are jointly responsible for management of, and expenditure from a common pool.
4 Independent management. This system is characterized by the absence of access to all household income by either partner. Each has a separate income and specifically designated areas of responsibility for expenditure.

It is not possible to reach any conclusive estimate of the incidence of these different types,[8] partly because researchers have used slightly different ways of classifying their material, and also because studies have often been of particular types of locality, or of populations which are particular in some other sense. In addition, shared management tends to be over-reported because of a common agreement *in principle* to the ideas of sharing and equality. The only reliable finding is the very low incidence of independent management, though the allowance system seems to be most common and the whole wage system fairly extensively used.

8 For a table giving the incidence of different types reported by different studies see Morris with Ruane (1988).

The Labour Market Connection

We may investigate the connection between the labour market and household finance along two different dimensions, first, how does labour market status affect the organization of finances, and secondly, how does finance management influence behaviour in the labour market?

The effect of labour market status. Jan Pahl's work in the area of household finance has distinguished between control, management and budgeting. Logically the control over income will lie with its direct recipient, for he or she will have power of disposal from the point at which money enters the household economy. It is still the case that this person is more likely to be a man than a woman, and the traditional association of women with activity in the domestic sphere seems likely to lead to female involvement in management and budgeting rather than control. Jan Pahl (1983: 244–5) offers the following definitions:

> 'Control' is primarily concerned with the way in which money is allocated within the household, and involves decisions about the distribution of income and responsibilities for different areas of expenditure.

> 'Management' refers to the process whereby control decisions are actually put into operation, primarily in the management of designated areas of expenditure.

> 'Budgeting' is the process of spending *within* particular expenditure categories, and the use of the resources available to achieve minimal consumption requirements.

The organization of these three functions will vary between the four basic household finance types listed above. The occurrence of the different types can be accounted for in a number of ways, often connected with labour market status.

The whole wage system in its commonest form, that is, the man handing over the full wage to the woman, seems to be associated both with low income (and therefore also a weak labour market position) and with traditional working-class culture. Examples are found in Dennis et al. (1956), Kerr (1958), Land (1969). Source of income also seems to have a bearing, with unemployment, or more precisely benefit dependence, consistently reported as leading to a 'whole wage' system. This association has been noted by Jan Pahl (1984), Land (1969) and Morris (1958b).

Land (1969) in her study of large families in London notes 'The primary responsibility for managing the household finances shifted from the father in the higher income families, to the mother in the low income families'. She explains this by the general pattern of responsibility by women for day-to-day expenditure, and the concentration of this category of spending in poorer homes. Morris (1984) has further argued the need for closer surveillance of spending where income is low and the consequent probability of unitary control. The woman's traditional association with the domestic sphere, and the priority commonly attached to food, fuel and accommodation, make her the most likely candidate.

Where income is higher, and labour market position stronger, retentions from the wage by the man are more likely, if only for his personal spending, an arrangement illustrated by Gray (1979), and Morris (1984). When this occurs the whole wage system shades over into the allowance system, a predominantly working-class arrangement. There is some evidence of a relationship between the allowance system and a variable wage, whether to secure the housekeeping allowance from fluctuations in the wage, as reported by Dennis et al. (1956) and Kerr (1958), or to secure for the main earner (usually the husband) any additional earnings by bonus or overtime. If the housekeeping allowance remains stable, additional earnings accrue to the employed worker. Examples of this pattern are found in Gray (1979) and Dennis et al. (1956).

There are several indications that *level* of income is also a factor in the adoption of the joint management system, though this system is often associated with two incomes, and with middle-class occupations, Just as Land (1969) has noted a shift from male to female control as income falls, management seems to become increasingly 'joint' as income rises, a point also made by Jan Pahl (1983) and Morris (1984). One explanation may be the converse of the whole wage system, that is, the higher the disposable income, the less need there is for tight control of spending and the more viable a joint system. Level of income can also be associated with sources of income, and Jan Pahl (1983), Edwards (1981) and Gray (1979) have all noted that joint management occurs most commonly with employment for the wife, though Morris (1984) stresses that in South Wales this occurred only where the woman's job was full-time. Jan Pahl (1980) makes the additional point that a tradition of secure employment for women has the opposite effect of the rigid sexual division of labour associated with the whole wage, and is more likely to produce a pooling of income.

While the joint arrangement described above is associated with relatively high income, and possibly as a result of this with female employment, the independent management system requires as a basic condition the existence of separate incomes for the couple involved. Though two earner couples will not necessarily adopt this system, independent management will depend on two incomes, a point noted by Jan Pahl (1983).

The influence of household finance systems. The suggestion that there may be some relationship between household finance management and labour market *behaviour*, however, raises the question of motivation to work, and requires some consideration of personal spending requirements, individual commitment to 'collective' expenditure, and individual access to 'household' income.

Assumptions about these issues have crept into an employment-related literature, often without being fully investigated. Shimmin (1962), for example, notes three different studies, all of which purport to show that hours of work increase with family responsibility (i.e. size of family), citing Walker (1961), Buck and Shimmin (1959) and Robertson (1960). But can it be assumed that the additional earnings of men with large families are spent on those families, and that this is necessarily their main motivation for additional earning?

One of the most detailed and readable accounts of the relationship between workplace, domestic life and community is still Dennis et al. (1956). This study of a traditional coal mining community reveals, among other things, a tension between the acknowledged male responsibility to cater for household needs, and the man's wish, supported by strong peer group norms, to have a good fund for personal spending. This personal fund is, in a sense, protected by the 'allowance' system of household finance. The man pays a set amount to his wife, and any additional earnings, for example, through overtime, will be disposed of at his discretion.

A clear illustration of the household influence on behaviour in the workplace is furnished by the case of male overtime working. Gray (1979) has usefully reported two contrasting patterns. Within a group of skilled workers she found long hours to be associated with high responsibility for 'collective' (home-based) expenditures. Among unskilled workers the pattern was the opposite, long hours being associated with minimal collective responsibility. The distinction suggests contrasting motivation to earn, and possibly even the influence of occupational status on financial arrangements.

Implicit in both Gray's and Dennis et al.'s account is the possibility that in some cases a whole wage system, in which the man hands over all his income, could deter him from overtime working, since he forgoes control of additional earnings. Parallel issues arise when we examine young people's contribution to household income. In a well-known study, Millward (1968) has shown a 'tipping-up' system, equivalent to the whole wage, reduced the effectiveness of an incentive bonus scheme but that once the girls were paying a set amount to their parents their efforts to earn increased.

Women's employment and finance management. If male breadwinners and young adults are struggling to resolve the tension between personal and collective calls on income, what is the position of married women, who have traditionally been identified with, and often responsible for, 'collective' expenditures?

It is important in this context to note the variations both in women's employment status and the function of the wife's income in the household's financial organization. Morris (1984) distinguishes between full-time and part-time employment for women, associating the former with joint financial management, but the latter with the whole wage or allowance systems. In these households, the use of the woman's wage was unfailingly to augment domestic income. Such an arrangement does not necessarily imply a substantial shift in the wife's influence over the operation of the financial system as a whole, and in the case of the allowance system can have the effect of reducing calls on the husband's wage, a phenomenon also noted by Jephcott et al. (1962), without challenging his 'breadwinner' role (cf. Morris, 1987b).

Jan Pahl (1983) and Land (1969) have raised the question of the woman's independent income in a similar context. Both report that mothers typically used their money for spending on children's needs and housekeeping expenses, although Land argues that the man's breadwinner role and degree of control was necessarily decreased.

Morris (1987b) has considered the role of women's earnings in the context of two earner households and the demise of the sole male breadwinner earning a 'family wage' in Hartlepool. She reports on wives reluctance to 'depend' on their husbands and a wish for their own income, but finds that the use of such income is commonly to contribute to housekeeping money, sometimes because of low male wages and sometimes because of male intransigence over the allowance. She goes on to argue that the importance of such contributions is rarely perceived by the husband, because of a rigid demarcation of financial and domestic responsibilities common to the region. The man's self-image thus remains unchallenged.

An interesting piece of research in the North West of England by Stamp (1985) sets out to test the 'resource theory of power' outlined by Pahl (1983), which suggests that the more income an individual brings into the home the greater his or her decision-making power. Examining financial arrangements in homes with a female main earner, she reports on the predominance of a whole wage arrangement, and the complete absence of an allowance system – generally speaking the *commonest* arrangement. This is explained by a distaste for the idea of a man receiving an 'allowance' from an woman, dealt with by joint or independent management (44 per cent) or male control of the whole wage. She notes throughout attempts by women to soften the impact of their role as main earner on the man's self-respect and stresses the importance of incidental earnings for men in these circumstances. In contrast to women's earnings such income is used entirely for personal spending. The general indications are that an income for women is not sufficient to overcome issues of gender role and identity in the management of household finance, but that inadequate housekeeping together with the woman's traditional responsibility for the domestic sphere may ironically drive her to seek paid employment.

The Specific Case of Male Unemployment

Unemployment tends to be accompanied by a whole wage system managed by the wife, with female employment discouraged by benefit regulations. This does not exclude the possibility of illicit earnings on the part of husband or wife. In so far as we can rely upon formal survey techniques to uncover data on this matter, then Ray Pahl's work indicates that the incidence of such income is low. Only 4 per cent of respondents admitted to receiving money for work 'on their own account', and a further 1 per cent received unrecorded payments from an employer (Pahl, 1984: 247). When translated into actual cases this means ten men in full-time employment and one unemployed man were in receipt of 'unofficial' income, and sixteen women, eight of whom were not otherwise gainfully employed earned such income. Ten of the women were in low-income households, which raises interesting questions about the other six (who were not in low-income households) in terms of resource allocation within the home.

Pahl's interpretation of the data suggests that involvement in informal work is easier for those already in employment, and also with the time and opportunity to take on extra tasks. In contrast, those without tools, transport or money (i.e. the unemployed) are severely handicapped in seeking or in carrying out informal work. It may of course be that those in receipt of benefit are not prepared to admit to involvement in such activity. However, Pahl's explanation seems to rest on the assumption that there are no social or economic resources which carry over from the employed to the unemployed state; that is, that tools, transport and customer networks disappear abruptly with the termination of formal employment. *Logically* this cannot be the case, although the extent to which such resources are in fact mobilized in informal work or atrophy with time is an open question.

Nevertheless, Pahl does convincingly argue that there is a limit to the potential for expansion of informal work, especially in times of general economic decline, although there may well be variation in type and level of demand between localities. Morris (1984), for example, has argued that the steel redundancies in Port Talbot created a particular combination of circumstances favouring opportunities for informal earning, with benefit claims in effect subsidizing the very low wages offered by some local contracting firms to temporary workers, though in such cases the work was often available only for a matter of a few days, or possibly weeks.

Whilst the question of the degree of involvement in informal earning remains unsolved, small-scale studies, such as that by Morris in South Wales, can examine the household implications of such income sources in cases of male unemployment (1984: 507). The research found that there are men for whom informal economic activity provides a source of income which is at their disposal in a way that benefit, at least normatively, is not. Money earned in the informal sector may be used to finance some kind of male social activity; may be earned with a view to meeting some particular domestic cost; may be handed over entirely to the wife, who would almost invariably hand some back; or may simply be divided in half.

More recent work in the North East of England (Morris 1987: 99) indicates that informal earning for men performs two functions which have the effect of supporting established gender roles. First, it provides some kind of activity outside the home, a dissociation from the wife and domestic activities during the day, and a substitution for employment. Secondly, it involves a fairly meagre amount of additional earnings which finance some degree of social activity without taking from the family purse. Given that male spending is usually accommodated by the woman from benefits received, if only to a minimal extent, then for a man to cater for his own spending represents a saving for her.

While 'informal' employment provides a means of bypassing the disincentive to work embodied in the low-earnings disregard for supplementary benefit claimants, women's earnings from this source are more likely than men's to be channelled into 'collective' spending. Thus, argues Morris (1987b: 101), female spending patterns are bound up with their association with the domestic sphere, and should be contrasted with men's perceived need for a 'public' identity achieved through social spending.

The Household in its Social Setting

The foregoing discussion has touched upon various factors which will mediate the translation of social and economic change into experience at the level of the household. Examples are the nature and structure of the local market for labour, both formal and informal; the mechanisms of access to work; and the nature of local beliefs about gender roles. What are the means by which these influences exert a differential impact on domestic life?

The notion of a 'survival strategy' was first introduced by a literature concerned with third world or ghetto poverty (e.g. Lomnitz, 1977; Peattie, 1968; Stack, 1974) which documents the routinized flow of information and aid across household boundaries. Such extra-household linkages have not been so central to current 'strategy' research in Britain. There is, however, wide popular acceptance of the importance of mutual aid, support networks and cross-generational assistance in working-class districts, and the transfer of resources across household boundaries within middle-class (extended) families has also been documented (Litwake, 1970; Bell, 1968). Grieco (1982: 702) brings an extra dimension to this data by emphasizing links between family structure and employment prospects. She cites evidence to support the transmission of 'occupational property', but observes that in contrast to the working-class emphasis in studies of informal aid, the literature concerned with employment opportunities was 'restricted almost exclusively to middle and upper-class families' (1982: 704). Her claim is that the transmission of occupational advantage also occurs within the working-class family.

If this insight is extended, of particular interest are the means by which different individuals are channelled into different sorts of jobs, or indeed into unemployment. Here information will play a critical role. Jobs which are formally advertised are, at least notionally, equally accessible to all potential applicants, although informal channels of influence can be brought to bear even in formal recruitment. Where jobs are not advertised then the dissemination of information and exertion of personal influence becomes crucial – even more so where illicit earnings are involved, that is, in the 'informal sector' of the economy. The realm of information and influence constitutes one area in which the 'social network' of a household or individual is an important factor in connecting the household and the labour market. An example is to be found in Harris et al. (1987).

The role of networks can be important in a number of other ways which will affect this relationship. Networks not only carry information and influence in connection with employment but also provide a source of support, both moral and material, in unemployment. Support networks can provide the childcare or domestic services which free many married women to take up employment, although they may act as a means of sanctioning and policing gender roles, thus constraining the sexual division of labour for many households. Whichever of these processes is uppermost, it is principally the social network that provides the mechanism by which the household is articulated with its social and economic environment.

It is in this area that Pahl and Gershuny are weakest, although they did move away from early speculation about freedom and innovatory work patterns (see Gershuny and Pahl, 1981) to make the point that unemployment is unequally distributed both geographically and socially, and that the decline in work opportunities is born disproportionately by low-skill and low-status groups. This is simply to recognize that household strategies cannot be understood in isolation from the labour market, but are closely tied to factors *external* to the home which structure the nature and distribution of 'work' opportunities. Arguably, to move beyond simply documenting variety in household employment structure, it is necessary to address the question of precisely how individual members of different households find themselves in different types of employment.

Access to Employment

The outcome of any given individual's efforts to find employment will be partly a product of history, for time of entry onto the labour market can have a strong influence on future prospects by virtue of the prevailing employment structure (e.g. Morris, 1987c). Granted this, it is also the case that informal influences via social networks can play an important role through what Grieco (1987: 33) describes as the interactions between job vacancy chains and social networks: 'grapevine recruitment'. Grieco argues that: 'Networks play an important role in the filling of vacancies, both over distance and in the local labour market . . . The existing workforce pass employment information on to other members of their network, and use influence to put network candidates at an advantage over other candidates for the vacancy' (1987: 36). She cites a number of studies which provide evidence of the 'capture' of opportunity through 'the annexing of an entire chain of employment', and also suggests its importance is greatest in blue-collar occupations. A detailed example of this process of 'annexation' can be found in Dick and Morgan's (1987) study of a Yorkshire textile mill, and Whipp (1985) reports more generally on the connection between labour markets and the communities in which they operate. He emphasizes the family's role in work orientation, socialization, skill inheritance, training and in the 'capture closure and control of job niches and pathways' (1985: 779).

The idea of preferential recruitment through informal channels has been taken up by Harris et al. (1987), and by Morris (1984) in a study of the South Wales steel redundancies. This work examines the means by which redundant workers gained access to new employment. The argument of the study is to suggest that methods of recruitment dictated not only which workers were successful in the search for employment, but also what kinds of work they eventually acquired.

Thus, to understand the 'strategies' of any given household it is insufficient to deploy a rational decision-making model which examines the labour power available and weighs the relative advantages of household members in domestic and paid work, an approach perhaps most clearly exemplified by Becker (1981). It remains to consider the way in which different individuals gain access to employment opportunities, and how that access relates to their location in a world of social contacts which, at least potentially, link the household with the labour market. Such an exercise requires a consideration of the nature of local employment opportunities, the varying types of social contact of prospective employees, and the differing recruitment strategies of employers.

Findings from the study of the Port Talbot steel redundancies indicate that a (relative) increase in short-term employment, largely as a result of reorganizing the production process around the increased use of contractors, created a concentration of jobs in which it suited employers to recruit through informal channels. Thus small-scale enterprise working to a contract and offering short-term employment, often for low pay and under poor conditions can adopt informal methods to minimize recruitment costs, avoid trouble makers and identify workers with an appropriate skill, while also fostering loyalty and co-operation by involving the existing work-force in selection.

The study argues that as a result the labour market prospects of individual workers will be strongly influenced by their location in a local social network of contact, information and influence. Those with a highly developed network will have most chance of finding employment, but because of an association between insecure jobs and informal recruitment methods, the work is unlikely to be long term. Those with less developed social networks are less likely to have informal access to employment, will be more reliant on formal means, and more likely to suffer long periods without work. Conversely, employment once acquired is more likely to be long term.

Gender Roles and Support Mechanisms

The South Wales study goes on to make other connections between the household division of labour and its location in a web of social influences, notably with reference to women's employment and gender roles. The suggestion here, closely related to Elizabeth Bott's (1957) early work on social networks and marital relations is that the influence of the social network is brought to bear both on beliefs about appropriate gender behaviour, and also on access to opportunities for employment.

Where there is a well-established pattern of female responsibility for domestic and childcare tasks, a women's paid work must either take account of her domestic obligations or those obligations must accommodate her paid employment. Broadly speaking, there are three possibilities:

1 Hours in paid employment must leave the woman free at the appropriate times for the fulfilment of domestic and childcare obligations.
2 An arrangement may be made with female friends or relatives whereby they assume some of the domestic labour, either for financial reward or on a reciprocal basis.
3 A husband may assume a share of the activities previously defined as the responsibility of his wife.

It is in deciding which of these possibilities is viable, and which easiest to realize, that the social network comes into play. This is not to suggest that there is no room for the notion of choice in our understanding of entry into paid employment by women; rather, decisions about work can only be fully understood in terms of constraints and possibilities which derive from the woman's location in a web of social contacts.

Entering paid work was found to be largely the result of exploiting informally acquired knowledge of suitable work opportunities; 'suitable' usually being defined as opportunities which did not interfere too severely with traditional patterns of domestic organization. Wives' participation was structured by their position in the traditional nuclear family household, and the ability of their social contacts to provide, minimally, information about the availability of suitable employment. Just as informal access to employment allows women with heavy domestic obligations who are seeking paid work to identify jobs which accommodate those obligations, so informal recruitment operates to the advantage of employers by encouraging the creation of low-cost, low-security, part-time work for women.

The nature of the social network, however, can act upon the content of gender roles in areas other than access to employment. Building on the original insights of Bott (1957), and following Fallding (1961) and Harris (1969), Morris (1985b) has argued that what is of particular importance is the potential for a social network of developing common norms and exercising some control over members' behaviour. Where a network is comprised by a predominantly single-sex peer group then rules and sanctions concerning gender roles are likely to develop.

The network may thus come to act not simply as a vehicle for information and influence on employment opportunities, but also on perceptions of an appropriate sexual division of labour. Data from South Wales are used to demonstrate that a rigid division of domestic labour is most likely to occur where there is a highly developed and interconnected social network, and that flexibility will be greatest where social contact is individualistic rather than collective, hence exerting minimal consensual influence.

Mutual Aid and Social Support

The household's location in a social milieu and the character of individual members' social networks can, then, affect both labour market prospects and attitudes towards gender roles. The network can also become a drain on household resources or provide much needed support, again depending upon the general character of social contact. Morris (1984), for example, has illustrated that a highly developed network may require financial expenditure by the man which places a strain on the domestic purse, and necessitates strict control of all household income by the woman, with predictable conflicts of interest.

It is also the cause, however, that the network can supply the resources which help to maintain a segregated male social life dependent on spending – either through access to opportunities for paid employment in either the formal or informal sector of the economy, or through supplying resources more directly. This pattern of aid is particularly important in cases of male unemployment, and has been noted both in Port Talbot and in Hartlepool (Morris, 1985b; 1987b). More generally this research has found that the source of aid and the use to which it is put tend to acknowledge the nature of the different constraints on men and women imposed by a low household or domestic income. A highly developed network may thus both prescribe and facilitate particular kinds of gender behaviour.

The nature or form of support from kin and friends in cases of poverty and unemployment has now begun to be documented. McKee (1987) notes variations in pattens of aid and in responses by the recipient. Binns and Mars (1984) note the importance of an extensive social network in fostering alternative values among the young (cf. Morris, 1987c): 'such networks help to sustain shared definitions of priorities which give primacy or at least legitimacy to non-work-oriented relationships and activities' (Binns and Mars, 1984: 686).

Morris has argued (1987c), using data from a small-scale study in Hartlepool, that high levels of long-term unemployment which show spatial concentrations *within* local labour markets, and which may also be concentrated within extended families will have a number of far-reaching implications. Access to informal channels of recruitment will become increasingly privileged, and potential sources of informal support limited to those in like circumstances, as a result of a growing segregation of the long-term unemployed from the rest of society.

The study concludes that the disadvantageous position of some households in declining local labour markets will have implications for access to work, socialization into different attitudes towards work, and the development of supportive networks. It seems likely that at the extreme positions we will find not just households in contrasting employment situations, but families of extended kin, and spatially grouped homes, increasingly interdependent and lacking any contact with those whose circumstances differ from their own (cf. Payne, 1987). The implications for future access to employment and sources of informal support are self-evident, and will serve to reinforce an already detectable trend towards the social segregation of the long-term unemployed.

Conclusion

This chapter has traced the current interest in 'household' studies to a number of sources: concern about the changing nature of work, the effects of increasing male unemployment, married women's rising labour market participation, and more broadly based concern about 'the family' and 'gender relations' in economic change.

The argument here has been that there are specific areas of enquiry directed to the dynamic of relationships within the household which have yielded important research findings, notably on the sexual division of labour and the management of household finance. These topics of enquiry, however, also served to demonstrate the limitations of too narrow a household focus. This approach can de-emphasize the fact that the household does not function as a 'collectivity' unproblematically. Divisions of labour, and the control of, and access to resources, are potential (and likely) sources of conflict where individual and collective interests will not necessarily coincide.

Nor do they represent actions based entirely on rational decision-making free of constraint. While none would argue explicitly that they do, the task of specifying constraints – their source and their effects – has only just begun. Areas of interest identified in this chapter have been the structuring of and access to employment opportunities; the operation of benefit rulings; the significance of local gender ideologies; the role of social networks in sanctioning gender roles; and their importance in providing support. Once such a framework for analysis has been established, we are then in a stronger position to fulfill the enormous promise of the 'household' perspective, which will only be made possible by the placing of household relations in their social context.

References

Bell, C. 1968. *Middle-class Families*. London: Routledge and Kegan Paul.
—— and McKee, L. 1985. 'Marital and Family relations in times of Male Unemployment'. *New Approaches to Economic Life*. Eds Roberts, B., Finnegan, R. and Gallie, D. Manchester: Manchester University Press.
Becker, G. 1981. *A Treatise on the Family*. Cambridge, Mass.: Harvard University Press.
Beechey, V. and Perkins, T. 1987. *A Matter of Hours*. Cambridge: Polity.
Binns, D. and Mars, G. 1984. 'Family, Community and Unemployment'. *Sociological Review*, 32, 662–95.
Bott, E. 1957. *Family and Social Network*. London: Tavistock.
Brenner, T. and Ramas, M. 1984, 'Rethinking Women's Oppression'. *New Left Review*, 144, 33–71.
Buck, L. and Shimmin, S. 1959. 'Overtime and Financial Responsibility'. *Occupational Psychology*, 3, 137–48.
Cooke, K. 1987. 'The Withdrawal from Paid Work of the Wives of Unemployed Men'. *Journal of Social Policy*. 16, 371–82.
Curran, M. 1984. *Recruiting Gender Stereotypes for the Office*. Manchester: EOC Research Bulletin.

Daniel, W. 1981. 'The Unemployed Flow Interim Report'. London: Policy Studies Institute.

—— and Stilgoe, S. 1977. *Where Are They Now?* London: PEP.

Dennis, M., Henriques, L. and Slaughter, C. 1956. *Coal is our Life*. London: Eyre and Spottiswoode.

Department of Health and Social Security. 1985. *Reform of Social Security*. Cmnd 9691. London: HMSO.

Dex, S. 1985. *The Sexual Division of Work*. London: Wheatsheaf Books.

Dick, B. and Morgan, G. 1987, 'Family Networks and Employment in Textiles'. *Work Employment and Society*, 1, 225–46.

Edgell, S.R. 1980. *Middle Class Couples*. London: Allen & Unwin.

Edwards, M. 1981. 'Financial Arrangements within Families'. *Social Security Journal* (December), 1–16.

Fallding, H. 1961. 'The Family and the Ideas of a Cardinal Role'. *Human Relations* 14, 329–50.

General Household Survey. 1984. London: HMSO.

Gershuny J.I. 1977. 'Post-industrial Society: The Myth of the Service Economy'. *Futures*, 10, 103–14.

—— 1979. 'The Informal Economy: Its Role in Post-Industrial Society'. *Futures*, 12.

—— and Jones, S. 1987. 'The Changing Work/Leisure Balance in Britain 1961–84'. *Sociological Review Monograph*, 33 (January), 9–50.

—— Miles, I., Jones, S., Mullins, C., Thomas, G. and Wyatt, S.M.E., 1986. 'Preliminary Analyses of the 1983/4 ESRC Time Budget Data. *Quarterly Journal of Social Affairs*, 2, 13–39.

—— and Pahl, R.E. 1979. 'Work Outside Employment: Some Preliminary Speculations'. *New University Quarterly*, 34, 120–35.

—— and Pahl, R.E. 1980. 'Britain in the Decade of the 3 Economies'. *New Society* (3 January), 7–9.

—— 1981. 'Work Outside Employment'. *Can I have it in Cash?* Ed. Henry, S. London: Astragal Books.

Goody, J. 1972. 'The Evolution of the Family'. *Household and Family in Past Time*. Ed. Laslett, P. Cambridge: Cambridge University Press.

Gray, A. 1979. 'The Working Class Family as an Economic Unit'. *The Sociology of the Family*. Ed. Harris, C.C. Social Review Monograph. Keele.

Grieco, M. 1981. 'The Shaping of a Workforce'. *International Journal of Sociology and Social Policy*, 62–88.

—— 1982. 'Family Structure and Industrial Employment: The Role of Information and Migration'. *Journal of Marriage and the Family*, 701–7.

—— 1987. 'Family Networks and the Closure of Employment'. *The Manufacture of Disadvantage*. Eds Lee, G. and Loveridge, R. Milton Keynes: Open University Press.

Hakim, K. 1987. 'Home-based Work in Britain'. Research Paper No. 60. London: Department of Employment.

Harris, C.C. 1969. *The Family*. London: Allen & Unwin.

—— 1983. *The Family and Industrial Society*. London: Allen & Unwin.

—— et al. 1987. *Redundancy and Recession in South Wales*. Oxford: Basil Blackwell.

—— and Morris, L.D. 1986. 'Households, Labour Markets and the Position of Women'. *Gender and Stratification*. Eds Crompton, R. and Mann, M. Cambridge: Polity.

Jephcott, P., Seear, N. and Smith, 1962. *Married Women Working*, London: Allen & Unwin.

Joshi, H. 1984. 'Women's Participation in Paid Work'. Research Paper No. 45. London: Department of Employment.

Kerr, M. 1958. *The People of Ship Street*. London: Routledge and Kegan Paul.

Laite, J. and Halfpenny, P. 1987. 'Employment, Unemployment and the Domestic Division of Labour'. *Unemployed People*. Eds. Fryer, D. and Ullah, P. Milton Keynes: Open University Press.

Land, H., 1969. *Large Families in London*. London: G. Bell and Sons.

—— 1976, 'Social Security and the Division of Unpaid Work in the Home and Paid Employment in the Labour Market'. *Social Security Research*. London: HMSO.

Litwake, E. 1970, 'Geographical Mobility and Extended Family Cohesion'. *Social Demography*. Eds. Ford, T.R. and Dejong, G.F. New York: Prentice-Hall.

Lomnitz, L. 1977. *Life in a Mexican Shanty Town*. London: Academic Press.

Mckee, L. 1987, 'Households during Unemployment: The Resourcefulness of the Unemployed'. *Give and Take in Families*. Eds Brannen, J. and Wilson, G. London: George Allen & Unwin.

Marsden, D. 1982. *Workless*. London: Croom Helm.

Martin, J. and Roberts, C. 1984. *Women and Employment*. Report on the DE/OPCS Survey. London: HMSO.

Massey, D. 1984. *Spatial Divisions of Labour*. London: Macmillan.

Millward, N. 1968. 'Family Status and Behaviour at Work', *Sociological Review*. 16, 149–64.

Molyneux, M. 1979. 'Beyond the Domestic Labour Debate'. *New Left Review*, 116, 3–27.

Morris, L.D. 1984. 'Redundancy and Patterns of Household Finance'. *Sociological Review*. 32, 492–523.

——1985a. 'Renegotiation of the Domestic Division of Labour'. *New Approaches to Economic Life*. Eds Roberts, B. et al. Manchester: Manchester University Press.

—— 1985b. 'Local Social Networks and Domestic Organisation'. *Sociological Review*, 33, 327–42.

—— 1987a. 'The Life Cycle and the Labour Market in Hartlepool'. *Rethinking the Life Cycle*. Eds Bryman, A., Bytheway, B., Allatt, T. and Keil, T. London: Macmillan.

—— 1987b. 'Constraints on Gender'. *Work Employment and Society*, 1, 85–106.

——1987c. 'Local Social Polarisation'. *International Journal of Urban and Regional Research*, 11, 333–52.

—— with Ruane, S. 1988. *Household Finance Management and the Labour Market*. Aldershot: Gower.

Moylan, S., Millar, S. and Davis, R. 1984. *For Richer For Poorer?* DHSS cohort study of unemployed men. London: HMSO.

Oakley, A. 1974. *The Sociology of Housework*. London: Martin Robertson.

—— 1976. *Housewife*. Harmonsdsworth: Penguin.

Pahl, J. 1980. 'Patterns of Money Management within Marriage'. *Journal of Social Policy*, 9, 313–35.

—— 1983. 'The Allocation of Money and the Structuring of Inequality within Marriage'. *Sociological Review*, 31, 235–62.

—— 1984. 'The Allocation of Money in the Household'. *State, Law and the Family*. Ed. Freeman, M. London: Tavistock.

Pahl, R.E. 1980. 'Employment, Work and the Domestic Division of Labour'. *International Journal of Urban and Regional Research*, 4, 1–20.

—— 1984. *Divisions of Labour*. Oxford: Basil Blackwell.

—— and Pahl, J. 1971. *Managers and their Wives*. London: Allen Lane.

—— and Wallace, C. 1984. 'Household Work Strategies in Economic Recession'. *Beyond Employment*. Eds. Mingione, E. and Redclift, N. Oxford: Basil Blackwell.

Payne, J. 1987. 'Does Unemployment Run in Families?'. *Sociology*, 21, 199–214.

Peattie, .R. 1968. *The View from the Bario*. Michigan: University of Michigan Press.

Rapoport, R. and Rapoport, R.N. 1971. *Dual Career Families*. London: Martin Robertson.

—— 1976. *Dual Career Families Re-examined*. London: Martin Robertson.

Redclift, N. 1984. 'The Contested Domain'. *Beyond Employment*. Eds Mingione, E. and Redclift, N. Oxford: Basil Blackwell.

Roberston, D. 1960. *Factory Wage Structures and National Agreements*. Cambridge: Cambridge University Press.

Shimmin, S. 1962. 'Extra-mural Factors Influencing Behaviour at Work'. *Occupational Psychology*, 36, 124–31.

Siltanen, J. and Stanworth, M. 1984. *Women and the Public Sphere*. London: Hutchinson.

Solien, N. 1960. 'Household and Family in the Caribbean'. *Social and Economic Studies*, 9, 101–6.

Stack, C. 1974. *All Our Kin*. New York: Harpers.

Stamp, P. 1985. 'Balance of Financial Power in Marriage'. *Sociological Review*, 33, 546–57.

Thomas, G., Wyatt, S. and Miles, I. 1985. 'Preliminary Analysis of the 1983/4 ESRC Time Budget Survey'. Brighton: SPRU, mimeo.

Townsend, A. 1986. 'Part-time Employment in the Northern Region'. *Northern Economic Review*, 12, 2–15.

Walby, S. 1987. *Patriarchy at Work*. Cambridge: Polity.

Walker, J. 1961. 'Shift Changes and Hours of Work'. *Occupational Psychology*, 35, 1–9.

Wheelock, J. 1986. 'Unemployment, Gender Roles and Household Work Strategies on Wearside'. Sunderland Polytechnic.

Whipp, R. 1985. 'Labour Markets and Communities'. *Sociological Review*, 33, 768–91.

Yeandle, S. 1984. *Women's Working Lives*. London: Tavistock.

Young, M. 1973. *The Symmetrical Family*. London: Routledge & Kegan Paul.

—— and Wilmott, P. 1957. *Family and Kinship in East London*. London: Routledge & Kegan Paul.

14 Educational Institutions, Youth and the Labour Market

David Ashton

Introduction

The study of the relationship between educational institutions and the labour market has its origins in the writings of the classical theorists, especially Durkheim and Marx. These two theoretical orientations still exert a powerful influence on contemporary approaches, but they have been supplemented by more recent developments in social theory, namely those concerned with exploring the experiential dimensions of human society. The first part of this chapter provides an explicit examination of the influence of these three schools of thought.

The second section deals with the form the relationship takes between educational institutions and the labour market since this varies from one society to another in accordance with conditions of historical development. An understanding of the historical conditions which helped shape the educational system and the labour market enables us to comprehend not only the distinctive from which the relationship takes in Britain, but also why the respective institutions and the functions they perform should change over time. It helps focus on the processional character of the relationship.

Empirical analysis of the relationship between educational institutions and the labour market in Britain started on a significant scale in the 1950s and 1960s. Although the research was often informed by a specific theoretical orientation, the problems tackled were strongly influenced by the prevailing social and economic conditions. For this reason the presentation of research results is organized in terms of two major research agenda. In the period 1950 to the late 1970s the focus was on problems of equality of opportunity, jobs choice and the trauma of the transition period. In the second period, the late 1970s onwards, the onset of mass youth unemployment created a new agenda in which questions of unemployment, broken transitions, training and the structure of the youth labour market came to the fore. This transformation of the research agenda forms the third major theme around which the chapter is organized.

Education and the Labour Market: Theoretical Perspectives

The Marxian Tradition: Education, Social Control and the Reproduction of the Labour Force

The main problem confronted by the Marxian tradition has been to explain the part played by social class in determining education, the state and the reproduction of the labour force. Class analysis has made a substantial contribution to our understanding of changes in educational provision. In historical analysis it has been used to show how the development of educational provision involved the imposition on the working class of a system of education and control which reflected the interests of the bourgeoisie and aristocracy. From this perspective, educational provision is seen as strongly contested. It was contested in the first place as the new entrepreneurial groups of the nineteenth century sought to replace an aristocratic concept of education with one more in keeping with the scientific and technical interests of the business class. Educational provision was later contested by the working class as it came to be used as a means of disciplining and controlling the new industrial work-force. This perspective continues to inform contemporary accounts of working-class experience of education and more recently the training measures which have been introduced for youths.

Class analysis has been further developed in two directions; one explaining how the educational system plays a vital role in the reproduction of the labour force, the other explaining why working-class children find it difficult to achieve within the educational system. Bowles and Gintis (1976) in the USA, took the former direction. They argue that the educational system has relatively little autonomy in relation to the class structure merely reproducing and legitimating class inequalities in the process of educating or training young people for their respective positions within the labour market.

Bourdieu (1977) pursued the matter of underachievement and was more concerned with analysing the ways in which the cultural forms in capitalist society generate and legitimate class domination. Within the school, he argues that it is the culture of the dominant class that is taught. Thus, those pupils who are socialized into that culture within the family carry with them greater amounts of cultural capital on entering the school and hence perform better in it.

Marxist ideas have also been influential in highlighting the role of the state in the reproduction of the labour force. In particular the actions of the state are seen as crucial in handling the crises of mass unemployment which occurred in the 1930s and 1980s. In both instances the state is seen as playing a vital role in ensuring that the political consequences of mass unemployment are contained and that measures are instituted to ensure the continued reproduction of the labour force. There is considerable disagreement however, as to the degree of autonomy exercised by the state in relation to the class structure, with some arguing that the measures introduced by the state merely reflect the immediate interest of the capitalist ruling class, whereas others argue that the state has a degree of autonomy in relation to the class struggle and hence may institute measures which may be at variance with the immediate interests of fractions of capital.

Marxist ideas have also been influential in the analysis of the labour market itself. Much of the work of radical economists (e.g. Gordon et al., 1982; Wilkinson, 1981) has been inspired by a dynamic form of class analysis. This work has shown how changes in the organization of production and the outcome of the continuing struggle between capital and labour have fragmented the working class, creating a series of labour market segments. In the course of this struggle employers use a number of techniques to further their control over the labour process including the technology of production and the imposition of internal labour markets. In this process they exploit gender and ethnic divisions to divide further the working class. Similarly, but usually less effectively groups of workers seek to maintain any privileges they have secured such as a higher or more secure income through techniques of closure which exclude outsiders.

The Durkheimian Heritage: Education and Equality of Opportunity

The ideas of Durkheim, outlined in *The Division of Labour* (1964), and concerned with the relationship between individual abilities and the allocation of occupational tasks, informed much of the earlier work on the functions of education as an agent of occupational selection and on the question of equality of educational opportunity. Durkheim argued that one of the problems with modern industrial society was what he referred to as the anomic division of labour. This occurs where there is a mismatch between the abilities and qualities of individuals and those required by the jobs they enter. If the society is to function effectively then it is important that the most able people are recruited to the most demanding jobs. This provides the intellectual justification for the ideal of equal opportunities. Unlike the Marxist heritage which stresses the ideal of equality of outcomes, the Durkheimian position assumes an inequality in the distribution of rewards and emphasizes the need for everyone to have equal access to these positions.

A precondition for the achievement of equal opportunities is that the disadvantage faced by the working class in the existing educational structure should be recognized and removed. The work of Halsey et al. (1961) demonstrates the extent to which, despite the provision of secondary education to the working class, inequalities in educational achievement persisted. Banks (1955), in revealing the links between changes in educational provision and changes in the occupational structure, shows how the introduction of secondary modern schools resulted in the working class receiving an education in institutions widely regarded as second class. Douglas (1964) identifies some of the possible mechanisms such as poor housing conditions, lack of resources and parental values, which were producing the lower levels of achievement found among working-class pupils. Bernstein (1971, 1973) takes this analysis further by pointing to the way in which the culture of certain sections of the working class, as manifest in their use of language, is different from that which operates within the school. Much of this work was used to argue the case for a system of comprehensive education to replace the division between the old grammar schools and the secondary moderns. It was argued that if the disadvantage that the working class faced in the educational system could be removed, then the allocation of people within the occupational structure could be based on merit.

The establishment of a comprehensive system of education did not resolve the problem. Research by Ford (1969) and others shows that working-class pupils underachieved within the new system. Some of the inequalities had been removed by the introduction of comprehensives but the persistence of forms of streaming, the labelling of pupils by teachers and young people's values were all seen as maintaining their disadvantaged position. More recently the idea of the hidden curriculum of the school has provided further insights into how the aspirations of working-class children are restricted by the organization of the curriculum and its delivery.

In the last decade this theoretical tradition has received a new impetus from two sources. The first is the need to explain the under-achievement of ethnic minorities in school and the second is the failure of the Youth Training Scheme to reduce inequalities in the labour market.

Experiential Theory: Education and the Experience of the Transition

Theoretical inspiration for studies of the experiential dimension has derived from a number of sources. Throughout the 1960s and 1970s psychological theories of occupational choice, with their origins in the work of Ginsberg and Super in the USA, tended to dominate the literature. In a period of unprecedented prosperity, when young people were confronted with a choice of jobs on leaving school, these theories appeared to make sense. In Britain these ideas were less readily accepted by sociologists and heavily criticized although they still provide the theoretical basis for much of contemporary careers guidance.

In the 1960s the impact of symbolic interactionism in Britain, combined with the use of ethnographic techniques, opened up new ways of exploring the experiential dimension. Instead of 'imposing' ideas about the mechanics of occupational choice on youth, researchers started to enquire into the ways in which young people actually experienced the transition. This work has identified important differences in the ways in which youths' experiences of the family, school and peer group generate different orientations to school and work. More recently the existence of mass unemployment among youth has led social psychologists to explore this dimension and study gender as well as the coping mechanisms which young people adopt to handle unemployment and problems associated with it.

Education, Social Context and the Reproduction of the Labour Market

The Historical Development of the Educational System

In the course of its historical development the relationship between the educational system and the labour market has undergone a number of significant changes. In the first half of the nineteenth century the provision of educational institutions and the content of the curriculum reflected the existing social divisions. Thus the Schools Inquiry Commission, reporting in 1868, distinguished three grades of secondary education which corresponded with separate grades of society. Schools of the first grade were used by 'men with considerable incomes independent of their own exertions', and 'the great body of professional men, especially the clergy, medical men and lawyers' who 'have nothing to look to but education to keep their sons on a high social level'. The special function of such (public) schools was 'the formation of a learned or literary, and a professional or cultural class'. Below these in status were the schools, used by men whose sons must leave at the age of sixteen either to enter immediately into employment or begin some special training, as, for example, the army and the highest branches of the medical and legal professions, civil engineering and so on. The function of such schools was to educate men with a view to some form of commercial or industrial life. Below these were the schools for the sons of small farmers, tradesmen and the superior artisans (Report of the Schools' Inquiry Commission, 1868: i, 20). The working classes were only provided with elementary education either through the Church schools or the private 'Dame' schools. Many did not receive any formal education. In this 'system' the relationship between the type of school and the type of work the pupils subsequently entered was unambiguous. Such an education prepared them explicitly for their function in the labour market and their place in the system of stratification.

The curricula of such schools were designed to meet the requirements of the different classes. That of the public schools integrated the new entrepreneurial ideals of competition and discipline into the traditional curriculum founded as it was on classics. The result was an education designed to prepare the sons of the aristocracy and of the more successful businessmen for the ruling positions.

The education provided for the working class through the Charity schools was no less 'vocational'. The ruling class, with the spectre of the French Revolution still prominent in its mind, was fearful of the new labouring masses, and significant elements within it saw them as a threat to society's stability. For this reason they attempted to use education to civilize the masses. Such an education consisted of a basic instruction in literacy together with an appropriate moral and religious education designed to ensure that they accepted their lot within the existing order and acquired discipline so essential to the factory system.

Not all sections of the working class accepted this type of education and during the first half of the nineteenth century many paid for their own education in the private 'Dame' schools. Castigated by the middle class as inefficient these schools provided a very basic education in literacy but under conditions controlled by working-class parents who paid for it. The child could attend the school during hours convenient for the parents and would cease to attend when they had acquired the basic rudiments of literacy (Gardner, 1984).

The introduction of compulsory state education at the end of the nineteenth century sought to extend education but also to integrate the working classes more effectively by exercising a greater degree of control over the socialization of their children. To achieve this goal the private schools were destroyed and replaced by state financed institutions, a process which engendered resistance on the part of sections of the working class to the new curriculum that was imposed upon them (Humphries, 1981).

With the development of a national system of state education and the growth of industry, sections of the working class, together with the lower middle class attempted to use the new educational system as an avenue of social mobility for their children. They adapted more readily to state education and it was their children who attended the higher grade schools which mushroomed in the late nineteenth century. These provided a modern, scientific and vocational curriculum for the 'bright' working-class youth. The growth of such schools and the demand which they symbolized for upward mobility posed a threat to the closure of the old social order in education based on separate schools for each of the social strata. The integration of the working class had resulted in sections of them competing for access to the expanding middle-class occupations.

The initial reaction of the state was to suppress the new vocationally oriented schools and incorporate the secondary grammar schools. These had a curriculum modelled on the classical tradition of the public schools (Eaglesham, 1967). By permitting a degree of selectivity some of the sons and daughters of the upper working class and lower middle class were provided with access to grammar schools and through them to clerical and administrative jobs, but only after a period of education or training in the classical tradition. Such schools provided their working-class pupils with the middle-class attributes necessary for success in their new careers.

This solution contained the problem for a period of time but representatives of the working class demanded access to a secondary education for all pupils, not just the chosen few. However, the ruling elites, with the support of the middle class, sought to maintain the distinctive ethos of the grammar schools which controlled access to white-collar and professional jobs. The solution to this problem was contained in the Education Act 1944. This provided secondary education for all but in three types of school: grammar, technical and secondary. The grammar schools for those with 'an academic mind'. the children of the middle class, were to be maintained. However, access to them, and the jobs they fed into, was to be opened up to the working class on a free basis, but the numbers involved were to be controlled through the use of selection (intelligence) tests. The technical schools were to provide a more vocational education for the working class but few of these were built. The majority of the working class, the non-academic and those of the lower middle class who failed the selection tests, were to be provided with a general secondary education in secondary modern schools, schools whose pupils were primarily destined for manual work.

With the establishment of this tripartite system the function of education as an avenue of social mobility was firmly recognized. Yet, as the system was being implemented, other changes were taking place which were starting to undermine it. The most significant of these was the increasing use of educational qualifications by employers in the 1960s and 1970s. In addition, the new secondary modern schools started to emulate the grammar schools and introduce elements of the same classical curriculum for working-class youth who sought educational credentials. As the link between educational qualifications and occupational entry strengthened, so the significance of the type of school attended decreased in importance. The introduction of the classical curriculum and the extension of secondary education continued to meet with resistance from sections of working-class youth, but a significant proportion adapted and acquired educational credentials.

During this period opposition to the selectivity of the tripartite system strengthened from working-class organizations and conditions were established for the introduction of the comprehensive system. When this occurred in the 1960s and 1970s, selection was abolished, together with the distinction between the different types of school. Thus the link between type of school and occupational placement which had been a characteristic feature of the British state educational system had become redundant. However, at the apex of the class structure the public schools still maintained their links with positions in the ruling class. For those lower down in the hierarchy educational credentials were now of major significance in determining access to the better jobs.

Education and Class Culture

It is against this background that a number of ethnographic studies were conducted in the 1970s into the experiential dimension of the educational process. In 1977 Willis produced his widely acknowledged attempt, utilizing Marxist theory, to establish the significance of the cultural determinants of working-class experience. Hargreaves (1967) had previously argued that the existence of a counter-culture within secondary modern schools was a consequence of the educational failure of working-class pupils. Their allocation to the lower streams labelled them as failures with a future limited to unskilled work. The pupils reacted by rejecting societal and teacher values, substituting for them a set of peer group values derived from conformity to a reversal of teacher values. Willis argues that on the contrary the development of a counter school culture is a cause not a consequence of educational failure. The working-class pupils draw on their own class culture and see through the ideology of the school. They do not evaluate their position in the school in terms of what the school might offer but in terms of what success within it might mean for being a working-class adult, and it is this which leads them to reject the school. To accept success at school would mean rejecting their class. The unintended consequence of this process is a future in manual labour, as their rejection of educational success means that they can only enter manual work. Willis is pointing out that sections of the working class are continuing to resist the imposition of a middle-class curriculum on them. However, they are only a minority, the majority of pupils who conform to the school are seen as having been duped by the system.

This was followed in 1979 by a similar study by Corrigan and in 1983 by Jenkins's study of youth in Northern Ireland. Jenkins sought to establish the patterned differences, cultural and material, within the working class and how such distinctions were reproduced especially in the transition from youth to adult and school to work. He identifies three distinct life-styles: 'the lads' who are more likely to come from a single-parent household, have a criminal record, possess no educational qualifications and enter unskilled work; the 'ordinary kids' who do better at school, are less likely to be unemployed or in unskilled work; and the 'citizens' who enter skilled manual or white-collar occupations. He distinguishes three dimensions to the reproduction of these life-styles: the practices of the youth themselves, derived in part from the conventional wisdom of parents and friends; the practices of significant others, such as housing officials, the police, teachers and employment recruiters, whose definitions of the world ensure the reproduction of these divisions, and, thirdly, the institutional context within which the other two sets of practices are located. In short, differences in life-styles are seen to stem from the differential allocation of resources within the working class.

More recently, Brown (1987) has identified three similar groups, the 'rems', 'ordinary kids' and 'swots'. He argues that each has a distinctive orientation which cannot be explained either by reference to selection processes within the school (Hargreaves, 1967) or by reference to a unitary working-class culture (Willis, 1977). While the organization of the school provides the raw material for the pupil subcultures they are imbued with cultural and social significance originating in the class culture of the immediate neighbourhood. In particular, he focuses on the 'ordinary kids' willingness to make a limited effort at school which is seen as part of an authentic attempt to maintain command of their own life and enhance their chances of making a working-class career. He characterizes such 'ordinary kids' as having an instrumental orientation to school. They conform and make an effort at school on the assumption this will pay off in the form of a good working-class job, a trade. This forms the basis of their compliance which is threatened in times of high unemployment when the chances of education paying-off in the labour market are reduced.

Assessment

In many respects the recent examination of the experience which working-class youth has of the educational system evokes strong parallels with the past. The work of Willis and Corrigan demonstrates how sections of the working class continue to resist the cultural dominance of the ruling class as imposed through the school curriculum. Yet both Jenkins and Brown have shown how material and cultural divisions within the working class continue to lead the 'swots' to use education as a means of getting out of the working class, while, for the majority, compliance is obtained by the promise of a good working-class job at the end.

It follows from this that the crude two class model that Willis worked with is no longer an appropriate conceptual tool for sociological analysis as there are significant sources of economic and cultural variation within the working class. It is also clear that sections of working-class youth reject school on the basis of their cultural resources which are drawn from outside school. However, as these cultural resources are differentially located throughout the middle and working class, so too are the resources on which pupils can draw to give meaning to their experiences within the school. Perhaps even more significantly it is now established that young people negotiate their way through the various institutional structures with which they are confronted and, through that process, contribute towards their reproduction and change.

Education and Equality of Opportunity

Educational Achievement and Occupational Opportunity

It has already been shown how there was a direct link between social origins, type of education and the occupation entered by young people in the nineteenth century. In these circumstances the occupational placement and subsequent job history of the young person was seen to be determined by their ascribed status. It was the circumstances of their birth which conditioned their subsequent status. With changes in the occupational structure associated with industrialism it was argued that achieved status, attained through education, becomes more important in determining a person's position within the social division of labour (Blau and Duncan, 1969). If people could be allocated to occupations on the basis of their ability rather than their parents' social status this opened up the possibility of achieving the ideal of equality of opportunity.

The work of Glass (1954) and the Oxford Social Mobility Group has enabled these ideas to be tested. Analysing data from cohorts of the general population interviewed in 1949 and 1972 it was found that, for those who grew up in the post-war era, education was of increased significance for the transmission of social standing from fathers to sons. Education, or more specifically formal educational qualifications, had a larger effect on occupational careers while the effect of father's occupation was reduced. However, the influence of social origins on educational attainment actually increased. Taken together, the overall association between origins and first job was effectively unchanged. It was not so much the extent of transmission as the mechanism that changed (Heath, 1981: 170). In fact, the first part of the twentieth century saw the British educational system become more rigid as the type of secondary school attended became increasingly important for determining success in the external examinations which were becoming ever more important in determining access to a wide range of jobs.

Results such as these gave credence to the thesis of a tightening bond between educational qualifications and occupational attainment. It was argued that with the development of more advanced technology an ever increasing proportion of occupations required educational qualifications for entry. However, the precise nature of the bond has been debated.

Some argue that the bond has tightened because educational qualifications are now necessary for entry to the more desirable occupations. This thesis has been challenged by Payne (1987) who argues that for the more desirable occupations a high level of educational achievement is a sufficient but not a necessary condition for entry. Analysing data over the four decades from 1930 onwards he found it was only the 1960s which showed any sign of the link tightening (Payne, 1987: 149).

Unfortunately all these studies were restricted to the period when selective schools operated and so the results can tell us little about any change which the introduction of non-selective education has brought about. In fact, the introduction of the comprehensive schools in the 1960s may have further tightened the bond.

Work on the relationship between the educational qualifications of school leavers and occupational attainment (Raffe, 1984; Payne, 1985; Payne and Payne, 1985) suggest that the link between the two has become stronger over the last decade. As unemployment levels rose those who obtain CSEs, GCEs, or their Scottish equivalents, stood a much better chance of avoiding unemployment and of obtaining the kind of work they wanted. The exception to this was in areas of very high unemployment where the relationship between educational achievement and the probability of securing employment broke down (Spilsbury, 1986). However, just what the links are which connect educational achievement with occupational attainment is still a subject of debate. Through a study of employers' recruitment practices, Ashton et al. (1988) argue that the functions of educational qualifications vary in accordance with the type of segment for which labour is recruited, while Jones (1985) argues that their primary effect is via young people's job-seeking behaviour. At this point in time it is difficult to establish whether the increasing importance of qualifications is a function of the growth of mass unemployment with employers using them as a screening device in the face of large numbers of applicants, or whether it represents a permanent shift in employers' practices. Certainly, if the demand for labour were to increase it is very likely that employers recruiting for skilled and unskilled jobs would become more flexible in their approach and recruit more of the unqualified. If this were to happen then the significance of qualifications would decrease.

The Social Determinants of Educational and Occupational Success

The early work on the determinants of educational success was done by Blau and Duncan (1969) in the USA. Their findings, based on path analysis, enabled some estimation to be made of the effects of different factors on occupational attainment. What they found was that father's occupation and father's education level influenced the son's educational achievement and that educational achievement and social origins influenced the type of job entered. Once in the labour market, the type of job entered, educational achievement and social origins all influenced subsequent career attainment. Later research extended this basic model to include additional variables such as occupational aspirations, peer group influence, sex and race.

The work of Halsey et al. (1980) adapted this form of analysis to the British context. Their results emphasize the continuing importance of class differentials; a boy from the service class had nearly forty times the chance of his working-class peer of entering one of the major private (public) schools. The likelihood of a working-class boy receiving a selective education in the mid-1950s and 1960s was very little different from that of his parents' generation thirty years earlier. They found that factors in the material and cultural background of the family were important in determining which sons went to private schools. Once in the school they found that the type of school entered has an independent effect on educational attainment. Thus, for two boys with identical social background, the one allocated to the grammar school did vastly better than the one sent to a secondary modern. Even when they introduced IQ as a variable this made little difference. The other factor which they found to be of significance as a determinant of school career was the material circumstances of the family.

As the type of school entered appeared to be such an important factor in determining educational success in Britain, it would be expected that changes in the organization of education, such as that associated with the introduction of comprehensive schools would have an effect. Initial results suggested that little had changed, but research conducted in Scotland, on samples of people who had started their education after the system of comprehensive schools was fully in place, indicates that, within a period of eight years, comprehensive schools had significantly reduced social class inequalities of attainment. They did this in two ways, by improving the average levels of school attainment and by reducing social class inequalities. However, the end of selection was not the only factor; the raising of the school leaving age to 16 meant that more pupils had to sit the examinations and general improvements in education, such as the improvements in the school's ability to learn how to raise standards were also thought to play a part (McPherson and Willms, 1987). Just how such changes in school organization affect the relationship between parental material circumstances, family culture and IQ as determinants of educational achievement remain to be seen.

Although occupational attainment was an integral element in Blau and Duncan's original status attainment model it has received less attention. Recently, Elias and Blanchflower (1987) found that occupational attainment is dominated by three influences: the work history pattern, the decision to leave school at 16 and mathematics and reading abilities.

As a number of writers have pointed out, the status attainment model has a poorly developed theoretical basis which assumes that individual characteristics are identified and rewarded according to their societal value. This has now been challenged by developments in labour market segmentation theory. Breen (1984), analysing Irish data, argues that although there is a strong relationship between the level of educational qualifications obtained and the likelihood of unemployment, this is because those who leave school with few qualifications are more likely to enter the secondary exposed sector of the labour force. This, together with other findings, such as Ashton et al. (1988) on the youth labour market, and Dex (1987) on the female labour market, suggest that differences in the structure of the labour market may have an independent effect on the attainment of young adults in a similar manner to that exercised by the type of school under the tripartite system.

Experience of the Transition

Job Choice or Allocation

The first research on the transition from school to work was characterized by an attempt to explore the ways in which young people (primarily males) experienced the transition. One of the major foci of research in this phase was the question whether young people chose to enter specific jobs or whether they were allocated to them. Psychologists argued that young people chose their jobs. Ginsberg identifies a number of stages during which the individual moves from fantasy choices to realistic choices. Super argues that the self-concept is crucial in influencing this process of occupational choice for it is from a growing awareness of the self that young people are able to seek out the appropriate choice of occupation which will enable them to implement their self-concept.

Early studies of the transition by Carter and Maizels reveal that even in the relatively affluent 1960s many young people did not actively choose jobs but rather appeared to drift into work. Drawing on these and other findings, Roberts (1975) argues that if we are to understand the job 'choices' made by youths we should focus not on the process of personal growth but on the structures of opportunity available to youths as they move from school to work. Young people acquire their aspirations and expectations not from a process of introverted reflection but from the type of school they enter and the kind of opportunities they know are available in their locality. It is these, the socialization processes in the school and in the labour market which shape their 'occupational choices'.

Research has continued in this tradition. In 1983 West and Newton examined the impact of different types of careers teaching on the formation of young people's aspirations and their subsequent experience of the labour market. They note how in a tight labour market those who have been subjected to the influence of a programme of careers teaching aimed at broadening their horizons find it more difficult to compromise and settle in jobs which do not meet their aspirations than those whose careers' programme is limited to the provision of labour market information.

Cultural Shock or Discontinuity

A second major focus of research in the first phase was centred around the thesis of the culture shock. Miller and Form (1951) in the USA had suggested that the transition would involve young people in a culture shock as they moved from the protected environment of the school, where they were treated as children, to the adult world of work where they were faced with the reality of adult life. The only evidence in Britain of such a gap between school and work came from the work of Bazalgette (1978), who examined the organization of both the school and work. He found that the two institutions emphasized different relationships, the comprehensive school had large unstable working groups and the pupils had hostile relationships to authority. In employment work was organized in small, stable and secure groups where supervisors were seen as supportive. In making the transition, he argued young people were exposed to very different types of relationships.

Apart from Bazalgette's work, most of the empirical studies of the transition (Carter, 1962; Maizels, 1970), found that the vast majority of young people in the 1950s and 1960s experienced few problems of adjustment to work. In fact the area where they encountered adjustment problems, if at all, was school. Most working-class youth were only too keen to get out of school and enter work, which was seen as offering independence and freedom. For them the transition represented a major landmark en route to adult status.

Using findings from a number of studies Ashton and Field (1976) sought to explain how it was possible that young people coming from very different social class backgrounds and with different experiences of school, some in secondary moderns, others in grammar schools or comprehensives, should adjust with such ease to working life. They argued that there was a broad structural correspondence between family background, type of school and type of work which created three main channels along which young people moved in their preparation for and entry into work. These were similar to the divisions which Brown and Jenkins later identified as the source of the distinctive life-styles and orientations of working-class and middle class youth. These three channels provided the young people who moved through them with a consistent set of relationships which reinforced distinctive frames of reference. Discontinuities were only experienced by those entering jobs providing a set of experiences which were in conflict with the frame of reference acquired in the family and reinforced by their experience of school.

Gender and the Experience of the Transition

Towards the end of the 1970s studies of the first phase came under increasing criticism. It was argued that many of them provided an inadequate understanding of the ways in which young people experienced the transition because they were primarily concerned with white male working-class youth. Indeed, while some of the studies cited above did include women in the sample, they were in many respects invisible in the subsequent analysis.

Work by McRobbie (1978), Deem (1978) and Griffin (1985) has brought the distinctive experience of young working-class women firmly to the forefront. McRobbie has shown how their reaction to school involves a different anti-school subculture which stresses having a good time, rather than achievement; how they resist a meaningless curriculum by talking back to teachers and among themselves and how this resistance sometimes takes the form of assertive impertinence.

Griffin highlights a number of aspects of the female experience of the transition which have been ignored. Women's responsibility is to the home. Unlike in the case of men, the commitment this involves plays an important part in shaping young women's entry to college and the job market. She argues that to understand the young women's experience it is important to locate it in the context of their simultaneous positions in the sexual, marriage and labour markets. For the young women the immediate problem is to manage the simultaneous pressures of finding a job and a boyfriend, both of which interact. Thus, pressures to get a man can influence the type of job they aim for. For example, office work is seen as particularly attractive because it offers young working-class women the chance to meet higher status middle-class males.

The Growth of Youth Unemployment and the Crisis of the Old Framework

The Growth of Youth Unemployment and the Changing Context of the Transition

Although Britain was still experiencing a period of full employment in the 1960s, levels of youth unemployment started to rise. In the 1970s youth unemployment started to grow more rapidly, especially in the latter part of the decade. However, at this stage it remained largely confined to unqualified school leavers in the depressed regions. It was in the early 1980s that the magnitude of the problem was transformed (Raffe, 1987a). In 1978, 85 per cent of 16 year olds found work on leaving school, by 1982 that figure had fallen to 50 per cent, and by 1985 to 27 per cent. Unemployment, which had previously been a regional problem, facing the unqualified, became a mass phenomenon facing the majority of school leavers.

The transformation of school leavers' prospects which this implied had an equally profound effect on the ways in which the transition was conceptualized. The old idea that young people faced one transition from school to work could no longer be sustained. Of course, some young people had always faced problems of unemployment on leaving school, but this now became a majority experience. In areas of high unemployment some youths now faced the prospects of never securing entry into permanent paid employment. The transition from school to work had been ruptured. For others, high levels of unemployment encouraged them to stay on at school while a few chose to return to college after a short spell in the labour market. This new context emphasized that young people were simultaneously undergoing a number of transitions, from youth to adult, from school to the labour market, from financial dependence to independence and from the family of origin to the family of procreation. This questioning of the traditional model of the transition resulted in a new research agenda, which focused on these broken transitions and the strategies young people have developed to cope with them.

The Experience of Youth Unemployment

Studies of youth unemployment in the initial phase of the 1980s recession (Roberts et al., 1981) found that most of it consisted of short spells and that exceptionally high levels of youth unemployment could be partly explained by the constant movement into and out of work by young people. Such findings also suggested that some young people actually preferred intermittent employment to continuous work in low-paid, unskilled jobs. As the general level of unemployment increased, so the spells of unemployment became longer (Ashton and Maguire, 1986). Meanwhile, more and more young people found their first experience of the labour market consisted of a spell on a government scheme. As Raffe (1987a) has shown the problem of unemployment changed from young people's failure to keep jobs to their being unable to obtain jobs.

Work by social psychologists (Banks and Jackson, 1982) on the effects of unemployment on young people has established that it lowers health scores and has a damaging effect on their self-esteem. A number of studies found that young people usually consider it an ordeal, while others have shown how it affects the ability of young people to 'go out' to acquire adult tastes and spending patterns (Gurney, 1980; Hendry et al., 1984). There are also clear gender differences in the impact of unemployment. For males, peer group activities remain an important source of support while females are more constrained by their domestic responsibilities and the need to preserve their reputation. The result is that they are more isolated than males (Wolverhampton Youth Review, 1985).

A number of researchers have argued that young people are in a better position to handle the effects of unemployment because for many it is part of their normal experience of the labour market and can be experienced as a break from the routine and boredom of the kind of jobs on offer to young people. In addition, young people do not have the financial responsibilities of adults (Watts, 1983; Warr, 1983; Roberts. 1984). Coffield et al. (1986) have challenged this view arguing that unemployed young people still have to secure an occupational identity and make the transition to adulthood; because they are unemployed that does not stop them becoming adults. The resolution of this debate will be advanced by making a distinction between short-term and long-term unemployment. In the case of short-term unemployment, many of the negative consequences, such as the effects on health scores and self-esteem can be ameliorated on securing employment. In the case of long-term unemployment the situation is different. Given that many of the long-term unemployed are concentrated in communities with very high levels of unemployment, the problems of boredom and deprivation associated with unemployment are compounded by those of poverty. For them, in the absence of a massive increase in the demand for labour, the acquisition of paid employment is not necessarily a realistic way out of their predicament.

Coffield et al. identify a number of survival tactics which young people use to handle long-term unemployment which range from changes in spending patterns to a blank refusal to talk to others about it.

However, their ability to handle it is constantly constrained by acute financial deprivation.

The implications of high levels of unemployment are not of course confined to the unemployed. The contraction of the youth labour market increases the competition for jobs throughout the labour market. A consequence of this is the threat which high levels of unemployment pose to those in school and about to enter the labour market. Brown (1987) argues that, given the prevalence of an instrumental orientation to school on the part of most working-class youth, high levels of youth unemployment threaten the basis of their compliance within the school. If, in exchange for their commitment to school and the acquisition of the requisite educational qualifications, they cannot obtain a job on leaving, then what is the point in ordinary working-class kids complying with the demands of the institution? In areas of high unemployment he argues, the legitimacy of the educational system is at stake.

Just what actually happens to youths when they enter the labour market under these new conditions has been the subject of a number of projects. Where unemployment is close to the national average, Furlong's (1987) results suggest that those who fail to secure an appropriate job adopt a number of strategies in order to maintain the self-image they have built up. One such strategy is to return to full-time education, another is to use the better YTS schemes as a means of securing some form of training which may enable them to achieve their original goal in the future, and another is to accept a job which they regard as inferior but to distance themselves from it by defining it as only a temporary stop gap until something better turns up. Young people are not passively accepting their fate on leaving school but are developing strategies to accommodate the new situation. By extending the transition, government schemes and the expansion of further education are providing time and space for them to do this.

In areas of high unemployment, Wallace (1987) suggests that a substantial proportion of the population has become marginalized as the sub-employed, a group who move into and out of low pay, casual or temporary employment and who exist on the margins of the labour market. This is a future which has become the lot of a large proportion of school leavers in areas of high unemployment (Ashton et al., 1988; Roberts et al., 1986). Wallace suggests that this is creating new life-styles and patterns of domestic career for the youths concerned. It is clear that the movement from school to government scheme, unemployment, temporary job and unemployment is a new condition which faces the 1980s' generation as they endeavour to make the transition.

Unemployment and the Diversification of the Transition

The magnitude of the changes which have taken place in the 1980s has upturned the close connection between the different types of educational experience or channels and the various segments of the labour market entered by youths, which existed in the 1960s. Wallace (1987) argues that the major difference is no longer between those destined for long-term or short-term careers and the careerless (Ashton and Field, 1976) but between those with permanent employment and those without. The crucial factors differentiating young people's experience of the transition are the length of time in employment and their sex. Similarly Roberts et al. (1986) have focused on the phenomenon of broken transitions which they see as characteristic of contemporary Britain.

The combined effect of unemployment and government schemes has been to extend the transition for many young people and keep them in a state of dependency. In the light of these trends Roberts (1984) suggests that it is no longer useful to base typologies on the official occupational classifications, but that new typologies should be developed to accommodate the new routes into the labour market. These he suggests as (a) traditional transitions, straight from school into primary occupations which can be practised into adulthood; (b) protracted transitions which lead into primary adult employment via various combinations of schemes, youth jobs and spells of unemployment; (c) early careers in which young people become trapped in special programmes, youth jobs and secondary labour markets, and (d) careers in which young people descend into long-term unemployment. While these developments provide a more adequate basis for a model of the transition in the 1980s they are not without problems. They undoubtedly provide a better understanding of the range of routes that are developing during the period of indeterminacy between leaving school and entering permanent employment. However, they only provide tenuous links with the 'real' labour market. At best, jobs are differentiated into primary and secondary; youth and adult; at worst the analysis of the transition tends to be conducted without reference to its outcomes in the labour market.

Youth Unemployment and Structural Change in the Youth Labour Market

During the first phase of empirical studies into the transition, the structure of the youth labour market and its relationship to that for adults remained something of a black box. With studies of employers by Ashton et al. (1982), Livock (1983), and of young people entering the labour market from the Scottish School Leavers' survey, two opposing schools of thought emerged on the structure of the youth labour market. Ashton et al. (1982) argue that employers' recruitment strategies suggest that the youth labour market is segmented in terms of skill levels, age and sex. For example, they find large parts of the general labour market closed to youths, with jobs concentrated in a limited part of the labour market. All this indicates that the youth labour market has distinctive characteristics. In a later paper (Ashton and Maguire, 1983) they identify a number of longer term processes of change which they argue are reducing the demand for youth labour, for example, the decline of manufacturing industry, qualification inflation and the increasing competition from married women returning to work.

Raffe (1986, 1987a, 1987b), using data from the Scottish School Leavers'

Survey argues to the contrary that the labour market is relatively open and that employers are selecting youths on the basis of their human capital as queue theory would predict. In his work on YTS he suggests that there is nothing specific to the demand for youth labour which distinguishes it from that for adults and therefore, until the general problem of unemployment is resolved there can be no solution to the problem of youth unemployment.

The debate on the structure of the youth labour market has recently been taken further by Roberts et al. (1986) who argue that, while the youth labour market has distinctive characteristics, in those areas where young people and adults do compete young people have been displaced by adults who are regarded by employers as more experienced. However, the appearance of jobless growth and the upgrading of jobs which has occurred during the recession does mean that important structural changes have taken place during the recession. Many of the new jobs being created are at professional, managerial and technician levels, for which most school leavers are not qualified, while the jobs which they traditionally entered have been destroyed by the recession. Further work on this problem by Ashton et al. (1988) has shown a number of different sources of change operating on the various segments which comprise the youth labour market. These range from changes in the structure of inter-national product markets, the impact of technology on the employment output relationship, and qualification inflation, to the effect of political intervention in the form of the Youth Training Scheme (YTS). They argue that the recession has involved a fundamental restructuring of the general labour market which has had a profound effect on the structure of the youth labour market, producing a differential impact on the male and female segments. These changes have not only caused the youth labour market to shrink, they have also changed the relative size of the various segments, as well as changing the content of many of the jobs which comprise them.

Locality and Variations in the Youth Labour Market

It has always been known that the labour market for school leavers is essentially a local labour market. However, this second phase of research has revealed new insights into the significance of local labour markets. Roberts et al. (1986), Coles (1986) and Stern and Turbin (1986). Have started to explore the relationship between local labour markets and the life chances of young people. Their results suggest that the structure of the local labour market is an important factor in determining life chances. Thus, Ashton and Maguire (1988) find that the sons of lower working-class parents in St Albans, where employment opportunities have been maintained throughout the recession, have a better chance of entering white-collar employment than the sons of middle-class parents in Sunderland, which has suffered severely from the recession. Roberts et al. find that the occupational returns from any set of qualifications differ considerably between local labour markets. They also find that recent changes in the structure of demand for youth labour has created serious imbalances in all three local labour markets they studied. Even in the more affluent context of the Chelmsford labour market, unskilled jobs have been lost, creating problems for unqualified school leavers. However, in Liverpool and Walsall the same processes have created mass youth unemployment affecting not only those without qualifications but the qualified as well. Taken together, all these findings suggest that young people's aspirations, chances of entering different types of jobs and training, as well as the risks of unemployment, differ according to their qualifications and where they live.

Youth Training and the Restructuring of the Transition

The Historical Specificity of the British Training System

While the question of youth training is very much a product of the second phase of research, to understand the system of training requires that a much longer time perspective is adopted. In fact, much of what we now refer to as the training system has its origins in the nineteenth century and before that in the remnants of the medieval guild system. While the main institutional framework of guilds was destroyed by the development of industrial capitalism, elements of it remained, especially in the form of the apprenticeship system which was used extensively in the training of artisans. This involved binding the young person for a period of years (usually from five to seven) to a master who promised to introduce the apprentice to the secrets of the trade. This was the way the trades had been reproduced before the establishment of the factory system and this was rapidly adapted by both workers and owners to the demands of industrial capitalism. Workers preserved it because it gave the tradesmen control over entrance to the trade and ensured the relative closure of the occupation. Early factory owners used it as a means of securing the labour of paupers to work in the factories. That development subsequently died out but apprenticeship was retained as the main means of organizing the training of youths (especially males) in manufacturing industry. While many modern apprenticeships are now shorter in duration and based on standards of achievement rather than the length of time served, they continue to form the basis of industrial training and play an important part in structuring the relationship between education and the labour market in contemporary Britain.

Important theoretical insights into the consequences of such a system of training have been pioneered in France, in the work of Maurice et al. (1986). They argue that collective entities such as the educational system, the system of industrial training and the organization of the firm must be studied in relation to each other as independent theoretical subjects. This is because the way in which the educational system is organized has important implications for the organization of training and both affect the ways in which management exercises its authority and structures relationships within the firm. Put simply, if the educational and training systems provide young recruits with a set of transferable skills, this limits the range of discretion available to management in organizing the internal labour market, that is, it cannot promote less skilled workers unless they undergo such a training. If the educational system provides only a general education then management can train recruits in firm-specific skills and organize the internal labour market as it sees fit. Marsden (1986) has advocated the adoption of this framework for the analysis of the youth labour market and has argued that in many respects the British apprenticeship system approximates to that of the German Model. He argues that the institutional structure through which the educational training and industrial systems are linked is crucial in influencing levels of youth wages, patterns of access to jobs and patterns of potential substitution between youths and adults. Thus, in Britain and Germany, the apprenticeship system provides special access channels to young workers, making it easier for unions to monitor substitution and hence more willing to accept lower youth rates. In France and Italy, where there is no apprenticeship system, this leaves skilled adults more open to substitution by the labour of school leavers and hence greater pressure is exerted on employers to exclude youth altogether.

Using a similar approach Ashton (1988) has argued that the inheritance of the apprenticeship system in Britain with its emphasis on recruiting 16 year olds, has created pressures on young people to curtail their education and to leave school early in order to gain entry to the most prestigious working-class jobs. By contrast in Canada and the USA, where recruitment to such skilled jobs is delayed until recruits are in their early twenties, there is more incentive for youths to continue in education. However, in Britain, the use of the apprenticeship system is limited to the manufacturing sector. In the service sector firms have taken the products of a general system of education and trained them in skills specific to the organization. Indeed, the industrial training boards which could have imposed a training system in this sphere were abandoned before such a system could be established.

The Creation and Expansion of YTS

It was against this background of extensive training for males entering manufacturing in the form of apprenticeships and relatively little general or occupational training for those, mostly females, entering the service sector, that YTS was created. It had its origins in a number of short-term measures instituted by various governments to combat the problems of youth unemployment in the late 1970s and early 1980s. During the period of relatively full employment in the 1960s and 1970s, the training of young people was not seen as problematic. As youth unemployment rose and affected the unqualified, some form of training was seen as a possible cure for the problem. This cure was advocated by the Manpower Services Commission as it sought to establish a national system of training in Britain. The opportunity to move towards this goal was provided after the youth riots of 1981 when, faced with the problem of mass youth unemployment, the government sought some means of removing youths from the streets.

The MSC provided the answer in the form of a youth training scheme. This was first introduced as a one-year scheme to provide an opportunity for all school leavers who were not successful in obtaining a job. However, in order to emphasize that this was more than just another unemployment scheme attempts were made to include some jobs. The number of young people involved was massive, although no larger than that catered for by its predecessor, the Youth Opportunities Programme. The number of entrants to YOP rose from 162,000 in 1979 to 553,000 in 1982. The numbers on YTS which started in 1984 was 354,000 rising to 430,000 in 1987 when the two-year scheme came into operation. The magnitude of the impact of YTS is indicated by the fact that in 1987 it catered for 27 per cent of all 16 year olds, a figure not far short of the 31 per cent who stayed on at school and much larger than the 17 per cent who found employment.

The growth of the MSC since its foundation in 1974 has stimulated concern about the provision of training in Britain. Work funded by the MSC has shown how far Britain is lagging behind its competitors in the provision of training. In comparison with West Germany, where in 1978 67 per cent of the population had some form of educational or vocational qualification, the figure in Britain was 36 per cent. The introduction of YTS will eventually close this gap, but even with YTS, Britain is still lagging behind other countries. Using Germany again as an example, in 1981, 84 per cent of 16–18 year olds there were participating in some form of education or training compared with 63 per cent in Britain. When it comes to participation in full-time education, the situation in Britain is even worse, for over half of all 16 year olds leave school compared with 5 per cent in Japan and between 10 and 20 per cent in Canada and the USA. Comparisons such as these have been used to argue the case for a more comprehensive system of training in Britain.

The Marxian Interpretation of YTS

The Marxian interpretation has developed in opposition to this official view of a 'training crisis'. Rees and Atkinson (1982) were among the first to challenge the official view in a collection of readings on state intervention in the youth labour market. The analysis they contain suggests that mass unemployment represents a crisis of capitalism, to which the state is responding in a number of ways. One is to blame the victim, a strategy which was adopted in the 1930s when the state introduced juvenile training centres for the long-term unemployed. In the late 1970s and early 1980s politicians were voicing a similar solution, arguing that in order to make them employable the state had to provide additional training which the schools had failed to provide. This strategy enables the state to deflect attention from the real problem of unemployment which in any case is disguised by the massaging of the unemployment figure.

It is also argued that the introduction of government schemes is part of a broader strategy to restructure the labour force and the education system. The function of the schemes is to maintain youth in a state of dependency, so extending the degree of control exercised by the state over the behaviour of young people. However, if they are to be of use to employers the schemes have also to maintain the commitment of youth to the work ethic and enforce their acceptance of industrial discipline so that this reserve army will be ready for employment as and when they are required.

While the virtue of this approach is that it raises to the centre of sociological enquiry the role of the state in mediating the relationship between education and the labour market, there are a number of problems associated with its reliance on traditional Marxist analysis of the state. There can be no doubt that the Thatcher government has developed a strategy for the restructuring of the educational service and that it has used the MSC to manage some of the social consequences of the recession it helped create. Yet much of that policy, such as the formation of the YTS, was just as much a stumbling response to a political crisis of youth employment, as part of a grand scheme aimed at restructuring the attitudes of the entire working class. In providing a conspiratorial account of it, the Marxist account also imbues the state with virtual omnipotence and takes no account of the different interests which are represented within the machinery of the state or of the unintended consequences of attempts to implement such policies.

YTS and Social Stratification

As the introduction of the YTS was seen by the government and the MSC partly as a response to the failure of the educational system, it was implemented through employers. Educational institutions which had participated in the previous schemes under YOP were largely excluded. One consequence of this was that the YTS tended to replicate and reinforce the existing pattern of training provision. It was integrated into some apprenticeship training and formed the first year of training. In occupations such as typist and shop assistant or cashier, where little training was given, it provided a minimum of training in general social skills. However, employers continued to meet most of the cost of training apprentices, and the state, through the educational system, met the cost of training females in clerical skills. The vast majority of the trainees' time on the YTS consisted of work experience, as it has done on its predecessor, YOP. Raffe (1987a) has argued that if the scheme is to become recognized as a training scheme rather than an unemployment measure it will have to pay more attention to the context within which the places are located rather than the content of the scheme. This is because some schemes clearly lead to recognized qualifications and jobs such as apprenticeships, while other schemes offer no guarantee of employment, merely holding young people off the dole. This had led Lee et al. (1987) to argue that the YTS represents no more than a surrogate labour market for youth.

The introduction of YTS has also been seen as part of a wider strategy to reintroduce selective education, with the Training Vocational Education Initiative (TVEI) and YTS as the provision for the working class, and some form of selective education and higher education for the middle class (Blackman, 1987). Finn (1987) argues that the introduction of these new educational initiatives together with the YTS represents an attempt to transform the relationship between education, training and work. It is an attempt which aims to restructure the attitudes and skills of the young working class to make them more acceptable to employers. The ruling class always had their own separate system of vocational education in the form of the public schools and Oxbridge.

YTS and the Experience of Transition

Concern with the way in which YTS has replicated the wider inequalities in the labour market has dominated studies of young people's experience of the various schemes which comprise it. Their response has differed according to the type of scheme they entered and the chances it offered of securing the type of work they wanted. Most regard YTS as second best and for that reason seek to enter full-time jobs on leaving school, only entering YTS after a period of unemployment (Roberts et al., 1986). Once on the scheme, whether they leave it for a full-time job depends on the type of scheme, where they live (the local labour-market), their social class background, educational qualifications, ethnic group membership and sex. The same factors influenced their school experience and performance.

The effect of locality on the chances of entering schemes is evidenced by the fact that 38 per cent of 16 year olds in Chelmsford entered them compared with 72 per cent in Liverpool. Within local labour markets, the better qualified avoid YTS. For those who go on it, although it is second best, it is better than the dole. Once on the scheme, the better qualified move onto the schemes which provide better training and chances of permanent employment, schemes which are more prevalent in areas of relatively full employment.

Not all school leavers accept YTS (Church and Ainley, 1987); a small group are hostile to the scheme and prefer to take on the risk of unemployment rather than accept what they see as meaningless 'training' which only leads back to the dole. YTS provides a holding operation, enabling some of those who enter to achieve their aspirations while taking large numbers of youth out of the 'real' labour market. While doing this it also plays an important role in aligning young people's expectations with the realities of opportunities in local labour markets.

Because YTS operates within the constraints of the local labour market, its organization reflects the sources of segmentation which operate within it. Cockburn (1987), in a study of young women's experience of YTS, has shown the way in which stereotypes and assumptions about women's position in society structure the movement of women through the scheme, which she describes as a system of two track training; males entering skilled manual, technician and manufacturing schemes, and females entering community and health care, administration, clerical and sales schemes. Her work is important in that she shows how the mechanisms involve far more than conscious discrimination.

Ethnicity is the other factor which has a powerful influence on young people's chances of obtaining work and on the type of scheme they enter.

Both Asian and black groups are overrepresented among the unemployed and in those YTS schemes which offer the worst prospects for jobs. Cross (1987) and others have argued that the introduction first of Mode B schemes on YTS and later of premium places for young people with special needs means the creation of a form of second-class training within the YTS for minorities. Yet research by Roberts et al. (1983) and Cross (1987), has shown that black unemployed youth are better qualified in educational terms than their white counterparts. Like Cockburn, Jenkins and Troyna (1983) argue that the main source of discrimination is located in the labour market, and so, irrespective of their personal achievements, members of the ethnic minorities will continue to be denied access to large parts of it. Overall, it appears that as it is presently instituted the YTS is merely reproducing inequalities that already exist within the labour market.

Conclusion

Throughout this analysis the transformation of the research agenda points to strong continuities in the field, in spite of the changes which have taken place over the last four decades. One such source of continuity has been in the persistence of forms of stratification in both the educational system and the labour market. Political attempts to reduce inequalities in education have been only partly successful while more recent changes have served to strengthen them. Attempts to reduce inequalities in the labour market have followed the same pattern. In view of this, inequality and political reaction to it can confidently be expected to remain at the centre of sociological enquiry in the foreseeable future.

As we have seen, the development of the relationship between educational institutions and labour markets is strongly conditioned by its historical context. Thus it has many features which are distinctively British, such as the nature of the educational curriculum, the form of the apprenticeship system and the structure of the Youth Training Scheme. If we are to develop our theoretical understanding of the relationships involved, the comparative study of educational institutions and labour markets is essential.

References

Ashton, D.N. 1988. 'Sources of Variation in Labour Market Segmentation: A Comparison of Youth Labour Markets in Britain and Canada'. *Work, Employment and Society*, 2 (March).
—— and Field, D. 1976. *Young Workers: From School to Work*. London: Hutchinson.

—— Maguire, M.J. and Garland, G. 1982. 'Youth in the Labour Market'. Research Paper No. 34. London: Department of Employment.

—— and Maguire, M.J. 1983. 'The Vanishing Youth Labour Market'. London: Youthaid.

—— and Maguire, M.J. 1986. 'Young Adults in the Labour Market'. Research Paper No. 55. London: Department of Employment.

—— and Maguire, M.J. 1988. 'Local Labour Markets and the Impact on the Life Chances of Youths'. *Young Careers.* Ed. Coles, R. Milton Keynes: Open University Press.

—— , Maguire, M.J. and Spilsbury, M. 1988. *Restructuring the Labour Market.* London: Macmillan.

Banks, M.H. and Jackson, P.R. 1982. 'Unemployment and Risk of Minor Psychiatric Disorders in Young People: Cross-sectional and Longitudinal Evidence'. *Psychological Medicine*, 11, 561–80.

Banks, O. 1955. *Parity and Prestige in English Secondary Education.* London: Routledge & Kegan Paul.

Bazalgette, J. 1978. *School Life and Work Life. A Study of the Transition in the Inner City.* London: Hutchinson.

Benstein, B. 1971, 1973. *Class, Codes and Control.* Volumes 1 and 2. London. Routledge & Kegan Paul.

Blackman, S.J. 1987. 'The Labour Market in School: New Vocationalism and Issues of Socially Ascribed Discrimination. *Education, Unemployment and Labour Markets.* Eds Brown, P. and Ashton, D.N. Lewes: Falmer Press.

Blau, P. and Duncan, O.D. 1969. *The American Occupational Structure.* New York: John Wiley.

Bourdieu, P. 1977. 'Cultural Reproduction and Social Reproduction'. *Power and Ideology in Education.* Eds Karabel, J. and Halsey, A.H. New York: Oxford University Press.

Bowles, S. and Gintis, H. 1976. *Schooling in Capitalist America.* London: Routledge & Kegan Paul.

Breen, R. 1984. 'Status Attainment or Job Attainment? The Effects of Sex and Class on Youth Unemployment'. *British Journal of Sociology*, 35 (September). 363–86.

Brown, P. 1987. *Schooling Ordinary Kids.* London: Tavistock.

Carter, M.P. 1962. *Home, School and Work.* London: Pergamon Press.

Church, A. and Ainley, P. 1987. 'Inner City Decline and Regeneration: Young People and the Labour Market in London's Docklands'. *Education, Unemployment and Labour Markets.* Eds Brown, P. and Ashton, D.N. Lewes: Falmer Press.

Cockburn, C. 1987. *Two-Track Training: Sex Inequalities and the YTS.* London: Macmillan.

Coffield, F., Borrill, S. and Marshall, S. 1986. *Growing Up at the Margins.* Milton Keynes: Open University Press.

Coles, R. 1986. 'School Leaver, Job Seeker, Dole Reaper: Young and Unemployed in Rural England'. *The Experience of Unemployment.* Eds Allen, S. et al. London: Macmillan.

Corrigan, P. 1979. *Schooling the Smash Street Kids.* London: Macmillan

Cross, M. 1987. 'Black Youth and YTS: The Policy Issues'. *Black Youth Futures.* Eds Cross, M. and Smith, D.I. Leicester: National Youth Bureau.

Deem, R. 1978. *Women and Schooling.* London: Routledge & Kegan Paul.

Dex, S. 1987. *Women's Occupational Mobility*. London: Macmillan.

Douglas, J.W.B. 1964. *The Home and the School*. London: MacGibbon & Kee.

Durkheim, E. 1964. *The Division of Labour*. London: Collier-Macmillan.

Eaglesham, E.J.R. 1967. *The Foundation of Twentieth-Century Education in England*. London: Routledge & Kegan Paul.

Elias, P. and Blanchflower, D.J. 1987. 'Who Gets the Jobs. Parental Background, Education, Work History as Factors in Early Career Formation'. Warwick: Institute for Employment Research.

Finn, D. 1987. *Training Without Jobs: New Deals and Broken Promises*. London: Macmillan.

Ford, J. 1969. *Social Class and the Comprehensive School*. London: Routledge & Kegan Paul.

Furlong, A. 1987. 'Coming to Terms with the Declining Demand for Youth Labour'. *Education, Unemployment and Labour Markets*. Eds Brown, P. and Ashton, D.N. Lewes: Falmer Press.

Gardner, P. 1984. *The Lost Elementary Schools of Victorian England*. London: Croom Helm.

Gordon, D.M., Edwards, R. and Reich, M. 1982. *Segmented Work, Divided Workers*. Cambridge: Cambridge University Press.

Glass, D.V. (ed.) 1954. *Social Mobility in Britain*. London: Routledge & Kegan Paul.

Griffin, C. 1985. *Typical Girls: Young Women from School to the Job Market*. London: Routledge & Kegan Paul.

Gurney, M. 1980. 'The Effects of Unemployment on the Psycho-social Development of School-leavers'. *Occupational Psychology*, 53, 205–13.

Halsey, A.H. Floud, J. and Anderson, C.A. (eds) 1961. *Education Economy and Society*. Glencoe, Ill: Free Press.

—— Heath, A.F. and Ridge, J.M. 1980. *Origins and Destinations: Family, Class, and Education in Modern Britain*. Oxford: Clarendon Press.

Hargreaves, D.H. 1967. *Social Relations in the Secondary School*. London: Routledge & Kegan Paul.

Heath, A.F. 1981. *Social Mobility*. Glasgow: Fontana.

Hendry, L.B., Raymond, M. and Stewart, C. 1984. 'Unemployment, School and Leisure: An Adolescent Study'. *Leisure Studies*, 3, 175–87.

Humphries, S.A. 1981. *Hooligans or Rebels?: An Oral History of Working Class Childhood and Youth, 1889–1939*. Oxford: Basil Blackwell.

Jenkins, R. 1983. *Lads, Citizens and Ordinary Kids*. London: Routledge & Kegan Paul.

—— and Troyna, B. 1983. 'Educational Myths and Labour Market Realities'. *Racism, School and the Labour Market*. Eds Troyna, B. and Smith D.I. Leicester: National Youth Bureau.

Jones, P. 1985. 'Qualifications and Labour Market Outcomes among 16-year Old School Leavers'. *British Journal of Guidance and Counselling*. 13.

Lee, D., Marsden, D., Hardey, M. and Penny, R. 1987. 'Youth Training, Life Chances and Orientations to Work: A Case Study of the Youth Training Scheme'. *Education, Unemployment and Labour Markets*. Eds Brown, P. and Ashton, D.N. Lewes: Falmer Press.

Livock, R. 1983. 'Screening in the Recruitment of Young Workers'. Research Paper No. 41. London: Department of Employment.

McPherson, A. and Willms, J.D. 1987. 'Equalisation and Improvement: Some Effects of Comprehensive Reorganisation in Scotland'. *Sociology*, 21 (November), 509–39.

McRobbie, A. 1978. 'Working Class Girls and the Culture of Femininity'. *Women Take Issue*. Ed. Women's Studies Group. London: Hutchinson.

Maizels, E.J. 1970. *Adolescent Needs and the Transition from School to Work*. London: Athlone Press.

Maurice, M., Sellier, F. and Silvertre, J. 1986. *The Social Foundations of Industrial Power*. London: MIT Press.

Marsden, D. 1986. *The End of Economic Man?* Brighton: Wheatsheaf.

Miller, D.C. and Form, W.H. 1951. *Industrial Sociology*. New York: Harper.

Payne, G. 1987. *Employment and Opportunity*. London: Macmillan.

Payne, J. 1985. 'Changes in the Youth Labour Market, 1974–1981'. *Oxford Review of Education*, 11, 167–79.

—— and Payne, C. 1985. 'Youth Unemployment 1974–1981: The Changing Importance of Age and Qualifications'. *Quarterly Journal of Social Affairs*, 1, 177–92.

—— 1986. 'Unemployment, Apprenticeships and Training – Does it Pay to Stay on at School?'. University of Oxford, Department of Social and Administrative Studies, mimeo.

Raffe, D. 1983. 'Can There be an Effective Youth Unemployment Policy?'. *In Place of Work*. Ed. Fiddy, D. Lewes: Falmer Press.

—— 1984. 'School Attainment and the Labour Market'. *Fourteen to Eighteen*. Ed. Raffe, D. Aberdeen: Aberdeen University Press.

—— 1986. 'Change and Continuity in the Youth Labour Market'. *The Experience of Unemployment*. Eds Allen, S. et al. London: Macmillan.

—— 1987a. 'Youth Unemployment in the United Kingdom 1979–84'. *Education, Unemployment and Labour Markets*. Eds Brown, P. and Ashton, D.N. Lewes: Falmer Press.

—— 1987b. 'The Context of the Youth Training Scheme: An Analysis of its Strategy and Development'. *British Journal of Education and Work*, 1: 1.

Rees, T. and Atkinson, P. 1982. *Youth Unemployment and State Intervention*. London: Routledge & Kegan Paul.

Roberts, K. 1975. 'The Developmental Theory of Occupational Choice: A Critique and an Alternative'. *People and Work*. Eds Esland, G., Salaman, G. and Speakman, M. Edinburgh: Holmes McDougall.

—— 1984. *School Leavers and their Prospect*. Milton Keynes: Open University Press.

—— Duggan, J. and Noble, M. 1981. 'Unregistered Youth Unemployment and Outreach Careers Work'. Research Paper No. 31. London: Department of Employment.

—— Noble, M. and Duggan, J. 1983. 'Young, Black and Out of Work'. *Racisms, School and the Labour Markets*. Eds Troyna, B. and Smith, D.I. Leicester: National Youth Bureau.

—— Dench, S. and Richardson, D. 1986. 'The Changing Structure of Youth Labour Markets'. Research Paper No. 59. London: Department of Employment.

Spilsbury, M. 1986. 'Individual Youth Unemployment and the Local Labour Market'. Working Paper No. 10. Leicester: Labour Market Studies.

Stern, E. and Turbin, J. 1986. *Youth Employment and Unemployment in Rural England*. London: Tavistock.

Troyna, B. and Smith, D.I. 1983. *Racism, School and the Labour Market*. Leicester: National Youth Bureau.

Wallace, C. 1987. 'From Generation to Generation: The Effects of Employment and Unemployment Upon the Domestic Life Cycle of Young Adults'. *Education, Unemployment and Labour Markets*. Eds Brown, P. and Ashton, D.N. Lewes: Falmer Press.

Warr, P. 1983. 'Work, Jobs and Unemployment'. *Bulletin of the British Psychological Society*, 36, 305–11.

Watts, A. 1983. *Education, Unemployment and the Future of Work*. Milton Keynes: Open University Press.

West, M. and Newton, P. 1983. *The Transition from School to Work*. Beckenham: Croom Helm.

Wilkinson, F. (ed.) 1981. *The Dynamics of Labour Market Segmentation*. London: Academic Press.

Willis, P. 1977. *Learning to Labour*. Farnborough: Saxon House.

Wolverhampton Youth Review. 1985. *The Social Condition of Young People in Wolverhampton in 1984*. Wolverhampton: Wolverhampton Borough Council.

PART III
Economic Change and Collective Organization

15 Ownership and Employer Control

John Scott

The large business enterprise is such a powerful force in people's lives that it has been a persistent subject of study by sociologists and economists. For many years, however, it has been assumed – even by many radical writers – that the control which employers can exercise over their work-force no longer rests upon share ownership. In consequence, the enterprise has been studied as a system of bureaucratic administration and as an unproblematic 'black box' from which rational market decisions emanate. This has been associated with a widely held belief that the business enterprise is no longer a *capitalist* enterprise: industrial society is a 'managerial' society. Marxist writers have, of course, rejected the claim that the capitalist enterprise has disappeared, but many Marxists have accepted that the issue of ownership is irrelevant to understanding the behaviour of large business enterprises. Whether controlled by 'owners' or 'managers', it is argued, the capitalist enterprise acts strictly in response to market forces. Control over the labour process can be studied as an inexorable consequence of capitalist development rather than in relation to varying forms of owner participation and control. Some Marxists, have proposed that ownership remains of crucial importance for employer control. These writers have claimed that the modern business enterprise is subject to the ownership and control of banks and bankers.

Thus, sociology and economics have come to be characterized by an implicit and taken-for-granted managerialism, countered principally by Marxist theories of bank control. I wish to argue that these are not the only alternatives open to us. Ownership, if properly understood, is an important issue for theoreticians and researchers interested in studying market, work and employment relations. The aim of this chapter is to review the debates surrounding this issue and to document an alternative approach to property ownership and control.

The Managerial Revolution and Social Theory

Despite Burnham's (1941) flamboyant and unconvincing statement of a theory of the 'managerial revolution', there has been a very widespread acceptance of a looser and narrower conception of the growth of management power. The research agenda of Berle and Means (1932) established the concept of 'management control' as the counterpoint to all forms of 'owner control', and by 1961 Florence (1961: 187) felt able to conclude that there were strong signs of a 'managerial evolution' in Britain. A stronger case was put for the USA, where a leading researcher claimed that 'it would appear that Berle and Means in 1929 were observing a "managerial revolution" in process. Now, thirty years later, that revolution seems close to complete' (Larner, 1966: 786–7). The clearest academic expressions of this thesis were those of Bell (1961) and Galbraith (1967). While Bell postulated the end of family capitalism alongside the end of ideology, Galbraith claimed that a managerial 'technostructure' now held sway in all the major business enterprises. Kerr and his associates embodied such assumptions in their theory of industrial convergence, which held that the inexorable trend in all industrial societies was towards the establishment of management control and an economic system which would shape the whole of the social structure in its own image. The nature of industrial technology was such as to require management control of industry and a pluralistic structure of political power (Kerr et al., 1960).

This set of assumptions became embodied in the mainstream writings of both sociology and economics, though their emphases and conclusions varied. For many sociologists, the managerial revolution was seen as involving a move away from the narrow criterion of profitability, to which capitalist owners had been committed, and towards a conception of the 'social responsibility' of business leadership. The declining significance of shareholders in terms of the *control* that they are able to exercise over business affairs, it is held, is reflected in the declining significance of shareholder *interests* for business practice. Managers are able to 'judge society's needs in a more conscious fashion . . . on the basis of some explicit conception of the "public interest" ' (Bell, 1974: 284). Economists, on the other hand, have tended to argue that the decline of shareholder control has led to a shift in business motivation from profit maximization to such things as growth and managerial remuneration. Managers pursue the sectional interests of their enterprise, their department, and their personal career, and this leads them to plough back profits in order to build up large and rapidly growing enterprises (Baumol, 1959; Marris, 1964). The common theme in both the 'sectionalist' and the 'non-sectionalist' variants of managerialism (Nichols, 1969) is the claim that professional managers pursue goals which are fundamentally at variance with those traditionally imputed to the capitalist.

Such arguments had important political consequences and were supportive of widely held beliefs among politicians and business men that old style capitalism was dead. Indeed, managerialist claims were the counterpart of the assumption of working-class 'embourgeoisement' (Zweig, 1952): the capitalist class of property owners, like the traditional proletariat, had become a declining social force of marginal political importance for many commentators. Britain's leading Fabian writer, for example, argued that power in industry had shifted into the hands of meritocratic career managers, and he concluded that the Labour Party should abandon its assumption of class warfare and seek to attract the electoral support of both the technically qualified managers and the newly affluent workers (Crosland, 1956). When in power, the Labour Party should seek to ensure that the state intervenes in the economy in such a way as to promote what Harold Wilson called the 'white heat of the technological revolution'. The technocratic managers were the agents of this revolution, and they should ensure that the consequent benefits of economic growth were widely shared.

Such beliefs have become progressively more difficult to sustain in a climate of economic decline and high unemployment, and their intellectual foundations have, in part, been challenged. The thesis of 'embourgeoisement' has been largely discredited by sustained critique and by the accumulation of contrary evidence (Goldthorpe et al., 1969; Marshall et al., 1988). The managerialist thesis, on the other hand, has survived largely intact. This survival reflects the apparent solidity of the original research of Berle and Means, which was largely responsible for the acceptance of 'management control' as an established fact. Despite the careful dissection of Burch (1972) and the devastating critique of Zeitlin (1974), the empirical basis of the claims made by Berle and Means have been widely ignored. As a result, managerialism prevails in many areas of the social sciences, and those few who do recognize its inadequacies have generally failed to pursue the implications of any of the alternative models of business organization which have emerged in the wake of Zeitlin's critique. In the light of the continued salience of the managerialist thesis, it is important to understand just what Berle and Means were claiming and exactly where they went wrong.

Theoretical Perspectives

The Managerialist Position

Berle and Means (1932) see the problem of control as one which arises with the expansion of joint stock enterprise in manufacturing and commerce. The joint stock company is the legal form through which the bulk of the modern business enterprises are organized. Whereas traditional enterprise was limited by the scale of the entrepreneur's own resources, the company form of organization allows enterprises to draw upon the resources of a large pool of investors. The capital of the enterprise comprises the funds which these investors jointly subscribe in the form of 'stocks' and 'shares'. Each investor has ownership rights in a particular number of shares in the company, but ownership of the business assets themselves is vested in the company. Berle and Means argue that this marks a 'dissolution' of traditional property rights, a separation of the 'passive' rights of the investor from the 'active' right to control the assets and operations of the company. The shareholder has purely nominal ownership rights in anything other than a share certificate; the only legally enforceable rights which a shareholder possesses are the rights to a dividend income from his or her investment and a corresponding right to a vote in the choice of the directors of the company (Berle and Means, 1932: 433ff.).

It is this voting right which constitutes the sole link between the shareholder and the powers of effective control over business affairs which are embodied in the board of directors and the executives which they appoint. Where one individual, or a group such as a family, own all the shares of a joint stock company, their voting rights give them equivalent powers of personal control to those exercised by the traditional owner-entrepreneur; all that has changed is that these powers are mediated through the legal form of joint stock capital. Berle and Means designate such control 'private ownership'. If the owner, or owners, of the shares of a privately owned company sell some of their holding or fail to buy all the new shares which the company issues to finance its activities, their percentage holding will fall and they will have mere 'majority ownership'. In practice, Berle and Means feel, the effective power associated with private ownership does not disappear until the controlling holding falls below 80 per cent, and it is only after this that the majority owners must begin to take some account of the wishes and interests of the other shareholders. So long as the dominant group holds a majority of the shares, however, they can be sure of carrying the day in any corporate decisions which come to a vote, and so majority ownership involves little real separation of nominal from effective ownership. This separation is a potential contained within the legal form of the joint stock company, and is realized in its fullest form only when no individual or group holds a majority of the shares.

It was of central importance to the argument of Berle and Means for them to show that the complete separation of the owners from control did not occur immediately that their holding fell below 50 per cent. There was no certainty that such shareholders would win each and every vote, but neither was there any certainty that they would lose. There was, in fact, a grey area of uncertainty between majority ownership and complete separation, and this was termed 'minority control' by Bere and Means. A situation of minority control exists where an individual or group holding less than 50 per cent of the shares has *de facto* 'working control' because of the absence of any other holdings large enough to oppose them. That is to say, any rivals have insufficient shares to mobilize a vote against the minority controllers. But the fact that a rival group may be able to gain sufficient support from 'uncommitted' shareholders to outvote the minority controllers means that a minority holding is a precarious basis for control.

Where the degree of dispersal in the ownership of the shares of a company is such that no individual or group is able to exercise the powers of minority control, Berle and Means talk of 'management control'. Control is dissociated from share ownership altogether, and passes to those who lack a substantial shareholding in the company. For the purposes of their research, Berle and Means set the threshold between minority and management control at 20 per cent. Below this level, they argue, the largest shareholder is simply one of a number of countervailing shareholders, no one of which can dominate the others. They go further than this, however, in arguing that in enterprises which have reached this stage it will typically be the case that no single shareholder will have anything approaching 20 per cent and that there will be simply an anonymous mass of small shareholders. Such shareholders can no longer be regarded as 'capitalists', as their sole remaining right to participate in corporate affairs – the right to vote at an Annual General Meeting – is all but worthless. Their vote is one in a large sea of votes and they can have no real control; ownership has been effectively separated from control and the shareholders have been left with only their right to a regular dividend. As a result, argue Berle and Means, the board of directors becomes a self-perpetuating group insulated from the pressures of ownership, and, while bankers and other 'outsiders' may be recruited to the board, the internal career managers are the most likely contenders to rise up and fill the power vacuum created by the absence of controlling shareholders.

Berle and Means demarcated minority from management control on the basis of a specified threshold level of shareholding, but this decision was made for practical research purposes and they recognized that its application to particular cases might be arbitrary. Although they saw the security of minority control as dependent upon the dynamics of the distribution of the vote, they were faced with the need for a general yardstick to apply in their research. The decision to follow this procedure is understandable when information on the overall distribution of shares is unavailable, but it has proved to be one of the most controversial elements in their thesis. Critics of the concept of management control have been able to argue that the effective threshold is much lower than the level at which it was set by Berle and Means. By lowering the threshold they have, definitionally, reduced the number of companies classified as subject to management control. The most commonly adopted threshold level in recent research has been 10 per cent. By suggesting that minority control is possible with a very low percentage shareholding – some have suggested as low as 5 per cent (Burch, 1972) – these critics have sought to defuse the managerialist thesis by enlarging the grey area between majority ownership and the complete separation of ownership from control. The price that has been paid, however, has been failure to reconsider the centrepiece of the Berle and Means thesis: the concept of management control itself. It will be shown in the following section that this is a precondition of fruitful research.

The central claim of Berle and Means – a claim which they believed that they had documented in their research – was the contention that the USA (and, by implication, all other capitalist societies) was undergoing a historical transformation in which the control of business operations was passing from private and majority ownership to management control, and that a transitional period such as they were studying would exhibit a mixture of all forms of control. Their research reported that only 11 per cent of the top 200 enterprises of 1929 were subject to private or majority ownership. Already 44 per cent were subject to management control, and the number was increasing (Berle and Means, 1932: 106). Such was the inevitability of this process that they felt themselves to be witnessing the demise of capitalism and the capitalist class.

John Scott

The Marxist Critique

The most systematic alternatives to managerialism have come from within the Marxist tradition, though these have not generally involved direct confrontation with the arguments of Berle and Means. Management control has, in general, been regarded as irrelevant or unimportant. Those who have rejected the thesis of the separation of ownership from control have argued that old style capitalist ownership has been supplemented by newer forms of 'bank control', which have reinforced the dominance of capital over production. Those who have accepted the idea that 'owners' have been displaced by 'managers' have gone on to claim that this has involved no departure from the criterion of profit maximization and that the expertise and professionalism of managers have been placed in the service of profitability. In either case, the logic of capital accumulation prevails. While the 'Marxist managerialism' of Baran and Sweezy (1966) has been an important influence on researchers, the predominant viewpoint has involved an acceptance of one or another variant of the model of 'finance capital' first formulated by Hilferding (1910).

According to Hilferding, the expanding scale of production means that enterprises grow beyond the ability of their individual owners to finance their operations and so have recourse to the stock exchange and the banking system, an assumption shared with the managerialist position. But Hilferding argues that a small circle of 'finance capitalists' who occupy key positions in the financial system are able to exercise virtually all the powers inherent in the capital mobilized. Individual capitalist owners are, indeed, squeezed out of positions of control, but they are replaced not by professional career managers but by the finance capitalists who embody the system of monopoly capital. Both industry and banking become progressively monopolized through increasing size and through the establishment of cartels, trusts, and interlocking directorships, and the two sectors become fused into a single system of 'finance capital'. Through the system of finance capital, enterprises become tied into financial groups, within each of which enterprises from banking, insurance, commerce and manufacturing are brought together and operated as a single unit of capital. As a result, the system of finance capital is structured into a number of competing financial groups, whose interplay determines the overall development of the economy.

Hilferding saw banks as the key institutions in the system of finance capital, both through their lending operations and through their direct share ownership, but a number of more recent Marxist writers have taken this further. They have argued that banks act as centres of control within the financial groups and are able to ensure that the activities of the enterprises which they control are guided in the interests of the banks. This position postulates a fundamental conflict of interest between 'banks' and 'industry' with the latter subordinate to the former, and has often involved the claim that the banks themselves remain subject to control by the major capitalist families. The link between ownership and control has not so much been broken as transformed, and now operates through a chain of intermediaries. In the USA, writers such as Rochester (1936) and Perlo (1957) have posited the existence of bank-centred financial groups controlled by such families as Morgan, Rockefeller, and Mellon, while the British Marxist Aaronovitch (1955) has claimed that the City of London is the hub of a system of finance capital divided into financial groups centred around the major clearing and merchant banks.

Zeitlin's (1974) critique of managerialism drew heavily on this Marxist position, and attempted to outline more fully the mechanisms of bank control. His argument was that the dispersal of share ownership observed by Berle and Means had been replaced by a move back towards share concentration, but that the shareholders in whose hands the shares had become concentrated were not individuals and families but financial intermediaries such as banks, insurance companies and pension funds. Banks, argues Zeitlin, play a key role as trustees and managers of insurance and pension funds, and so come to control large blocks of shares in virtually all large business enterprises. As more and more shares come into the hands of the banks, so the level of control which they can exercise over business operations increases. Where Zeitlin and similar writers such as Kotz (1978) differ from the earlier advocates of bank control is in their recognition that it may often be necessary for two or more banks to co-operate in order to mobilize a controlling block. The system of finance capital, it is argued, involves the coexistence of financial groups subject to bank control and 'independent' enterprises controlled by coalitions of banks.

A major problem with this position, however, is an implicit assumption that the distinction between 'management control' and 'minority control' can be used in the way in which it was originally formulated by Berle and Means. Whereas Berle and Means argued that there was a move from minority to management control, their critics have argued that there has been a move back from management to minority control. The marxist critics of managerialism as an *empirical* thesis have not questioned its *conceptual* basis: they have not asked whether new concepts may be required to supplement the original schema. A more satisfactory alternative to managerialism must reconsider the conceptual basis of the whole debate.

An Alternative to Marxism and Managerialism

The evidence to be reviewed later in this chapter will show that there has been a general move away from personal forms of ownership and towards more impersonal forms in all the major capitalist economies. While individuals and families have, in a number of cases, been able to maintain or attain control of large enterprises through their personal shareholdings, a greater and greater proportion of company shares have come into the hands of corporate shareholders and financial intermediaries. As a result, chains of intercorporate shareholdings tie enterprises together into a largely depersonalized structure of property ownership. There is an element of truth in the argument that *personal* ownership has become increasingly separated from corporate control. At the same time, there is much truth in the view that a system of 'finance capital' prevails in the major capitalist economies. But this claim must be separated from the argument that the impersonal possession characteristic of finance capital always and necessarily involves the control of banks over industry. Indeed, the most characteristic pattern of impersonal possession is one in which banks play an important but not overwhelming role, though the system of finance capital in Britain and the USA involves the generalized hegemony of 'institutional' shareholders.

Any comparative account of corporate control must recognize that, while there are certain uniformities of technology and business practice in all the major capitalist economies, there are equally important divergencies arising from specific historical experiences and differing cultural and legal system. These national variations shape the constraints which operate on the actions and orientations of business leaders and result in the existence of a number of alternative patterns of capitalist development. The pattern taken by impersonal possession in Britain, the USA and certain other economies is to be seen as the outcome of a specific convergence of national and international forces in the Anglo-American, English-speaking world. In other parts of the world, and under the impact of other forces, different patterns of impersonal possession will be apparent.

In order to develop this thesis more fully, some of the more important inadequacies in the conventional understanding of minority and management control must be reviewed.[1] In the discussion which follows, a threshold level of 10 per cent is assumed, below which level minority control is not generally possible. This assumption has been justified elsewhere (Scott, 1986: 54–65). The concept of management control, as outline by Berle and Means, involved a claim that, as share ownership became more and more dispersed, the internal managers of an enterprise would achieve a greater autonomy from the interests and influence of its numerous individual shareholders. Management control exists where no individual or group of associates holds sufficient shares to exercise any real influence over the managers. The concept of minority control, on the other hand, depends upon the existence of a small group of shareholders who are willing and able to determine the composition of the board of directors and, therefore, to shape the decisions which are made by the directors and top management. Where financial intermediaries become the holders of large numbers of shares, and play an additional role through their lending operations, neither of these conditions holds and a new concept is required to grasp the mechanisms of corporate control.

The concept which has been introduced to apply to just such circumstances is 'control through a constellation of interests' (Scott, 1985: 49–51). This concept describes the situation in which a small but diverse group of corporate shareholders owns sufficient shares to exercise minority control, but does not have the capacity or willingness to act in concert which this requires. This group of shareholding interests does not constitute a unified coalition of associates, but neither does it constitute an anonymous mass of small shareholders. The dominant shareholders comprise a diverse

1 The discussion which follows draws upon Scott (1985: ch. 2 ; 1986: ch. 2).

constellation of capitalist interests, whose conflicting interests provide the space for some autonomy on the part of directors and top executives. On the other hand, their inability to sustain long-term co-operation does not mean that the members of the constellation are not able to achieve enough co-operation to determine the composition of the board of directors and to supervise its activities (Scott, 1986: 54–7). Following Florence's (1961) argument, the concept of control through a constellation of interests has been operationalized as that situation in which the twenty largest shareholders in an enterprise collectively hold 10 per cent or more of the shares, but where no individual shareholder has sufficient shares to exercise minority control. This, it will be shown, is the characteristic form of impersonal possession in the Anglo-American economies of Britain, the USA, Canada, Australia and New Zealand, where share ownership is structured by the hegemonic role of financial intermediaries.

The situation just described depends upon the existence of large corporate shareholders in competition with one another, and the concept of control through a constellation of interests will not be appropriate where this condition does not hold. For enterprises whose largest shareholders are non-competing *coalitions* of associates the category of minority control may sometimes be appropriate. But, where these coalitions are involved in circular chains of mutual shareholding, reinforced by preferential trading, joint ventures and mutual lending arrangements, an alternative concept is required. Such a situation corresponds closely to the 'financial group' depicted in Marxist theories, and the form of impersonal possession which it involves must be clearly distinguished both from control through a constellation of interests and from minority control. The concept of 'aligned interests' has been proposed (Scott, 1985: 146) to designate the situation where controlling blocks are held by coalitions of industrial and financial associates, each member of which is itself controlled by the remaining members of the coalition. The coalitions, therefore, form co-ordinated groups of enterprises in which there may or may not be a dominant enterprise. It will be shown that this concept has little application to the largest enterprises in Britain and the USA. In Japan, however, the dominant form of corporate control involves acephalous coalitions of aligned interests.

Control through a constellation of interests and control by coalitions of aligned interests are the two main forms taken by impersonal possession. Together, these concepts supplement the battery of concepts bequeathed to researchers by Berle and Means, and they make possible a comparative investigation of ownership and employer control. In the following sections, the patterns of control which can be found in the major capitalist economies will be explored.

Ownership and Employer Control in Britain

The only sustained investigation into the ownership and control of British companies has, until recently, been that of Florence (1961), who undertook his investigations in the 1930s and 1950s and sought evidence of

TABLE 15.1   *Type of controller in Britain (1976)*

Type of controller	Number of companies
Personal	46
British corporate	25
Foreign corporate	43
State	18
Mixed	10
No dominant interest	108
Total	250

Source: Project data. The 'top 250' companies analysed are the 200 largest non-financials (ranked by turnover) and the largest financials in each of a number of sectors (ranked by assets)

any trends over that period. Only since the late 1960s has the issue been accorded any real importance in economies or industrial sociology, and it is only in the 1980s that there has been any serious attempt to explore the implications of the massive growth in 'institutional' share ownership in the post-war period. Nevertheless, it is possible to piece together an account of trends in the first part of the century and to combine this with the results of the major study which was carried out in order to update and extend the work of Florence (Scott, 1986).

The broad picture of corporate control today is clear enough: in over a half of the largest enterprises there is a single controlling interest, and in the remainder there is some form of impersonal possession. Outside the system of impersonal possession the controlling interests comprise the families, entrepreneurs and tycoons which make up the surviving elements of 'personal possession' in the British economy, together with corporate controllers and the state. As can be seen in table 15.1, in the 250 largest enterprises of 1976 there were forty-six enterprises controlled by families and individuals, forty-three controlled by foreign corporations, twenty-five controlled by other British corporations, and eighteen controlled by the state – and a further ten were controlled by mixed alliances of entrepreneurial, corporate and state capital (Scott, 1986; table 4.2).

The public sector comprises large public corporations as well as joint stock companies in which ministries and state agencies are the dominant shareholders, though the extent of state control has been reduced through the denationalization of state assets. By 1988 this 'privatization' had affected British Airways, British Gas, British Telecom (formerly an integral part of the Post Office) and National Freight. The dismantling of the National Enterprise Board and the sale of its subsidiaries, such as Rolls-Royce, further diminished the state sector of the economy. The largest block of foreign corporate capital was American, companies based in the USA owning a half of the large foreign-owned enterprises operating in Britain in 1976. Next in importance in the foreign sector was the European block, with French interests predominating through the ownership of such companies as Michelin, Total and Louis Dreyfus, as well as through

TABLE 15.2   *Modes of control in Britain (1976)*

Mode of control	Number of companies
Public corporations	13
Majority control	78
Minority control	51
Non-proprietary	8
Constellation of interests	100
Total	250

Source: Project data. 'Non-proprietary' refers to building societies and mutual insurance companies which have no share capital *per se* and are controlled by their depositors and policy holders

holdings in Lead Industries and Cavenham. The only other countries in which two or more controlling interests were based were Canada and South Africa.[2] While foreign capital was predominantly involved in the manufacturing sector (especially in vehicles, metals, electronics and chemicals) and in oil distribution, British corporate controllers prevailed in the financial sector. More than this, the British corporate controllers were themselves financial enterprises. The big clearing banks were involved in exclusive and shared control of Scottish and overseas banks, specialist banking and investment companies and overseas trading enterprises.

Berle and Means (1932) distinguished 'ultimate' from 'immediate' control in an attempt to deal with the true control status of those enterprises which had other enterprises as their dominant controllers. It is clear that where an enterprise is subject to the immediate control of another enterprise it is important to push the analysis back to the ultimate controllers of the parent itself. There are often insuperable problems of data availability in discovering the ownership of foreign parents, but it was discovered that the majority of the American and European parents in the 1976 study were themselves characterized by forms of impersonal rather than personal possession. This implies that when an international perspective is taken the significance of impersonal possession is greater than is apparent from analyses limited to particular national economies.

Entrepreneurial capital of various kinds was especially important in the financial and commercial sectors (especially merchant banking and retail distribution), in construction, and in food and drink. Very few family-controlled enterprises operated in the mainstream of manufacturing industry. Enterprises controlled by personal interests were evenly divided between the categories of majority and minority control, and comprised a mixture of both 'old' and 'new' capital. Some minority-controlled enterprises, for example, could be seen as the surviving residue of enterprises which were, at one time, wholly owned by their controlling

2 Shell and Unilever were parts of Anglo-Dutch combined enterprises, but were not themselves foreign owned.

families. Guinness, Rowntree Mackintosh, W.H. Smith, Whitbread and Pilkington, for example, could all be seen in this light, and they might be expected to show a continued long-term decline in the proportional size of the family holding. Many enterprises now subject to impersonal possession are the end result of just such a process of dispersal and dilution. On the other hand, there is considerable evidence that, despite the expectations of the proponents of the managerialist thesis, new entrepreneurs have been able to acquire substantial controlling holdings in large enterprises and that new family firms have been established. Typical of these were Tesco, Ladbroke, GUS, Marley and Lonrho. A number of old family-controlled enterprises have shown little or no sign of any dispersal in the family holding: the Baring and Rothschild banks, for example, remained wholly owned by their families, as they had been in the eighteenth century.

Tables 15.1 and 15.2 summarize these conclusions. One hundred of those enterprises with no single controlling interest can be characterized by the dispersed form of ownership control called 'control through a constellation of interests'. The extent of share concentration in these enterprises is not such that minority control can be exercised by a single shareholder, or even by a coalition, but neither is the level of dispersal as great as is required by Berle and Means's concept of management control. The present level of dispersal results from the massive growth in institutional funds since the inter-war period, and especially after the Second World War. Insurance companies, investment trusts, unit trusts, and, most recently, pension funds bought company shares on a large scale at precisely the time when many enterprises were growing beyond the bounds of the capital which could be subscribed by their controlling families.

In the late nineteenth century and before the First World War, the majority of large enterprises were family owned. The large banks, insurance companies, railways and industrials which were not owned by particular families or family groups were owned by syndicates of family-owned financials or by coalitions of large shareholding families. A gradual dispersal of shareholdings occurred as many of these families reduced or diversified their holdings and it is clear that the predominant pattern was a U-curve of dispersal followed by reconcentration. In the financial and transport sectors, family control weakened early in the century and their shares remained relatively dispersed until the rapid growth of institutional funds in the post-war period. Family holdings in manufacturing and commercial enterprises were diluted much later – mainly during the inter-war years – but these enterprises experienced the same post-war reconcentration of shareholding (Scott, 1986: 96–8).

Families sought to spread their investments by reducing their dependence on particular enterprises, and once their stake in a 'family firm' had fallen below the majority level the barrier to further reduction was broken. A large number of family enterprises, however, survived until well into the 1950s, only the challenge of American competition forcing reconstructions which pushed many families into the back seat. As a result, many of the former controlling families became *rentiers* with a much attenuated participation in the control of the enterprises which they once owned. The shares

TABLE 15.3   *The controlling constellation of General Electric (1976)*

Shareholder		%
1	Prudential Assurance	6.5
2	Weinstock and allied families	2.8
3	Commercial Union Assurance	1.4
4	National Coal Board	1.3
5	Imperial Chemical Industries	1.2
	Top 5	13.2
6	Royal Insurance	1.0
7	Standard Life Assurance	1.0
8	Co-operative group	0.9
9	Pearl Assurance	0.9
10	Royal London Mutual Insurance	0.8
	Top 10	17.8
11	'Shell' Transport and Trading	0.6
12	Norwich Union	0.6
13	Morgan-Grenfell	0.6
14	Legal and General Assurance	0.6
15	N.M. Rothschild	0.6
	Top 15	20.8
16	Britannic Assurance	0.6
17	British Steel	0.6
18	Mercury Securities	0.6
19	Robeco group, Netherlands	0.6
20	Unilever	0.6
Total of top 20 shareholders		23.8

Source: Scott, 1984 (figures are rounded from the original source)

which were sold by these families came into the hands of the institutional funds which had, by the 1950s, become the dominant force in the stock market. In 1957 the proportion of all company shares held by individuals and families was still at the relatively high level of 66 per cent, but by 1975 this had fallen to 38 per cent. By the beginning of the 1980s personal share ownership had fallen below 30 per cent, and by 1984 it stood at 22 per cent. Over the period 1957–81 the proportion of shares held by insurance companies had risen from 9 per cent to 21 per cent, and the proportion held by pension funds rose from 3 per cent to 27 per cent (Scott, 1985: table 16). Many of the largest enterprises, therefore, became subject to the control of the diverse group of competing financial institutions which comprised their major shareholders. In other enterprises the institutional funds became essential supports of the surviving blocks of family ownership and influence.

The outcome of this process is a situation of dispersed ownership in which the twenty largest shareholders in an enterprise collectively occupy a dominant position in the ownership of the voting shares, the remaining thousands of shareholders each owning only minute fractional parts (Scott, 1986: table 5.2). In 1976 there was no enterprise among the hundred in question which had less than 10 per cent of its shares held by the twenty largest shareholders, but there was no enterprise in which they held more than 50 per cent. The largest single shareholder in such an enterprise, invariably the Prudential Assurance, would normally have a direct stake of between 2 per cent and 6 per cent – generally around 2 or 3 per cent – and the smallest participant in the twenty member constellation would normally hold around 0.4 per cent or 0.5 per cent. Shareholdings outside this 'top twenty' tail off rapidly to negligible levels, and it is clear that Florence was correct in seeing the twenty largest voting shareholders as the crucial group in corporate control. Enterprises which were controlled through constellations of interests in 1976 included many of the very largest British enterprises: for example, Barclays, Lloyds, Midland Bank, National Westminster, Prudential and Commercial Union in the financial sector and ICI, Imperial Group, Shell, GEC and Boots in the non-financial sector.[3]

An example can illustrate the balance of power among the top twenty shareholders of such an enterprise (see table 15.3). GEC's controlling constellation held 23.8 per cent of its shares, putting it into the modal category of dispersed ownership: in sixty-one of the hundred enterprises the top twenty held between 20 per cent and 29 per cent. Insurance companies, led by the Prudential, held 14.3 per cent of GEC's voting capital, while the pension funds of non-financial enterprises held 4.3 per cent; the remainder of the institutional holdings were those of merchant banks and investment trust groups. But any such classification must be treated with care, as a number of the large insurance companies and all the merchant banks were engaged in pension management business. Indeed, the substantial growth in bank holdings observed in many enterprises is largely due to their involvement in the running of pension schemes and other trustee business on behalf of their clients. Although the names of the 'big four' clearing banks (Barclays, Lloyds, Midland, National Westminster) did not appear among GEC's largest shareholders, they held, for example, 3.3 per cent of AE, 2.0 per cent of Chloride Group, 2.7 per cent of Imperial Group, 2.0 per cent of Prudential Assurance and 2.4 per cent of Tarmac. The big four banks were also substantial holders of their own capital, holding 1.4 per cent of Barclays, 1.1 per cent of Lloyds, 1.7 per cent of Midland and 0.5 per cent of National Westminster.[4] It is, therefore, the institutional funds of the insurance, pension and investment sector, whatever the names under which they appear, which predominate in the ownership of companies with dispersed capital, and the current changes in the City of London – discussed more fully below – are reinforcing this trend by creating large diversified financial conglomerates involved in all spheres of banking and fund management.

It is important to realize, however, that GEC's controlling constellation includes a substantial 'family' shareholding. Sir Arnold Weinstock, now

3 Full details of the large shareholders in the 100 companies can be found in Scott (1984). In addition to the case of GEC discussed in this chapter, certain other lists have been published: that for Imperial Group can be found in Scott (1986: table 5.2, 94), and those for ICI and Prudential Assurance in Scott (1985: table 19, 82).

4 The holdings counted in these totals are only those which appear among the twenty largest shareholders in each company.

Lord Weinstock, was GEC's chief executive and inherited a stake in one of the constituent companies of GEC. In 1976 he and his family held 2.8 per cent of the shares in his own name and in a number of trustee accounts, and it is believed that some of the holdings managed by Morgan Grenfell were also those of his family.[5] This ability of a family to retain considerable influence over the control of an enterprise with a substantially reduced shareholding stake is far from unusual in business: one-third of the one hundred enterprises with dispersed ownership had family participants in their controlling constellations, and the bulk of these families also had at least one seat on the board of directors. The total figure for both family *control* (majority or minority) and family *participation* in the controlling constellations was eighty-five in the top 250 enterprises, a remarkably high figure in the face of the expectations of the managerialist thesis (Scott, 1986: 75–8).

The system of impersonal possession in Britain, therefore, takes the form of control through a constellation of interests, with a substantial level of family participation. The system is dominated by institutional funds, and families have retained a considerable role in this key sector. Seven merchant banks, all involved in fund management, were controlled by family groups, often of long standing (Baring, Fleming, Rothschild, Hambro, Kleinwort, Warburg, Samuel). Families had control or influence in other enterprises with a fund management role, operating mainly in the insurance and insurance broking sectors. The two sectors of entrepreneurial capital and impersonal possession are interdependent, and it would be misleading to regard them as sharply separated. Families are constantly reducing their ownership stakes, most typically as the result of a company takeover which leaves them with a smaller stake in a larger enterprise. At the same time, other enterprises are being built up or acquired by new entrepreneurs or tycoons concerned to establish a patrimony which can be passed on to their heirs. There seems no reason to believe that the level of family control and influence will fall substantially below its present level, unless something radical happens in the legal and political environment in which British business operates. Short of radical changes in the system of wealth taxation or a deliberate government policy of dispossession, for example, it is difficult to see how or why there should be any further secular decline in family control. The composition of the sector may alter over time, but its size should remain constant.

The decline in personal shareholdings has been largely at the expense of the small and medium-sized shareholder. Although the publicity campaigns associated with the privatization of state shareholdings has resulted in an increase in the number of individuals who hold shares, the rump of private shareholdings is largely in the hands of Britain's wealthiest families. Most of the 'new' personal shareholders in such privatized companies as British Telecom and British Gas hold very small numbers of shares, and many shares issued to individuals were rapidly sold again in the stock market. Big financial intermediaries were willing buyers of these shares as additions to their long-term portfolios, while individual

5 These Weinstock family holdings include those in the name of the Sobell family.

shareholders were willing sellers attracted by a short-term capital gain. There is no sign that those individuals who have been encouraged to speculate on a privatization issue were subsequently attracted to long-term stock exchange investment. Gambling on the re-sale of privatized shares is regarded as a one-off speculation, in much the same way as many people regard a bet on the Grand National (Labour Research, 1987: 7–8) The concentration of shareholdings in institutional hands has, paradoxically, helped to concentrate the remaining personally owned shares in the hands of the wealthy. The unity of interest between the institutional funds and their managers, on the one hand, and the wealthy *rentier* families, on the other, can clearly be seen in the patterns of recruitment to the boards of directors of companies operating in the sector of impersonal possession.

The boards of large business enterprises embody the 'dominant coalition' (Child, 1972) which exercises active business leadership within the constraints set by the capital and property markets. Active business leadership involves the exercise of 'strategic control', participation in the making of the decisions which set or alter the basic structural parameters within which a particular enterprise must act. Strategic issues concern such matters as patterns of product investment, executive recruitment, company acquisitions, and reconstructions, and these have increasingly come to be differentiated from the lower level operational decisions involved in the implementation of a strategy (Scott, 1985: 44–5, chapter 6 passim). The tasks undertaken by directors, therefore go beyond the minimum legal requirements of ensuring that a company meets its obligations under company law, and the board of directors is an arena within which struggles to determine strategic decisions take place. Leading shareholders, providers of credit, and internal executives all have an interest in the fate of the particular enterprises with which they are associated. These protagonists seek to enhance their positions by securing the election of themselves and of sympathetic outsiders to company boards and by furthering their interests once elected.

While it is undoubtedly true that overt boardroom struggles are rare – though perhaps increasing in number – it is important to appreciate the role played by the presence of a latent conflict of interest among these contenders for control. Recruitment to the board reflects the struggle, antagonism and competition between shareholders financiers and executives; and corporate strategy is an outcome of the balance of power which they are able to establish among themselves. It is in this sense that one must talk of control *through* a constellation of interests: the board has an autonomy which is not possible when there are majority or minority shareholders, but those who seek to participate in the decision-making powers of the board must take account of the wishes and interests of the constellation of leading shareholders. In order to monitor and supervise board decision-making, one or more of these shareholders may seek to be represented on the board and will try to build up support from other leading shareholders and from those who are already board members. In many circumstances, however, shareholders will not seek such direct representation but will be happy so long as the board includes a number of people of accepted standing in the financial world and on whom it is felt they can rely. For this reason, bank directors – whether executives of a bank or industrial executives who sit on a bank board – are in great demand by company boards. To be a director of a bank, an institution extensively involved in fund management, is to receive the imprimatur of financial probity, and so bank directors come to be regarded by other directors as acceptable trustees of the interests of the institutional funds as a whole.

This is clearly brought out by the fact that the directors of the big four banks and the Bank of England comprised almost a half of all multiple directors and accounted for almost one-third of the directorships held by multiple directors. When directors of the Scottish clearing banks, the specialist lending banks, and the merchant banks are included in the calculation, the pre-eminence of bank directors is overwhelming. In fact, 70 per cent of all multiple directors had at least one directorship within the financial sector, and for many of these people the financial sector comprised their primary business interest. One-third of the multiple directors were executive directors of financial enterprises in the top 250 and a further 8 per cent were retired financial executives or had their primary interest in a smaller financial concern (Scott, 1985: table 44). The directorships held by the multiple directors generated a network of interlocking directorships within which the multiple directors could be seen as an 'inner circle' of finance capitalist (Useem, 1984).

Perhaps the most striking feature of the inner circle was that it was exclusively male: not a single woman held more than one directorship in the top 250 enterprises of 1976. Indeed, the number of women in the directorate as a whole was extremely low. Just eleven women appeared among the 2,682 directors of large companies (0.4 per cent).[6] Five of these women sat on public sector boards (two of them on the board of the BBC), and just two appeared to sit on private sector boards in their own right rather than as members of family groups: Muriel Downs sat as a director of the American-owned Woolworth group, and Daisy Hyams, chief buyer, sat as a director of Tesco.[7] In the numerous cases where women appeared as members of family shareholding blocks it was unusual for them to have a directorship in the family firm. This was the case in only three of the family-controlled enterprises, though one (Guinness) did have two women on its board.

The men of the inner circle were drawn from a very restricted social background as measured by the conventional indicators of public school attendance and possession of an hereditary title. Many of those without hereditary titles had been awarded life titles of knighthood or peerage, and a total of 131 of the 282 multiple directors were titled. The larger the number of directorships a man held, the more likely he was to be titled, both because prominent businessmen tended to be awarded titles and because those with titles were more likely to achieve prominence (Scott and Griff, 1984: table 5.5). The titled directors were, furthermore, more likely to hold directorships in the financial sector

6 The gender of a director could not always be inferred from a list of names when people were listed by initials, but most enterprises followed the practice of listing men by their initials and women by their title and first name.

7 Although she was a long-time associate of Sir Jack Cohen, whose family owned Tesco, Miss Hyams was not herself a members of the family.

and to play a key role in linking the financial and industrial sectors: titled directors held 47 per cent of all clearing bank directorships in 1976.

These men were also linked together through kinship ties. While kinship might be expected to play, by definition, an important role in companies under family control, it was also of considerable importance within the system of impersonal possession. Lupton and Wilson (1959) and Whitley (1974) have shown the great importance of kinship links within the City of London. My own research has confirmed this picture and has also shown that the present level of integration through kinship is far lower than was the case in the inter-war period. Kinship has tended to survive most strongly as a factor in linking the merchant and clearing banks of the City with other enterprises. Many of the Jewish merchant banks remain family controlled, and the extensive 'cousinhood' of Jewish families links them to numerous other companies. The strong tradition of endogamy within the Jewish community reinforced by the exclusionary practices of non-Jews, has tended to ensure that a web of kinship links continues to stretch beyond the confines of the family firms themselves.

A similar situation of endogamy and exclusion was characteristic of the early Quaker families and, while a number of the Quaker business families became Anglicans in the late nineteenth century, the established kinship links continue to tie the originally Quaker banks of Barclays and Lloyds to the wider corporate system. Barclays Bank, for example, was controlled through a constellation of interests and had no individuals or families among its largest shareholders, yet eight of its directors in 1976, including the chairman, were members of the intermarried Quaker cousinhood (Scott and Griff, 1984: table 4.4).[8] The Quaker cousinhood had, in fact, become a part of the more extensive city establishment which has played such an important role in the British economy since the nineteenth century (Lisle-Williams, 1984). Virtually all the major city enterprises are connected through kinship links as well as through interlocking directorships, and this has traditionally played a large part in the 'trust' which was central to City business practice. The kinship and friendship links of the establishment create a nexus of informality which reinforces formal interlocking directorships and allows business transactions to proceed more smoothly.

The network of interlocking directorships in 1976 included three-quarters (189) of the top 250 enterprises, the level of interlocking being especially high for the financials (forty-seven out of fifty) and enterprises controlled through constellations of interests (eighty-eight out of one hundred). These figures reflect the hegemonic position of financial institutions in the mobilization of capital, but it should be emphasized that particular shareholding relations are rarely reflected in interlocking directorships. The fact of investing in an enterprise, even as a member of the controlling constellation is not generally regarded as a necessary or sufficient reason for board representation. Board members are recruited from the general pool of those who represent financial interests, but their recruitment depends upon expertise and their position in social networks rather than on the presence of a shareholding between the companies concerned. The fact that there is no one-to-one relationship between capital relations and interlocking directorships emphasizes the relative autonomy of boards from their particular controlling constellations.

When the network of shareholdings generated by the investments of the various controlling constellations is examined, a clear hierarchy emerges. The central and, therefore, dominant enterprises are the insurance companies and pension funds. The Prudential alone was a member of eighty-eight constellations, while the NCB pension fund was a member of seventy-five. The Co-operative group, Legal and General, Norwich Union, and Pearl Assurance were each members of sixty-four constellations (Scott, 1986: table 5.3). None of these institutions, however, was at all central in the network of interlocking directorships. The Prudential, for example, was interlocked at board level with only five of the top 250 enterprises, and three of these were American subsidiaries. The practice of regarding bank directors as 'representatives' of the financial community as a whole meant that banks occupied a central position in the network of interlocking directorships, giving them a position out of all proportion to their direct shareholdings and their managed funds (Scott and Griff, 1984: table 6.2). Interlocks become structured around the big banks, and this enables the insurance companies and pension funds to remain relatively passive. The institutions allow bank directors to safeguard and give voice to their interests at the board meetings which they attend. To the extent that banks enter, in their own right, into capital, commercial and personal relations with particular customers and client enterprises, they will tend to form loose knots of connection. Banks tend to recruit their own directors from among their most important clients and associates, while industrial boards which seek and recruit a bank director will look, in the first instance, to their primary bank. It is this two-way exchange of directors which is responsible for the formation of bank-centred 'spheres of influence', and it is through these spheres – loose and overlapping as they are – that the interests of the institutional fund managers in the system of impersonal possession are secured.

Given the centrality of the City of London and its financial institutions in the British corporate economy, it is of obvious importance to discuss the development of the City and to examine some of the recent trends in the organization of its financial and commercial markets. Towards the end of the nineteenth century the banking system crystallized around a split between the smaller 'country banks' which were concerned with personal, agricultural and industrial finance on a long-term basis and the 'City banks' which concerned themselves with short-term loans and with the discounting of bills of exchange. As the country banks later became incorporated into the City-based national banking chains, so a split developed between the City banks and the provincial manufacturing enterprises which could formerly rely on local banking support. The growing scale of industrial enterprise led, as has been seen, to a closer relationship between the City and industry, and Britain's largest industrials found themselves under increasing pressure to adapt to the established practices of the City banks. The growth of interlocking directorships and institutional shareholdings produced a fusion of banking and industry within which the City banks held a central place (Scott and Griff, 1984: chapter 6; Scott, 1985: 95–102).

This system of 'finance capital', however, did not involve the dominance of banks over industry, as was the case in countries such as Germany. Rather, the big City banks became arenas in which the controllers of the huge institutional funds, including the pension funds of the large *industrial* enterprises, could come together and determine the policies which would shape corporate decisions throughout the economy. Those who sit on the bank boards and formulate their policies are drawn disproportionately from the banking and investment sectors, but they include, also, a large number of directors and executives of the chief industrial enterprises. It is in this sense that the inner circle of multiple directors, recruited from all areas of the economy, can be defined as a group of 'finance capitalists' operating through the boards of the banks on whose boards they sit.

Ingham (1984) has criticized the conventional Marxist view of finance capital on the grounds that British capitalism remains divided between its 'City' and 'industrial' wings. His argument, however, is not necessarily incompatible with the view that have been put forward in this chapter. According to Ingham, the City banks and investment institutions act as commercial intermediaries between lenders and borrowers and between buyers and sellers. That is to say, they act mainly as traders in commodities, whether these be coffee futures, eurodollars or company shares. They have not, Ingham argues, bought shares as long-term investments or as a way of influencing industrial strategy. The City, therefore, is characterized by the predominance of short-term commercial practices. While the City and productive industry have come closer together in *quantitative* terms – through shareholdings and board memberships – there remains a *qualitative* separation between 'commercial' and 'productive' concerns. The City institutions are interested in the short-term gains to be made in share dealing and, particularly, in the large profits that can be made in takeovers and mergers (Ingham, 1984: 62, 70). The proportion of institutional funds invested in company shares, though of crucial significance to the industrial sector, is only a small part of institutional capital and so companies making share issues must compete against the returns available from real property, overseas investment, government stocks, and local authority bonds. Where there is strong pressure on institutions to perform at a very high level in the short term, as in the merchant banks involved in managing the pension funds of the large industrials, there is a very rapid turnover in the ownership of shares. The consequences of this complex of factors, argues Ingham, are that the City institutions show little long-term stability in their patterns of share ownership and that they put great pressures on industrial enterprises to make short-term profits. Industrials are forced to declare high profits in order to bolster their own share prices and so are less able to plough back their earnings into new productive investments (Ingham, 1984).

None of this contradicts the view put forward in this chapter.The inner circle of finance capitalists, the multiple directors, are the embodiment of this short-term commercial orientation. The board level links between the City and the large industrials encourage industrial companies to invest their surplus capital in the money, currency and security markets rather than in refinancing their own activities. The underfinancing of British industry is a consequence of the particular form of *fusion* that exists between the City and industry. Industrialists who sit on bank boards espouse the same commercial viewpoint as do the City men who sit on industrial boards (Ingham, 1984: 77–8). The fusion of banking and industry through shareholding and interlocking directorships that has been described as a system of finance capital involves the acceptance of the 'City view' by bankers, fund managers, and industrialists alike.[9]

The split at the heart of British capital is a division *within* finance capital, but the banking and manufacturing sectors of big business are not divided from one another. There is, however, an important element of truth in the conventional view of the separation of banking and industry in Britain. This separation is not to be found within big business or within finance capital, but between finance capital and the operations of the small and medium-sized businesses subject to personal ownership. Those enterprises which received substantial institutional investment and are locked into the City viewpoint are the profitable large companies which are tied together into the system of impersonal possession. Entrepreneurial capitalists in the smaller enterprises, on the other hand, are able to take a long-term perspective because of their relative isolation from City practices (Scase and Goffee, 1982). Entrepreneurial capitalists in the larger enterprises described in this chapter are in an intermediate situation. The pattern of personal possession ensures them a degree of autonomy from the big institutional funds, but they must still accommodate to the short-term commercial orientation of the City if they are to avoid becoming the targets of takeover bids. The increase in the number of takeovers since the 1950s, resulting in the disappearance of many family-owned enterprises, is a consequence of the dominance of the system of impersonal possession and finance capital characterized by the acceptance of the commercial practices of the 'City'.

Despite the short-term orientation of finance capital, there has been an increasing tendency for institutions to intervene in corporate affairs to make their control effective. In part this is due to the fact that short-term trading takes place mainly at the margins of a holding: an institution will tend to adjust the *size* of its holding in a particular company rather than to sell out completely. Institutional holdings are of such a scale that they cannot be significantly reduced in the short term without causing a drastic fall in the share price. As a result, large institutions are 'locked in' to the fate of the companies in which they invest, and they must protect their investments, when necessary, through intervention. Institutions, therefore, retain a substantial commitment even to institutions whose stock they are selling. The bulk of institutional holdings are retained for five years or more, only about 20 per cent being turned over in the short term (Briston and Dobbins, 1978: 48–51, 194).

The other factor leading to increased institutional intervention is a shift in the nature of institutional fund management resulting from increased levels of competition within the City. Prior to the 1970s the

9 I am grateful for comments raised in a seminar at Hull University which helped me to clarify this point.

level of turnover in share ownership was lower and institutional holdings were more stable. The higher rates of turnover have resulted mainly from the huge expansion of pension funds in the last fifteen years (Minns, 1980; Hannah, 1986; Schuller, 1986). Where trustees of pension funds (industrialists and, sometimes, trades unionists) farm out the management of the fund to merchant banks there is a tendency towards very short-term gains as a way of monitoring their performance. Many trustees aim to switch the management of their fund from one bank to another if the fund does not produce good results over a period of three to six months, resulting in the present high levels of share turnover.

The recent liberalization of the various City markets – the so-called 'Big Bang' – has opened institutional fund managers to foreign competition and may tend to increase the level of share turnover and the orientation of industry towards short-term gains as a way of avoiding takeover. One way of ensuring such short-term gains is to become an active agent in a takeover. The City's 'star performers' over the last decade have been the conglomerates which have undertaken asset-stripping acquisitions of other companies. But the path of corporate acquisitions can only be successfully taken if the support of the institutions can be ensured, and this has required a greater degree of consultation between the management of enterprises and their leading shareholders. Such interventions only rarely become a matter of public knowledge, though they tend to become rather more visible through a concern for such matters as 'insider dealing', 'acting in concert' and the weakness of traditional forms of self-regulation in the City (Clarke, 1986).

National Variations in Impersonal Possession

It has been argued that a move from personal to impersonal forms of possession is characteristic of all the major capitalist economies. The form taken by this transition and the system of impersonal possession which results in any particular country reflects its national experience of industrialization. The specific complex of national and international constraints which exists at a particular time is able to shape the ways in which culturally conditioned economic actions develop. This can be illustrated by an examination of the current distribution of the main forms of impersonal possession. Control through a constellation of interests, the predominant pattern in Britain, is most prevalent in those countries which share an 'Anglo-American' cultural heritage and set of legal institutions; control by aligned interests prevails outside this cultural and legal context and, especially, where industrialization took place under the sponsorship of the state or of established financial interests (Scott, 1988).

Large enterprises in the USA began to show a high level of dispersal in their share ownership during the 1920s, as the massive scale of production for the American and international markets forced them beyond the confines of family capital. It was their observation of the early stages of this process that led Berle and Means (1932) to formulate the thesis

TABLE 15.4   *Patterns of ownership in selected economies (1974–84)*

			Number of companies			
Ownership	USA 1980	Canada 1975	Australia 1975	New Zealand 1974	South Africa 1984	Japan 1980
Majority	8	140	48	3	72	5
Minority	53	43	99	16	28	69
Limited minority	0	2	–	3	–	0
No dominant interest	165	20	79	21	0	169
Not						7
known	26	0	0	0	0	
Totals	252	205	226	43	100	250

Note: The cut-off point for minority control was 10 per cent. 'Limited minority control' is used in some studies to refer to the situation where a particular shareholder has just below 10 per cent but is actively involved on the board.
Sources: USA from Scott (1986: table 6.1); Canada and Australia from Scott (1985: tables 26, 28); New Zealand from Fogelberg (1980: 69); South Africa from Savage (1985: table 5); Japan from Scott (1986: table 7.1). Each study has adopted slightly different selection criteria, detailed in the original sources, and this must be borne in mind in interpreting the data

of the separation of ownership from control. It is clear, however, that the result of this dispersal of shareholdings was, certainly, a situation of weakened family control, but also a situation in which competing financial institutions became the major providers of capital. By the 1970s the pension funds had become the largest single source of new investment capital, much of this being handled by the trust departments of the big banks. In 1980 (see table 15.4) most of the largest American enterprises had no single dominant shareholding.

International comparisons are, of course, extremely difficult to make with any precision, as definitions and criteria vary from one study to another. It is possible, however, to get a general picture of the main patterns of variation in corporate control. Table 15.4 shows how the American situation compares with that in Canada, Australia and New Zealand. The bulk of the large Canadian enterprises in 1975 were foreign owned, a consequence of Canada's dependence on the American and wider world economy. As a result, very few large enterprises in Canada showed any degree of share dispersal. The enterprises which had moved in this direction, however, were controlled through constellations of interests and formed the core of a network of interlocking directorships. Canadian-controlled financial institutions were central to this network and formed 'points of articulation' which linked the domestic and foreign sectors of the economy (Carrol et al., 1982: 49–50). Australia and New Zealand are less dependent on the American economy and so show lower levels of foreign ownership. In both countries the domestic sector of ownership was more important and showed a similar trend to control through a constellation of interests as that found in Britain. Banks and insurance companies were important in the networks of interlocking directorships, with the level of interlocking in Australia being comparable with that found in Britain and the USA (Stening and Wan, 1984; Davison et al., 1984).[10]

South Africa, with its high level of foreign ownership and close links to the Anglo-American economies, shows a superficially similar pattern to that found in Canada. There were, however, no cases of dispersed ownership among the hundred largest South African enterprises of 1984.[11] In fact, the predominant pattern in South Africa was a pyramidding of majority and minority holdings into a small number of enterprise groups. The Oppenheimer group and its associated Barlow Rand group dominated the economy in this way, and used interlocking directorships to tie their holdings into tight interest groups. The Oppenheimer, Barlow Rand, Anglo-Vaal, Rembrandt and Sanlam groups together accounted for half the top hundred enterprises (Savage, 1984). This pattern is therefore, intermediate between control through a constellation of interests and control by aligned interests. The latter form of impersonal possession involves the formation of interest groups through interweaving share participations and is epitomized by Japan.

The numerous enterprises with dispersed ownership in Japan (again see table 15.4) were, together with some of those subject to majority or minority control, elements in a structure of impersonal possession which differs radically from that found in Britain and the USA (Scott, 1986: chapter 7). Six large combines (Mitsubishi, Mitsui, Sumitomo, Sanwa, DKB and Fuyo) and a number of smaller groups together accounted for 153 of the top 250 enterprises in 1980. In none of these groups was there a dominant 'parent' company. There were mutual share participations among the leading group members, making them subordinate elements in the larger group. Strategic control over all group enterprises was vested in an informal committee recruited from the chief executives of the leading group companies. These coalitions of aligned participations, therefore, differed sharply from the constellations of financial institutions which structured the system of impersonal possession in the Anglo-American economies.

Enterprise group members in Japan engaged in preferential trading, joint ventures, technical integration, and common banking arrangements, and they corresponded closely to the financial groups depicted in the

10 The figures for New Zealand in table 15.4 involve some calculations from the Appendix of Fogelberg (1980), and this led to the discovery of an error in his paper. New Zealand News was not included in his list on p. 67 but has been included in my tabulation. See also Fogelberg (1978) and Chandler (1982). Table 2 in Stening and Wan (1984) had a misprinted date, which has been corrected here.

11 The figures in table 15.4 are calculated from the lists in Savage (1985) and involve a different treatment of joint ownership. I have used categories comparable with those of other studies and so my tabulation differs from his.

Marxist model of finance capital. They did not, however, involve bank dominance of the kind that is often implied in that model. In Germany and, to a lesser extent, in Switzerland and Italy there was a closer approximation to this notion of bank domination, though the bank groups which did exist were not so tightly integrated as in Japan. In France and Belgium investment banks have tended to form relatively tight groups, but they are separate from the main business of deposit banking. As a result, the banks of France and Belgium are far less powerful than the so-called 'universal banks' of Germany which combine investment and deposit banking (Scott, 1985: chapter 5; Stokman et al., 1985).

Outside the Anglo-American economies, therefore, impersonal possession is found to take a number of variant forms involving different patterns of aligned interests. The important role of banks and investment companies in industrial enterprise reflects their importance in the funding of industrialization in these countries. The separation of the big banks from industry, which for a long time characterized the British economy and was an important example for countries within the British sphere of influence, never developed in Japan or continental Europe. In these areas, often with the support of the state, banks took long-term investment stakes in industrial enterprises and have continued to play an important role in direct industrial finance. It is for this reason that the trend towards impersonal possession takes differing forms in the various economies considered in this chapter.

Conclusion

This chapter has argued that the managerialist thesis and the rival thesis of bank control must both be rejected, though the abandonment of widely accepted theories is rarely that easy. The managerialist assumption that the large business enterprise is, *ipso facto*, a 'managerial' enterprise is so deeply entrenched that it is unlikely to be cast aside immediately. It remains important not only as a taken-for-granted assumption in sociology and economics, but also for business men in their day-to-day actions. But an attempt has been made to show that there is no evidence to support it from any of the research carried out during the last decade or so. Even Herman (1981), in his sophisticated attempt to reaffirm the theory, recognized that the form of 'management control' which he discovered in the USA involves a considerable degree of 'constraint' over managerial actions by the financial institutions. In view of the unacceptable theoretical and political baggage which is inherent in the term 'management control', the term 'control through a constellation of interests' is not only more accurate but is also less likely to allow researchers to smuggle in unwarranted assumptions about managerial motivation and behaviour. It also provides a more fruitful interpretation of the evidence on bank share ownership than does the Marxist theory of bank control.

Patterns of share ownership may have a considerable impact on business decision-making, control over the labour process and the exercise of class power (Scott, 1985: chapters 6, 7). There is an acute need of more research on these linkages; there is now sufficient evidence on share ownership and control, as far as Britain is concerned, for research to move to the next stage of exploring its impact on work and employment relations in modern organizations.

References

Aaronovitch, S. 1955. *Monopoly: A Study of British Monopoly Capitalism*. London: Lawrence and Wishart.
Baran, P. and Sweezy, P.M. 1966. *Monopoly Capital*. Harmondsworth: Penguin.
Baumol, W.J. 1959. *Business Behaviour*. New York: Macmillan.
Bell, D. 1961. *The End of Ideology*. New York: Collier-Macmillan.
—— 1974. *The Coming of Post-Industrial Society*. London: Heinemann.
Berle, A.A. and Means, G.C. 1932, *The Modern Corporation and Private Property*. New York: Macmillan. 1947.
Briston, R.J. and Dobbins, R. 1978. *The Growth and Impact of Institutional Investors*. London: Institute of Chartered Accountants.
Burch, P.H. 1972. *The Managerial Revolution Reassessed*. Massachusetts: Lexington Books.
Burnham, J. 1941, *The Mangerial Revolution*. Harmondsworth: Penguin. 1945.
Carroll, W.K., Fox, J. and Ornstein, M.D. 1982. 'The Network of Directorate Links Among the Largest Canadian Firms'. *Canadian Review of Sociology and Anthropology*, 19.
Chandler, R.F. 1982. 'The Control and Accountability of New Zealand's Public Corporations'. *New Zealand Journal of Business*, 4.
Child, J. 1972. 'Organisational Structure, Environment and Performance'. *Sociology*, 6.
Clarke, M. 1986. *Regulating the City*. Milton Keynes: Open University Press.
Crosland, C.A.R. 1956. *The Future of Socialism*. London: Cape.
Davison, A.G., Stening, B.W. and Wan, T.N. 1984. 'Auditor Concentration and the Impact of Interlocking Directorates'. *Journal of Accounting Research*, 22.
Florence, P.S. 1961. *Ownership, Control, and Success of Large Companies*. London: Sweet and Maxwell.
Fogelberg, G. 1978. 'Changing Patterns of Share Ownership in New Zealand's Largest Companies'. Research Paper No. 15. Victoria University of Wellington.
—— 1980. 'Ownership and Control in 43 of New Zealand's Largest Companies'. *New Zealand Journal of Business*, 2.

Galbraith, J.K. 1967. *The New Industrial State*. London: Hamish Hamilton.

Goldthorpe, J.H., Lockwood, D., Bechhofer, F. and Platt, J. 1969. *The Affluent Worker in the Class Structure*. Cambridge: Cambridge University Press.

Hannah, L. 1986. *Inventing Retirement*. Cambridge: Cambridge University Press.

Herman, E.O. 1981. *Corporate Control, Corporate Power*. Cambridge: Cambridge University Press.

Hilferding, R. 1910, *Finance Capital*. London: Routledge & Kegan Paul. 1981.

Ingham, G.K. 1984. *Capitalism Divided?* London: Macmillan.

Kerr, C., Dunlop, J.T., Harbison, F. and Myers, C.A. 1960. *Industrialism and Industrial Man*. Cambridge, Mass: Harvard University Press.

Kotz, D.M. 1978. *Bank Control of Large Corporations in the United States*. Berkeley: University of California Press.

Labour Research. 1987. 'Big Fish Grab Sell-Off Shares'. *Labour Research*, September.

Larner, R.J. 1966. 'Ownership and Control in the 200 Largest Non-Financial Corporations: 1929 and 1965'. *American Economic Review*, 56.

Lisle-Williams, M. 1984. 'Beyond the Market'. *British Journal of Sociology*, 35, 2.

Lupton, T. and Wilson, C.S. 1959, 'The Social Background and Connections of Top Decision Makers'. *Power in Britain*. Eds Urry, J. and Wakeford, J. London: Heinemann. 1973.

Marris, R. 1964. *The Economic Theory of 'Managerial' Capitalism*. London: Macmillan.

Marshall. G., Newby, H., Rose, D. and Vogler, C. 1988. *Social Class in Modern Britain*. London: Hutchinson.

Minns, R. 1980. *Pension Funds and British Capitalism*. London: Heinemann.

Mizruchi, M. and Schwartz, M. (eds) 1988. *The Structural Analysis of Business*. Cambridge: Cambridge University Press.

Nichols, T. 1969. *Ownership, Control and Ideology*. London: Allen & Unwin.

Perlo, V. 1957. *The Empire of High Finance*. New York: International Publishers.

Rochester, A. 1936. *Rulers of America*. New York: International Publishers.

Savage, M. 1984. 'An Anatomy of the South African Corporate Economy'. University of Capetown Africa Seminar.

Scase, R. and Goffee, R. 1982. *The Entrepreneurial Middle Class*. London: Croom Helm.

Schuller, T. 1986. *Age, Capital and Democracy*. Farnborough: Gower.

Scott, J.P. 1984. 'The Controlling Constellations'. Working Paper for the Company Analysis Project, University of Leicester.

—— 1985. *Corporations, Classes, and Capitalism*. Second edition. London: Hutchinson.

—— 1986. *Capitalist Property and Financial Power*. Brighton: Wheatsheaf.

—— 1988. 'Intercorporate Structure in Western Europe'. *The Structural Analysis of Business*. Eds Mizruchi, M. and Schwartz, M. Cambridge: Cambridge University Press.

—— and Griff, C. 1984. *Directors of Industry*. Cambridge: Polity.

Stening, B.W. and Wan, T.W. 1984. 'Interlocking Directorates Among Australia's Largest 250 Corporations'. *Australia and New Zealand Journal of Sociology*, 20.

Stokman, F.N., Zeigler, R. and Scott, J.P. (eds.) 1985. *Networks of Corporate Power*. Cambridge: Polity.

Useem, M. 1984. *The Inner Circle*. New York: Oxford University Press.

Whitley, R. 1974. 'The City and Industry'. *Elites and Power in Britain*. Ed. Stanworth, P. and Giddens, A. Cambridge: Cambridge University Press.

Zeitlin, M. 1974. 'Corporate Ownership and Control'. *American Journal of Sociology*, 79, 5.

Zweig, F. 1952. *The British Worker*. Harmondsworth: Penguin.

16 Employment, Unemployment and Social Stratification

Duncan Gallie

In the past three decades major changes have occurred in the British employment structure, involving the expansion of non-manual occupations, the diffusion of automation both on the shopfloor and in the office, the changing gender composition of the employed population and the growth of mass unemployment. A central issue of sociological inquiry has been the impact of these changes on patterns of social stratification. Have they affected significantly the major lines of social division and have they had implications for the nature and extent of collective organization? This chapter will focus on three issues that have been particularly central to theoretical debate and research. The first is the view that the most significant source of change in the stratification system has been the growth of an underclass that cuts across traditional class divisions. The second is the thesis that changes in the work and labour market situation of manual workers have led to a decline in resentments about class inequality and hence to an erosion of manual workers' commitment to the collective defence of their interests. The third is the argument that there has been a marked change in the experience of employment of non-manual workers that has led to the growth of more radical attitudes to work and to society.

The Growth of an Underclass?

In describing the changing class structure of the advanced societies Giddens (1973) argued that the most fundamental long-term change in the pattern of social division was the emergence of an underclass. This, he maintained, was leading to the fragmentation of the manual working class and to growing polarization between a radicalized underclass and a more conservative traditional working class. The 'underclass' is composed of people that are concentrated among the lowest paid occupations, or are chronically unemployed or semi-employed, as a result of a 'disqualifying' market capacity of a primarily cultural type. Its principal economic basis is a general process of economic differentiation in advanced capitalist societies, leading to the creation of a dual labour market. This divides workers between a primary market, where wages, job security and career opportunities are good and a secondary market where they are poor.

An underclass is formed where common economic experiences in the secondary market overlap with sources of distinctiveness of an ethnic or cultural type. The principal examples of categories that suffer from such disqualifying market capacities are women and the ethnic minorities. Once people have entered a disadvantageous labour market position they tend to become trapped into a 'vicious cycle of underprivilege'. This produces considerable continuity of experience over time and a basis for distinctive types of attitudes, beliefs and styles of life (Giddens, 1973: 111–12; 215–20).

The growth of an underclass, Giddens argues, is likely to have profound implications for class conflict. Whereas the underclass may well become radicalized as a result of its experience of deprivation, this radicalism is unlikely to be shared by the working class as a whole and will almost certainly produce a conservative reaction.[1] It is evident, he writes, 'that there is a basic division of interest, which in all probability will become more and more pronounced in the future between those in the new "reserve army" of capitalism, in insecure occupations yielding only a low rate of economic return, and those in the more stable, high-yielding manual occupations' (Giddens, 289).

This interpretation of the changing pattern of social divisions raises a number of key issues. First, how convincing is the argument that there is a distinctive economic basis for an underclass? Secondly, what is the relationship between labour market disadvantage and characteristics such as ethnicity and gender? And, finally, what are the implications of such disadvantages for social attitudes and behaviour?

The theory of the underclass, as advanced by Giddens, is rooted in a 'dualist' conception of the evolution of the employment structure. It relates, then to an important current of theory that has argued that as a result of changes in the product market, in technology, in employer labour management policies and in the strength of the trade-union organization, there has emerged a sharp and growing distinction between primary and secondary sector employment opportunities (among later formulations, see Edwards, 1979; Berger and Piore, 1981). In the primary sector, employers are concerned to retain labour for a long period and thus provide particularly favourable employment conditions in terms of income, security, opportunities for advancement and the degree of individual discretion and autonomy allowed in work. In the secondary sector, the emphasis in employer policies is on low cost and on being able to hire and fire labour easily. These tend to be poorly paid, short-term jobs where relatively untrained labour is subject to tight forms of direct supervision. It is the growth of these secondary sector jobs that provides the principal economic basis for an underclass.

More recent research evidence has cast considerable doubt upon the empirical validity of this dualist description of labour market stratification.

---

1 The degree of radicalism to be expected from the underclass is a little unclear in Gidden's argument. At one point (Giddens, 1973: 289) he argues that its members 'constitute a possible source of an upsurge in revolutionary consciousness'. At another, he recognizes that, at least in the USA, the evidence for any widespread revolutionary ideology among black workers is not compelling. However, he definitely anticipates chronic 'hostile outbursts' on the part of members of the underclass, so long as they are denied equal rights (1973: 218).

Central to the idea of a 'primary' market is the growing importance of internal labour markets. As has been shown in chapter 9, however, there is little evidence that these have become widespread in British industry. Further, while some employers have sought to increase flexibility through the use of 'secondary sector' temporary jobs, the overall extent of this development would appear to be limited and there is little evidence of the major expansion of this sector suggested by theories of the underclass. The overall proportion of the employed population in Britain involved in temporary work in 1986, including people working on training schemes for the unemployed, was around 7 per cent. This was the same proportion as in 1975 (Hakim, 1987: 557).

The attempt to root the concept of the underclass in a dualist conception of the structure of employment must, then, be regarded as unconvincing. The concept might still be of value, however, even if these theoretical underpinnings are rejected. A significant sector of the employed population receives pay close to or below the official poverty line and there are marked inequalities of pay by race and gender. There has been a substantial increase in the proportion of part-time rather than full-time work. Perhaps most important of all, there has been a substantial increase in the 1980s of the most severe type of labour-market disadvantage, the experience of unemployment. Precise estimates of changes in the level of unemployment depend upon the measures used. But, even on a conservative estimate, the proportion of the labour force unemployed doubled between 1979 and 1983. By January 1988, there were 2.7 million claiming unemployment benefit, 9.8 per cent of the working population. Moreover, over 1 million of the unemployed had been without work for six months or more (*Employment Gazette*, May 1988). The experience of unemployment, both because of its extensiveness and its distinctiveness as a labour market situation, would appear to provide a potentially more significant economic basis for the formation of an underclass than employment in 'secondary sector' jobs. In short, a number of different types of labour market marginality has persisted and even increased in the 1980s, in a way that has continued to encourage debate about an underclass.

An underclass emerges, it is argued, when labour market disadvantage is associated in an enduring way with specific cultural characteristics. It is with regard to the position of ethnic minorities that the concept has been most systematically elaborated. Rex and Tomlinson (1979) used it to describe the position of Asians and West Indians in Britain. It suggested the possibility that 'these minorities were systematically at a disadvantage compared with working-class whites and that, instead of identifying with working-class culture, community and politics, they formed their own organizations and became in effect a separate underprivileged class' (1979: 275). On the basis of their study in the Handsworth area of Birmingham, they suggest that West Indian and Asian immigrants not merely do worse than white people in quantitiative terms, but may be thought of as living in different labour markets and in different kinds of housing situations from comparable white groups. They point to the development of forms of radical consciousness – indicated by the increasing independence of Asians from the organized labour movement and by the growth of revolutionary black consciousness

– which has effectively displaced simple working-class consciousness amongst West Indians (1979: 292). At the same time, white racism, rooted in identities moulded by an imperial past, is becoming sharper. There is, the authors conclude, 'an increasing polarization between the vast majority of whites, including especially the working class, and the West Indian and Asian immigrant and British-born black communities' (1979: 282).

A central issue raised by this analysis is the assumption that the ethnic minorities share a sufficiently similar employment situation for a sense of common economic interests to develop. As Richard Jenkins has outlined in chapter 11, there can be no doubt about the sharpness of the labour market disadvantages experienced by the ethnic minorities. Moreover, there is a particularly striking difference between black and white workers in their vulnerability to unemployment, an aspect of labour market disadvantage that is central to underclass theory. Yet, as Rex and Tomlinson (1979: 279) point out, their evidence does not clearly demonstrate the existence of the type of qualitatively different labour market situation that is implied by their argument. A more detailed examination (Brown, 1984), based on a large-scale survey in 1982, has shown that, although the overall job levels of white workers are much higher than those of black workers, the ethnic minorities are dispersed across the occupational structure and there are very substantial variations between different ethnic groups. For instance, while, overall, white males are more likely to be in non-manual occupations than black males, the African Asians are more likely to be in non-manual work than white males. Although 70 per cent of Bangladeshi employees are in the types of semi-skilled and unskilled manual occupations that are often associated with the concept of an 'underclass', this is the case for 40 per cent of Indian and Pakistani employees and for only 25 per cent of African Asians (1984: 197). Black women are more heavily concentrated in particular job levels than men, but at the same time they are much closer in their occupational profile to white women (1984: 157). There are also important differences in the extent to which people are self-employed: 18 per cent of Asian men in employment, compared with 7 per cent of West Indians and 14 per cent of white men, are self-employed (1984: 165). In short, while finer measures might well reveal further inequalities within job levels. the employment pattern of the ethnic minorities has a degree of internal differentiation that is unlikely to encourage collective class formation or the development of a generalized form of underclass consciousness.

Moreover, the extent to which there is felt to be a divergence of interests between white workers and the ethnic minorities within the employment situation is likely to depend upon the recruitment strategies and policies of the trade unions. The evidence to date suggests that Asian and West Indian employees are being integrated within the existing framework of trade unionism. Indeed, Asian and West Indian employees are more likely to be in trade unions than white employees (Brown, 1984: 169). This partly reflects differences in occupational distribution, but, even within job levels, Asian and West Indian male employees are at least as likely, and women employees are more likely, to be union members than their white equivalents. Attendance levels at union meetings are broadly similar; the major respect in which the integration of black workers within the union movement remains very restricted is in the holding of elected posts (Brown, 1984: 170–1).

The political allegiances of the ethnic minorities also suggest that there are stronger trends towards integration than towards separatism. There may be some evidence of greater withdrawal among black minorities in their lower levels of registration and, at least for West Indians, in their lower turnout for voting. Underregistration declined in the 1970s, however, and, given the potentially diverse reasons for non-registration, must be treated with caution as an indicator of political attitudes (Community Relations Commission, 1975: 14; Anwar, 1980: 35–6). The most striking finding from studies of voting intentions is that black people give overwhelming support to the Labour Party. Ethnic minority status reinforces class support for Labour among black manual workers and it also gives Labour a majority among black non-manual workers (Layton-Henry, 1984: 170–5). While the heavy concentration of black workers in particular communities has been associated with some political activity on a communal basis, it is relatively rare; there is little cross community organization, and relations between ethnic minorities within local communities can produce strains that make a scenario of extensive united black action in the near future unlikely (Layton-Henry, 1984: 176–7).

There can be little doubt, then, about the extent of disadvantage experienced by the ethnic minorities. Moreover, whether in terms of trade-union adherence or political orientation, the black minorities appear significantly more radical. To date, however, this radicalism has been assimilated into the traditional organizational forms of the Labour movement and there is little evidence of any widespread growth of 'revolutionary' consciousness or indeed of well-supported independent political organization of the type indicated by some versions of underclass theory.

The second source of cultural distinctiveness linked to labour market disadvantage that is highlighted by underclass theory is gender. There has been a sustained debate in the literature about the relative merits of defining the class position of women in terms of their own employment position or that of their husbands (Crompton and Mann, 1986; Goldthorpe, 1983, 1984; Stanworth, 1984). Underclass theory focuses on women's personal employment experience. This approach has the advantage of highlighting the extent of gender inequalities at work. As Shirley Dex has emphasized in chapter 10, women suffer from disadvantages in pay levels that cannot be adequately accounted for solely in terms of their qualifications or experience. Moreover, women are disproportionately concentrated in routine non-manual work and in lower skilled manual work, whereas men are heavily overrepresented in the managerial and professional non-manual categories and in higher skilled manual work. As with the ethnic minorities, however, the high degree of internal differentiation within women's employment is likely to discourage a sense of common economic interest. Moreover, at least in Britain, women do not suffer disproportionately in one aspect of labour market disadvantage that is central to underclass theory: the experience of unemployment. Whether one examines unemployment levels in terms of the 'official' definition of unemployment or in terms of the International Labour Organization (ILO) criteria of being without work, available for work and wanting work, the evidence is remarkably consistent that women are less likely to be unemployed than men.

The argument about women's greater marginality to employment has focused primarily on the high proportion of women in part-time work or outside the labour market altogether. This is certainly integrally linked to cultural definitions of gender roles and, in particular, to responsibilities for childrearing (see Morris in chapter 13). The majority of women, however, would appear to regard the marginalization of their labour market situation during this period of the life cycle as basically legitimate. In 1980, 60 per cent of women were of the view that a woman should stay at home rather than go out to work if her children were under school age, and a further 25 per cent thought that she should only go out to work if there was strong financial necessity (Martin and Roberts, 1984: 177).

This conception of gender roles is also likely to be a crucial factor accounting for women's attitudes to part-time work. The major expansion in women's employment has been linked to the growth of part-time employment. Since only 16 per cent of part-time workers are in temporary jobs, they cannot easily be equated with the type of secondary sector work force postulated by dualist theory. Part-time work, however, has been an important factor in maintaining inequalities of pay (see chapter 10) and involves substantial disadvantages in terms of pension and sick pay provision, training opportunities and promotion (Martin and Roberts, 1984: ch. 5). Yet the evidence suggests that women involved in such work have high levels of satisfaction with their employment situation. There is little sign that it is regarded as a poor substitute for full-time employment: 94 per cent of part-timers, compared with 89 per cent of those in full-time work, are satisfied with their hours of work. Part-timers are significantly more likely to be satisfied with their rate of pay and they are marginally more satisfied with their job as a whole (Martin and Roberts, 1984: 73–4). These high levels of satisfaction are likely to be related to the primacy given to domestic responsibilities by part-timers, the majority of whom are married women with children under 16 (Martin and Roberts, 1984: 15).

Hence, despite its considerable long-term implications for pay and career opportunities (Joshi, 1984), women's subemployment in this phase of the life cycle does not appear to be an experience that generates strong resentment about the employment structure. Instead of leading to more radical attitudes, it may be associated with a lower level of collective organization at work. While female union density has increased markedly over the post-war period from 24.3 per cent in 1948 to 39.5 per cent in 1979, this was still only 60 per cent of the level for men (Price and Bain, 1983: 50). As the Women and Employment Survey has shown, this is strongly linked to the prevalence of part-time work (Martin and Roberts, 1984: 54–5). Part-time workers were certainly less likely to have a union to join, but this is not a sufficient explanation of their lower membership. They were also less likely to be union members when there was a union at their place of work. It might be argued that this reflects an inadequate welcome by the unions. But it is notable that where women were employed in a workplace without a union, only 28 per cent of part-timers, compared with 51 per cent of full-time employees, wanted one.

Further, there is little evidence that women's greater marginality in employment leads to distinctive political attitudes. Perhaps the most interesting data on the importance of labour market position for women's political attitudes come from Marshall et al. (1988). Their analysis of cross-class families reveals rather clearly that women's voting is less affected by their personal position than by that of their husband (1988: 70–1, 239–40).

Although a focus on individual class position reveals substantial inequalities in women's employment situation, their impact on social attitudes is heavily mediated by the social relations of the household. Far from a more marginal position in the labour market leading to a distinct category-consciousness among women, it appears to make their personal employment experiences a less important determinant of their political attitudes.

The diverse nature of the forms of disadvantage experienced by the cultural groups at the centre of underclass theory undermines the likelihood of the development of alternative collective identities to those of class. It might be argued, however, that the concept is still of use in highlighting the social situation and attitudes of a more restricted category: that of the unemployed. The emergence of mass unemployment in the 1980s appeared to many to indicate that a major new line of social cleavage was opening up between those in employment, who were reaping the benefits of technological progress and rising real incomes, and a growing sector of people excluded from employment and condemned to impoverishment. This view was reinforced by the fact that unemployment appears to run in families (Payne, 1987) and by the consistent finding that the wives of unemployed men are very much less likely to be in employment than those of employed men (Daniel and Stilgoe, 1977: Wood, 1982; Moylan et al., 1984: 114–32). As Pahl discovered in his research on the Isle of Sheppey, the deprivations of unemployment are not mitigated by substantial opportunities to carry out informal work. Rather, the benefits of self-provisioning, informal exchange and paid work in the black economy would appear to go primarily to those in employment, generating patterns of cumulative advantage and disadvantage. Pahl (1984) concludes that:

A process of polarization is developing, with households busily engaged in all forms of work at one pole and households unable to do a wide range of work at the other . . . The division between the more affluent home-owning households of ordinary working people and the less advantaged underclass households is coming to be more significant than conventional divisions based on the manual/non-manual distinction. (1984: 313–14)

There can be little doubt that unemployment involves very sharp deprivations both in terms of loss of income and in psychological strain. Despite claims to the contrary, welfare benefits fall far short of compensating for lost earnings (Moylan et al., 1984) and a wide range of studies have shown that the unemployed suffer from higher levels of anxiety and depression (Warr, 1987). The central question, however, for theories of the underclass is the extent to which this situation of economic disadvantage leads to the creation of a social stratum with sufficient stability of composition over time and internal homogeneity to produce a distinctive set of attitudes towards society.

To take first the issue of stability, Marsh has shown in chapter 12 that relatively stable levels of unemployment conceal huge flows into and out of the stock of the unemployed each month. Indeed, in 1985, approximately half the people becoming unemployed found work again within three months. The high prevalence of relatively short periods of unemployment may well conceal longer-term patterns of labour market disadvantage. It has been shown that a significant proportion of people are trapped into cycles of recurrent unemployment (Daniel, 1983; Harris, 1987). But while this is likely to run down family resources over time, it is unlikely to encourage the formation of a sense of collective identity among the unemployed or the establishment of stable forms of collective organization. The category that does come close to the stable conditions assumed by underclass theory is that of the long-term unemployed. This was a sizeable category: by January 1988 some 1.1 million people had been registered unemployed for at least a year (*Employment Gazette*, May 1988). It had also increased significantly as a proportion of all unemployed between 1984 and 1987 (*Social Trends*, 1988:78). As White (1983: 143ff.) has shown, the long-term unemployed experience acute economic and psychological deprivations. Yet they share with the unemployed as a whole a number of characteristics that make it highly unlikely that they will develop a strong sense of collective identity or capacity for radical action.

In the first place, the unemployed are very heterogeneous in terms of the circumstances that brought them into unemployment, their personal characteristics and their position in the life cycle. A study of the stock of unemployed in 1986 showed that while 71 per cent of unemployed men had been in a job before becoming unemployed, this was the case for only 36 per cent of women. A high proportion of the unemployed women (37.7 per cent) had been previously looking after their family or home. Similarly, there are major variations by gender in the reasons why people had left their last job. The single most important reason for men is that they had been made redundant, while this was much less important for women than family or personal reasons (Department of Employment, 1988). To this can be added a further stratification of the unemployed in terms of career position, ranging from school leavers to those close to retirement age. It is clear that the experience of unemployment is likely to vary substantially between groups and that the various subcategories of the unemployed are likely to adopt rather different coping strategies. -

As well as the high level of instability and internal heterogeneity of the unemployed, there is now substantial evidence that it is a type of experience that makes effective collective action extremely difficult. Along with anxiety and depression, it engenders a loss of the sense of self-efficacy that has been shown to be one of the most important psychological underpinnings of political participation. It appears to lead, at least among men, to social withdrawal and to the collapse of the types of networks that could sustain organized activity. Finally, lack of financial resources places heavy restrictions on collective action, in a situation where few established institutions are prepared to bear the organizational costs of such activity. Certainly there has been a marked lack of political activity by the unemployed of the type that would be anticipated on the basis of underclass theory, despite very high concentrations of the unemployed in particular communities.

Moreover, there is little evidence that unemployment generates the sharp division of attitudes within the population implied by the theory. Rather it would appear to be a 'valence' or consensus issue, to which the great majority of the population, irrespective of party and class, attach considerable importance (Dunleavy and Husbands, 1985: 50; Heath, et al. 1985: 109, 125). The evidence indicates rather clearly that, in a situation of mass unemployment, the employed do not generally blame the victims or react to them aggressively as potential low-cost competitors for their own jobs. Rather they see unemployment as a result of structural circumstances and government policies, and their primary concern is that it should be reduced (Fraser et al., 1985: 362; Dunleavy and Husbands, 1985: 157). This may well reflect the fact that, despite the concentration of unemployment in specific families, its effects are felt much more widely through the anxieties and responsibilities it generates for family networks.

The general conclusion that emerges from a consideration of the marked labour disadvantages experienced by women, members of the ethnic minorities and the unemployed is that in each case they are of a type that provides little basis for the emergence of an underclass that could lead to major changes in the class structure. In part this reflects rather fundamental flaws in the nature of the theory. First, its picture of the emergence of an underclass consisting of a substantial proportion of the population was constructed by aggregating together what are in fact very dissimilar types of labour market disadvantage, thereby underestimating the internal heterogeneity of the categories concerned and the likely diversity of their interests. Secondly the assumption that the conjunction of labour market disadvantage with a distinctive cultural identity would generate social radicalism is ultimately implausible. For what is crucial is not the distinctiveness of cultural identity *per se*, but its nature. It may be conducive to be the fatalistic acceptance of inequalities or, as would appear to be the case of the subemployment of women, to their legitimation. Thirdly, it takes little account of the capacity of established institutions to adapt to and to contain new types of demand within the existing institutional framework. In part this was because the theory assumed that secondary, subemployed or unemployed workers would be in competition with those in full-time employment, thereby generating an inevitable clash of interests. This attempt to blend in theory of the 'reserve army' with a theory of 'segmentation' had little theoretical coherence. In practice it is clear that labour market competition was unlikely to be threatening for most employees.

The one case where the concept of an underclass would appear to have some relevance is that of the long-term unemployed. Their deprivations are distinctive from those generated directly by the employment relationship and they have the type of stability over time that is assumed by underclass theory. It is essential, however, to bear in mind that long-term unemployment can be regarded as an inequality linked to class position, in that it affects primarily manual workers (White, 1983: 33). Further, this use of the concept would appear to have none of the wider implications for the dynamics of the class structure anticipated by writers such as Giddens and Rex. While the long-term unemployed may be distinctive in terms of their social attitudes, this does not result in a greater propensity for radical action, but in greater psychological demoralization and social withdrawal. Further, there is no evidence at all that an underclass of this type produces a conservative backlash that fundamentally alters the character of the manual working class.

The Decline of Manual Worker Collectivism?

An influential early formulation of the argument that structural changes were affecting the nature of British working-class culture was David Lockwood's 'Sources of Variation in Working-Class Images of Society' (1966). Transferring many of the arguments of the theory of industrialism to the analysis of structural changes at the local level, Lockwood depicted a long-term trend towards the dissolution of the kinds of social structures that had sustained traditional class solidarities. The developing conditions of production, he argued, led to the weakening of worker solidarities, psychological withdrawal from the work situation and the replacement of work by the family as the central life interest. In part, this was the result of the growth of large-scale, bureaucratically organized factories utilizing mass production technologies. These were associated with specialized, repetitive work and with the dissolution of traditional types of work group. Such conditions were unlikely to make people feel strong commitment to their workmates or deep hostility to their employer. The privatized character of community relations reinforced those of the workplace by undercutting communal solidarities. The overall effect of these changes was to encourage a shift in worker consciousness from a 'class-divided' conception of society to a 'pecuniary' model, in which the class structure is perceived in terms of finely graded income strata, the distinction between manual and non-manual work loses its significance and conflicts of power between classes have little salience. Although there was a distinct shift in explanatory emphasis, the programme of empirical research that was associated with these ideas (Goldthorpe et al., 1969) drew a very similar picture of the direction of social change. The new type of worker, it was argued, had a primarily instrumental orientation to work. He continued to adhere to trade unions and to support the Labour Party, but only because these were seen to be the most effective vehicles for realizing the individual's private goals as consumer.

Lockwood's work had emphasized the diversity of class attitudes depending on the nature of local work and community settings. This conception of the determinants of working-class culture influenced research for the next decade. Sociologists set out to the docks, to shopyards and to farming communities to tease out the intricacies of the local structural milieux of diverse types of 'traditional' worker and to chart their impact upon conceptions of the class structure. As the evidence accumulated, Lockwood's emphasis on the importance of local structural factors appeared less and less plausible. Studies of manual workers in traditional industries, such as the docks and shipbuilding, revealed attitudes to work and to society that bore a remarkable affinity to the attitudes of workers in the more advanced industrial sectors (Bulmer, 1975; Hill, 1976). There was little indication of strong class resentment either with respect to the employer or to the wider structure of inequality. Much like the 'affluent' workers, the majority had an image of the class structure that de-emphasized the distinction between manual and non-manual workers, that saw class differentiation largely in terms of income differences and that revealed few traces of class antagonism. The description that had been given of the social attitudes of the 'affluent worker' appeared to reflect less the specific context of work and community in the advanced sectors of production than the more general characteristics of British working-class culture.

Thus a striking finding of this phase of research was the essential homogeneity of British working-class culture. Further, one of its most notable features was the very low level of resentment about wider inequalities of income and wealth. Runciman (1966) had shown that when asked what sort of people were doing noticeably better than themselves, less than a quarter of manual respondents chose an explicitly non-manual reference group. Studies replicating Runciman's methodology in the 1970s came to virtually identical conclusions (Daniel, 1975; Scase, 1977). The low level of class radicalism in Britain emerged particularly sharply when British manual workers were compared with French. Surveys of British manual workers have repeatedly shown that a majority feel no clear sense of class identification. For instance, in February 1974, at the height of the crisis of the miners' strike, a mere 35 per cent of British manual workers felt that they belonged to the working class. In contrast, a survey in France in 1976 showed that some 56 per cent spontaneously thought of themselves as belonging to the working class. There were equally important differences in the importance that manual workers attached to reducing inequalities between rich and poor. For instance, in 1978, a cross-cultural survey showed that 68 per cent of French manual workers, but only 20 per cent of British, thought that it was very important to 'try and reduce the number both of very rich people and of very poor people' (Gallie, 1983: 157ff.).

By the 1980s, however, it could be argued that the economic and political landscape in Britain was changing fundamentally. In the first place, major changes were occurring in the technology of work, with the rapid diffusion of automation. While mass unemployment reached heights that were unprecedented since the depression of the inter-war years, those in employment saw a steady rise in their real incomes, producing an increased polarization within the working class. The growth of personal wealth among an important sector of manual workers was reinforced by the spread of home-ownership. For some writers (Saunders,

1981; Dunleavy and Husbands, 1985), this was seen as leading to the growth of 'consumption sector' cleavages, whereby factors such as housing tenure generated quite different interests between different groups of manual workers with regard to taxes and state subsidies.

Within the context of these changes in employment and living conditions, there appeared to be considerable grounds for doubt about the tenacity of collectivist orientations within the working class. In the 1970s there was some evidence of increasing hostility to the trade unions, reflected in the rising proportion of people that regarded the unions as having too much power. More fundamentally, from the late 1970s, the British trade unions entered a phase of severe decline. Between 1979 and 1984, they lost over two million members and union density fell from some 54 per cent of the work-force to 45 per cent. At the same time, the successive electoral victories of the Conservative Party and the apparent erosion of skilled working-class support for the Labour Party suggested a marked erosion of even rather moderate types of class solidarity. In 1966 some 69 per cent of manual workers had voted for the Labour Party, by 1983 it was a mere 42 per cent. In terms not dissimilar from those that had launched the first embourgeoisement debate in the late 1950s and early 1960s, researchers began to consider whether or not changes in employment conditions were leading to a marked diversification of the working class involving, at least in some sectors, major changes in traditional working-class values. There is still relatively little evidence with which to assess this argument, but it is possible to take an initial look at its plausibility.

A first point to consider is the striking decline of British trade-union strength. To what extent does this suggest a major erosion of workplace collectivism? The major sources of evidence on this are the British Workplace Industrial Relations surveys. These provide comparable information for 1980 and 1984, based on interviews with national samples of employers. In their analysis of this data, Millward and Stevens (1986: 52–3) found that the major decline in the proportion of workplaces with trade-union members was in private manufacturing, but argued that the most plausible explanation of the fall of membership was the disproportionate closure of large workplaces over the period. Further they found a strong negative association between union density and employment growth. They concluded that: 'The disproportionate loss of employment among highly unionized establishments that have remained in existence throughout the period must surely be largely responsible for the aggregate decline in union membership numbers' (1986: 60). This suggests that the major source of trade-union decline can be attributed to structural constraint rather than to any significant erosion of allegiances to trade unions on the part of employees. The major trend in work organization that would appear to pose a substantial threat to trade-union strength is the shift towards smaller sizes of establishment. This may make it substantially more difficult for the unions to organize manual workers and may prevent any easy recovery of union strength with a major recovery of manufacturing industry.

The albeit rather restricted survey evidence would appear to suggest the growth of somewhat more favourable attitudes to trade unions in the 1980s, rather than any erosion of trade-union support. In the 1970s there had certainly been a sharp increase, even among manual workers, in the belief that the trade unions had become too powerful. In 1970 some 53 per cent of manual workers felt that the unions had too much power; by October 1974 the proportion had risen sharply to 68 per cent and, by the election of 1979, it had reached 72 per cent (Gallie, 1983: 74). The early 1980s, however, would appear to have seen a marked reversal of this trend, despite a much more aggressive critique of the power of the unions by the government. Indeed, by 1983 the proportion of manual workers that considered the unions too powerful had fallen to 63 per cent, which was below its level in 1974. This confirms the view that the decline in trade-union membership reflected primarily the collapse of employment in the traditionally highly unionized sectors of British industry, rather than any growing crisis of manual workers' commitment to the unions. In the bleaker economic climate of the 1980s, manual workers' awareness of the importance of trade-union organization may well have become stronger.

If there is little convincing evidence of an erosion of workplace collectivism, have there been changes in manual workers' sense of class identity and in their attitudes to inequalities in the distribution of income? It is commonly believed that this was a period when the restructuring of employment was heavily undercutting class solidarities. Yet, the data from the General Election survey of 1983 suggest that it was a period that, if anything, sharpened manual workers' sense of class membership. Whereas in 1979 only 38 per cent of manual workers had any strong sense of working-class identity, by 1983 the proportion had risen to 45 per cent. Further there is some evidence of an increased resentment about social inequality. The proportion of manual workers that thought that it was very important to try to reduce the number both of very rich and of very poor people rose from 20 per cent in 1978 to 33 per cent in 1983 (Gallie, 1988). These differences are not very substantial and the overwhelming impression remains one of very low levels of class identity and class resentment. There may also be significant time-lag effects before the full implications of patterns of economic and institutional change become apparent. The available data, however, provide little support for the view that there has been a significant erosion of class identities or concern about social inequalities in the early 1980s.

If there is little evidence that manual workers' attachment to trade unions or resentment about inequalities have changed substantially, a number of analysts do claim to have found significant signs of change in their attitudes to the political representation of their interests. For instance, Sarlvik and Crewe (1983) argued that, from the mid 1960s, there had been a marked process of class dealignment in which both the Labour Party and the Conservative Party had lost support from their natural class bases and class itself had become a less significant source of political division. Dunleavy and Husbands (1985) provided an account of the changing political allegiances of manual workers in terms of the influence of 'consumption sector' cleavages that cut across the class interests that derive from people's employment situation and internally divide the manual working class. They point to the substantial differences in the voting behaviour of manual workers depending upon their degree of integration into processes of privatized consumption. For instance, in 1983, whereas 54 per cent of council tenants voted Labour, this was the case for only 36 per cent of home-owners (1985: 138).

Heath et al. (1985), however, have shown that there must be severe doubts about whether the loss of working-class support can be attributed to changes in the structural conditions of working-class life. They find no clear trend over the period 1964 to 1983 towards a decline in relative class voting (1985: 35). Labour did less well in securing working-class support in 1983 than it had in the past, but this was not a problem that was distinctive to the working class, but was part of a general loss of support among all classes. The explanation has, then, to be sought in more general political factors rather than in changes in the employment or living conditions of manual workers. In particular they are critical of the interpretation that is usually given to the association between consumption patterns and voting. On the key issue of housing, they argue that the evidence supports the view that more conservative social values may have determined tenure choice, rather than a person's voting choice being the result of consumption sector location. Marshall et al. also conclude from their analysis of a large-scale survey carried out in 1984 that: 'in so far as sectoral cleavages in housing and employment are associated with voting intention, these are merely surrogates for social class' (1988: 251).

In accounting for changes in political loyalties, Heath et al. place primary emphasis on the influence of more specifically political factors. At one level, this reflects a shift in general values away from adherence to the virtues of state intervention and towards support for the values of free enterprise. This shift, they suggest, must be in part understood as a result of the longer-term influence of political parties on general ideologies (1985: 112, 133–4, 174). However, they also attribute an important role, in the shorter term, to the way in which parties present their political ideas. The Labour Party suffered from assuming that resentment about class inequalities was more salient than it was and from thereby presenting a sectionalist image of its political objectives (1985: 166).

Overall, the evidence for a major shift in manual worker values as a result of economic change in the 1980s is very thin. Support for trade unionism did not decline and indeed may well have increased, despite heavy membership losses arising from the closure of firms. The principal sign of a shift in the attitudes of manual workers would appear to be the loss of support for the Labour Party. This was not, however, a result of changes that were specific to the manual working class and can scarcely be treated as an indication of a major shift in values. For the period for which there is satisfactory data, there is no evidence that the Labour Party was supported out of attachment to values of redistribution or out of any strong sense of class solidarity. The notable feature of British working-class culture throughout this period has been the very low salience of issues of class inequality. Support for the Labour Party was based primarily on instrumental motives and hence was always vulnerable to erosion if manual workers could be persuaded that their personal economic interests lay elsewhere.

The Radicalization of Non-manual Workers?

The long-term pattern of occupational change has been towards an increase in the various social strata that have been conventionally labelled as the 'middle classes'. Indeed, these now represent roughly half the overall active population and a majority of those currently in employment. Increasingly, then, sociological interest has focused on the implications of the growth of non-manual occupations for traditional forms of class organization and for the legitimacy of the reward structure of capitalist societies. There is a quite remarkable diversity of views in the literature about the nature of these occupational categories, their location within the class structure and the direction in which they may be changing (see, for instance, Abercrombie and Urry, 1983). Moreover, an interesting feature of this 'boundary debate' is the extent to which it cuts across conventional theoretical divisions. At a general level, it is possible to distinguish three positions that have been particularly influential.

The first depicts the expanding 'new middle classes' as benefiting from a relatively advantageous position in the structure of social inequality. This derives primarily from their higher levels of education and their closer association with the exercise of authority. While distinct from the dominant class of employers, they are none the less occupational groups that have a substantial stake in the status quo and that are likely to be supportive of the existing institutional framework. This view underlay the scenario of growing social consensus developed by the theorists of industrialism (see, for instance, Lipset, 1969). It also has, however, its Marxian variants. For instance, Poulantzas (1975) argued that the growth of white-collar employees, technicians and supervisors has created a 'new petty bourgeoisie' that is quite distinct from the working class as a result of its involvement in unproductive labour, its supervisory responsibilities and the mental rather than manual character of the work. Its structural position results in ideological beliefs that have a close affinity to those of the traditional petty bourgeoisie, to the extent that the two can be regarded as part of a single social class (1975: 287).

The strongest form of the argument is perhaps that developed by Bell (1974), who predicted that the expansion of these strata would create major problems for the trade unions in maintaining their membership (1974: 40–2). This was not due just to the traditional sense of superiority of status and the individualistic ethos of non-manual workers, but also reflected the fact that the expansion of these categories had been largely based on the increased labour market participation of women. Women, he argued, feel less committed to the labour market and therefore have much less incentive to become involved in trade unions (1974: 146). The one area in which Bell anticipated the development of strong types of middle-class organization was among professional employees. However, in terms of the traditional labour movement, such associations are inherently ambivalent. They share with trade unions a concern to defend the income of their members and, in the context of tight government budgetary controls, this could lead to greater militancy (1974: 144). At the same time, however, they are bastions of the defence of privilege and are concerned to maintain the distinctiveness of their professional status through clearly differentiating themselves from other social groups. For Bell, the most plausible future scenario is the growing assertion of a professional ethos that makes it very unlikely that such organizations will form any close alliance with traditional organized labour (1974: 153–4).

In contrast to the view that the growth of the non-manual work-force would lead to a decline in class-based conflicts and in forms of collective employee organization, a number of theorists suggested that changes occurring in the nature of non-manual work created a new basis for a solidarity of interests between the manual and non-manual work-force, One version of this argument stressed the importance of the deskilling of non-manual occupations. Already developed in the inter-war period by a number of writers (see, for instance, Klingender, 1935), this thesis gained new impetus from the work of Braverman (1974). Although he developed the argument most systematically with respect to clerical work, Braverman believed that similar processes were beginning to affect most of the 'middle layers' of employment, including the 'mass employments of draftsmen and technicians, engineers and accountants, nurses, teachers and the multiplying ranks of supervisors, foremen, and petty managers'. This process of deskilling would have significant implications for employee attitudes: 'In such occupations, the proletarian form begins to assert itself and to impress itself upon the consciousness of these employees' (1974: 407–8). For Braverman, the development of capitalism was associated with the long-term proletarianization of the greater part of non-manual workers, who, as members of an undifferentiated 'working class', would have interests identical to those of manual workers.

A broadly similar scenario was depicted by Wright (1979). While elaborating a broader conception of the class structure that explicitly allowed for the existence of 'contradictory class locations', Wright none the less emphasized the 'constant proletarianization of the working conditions of white-collar labour'. He concluded that 'it seems almost certain that the large majority of white-collar employees, especially clerical and secretarial employees, have – at most – trivial autonomy on the job and thus should be placed within the working class itself' (1979: 81). While neither Wright nor Braverman were notable for their elucidation of the links between class position and collective action, the clear presumption was that similar forms of class position should be conducive to similar forms of social consciousness.

A third set of theories anticipated not only the emergence of new forms of social radicalism among the rapidly expanding sectors of the non-manual work-force, but argued that non-manual workers rather than manual would become the major force for structural change. One of the most influential early versions of this argument was developed by Gorz (1967). Much like the liberal theorists, Gorz sees a long-run tendency towards rising levels of skill and education among non-manual workers. This was reflected in the growing importance of technicians, engineers and scientific researchers who have been trained to think creatively and with a longer-term perspective. Unlike the liberal theorists, however, Gorz anticipates that the structures of the capitalist enterprise, with their emphasis on short-term profitability, will generate deep dissatisfaction among employees by frustrating the use of their creative abilities. According to Gorz:

> The industry of the second half of the twentieth century increasingly tends to take men from the universities and colleges, men who have been able to acquire the ability to do creative or independent work; who have curiosity, the ability to synthesize, to analyze, to invent, and to assimilate, an ability which spins in a vacuum and runs the risk of perishing for lack of an opportunity to be usefully put to work. (1967: 104-6)

This tension will heighten awareness of the need for social change and give rise to conflicts centred on the issue of the democratization of decision-making processes. Similar views to Gorz's were developed by Mallet (1969) and Touraine (1968, 1969), who argued that the fact that the new radicalism is directed against the constraints of capitalist institutions opens up the possibility of an alliance between sectors of the non-manual work-force and at least certain categories of manual workers. They point to the emergence of a new contesting class that embraces professionals, technicians and manual workers in the more technologically advanced sectors of industry and that will focus its demands primarily on issues of participation and control.

We have then quite diverse interpretations of the implications of the growth of the non-manual strata for patterns of social division and the nature of conflict. These range from the view that the pattern of occupational change is heightening the social integration of society and undercutting forms of collective organization through to the belief that it will lead to a more radical contestation of the existing institutional framework of society. It is notable, however, that the categories of non-manual worker that lie at the centre of the analysis are rather different depending on the particular view that is being advocated. The proletarianization thesis is elaborated most systematically for clerical and service workers, whereas its extension to other categories is a little more tentative. In contrast, the 'liberal' theorists and writers such as Gorz and Touraine focus primarily on scientific workers and technicians.

The longest standing debate has been about the evolution of clerical work. Inter-war Marxian theorists had stressed the proletarianization of the clerical work task, but had encountered difficulties in explaining the persistence of decidedly non-socialist forms of consciousness. Lockwood (1958) argued that the continuing differences in consciousness between clerical and manual workers could only be accounted for in terms of significant remaining differences in their work and labour market situation. Clerical workers still tended to work in small units and had close contacts with management, there was a lower level of standardization in work tasks and mechanization was less pervasive. While income differentials with manual workers had narrowed, the conditions of work, job security and opportunities for advancement remained substantially better. In short, while recognizing that major changes had occurred in the employment conditions of clerical workers, Lockwood contested the view that this involved the type of proletarianization that had been claimed by Marxian writers. These arguments have been heavily criticized by Crompton and Jones (1984), who argued that they were based on an analysis of clerical work before the widespread diffusion of computerization in the office. Their own research into clerical work in banking, life assurance and local government suggested that fully 91 per cent of those on clerical grades exercised no control in their work and hence could be said to have very little skill (1984: 61).

The study by Crompton and Jones was based on a rather small sample (262 clerical workers) and statements about relative employment conditions were hampered by the absence of any comparison of clerical workers with manual workers. A rather more comprehensive study of the work and market situation of employees by Marshall et al. (1988), using a large-scale national sample, provides very little support for the view that there has been a sharp deterioration in the work situation of routine white-collar workers or for the argument that their employment conditions have become assimilated to those of manual workers. For instance, among female employees in Class IIIa (white-collar clerical and secretarial) full 66 per cent were of the view that their present jobs required more skill than when they first started to do them and a mere 4 per cent felt that they had been deskilled. This contrasted sharply with the situation among unskilled manual workers, where the great majority (71 per cent) felt that their skill levels had remained unchanged (1988: 116–17). In terms of their autonomy and self-control in work (a concept of skill similar to that deployed by Crompton and Jones), clerical and secretarial employees were substantially more likely to feel that their job allowed them to design and plan important aspects of their work than skilled or semi-skilled manual workers and indeed came close to the level characteristic of the supervisors of manual workers (1988: 118). The pattern remains remarkably consistent across a range of questions exploring different aspects of autonomy and discretion.

The Essex study does not explicitly examine the impact of computerization. The 1984 Workplace Industrial Relations Survey, however, reveals that 55 per cent of managers in establishments that had experienced office automation thought that the level of skill involved in office workers' jobs had increased, while only 2 per cent thought that it had decreased. Similarly, 59 per cent thought that the range of activity in the job had increased, compared with 8 per cent that felt that it had diminished (Daniel, 1987: 161). Further, automation of the office was substantially more likely to improve the interest, skill and variety of tasks than was automation affecting manual workers (1978: 161–3). Far from leading to the proletarianization of white-collar work, advanced technology would appear to have increased the differences between the work situation of office and manual workers.

A second group that has been central to the debate about the implications of employment changes for class boundaries is that of technicians. While the available evidence is fragmentary, the general picture it provides reinforces the conclusions reached by research into clerical work. The study by Roberts et al. (1972) of 1,167 technicians emphasized the sheer diversity of work tasks that technicians carried out and the low level of standardization across companies of the nature of technicians' role (1972: 40–8). A notable finding across the various categories of technician, however, was the high degree of interest that technicians found in their work. While there was some feeling of underutilization of skills, this had to be seen in the context of high aspirations for promotion. Overall, the authors conclude: 'their interest in their work appears to provide a major source of psychic rewards, a source which contrasts quite markedly with the degree of job satisfaction derived from more extrinsic aspects of their position in the firm such as salary and fringe benefits' (1972: 138). Moreover, the majority of technicians felt that they could influence their superiors in terms of technical decisions about the job and continued to work within small work groups in an unbureaucratized work setting. While the type of production technology appeared to make very little difference to technicians' attitudes, those involved in advanced technological settings appeared generally more satisfied about existing communications with management than technicians in more traditional unit and small batch settings (1972: 164). This is scarcely encouraging for the view that there is an on-going process of proletarianization of technical work.

A study in the late 1970s of the work situation of technicians in a British aerospace factory (Smith, 1986, 1987) confirmed this general picture of the nature of technical work in an advanced sector of production. While stressing the diversity of occupations within this general category, Smith noted that there were a number of general elements within the work situation of most middle-range technical workers. These included the exercise of a high degree of individual autonomy on the job, effective self-supervision, a freedom of movement that was quite distinct from that accorded to manual workers, an informal work atmosphere and a high degree of job satisfaction (Smith, 1986: 84–5; 1987, ch. 4). While there may be an increase in time consciousness and possible future threats to the role of lower technicians, depending upon the way in which Computer Aided Design is implemented, it is clear that the 'conceptual' elements of work remain central to the work tasks of technicians. Although it emphasizes the continuities both in terms of craft ethos and of social relations between technicians and skilled manual workers, there is little in Smith's account that points towards proletarianization. This is confirmed by the national study of the class structure by Marshall et al. (1988), which shows that those in the general 'class' category of lower-grade technicians and supervisors of manual workers were even more likely to have experienced an increase in skill than clerical and secretarial workers. Fully 76 per cent of men and 56 per cent of women thought that the job needed more skill than when they first took it. In contrast, only 4 per cent of the men and none of the women reported a decrease in skill.

There seems little doubt, then, that both clerical workers and technicians have continued to have a very different work situation from that of both skilled and non skilled manual workers. On almost all measures of autonomy and decision-making in work they fall between the conditions that characterize manual workers on the one hand and the higher 'service' occupations on the other (Marshall et al., 1988: 118–19). There are, then, strong grounds for considering them as distinct occupational strata from those of manual workers and there is little sign of any generalized tendency to deskilling.

A number of researchers have advanced the further argument that, whatever the trends in the evolution of the characteristics of lower white-collar work, the members of these intermediate strata are very unlikely to develop a common set of attitudes to their situation due to the heterogeneity of their social origins and career trajectories. The case was developed with particular force by Stewart et al. (1980) in their discussion of the 'class' situation of clerical workers. The fundamental flaw with theories of proletarianization, they suggested, is that they assume a work-force that is stable over time and homogeneous in terms of its work histories. In practice, the clerical work-force is highly diverse, consisting of a mixture of older manual workers who had reached non-manual jobs as the concluding phase of their careers, of young male clerical workers for whom the job was a temporary staging post before promotion, and of women who were likely to regard the job as short term or as secondary to their domestic commitments. Given their very diverse backgrounds, these different types of clerical workers were unlikely to respond to the objective nature of the work in a similar way and, for the greater part, they were unlikely to hold their jobs for sufficient time to experience personally marked changes in job content. It was rather unlikely, then, that changes in the employment conditions of clerical work would generate any coherent form of consciousness, let alone produce a systematic pattern of growing identification with the manual working class.

A picture of considerable diversity in social origins also emerges from the work on technicians. Roberts et al. (1972: 130–1) report that among their draughtsmen, laboratory staff, planning and production engineers roughly half came from manual and half from non-manual and self-employed families. Moreover, they had arrived as technicians by very different routes: 30 per cent had been originally craft apprentices, 31 per cent had taken technician training of an apprenticed form and 25 per cent had no kind of apprenticeship whatsoever (1972: 40). Similarly, Smith (1986: 95) reports that: 'It was common in estimating, planning and many draughting departments for over half of the office to have entered via a skilled shopfloor position.'

The evidence from these case studies is confirmed by Goldthorpe's (1980) analysis of national social mobility patterns among men. The intermediate classes are characterized by much more diverse patterns of recruitment in terms of family origins than the manual working classes. Further, even where people appear to have been intergenerationally stable in these classes, they are in fact much more likely to have experienced substantial mobility in the course of their work lives. He concludes that 'within the range of intermediate-class positions that we have distinguished, the extent and nature of mobility is such that the existence of classes as collectivities that retain their identity through time is for the most part highly problematical' (1980: 262).

This combination of relatively advantageous employment conditions with a highly diverse and fluid pattern of recruitment might be thought to have created the perfect conditions for discouraging the growth of collective organization among non-manual workers. Yet one of the most notable developments of British industrial relations in the 1970s was the marked growth in white-collar trade union membership. Whereas in 1969 union density among white-collar workers was 32 per cent, by 1979 it had risen to 44 per cent. Indeed, the growth of white-collar membership accounted for more than two-thirds of total union growth over this period and by 1979 non-manual workers represented 40 per cent of all trade-union members (Price and Bain, 1983: 50).

One explanation of this apparent paradox might be to see white-collar trade unionism not as a result of the growth of resentments about the employment relationship, but as the product of institutional constraints. In his early work on the historical growth of white-collar trade unionism, Bain (1970: 183) developed a thesis that pointed in this direction. He suggested that there was no significant relationship between the growth of white-collar unionism and factors such as the socio-demographic characteristics of white-collar workers, their earnings, conditions of employment, employment security or the technical nature of their work. Unionization was facilitated by higher levels of employment concentration, but the critical explanatory factor, he argued, lay in the nature of employer policies. Union membership had expanded where employer associations had taken the initiative of granting recognition on behalf of their member firms or had provided a framework facilitating recognition. The role of government had been crucial both directly as employer and through the influence it could bring to bear on the policies of private employers. In a sharp attack on 'stratification' explanations of trade unionism, Bain et al. argued that 'the decision to join a union is generally not a completely voluntary act, but is, to a greater or lesser extent, constrained by the institutionalization of unions' (1973: 57).

However, dismissal of the importance of the commitment to trade unionism of white-collar workers themselves is problematic. In contrast to the situation among manual workers, the level of institutionally constrained union membership among white-collar workers is likely to be low. For instance, in 1984, while 30 per cent of manual workers in establishments with twenty-five or more employees were covered by closed shop provisions, the proportion of non-manual workers was a mere 8 per cent. In the public services, where levels of white-collar trade unionism were exceptionally high, only 5 per cent of non-manual workers were in a closed shop (Millward and Stevens, 1986: 102). A comparison of white-collar and blue-collar workers' reasons for joining trade unions by Roberts et al. (1977: 130) showed that while 49 per cent of manual workers had joined because they were in a closed shop, this was the case for only 22 per cent of white-collar workers. The predominant reason for membership given by white-collar workers (54 per cent) was 'the pursuit of specific occupational interests'. In short, while employer policies could certainly make it easier or more difficult for employees to join unions where they wished to do so, they did not create conditions where membership was heavily 'constrained'. Nor, as Price (1983) has pointed out, can an explanation focusing primarily on employers' recognition policies account very effectively for fluctuations in membership after recognition. This poses particular problems for the analysis of the growth of white-collar unionism in the 1970s where 'well over one-half of the total increase in white-collar membership occurred in industries and sectors where recognition had been achieved for the unions concerned many years previously' (Price, 1983: 156). A satisfactory explanation of growth of white-collar unionism must account, then, both for the policies of employers and for the sources of commitment to trade unionism of white-collar workers themselves.

The most plausible explanation for the growth of white-collar workers' commitment to collective organization lies in changes in their labour market position. Prandy et al. (1982: 163) found that the major determinant of clerical workers' commitment to collective organization in the enterprise and their preparedness to engage in industrial action was their income and their degree of dissatisfaction with their income. Apart from income the main influences related to job security. Similarly, the study of Roberts et al. (1972: 320–2) of technicians emphasizes the significance of declining promotion opportunities and the perception of diminishing earnings differentials in relation to manual workers in generating collective resentment. They found that 'The most important factors leading to unionization were the ambiguity and uncertainty felt by many technicians about their career pattern and their future place in the labour market' (1972: 323). Kelly (1980: 94–7), in a study of British civil servants, underlines the central importance of resentments over pay and work hours in building up union membership – particularly in the favourable context provided by the First World War. Further, it was the real and perceived decline of salaries that moved the Civil Service clerical workers away from the 'ethic of harmony' to industrial militancy in the 1970s. Price and Bain (1983), in seeking to account for the marked increase in union density in almost every industry in the 1970s, argue that 'a large part of the answer to this question is provided by economic factors'. It was a period of rapid inflation combined with a marked slowing down of the increase in real earnings.

> White-collar workers were particularly hard hit relative to manual workers. Whereas increases in white-collar earnings generally kept up with and even exceeded increases in manual earnings prior to 1968, the reverse was true during 1969–79: primarily as a result of the flat-rate characteristics of a series of incomes policies, the white collar/manual earnings differential was severely squeezed. (1983: 55)

The growth of the commitment to collective organization of white-collar workers was then closely connected to changes in labour market position and reflected increased tensions within the employment relationship. Further, the growing militancy of many white-collar unions in the 1970s and 1980s, and their increasing affiliation to the TUC, suggests that there is little significant difference in union character between manual and white-collar unions as such, although there is considerable diversity among unions representing both categories of workers. Can the rise in white-collar collective organization, then, be held to be a sign of the growth of more radical attitudes to society, along the lines suggested by authors such as Gorz, Mallet and Touraine?

Empirical inquiry into the social attitudes of the 'middle classes' is still very underdeveloped. The evidence available, however, offers little support for the view that there has been a general process of social radicalization. It has been seen already that the motives behind unionization were typically of a sectionalist type. Roberts et al. (1977: 130) found that only 11 per cent of their white-collar trade unionists had joined for ideological or ethical reasons. A large-scale study of technicians found that, when asked whether technical staff had an outlook more in common with management or with shopfloor workers, technicians of all categories were more than twice as likely to cite management as they were to identify with manual workers (Roberts et al., 1972: 145). More generally, it is notable that middle-class political attitudes have remained predominantly favourable to the Conservative Party or to the centre. In the election of 1983, Labour secured the support of a mere 25 per cent of routine non-manual workers and 26 per cent of technicians and foremen, compared with 49 per cent of manual workers (Heath et al, 1985: 32–3). These strata were also markedly to the right of the manual working classes in their attitudes to the ownership of industry, income distribution and support for private education (1985:18). The growth of a more aggressively individualistic Conservatism may have increased differences within the middle classes, between those with higher levels of education and greater involvement in the public sector, who favour the retention of the post-war institutional framework, and those more directly in the market economy, who endorse the values of selfhelp. There has also been a long historical tradition of support among a significant sector of the middle classes for policies of social reform. But, while the evidence about patterns of change is still very imperfect, there is little sign that economic change over the last two decades has led to a growing radicalization of attitudes towards wider social inequalities.

The implications of the growth of the non-manual strata in Britain do not correspond closely to any of the main scenarios of social change that were considered earlier. The shift in the occupational structure has not produced the type of social consensus envisaged by the theorists of industrialism and it has not precipitated a major decline of trade unionism. Instead, there has been a growth in the level of collective organization and increased militancy. This cannot be accounted for, however, in terms of the proletarianization of the work situation of white-collar workers, for there is little evidence that any general process of proletarianization has occurred. Rather, the major factor would appear to have been heightened conflict over pay, resulting partly from the increased importance of the white-collar work-force within the occupational structure and partly from its close association with the public sector, where governments could seek most directly to implement policies of pay

control. Thus increased unionization would not appear to reflect the growth
of wider social radicalism. It is a unionism concerned to defend specific
occupational interests. As such, it built upon, and reinforced, the model
of trade unionism that had been developed by manual workers, a model
characterized by relatively limited objectives for wider social change.

Conclusion

The changes in economic structure over the last two decades have
modified, but have not altered in any fundamental way, the contours
of social stratification in Britain. Predictions of the development of a
radical underclass that would create a major new line of division within
the British class structure and that would lead to the growth of aggressive
conservative attitudes in the employed manual working class have proved
largely unfounded. They were based upon unsound assumptions about the
way in which labour markets were developing, they greatly overestimated
the homogeneity of the categories that lay at the centre of the analysis and
they took little account of the capacity of existing institutions to adapt to
and to channel new sources of tension. The principal economic category
to which the concept of an underclass may have relevance is that of the
long-term unemployed. But the long-term unemployed have not been
noted for their radicalism and their plight has engendered sympathy rather
than hostility among the greater part of employed manual workers.

Moreover generally, there is notably little evidence of major shifts
in the values and beliefs of the manual working classes, despite significant
changes in the technology of work and in levels of consumption. In part,
this reflects the fact that the relative disadvantages of manual workers have
not significantly changed and there is a very high level of intergenerational
continuity in class composition. It is also the case, however, that speculation about long-term changes in manual worker attitudes frequently rely
on a largely mythical conception of earlier forms of working-class culture.
There is, in fact, little evidence that the British working class has been
markedly class conscious – in the sense of attaching great importance
to wider issues of social inequality – for any significant period in the
twentieth century. Its members have been concerned to protect and to
advance their more immediate material interests and their attachments to
both trade unions and to political parties have been primarily a reflection
of this. Commitment to trade unionism would appear to have altered little
even over the difficult economic period of the 1980s and shifts in party
support are most likely to reflect the ability of the parties to demonstrate
the relevance of their policies to workers' economic interests, rather
than deeper value change on the part of manual workers themselves.

The most significant modification of the stratification system has been
the long-term shift in the relative weight in the occupational structure of
the manual and non-manual work-forces. This has not led, however, to
fundamental change in patterns of collective organization or the nature of

social attitudes. Contrary to the expectations of some theorists, a notable feature of recent decades has been the increasing strength and militancy of the non-manual strata. This has not been due to the proletarianization of the work situation of non-manual workers, since there is little evidence that any general process of proletarianization has in fact occurred. Rather, it has been a result of increasing conflict over pay regulation. The form taken by the collective organization of non-manual workers has developed in the context of, and has been heavily influenced by, the powerful traditions of trade unionism among British manual workers. It has not been the reflection of the growth of wider social radicalism; it has been a form of unionism concerned with the defence of categorial interests and with relatively moderate objectives for social change. It has reinforced rather than transformed the traditional patterns of class organization in Britain.

References

Abercrombie, N. and Urry, J. 1983. *Capital, Labour and the Middle Classes*. London: Allen & Unwin.
Anwar, M. 1980. *Voting and Policies: Ethnic Minorities and the General Election 1979*. London: Commission for Racial Equality.
Bain, G. 1970. *The Growth of White-Collar Unionism*. Oxford: Clarendon Press.
—— Coates, D. and Ellis, V. 1973. *Social Stratification and Trade Unionism*. London: Heinemann Educational.
Bell, D. 1974. *The Coming of Post-Industrial Society*. London: Heinemann.
Berger, S. and Piore, M. 1981. *Dualism and Discontinuity in Industrial Societies*. Cambridge: Cambridge University Press.
Braverman, H. 1974. *Labor and Monopoly Capital*. New York: Monthly Review Press.
Brown, C. 1984. *Black and White Britain. The Third PSI Survey*. London: Heinemann Educational.
Bulmer, M. (ed.) 1975. *Working Class Images of Society*. London: Routledge & Kegan Paul.
Community Relations Commission. 1975. *Participation by the Ethnic Minorities in the General Election October 1974*. London: Community Relations Commission.
Crompton, R. and Jones, G. 1984. *White-Collar Proletariat*. London: Macmillan.
—— and Mann, M. 1986. *Gender and Stratification*. Cambridge; Polity.
Daniel, W.W. 1975. *The P.E.P. Survey on Inflation*, XLI, Broadsheet No. 553.

—— 1983. 'How the Unemployed Fare After They Find New Jobs'. *Policy Studies*, 3 (April).

—— 1987. *Workplace Industrial Relations and Technical Change.* London: Frances Pinter.

—— and Stilgoe, E. 1977. *Where Are They Now? A Follow-Up Study of the Unemployed.* London: Political and Economic Planning.

Department of Employment. 1988. *Employment Gazette*, January.

—— 1988. *Employment Gazette, May.*

Dunleavy, P. and Husbands, C.T. 1985. *British Democracy at the Crossroads.* London: Allen & Unwin.

Edwards, R. 1979. *Contested Terrain: The Transformation of the Workplace in the Twentieth Century.* London: Heinemann.

Fraser, C., Marsh, C. and Jobling J. 1985. 'Political Responses to Unemployment' *New Approaches to Economic Life.* Eds Roberts, B., Finnegan, R. and Gallie, D. Manchester: Manchester University Press.

Gallie, D. 1983. *Social Inequality and Class Radicalism in France and Britain.* Cambridge: Cambridge University Press.

—— 1988. 'Social Inequality and Class Consciousness: Patterns of Change in France and Britain'. Paper to the Southwestern Sociological Association, Houston.

Giddens, A. 1973. *The Class Structure of the Advanced Societies.* London: Hutchinson.

Goldthorpe, J.H. 1980. *Social Mobility and Class Structure in Modern Britain.* Oxford: Clarendon Press.

—— 1983. 'Women and Class Analysis: In defence of the Conventional View'. *Sociology*, 17, 465–88.

—— 1984. 'Women and Class Analysis: Reply to the Replies'. *Sociology*, 18, 491–9.

—— Lockwood, D., Bechhofer, F. and Platt, J. 1969. *The Affluent Workers in the Class Structure.* Cambridge: Cambridge University Press.

Gorz, A. 1967. *Strategy for Labor.* Boston, Mass.: Beacon Press.

Hakim, C. 1987. 'Trends in the Flexible Workforce'. *Employment Gazette* (November), 549–60.

Harris, C.C. 1987. *Redundancy and Recession.* Oxford: Basil Blackwell.

Heath, A., Jowell, R. and Curtice, J. 1985. *How Britain Votes.* Oxford: Pergamon.

Hill, S. 1976. *The Dockers.* London: Heinemann.

Joshi, H. 1984. 'Women's Participation in Paid Work'. Research Paper No. 45. London: Department of Employment.

Kelly, M.P. 1980. *White-Collar Proletariat: The Industrial Behaviour of British Civil Servants.* London: Routledge & Kegan Paul.

King, S. 1988. 'Temporary Workers in Britain'. *Employment Gazette* (April) 238–47.

Klingender, F.D. 1935. *The Condition of Clerical Labour in Britain.* London: Martin Lawrence.

Layton-Henry, Z. 1984. *The Politics of Race in Britain.* London: Allen & Unwin.

Lipset, S.M. 1969. 'The Modernization of Contemporary European Politics'. *Revolution and Counter-revolution.* London: Heinemann.

Lockwood, D. 1958. *The Blackcoated Worker.* London: Allen & Unwin.

—— 1966. 'Sources of Variation in Working-Class Images of Society'. *Sociological Review*. 14.

Mallet, S. 1969. *La nouvelle classe ouvrière*. Paris: Seuil.

Marshall, G., Newby, H., Rose, D. and Vogler, C. 1988. *Social Class in Modern Britain*. London: Hutchinson.

Martin, J. and Roberts, C. 1984. *Women and Employment: A Lifetime Perspective*. London: HMSO..

Millward, N. and Stevens, M. 1986. *British Workplace Industrial Relations 1980–1984*. Aldershot: Gower.

Moylan, S., Millar, J. and Davies, R. 1984. *For Richer, For Poorer? DHSS Cohort Study of Unemployed Men*. London: HMSO.

Pahl, R. 1984. *Divisions of Labour*. Oxford: Basil Blackwell.

Payne, J. 'Does Unemployment Run in Families? Some Findings from the General Household Survey'. *Sociology*, 21, 199–214.

Poulantzas, N. 1975. *Classes in Contemporary Capitalism*. London: New Left Books.

Prandy, K., Stewart, A. and Blackburn, R.M. 1982. *White-Collar Work*. London: Macmillan.

—— ——and —— 1983. *White-Collar Unionism*. London: Macmillan.

Price, R. 1983. 'White-Collar Unions: Growth Character and Attitudes in the 1970s' *The New Working Class? White-Collar Workers and their Organizations*. Eds Hyman, R. and Price, R. London: Macmillan.

—— and Bain, G. 1983. 'Union Growth in Britain: Retrospect and Prospect'. *British Journal of Industrial Relations*, 21, 46–68.

Rex, J. and Tomlinson, S. 1979. *Colonial Immigrants in a British City: A Class Analysis*. London: Routledge & Kegan Paul.

Roberts, B.C., Loveridge, R. and Gennard, J. 1972. *Reluctant Militants*. London: Heinemann Educational.

Roberts, K., Cook, F.G., Clark, S.C. and Semeonoff, E. 1977. *The Fragmentary Class Structure*. London: Heinemann.

Runciman, W.G. 1966. *Relative Deprivation and Social Justice*. London: Routledge & Kegan Paul.

Sarlvik, B. and Crewe, I. 1983. *Decade of Dealignment – The Conservative Victory of 1979 and Electoral Trends in the 1970s*. Cambridge: Cambridge University Press.

Saunders, P. 1981. 'Beyond Housing Classes: The Sociological Significance of Private Property Rights in Means of Consumption'. *International Journal of Urban and Regional Research*, 8, 207–27.

Scase, R. 1977. *Social Democracy in Capitalist Society*. London: Croom Helm.

Smith, C. 1986. 'Class Relations, Diversity and Location – Technical Workers'. *White-Collar Workers, Trade Unions and Class*. Eds Armstrong, P., Carter, B., Smith, C. and Nichols, T. London: Croom Helm.

—— 1987. *Technical Workers, Class, Labour and Trade Unionism*. London: Macmillan.

Social Trends, 1988. London: HMSO.

Stanworth, M. 1984. 'Women and Class Analysis: A Reply to Goldthorpe'. *Sociology*, 18, 159–70.

Stewart, A., Prandy, K. and Blackburn, R.M. 1980. *Social Stratification and Occupations*. London: Macmillan.

Touraine, A. 1968. *Le mouvement de mai ou le communisme utopique.* Paris: Seuil.

—— 1969. *La société post-industrielle.* Paris: Éditions Denoel.

Warr, P. 1987. *Work, Unemployment and Mental Health.* Oxford: Clarendon Press.

White, M. 1983. *Long-Term Unemployment and Labour Markets.* London: Policy Studies Institute.

Wood, D. 'Men Registering as Unemployed in 1978 – A Longitudinal Study' *DHSS Cohort Study of Unemployed Men, Working Paper No. 1.* London: DHSS.

Wright, E.O. 1979. *Class, Crisis and the State.* London: Verso.

17 Sectoral Change and Trade-Union Organization

David Winchester

Trade-union organization has always been influenced by the character of the employment relationship, the structure of industry and labour markets, and the composition of the labour force. This is because trade unions are 'secondary' organizers; their members have already been 'organized' into distinctive groups and relationships by employers (Offe and Wiesenthal, 1985: 176). The history of trade-union organization thus centres on the willingness and ability of trade-union members and leaders to adapt their organization and methods to the constantly changing methods of production and the structure of employment.

In the 1980s, British trade unions have been confronted by a more powerful set of environmental constraints and challenges than at any time since the inter-war years. After twenty years in which the 'problem of trade union power' had encouraged an erratic series of government interventions, the election of three Conservative governments has decisively buried what was left of the 'post-war compromise' in industrial relations. The explicit commitment to reduce trade-union influence at the workplace, and to exclude it from national political representation, has been vigorously pursued. Macroeconomic policies designed to restructure international and domestic capital, privatization and expenditure controls in the public sector, and a more restrictive legal regulation of trade-union activities, have been combined with other policies to expose the fragility of trade-union organization at a time of very high unemployment.

The main expressions of union weakness are well known. In the seven years from 1979, unions affiliated to the Trades Union Congress (TUC) lost nearly 3 million members, many of whom had been employed in the strongly organized manufacturing and nationalized industry sectors. This decline in union membership and resources exposed weaknesses in traditional patterns of union organization. Inter-union conflict and increasing problems of co-ordination and communication within individual unions were exacerbated by a number of highly publicized employers' initiatives designed to weaken or neutralize union influence. The imposition of 'flexible' working practices, the negotiation of 'no strike agreements', and government-supported employers' victories in major disputes, most notably in the printing industry and coal mining, added to the demoralizing effect of job losses and factory closures, and the political defeat of the labour movement in three General Elections. The impact of these organizational problems on the capacity of unions to represent and protect their members' interests, however, remains a matter of dispute.

Within the trade-union movement, arguments in favour of a 'new realism' emerged in the early 1980s; prominent leaders advocated a more modest programme of industrial and political goals, and more collaborative methods of pursuing them. These views were based on the assumption that changes in the labour market, reflecting new government policies, management strategies and members' (and potential members') attitudes, required a substantial shift in trade-union practice. Expressions of 'new realism' have taken a number of different forms in the last few years. They have been advocated or contested for a variety of motives, some of which reflect long-established ideological divisions. The debates within the outside the trade-union movement have also revealed conflicting assessments of the scale of the changes confronting unions. Three issues of importance for the following discussion can be noted here.

The first recognizes that economic restructuring and changes in the political environment may have a very uneven impact on trade-union organization in different occupations, establishments, regions and sectors. Traditional and secure forms of trade-union practice have always existed alongside fragile and vulnerable organization, so it is important to assess whether an increasing differentiation in union practice has occurred.

The second issue concerns the variety of data, and the alternative analytical assumptions, typically employed in the evaluation of changes in trade-union power. Survey data on union organization, such as membership density, collective bargaining coverage and shop steward facilities, and data on bargaining outcomes, such as the increase in average earnings, productivity growth and strike frequency, have often been combined to explore changes in trade-union power at the workplace (Terry, 1986). The conclusions to be drawn from such analysis remain uncertain. As Kelly (1987) has shown, assessments of unions' and employers' bargaining power have to confront formidable methodological problems, and require additional data on specific labour and product markets that shape the interests and the patterns of conflict and co-operation between the parties.

The third issue of analytical importance concerns the periodization of sectoral change and trade-union organization. The pace and direction of change in the economic and political environment facing unions may have shifted significantly in recent years, but current changes in union organization and practice may also express a delayed response to earlier pressures, or a continuing adjustment to long-term trends. For this reason, though the following discussion is focused on recent changes, it is preceded by an historically grounded framework for understanding the development of trade-union organization.

An Historical and Analytical Perspective

The timing, pace and unevenness of the industrialization process produced considerable variation in the strength and organizational forms of trade unionism in different countries, and distinctive and diverse patterns of trade-union practice have survived the transformation of capitalist economies over the last century. It is possible, none the less, to outline a number of common pressures and constraints that have influenced trade unionism in most countries, to identify variations in the nature of the problem they posed for national union movements, and to note some of the distinctive features of British trade-union development. The discussion focuses on three broad issues: changes in union structure and policy-making procedures brought about by an increasingly heterogeneous membership; the impact of collective bargaining on trade-union practice; and the response of trade unions to the growing economic intervention of the state.

First, in most countries, trade unionism began with the local organization of skilled workers in the nineteenth century. Their collective capacity to improve members' terms and conditions of employment by limiting the supply of labour was eventually undermined by technological change, the growth of mass markets and large industrial enterprises, counterorganization by employers, and the development of more 'scientific' management. The subsequent amalgamation of craft unions, and the formation of industrial and general unions to represent less skilled workers, varied in pace and precise organizational form between different industries in Britain, and in other countries. In general, however, trade unions became much larger organizations with a more heterogeneous membership.

The increasing concentration of union organization typically encouraged more centralized policy-making, a growth in the number of full-time officials and the bureaucratization of union administration. At the same time, the increasing heterogeneity of membership required the development of organizational procedures to reconcile the sectional interests of members and to identify more general common interests that could be expressed in union policies (Müller-Jentsch, 1985: 6). These developments inevitably influenced the perennial and related problems of internal union democracy and inter-union relations.

In many countries, a commitment to the principle of industrial unionism facilitated more centralized union co-operation and limited inter-union competition. In Britain, however, the emergence of two major general unions in the 1920s, and the survival of a strong craft tradition, prevented the rationalization of union structure along industrial lines, and limited the authority of the TUC. Inter-union competition developed alongside an extremely diverse pattern of internal trade-union government in which the tension between national policy and workplace trade-union initiative was often unresolved. It will be argued below that these characteristic problems of British trade unionism have been exacerbated by the scale and pace of change in the labour market in the last few decades; the sectoral, occupational and gender changes in the labour force have highlighted weaknesses in methods of union organization and representation.

Secondly, the evolution of trade-union organization and policy was crucially influenced by the development of collective bargaining. The struggle to achieve union recognition invariably involved intense and protracted disputes with employers, and often brought unions into conflict with governments and the courts. The eventual acceptance of collective bargaining by employers, and its regulation by the state, often transformed the pattern of industrial conflict and the character of trade-union organization. The willingness of employers to concede union recognition, and the level, scope and form of bargaining that developed, varied enormously between countries. In many countries, however, the legal framework of bargaining increased the tendency towards centralization and professionalization of union leadership.

The development of collective bargaining in Britain was a more gradual process than elsewhere. Employers' resistance to unions was less intense than in many countries, and collective bargaining was therefore less dependent on legal support and regulation. The pattern of industry-wide bargaining that emerged in the early years of the century, and which was consolidated by broad public policy support in the late 1940s, none the less encouraged fairly centralized union policy-making and low levels of conflict. It also left an institutional vacuum at the workplace that was gradually filled by the growth of fragmented and informal bargaining in the tight labour market conditions of the 1960s, and the formalization of plant bargaining initiated by management in the following decade.

Recession and economic restructuring have led to a significant revision of employers' commitment to collective bargaining in all countries. In Britain the central importance of collective bargaining has been challenged by the growth of non-union firms in expanding sectors of employment, and by the more confident insistence on management discretion to increase labour flexibility and to introduce new forms of consultation in organized firms. These initiatives threaten the procedural and substantive functions of collective bargaining, and they may also encourage a form of 'enterprise unionism' that further fragments union organization.

Thirdly, the growth of a more active state intervention in economic and social policy, and in the regulation of industrial relations, has posed common problems for all trade-union movements. Increasing state intervention, especially in the post-war years, emphasized the need for more authoritative confederations to co-ordinate trade-union responses to the threats or opportunities provided by government initiatives. These centralizing tendencies often produced problems for the established authority relations between different levels of trade-union organization and policy-making.

The considerable variation in the scope and direction of state intervention in economic policy and industrial relations has influenced the structure and ideology of trade unionism in each country since the outset of industrialization. In the post-war years, the extent to which governments have chosen to directly involve union leaders in 'corporatist' policy-making arrangements, or to exclude them from the political arena, has varied between countries, and within each country has shifted over time in response to changing economic and political conditions. Trade-union leaders naturally seek to influence the direction of government economic intervention: they rarely refuse invitations to participate in 'corporatist' representational structures, whilst formal exclusion from policy-making may encourage more direct forms of political and industrial mobilization.

Until the 1970s, British trade unions were offered only marginal forms of tripartite consultation with government. Keynesian economic policies had sustained labour market conditions that were favourable to unions' collective bargaining policies. In the critical economic and political conditions of the mid-1970s, TUC leaders briefly enjoyed a more direct involvement in the formulation and implementation of government policy than hitherto. The 'social contract' began with an explicit agreement between the TUC and the Labour Party on a range of economic and social policies. It soon produced more favourable labour legislation and a more extensive union leadership representation in state agencies. It collapsed, however, because the TUC was unable to influence government economic policy, and was unwilling to sustain its role in the implementation of pay restraint policies beyond a few years.

The fragility of this 'corporatist' initiative paved the way for the almost complete exclusion of trade-union leaders from the political processes of government after 1979. It also revealed the organizational and ideological constraints on the TUC in attempting to create and sustain an active trade-union role in economic policy. In comparison with Sweden or West Germany, for example, the degree of inter-union rivalry, the pursuit of sectional bargaining, and the scope of unresolved ideological conflicts between unions, limited the capacity of the central confederation to mediate between unions and the state.

It has been suggested that broadly similar pressures on trade-union organization, partly shaped by their involvement with management in the process of collective bargaining, and with government in the attempt to influence economic policies, occurred in all countries. A distinctive pattern of trade-union organization and practice developed in Britain in response to the particular characteristics of economic and political development. This chapter explores the capacity of unions to adapt to recent changes in the structure of employment in Britain.

Union Membership Growth and Decline

Aggregate Change in Historical Perspective

Over the last century, there have been considerable fluctuations in trade-union membership in Britain. Periods of growth and decline can be broadly explained by changes in the political and economic context; in particular, by the way in which they have changed industrial structure, and helped to shape employees' attitudes to collective organization, employers' policies to trade union recognition, and unions' recruitment and organization initiatives. The decline of trade-union membership since 1979, after a decade of rapid growth, is the central focus of discussion, but a brief consideration of earlier periods of union growth and decline will help to place more recent changes in perspective.

In the two decades from 1892, trade-union membership increased gradually as groups of less skilled workers, employed in larger firms, achieved some success in their recognition struggles with employers. From 1912 to 1920, union growth was very rapid; the economy expanded to meet the needs of wartime production and the public status of trade unionism was enhanced through the involvement of its leaders in government policy-making. This phase of growth, resulting in a total membership of 8 million, was quickly reversed in the inter-war years. There was a dramatic slump during the recession of the early 1920s, and a more gradual further decline until the mid-1930s. High levels of unemployment, and the political defeat of unions in the General Strike in 1926, generated a more hostile climate for union organization, and membership was halved to 4 million.

These losses were gradually regained during the fifteen years up to 1948 when membership was in excess of 9 million, and trade-union *density* was 45 per cent (see table 17.1 for definition). The growth in employment arising from the preparation for war, and the extensive economic intervention of the wartime coalition government (which included Ernest Bevin, leader of the TGWU, as Minister of Labour) created a more positive organizing environment. Indirect legislative support for union organization and collective bargaining was introduced and trade-union membership spread into the rapidly expanding 'new' industries, such as chemicals, electrical goods and motor manufacturing.

Fluctuations in union membership have been less severe in the post-war years, but three distinct periods can be identified. During the two decades from 1948, aggregate membership was more or less stable at around 9 to 10 million members, a density of 43–5 per cent. A decade of exceptional growth followed, with membership peaking at more than 13 million (54 per cent) in 1979. Since then, a period of rapid decline has wiped out all the previous decade's membership gains, resulting in a total membership of less than 11 million, 42 per cent density, in 1986.

Explanations of shifts in aggregate union membership and density rely heavily on changes in the economic and political environment. The high levels of unemployment in the inter-war years, and in the 1980s, have been associated with periods of declining membership, but, at lower levels of unemployment, small changes may not influence union growth; for example, membership increases accompanied the rise in unemployment throughout the 1970s. The rate of change in prices and money incomes can be closely linked with membership trends. Employees will view rapid price rises as a threat to their living standards and may believe that rapid increases in money income can be credited to union bargaining activities. In combination, the 'threat' and 'credit' effect of rapid inflation offers a convincing, if partial, explanation of membership growth in the 1970s; levels and changes in the rate of inflation were much lower and smaller in the earlier period of membership stagnation and the later, more recent, period of decline (Price and Bain, 1983: table 7).

The availability of time series data has encouraged the development of econometric models to test the relationship between aggregate union membership and changes in prices, money incomes and unemployment (Bain and Elsheikh, 1976). While government policies may have a vital influence on the economic context, the impact of other changes in the political environment is not so easily specified (see Carruth and Disney (1988) for an interesting attempt to include a proxy for political climate in their model). Legislation may be designed to support or discourage trade-union organization and other policies may seek to influence public opinion and the attitudes of employers to union recognition. The evaluation of such initiatives is notoriously difficult; policies often generate unintended consequences and the impact of particular policies can rarely be isolated from that of other influences. Despite these analytical problems, it can be safely asserted that changes in the political context contributed substantially to the growth of aggregate union membership from 1968 to 1979, and its decline since then.

Throughout most of the former period, Labour governments introduced voluntary and statutory support for union organization and collective bargaining. In the late 1960s, government initiatives encouraged managers 'to view the growth of union organisation among virtually all levels of employees as, if not desirable, at least inevitable. As a result many employers recognised trade unions as part of a more general restructuring of industrial relations within their firms and industries' (Bain and Price, 1983: 19). This development seems to have been little affected by the Industrial Relations Act introduced by the 1970–4 Conservative government, according to the authoritative evaluation of Weekes et al. (1975: 232). Its repeal by the returning Labour government cleared the way for a set of legislative initiatives that were all favourable to union organization; recognition procedures, provisions for shop steward facilities, disclosure of information, health and safety representation, and the removal of legal constraints on the closed shop were enacted. These procedures rarely worked as effectively as their advocates had hoped. They contributed, none the less, to a consolidation of the process of bargaining reform initiated in the late 1960s, in which secure trade-union organization was seen as an essential component of stable industrial relations. The Labour government's 'social contract' with trade unions, moreover, offered leaders a more visible and direct 'partnership' in policy-making than hitherto.

Since 1979, three Conservative governments have enacted a series of legislative constraints on union organization and abandoned the post-war public policy commitment in favour of collective bargaining. The development of a 'right to dissociate' from trade-union membership extends far beyond the severe constraints on the closed shop (union membership agreements) and the ban on union-only practices, and it has been accompanied by an unprecedented degree of interference in trade-union government, and a substantial restriction on the ability of trade unions to organize lawful industrial action. As Lewis (1986: 31) argues, the legal regulation of trade unions is designed to free employers from the constraints of union power; it thus complements a range of other 'free market' economic and social policies of deregulation. It has also been accompanied by a systematic exclusion of trade-union representation from public policy-making.

Aggregate union membership trends can be explained by distinct conjunction of economic and political forces. From 1968 to 1979, and in the

TABLE 17.1   *Union membership and density in Great Britain, 1948–79*

	Union membership ('000s) and trade-union density (%)					
	1948		1968		1979	
Aggregate	9,363	(45)	10,200	(44)	13,447	(55)
Sectoral						
Public sector	3,279	(71)	3,661	(66)	5,190	(82)
Manufacturing	3,720	(51)	4,138	(50)	5,157	(70)
Manual	3,567	(58)	3,808	(62)	4,235	(80)
White-collar	154	(13)	330	(15)	923	(44)
Construction	611	(46)	472	(30)	520	(37)
Private services	665	(15)	768	(13)	1,215	(17)
Occupational						
Manual	7,056	(50)	6,637	(50)	7,578	(63)
White-collar	2,062	(33)	3,056	(33)	5,125	(44)
Gender						
Male	7,468	(55)	7,428	(51)	8,866	(63)
Female	1,650	(24)	2,265	(28)	3,837	(40)

Source: Bain and Price, 1983. Selected and rounded data from tables 1.1, 1.2, 1.3 and 1.4.
Trade-union *density* is actual union membership as a percentage of 'potential union
membership': the latter is the labour force minus employers, the self-employed, and members
of the armed forces – it thus includes the registered unemployed (Price and Bain, 1983: 47)

period since then, they have exerted a positive and negative impact on
aggregate union membership respectively. These trends inevitably conceal
important changes in the composition of trade unions, some of which cannot satisfactorily be explained by general economic and political factors.

Change in Membership Distribution

Important shifts have occurred in the sectoral, occupational and gender
composition of trade-union membership, especially during the last twenty
years. It is interesting to note first, however, that the relative stability, or
stagnation, of union density over the period 1949–68 survives disaggregation
be sector. Table 17.1 shows a marginal decline in all four sectors and
only small changes in union membership. It conceals, however, industrial
shifts of some magnitude. In the public sector, for example, half-a-million
trade-union members left the railways and coal-mining industries and a
comparable gain in membership took place in local government and
education, while trade-union density remained much the same (Bain and
Price, 1983: 15–5). In the same period, white-collar membership increased
by 1 million (30 per cent), but unions failed to organize an increasing
proportion of the fast-growing white-collar labour force. Finally, a small
shift in the gender composition of trade unions occurred over this twenty
year period; the 4 per cent decline in male union density was accompanied

by a similar rise in the figure for women. As Bain and Price note, 'changes in the sexual, occupational, and industrial composition of potential union membership are interrelated' (1983: 13); the same is, of course, true of actual membership, as the period of rapid growth from 1968–79 reveals.

Table 17.1 indicates that the already well-organized manufacturing and public sectors accounted for most of the rapid increase in trade-union membership between 1968 and 1979. In contrast, though membership and density increased in the private sector, they remained low in the large distribution sector, and very low in the growing miscellaneous services sector. As Bain and Price argue, 'the poorly unionised sectors showed little sign of producing a significant expansion of the base of unionization in Britain in this period' (1983: 10).

The sectoral composition of union growth can be linked closely with occupational and gender changes. The rapid increase in white-collar union membership to more than 5 million, and the rise in density to 44 per cent, arose from a decisive breakthrough in manufacturing (where white-collar employment had slightly declined) and a consolidation of the relatively high levels of membership and density in the public sector (where employment had increased considerably). These sectoral and occupational trends overlap with the growth of trade-union membership among women in this period; it exceeded their higher labour force participation rate, resulting in a sharp rise in female union density to 40 per cent.

How can these sectoral, occupational and gender variations in union density and growth be explained? The single most important factor appears to be employment concentration; unionization tends to increase with the size of establishments. Variations in union density within and between industries, for manual and white-collar workers, are closely associated with employment concentration. Similarly, the lower density of women compared with men, and white-collar employees compared with manual workers, arises largely from their location in smaller establishments (Bain and Price, 1983: 27).

Workers' inclination to join, employers' willingness to recognize, and unions' capacity to organize, can all be clearly linked to establishment size. Generally, though not invariably, bureaucratic rules and standardized procedures replace personal and individual management-employee relations as the size of work establishments increases; thus the 'collectivist' inclinations of workers will be encouraged. At the same time, and for similar reasons, employers' resistance to trade unionism may decline with increasing establishment size. The involvement of union representatives in the joint regulation of pay and conditions may appear less threatening; indeed, it may be viewed as a positive value, once bureaucratic rules and standardized procedures have been introduced. Finally, and most obviously, trade unions face fewer recruitment and representation costs in dealing with larger, rather than smaller, groups of members.

The growth of membership and density from 1968 to 1979 – located in the already well-unionized manufacturing and public sectors – was also related to employment concentration. In this period, company mergers and reorganization in manufacturing significantly increased the proportion of employees working in establishments with more than 500 employees and the proportion of employees in multi-establishment enterprises. In the latter case, the survey evidence suggests that corporate personnel managers pursued more positive recognition policies, especially in relation to white-collar employees, than managers in independent establishments, who often retained more paternalistic attitudes (Bain and Price, 1983: 29). In the public sector, the reorganization of local government and the health service in the mid-1970s added to the characteristically high level of employment concentration and the tendency towards bureaucratic forms of management.

Finally, the growth in union membership and density was probably influenced by the spread of closed shop agreements and other union security provisions. Dunn and Gennard (1984: 17) estimated that there were more than 5 million workers in closed shops in 1978; in the 1970s, post-entry closed shops became more widespread in large-scale manufacturing, local authorities and nationalized industries where union density was already high. They argue that previous management hostility to the practice diminished in two phases. Managers' initial belief that the concession of a post-entry closed shop would contribute positively to the process of bargaining reform, and thus encourage greater order and stability, later gave way to a more modest assessment; namely, that union membership agreements had no apparent disadvantages (1984: 89). Alongside the extension of the closed shop, the increasing willingness of employers to deduct union membership contributions directly through 'check-off' arrangements may have contributed to union growth in the 1970s. With the help of managers, unions were able to increase membership where they were already strong, and reduce turnover and loss of membership income where they were administratively weak.

It has been argued that the aggregate loss of trade-union membership since 1979, broadly equal to the gains of the previous decade, can be explained partly be higher levels of unemployment, lower inflation and more hostile government policies towards trade unions. The changing structure of employment provides a clear indication of the sectoral and spatial distribution of membership losses.

The deep recession of 1980–2 accelerated the process of long-term decline in manufacturing employment; 1.5 million jobs disappeared in three years. The most substantial decline occurred in highly unionized large establishments, and thus the extent and coverage of the closed shop was significantly reduced (Millward and Stevens, 1986). In the well-organized public sector, considerable variations in employment trends occurred in the 1980s. The long-term decline of employment in the nationalized industries continued, and the Conservative government's target of a reduction of 14 per cent in civil service employment between 1979 and 1984 was exceeded. In contrast, job losses in some areas of local authority employment (mainly manual workers) were marked by gains in others, and employment in the National Health Service increased throughout the period (Camley, 1987).

While factory closures and redundancies affected most parts of manu-facturing and all regions, the uneven 'recovery' of employment since 1983 has been in areas of union weakness. The long-term growth of employment in private services (and women's and part-time employment) resumed after the recession, and there has been an increase in self-employment. The overall decline in manufacturing employment has continued at a slower pace, and there have been shifts 'from older heavier industries to newer lighter ones, often in new geographical areas away from urban centres, often in newer smaller premises' (MacInnes, 1987: 73).

The restructuring of the labour force appears to embody sectoral, geographical, occupational, gender and other characteristics, such as part-time employment in small establishments, that have been associated with trade-union weakness in the past. Some of the changes have undoubtedly arisen from employers' intentions to undermine trade-union organization. The decline in membership, and other expressions of union weakness, are unlikely to be reversed without significant change in trade-union organization, policies and practice.

Union Structure and Organization

Trade-union structure refers to the industrial and occupational coverage of individual unions, and the relationships between them. The changing structure of British trade unionism can be explored, therefore, by analysing the way in which union organization and policy have responded to the changing composition of the labour force and the other external pressures that account for the aggregate membership trends discussed above. The analysis has to confront the complexity and variety of organizational forms that distinguish British trade unions from their counterparts in other coun-tries. Trade-union organization developed with greater continuity, over a longer period of time, and with less central direction than elsewhere.

Four themes will be discussed in this section. First, it will be argued that few trade unions can be classified according to a single organizational principle, and thus generalizations about variations in union character and practice between different types of union have a limited and diminishing validity. Secondly, the increasing concentration and diversification of membership resulting from the uneven growth of individual unions and the impact of amalgamations will be explored. Thirdly, the implications of these developments for trade-union unity will be considered. It will be argued that more pronounced expressions of inter-union competition have recently inhibited national policy co-ordination. Finally, and directly arising from the above issues, the ability of unions 'democratically' and effectively to represent the heterogeneous and changing interests of their members in the workplace and in the national political system will be examined.

Organizational Principles and Union Character

By the end of the nineteenth century, the differences between the established craft unions, and the 'new unionism' that aspired to industrial or general organizational principles, were sufficiently clear for the Webbs to advance a general theory of union organization and behaviour in *Industrial Democracy* (1897). The Webbs suggested an unambiguous definition of union objectives: a trade union was 'a continuous association of wage earners for the purpose of improving the conditions of their working lives'. They were then able to differentiate three principal trade-union methods: the unilateral trade-union regulation of labour supply and wage rates developed by craft unions; the combination of union-imposed promotion rules and collective bargaining developed by unions representing members with industry-specific skills; and the reliance on a combination of collective bargaining and statutory regulation developed by unions representing less-skilled workers. Differences in the way in which unions attempted to regulate their members' terms of employment largely explained, 'the grades of employee which were included in each type of union, its form of government, and the pattern of its strikes' (Clegg, 1976: 1–4).

The diminishing relevance of unilateral regulation, the variety of forms of collective bargaining, and the uncertain commitment to statutory regulation, present formidable barriers to any attempts to establish such clear links between union objectives, methods and organization in Britain today. While it is sometimes useful to differentiate between craft, industrial, general and white-collar unions, it is rarely justifiable to infer that unions within one of these categories share characteristics that differentiate their policies and members' behaviour and attitudes from those in the others. These problems of generalization arise for two reasons. First, there are considerable variations in union character within each category, partly arising from the sectoral and functional location of members; and, secondly, many unions now organize an increasingly heterogeneous membership, having extended their areas of recruitment, or merged with other unions, beyond their original industrial and occupational territory.

The literature on the 'character' of white-collar unionism provides a good example of the former issue. The limited growth of white-collar union membership until the late 1960s, and empirical studies of variations in the organization, policies and affiliations of staff associations and white-collar unions, encouraged an analytical focus that explored the degree to which particular white-collar unions resembled traditional manual trade unionism. Blackburn and Prandy, for example, argued that the degree of similarity and difference between white-collar and manual unions could be measured along seven dimensions; unions were more or less 'unionate', defined as 'the commitment of a body to the general principles and ideology of trade unionism', and thus expressed a greater or lesser degree of class consciousness (1965: 112).

The conceptual limitations of Blackburn and Prandy's framework, and other attempts to compare the character of white-collar unions with a stereotypical model of manual trade unionism, have been explored in a wide range of more recent literature. In his review essay, Price suggests that 'the critical question is no longer whether white-collar unions are "different" . . . but *how* and *why* they differ, and the exploration of the structural and contextual factors which determine their behaviour' (1983: 181). The same question must, of course, be asked about the character of manual unions and their members' attitudes, both of which long ago ceased to conform to any stereotypical model.

The rapid growth and more extensive occupational and sectoral coverage of white-collar unions have encouraged more focused research in this area. In place of the implied homogeneity of 'white-collar' employees, work or unions, analysis now more often focuses on specific groups and their functions. Clerical, supervisory, technical and managerial employees occupy different hierarchical positions within the division of labour, and perform different functions within the labour process. Their sectoral location – in manufacturing, the public sector or private services (and in subsectors within these broad groupings) – may significantly inhibit or facilitate their trade-union organization. The occupational segregation of women's and men's employment may also reinforce broader expressions of women's subordination at work and influence their involvement in trade unions.

These factors may account for variations in the behaviour and attitudes of different groups of members within large 'open' unions. They also partly explain, for example, the survival of six separate school-teachers' unions, each organized around a distinctive conception of occupational interest and trade-union or professional practice. A recognition of these distinctions creates problems for both Weberian and Marxist theoretical interpretations of the link between trade unionism and social stratification or class analysis that cannot be pursued here (see, e.g., Hyman and Price, 1983; Crompton and Jones, 1984; Armstrong et al., 1986; and Smith, 1987). More simply, variations in the character of white-collar and manual unions should discourage frequent use of the categories, and the assumption that they refer to distinctive patterns of union organization and practice.

Concentration and Diversification

In recent decades, the British trade-union movement has become more concentrated. Although the Certification Officer recorded 375 separate trade unions at the end of 1986, the smallest 300 organized only 3 per cent of the total membership. The twenty-four unions with more than 100,000 members organized over 80 per cent of the total and half of the trade unionists in Britain were members of only eight unions. As table 17.2 shows, all but three of these large unions were affiliated to the Trades Union Congress, which, in 1987, represented eighty-seven union with a total membership of 9,243,297 (the exceptions were the Royal College of Nursing, the Police Federation, and the Assistant Masters and Mistresses Association).

The increasing concentration of membership into fewer unions, and thus the greater heterogeneity of membership interests within many unions, have resulted from two processes: there has been an uneven

TABLE 17.2   *Membership of major TUC affiliated unions: 1969, 1979 and 1986*

	Membership '000s		
	1969	1979	1986
Transport and General Workers (TGWU)	1,532	2,086	1,378
Amalgamated Engineering Union (AEU)	1,196	1,299	858
General, Municipal, and Boilermakers (GMB)	804	967	814
National and Local Government Officers (NALGO)	397	753	750
National Union of Public Employees (NUPE)	305	692	658
Scientific, Technical and Managerial Staff (ASTMS)	124	491	390
Shop, Distributive and Allied Workers (USDAW)	316	470	382
Electrical, Electronic, Telecom and Plumbing (EETPU)	392	420	336
Construction, Allied Trades and Technicians (UCATT)	–	348	249
Technical, Administrative and Supervisory (TASS)	87	201	241
Confederation of Health Service Employees (COHSE)	78	213	212
Society of Graphical and Allied Trades '82 (SOGAT)	236	206	200
Union of Communications Workers (UCW)	198	203	192
National Union of Teachers (NUT)	290	249	184
Banking, Insurance and Finance Union (BIFU)	87	132	159
National Communications Union (NCU)	112	126	156
Civil and Public Services Association (CPSA)	181	224	151
National Graphical Association (1982) (NGA)	106	111	126
National Union of Railwaymen (NUR)	191	180	125
Schoolmasters and Women Teachers (NAS/UWT)	45	122	124
National Union of Mineworkers (NUM)	297	253	105

Source: TUC Annual Reports

pattern of membership growth and decline in major unions, and the rate of mergers and 'transfers of engagements' has substantially increased over the last few decades. While the two developments often have been closely interrelated, they raise analytically distinct questions about trade-union organization and practice, as Undy et al. (1981) have shown.

The differences in the rate of membership growth of individual unions from 1969 to 1979, and variations in the decline of membership since then (shown in table 17.2), can be explained partly by changes in the structure of employment. The expansion of the public service sector, for example, created a favourable organizing environment for NUPE and NALGO; the growth of white-collar occupations in general, and in financial services in particular, helped ASTMS and BIFU respectively; and the decline in coal-mining employment largely explains the long-term decline in the NUM's membership.

Trade unions do not, however, simply and passively receive the benefits or losses arising from the changing pattern of employment; leaders and activists can mobilize organizational resources to influence growth in several ways. They can seek to alter the scope of their recruitment by moving from 'closed' to more 'open' occupational and industrial 'job territories'. It has already been argued that there is a universal, long-term tendency towards larger, more open, unions with a greater heterogeneity of membership, and there is little doubt that the pace of this development has increased in the last few decades.

Different trade unions have pursued membership growth with varying degrees of commitment and success. The rapid growth of ASTMS in comparison with other non-manual unions, or the TGWU in comparison with its rival general union, the GMB, can be explained by variations in leadership strategies and organizational changes. These unions, and others with higher than average growth rates, demonstrated a positive and expansionist national leadership commitment to growth, embarked on selective and well-resourced recruitment campaigns, developed more participative and decentralized forms of collective bargaining, and projected an image of 'delivering the goods', by using the mass media and their own methods of communication more effectively in highlighting membership gains from successful negotiations and disputes (Undy et al., 1981: 161–3).

The extension of recruitment boundaries, and uneven growth between rival unions, inevitably generated an increase in inter-union competition. The restrictions imposed by the TUC on recruitment in areas where other affiliates had members and recognition agreements, and the rules against poaching other unions' members, came under increasing strain in the decade of rapid growth and, as will be shown below, could not resolve the more intense expressions of inter-union conflict during the more recent period of membership decline.

The increasing pace of union amalgamations since the 1960s has reinforced the pattern of uneven 'natural' growth in generating a more concentrated and diversified trade-union structure in Britain. The motivation of union leaders in seeking mergers, and the response of activists and members in confirming or undermining their initiatives, have varied in ways that are not fully captured in the distinction between 'defensive', 'consolidatory' and 'aggressive' mergers made by Undy et al. (1981: 74).

Small trade unions, and those faced with declining membership, have agreed to merge with larger unions for primarily 'defensive' reasons. The particular and immediate pressures, however, have varied enormously. Technological change and industrial decline may have undermined the union's present and potential membership and bargaining power, for example, in the textiles, shipbuilding and printing industries. In other cases, notably in the financial services sector, members of staff associations have been persuaded that larger, TUC-affiliated unions could represent their interests more effectively at a time of rapid structural change in the sector. Other mergers have developed from the co-operative working relationships and close political ties of union leaders.

More generally, there has been 'an apparent rise in the threshold of union solvency' (Hyman, 1983: 38); low subscription income at a time of increasing inflation made it more difficult for small unions, or relatively large ones with declining membership, to pay for an expanding range of union services and activities. This was exploited by larger unions seeking to consolidate their influence in sectors where they already had substantial membership, and to extend their membership into new sectors or occupations.

The two unions with the strongest leadership orientation to growth, the TGWU and the ASTMS, pursued the most aggressive merger policies. They were able to outbid rival unions in the competitive scramble for members in the 1960s and 1970s for similar reasons; they were the most influential unions with the best-known national leaders (Jack Jones and Clive Jenkins) in the manual and white-collar union sectors respectively, and their flexible and decentralized systems of policy-making on bargaining issues seemed to offer potential partners a greater degree of independence and a stronger sense of identity than would have been possible if they merged with other large unions (Undy et al., 1981: chapter 6).

Competition and Co-ordination

The combined impact of uneven growth and union amalgamations has not significantly reduced the complexity of British trade-union structure. A degree of rationalization has occurred in parts of printing and publishing, telecommunications and the civil service. Moreover, the merger between ASTMS and TASS in 1988, creating a new union, Manufacturing, Science, Finance (MSF), with over 600,000 members and negotiating rights in 8,000 companies, offers the prospect of further rationalization in white-collar union organization. Other mergers, and the opportunistic extension of recruitment into areas previously regarded as closed territory, however, have led to 'the further diversification of the conglomerates' (Clegg, 1979: 177). The response of many unions to the substantial membership losses of the early 1980s have also highlighted the fragility of inter-union co-ordination and the increasing pressures towards competition and conflict.

In comparison with the exclusive jurisdiction of North American unions in each plant, or the structure of industrial unionism and works council representation in West Germany, traditional patterns of competitive multi-unionism have frequently attracted criticism in Britain. From a managerial perspective, multi-unionism has usually been associated with demarcation rules that reduce labour flexibility and manpower utilization, and with 'unnecessary' inter-union disputes over recognition and bargaining policies. Such criticism often exaggerates past problems by generalizing from the distinctive circumstances of a few craft-based industries, for example, shipbuilding and printing. It also fails to recognize the extent to which many managers and union representatives developed informal or formal procedures to co-ordinate multi-union representation in joint shop stewards committees or joint industrial councils.

In the hostile political and economic environment of the 1980s, however, the structure of British trade unionism has been exposed as a major source of weakness for union members, and an opportunity for employers and the government to exploit divisions and conflicts of interest. In the well-organized public sector, positive examples of inter-union co-operation and common action around pay campaigns developed in the civil service in 1981 and in the National Health Service a year later. They have rarely been sustained long enough, however, to conceal competition for members and the tactical pursuit of sectional interests in pay bargaining.

The rivalry and conflict between school-teachers' unions is unusually pronounced. Six separate unions imperfectly reflect and reinforce old status distinctions between types of school, teachers' qualifications and gender, and the different role of classroom teachers and senior staff. The lengthy pay and conditions dispute in the mid-1980s offered countless examples of NUT and NAS–UWT initiatives designed to achieve some tactical advantage over the other. The dispute also revealed the continuing division between 'professional' and 'militant union' practice, and between TUC unions and non-affiliated staff associations. Moreover, the 'resolution' of the dispute, involving the abolition of the collective bargaining machinery and the government imposition of a new salary structure and teachers' contract in 1987, provided the most eloquent testimony to the depth of union divisions, and the willingness of government ministers to exploit them.

The current structure of trade unions poses even greater problems in the attempt to organize workers in the expanding services sector, and in firms located in new towns and industrial estates with no tradition of union organization. The difficulties encountered in recruiting, retaining and effectively representing part-time employees, often located in geographically dispersed and small establishments, have been recognized for a long time. The recent campaigns of the two largest general unions (the GMB and the TGWU), though they signified a more urgent commitment to the recruitment of service sector workers, seemed unable to confront the source of past failures; they continued to duplicate organizational initiatives and dilute resources, and in the case of the hotel and catering industry, for example, were unable to present potential members with a single, and clearly indentifiable, 'appropriate' union.

In 1987, very tentative proposals to deal with these problems were considered by union leaders. The General Secretary of the TUC submitted a discussion paper to the General Council that outlined the possibility of an innovative TUC role; the creation of a TUC Organising Fund, the co-ordination of multi-union recruitment campaigns in new towns, and 'a system for designating on a temporary basis particular unions as appropriate for particular organising areas' (TUC, 1987: 17). The initial response of most union leaders was not positive. They accepted the analysis of the problem, but resisted the proposals for a more intrusive TUC role in union organization. In confirming the traditional constraints on the capacity of the TUC to co-ordinate the recruitment activities of individual unions, the response of some union leaders suggested either that they underestimated the severity of the organizational problems in growth sectors of employment, or that they preferred to confront the difficulties by means of more intense competition between a handful of conglomerate unions.

The initiative occurred, moreover, at a critical moment for the TUC leadership. Its limited influence on the conduct and outcome of the 1984–5 coal mining dispute had been quickly followed by inter-union conflicts over the negotiation of 'single-union' agreements. Management recognition of a single union on greenfield sites is not, of course, unusual in Britain. The association of sole representation rights with so-called 'no-strike' agreements, however, especially when linked with new employment practices designed to produce a high degree of labour flexibility, and new forms of employee representation and involvement, generated an acrimonious debate between major TUC affiliates. The most widely publicized competition for single-union recognition accompanied the Nissan investment in the North East of England, but the TUC faced a much more severe challenge in attempting to deal with the EETPU involvement in the traumatic developments in the national newspaper industry which began in late 1985.

The chairman of News International, Rupert Murdoch, was able to relocate his newspaper production from Fleet Street to Wapping, introduce the latest electronic production processes and radically different working practices, dismiss his former employees, and defeat the print unions' prolonged and bitter dispute with the help of a series of legal actions that culminated in a threat to seek the sequestration of the assets of two print unions. Local officials of the EETPU had helped to organize the recruitment of the new labour force at Wapping, and throughout the fifteen month dispute, leaders of the Electricians' Union exposed the limitations of TUC machinery in resolving such intense inter-union conflict.

The General Council had been advised that it would be unlawful to issue a direction to the EETPU 'to inform their members to refrain from undertaking work normally done by members of the print unions'. It could only conclude that the activities of the EETPU 'were detrimental to the interests of the trade union movement' and accept the undertaking of the EETPU Executive that it accepted the rather vacuous directions of the General Council (TUC, 1986: 55). The internal authority of the TUC has always been limited by the competition between major affiliated unions, and the questionable value of expulsion – its ultimate sanction. The concentration of membership into fewer conglomerate unions, engaged in more intense membership competition, and willing to project ideological divisions in a more provocative manner, however, has exposed the minimal influence of TUC in a sharper light.

Participation and Democracy

The extent to which trade-union policy and practice adequately reflects and represents the workplace interests and political values of membership is a matter of perennial debate within, and outside, the trade-union movement. In the last twenty years, however, the issue of trade-union democracy has assumed much greater importance.Repeated government intervention to deal with the alleged excesses of trade-union industrial and political power, culminating in direct legal regulation of internal trade-union affairs, has attempted to influence members', and potential members', attitudes towards union organization and practice; the legitimacy of trade unionism has been questioned more directly than at any time in the last fifty years.

Trade-union democracy concerns the relationship between three groups: the full-time officials and executive members that constitute union leadership; the shop stewards, conference delegates, branch officers and others who comprise the lay activists; and the majority of members who take little part in union activities outside their workplace for most of the time. The assumption that union leaders are preoccupied with institutional goals, activists with ideological values and objectives, and members with limited instrumental interests is widespread, but misleading. As Undy and Martin (1984: 185–9) have argued, conflicting interests and ideology can be observed within each of the groups, as well as between them. Moreover, the degree of conflict, and the forms in which it is expressed and reconciled, vary between unions and over time.

Much of the extensive literature on union democracy has focused on internal government and administration. As Hyman (1983: 62) has noted, the emphasis on *internal* and formal sources of policy-making, and their separation from the formidable *external* material and ideological constraints on union democracy, can be traced back to Michels's *Political Parties* (1915). His polemical argument that large-scale organization inevitably leads to oligarchic control, also influenced the direction of most research; namely, what constraints, if any, undermine the tendency towards leadership domination and membership apathy in trade unions?

Empirical studies have thus focused on the degree of participation and competition in elections, the extent and nature of organized opposition to leadership, the constitutional relationship between full-time officers and the elected executive and conference, and the balance between centralized and devolved power in decision-making (Undy and Martin, 1984: 190). The research data have been subject to conflicting interpretations; no consensus exists on the legitimate scope of union objectives and methods, or the most appropriate definition of democracy. Some of these issues can be explored by analysing how the changes in union membership and organization – shaped by the actions of governments and employers and the changing economic and political environment discussed earlier – have generated new tensions in union policy-making, and partly redefined the problem of union democracy.

From the mid-1960s, changes in the structure and process of collective bargaining introduced a new dimension into the discussion. The growth of workplace bargaining reflected and reinforced the devolution of power from union officials to a rapidly expanding, more self-reliant and confident group of shop stewards and lay activists. Changes in the level and scope of bargaining varied considerably between industries and sectors, and the leadership of different unions responded with contrasting degrees of enthusiasm in seeking to accommodate shop steward in the formal structures of union decision-making. None the less, as Clegg (1979: 220) argued,

> Trade union workplace organizations have therefore promoted democracy within British trade unions by bringing important decisions closer to the members; by exercising a direct influence over their trade union leaders; and by assisting in the development of factions. In addition a number of important unions have adapted their constitutions to give workplace organizations a recognized place within the machinery of government.

By the late-1970s, academic debate began to focus on the degree to which the 'bureaucratization of the rank-and-file' had taken place. It was argued that the reform of collective bargaining initiated by management, especially in medium and large manufacturing plants, had encouraged centralization and hierarchy in shop steward organization, and thus a separation of senior stewards from less involved activists and members. This process was compounded by the partial integration of senior stewards into national levels of union policy-making and confirmed by the limited shopfloor opposition to the policy of pay restraint agreed between TUC leaders and the Labour government between 1975 and 1978 (Hyman, 1979: 58).

As England (1981: 17) stressed in his critique of the 'bureaucratization' or 'incorporation' thesis, the external pressures on union democracy had changed dramatically since the 1960s. They included unprecedented levels of inflation, rising unemployment, and a public expenditure crisis that, in turn, reshaped both the political relationship between union leaders and the government, and the expectations of union members. More generally, there were still enormous variations in trade-union government and collective bargaining practices. The 1978–9 'winter of discontent' highlighted the uncertain and changing patterns of control within unions, and decisively shifted the parameters of subsequent debate on union democracy.

The widespread industrial disruption and the tensions between union leaders and the Labour government that preceeded the 1979 Conservative Party's election victory, inevitably strengthened the new government's commitment to reduce the power of trade unions. Over the next four years, this objective was undoubtedly achieved. Legislative restrictions on trade-union strike immunities and the operation of the closed shop were probably less significant than other factors: the membership losses caused by the collapse of manufacturing employment; the government's determination to defeat union wage campaigns in the public sector; a more assertive management attack on 'restrictive practices'; and internal conflict in the Labour Party that involved, and partly demoralized, union leaders and activists. In this context, and following its victory in the June 1983 election, the Conservative government elevated trade-union democracy to the pivotal position in its legislative programme.

The January 1983 Green Paper, *Democracy in Trade Unions*, had outlined the three main targets for legislation and the populist and assertive justification for choosing individual, secret ballots as the most appropriate weapon. First, low turn-out, obscure rule books, and the suspicion of electoral malpractice had resulted in the election of union leaders who were 'neither representative of the majority of their members nor directly responsible to them' (para. 7). Secondly, secret ballots before strikes were necessary because 'the methods trade unions use to consult their members are often totally inadequate. Few things have done more to lower public regard for trade unions than the spectacle of strike decisions being taken by a show of hands at stage-managed mass meetings to which outsiders may be admitted and where dissenters may be intimidated' (para. 56). Thirdly, reform of the law on union political funds and affiliation was necessary to ensure that 'the proclaimed views of their leaders reflect their members' wishes and interests' (para. 74).

The legislative intentions of the 1984 Trade Union Act were unambiguous and the broad measure of public support for the extension of ballots suggests that the timing of the legislation was propitious. Trade unions could not easily, or convincingly, oppose the principle of secret ballots, not least because some unions already used them. In particular, the engineers' and the electricians' unions had introduced postal ballots in union elections and, more damaging to the prospects of TUC opposition to the legislation, the NUM leadership decided not to follow its traditional practice (under Rule 43) and call a national ballot at the outset of the 1984–5 strike. This decision had a crucial bearing on the conduct of the dispute and on wider public perceptions of 'the democracy of the ballot box' (Adeney and Lloyd, 1986: chapter 5).

It was clear that the legislation, and the barrage of rhetoric that accompanied it, was designed to promote a 'representative', or 'parliamentary' model of democracy. This emphasizes the rights of individual union members, argues that they should be expressed through secret ballots, and envisages a relatively passive process of decision-making in which representatives, once elected, are accountable to their members only periodically. It contrasts with, and seeks to undermine, the alternative 'participatory' model of union democracy: one that emphasizes collective interests, active participation and involvement, and the direct and continuous accountability of delegates to the membership. In his advocacy of the latter conception of union democracy, Fairbrother (1984: chapter 3) argued that it had been seldom achieved in practice; thus he exposed the vulnerability of recent trade-union policy-making and practice to criticism from the left within the movement.

The Conservative government's policy rested on the questionable premise that secret ballots would increase industrial and political 'moderation' in the trade-union movement (Undy and Martin, 1984: 210). In the period immediately following the legislation, some notable examples of leadership recommendations for industrial action being defeated in strike ballots were used in support of the industrial 'moderation thesis'. By the end of 1986, however, it was clear that many trade-union negotiators had adjusted their bargaining tactics to accommodate the balloting requirements; of the 246 ballots reported to the Advisory, Conciliation and Arbitration Service (ACAS), 189 resulted in majorities in favour of industrial action, twenty of which led to strikes (ACAS, 1986). The increase in the number of wage disputes in early 1988, and the widespread assumption that union negotiators had been able to use ballots to strengthen their bargaining position, confirmed Undy and Martin's argument that the effect of ballots on bargaining outcomes was unpredictable, and depended more on product and labour market conditions than union decision-making processes.

The attention given to the effect of ballots has partly concealed the implications of the changes in union membership and organization, discussed earlier. The increasing concentration of membership in conglomerate unions remains a formidable obstacle to the development of representative and effective methods of union policy-making. Large unions with heterogeneous membership face a continuous problem in identifying and reconciling the different interests of members. There is some evidence that the balance has shifted from national policy co-ordination and the pursuit of general interests towards greater local discretion and the recognition of separate interests in some unions.

The coal mining industry offers an exceptional and dramatic example of trade-union fragmentation resulting from an attempt to pursue forceful national policies against the wishes of a substantial group of members. The breakaway Union of Democratic Mineworkers, based largely around the coal miners who worked throughout the 1984–5 strike, embodies a set of related interests – based on working conditions, job security, geography, political traditions and values – that divide its members from the majority of others in the NUM. The origins of the split have no direct counterpart in other trade unions, but most have to confront the disparate demands of a far more heterogeneous membership.

The uncertain and changing pressures faced by different groups of members arise partly from the uneven impact of the 1980–2 recession and the pattern of economic growth since 1983. More specifically, product and labour market variations, within and between different sectors, have led to a wider range of management policies towards work organization, wage and salary structures, patterns of working time and trade-union facilities. Managers have always had the opportunity to facilitate or impede trade-union workplace organization; it is now clear that many are choosing to influence the character of union representation directly. Innovative, and enterprise-specific, employment practices, methods of communication and additional channels of employee participation can only add to the fragmentation of union members' interests and the problems of union co-ordination.

These constraints have challenged the 1970s pattern of union democracy developed by well-organized, male full-time workers, employed in large manufacturing plants. The organization and effective representation of women workers, often employed part-time and located in small and dispersed workplaces in the expanding service sector, presents even greater problems. Over the last decade, the leaders of several major unions have responded to the demands of their more active women members; women's distinctive interests have been more clearly recognized, some of the obstacles to women's participation in union meetings have been removed, and reserved seats for women have been created on executive committees. This progress, however, has been uneven, and it has coincided with a deterioration in the quality of employment opportunities, working conditions and welfare state provision available to many women.

Future Prospects

This chapter has identified a number of weaknesses in trade-union organization that have been exposed by the force of economic and political change in the 1980s. The loss of membership and political influence has been accompanied by increasing tensions in the relationships between major unions and by the growing problems each faces in trying to represent the heterogeneous interests of its members effectively. Traditional forms of trade-union organization and practice seem inadequate to meet the challenge posed by government hostility, management reappraisal of the value of union representation and collective bargaining, and the uncertain interests of potential members facing a variety of rapidly changing employment and labour market conditions.

In the current debate on the future of British trade unions, there is some consensus that the conditions that generated the high level of industrial and political mobilization in the 1970s are unlikely to reappear. Since the coal-mining strike and the third Conservative Party election victory, fewer voices are raised in support, or in the expectation, of a return to 'class politics' and industrial militancy. Conflicting assessments, however, have been made of the scale, impact and pervasiveness of economic and political changes, and of the organizational capacity of unions to adapt to the current conditions. Much of the debate has focused on two separate issues: the legitimacy of 'market-based' unionism, exemplified in the ideology and practice of the leadership of the EETPU; and the prospects for a new union strategy to organize the fragmented work-force in the service sector, advocated most consistently by the leader of the GMB.

The EETPU has developed a version of 'market-based' trade unionism, and projected it in a more coherent and provocative manner than other unions (Lloyd, 1986). In ideological terms, it espouses an unambiguous acceptance of the capitalist market economy and the belief that harmonious industrial relations with employers are more likely to generate improved pay and conditions and job security for its members. The EETPU offers employers the prospect of collaboration through its advocacy of single-union and 'no-strike' agreements, and a willingness to accept flexible working arrangements. Potential members are offered the prospect of a harmonious workplace, the possibility of 'single-status' agreements with conditions of service that reduce the division between manual workers and staff, and the commitment to individual, secret ballots in union decision-making. They can also take advantage of a package of consumer-oriented membership benefits, such as car insurance and financial advice.

The main features of 'market-based' unionism are not new; most unions are involved in co-operative relationships with management for most of the time, and few unions have ever rejected employers' offers of sole representation rights. The acrimonious debate over the legitimacy of single-union agreements within the TUC has been fueled by the ideological stance and style of the EETPU leadership; its role in the News International dispute at Wapping was merely its most audacious initiative in a series of confrontations within the TUC. More generally at a time of relative union weakness, employers have exploited and intensified inter-union rivalry by inviting union officials to outbid each other in competition for recognition rights on greenfield sites. This raises several potential problems for TUC unions: the employer may favour a union with limited experience in the sector and thus undermine the agreed spheres of influence between affiliated unions; the draft agreement may embody significant procedural and substantive concessions that undermine collective bargaining elsewhere; and the recognition of a single union may be followed by very low levels of union membership, as at Nissan, for example.

In practice, the leaders and activists of most unions have developed a more cautious and moderate style of trade unionism that implicitly accepts, even if it does not celebrate, the shift in power to employers. Some variant of 'market-based' unionism can therefore be seen as the most likely response of any union seeking membership in new areas of manufacturing employment, or in attempting to adjust its bargaining tactics in existing areas of manual and non-manual membership, in the public and private sector.

The failure of trade unions to recruit a significant membership in the growing service sector clearly exposes the limitations of traditional forms of organization and representation. In the decade of rapid union growth from the late-1960s, only marginal gains were made in parts of the service sector. Since that time, government policies designed to deregulate the labour market – the removal or dilution of protective employment legislation and the contracting-out of well-organized public service work to non-union private sector companies – have encouraged more extreme forms of exploitation and created additional obstacles to union organization.

The leaders of several unions have focused attention on the urgent need to develop new forms of trade unionism that would overcome their past organizational failures in this area. The General Secretary of the GMB has most clearly articulated the enormity of the challenge and the broad outlines of a strategy designed to offer trade-union protection to 'millions of exploited workers – overwhelmingly women working part-time in service industries or service occupations in other industries' (Edmonds, 1986: 18).

The central feature of his strategy is a trade-union campaign for a new legal framework of employment protection covering equal rights, health and safety, employment security and minimum pay and conditions. In order to attract workers into membership, Edmonds argues that trade unions will have to adapt their organization to bring together isolated and fragmented groups of workers, so that officials and activists can help members to enforce their rights against employers. A more extensive trade-union role in campaigns and community activities outside the workplace will also be required to offer the prospect of collective solutions to the problems of individually vulnerable workers and consumers.

This emphasis on the importance of legal protection, and the need for a new form and style of union representation, clearly envisages a radical departure from the 'voluntarist' traditions that prioritized collective bargaining as the essence of trade-union practice in Britain. If unions are unable to achieve such a change, then, at best, they are likely to represent a declining and relatively privileged segment of the working population.

References

Adeney, M. and Lloyd, J. 1986. *The Miners' Strike 1984–5: Loss Without Limit*. London: Routledge & Kegan Paul.
Advisory Conciliation and Arbitration Service. 1986. *Annual Report 1986*. London: ACAS.
Armstrong, P., Carter, B., Smith, C. and Nichols, T. 1986. *White Collar Workers, Trade Unions, and Class*. London: Croom Helm.
Bain, G.S. and Elsheikh, F. 1976. *Union Growth and the Business Cycle: An Econometric Analysis*. Oxford: Basil Blackwell.
—— and Price, R. 1983. 'Union Growth: Dimensions, Determinants, and Destiny'. *Industrial Relations in Britain*. Ed. Bain, G.S. Oxford: Basil Blackwell.
Blackburn, R.M. and Prandy, K. 1965. 'White-Collar Unionization: A Conceptual Framwork'. *British Journal of Sociology*, 16 (June), 111–22.
Camley, M. 1987. 'Employment in the Public and Private Sectors 1980 to 1986'. *Economic Trends*, 398 (December), 88–96.
Carruth, A. and Disney, R. 1988. 'Where Have Two Million Trade Union Members Gone?' *Economica*, 55 (February), 1–19.
Clegg, H.A. 1976. *Trade Unionism under Collective Bargaining: A Theory Based on Comparisons of Six Countries*. Oxford: Basil Blackwell.
—— 1979. *The Changing System of Industrial Relations in Great Britain*. Oxford: Basil Blackwell.
Crompton, R. and Jones, G. 1984. *White Collar Proleteriat: Deskilling and Gender in Clerical Work*. London: Macmillan.
Department of Employment, 1983. *Democracy in Trade Unions*. Cmnd 8778. London: HMSO.
Dunn, S. and Gennard, J. 1984. *The Closed Shop in British Industry*. London: Macmillan.
Edmonds, J. 1986. 'Uniting the Fragments'. *New Socialist* (June), 18–9.
England, J. 1981. 'Shop Stewards in Transport House: A Comment on the Incorporation of the Rank and File'. *Industrial Relations Journal*, 12 (September), 16–29.
Fairbrother, P. 1984. *All Those in Favour: The Politics of Union Democracy*. London: Pluto Press.
Hyman, R. 1979. 'The Politics of Workplace Trade Unionism'. *Capital and Class*, 8 (Summer), 54–67.
—— 1983. 'Trade Unions: Structure, Policies, and Politics'. *Industrial Relations in Britain*. Ed. Bain, G.S. Oxford: Basil Blackwell.
—— and Price, R. (eds) 1983. *The New Working Class? White-Collar Workers and their Organizations*. London: Macmillan.
Kelly, J. 1987. 'Trade Unions Through The Recession 1980–1984'. *British Journal of Industrial Relations*, 25 (July), 275–82.
Lewis, R. 1986. 'The Role of Law in Employment Relations'. *Labour Law in Britain*. Ed. Lewis, R. Oxford: Basil Blackwell.
Lloyd, J. 1986. 'The Sparks are Flying'. *Marxism Today* (March), 12–17.
MacInnes, J. 1987. *Thatcherism at Work: Industrial Relations and Economic Change*. Milton Keynes: Open University Press.
Michels, R. 1915. *Political Parties*. New York: Hearsts.

Millward, N. and Stevens, M. 1986. *British Workplace Industrial Relations 1980–1984*. Aldershot: Gower.

Müller-Jentsch, W. 1985. 'Trade Unions as Intermediary Organizations'. Economic and Industrial Democracy, 6, 3–33.

Offe, C. and Wiesenthal, H. 1985. 'Two Logics of Collective Action'. *Disorganized Capitalism: Contemporary Transformations of Work and Politics*. Ed. Offe, C. Cambridge: Polity.

Price, R. 1983. 'White-Collar Unions: Growth, Character, and Attitudes in the 1970s'. *The New Working Class?: White-Collar Workers and their Organizations*. Eds. Hyman R. and Price, R. London: Macmillan.

—— and Bain, G.S. 1983. 'Union Growth in Britain: Retrospect and Prospect'. *British Journal of Industrial Relations*, 21 (March), 46–68.

Smith, C. 1987. *Technical Workers: Class, Labour and Trade Unionism*. London: Macmillan.

Terry, M. 1986. 'How Do We Know If Shop Stewards Are Getting Weaker?'. *British Journal of Industrial Relations*, 24 (July), 169–79.

Trades Union Congress. 1986. *Annual Report 1986*. London: TUC.

—— 1987. *General Council Report*. London: TUC.

Undy, R., Ellis, V., McCarthy, W. and Halmos, A. 1981. *Change in Trade Unions: The Development of UK Unions since 1960*. London: Hutchinson.

—— and Martin, R. 1984. *Ballots and Trade Union Democracy*. Oxford: Basil Blackwell.

Webb, S. and Webb, B. 1897. *Industrial Democracy*. London: Longman.

Weckes, B., Mellish, M., Dickens, L. and Lloyd, J. 1975. *Industrial Relations and the Limits of the Law: The Industrial Effects of the Industrial Relations Act, 1971*. Oxford: Basil Blackwell.

Index

Index by Jackie McDermott